THE ANALYSIS OF FREQUENCY DATA

STATISTICAL RESEARCH MONOGRAPHS

VOLUME IV

SPONSORED JOINTLY BY THE INSTITUTE OF MATHEMATICAL STATISTICS

AND THE UNIVERSITY OF CHICAGO

SHELBY J. HABERMAN

THE ANALYSIS OF FREQUENCY DATA

THE UNIVERSITY OF CHICAGO PRESS
CHICAGO AND LONDON

The University of Chicago Press, Chicago 60637
The University of Chicago Press, Ltd., London

Published 1974. Midway Reprint 1977
Printed in the United States of America

ISBN: 0-226-31185-6
Library of Congress Catalog Number: 74-7558

CONTENTS

List of tables vii

Preface ix

1. Basic properties of log-linear models 1

2. Maximum-likelihood estimation 34

3. Numerical evaluation of maximum-likelihood estimates 46

4. Asymptotic properties 74

5. Complete factorial tables 147

6. Social-mobility tables 215

7. Incomplete contingency tables 228

8. Quantal-response models 303

9. Some extensions 374

Appendix A: Basic mathematical and statistical results used in the monograph 387

Appendix B: Procedures for verification that maximum-likelihood estimates exist 395

Appendix C: Proof of theorem 3.1 405

References 408

Index 415

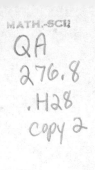

TABLES

1.1	Ratio of males to females in newborn babies	1
1.2	Mothers with previous infant losses	2
1.3	Injection of digitalis in lymph sac of frogs	5
3.1	Parole violators	51
3.2	Presence or absence of *torus mandibularis*	54
3.3	Maximum-likelihood estimates of means for eskimo groups	57
4.1	Attitudes toward Negroes of white women in public housing projects	120
4.2	Relation between teacher's rating and homework conditions	140
5.1	Maximum-likelihood estimates for racial attitudes study	204
5.2	Estimated interactions in racial attitudes study	205
5.3	Asymptotic covariances of interactions in racial attitudes study	207
6.1	British social mobility: fixed distances	218
6.2	Parameter estimates for British fixed-distance model	219
6.3	British social mobility: variable distances	220
6.4	Parameter estimates for British variable-distance model	221
6.5	Danish social mobility: fixed distances	223
6.6	Parameter estimates for Danish fixed-distance model	224
6.7	Danish social mobility: variable distances	225
6.8	Parameter estimates for Danish variable-distance model	226
7.1	Number of progeny from mating translocation-bearing males to attached-X females	229
7.2	Radial asymmetry and locular composition in staphylea (series A)	230
7.3	Elements $\lambda_{i_1i_2i_3i_4}^{(k,0)}$ of spanning vectors in example 7.4	238
7.4	Elements $\lambda_{i_1i_2i_3i_4}^{(k,5)}$ of spanning vectors after 5 iterations	239

7.5 Elements $\lambda^{(k,11)}_{i_1 i_2 i_3 i_4}$ of spanning vectors after 11 iterations 240

7.6 Spanning vectors $\underline{\lambda}^{(k,0)}$ for example 7.5 241

7.7 Elements $\bar{\lambda}^{(k,19)}_{i_1 i_2 i_3}$ of spanning vectors modulo 254,039 obtained after final iteration 242

7.8 Maximum-likelihood estimates for staphylea data 248

7.9 Components of X^2 for birth order data 261

7.10 Initial and final ratings of stroke patients 269

7.11 Simultaneous confidence intervals based on $\log p(j|i)$ for conditional probabilities in table 7.10 of final states given initial states 291

7.12 Simultaneous confidence intervals based on $p(j|i)$ for conditional probabilities in table 7.10 of final states given initial states 292

7.13 Maximum-likelihood estimate $\hat{\underline{m}}(\underline{n},I,E)$ for table 7.1 if $E = \{\{1\},\{2\},\{3\},\{4\}\}$ 294

7.14 Maximum-likelihood estimate $\hat{\underline{m}}(\underline{n},I,E')$ for table 7.1 if $E' = \{\{1\},\{2\},\{3,4\}\}$ 295

7.15 Elements $c^{(k)}_{i_1 i_2 i_3 i_4}$ of vectors spanning $[M(E)]^{\perp}$ in example 7.37 298

7.16 Components of estimated log-mean vector for data in table 7.1 300

7.17 Estimated interactions in table 7.1 300

8.1 Results of games between American league teams in 1948 305

8.2 Frequency of mutants with two methods of irradiation 306

8.3 Estimates of $\hat{\underline{\lambda}}$ for baseball data 329

8.4 Maximum-likelihood estimate of mean vector $\underline{m}^{(L)}(\underline{N},\hat{\underline{\lambda}})$ for baseball data 329

8.5 Coordinates $\lambda^{(t)}_{ij}$ for logit model of data in table 8.2 332

8.6 Maximum-likelihood estimates $\hat{m}^{(L)}_{ijk}$ for data in table 8.2 332

8.7 Relative team strengths for American league teams in 1948 343

8.8 Toxicity of ethylene oxide 350

8.9 Variables in Framingham study 353

8.10 Parameter estimates for Framingham study 370

9.1 Observed frequencies in 5% sample of native white persons of native white parentage attending school in New England in 1930 378

9.2 Employment status according to age of rural non-farm males in a 20% sample for New Jersey and the corresponding census counts by age and by employment status from the 1950 census of population 379

9.3 Estimated and true population totals for data in table 9.1 384

9.4 Estimated employment status according to age for population of non-farm males in New Jersey 385

9.5 Estimated asymptotic standard deviations for entries in table 9.3 385

Preface

Although log-linear models have received considerable attention recently from specialists in contingency table analysis, most statisticians are unfamiliar with these models. Even specialists in the area have often suffered from lack of a comprehensive theory concerning log-linear models. This monograph provides a rigorous general presentation of log-linear models. The specialists will find a number of new results concerning familiar models and some new models to consider. The general reader may regard the monograph as an introduction to the analysis of counted data.

The models proposed in this monograph are defined on linear manifolds. Coordinate-free methods of linear algebra and differential calculus provide the necessary mathematical tools for their treatment, just as coordinate-free linear algebra has contributed to analysis of variance and regression analysis (see Kruskal 1968a,1968b). This method of definition permits development of a general theory which applies equally well to complete factorial tables, incomplete tables, and quantal response models. Previous studies have had a much more limited scope. Each new type of model has required a new examination of the properties of maximum-likelihood estimates and a new computational procedure to find them. Statisticians desiring rigorous results have had to devise new proofs of the uniqueness and existence of their estimates. They have had to show that their algorithms converged, and asymptotic theory has been needed. The general log-linear model eliminates these problems for a large class of models for frequency data. This class is large enough, in fact, to include any log-linear model which corresponds to a model used in regression or analysis of variance.

General theories often involve powerful proofs of trivial results; however, the general theory of the log-linear model provides simpler proofs than those previously available. No longer are elaborate procedures required to take account of particular coordinate systems involving multiply subscripted arrays. Nevertheless, this treatment may pose a problem for the statistician unfamiliar with linear manifolds and linear operators. Consequently, an appendix is included which summarizes the basic mathematical results used. More detailed discussions of linear algebra are provided by Halmos (1958) and Hoffman and Kunze (1961). Fleming (1965) and Loomis and Sternberg (1968) discuss coordinate-free methods of differential calculus.

Optimal use of the book depends somewhat on the background of the reader. Many proofs require a knowledge of mathematical statistics comparable to that represented by familiarity with Rao (1965) or some similar work. Even then, some proofs are rather difficult. The reader who either is not mathematically inclined or is primarily interested in applications may prefer to omit proofs of theorems and instead concentrate on statements of results and worked examples. A mathematical statistician may be more interested in the proofs but may wish to skip certain sections. The following summary of the contents of the monograph should serve as a guide for the various possible readers.

Chapter 1 provides a general definition of the model and presents examples of familiar contingency table models included in the definition. The Poisson, multinomial, and conditional Poisson sampling methods are introduced. Complete minimal sufficient statistics are presented, and fundamental asymptotic results are stated. The chapter closes with a discussion of exact procedures for testing and estimation. Readers unfamiliar with the concept of completeness may ignore the results on complete minimal sufficient statistics without harm. The sections on the conditional Poisson model and exact procedures can be ignored if desired. In particular, the convergence proof in the conditional Poisson case is of interest to mathematical statisticians and probabilists, but it is quite complicated.

Chapter 2 considers some basic properties of maximum-likelihood estimates. In the Poisson and multinomial cases, they are shown to be unique when they exist, and necessary and sufficient conditions are given for their existence. Poisson and multinomial estimates are shown to be equivalent, and equations for maximum-likelihood estimates are stated. Several proofs require use of differentials. These functions are defined in the text, but many readers may still have some difficulty with some proofs. The statements of theorems and corollaries and the worked examples should permit the reader to develop some understanding of problems of existence of estimates. The sections on conditional Poisson models and extended maximum-likelihood estimates are less important than the earlier sections. It may be reasonable to omit them at a first reading.

Chapter 3 considers numerical determination of maximum-likelihood estimates. Basically this is a chapter on the maximization of concave functions. Results apply to problems other than the particular maximizations considered in the monograph. Two algorithms are proposed. The first is a modification of the classical Newton-Raphson procedure which provides excellent limiting convergence properties but requires extensive computations at each iteration. The second is the cyclic coordinate ascent algorithm. This technique is simpler to implement than the other algorithm but has a slower limiting convergence rate except in special cases. It is shown that the cyclic coordinate ascent method is equivalent to the iterative proportional fitting of Deming and Stephan (1940). Choice of algorithms depends primarily on the dimension of the manifold considered. The larger the dimension, the more attractive cyclic coordinate ascent becomes. This chapter makes extensive use of second and third differentials. These mappings are carefully defined, but statisticians not accustomed to manipulations with such functions may find some proofs difficult. Some readers may wish to read only the statements of the algorithms and the examples of their application to log-linear models.

Asymptotic properties are the subject of chapter 4. Asymptotic distributions are determined for maximum-likelihood estimates and test statistics, and simultaneous testing and estimation are examined. Familiarity with convergence in probability and convergence in distribution is necessary for an understanding of this chapter. Repeated references to Rao (1965) are made when test statistics are considered. The worked examples, however, only require familiarity with chi-square tests and regression theory.

The next four chapters apply the general results of chapters 1 through 4 to specific types of tables encountered in statistical work. In chapter 5, complete factorial tables are investigated by use of linear manifolds. Hierarchical analysis of variance models receive special attention. The Deming-Stephan algorithm is described in detail, and the relationship between convergence of this algorithm in one cycle and the existence of closed-form maximum-likelihood estimates is investigated. The chapter closes with a discussion of model selection and construction of special models. Proofs which involve determination of closed-form estimates are illuminating but rather more difficult to understand than the examples of common closed-form estimates. It may be useful to read the theorem statements, the examples, and then the proofs.

Chapter 6 considers a special complete table, the social mobility table. Log-linear models based on distance measures are constructed which provide good fits for the classical Danish and British mobility tables. This chapter is the most extended analysis of a model in the book. It should be of particular interest to applied statisticians, especially those in the social sciences.

Incomplete tables are the subject of chapter 7. The Deming-Stephan algorithm again receives a detailed discussion, and some closed-form estimates are presented. In incomplete tables, the correct number of degrees of freedom for chi-square tests becomes difficult to determine. Separability and special elimination methods are used to remove this difficulty. Several collections of data are analyzed by means of incomplete tables. No special mathematical difficulties are found in this chapter, but the models can be rather difficult to visualize in several dimensions. Consequently, this chapter may be more difficult than chapter 5.

Quantal response analysis is explored in chapter 8. Logit models are shown to be examples of log-linear models for which the Newton-Raphson algorithm is the proper method for computation of maximum-likelihood estimates. The proposed algorithm is related to the conventional procedure based on working logits, and some numerical examples are provided. Both binomial and multinomial responses are examined, and multiple dosage situations are considered. This chapter should be of greatest interest to biometricians, although it does not supersede book-length treatments of quantal response analysis such as that of Finney (1971).

The last chapter, chapter 9, considers models for flats. Applications are made to survey sampling. This chapter briefly introduces some specialized topics. It is not essential for understanding the rest of the book, but it may help the statistician with an unusual model. No special mathematical difficulties are encountered in this chapter.

This monograph is based on a dissertation written while the author was a graduate student at the University of Chicago. Research leading to this dissertation was generously supported by a John and Fannie Hertz Foundation Fellowship. Subsequent research incorporated in this monograph was partially supported by National Science Foundation grants NSF GP-25911 and NSF GS-2818.

My colleagues in the Department of Statistics at the University of Chicago have provided considerable assistance in the preparation of this manuscript. Particular acknowledgment must be given to Professor Leo Goodman, who was my dissertation advisor, and to Professors Stephen Fienberg, Morris Eaton, Paul Meier, and David Wallace.

Chapter 1

BASIC PROPERTIES OF LOG-LINEAR MODELS

DEFINITION OF THE MODEL

A contingency table may be regarded as a collection $\underline{n}$ of frequencies $\{n_i: i \in I\}$ indexed by a finite nonempty set I containing q elements. Given this definition, the following examples are contingency tables.

Example 1.1. Suppose that N tosses of a coin result in n_H heads and n_T tails. Then the set $\{n_H, n_T\}$ is a contingency table with index set $I = \{H,T\}$.

Example 1.2. The relationship between toxemia and the sex ratio of newborns was examined by Toivanen and Hirvonen (1970), who compiled table 1.1.

TABLE 1.1

RATIO OF MALES TO FEMALES IN NEWBORN BABIES

Group	Males	Females
Toxemia	588	473
Control	4196	4061

The table is an example of a 2 × 2 contingency table. The index set I consists of the four pairs $\langle 1,1\rangle$, $\langle 1,2\rangle$, $\langle 2,1\rangle$, and $\langle 2,2\rangle$. Here $\langle 1,1\rangle$ represents the combination of toxemia and males, $\langle 1,2\rangle$ represents toxemia and females, $\langle 2,1\rangle$ represents controls and males, and $\langle 2,2\rangle$ represents controls and females. The set I may be written as $\langle 1,2\rangle \times \langle 1,2\rangle = \overline{2} \times \overline{2}$, where for all integers k, $\overline{k}$ is the set of positive integers less than or equal to k. The table $\underline{n} = \{n_{ij}: \langle i,j\rangle \in \overline{2} \times \overline{2}\}$. Here n_{ij} can be considered an abbreviation for $n_{\langle i,j\rangle}$. If the tabular structure of I is to be emphasized but the interpretations of the elements of I are not of interest, one may write

$$\underline{n} = \begin{array}{|cc|} n_{11} & n_{12} \\ n_{21} & n_{22} \end{array} \quad (1.1)$$

Example 1.3. Snedecor and Cochran (1967) report on mothers with previous infant losses in table 1.2.

TABLE 1.2

MOTHERS WITH PREVIOUS INFANT LOSSES

Birth Order	Type of Children	No. of Mothers with Losses	No. of Mothers with No Losses
2	Problems	20	82
	Controls	10	54
3-4	Problems	26	41
	Controls	16	30
5+	Problems	27	22
	Controls	14	23

This table may be described as a 3 x 2 x 2 contingency table. The set I consists of all possible triples of birth order, type of children, and type of mother. If the birth order categories are numbered from 1 to 3, type of children is numbered from 1 to 2, and type of mother is numbered from 1 to 2, then $I = \overline{3} \times \overline{2} \times \overline{2}$. The table may be written as $\{n_{ijk}: \langle i,j,k\rangle \in \overline{3} \times \overline{2} \times \overline{2}\}$.

The table $\underline{n}$ is an element of the q-dimensional vector space R^I of real I-tuples $\underline{x} = \{x_i: i \in I\}$. This space may also be regarded as the space of functions from I to R (see Loomis and Sternberg 1968). If the index set I is understood from context, an element $\underline{x}$ may be written as $\{x_i\}$. For example, the 2 x 2 table $\underline{n}$ may be written as $\{n_{ij}: \langle i,j\rangle \in \overline{2} \times \overline{2}\}$ or as $\{n_{ij}\}$. The space R^I has the standard inner product $(\cdot,\cdot)$ such that

$$(\underline{x},\underline{y}) = \sum_{i \in I} x_i y_i \quad (1.2)$$

and the standard basis $\{\underline{\delta}^{(j)}: j \in I\}$, where $\delta_i^{(j)} = \delta_{ij}$, the Kronecker delta.

If $I = \overline{q}$, it is customary to write R^q rather than $R^{\overline{q}}$. If $q = 3$, then $\underline{x} = \langle x_1,x_2,x_3\rangle \in R^3$ and

$$(\underline{x},\underline{y}) = \sum_{i=1}^{3} x_i y_i \ . \quad (1.3)$$

The standard basis elements $\underline{\delta}^{(1)}$, $\underline{\delta}^{(2)}$, and $\underline{\delta}^{(3)}$ are respectively $\langle 1,0,0\rangle$, $\langle 0,1,0\rangle$, and $\langle 0,0,1\rangle$.

In a log-linear model, $\underline{n}$ is assumed to be a random vector with mean $\underline{m}$, where m_i is positive for each $i \in I$. Thus for each $i \in I$, $\log m_i$ is well defined. Therefore, if $\underline{\mu} = \{\log m_i\}$, then $\underline{\mu} \in R^I$. In a log-linear model, it is assumed that $\underline{\mu} \in M$, where M is a p-dimensional linear manifold contained in R^I and $0 < p \leq q$, where q is the number of elements in I.

Example 1.4. Consider the N coin tosses of Example 1.1. If the coin is fair, $m_H = m_T = N/2$. Thus $\mu_H = \mu_T = \log (N/2)$. If $M = \{\underline{\mu} \in R^{\{H,T\}}: \mu_H = \mu_T\}$, then $\underline{\mu} \in M$.

Example 1.5. Let $I = \overline{2} \times \overline{2}$. Then $R^I = R^{\overline{2} \times \overline{2}}$ is spanned by the four orthogonal vectors $\{\underline{\mu}^{(k)}: k \in \overline{4}\}$, where

(1.4) $$\underline{\mu}^{(1)} = \boxed{\begin{array}{cc} 1 & 1 \\ 1 & 1 \end{array}},$$

(1.5) $$\underline{\mu}^{(2)} = \boxed{\begin{array}{cc} 1 & 1 \\ -1 & -1 \end{array}},$$

(1.6) $$\underline{\mu}^{(3)} \quad \boxed{\begin{array}{cc} 1 & -1 \\ 1 & -1 \end{array}},$$

(1.7) $$\underline{\mu}^{(4)} \quad \boxed{\begin{array}{cc} 1 & -1 \\ -1 & 1 \end{array}}.$$

Bishop and Fienberg (1969) consider a model such that $M = \text{span}\ \{\underline{\mu}^{(1)}, \underline{\mu}^{(2)}, \underline{\mu}^{(3)}\}$. In this case a, b_1, b_2, c_1, and c_2 may be chosen so that

(1.8) $$\log m_{ij} = a + b_i + c_j, \quad i \in \overline{2},\ j \in \overline{2},$$

and

(1.9) $$\sum_{i=1}^{2} b_i = \sum_{j=1}^{2} c_j = 0.$$

Suppose that

$$(1.10)\qquad m_{i+} = \sum_{j=1}^{2} m_{ij}, \quad i \in \overline{2},$$

$$(1.11)\qquad m_{+j} = \sum_{i=1}^{2} m_{ij}, \quad j \in \overline{2},$$

$$(1.12)\qquad m_{++} = \sum_{i=1}^{2} \sum_{j=1}^{2} m_{ij}.$$

Then

$$(1.13)\qquad m_{i+} = e^{a}e^{b_i}(e^{c_1} + e^{c_2}), \quad i \in \overline{2},$$

$$(1.14)\qquad m_{+j} = e^{a}(e^{b_1} + e^{b_2})e^{c_j}, \quad j \in \overline{2},$$

$$(1.15)\qquad m_{++} = e^{a}(e^{b_1} + e^{b_2})(e^{c_1} + e^{c_2}).$$

Hence

$$(1.16)\qquad m_{ij} = \frac{m_{i+}m_{+j}}{m_{++}}.$$

Thus the model is additive in $\log m_{ij}$ and multiplicative in m_{ij}. Since $\underline{\mu}^{(4)}$ is orthogonal to $\underline{\mu}^{(1)}$, $\underline{\mu}^{(2)}$, and $\underline{\mu}^{(3)}$, $\underline{\mu}^{(4)}$ is orthogonal to M. It follows that

$$(1.17)\qquad \begin{aligned}(\underline{\mu},\underline{\mu}^{(4)}) &= \log m_{11} - \log m_{12} - \log m_{21} + \log m_{22} \\ &= \log (m_{11}m_{22}/m_{12}m_{21}) \\ &= 0.\end{aligned}$$

The cross-product ratio $m_{11}m_{22}/m_{12}m_{21}$ is therefore 1 whenever $\underline{\mu} \in M$. Since M is the orthogonal complement of $\{\underline{\mu}^{(4)}\}$, (1.17) implies that $\underline{\mu} \in M$ whenever the cross-product ratio is 1. In Example 1.2, the sex ratio for the toxemia group is m_{11}/m_{12}. The ratio for the control group is m_{21}/m_{22}. The hypothesis that the ratios are equal is equivalent to the hypothesis that

$$(1.18)\qquad \frac{m_{11}m_{22}}{m_{12}m_{21}} = 1.$$

This hypothesis is equivalent to the condition $\underline{\mu} \in M$.

Example 1.6. Miller, Bliss, and Braun (1939) and Finney (1947) consider an experiment in which digitalis is injected into the lymph sacs of frogs. Three dosage levels were each administered to 15 frogs. Their results are given in table 1.3.

TABLE 1.3

INJECTION OF DIGITALIS IN LYMPH SAC OF FROGS

Log Dose	No. Killed	No. Surviving
0.75	2	13
0.85	5	10
0.95	8	7

In this table $I = \overline{3} \times \overline{2}$, and row i, column j, contains the number of frogs receiving log dosage t_i who have outcome j. The outcome is known as a quantal response. If outcome 1 is death and outcome 2 is survival, then one may write p_{i1} as the probability that a frog dies if it receives log dosage t_i and $p_{i2} = 1 - p_{i1}$ as the corresponding probability of survival. In a logit model, it is assumed that the logit $\log (p_{i1}/p_{i2})$ is a linear function of the log dose t_i. Thus for some a and b, the log odds $\log (p_{i1}/p_{i2})$ satisfy

$$\log (p_{i1}/p_{i2}) = a + bt_i \tag{1.19}$$

for $i \in \overline{3}$. Since $m_{ij} = 15\, p_{ij}$, it follows that

$$\begin{aligned} \log (p_{i1}/p_{i2}) &= \log (m_{i1}/m_{12}) \\ &= \mu_{i1} - \mu_{i2} \\ &= a + bt_i. \end{aligned} \tag{1.20}$$

Equation (1.20) places linear restrictions on $\underline{\mu}$. The set M of all vectors $\underline{\mu} \in R^{\overline{3} \times \overline{2}}$ such that there exist a and b for which (1.20) holds for all $i \in \overline{3}$ is a linear manifold. The independent vectors $\{\underline{\mu}^{(k)}: k \in \overline{5}\}$ are all contained in M, where

$$\underline{\mu}^{(1)} = \begin{bmatrix} 1 & 1 \\ 0 & 0 \\ 0 & 0 \end{bmatrix}, \tag{1.21}$$

$$\underline{\mu}^{(2)} = \begin{bmatrix} 0 & 0 \\ 1 & 1 \\ 0 & 0 \end{bmatrix}, \tag{1.22}$$

$$\underline{\mu}^{(3)} = \begin{bmatrix} 0 & 0 \\ 0 & 0 \\ 1 & 1 \end{bmatrix}, \tag{1.23}$$

$$\underline{\mu}^{(4)} = \begin{bmatrix} 1 & -1 \\ 1 & -1 \\ 1 & -1 \end{bmatrix}, \tag{1.24}$$

$$\underline{\mu}^{(5)} = \begin{bmatrix} 1 & -1 \\ 0 & 0 \\ -1 & 1 \end{bmatrix}. \tag{1.25}$$

The vector $\underline{\mu}^{(6)}$ is orthogonal to any vector in M, where

$$\underline{\mu}^{(6)} = \begin{bmatrix} -1 & 1 \\ 2 & -2 \\ -1 & 1 \end{bmatrix}. \tag{1.26}$$

Since $\{\underline{\mu}^{(j)}: j \in \bar{6}\}$ is independent and $\bar{3} \times \bar{2}$ has 6 elements, these six vectors span $R^{\bar{3} \times \bar{2}}$, where M is $\text{span}\{\underline{\mu}^{(j)}: j \in \bar{5}\}$ and $M^{\perp}$, the orthogonal complement of M, is $\text{span}\,\{\underline{\mu}^{(6)}\}$.

Other examples may be constructed. The important point is that M is an arbitrary linear manifold; therefore, any linear model appropriate for linear regression or analysis of variance corresponds to a log-linear model.

No specification has been made yet concerning the underlying distribution of $\underline{n}$. In this monograph, the principal probability models considered are the Poisson and multinomial models. A generalization of these models which is of some interest is the conditional Poisson model. These models are described in the next three sections of this chapter.

THE POISSON MODEL

In the Poisson model, the elements of $\underline{n}$ are independent Poisson random variables with $E(n_i) = m_i$ for every $i \in I$ and $m_i > 0$ for each $i \in I$. If $\underline{m}(\underline{\mu}) = \{e^{\mu_i}\}$, then the log likelihood may be written as

$$(1.27)\qquad \ell(\underline{n},\underline{\mu}) = \sum_{i\in I} [n_i \log m_i(\underline{\mu}) - m_i(\underline{\mu}) - \log n_i!]$$

$$= (\underline{n},\underline{\mu}) - \sum_{i\in I} m_i(\underline{\mu}) - \sum_{i\in I} \log n_i!$$

$$= (\underline{n},\underline{\mu}) - \sum_{i\in I} e^{\mu_i} - \sum_{i\in I} \log n_i!\ .$$

In this equation, $\underline{n}$ is regarded as fixed and $\ell(\underline{n},\underline{\mu})$ is a function defined for $\underline{\mu} \in M$.

If P_M is the orthogonal projection from R^I to M, then since $\underline{\mu} \in M$ and P_M is a symmetric operator,

$$(1.28)\qquad (\underline{n},\underline{\mu}) = (\underline{n},P_M\underline{\mu}) - \sum_{i\in I} e^{\mu_i} - \sum_{i\in I} \log n_i!$$

$$= (P_M\underline{n},\underline{\mu}) - \sum_{i\in I} e^{\mu_i} - \sum_{i\in I} \log n_i!\ .$$

Therefore, the family of Poisson models such that $\underline{\mu} \in M$ is an exponential family. Since M and R^p are isomorphic (see Halmos 1958), $P_M\underline{n}$ is a complete minimal sufficient statistic for $\underline{\mu}$ (see Lehmann 1959). In addition, any nonsingular linear transformation of $P_M\underline{n}$ is a complete minimal sufficient statistic. For example, if $\{\underline{\mu}^{(j)}: j \in \overline{s}\}$ spans M, then $\{(\underline{\mu}^{(j)},\underline{n}): j \in \overline{s}\}$ is a complete minimal sufficient statistic.

The vector $\underline{n}$ has mean $\underline{m}(\underline{\mu})$ and covariance operator $D(\underline{\mu})$, where $D(\underline{\mu})\{x_i\} = \{m_i(\underline{\mu})x_i\}$ if $\underline{x} \in R^I$. Using the notation of Kruskal (1968b),

$$(1.29)\qquad \text{Cov}\ [(\underline{x},\underline{n}),(\underline{y},\underline{n})] = (\underline{x},D(\underline{\mu})\underline{y}) = \sum_{i\in I} x_i m_i(\underline{\mu}) y_i .$$

If $\{\underline{n}^{(N)}: N > 0\}$ is a sequence of random vectors from Poisson models with respective means $\{\underline{m}^{(N)}: N > 0\}$ and if $N^{-1}\underline{m}^{(N)} \to \underline{m}(\underline{\mu})$, then

$$(1.30)\qquad \frac{1}{N}\,\underline{n} \xrightarrow{P} \underline{m}(\underline{\mu})$$

and

$$(1.31)\qquad N^{-\frac{1}{2}}(\underline{n}^{(N)} - \underline{m}^{(N)}) \xrightarrow{\mathcal{D}} N(\underline{0}, D(\underline{\mu})).$$

In (1.30), the symbol $\xrightarrow{P}$ represents convergence in probability. In (1.31), $\xrightarrow{\mathcal{D}}$ represents convergence in distribution. Both results follow from Rao (1965). They are used in chapter 4.

Example 1.7. Suppose two independent Poisson random variables n_1 and n_2 are observed. If $M = \{\underline{\mu} \in R^2: \mu_1 = \mu_2\}$, then the vector $\underline{e} = \langle 1,1\rangle$ spans M. The inner product $(\underline{e},\underline{n}) = n_1 + n_2$, so $n_1 + n_2$ is a complete minimal sufficient statistic for $\underline{\mu} \in M$. The variance of $n_1 + n_2$ may be determined from (1.29). Thus

$$\text{Var}\,(n_1 + n_2) = \text{Cov}\,[(\underline{e},\underline{n}),(\underline{e},\underline{n})] = \sum_{i=1}^{2} m_i(\underline{\mu}). \tag{1.32}$$

Under the hypothesis $\underline{\mu} \in M$, $n_1 + n_2$ and $n_1 - n_2$ are uncorrelated, for

$$\text{Cov}\,[n_1+n_2,n_1-n_2] = \text{Cov}\,[(\langle 1,1\rangle,\underline{n}),(\langle 1,-1\rangle,\underline{n})] = m_1(\underline{\mu}) - m_2(\underline{\mu}) = 0. \tag{1.33}$$

Example 1.8. Table 1.1 may be an example of Poisson sampling. Suppose that the total number N of babies in the study is a Poisson random variable with mean M and there is a probability p_{ij} that a given baby is in group i and has sex j. The probability that the given table is observed is then

$$\begin{aligned} p(\underline{n}) &= p(N)\,p(\underline{n}|N) \\ &= \frac{e^{-M}M^N}{N!}\;\frac{N!}{\prod_{i=1}^{2}\prod_{j=1}^{2} n_{ij}!}\;\prod_{i=1}^{2}\prod_{j=1}^{2} p_{ij}^{\,n_{ij}} \\ &= \prod_{i=1}^{2}\prod_{j=1}^{2} \frac{e^{-Mp_{ij}}}{n_{ij}!}(Mp_{ij})^{n_{ij}} \\ &= \prod_{i=1}^{2}\prod_{j=1}^{2} \frac{e^{-m_{ij}}m_{ij}^{\,n_{ij}}}{n_{ij}!} \end{aligned} \tag{1.34}$$

Here $m_{ij} = Mp_{ij}$. The last two equalities are based on the observations that

$$\sum_{i=1}^{2}\sum_{j=1}^{2} p_{ij} = 1 \tag{1.35}$$

and

$$\sum_{i=1}^{2}\sum_{j=1}^{2} n_{ij} = N.$$

The last equality in (1.34) shows that the table $\underline{n}$ is derived from a Poisson model. The distribution of N would be Poisson if the study was made by examining births occurring in some fixed time interval $[t_1, t_2]$ if the probability of observing a birth between times t and $t + dt$, $t_1 \le t \le t + dt \le t_2$, depends only on dt (see Feller 1966).

Suppose M is the additive manifold considered in Example 1.2. Then $M = \text{span}\,\{\underline{\mu}^{(1)}, \underline{\mu}^{(2)}, \underline{\mu}^{(3)}\}$, where $\underline{\mu}^{(1)}$, $\underline{\mu}^{(2)}$, and $\underline{\mu}^{(3)}$ are respectively defined by (1.3), (1.4), and (1.5), and $\{(\underline{n},\underline{\mu}^{(1)}),(\underline{n},\underline{\mu}^{(2)}),(\underline{n},\underline{\mu}^{(3)})\}$ is a complete minimal sufficient statistic. If n_{i+}, n_{+j}, and n_{++} are defined in the same manner as m_{i+}, m_{+j}, and m_{++}, then

(1.37) $$(\underline{n},\underline{\mu}^{(1)}) = n_{++},$$

(1.38) $$(\underline{n},\underline{\mu}^{(2)}) = n_{1+} - n_{2+},$$

and

(1.39) $$(\underline{n},\underline{\mu}^{(3)}) = n_{+1} - n_{+2}.$$

An equivalent complete sufficient statistic is the set of marginal totals $\{n_{1+}, n_{2+}, n_{+1}, n_{+2}\}$.

THE MULTINOMIAL MODEL

In the multinomial model, the vector $\underline{n}$ consists of one or more independent multinomial random vectors $\{n_i : i \in I_k\}$ with mean $\{m_i : i \in I_k\}$. Thus $k \in \overline{r}$, $r \ge 1$, and the sets I_k, $k \in \overline{r}$, are disjoint and have union I. For each $k \in \overline{r}$, it is assumed that M is chosen so that

(1.40) $$\underline{\nu}^{(k)} = \{\chi_{I_k}(i) : i \in I\} \in M,$$

where χ_{I_k} is the characteristic function of I_k. This condition prevents unwanted restrictions on the possible values of $\underline{\mu}$. The range of $\underline{\mu}$ is not now equal to M; but as shown in this section, it does correspond to a linear manifold. This result is important in determination of complete minimal sufficient statistics, maximum-likelihood estimates, and asymptotic properties.

Example 1.9. The study considered in Example 1.8 could have been conducted in a number of different ways. One possibility would be to obtain a random sample of

$N = 10{,}000$ babies. In this case, $r = 1$ and $\underline{\nu}^{(1)} = \{1: \langle i,j\rangle \in \overline{2} \times \overline{2}\}$. If M is defined as in Example 1.8, then $\underline{\nu}^{(1)} \in M$. The study might also be conducted by selecting 2000 toxemia babies and 8000 controls and recording their sex. Now $r = 2$, $I_1 = \{\langle 1,1\rangle, \langle 1,2\rangle\}$ and $I_2 = \{\langle 2,1\rangle,\langle 2,2\rangle\}$. Thus

(1.41) $$\underline{\nu}^{(1)} = \begin{bmatrix} 1 & 1 \\ 0 & 0 \end{bmatrix}$$

and

(1.42) $$\underline{\nu}^{(2)} = \begin{bmatrix} 0 & 0 \\ 1 & 1 \end{bmatrix}$$

Both $\underline{\nu}^{(1)}$ and $\underline{\nu}^{(2)}$ are contained in M. A third way to conduct the study would be to sample 5000 male babies and 5000 female babies and determine whether toxemia is present. In this case, $r = 2$, $I_1 = \{\langle 1,1\rangle,\langle 2,1\rangle\}$, and $I_2 = \{\langle 1,2\rangle,\langle 2,2\rangle\}$. The indicator vectors $\underline{\nu}^{(1)}$ and $\underline{\nu}^{(2)}$ are both in M, where

(1.43) $$\underline{\nu}^{(1)} = \begin{bmatrix} 1 & 0 \\ 1 & 0 \end{bmatrix}$$

and

(1.44) $$\underline{\nu}^{(2)} = \begin{bmatrix} 0 & 1 \\ 0 & 1 \end{bmatrix}.$$

Complete sufficient statistics may be found by considering a direct sum decomposition of M into N and $M - N$, where N is the manifold generated by $\{\underline{\nu}^{(k)}: k \in \overline{r}\}$ and $M - N$ is the orthogonal complement of N relative to M (see Kruskal 1968). Suppose that the sample size for $\{n_i: i \in I_k\}$ is N_k. Since the expected value of $\Sigma_{i \in I_k} n_i$ is N_k, the vector $\underline{\mu} \in M$ must satisfy the equation

(1.45) $$(\underline{m}(\underline{\mu}),\underline{\nu}^{(k)}) = \sum_{i \in I_k} m_i(\underline{\mu}) = E(\sum_{i \in I_k} n_i) = N_k.$$

For $\underline{x}$ and $\underline{y}$ in R^I, define $\underline{x} \# \underline{y}$ by $\{x_i y_i\}$. Then

(1.46) $$\underline{m}(\underline{\mu}) = \underline{m}(P_N \underline{\mu}) \# \underline{m}(P_{M-N} \underline{\mu}).$$

For some $\{c_k: k \in \overline{r}\}$, (1.40) and the fact that each i is an element of exactly one I_k, where $k \in \overline{r}$, imply that

$$(1.47)\qquad P_N\underline{\mu} = \sum_{k=1}^{r} c_k\, \underline{\nu}^{(k)}$$

$$= \{\sum_{k=1}^{r} c_k\, \chi_{I_k}(i) : i \in I\}$$

$$= \{c_k : i \in I_k \text{ and } k \in \overline{r}\} .$$

Thus

$$(1.48)\qquad \underline{m}(P_N\underline{\mu}) = \{e^{c_k} : i \in I_k \text{ and } k \in \overline{r}\}$$

and

$$(1.49)\qquad (\underline{m}(\underline{\mu}),\underline{\nu}^{(k)}) = (\underline{m}(P_N\underline{\mu}) \# \underline{m}(P_{M-N}\underline{\mu}),\underline{\nu}^{(k)})$$

$$= \sum_{i\in I_k} m_i(P_N\underline{\mu})\, m_i(P_{M-N}\underline{\mu})$$

$$= \sum_{i\in I_k} e^{c_k}\, m_i(P_{M-N}\underline{\mu})$$

$$= e^{c_k}\, (\underline{m}(P_{M-N}\underline{\mu}),\underline{\nu}^{(k)}).$$

If $i \in I_k$, then $m_i(P_N\underline{\mu}) = e^{c_k}$ and (1.41) and (1.49) imply that

$$(1.50)\qquad m_i(P_N\underline{\mu}) = \frac{N_k}{(\underline{m}(P_{M-N}\underline{\mu}),\underline{\nu}^{(k)})} .$$

Thus $P_N\underline{\mu}$ is a function of $P_{M-N}\underline{\mu}$. Since $\underline{\mu}$ is $P_N\underline{\mu} + P_{M-N}\underline{\mu}$, $\underline{\mu}$ is a function of $P_{M-N}\underline{\mu}$. A complete minimal sufficient statistic for $P_{M-N}\underline{\mu}$ is consequently á complete minimal sufficient statistic for $\underline{\mu}$.

The log likelihood function is

$$(1.51)\qquad \ell^{(m)}(\underline{n},\underline{\mu}) = \sum_{k=1}^{r} \left\{ \sum_{i\in I_k} n_i \log \frac{m_i(\underline{\mu})}{(\underline{m}(\underline{\mu}),\underline{\nu}^{(k)})} + \log N_k! - \sum_{i\in I_k} \log n_i! \right\}$$

$$= \sum_{k=1}^{r} \left\{ \sum_{i\in I_k} n_i \log \frac{m_i(P_{M-N}\underline{\mu})}{(m(P_{M-N}\underline{\mu}),\underline{\nu}^{(k)})} + \log N_k! - \sum_{i\in I_k} \log n_i! \right\}$$

$$= (\underline{n},P_{M-N}\underline{\mu}) - \sum_{k=1}^{r} N_k \log (\underline{m}(P_{M-N}\underline{\mu}),\underline{\nu}^{(k)}) + \sum_{k=1} \log N_k! - \sum_{i\in I} \log n_i!$$

$$= (P_{M-N}\underline{n},P_{M-N}\underline{\mu}) - \sum_{k=1} N_k \log (\underline{m}(P_{M-N}\underline{\mu}),\underline{\nu}^{(k)}) + \sum_{k=1} \log N_k! - \sum_{i\in I} \text{lo}$$

If $p = \dim M > r$, then $M - N$ is isomorphic to R^{p-r}. The family of distributions such that $\underline{\mu} \in M$ and for each $k \in \overline{r}$, $(\underline{m}(\underline{\mu}),\underline{\nu}^{(k)}) = N_k$, is then an exponential family with $P_{M-N}\underline{n}$ as a complete minimal sufficient statistic for $P_{M-N}\underline{\mu}$. If $p = r$, then the family contains only one distribution. As in the Poisson model, alternate complete sufficient statistics may be obtained by use of nonsingular linear transformations. In particular, $P_M\underline{n}$ is a complete minimal sufficient statistic.

Example 1.10. In Example 1.6, multinomial sampling is present with $r = 3$ and $I_k = \{\langle k,1\rangle,\langle k,2\rangle\}$ for each $k \in \overline{3}$. If $\{\underline{\mu}^{(k)}: k \in \overline{5}\}$ is defined by (1.21)-(1.25), then $\underline{\nu}^{(k)} = \underline{\mu}^{(k)}$ for $k \in \overline{3}$. The vectors $\underline{\mu}^{(4)}$ and $\underline{\mu}^{(5)}$ are contained in M but are orthogonal to $N = \text{span}\,\{\underline{\mu}^{(k)}: k \in \overline{3}\}$. Thus $M - N = \text{span}\,\{\underline{\mu}^{(4)}, \underline{\mu}^{(5)}\}$, and $\{(\underline{n},\underline{\mu}^{(4)}),(\underline{n},\underline{\mu}^{(5)})\}$ is a complete minimal sufficient statistic for $\underline{\mu}$. Since

$$(1.52)\qquad (\underline{n},\underline{\mu}^{(4)}) = \sum_{i=1}^{3} (n_{i1} - n_{i2}) = \sum_{i=1}^{3} (2n_{i1} - 15) = 2n_{+1} - 45$$

and

$$(1.53)\qquad \begin{aligned}(\underline{n},\underline{\mu}^{(5)}) &= (n_{11} - n_{12}) - (n_{31} - n_{32})\\ &= (2n_{11} - 15) - (2n_{31} - 15)\\ &= 2(n_{11} - n_{31}),\end{aligned}$$

$\{n_{+1},n_{11} - n_{31}\}$ is also a complete minimal sufficient statistic.

The random vector $\underline{n}$ has mean $\underline{m}(\underline{\mu})$ and covariance operator $\ddagger(\underline{\mu})$, where

$$(1.54)\qquad \begin{aligned}\ddagger(\underline{\mu}) &= D(\underline{\mu}) - \sum_{k=1}^{r} \frac{1}{N_k} [D(\underline{\mu})\underline{\nu}^{(k)}] \bullet [D(\underline{\mu})\underline{\nu}^{(k)}]\\ &= D(\underline{\mu})[I - P_N^*(\underline{\mu})].\end{aligned}$$

In this equation, the symbol $\underline{x} \bullet \underline{y}$ denotes the outer product of $\underline{x} \in R^I$ and $\underline{y} \in R^I$. The outer product is the linear transformation on R^I defined by

$$(1.56)\qquad (\underline{x} \bullet \underline{y})(\underline{z}) = (\underline{y},\underline{z})\underline{x},$$

where $\underline{z} \in R^I$ (see Eaton 1970). The linear transformation $P_N^*(\underline{\mu})$ is the projection from R^I onto N which is orthogonal with respect to the inner product $((\cdot,\cdot))$, where if $\underline{x} \in R^I$ and $\underline{y} \in R^I$, then

$$((\underline{x},\underline{y})) = (\underline{x}, D(\underline{\mu})\underline{y}). \tag{1.56}$$

To show that the second equation is valid, it should be noted that N_k is $(\underline{\nu}^{(k)}, D(\underline{\mu})\underline{\nu}^{(k)})$ and $(\underline{\nu}^{(k)}, D(\underline{\mu})\underline{\nu}^{(j)}) = 0$ if $j \neq k$. Equality follows from Hoffman and Kunze (1961).

The first equation is an adaptation of a standard formula. This equation is easily verified if r is 1 and $\underline{\nu}^{(1)}$ is $\underline{e}$, where $\underline{e} = \{1 \colon i \in I\}$. If N is $(\underline{n},\underline{e})$, then

$$\Sigma(\underline{\mu}) = D(\underline{\mu}) - \frac{1}{N}\,\underline{m}(\underline{\mu}) \otimes \underline{m}(\underline{\mu}). \tag{1.57}$$

If $\underline{p} = N^{-1}\,\underline{m}(\underline{\mu})$ and $P = N^{-1}\,D(\underline{\mu})$, then

$$\Sigma(\underline{\mu}) = N(P - \underline{p} \otimes \underline{p}). \tag{1.58}$$

Thus the covariance matrix with respect to $\{\underline{\delta}^{(j)} \colon j \in I\}$ satisfies

$$[\Sigma(\underline{\mu})]_{ij} = N[\delta_{ij}\,p_i - p_i p_j]. \tag{1.59}$$

This equation may be found in Wilks (1962). It should be noted that

$$\Sigma(\underline{\mu})\underline{e} = D(\underline{\mu})\underline{e} - \frac{1}{N}\,[\underline{m}(\underline{\mu}) \otimes \underline{m}(\underline{\mu})]\underline{e} = \underline{m}(\underline{\mu}) - \underline{m}(\underline{\mu}) = \underline{0}. \tag{1.60}$$

In the chapter on asymptotic theory, two simple convergence results are employed. If $\{\underline{n}^{(N)} \colon N > 0\}$ is a sequence of multinomial models with constant partition $\{I_k \colon k \in \overline{r}\}$ and respective means $\{\underline{m}^{(N)} \colon N > 0\}$ such that $N^{-1}\underline{m}^{(N)} \longrightarrow \underline{m}(\underline{\mu})$, then

$$\frac{1}{N}\,\underline{n}^{(N)} \xrightarrow{P} \underline{m}(\underline{\mu}) \tag{1.61}$$

and

$$N^{-\frac{1}{2}}\,(\underline{n}^{(N)} - \underline{m}^{(N)}) \xrightarrow{\mathcal{D}} N(\underline{0},\, D(\underline{\mu})[I - P_N^{*}(\underline{\mu})]) \tag{1.62}$$

(see Rao 1965).

The multinomial and Poisson models are closely related. In fact, suppose $\underline{n}$ is a random vector with mean $\underline{m}$ such that $\underline{n}$ satisfies a Poisson model. Then the conditional distribution of $\underline{n}$ given $\{(\underline{n},\underline{\nu}^{(k)}) \colon k \in \overline{r}\}$ is the distribution of the multinomial model with partition $\{I_k \colon k \in \overline{r}\}$ and mean $\underline{m}^{*}$, where for each $i \in I_k$,

(1.63) $$m_i^* = \frac{(\underline{n},\underline{\nu}^{(k)})}{(\underline{m},\underline{\nu}^{(k)})} m_i .$$

Details may be found in Lehmann (1959) and Bishop (1967). Of particular interest is the fact that if $\underline{\mu}^*$ is $\log m_i^*$, then $\underline{\mu}^* \in M$ if and only if $\underline{\mu} \in M$.

Similarly, if the conditional distribution of $\underline{n}$ given $\{(\underline{n},\underline{\nu}^{(k)}): k \in \overline{r}\}$ is that of a multinomial model with partition $\{I_k: k \in \overline{r}\}$ and mean $\underline{m}^*$, where $\underline{m}^*$ satisfies (1.63), and each $(\underline{n},\underline{\nu}^{(k)})$ for $k \in \overline{r}$ is an independent Poisson random variable with mean $(\underline{m},\underline{\nu}^{(k)})$, then the unconditional distribution of $\underline{n}$ is that of a Poisson model with mean $\underline{m}$.

Example 1.11. Consider the 2 x 2 table of Example 1.8. The conditional distribution given N is multinomial and the unconditional distribution of $N = (\underline{n},\underline{e})$ is Poisson; hence, the unconditional distribution of $\underline{n}$ is Poisson. Suppose M is the additive manifold of Example 1.5. Since $m_i^* = (N/M)m_i$,

(1.64) $$\underline{\mu}^* = \underline{\mu} + [\log (N/M)]\underline{e},$$

where $\underline{e} = \{1\} \in M$. Thus $\underline{\mu}^* \in M$ is equivalent to $\underline{\mu} \in M$.

CONDITIONAL POISSON MODELS

Since a multinomial model may be derived from a Poisson model by conditioning, it is reasonable to consider more elaborate conditional distributions based on the Poisson model. In a conditional Poisson model, $\underline{n}$ is a vector of independent Poisson random variables such that $\underline{n}$ has mean $\underline{m}$, where $m_i > 0$ for every $i \in I$. Sampling is conditional on $P_N\underline{n} = \underline{c}$, where N is a linear manifold contained in M of dimension $r < q$. An alternative description of the sampling method may be obtained by considering a set $\{\underline{\nu}^{(k)}: k \in \overline{s}\}$ of vectors which span N. Sampling may be considered conditional on $\{(\underline{n},\underline{\nu}^{(k)}): k \in \overline{s}\} = \{b_k: k \in \overline{s}\}$, where for $k \in \overline{s}$,

(1.65) $$b_k = (\underline{c},\underline{\nu}^{(k)}) .$$

Sampling may also be regarded as conditional on $\underline{n} \in S(\underline{c})$, where

(1.66) $$S(\underline{c}) = \{\underline{n} \in Z^I: n_i \geq 0 \ \forall i \in I,\ P_N\underline{n} = \underline{c}\}.$$

Here Z is the set of integers and Z^I is the set of functions from I to Z. In order to ensure that conditional probabilities are meaningful, it is assumed that $S(\underline{c})$ is nonempty. If $\underline{e} \in N$, $S(\underline{c})$ is finite. In fact, if $\underline{n} \in S(\underline{c})$, then

(1.67) $$(\underline{n},\underline{e}) = \sum_{i \in I} n_i = (\underline{c},\underline{e}).$$

There exist only a finite number of $\underline{n}$ such that (1.67) holds, $n_i \geq 0$ for every $i \in I$, and n_i is an integer for every $i \in I$.

Conditional Poisson sampling may be derived from an actual sampling situation or it may be used for conditional inference. Both applications were considered by Fisher. In Fisher (1935a), an experiment is proposed to test the ability of a lady to determine by taste whether tea or milk was first added to a cup. In this experiment, eight cups are used, four with milk added first and four with tea added first. The lady is informed of the distribution but is not told which cups have tea added first. Thus the experiment leads to a two-way table in which row and column totals are fixed. If the lady cannot distinguish between the two types of cups, then the vector $\underline{\mu}$ lies in the additive manifold M, where $\underline{\mu} \in M$ satisfies (1.8). The relevant sampling distribution may be regarded as a conditional Poisson distribution, although Fisher himself does not make this argument. In Fisher (1935b), twin brothers of known criminals are examined. The twins are monozygotic or dizygotic and have been convicted or have never been convicted of a crime. Thus a 2×2 table is considered. Fisher performs the analysis conditional on the row and column totals, even though no such conditioning was used in the original sampling. This approach to inference is discussed also by Cochran (1952) and Cox (1958a).

The conditional distribution of $\underline{n}$ follows by elementary arguments. If $p(\underline{n},\underline{\mu},\underline{c})$ is the probability of $\underline{n}$ given $P_N\underline{n} = \underline{c}$, then since $[m_i(\underline{\mu})]^{n_i} = e^{n_i\mu_i}$,

(1.68) $$p(\underline{n},\underline{\mu},\underline{c}) = \frac{\prod_{i \in I} \left(\frac{[m_i(\underline{\mu})]^{n_i}}{n_i! e^{m_i(\underline{\mu})}} \right)}{\sum_{\underline{n}' \in S(\underline{c})} \left\{ \prod_{i \in I} \left(\frac{[m_i(\underline{\mu})]^{n_i'}}{n_i'! e^{m_i(\underline{\mu})}} \right) \right\}}$$

$$= \frac{(1/\prod_{i \in I} n_i!) \exp[(\underline{n},\underline{\mu})]}{\sum_{\underline{n}' \in S(\underline{c})} (1/\prod_{i \in I} n_i'!) \exp[(\underline{n}',\underline{\mu})]} .$$

If $\underline{n} \in S(\underline{c})$ and $\underline{\mu} \in M$, then

$$(\underline{n},\underline{\mu}) = (\underline{n},P_{M-N}\underline{\mu}) + (\underline{n},P_N\underline{\mu}) \tag{1.69}$$
$$= (P_{M-N}\underline{n},P_{M-N}\underline{\mu}) + (P_N\underline{n},\underline{\mu})$$
$$= (P_{M-N}\underline{n},P_{M-N}\underline{\mu}) + (\underline{c},\underline{\mu}).$$

It therefore follows that

$$p(\underline{n},\underline{\mu},\underline{c}) = \frac{(1/\prod_{i\in I} n_i!)\exp[(P_{M-N}\underline{n},P_{M-N}\underline{\mu})]}{\sum_{\underline{n}'\in S(\underline{c})}(1/\prod_{i\in I} n_i!)\exp[(P_{M-N}\underline{n}',P_{M-N}\underline{\mu})]} \tag{1.70}$$

The log likelihood $\ell^{(c)}(\underline{n},\underline{\mu},\underline{c})$ is $\log p(\underline{n},\underline{\mu},\underline{c})$. If $r = p$, then only one distinct distribution exists for $\underline{\mu} \in M$. If $r < p$, then the family of distributions is an exponential family such that $P_{M-N}\underline{n}$ is a complete minimal sufficient statistic for $P_{M-N}\underline{\mu}$. Since $P_N\underline{n}$ is constant, $P_N\underline{n}$ is also a complete minimal sufficient statistic.

Example 1.12. In the Fisher example of the lady tasting tea, $I = \overline{2} \times \overline{2}$ and $n_{1+} = n_{2+} = n_{+1} = n_{+2} = 4$. This condition is equivalent to $(\underline{n},\underline{\mu}^{(k)}) = 4$ for $k \in \overline{4}$, where

$$\underline{\nu}^{(1)} = \begin{array}{|cc|}\hline 1 & 1 \\ 0 & 0 \\ \hline\end{array}, \tag{1.71}$$

$$\underline{\nu}^{(2)} = \begin{array}{|cc|}\hline 0 & 0 \\ 1 & 1 \\ \hline\end{array}, \tag{1.72}$$

$$\underline{\nu}^{(3)} = \begin{array}{|cc|}\hline 1 & 0 \\ 1 & 0 \\ \hline\end{array}, \tag{1.73}$$

$$\underline{\nu}^{(4)} \quad \begin{array}{|cc|}\hline 0 & 1 \\ 0 & 1 \\ \hline\end{array} \tag{1.74}$$

If M is the additive manifold for the 2×2 table, then $M = N = \text{span}\,\{\underline{\nu}^{(k)}: k \in \overline{4}\}$. Thus the conditions of the conditional Poisson model are satisfied.

The vector $\underline{c} = 2\underline{e}$ and $S(2\underline{e})$ is $\{2\underline{e} + (j-2)\,\underline{\mu}^{(4)}: j \in \overline{4}\}$, where $\underline{\mu}^{(4)}$ satisfies (1.7). If $M = N$, then $p(\underline{n},\underline{\mu},\underline{c})$ is independent of $\underline{\mu}$ and N_{11} has a hypergeometric distribution. If $M = R^I$, then $(\underline{n},\underline{\mu}^{(4)}) = n_{11} - n_{12} - n_{21} + n_{22}$ is a complete sufficient statistic. Given the restraints on $\underline{n}$, n_{11} determines $\underline{n}$. Thus n_{11} is also a complete sufficient statistic.

Example 1.13. When a classified variable is randomly sampled without replacement from a finite population, the resulting distribution of sample frequencies is related to the conditional Poisson distribution. In this example, a population of size N and a sample of size n exist such that N_j members of the population and n_{j1} members of the sample belong to class $j \in J$. If n_{j2} is the number of members of class $j \in J$ that are in the population but not in the sample, then $n_{j2} = N_j - n_{j1}$. If $I = J \times \overline{2}$ and $\underline{n} = \{n_{jk}: \langle j,k\rangle \in J \times \overline{2}\}$, then the probability of a particular value of $\underline{n}$ is

$$(1.75)\qquad \binom{N}{n}^{-1} \prod_{j\in J} \binom{N_j}{n_{j1}} = \frac{\prod_{j\in J} \prod_{k=1}^{2} \frac{1}{n_{jk}!}}{\sum_{\underline{n}'\in S} \prod_{j\in J} \prod_{k=1}^{2} \frac{1}{n'_{jk}!}}$$

where

$$(1.76)\qquad S = \{\underline{n} \in Z^{J\times\overline{2}}: n_{j1} + n_{j2} = N_j, \sum_{j\in J} n_{j1} = n, n_{jk} \geq 0 \ \forall \langle j,k\rangle \in J \times \overline{2}\}$$

(see Wilks 1962). Since the elements of S satisfy linear constraints, $\underline{n}$ is distributed as a conditional Poisson random variable such that $\underline{\mu} \in N$, where

$$(1.77)\qquad N = \text{span}\,[\{\underline{\nu}^{(j)}: j \in J\} \cup \{\underline{\lambda}\}]\ ,$$

$$(1.78)\qquad \underline{\nu}^{(j)} = \{\delta_{jj'}: \langle j',k\rangle \in J \times \overline{2}\},\ j \in J,$$

and

$$(1.79)\qquad \underline{\lambda} = \{\delta_{1k}: \langle j,k\rangle \in J \times \overline{2}\}.$$

Since n_{j1} determines n_{j2}, if $\underline{n}^* = \{n_{j1}: j \in J\}$, then

$$(1.80)\qquad P\{n_j^* = k_j \ \forall j \in J\} = \binom{N}{n}^{-1} \prod_{j\in J} \binom{N_j}{k_j}.$$

If $J = \overline{2}$, n_1^* determines n_2^* and the distribution of n_1^* is hypergeometric.

The parameter $P_N\underline{\mu}$ cannot be estimated from the data unless $P_N\underline{m}$ is known. In this case, estimation of $P_N\underline{\mu}$ is possible by use of the methods of chapters 2 and 3. It is shown in chapter 2 that if $P_N\underline{m}$ is known, then $P_N\underline{\mu}$ is a well-defined function of $P_{M-N}\underline{\mu}$.

In general, the conditional mean and conditional covariance operator of $\underline{n}$ cannot be expressed in a convenient manner. One can only state that the conditional mean is

$$\underline{m}(\underline{c}) = \sum_{\underline{n}\in S(\underline{c})} \underline{n}\, p(\underline{n},\underline{\mu},\underline{c}) \tag{1.81}$$

$$= \sum_{\underline{n}\in S(\underline{c})} (\underline{c} + Q_M \underline{n})\, p(\underline{n},\underline{\mu},\underline{c})$$

$$= \underline{c} + \sum_{\underline{n}\in S(\underline{c})} (Q_M \underline{n})\, p(\underline{n},\underline{\mu},\underline{c})$$

$$= \underline{c} + Q_M\, \underline{m}(\underline{c}) ,$$

where $Q_M = I - P_M$. The covariance operator is then

$$\ddagger(\underline{c}) = \sum_{\underline{n}\in S(\underline{c})} \{[\underline{n} - \underline{m}(\underline{c})] \bullet [\underline{n} - \underline{m}(\underline{c})]\}\, p(\underline{n},\underline{\mu},\underline{c}) \tag{1.82}$$

$$= \sum_{\underline{n}\in S(\underline{c})} [Q_M\, \underline{n} - Q_M\, \underline{m}(\underline{c})] \bullet [Q_M\, \underline{n} - Q_M\, \underline{m}(\underline{c})]\;\; p(\underline{n},\underline{\mu},\underline{c}).$$

Asymptotic properties of the conditional Poisson model are comparable to those of the Poisson and multinomial models; however, derivations are far more complicated in the conditional Poisson case. The following theorem may be proven:

THEOREM 1.1. *Suppose that* N *has a basis* $\{\underline{\nu}^{(k)}: k \in \overline{s}\}$ *such that if* $k \in \overline{s}$ *and* $i \in I$, $\nu_i^{(k)}$ *is an integer. Suppose* $\{\underline{n}^{(N)}: N > 0\}$ *is a sequence of vectors such that the elements are independent Poisson variables. For each* $N > 0$, *suppose that* $\underline{n}^{(N)}$ *has mean* $\underline{m}^{(N)}$, *where* $N^{-1}\, \underline{m}^{(N)} \longrightarrow \underline{m}(\underline{\mu})$ *and for* $N > 0$, $S(P_N \underline{m}^{(N)})$ *is not empty. Then the distribution of* $N^{-\frac{1}{2}}\, (\underline{n}^{(N)} - \underline{m}^{(N)})$ *given* $P_N \underline{n}^{(N)} = P_N \underline{m}^{(N)}$ *converges to* $N(\underline{0},D(\underline{\mu})[I - P_N^{*}(\underline{\mu})])$, *and under this sequence of conditions,*

$$\frac{1}{N}\, \underline{n}^{(N)} \xrightarrow{P} \underline{m}(\underline{\mu}). \tag{1.83}$$

Remark. The distribution $N(\underline{0},D(\underline{\mu})[I - P_N^{*}(\underline{\mu})])$ is the conditional distribution of a normal random vector $\underline{x}$ with mean $\underline{0}$ and covariance operator $D(\underline{\mu})$ given the condition $P_N \underline{x} = \underline{0}$.

Proof. The first step in the proof is selection of a basis $\{\underline{\nu}^{(k)}: k \in \overline{q}\}$ for R^I such that $\{\underline{\nu}^{(k)}: k \in \overline{q} - \overline{r}\}$ is a basis for $N^{\perp}$ and for each $i \in I$ and $k \in \overline{q}$, $\nu_i^{(k)}$ is an integer.

To find such a basis, consider the vector space F^I defined over the field F of rationals. Here F^I is the set of functions from I to F. This space is q-dimensional. It includes the r-dimensional manifold R, where

(1.84) $$R = \{\sum_{k=1}^{r} f_k \underline{\nu}^{(k)}: f_k \in F \ \forall k \in \overline{r}\}.$$

A $(q - r)$-dimensional manifold S exists such that

(1.85) $$S = \{\underline{\mu} \in F^I: (\underline{\mu}, \underline{\nu}^{(k)}) = 0 \ \forall k \in \overline{r}\}.$$

Suppose that $\{\underline{\xi}^{(k)}: k \in \overline{q} - \overline{r}\} \subset S$ and

(1.86) $$S = \{\sum_{k=r+1}^{q} f_k \underline{\xi}^{(k)}: f_k \in F \ \forall k \in \overline{q} - \overline{r}\}.$$

Then the set $\{\underline{\xi}^{(k)}: k \in \overline{q} - \overline{r}\}$ is independent relative to the vector space R^I defined over R. In fact, if for some $\{c_k: k \in \overline{q} - \overline{r}\} \in R^{\overline{q}-\overline{r}}$,

(1.87) $$\sum_{k=r+1}^{q} c_k \underline{\xi}^{(k)} = 0$$

and $c_k \neq 0$ for any $k \in \overline{q} - \overline{r}$, then

(1.88) $$\{\underline{\mu} \in F^I: (\underline{\mu}, \underline{\nu}^{(k)}) = 0 \ \forall k \in \overline{r} \text{ and } (\underline{\mu}, \underline{\xi}^{(k)}) = 0 \ \forall k \in \overline{q} - \overline{r}\}$$

$$= \{\underline{\mu} \in F^I: (\underline{\mu}, \underline{\nu}^{(k)}) = 0 \ \forall k \in \overline{r} \text{ and } (\underline{\mu}, \underline{\xi}^{(k)}) = 0 \ \forall k \in \overline{q - 1} - \overline{r}\}.$$

Since the right-hand side of (1.88) includes all elements of F^I orthogonal to $q - 1$ vectors, this set is nonempty, orthogonal to S, and contained in S. Since this combination of conditions is impossible, $\{\underline{\xi}^{(k)}: k \in \overline{r}\}$ is an independent set of vectors in $N^{\perp}$. Thus $N^{\perp} = \text{span}\,\{\underline{\xi}^{(k)}: k \in \overline{r}\}$. Suppose r_k is an integer such that $r_k \xi_i^{(k)}$ is a positive integer for every $i \in I$. Then it is sufficient to set $\underline{\nu}^{(k)} = r_k \underline{\xi}^{(k)}$ for $k \in \overline{q} - \overline{r}$ in order to obtain the desired basis.

Given the basis $\{\underline{\nu}^{(k)}: k \in \overline{q}\}$, a useful partition of $N^{\perp}$ is available. Suppose that $Z^{\overline{q}-\overline{r}}$ is the set of functions from $\overline{q} - \overline{r}$ to Z, the set of integers. If $\underline{z} \in Z^{\overline{q}-\overline{r}}$, let

(1.89) $$A(\underline{z}) = \{\underline{x} \in R^I: \underline{x} = \sum_{k=r+1}^{q} b_k \underline{\nu}^{(k)} \text{ and}$$

$$\forall k \in \overline{q} - \overline{r},\ b_k \in [z_k - \tfrac{1}{2}, z_k + \tfrac{1}{2})\}.$$

If $\underline{z} \neq \underline{z}'$, $A(\underline{z})$ and $A(\underline{z}')$ are disjoint. In addition,

(1.90) $$N^{\perp} = \cup \{A(\underline{z}): \underline{z} \in Z^{\overline{q}-\overline{r}}\}.$$

This formula states that $N^{\perp}$ is the union of all $A(\underline{z})$ such that $\underline{z} \in Z^{\overline{q}-\overline{r}}$. Thus $\{A(\underline{z}): \underline{z} \in Z^{\overline{q}-\overline{r}}\}$ is a partition of $N^{\perp}$. This partition is particularly useful because if $\mu_{N^{\perp}}$ is Lebesgue measure over $N^{\perp}$, then $\mu_{N^{\perp}}(A(\underline{z}))$ is independent of $\underline{z}$.

A second feature of this partition is that the number $k(\underline{z})$ of elements of Z^I contained in $A(\underline{z})$ is constant for $\underline{z} \in Z^{\overline{q}-\overline{r}}$. In fact, suppose that

(1.91) $$C(\underline{z}) = \{\overline{\underline{z}} \in Z^I: \overline{\underline{z}} \in A(\underline{z})\}.$$

Let $\overline{\underline{z}}^{(j)} = \sum_{k=r+1}^{q} z_k^{(j)}\underline{v}^{(k)}$, where $j \in \overline{2}$ and $\underline{z}^{(j)} \in Z^{\overline{q}-\overline{r}}$ for each j. If $\overline{\underline{z}} \in C(\underline{z}^{(1)})$, then $\overline{\underline{z}} + \overline{\underline{z}}^{(2)} - \overline{\underline{z}}^{(1)} \in C(\underline{z}^{(2)})$. Therefore, $k(\underline{z}^{(1)}) \leq k(\underline{z}^{(2)})$. By symmetry, $k(\underline{z}^{(1)}) = k(\underline{z}^{(2)})$. Thus $k(\underline{z})$ equals some constant k for all $\underline{z} \in Z^{\overline{q}-\overline{r}}$. Since $\overline{\underline{z}}^{(1)} \in C(\underline{z}^{(1)})$, it follows that k is positive.

To prove that $N^{-\frac{1}{2}}(\underline{n}^{(N)} - \underline{m}^{(N)})$ has the desired conditional asymptotic distribution, it is sufficient to show that given the condition $P_N\underline{n}^{(N)} = P_N\underline{m}^{(N)}$, $(\underline{c}, N^{-\frac{1}{2}}(\underline{n}^{(N)} - \underline{m}^{(N)}))$ converges in distribution to $N(0,(\underline{c},D(\underline{\mu})[I - P_N^*(\underline{\mu})]\underline{c}))$, where $\underline{c}$ is an arbitrary vector in R^I. It follows from Curtiss (1942) that it is only necessary to show that the moment generating function $\phi^{(N)}(s)$ converges to $\phi(s)$ for s in a neighborhood of 0, where

(1.92) $$\phi^{(N)}(s) = E\{\exp[s(\underline{c},N^{-\frac{1}{2}}(\underline{n}^{(N)} - \underline{m}^{(N)}))]|P_N\underline{n}^{(N)} = P_N\underline{m}^{(N)}\}$$

and

(1.93) $$\phi(s) = E\exp(sX),$$

where $X \sim N(0,(\underline{c},D(\underline{\mu})[I - P_N^*(\underline{\mu})]\underline{c}))$. Since $\underline{c}$ is arbitrary and $s\underline{c} \in R^I$, it is sufficient to show that

(1.94) $$E^{(N)} = E\{\exp[(\underline{c},N^{-\frac{1}{2}}(\underline{n}^{(N)} - \underline{m}^{(N)}))]|P_N\underline{n}^{(N)} = P_N\underline{m}^{(N)}\} \to E\exp(X).$$

To prove (1.94), $E^{(N)}$ is expressed as a quotient $B^{(N)}(\underline{c})/B^{(N)}(\underline{0})$, where

(1.95) $$B^{(N)}(\underline{c}) = N^{r/2}\sum_{\underline{y}\in S^{(N)}} f^{(N)}(\underline{y})\exp[N^{-\frac{1}{2}}(\underline{c},\underline{y} - \underline{m}^{(N)})].$$

In (1.95), $S^{(N)} = S(P_N \underline{m}^{(N)})$, the set of possible values of $\underline{n}^{(N)}$, and $f^{(N)}(\underline{y})$, the probability that the unconditional random vector $\underline{n}^{(N)} = \underline{y}$, satisfies

$$(1.96) \qquad f^{(N)}(\underline{y}) = \prod_{i \in I} [m_i^{(N)}]^{y_i} \exp(-m_i^{(N)})/y_i!$$

for $\underline{y} \in Z^I$ such that $y_i \geq 0$ for each $i \in I$. If for each $\underline{c} \in R^I$, $B^{(N)}(\underline{c}) \to B(\underline{c})$, where

$$(1.97) \qquad B(\underline{c}) = a \int_{N^{\perp}} \exp[(\underline{c},\underline{x})]\exp[-(\underline{x},D^{-1}(\underline{\mu})\underline{x})/2]d\mu_{N^{\perp}}(\underline{x})$$

and a is a constant independent of $\underline{c}$, then $E^{(N)} \to E\exp\{X\}$, where $X \sim N(0,(\underline{c},D(\underline{\mu})[I - P_N^*(\underline{\mu})]\underline{c}))$. Thus it suffices to prove that $B^{(N)}(\underline{c}) \to B(\underline{c})$ for an arbitrary $\underline{c}$.

The proof that $B^{(N)}(\underline{c}) \to B(\underline{c})$ is quite involved. The first part of the proof involves expression of $B^{(N)}(\underline{c})$ as a Lebesgue integral $b \int_{N^{\perp}} h^{(N)}(\underline{x})d\mu_{N^{\perp}}(\underline{x})$. Given this integral, it is then necessary to show that $h^{(N)}(\underline{x})$ converges to $(a/b)\exp[(\underline{c},\underline{x})]\exp[-(\underline{x},D^{-1}(\underline{\mu})\underline{x})/2]$. To prove that $B^{(N)}(\underline{c}) \to B(\underline{c})$, an integrable function $h(\underline{x})$ is found such that for some $N(\underline{c})$, if $N > N(\underline{c})$, $h^{(N)}(\underline{x}) \leq h(\underline{x})$ for all $\underline{x} \in N^{\perp}$. By the dominated convergence theorem, $B^{(N)}(\underline{c})$ then converges to $B(\underline{c})$.

To define $h^{(N)}(\underline{x})$, it is necessary to select an element $\underline{y}^{(N)}$ of Z^I such that $\underline{y}^{(N)} - \underline{m}^{(N)} \in A(\underline{0})$. Such a selection is possible since $S^{(N)}$, which is nonempty, must contain some element $\overline{\underline{y}}^{(N)}$. Since $P_N\overline{\underline{y}}^{(N)} = P_N\underline{m}^{(N)}$, $\overline{\underline{y}}^{(N)} - \underline{m}^{(N)} \in N^{\perp}$. By (1.90), there exists $\underline{z}^{(N)} \in Z^{\overline{q}-\overline{r}}$ such that $\overline{\underline{y}}^{(N)} - \underline{m}^{(N)} \in A(\underline{z}^{(N)})$. If $\underline{y}^{(N)} = \overline{\underline{y}}^{(N)} - \sum_{k=r+1}^{q} z_k^{(N)}\underline{\nu}^{(k)}$, then $\underline{y}^{(N)} - \underline{m}^{(N)} \in A(\underline{0})$.

Given $\overline{\underline{y}}^{(N)}$, $h^{(N)}(\underline{x})$ may be defined for each $\underline{x} \in N^{\perp}$. If $Z^{(N)}(\underline{x})$ is the unique element of $Z^{\overline{q}-\overline{r}}$ such that $N^{\frac{1}{2}}\underline{x} \in A(\underline{z}^{(N)}(\underline{x}))$ and

$$(1.98) \qquad H^{(N)}(\underline{x}) = S^{(N)} \cap [C(\underline{z}^{(N)}(\underline{x})) + \underline{y}^{(N)}]$$

$$= \{\underline{y} \in Z^I: P_N\underline{y} = P_N\underline{m}^{(N)}, \underline{y} - \underline{y}^{(N)} \in A(\underline{z}^{(N)}(\underline{x}))\},$$

then $h^{(N)}(\underline{x})$ may be defined as

$$(1.99) \qquad h^{(N)}(\underline{x}) = N^{q/2}\,\Sigma\{f^{(N)}(\underline{y})\exp[(\underline{c},\underline{y} - m^{(N)})/N^{\frac{1}{2}}]: \underline{y} \in H^{(N)}(\underline{x})\},$$

where the right-hand side is the sum of all terms $f^{(N)}(\underline{y})\exp[(\underline{c},\underline{y} - \underline{m}^{(N)})/N^{\frac{1}{2}}]$ such that $\underline{y} \in H^{(N)}(\underline{x})$.

The function $h^{(N)}(\underline{x})$ is constant over subsets $T^{(N)}(\underline{z})$ of $N^{\perp}$, where $\underline{z} \in Z^{\overline{q}-\overline{r}}$ and

(1.100) $$T^{(N)}(\underline{z}) = \{\underline{x} \in N^{\perp}: N^{\frac{1}{2}}\underline{x} \in A(\underline{z})\}.$$

Since $\mu_{N^{\perp}}(T^{(N)}(\underline{z})) = \mu_{N^{\perp}}(A(\underline{0}))/N^{(q-r)/2}$ for each $\underline{z} \in Z^{\overline{q-r}}$,

(1.101) $$B^{(N)}(c) = N^{r/2} \sum_{\underline{z}\in Z^{\overline{q-r}}} \sum\{f^{(N)}(\underline{y})\exp[(\underline{c},\underline{y} - \underline{m}^{(N)})/N^{\frac{1}{2}}]: \underline{y} - \underline{y}^{(N)} \in A(\underline{z}), \underline{y} \in S^{(N)}\}$$

$$= N^{r/2} \sum_{\underline{z}\in Z^{\overline{q-r}}} h^{(N)}(\underline{x}^{(N)}(\underline{z}))\mu_{N^{\perp}}(A(\underline{0}))/N^{q/2}$$

$$= N^{(r-q)/2} \sum_{\underline{z}\in Z^{\overline{q-r}}} \int_{T^{(N)}(\underline{z})} h^{(N)}(\underline{x})d\mu_{N^{\perp}}(\underline{x})/\mu_{N^{\perp}}(T^{(N)}(\underline{z}))$$

$$= \int_{N^{\perp}} h^{(N)}(\underline{x})d\mu_{N^{\perp}}(\underline{x})/\mu_{N^{\perp}}(A(\underline{0}))$$

where $\underline{x}^{(N)}(\underline{z})$ is an arbitrary element of $T^{(N)}(\underline{z})$. Thus $b = 1/\mu_{N^{\perp}}(A(\underline{0}))$.

The limiting behavior of the integrand $h^{(N)}(\underline{x})$ must now be considered for a fixed $\underline{x} \in N^{\perp}$. Since $\underline{y}^{(N)}/N \to \underline{m}(\underline{\mu})$, $y_i \geq 0$ for each $i \in I$ and for each $\underline{y} \in C(\underline{z}^{(N)}(\underline{x})) + \underline{y}^{(N)}$, provided that N is sufficiently large. Thus for N sufficiently large, $H^{(N)}(\underline{x}) = C(\underline{z}^{(N)}(\underline{x})) + \underline{y}^{(N)}$, a set which contains k elements. It follows from the version of Stirling's formula given by Cramer (1946) that

(1.102) $$h^{(N)}(\underline{x}) = \sum_{\underline{y}\in H^{(N)}(\underline{x})} \exp[(\underline{c},\underline{y} - \underline{m}^{(N)})/N^{\frac{1}{2}}]$$

$$\times \prod_{i\in I} N^{\frac{1}{2}}\exp[-m_i^{(N)} + y_i\log m_i^{(N)} - (y_i + \tfrac{1}{2})\log(y_i+1)$$

$$+ (y_i+1) - \tfrac{1}{2}\log 2\pi - \Theta(y_i+1)],$$

where $0 < \Theta(y_i+1) < 1/[12(y_i+1)]$. By Taylor's theorem,

(1.103) $$- m_i^{(N)} + y_i\log m_i^{(N)} - (y_i + \tfrac{1}{2})\log(y_i + 1) + (y_i + 1)$$

$$= y_i + 1 - m_i^{(N)} + (y_i + 1)\log[m_i^{(N)}/(y_i + 1)] + \tfrac{1}{2}\log(y_i + 1) - \log m_i^{(N)}$$

$$= \tfrac{1}{2}\log(y_i + 1) - \log m_i^{(N)} - \tfrac{1}{2}[(y_i + 1 - m_i^{(N)})^2/(y_i + 1)]\,\Theta_1(y_i,m_i^{(N)}),$$

where $\Theta_1(y_i,m_i^{(N)})$ is between 1 and $(y_i + 1)/m_i^{(N)}$. Thus

(1.104) $$h^{(N)}(\underline{x}) = \sum_{\underline{y}\in H^{(N)}(\underline{x})} \exp[(\underline{c},\underline{y} - \underline{m}^{(N)})/N^{\frac{1}{2}}]\prod_{i\in I}\left[\frac{y_i N}{2\pi(m_i^{(N)})^2}\right]^{\frac{1}{2}}$$

$$\times \exp[-\tfrac{1}{2}\Theta_1(y_i,m_i^{(N)})(y_i + 1 - m_i^{(N)})^2/(y_i + 1) - \Theta(y_i + 1)].$$

For all $\underline{x} \in N^{\perp}$ and $N > 0$,

(1.105) $$\sup_{\underline{y}\in H^{(N)}(\underline{x})} \sup_{i\in I}|y_i - m_i^{(N)} - N^{\frac{1}{2}} x_i| < w,$$

where w is a constant independent of $\underline{x}$ and N. It follows from (1.102), (1.104), and (1.105) that

(1.106) $$h^{(N)}(\underline{x}) \to k \exp[(\underline{c},\underline{x})]\exp[-(\underline{x},D^{-1}(\underline{\mu})\underline{x})/2]/\prod_{i\in I}[2\pi m_i(\underline{\mu})]^{\frac{1}{2}} .$$

Thus $a/b = k/\prod_{i\in I}[2\pi m_i(\underline{\mu})]^{\frac{1}{2}}$.

To complete the proof, an integrable function $h(\underline{x})$ is required such that $h^{(N)}(\underline{x}) \le h(\underline{x})$ for N greater than some integer $N(\underline{c})$ and all $\underline{x} \in N^{\perp}$. Given any real $z > 0$, $N(\underline{c})$ may be selected so that for some d

(1.107) $$h^{(N)}(\underline{x}) < d \exp[(\underline{c},\underline{x})] \prod_{i\in I}\left(\frac{1 + 2x_i^{+}}{2\pi m_i^{*}}\right)^{\frac{1}{2}} \exp[- x_i^2/2(1 + zx_i^{+})m_i^{*}],$$

where $m_i^{*} = \inf_{N>0} m_i^{(N)}/N > 0$ and $x_i^{+} = \max(0,x_i)$. This result follows from (1.104), (1.105), and the definitions of $\Theta(y_i + 1)$ and $\Theta_1(y_i,m_i^{(N)})$. If $1/z > \max_{i\in I} c_i$, where $\underline{c} = \{c_i\}$, then the right-hand side is integrable, for if x_i is sufficiently large,

(1.108) $$\exp(c_i x_i)\exp[-x_i^2/(1 + zx_i)] < 2 \exp[(c_i - 1/z)x_i].$$

Thus $h(\underline{x})$ may be selected as the right-hand side of (1.107).

COROLLARY 1.1. *Under the conditions of Theorem 1.1,*

(1.109) $$\frac{1}{N} E(\underline{n}^{(N)}|P_N\underline{n}^{(N)} = P_N\underline{m}^{(N)}) \to \underline{m}(\underline{\mu})$$

and

(1.110) $$\frac{1}{N} \mathrm{Cov}(\underline{n}^{(N)}|P_N\underline{n}^{(N)} = P_N\underline{m}^{(N)}) \to D(\underline{\mu})[I - P_N^{*}(\underline{\mu})].$$

Proof. Since (1.94) holds for any $\underline{c}$, the conditional moments of $(\underline{c}, N^{-\frac{1}{2}}(\underline{n}^{(N)} - \underline{m}^{(N)}))$ given $P_N\underline{n}^{(N)} = P_N\underline{m}^{(N)}$ converge to the moments of $(\underline{c},\underline{X})$, where $\underline{X} \sim N(\underline{0},D(\underline{\mu})[I - P_N^*(\underline{\mu})])$ (see Curtiss 1942). Consequently, (1.109) and (1.110) follow.‖

Example 1.14. Consider the 2 x 2 table with rows and columns fixed. To find $I - P_N^*(\underline{\mu})$, observe that $P_N^*(\underline{\mu})$ has rank 3 and $R^{\overline{2}\times\overline{2}}$ has dimension 4. Thus $I - P_N^*(\underline{\mu})$ is a rank 1 projection. For some $\underline{\lambda} \in R^{\overline{2}\times\overline{2}}$,

$$I - P_N^*(\underline{\mu}) = \underline{\lambda} \otimes D(\underline{\mu})\underline{\lambda}/(\underline{\lambda},D(\underline{\mu})\underline{\lambda}), \tag{1.111}$$

where $D(\mu)\underline{\lambda}$ is orthogonal to N. Now the orthogonal complement of N is span $\{\underline{\mu}^{(4)}\}$, where $\underline{\mu}^{(4)}$ satisfies (1.7). Thus one may let

$$\underline{\lambda} = \boxed{\begin{matrix} 1/m_{11} & -1/m_{12} \\ -1/m_{21} & 1/m_{22} \end{matrix}}\ . \tag{1.112}$$

Then

$$(\underline{\lambda},D(\underline{\mu})\underline{\lambda}) = \sum_{i=1}^{2} \sum_{j=1}^{2} 1/m_{ij}. \tag{1.113}$$

The asymptotic covariance operator thus satisfies

$$\begin{aligned} D(\underline{\mu})[I - P_N^*(\underline{\mu})] &= [D(\underline{\mu})\underline{\lambda}] \otimes [D(\underline{\mu})\underline{\lambda}]/(\underline{\lambda},D(\underline{\mu})\underline{\lambda}) \\ &= \underline{\mu}^{(4)} \otimes \underline{\mu}^{(4)}/ \sum_{i=1}^{2} \sum_{j=1}^{2} \frac{1}{m_{ij}}\ . \end{aligned} \tag{1.114}$$

In this formula, it should be noted that $D(\underline{\mu})\underline{\lambda} = \underline{\mu}^{(4)}$. If the asymptotic variance associated with n_{11} is desired, it is only necessary to observe that $n_{11} = (\underline{n},\underline{\delta})$, where

$$\underline{\delta} = \boxed{\begin{matrix} 1 & 0 \\ 0 & 0 \end{matrix}}\ . \tag{1.115}$$

The asymptotic variance then satisfies

$$\begin{aligned} (\underline{\delta},D(\underline{\mu})[I - P_N^*(\underline{\mu})]\underline{\delta}) &= (\underline{\delta},\underline{\mu}^{(4)})^2/ \sum_{i=1}^{2} \sum_{j=1}^{2} \frac{1}{m_{ij}} \\ &= 1/ \sum_{i=1}^{2} \sum_{j=1}^{2} \frac{1}{m_{ij}}\ . \end{aligned} \tag{1.116}$$

Thus $(n_{11} - m_{11})(1/m_{11} + 1/m_{12} + 1/m_{21} + 1/m_{22})^{\frac{1}{2}}$ has an asymptotically normal distribution with mean 0 and variance 1.

If $\underline{\mu} \in M$, the additive manifold, then

$$\sum_{i=1}^{2}\sum_{j=1}^{2}\frac{1}{m_{ij}} = \sum_{i=1}^{2}\sum_{j=1}^{2}\frac{m_{++}}{m_{i+}m_{+j}} = \sum_{i=1}^{2}\frac{m_{++}}{m_{i+}}\left(\frac{m_{++}}{m_{+1}m_{+2}}\right) = \frac{m_{++}^{3}}{m_{1+}m_{2+}m_{+1}m_{+2}} . \tag{1.117}$$

Now $p_{i+} = m_{i+}/m_{++}$ is the probability that a randomly selected element of the table comes from row i, and $p_{+j} = m_{+j}/m_{++}$ is the probability that a randomly selected element comes from column j. Since $m_{i+} = n_{i+}$ and $m_{+j} = n_{+j}$, p_{i+} and p_{+j} are known quantities. In addition, $m_{++} = n_{++}$ is known from the sampling method used. Thus the asymptotic variance is $n_{++}p_{1+}p_{+2}p_{+1}p_{+2}$. The exact variance is $n_{++}^{2}p_{1+}p_{2+}p_{+1}p_{+2}/(n_{++} - 1)$ (see Cochran 1963). In addition, $(n_{ij} - m_{ij})^{2}$ is constant for $i \in \overline{2}$ and $j \in \overline{2}$ if $\underline{\mu} \in M$. Thus

$$\sum_{i=1}^{2}\sum_{j=1}^{2}(n_{ij} - n_{++}n_{+j}/n_{++})^{2}/(n_{i+}n_{+j}/n_{++})$$

has an asymptotic chi-square distribution with 1 degree of freedom. This statistic is the classical Pearson test statistic for independence in a 2 x 2 table.

Example 1.15. Theorem 1.1 can be used to find the asymptotic distribution of the sample $\underline{n}^{*} = \{n_{j1}: j \in J\}$ derived in Example 1.12 from a finite population with N_j elements in class $j \in J$. Suppose that a sequence of populations is considered such that $N_j^{(N)}$ elements are in class $j \in J$,

$$\sum_{j \in J} N_j^{(N)} = N; \tag{1.118}$$

and for each $j \in J$,

$$N_j^{(N)}/N \longrightarrow p_j. \tag{1.119}$$

Let $\underline{n}^{(N)}$ be a sequence of vectors in $R^{J \times \overline{2}}$ such that $n_{j1}^{(N)} + n_{j2}^{(N)} = N_j^{(N)}$ for each $j \in J$, $\sum_{j \in J} n_{j1}^{(N)} = n^{(N)}$, and $n^{(N)}/N \longrightarrow f$. Then the asymptotic distribution of $\underline{n}^{*(N)} = \{n_{j1}^{(N)}: j \in J\}$ is sought.

To find this distribution, define $\underline{m}^{(N)}$ by the condition

$$\begin{aligned} m_{jk}^{(N)} &= N_j^{(N)}n^{(N)}/N, \qquad j \in J,\ k = 1, \\ &= N_j^{(N)}(N - n^{(N)})/N,\ j \in J,\ k = 2. \end{aligned} \tag{1.120}$$

Then $N^{-1}\,\underline{m}^{(N)} \longrightarrow \underline{m}^*$, where

(1.121)
$$m^*_{jk} = p_j f, \qquad j \in J,\ k = 1,$$
$$= p_j(1 - f),\quad j \in J,\ k = 2.$$

It should be noted that since $m^{(N)}_{j+} = n^{(N)}_{j+} = N^{(N)}_j$ for each $j \in J$ and $m^{(N)}_{+1} = n^{(N)}_{+1} = n^{(N)}$, it follows that $P_N\,\underline{m}^{(N)} = P_N\underline{n}^{(N)}$. Since $\underline{\mu}^{(N)} \in N$ for each $N > 0$, the conditions of Theorem 1.1 are all satisfied. Therefore,

(1.122)
$$N^{-\frac{1}{2}}\,(\underline{n}^{(N)} - \underline{m}^{(N)}) \xrightarrow{\mathcal{D}} N(\underline{0}, D(\underline{\mu}^*)[I - P^*_N(\underline{\mu})]).$$

A Gram-Schmidt orthogonalization may be used to obtain $I - P^*_N(\underline{\mu}^*)$. With respect to the inner product defined by $D(\underline{\mu}^*)$, the vectors $\{\underline{\nu}^{(j)}: j \in J\}$ are already orthogonal. One then has $N = \text{span}\,[\{\underline{\nu}^{(j)}: j \in J\} \cup \{\underline{\lambda}^*\}]$, where

(1.123)
$$\underline{\lambda}^* = \underline{\lambda} - \sum_{j\in J} \frac{(\underline{\lambda}, D(\underline{\mu}^*)\underline{\nu}^{(j)})}{(\underline{\nu}^{(j)}, D(\underline{\mu}^*)\underline{\nu}^{(j)})}\,\underline{\nu}^{(j)}$$
$$= \underline{\lambda} - \sum_{j\in J} \frac{p_j f}{p_j}\,\underline{\nu}^{(j)}$$
$$= \underline{\lambda} - f\,\underline{e}$$

and $\underline{e}$ is the unit vector. It now follows that

(1.124)
$$D(\underline{\mu}^*)[I - P^*_N(\underline{\mu}^*)] = D(\underline{\mu}^*) - \sum_{j\in J} \frac{D(\underline{\mu}^*)\underline{\nu}^{(j)} \otimes D(\underline{\mu}^*)\underline{\nu}^{(j)}}{(\underline{\nu}^{(j)}, D(\underline{\mu}^*)\underline{\nu}^{(j)})} - \frac{D(\underline{\mu}^*)\underline{\lambda}^* \otimes D(\underline{\mu}^*)\lambda^*}{(\underline{\lambda}^*, D(\underline{\mu}^*)\underline{\lambda}^*)}$$
$$= D(\underline{\mu}^*) - \sum_{j\in J} \frac{1}{p_j} D(\underline{\mu}^*)\underline{\nu}^{(j)} \otimes D(\underline{\mu}^*)\underline{\nu}^{(j)}$$
$$- \frac{1}{f(1 - f)} D(\underline{\mu}^*)\underline{\lambda}^* \otimes D(\underline{\mu}^*)\underline{\lambda}^*.$$

If $\underline{x}^{(j')} \in R^{J\times\overline{2}}$ satisfies

(1.125)
$$x^{(j')}_{jk} = 1,\quad j = j',\ k = 1,$$
$$= -1,\quad j = j',\ k = -1,$$
$$= 0,\quad j \neq j',$$

then it is readily verified that

$$D(\underline{\mu}^*)[I - P_N^*(\underline{\mu}^*)] = \sum_{j\in J} p_j(1 - p_j)f(1 - f)\, \underline{x}^{(j)} \otimes \underline{x}^{(j)} - \sum_{j\in J} \sum_{j'\neq j} p_j\, p_{j'}\, f(1 - f)\, \underline{x}^{(j)} \otimes \underline{x}^{(j')}. \tag{1.126}$$

The sample $\underline{n}^{*(N)}$ is a linear function of $\underline{n}^{(N)}$, so in analogy to (1.58), one can state that

$$N^{-\frac{1}{2}}(\underline{n}^{*(N)} - \underline{m}^{*(N)}) \xrightarrow{\mathcal{D}} N(\underline{0}, f(1 - f)[P - \underline{p} \otimes \underline{p}]), \tag{1.127}$$

where $\underline{m}^{*(N)} = \{m_j^{(N)}: j \in J\}$, P is an operator with $[P]_{jj'} = p_j\delta_{jj'}$, and $\underline{p} = \{p_j: j \in J\}$. The conventional estimate $\hat{\underline{p}}^{(N)} = \{n_{j1}^{(N)}/n^{(N)}\}$ of $\underline{p}^{(N)} = \{N_j/N\}$ thus satisfies the conditions

$$\hat{\underline{p}}^{(N)} \xrightarrow{P} \underline{p} \tag{1.128}$$

and

$$(n^{(N)})^{\frac{1}{2}} (\hat{\underline{p}}^{(N)} - \underline{p}^{(N)}) \xrightarrow{\mathcal{D}} N(\underline{0}, (1 - f)[P - \underline{p} \otimes \underline{p}]). \tag{1.129}$$

The term $1 - f$ is a correction for finite sampling. If $\underline{n}^{*(N)}$ were multinomial and had mean $\underline{m}^{*(N)}$, (1.129) would hold with $1 - f$ equal to 1. If a particular $p_j^{(N)}$ is of interest, then

$$(n^{(N)})^{\frac{1}{2}} (\hat{p}_j^{(N)} - p_j^{(N)}) \xrightarrow{\mathcal{D}} N(0, (1 - f)\, p_j(1 - p_j)) \tag{1.130}$$

(see Cochran 1963). These results coincide with those of Van Eeden (1963), who indicates that they may be derived by the same argument as that used by Van Eeden and Runnenburg (1960). The authors also consider asymptotic distributions produced under conditions somewhat different from those in Theorem 1.1.

EXACT METHODS

Complete sufficient statistics are associated with minimum-variance unbiased estimates and uniformly most accurate unbiased confidence intervals (see Rao 1965). In the Poisson and multinomial cases, a minimum variance unbiased estimate for $\underline{m}$ may be obtained. In any of the cases considered, uniformly most accurate confidence intervals for linear functions $(\underline{c}, \underline{\mu})$ may be obtained. However, these estimates and confidence intervals are rarely useful.

To find the minimum-variance unbiased estimate of $\underline{m}$, suppose that

$$S = \{\underline{\bar{n}}: \underline{\bar{n}} \in Z^I, \bar{n}_i \geq 0 \ \forall i \in I, P_M\underline{\bar{n}} = P_M\underline{n}\}.$$

Since $E(\underline{n}) = \underline{m}$ and $P_M\underline{n}$ is a complete minimal sufficient statistic for any model considered, it follows by Lehmann and Scheffé (1950) that the minimum-variance unbiased estimate is unique and is given by

$$E(\underline{n}|\underline{\bar{n}} \in S) = \sum_{\underline{\bar{n}} \in S} \underline{\bar{n}} \prod_{i \in I} \frac{1}{\bar{n}_i!} \Big/ \sum_{\underline{\bar{n}} \in S} \prod_{i \in I} \frac{1}{\bar{n}_i!} . \tag{1.131}$$

This estimate has three unsatisfactory properties. Although $E(\underline{n}|\underline{n} \in S)$ is an unbiased estimate of $\underline{m}$, $\{\log E(n_i|\underline{n} \in S)\}$ is not an unbiased estimate of $\underline{\mu}$, and in general, $\{\log E(n_i|\underline{n} \in S)\} \notin M$. Thus the estimate need not correspond to a reasonable estimate of $\underline{\mu}$. If S has only one element, the estimate reduces to $\underline{n}$. In such a case, unbiasedness is obtained at the cost of excessive variability. In addition, the estimate is often difficult to compute when M has a basis of vectors with integral elements. The difficulty generally increases as the dimension of M and the size of the n_i increase.

Example 1.16. Consider the logit model of Examples 1.6 and 1.10. To find the minimum-variance unbiased estimate of $\underline{m}$, it suffices to note that S consists of those vectors $\underline{n}^{(k)}$ such that $\underline{n}^{(k)} = \underline{n} + (k - 3)\underline{\mu}^{(6)}$, where $k \in \bar{5}$ and $\underline{\mu}^{(6)}$ is defined by (1.26). Thus

$$\underline{n}^{(1)} = \begin{bmatrix} 0 & 15 \\ 9 & 6 \\ 6 & 9 \end{bmatrix}, \tag{1.132}$$

$$\underline{n}^{(2)} = \begin{bmatrix} 1 & 14 \\ 7 & 8 \\ 7 & 8 \end{bmatrix}, \tag{1.133}$$

$$\underline{n}^{(3)} = \begin{bmatrix} 2 & 13 \\ 5 & 10 \\ 8 & 7 \end{bmatrix}, \tag{1.134}$$

$$\underline{n}^{(4)} = \begin{bmatrix} 3 & 12 \\ 3 & 12 \\ 9 & 6 \end{bmatrix}, \tag{1.135}$$

and

(1.136) $$\underline{n}^{(5)} = \begin{array}{|cc|} 4 & 11 \\ 1 & 14 \\ 10 & 5 \end{array}\ .$$

The estimate $E(\underline{n}|\underline{n} \in S)$ then satisfies

(1.137) $$E(\underline{n}|\underline{n} \in S) = \begin{array}{|cc|} 2.127 & 12.871 \\ 4.742 & 10.258 \\ 8.127 & 6.871 \end{array}\ .$$

In this example, no computational difficulties arise. However, if $\overline{\underline{m}} = E(\underline{n}|\underline{n} \in S)$ and $\overline{\underline{\mu}} = \{\log \overline{m}_i\}$, then

(1.138) $$\overline{\underline{\mu}} = \begin{array}{|cc|} 0.756 & 2.554 \\ 1.556 & 2.328 \\ 2.095 & 1.927 \end{array}\ .$$

The inner product $(\overline{\underline{\mu}},\underline{\mu}^{(6)}) = 0.086$, which is small but not negligible. Thus $\overline{\underline{\mu}}$ has the unfortunate property that it is not in the same manifold M that $\underline{\mu}$ is presumed to be in.

Nevertheless, a few simple cases do exist where the minimum-variance unbiasedness estimate is useful. If $M = R^I$, then $S = \{\underline{n}\}$ and the estimate is $\underline{n}$. If $M = \text{span}\ \{\underline{e}\}$, $S = \{\overline{\underline{n}} : \overline{n}_i \geq 0\ \forall i \in I, \sum_{i\in I} \overline{n}_i = \sum_{i\in I} n_i\}$. Since the conditional distribution is multinomial, for $j \in I$,

(1.139) $$E(n_j|\underline{n} \in S) = \frac{1}{q} \sum_{i\in I} n_i,$$

the mean of the observations. This result is reasonable, for $\underline{\mu} \in M$ implies that m_i is constant for $i \in I$.

If Poisson sampling is used or if $\underline{c} \in M$ is orthogonal to N, uniformly most accurate unbiased confidence intervals for $(\underline{c},\underline{\mu})$ may be derived by considering the distribution of $(\underline{c},\underline{n})$ given $P_R\underline{n}$, where $R = M - \{\underline{c}\}$, the orthogonal complement of $\underline{c}$ relative to M. This distribution does not depend on the original sampling method used. If $T = \{\overline{\underline{n}}: \overline{\underline{n}} \in Z^I, \overline{n}_i \geq 0\ \forall i \in I, P_R\overline{\underline{n}} = P_R\underline{n}\}$, then

(1.140) $$p(\underline{n}|\underline{n} \in T) = \frac{\left(\prod_{i\in I} \frac{1}{n_i!}\right) \exp\,[(\underline{c},\underline{n})(\underline{c},\underline{\mu})/(\underline{c},\underline{c})]}{\sum_{\underline{n}'\in T} \left(\prod_{i\in I} \frac{1}{n_i!}\right) \exp\,[(\underline{c},\underline{n}')(\underline{c},\underline{\mu})/(\underline{c},\underline{c})]}\ .$$

The conditional distribution of $(\underline{c},\underline{n})/(\underline{c},\underline{c})$ then belongs to a one-parameter exponential family. As shown in Lehmann (1959), uniformly most accurate unbiased confidence intervals based on the conditional distribution given by (1.140) yield uniformly most accurate unbiased confidence intervals for the unconditional distribution.

Unfortunately, computations are generally tedious, and the resulting confidence intervals are randomized. Thus these confidence intervals are impractical even in rather simple cases, although tables do exist for simple Poisson and binomial random variables (see Blyth and Hutchinson 1960, 1961). In addition, the conditional distribution of $\underline{n} \in T$ may reduce to a single point. In this case, a sensible confidence interval cannot be obtained by these methods.

Nonrandomized intervals for $(\underline{c},\underline{\mu})$ may be obtained such that the probability is no greater than $\alpha/2$ that $(\underline{c},\underline{\mu})$ is to any given side of the interval; however, computations are still rather tedious. Confidence intervals are commonly obtained by this method only for simple Poisson and binomial random variables. Tables and charts are given by Pearson and Hartley (1966). Neither randomized nor nonrandomized confidence intervals for the cross product ratio of a 2 x 2 table are often derived by use of (1.140), but it is not unusual in small samples to use a nonrandomized test derived by Fisher (1935a) for the hypothesis that the cross-product ratio is 0. Tables for this test are also found in Pearson and Hartley (1966).

Example 1.17. On the basis of the logit model for the data in table 1.3, one might wish to construct a 95% confidence interval for the probability of death for a frog given a log dose of 0.85. To assess this probability, it is necessary to construct a confidence interval for the log odds $\nu_2 = \log (p_{21}/p_{22})$. The probability p_{21} of death satisfies

$$p_{21} = e^{\nu_2}/(1 + e^{\nu_2}). \tag{1.141}$$

To obtain the confidence interval for $\log(p_{21}/p_{22})$, it should be noted that

$$\begin{aligned} \log (p_{21}/p_{22}) &= \log m_{21} - \log m_{22} \\ &= \mu_{21} - \mu_{22} \\ &= (\underline{c},\underline{\mu}), \end{aligned} \tag{1.142}$$

where

(1.142) $$\underline{c} = \begin{array}{|cc|} 0 & 0 \\ 1 & -1 \\ 0 & 0 \end{array} .$$

Since $\underline{\mu} \in M$,

(1.144) $$\log (p_{21}/p_{22}) = (P_M \underline{c}, \underline{\mu}) = \tfrac{1}{3}(\underline{\mu}^{(4)}, \underline{\mu}),$$

where $\underline{\mu}^{(4)}$ satisfies (1.24).

The manifold R is then equal to span $\{\underline{\mu}^{(1)}, \underline{\mu}^{(2)}, \underline{\mu}^{(3)}, \underline{\mu}^{(5)}\}$, and the set T is $\{\underline{n} \in Z^{\overline{3}\times\overline{2}}: n_{ij} \geq 0\ \forall \langle i,j\rangle \in \overline{3} \times \overline{2},\ n_{i+} = 15\ \forall i \in \overline{3},\ n_{11} - n_{12} - n_{13} + n_{32} = -12\}$. Since $(\tfrac{1}{3}\underline{\mu}^{(4)}, \tfrac{1}{3}\underline{\mu}^{(4)}) = 2/3$ and $(\tfrac{1}{3}\underline{\mu}^{(4)}, \underline{n}) = \tfrac{1}{3}(n_{+1} - n_{+2})$,

(1.145) $$p(\underline{n}|\underline{n} \in T) = \frac{\left(\prod_{i=1}^{3} \prod_{j=1}^{2} \frac{1}{n_{ij}!}\right) \exp[\nu_2(n_{+1} - n_{+2})/2]}{\sum_{\underline{n}' \in T} \left(\prod_{i=1}^{3} \prod_{j=1}^{2} \frac{1}{n'_{ij}!}\right) \exp[\nu_2(n'_{+1} - n'_{+2})/2]} .$$

Confidence intervals are based on the conditional distribution of $n_{+1} - n_{+2}$, so it should be noted that if $U(k)$ is $\{\underline{n} \in T: n_{+1} - n_{+2} = k\}$ and k is odd, then $U(k)$ consists of those $\underline{n} \in Z^{\overline{3}\times\overline{2}}$ such that

(1.146) $$\max(0, \tfrac{3 + k}{4}) \leq n_{11} \leq \min(\tfrac{33 + k}{4}, 9)$$

and

(1.147) $$\underline{n} = \begin{array}{|cc|} n_{11} & 15 - n_{11} \\ \frac{33 + k}{2} - 2n_{11} & 2n_{11} - \frac{3 + k}{2} \\ n_{11} + 6 & 9 - n_{11} \end{array} .$$

The set $U(k)$ is nonempty if $-33 \leq k \leq 33$. After minor manipulations, one may write

(1.148) $$P_{\nu_2}\ n_{+1} - n_{+2} = k|\underline{n} \in T$$

$$= \frac{g(k) \exp(\nu_2 k/2)}{\sum_{p=-17}^{16} g(2p + 1)\exp[\nu_2(2p + 1)/2]} ,$$

where

$$g(k) = \sum_{n_{11}=\max(0,\frac{3+k}{4})}^{\min(\frac{33+k}{4},9)} \binom{15}{n_{11}} \binom{15}{2n_{11} - \frac{3+k}{2}} \binom{15}{n_{11}+6}, \tag{1.149}$$

and the subscript ν_2 indicates that the probability in (1.148) depends on ν_2. Since $n_{+1} - n_{+2} = -15$, the nonrandomized 95% confidence interval $[a,b]$ for ν_2 satisfies the equations

$$\begin{aligned} P_b\{n_{+1} - n_{+2} \le -15 \; \underline{n} \in T\} &= \sum_{p=-17}^{-8} g(2p+1)\exp[b(2p+1)/2] \Big/ \sum_{p=-17}^{16} g(2p+1)\exp[b(2p+1)/2] \\ &= 0.025 \end{aligned} \tag{1.150}$$

and

$$\begin{aligned} P_a\{n_{+1} - n_{+2} \ge -15 \; \underline{n} \in T\} &= \sum_{p=-8}^{16} g(2p+1)\exp[a(2p+1)/2] \Big/ \sum_{p=-17}^{16} g(2p+1)\exp[a(2p+1)/2] \\ &= 0.025 \end{aligned} \tag{1.151}$$

(see Hoel 1962). This interval satisfies the relationships $P\{\nu_2 < a|\underline{n} \in T\} \le 0.025$ and $P\{\nu_2 > b|\underline{n} \in T\} \le 0.025$. Since these relationships hold conditionally for any set T corresponding to a possible value of $P_{\underline{R}}\underline{n}$, they also hold unconditionally. Thus $P\{\nu_2 < a\} \le 0.025$, $P\{\nu_2 > b\} \le 0.025$, and $P\{a \le \nu_2 \le b\} \ge 0.95$.

Equations (1.150) and (1.151) may be solved by use of any standard technique for solution of nonlinear equations in one variable (see Ralston 1965). The resulting interval $[a,b]$ for ν_2 is $[-1.570,-0.077]$, while the corresponding confidence interval for p_2 is $[0.172,0.481]$. These results are rather similar to those found in Example 4.5 by use of techniques based on asymptotic theory; however, the approximate intervals derived in chapter 4 are far easier to compute than the intervals considered in this example.

If randomized intervals are desired, then computations are substantially more difficult. By Lehmann (1959), the 95% uniformly most accurate confidence interval for ν_2 consists of those ν for which

(1.152) $$a(\nu) \le -15 + 2\varepsilon \le b(\nu),$$

where ε is a uniform random number between 0 and 1 and $a(\nu)$ and $b(\nu)$ satisfy the equations

(1.153) $$P_\nu\{a(\nu) \le n_{+1} - n_{+2} + 2u \le b(\nu) | \underline{n} \in T\} = 0.95$$

and

(1.154) $$E_\nu\{(n_{+1} - n_{+2} + 2u)\chi_{[-a(\nu),b(\nu)]}(n_{+1} - n_{+2} + 2u)]\}$$
$$= 0.95\ E_\nu\{(n_{+1} - n_{+2} + 2u)\},$$

where u is a uniform random variable with range from 0 to 1 which is independent of $\underline{n}$. The set of ν which satisfy (1.152), (1.153), and (1.154) is an interval which can be computed by solving two sets of two simultaneous equations; however, the calculations required are too difficult for these intervals to be considered of practical value.

Since exact methods are usually impractical, approximate methods must be tried. One such method, that of maximum likelihood, provides estimation and test procedures which involve simple computational methods and which have optimal large sample properties. This method is the subject of the remainder of the monograph.

Chapter 2

MAXIMUM-LIKELIHOOD ESTIMATION

It is convenient to begin consideration of maximum-likelihood estimation with an examination of the Poisson model. Results for the multinomial model follow directly. The conditional Poisson model involves special difficulties which make maximum-likelihood estimates costly to calculate on a computer in this case. In this chapter, existence and uniqueness of estimates is investigated. This topic has been considered by Birch (1963) in connection with the hierarchical models for complete factorial tables which are discussed in chapter 5. More recently, Fienberg (1970) has considered the problem in the case of incomplete two-way tables. Results in this chapter are more general and sharper than those previously derived.

THE POISSON MODEL

In the maximum-likelihood estimation problem for the Poisson model, an element $\hat{\underline{\mu}}$ of M is sought such that

$$\ell(\underline{n},\hat{\underline{\mu}}) = \sup_{\underline{\mu} \epsilon M} \ell(\underline{n},\underline{\mu}). \tag{2.1}$$

If $\hat{\underline{\mu}}$ exists, then $\hat{\underline{\mu}}$ is a maximum-likelihood estimate of $\underline{\mu}$. The vector $\hat{\underline{m}} = \{e^{\hat{\mu}_i}\}$ is a maximum-likelihood estimate of $\underline{m}$.

Even if $\hat{\underline{\mu}}$ does not exist, $\sup_{\underline{\mu} \epsilon M} \ell(\underline{n},\underline{\mu})$ is finite. This result follows by considering $n\mu - e^{\mu}$ for fixed n. If $n \le 0$, then $n\mu - e^{\mu} < 0$ for all $\mu \epsilon R$. If $n > 0$, then $n\mu - e^{\mu}$ is a strictly concave function with a maximum when $\mu = \log n$. Thus $\ell(\underline{n},\underline{\mu})$ is bounded above.

In order to examine the properties of $\hat{\underline{\mu}}$, it is necessary to consider the first and second differentials of $\ell(\underline{n},\underline{\mu})$. The first differential at $\underline{\mu}$ is a linear function $d\ell_{\underline{\mu}}(\underline{n},\underline{\nu})$ defined for $\underline{\nu} \epsilon M$ such that

(2.2) $$\ell(\underline{n},\underline{\mu}+\underline{\nu}) = \ell(\underline{n},\underline{\mu}) + d\ell_{\underline{\mu}}(\underline{n},\underline{\nu}) + o(\underline{\nu}),$$

where $o(\underline{\nu})/\|\underline{\nu}\| \longrightarrow 0$ as $\underline{\nu} \longrightarrow 0$. By elementary calculus,

(2.3) $$n(x+y) - e^{x+y} = (nx - e^{x}) + (ny - e^{x}y) + o(y),$$

where $y^{-1}\, o(y) \longrightarrow 0$ as $y \longrightarrow 0$. Therefore,

(2.4) $$d\ell_{\underline{\mu}}(\underline{n},\underline{\nu}) = (\underline{\nu},\underline{n} - \underline{m}(\underline{\mu})).$$

The second differential $d^2\ell_{\underline{\mu}}(\underline{n},\underline{\xi})(\underline{\nu})$ of $\ell(\underline{n},\underline{\mu})$ at $\underline{\mu}$ is a linear function from M to the space M^* of linear functions on M. This differential satisfies

(2.5) $$d\ell_{\underline{\mu}+\underline{\xi}}(\underline{n},\underline{\nu}) = d\ell_{\underline{\mu}}(\underline{n},\underline{\nu}) + d^2\ell_{\underline{\mu}}(\underline{n},\underline{\xi})(\underline{\nu}) + o_{\underline{\xi}}(\underline{\nu}),$$

where

(2.6) $$\lim_{\underline{\xi}\to 0} \frac{1}{\|\underline{\xi}\|} \sup_{\|\underline{\nu}\|=1} \|o_{\underline{\xi}}(\underline{\nu})\| \longrightarrow 0.$$

Since

(2.7) $$d\ell_{\underline{\mu}+\underline{\xi}}(\underline{n},\underline{\nu}) - d\ell_{\underline{\mu}}(\underline{n},\underline{\nu}) = \sum_{i\in I} \nu_i(e^{\mu_i} - e^{\mu_i+\xi_i}) = -\sum_{i\in I} \nu_i\xi_i e^{\mu_i} + (\underline{\nu},\underline{o}(\underline{\xi})),$$

where $\frac{1}{\|\underline{\xi}\|}\|\underline{o}(\underline{\xi})\| \longrightarrow 0$ as $\|\underline{\xi}\| \longrightarrow 0$, it follows that

(2.8) $$d^2\ell_{\underline{\mu}}(\underline{n},\underline{\xi})(\underline{\nu}) = -\sum_{i\in I} \nu_i\xi_i e^{\mu_i} = -\sum_{i\in I} \nu_i\xi_i m_i(\underline{\mu}).$$

If $D(\underline{\mu})\{x_i\} = \{e^{\mu_i}x_i\}$, then one may write

(2.9) $$d^2\ell_{\underline{\mu}}(\underline{n},\underline{\xi})(\underline{\nu}) = -(\underline{\nu},D(\underline{\mu})\underline{\xi}).$$

If $\underline{\nu} \neq \underline{0}$, $\underline{\nu} \in M$, and $\underline{\mu} \in M$, then

(2.10) $$d^2\ell_{\underline{\mu}}(\underline{n},\underline{\nu})(\underline{\nu}) = -\sum_{i\in I} \nu_i^2 e^{\mu_i} < 0.$$

Thus $\ell(\underline{n},\underline{\mu})$ is a strictly concave function of $\underline{\mu}$.

Given the results of the preceding paragraph, the following theorem can be proven:

THEOREM 2.1. *If a maximum-likelihood estimate* $\hat{\underline{\mu}}$ *exists, then it is unique and satisfies the equation*

(2.11) $$P_M\hat{\underline{m}} = P_M\underline{n}.$$

Conversely, if for some $\hat{\underline{\mu}} \in M$ *and* $\hat{\underline{m}} = \{e^{\hat{\mu}_i}\}$, *equation (2.11) is satisfied, then* $\hat{\underline{\mu}}$ *is the maximum-likelihood estimate of* $\underline{\mu}$.

Proof. Since $\ell(\underline{n},\underline{\mu})$ is strictly concave, at most one critical point exists. If a critical point does exist, this point is a maximum. Therefore, only one maximum-likelihood estimate can exist. If the maximum-likelihood estimate $\hat{\underline{\mu}}$ exists, then for every $\underline{\nu} \in M$,

$$d\ell_{\hat{\underline{\mu}}}(\underline{n},\underline{\nu}) = (\underline{\nu},\underline{n} - \hat{\underline{m}}) = 0. \tag{2.12}$$

Therefore, $\underline{n} - \hat{\underline{m}} \in M^{\perp}$. Thus equation (2.11) must hold. On the other hand, if $\hat{\underline{\mu}}$ satisfies equation (2.11), then

$$d\ell_{\hat{\underline{\mu}}}(\underline{n},\underline{\nu}) = (\underline{\nu},\underline{n} - \hat{\underline{m}}) = (P_M\underline{\nu},\underline{n} - \hat{\underline{m}}) = (\underline{\nu},P_M\underline{n} - P_M\hat{\underline{m}}) = 0 \tag{2.13}$$

for every $\underline{\nu} \in M$. Thus a critical point exists at $\hat{\underline{\mu}}$. Since $\ell(\underline{n},\underline{\mu})$ is strictly concave, this point must be a maximum. ||

The likelihood equation (2.11) requires that $\hat{\underline{m}}$ fit the sufficient statistic $P_M\underline{n}$. If $\{\underline{\mu}^{(j)}: j \in \overline{s}\}$ spans M, then equation (2.11) is equivalent to the condition

$$(\hat{\underline{m}},\underline{\mu}^{(j)}) = (\underline{n},\underline{\mu}^{(j)}) \tag{2.14}$$

for every $j \in \overline{s}$. This equation is particularly suggestive if

$$\begin{aligned} \mu_i^{(j)} &= 1, \quad i \in I_j, \\ &= 0, \quad i \in I - I_j. \end{aligned} \tag{2.15}$$

Then

$$\sum_{i \in I_j} \hat{m}_i = \sum_{i \in I_j} n_i. \tag{2.16}$$

Thus certain marginal totals must be equal for $\hat{\underline{m}}$ and $\underline{n}$. This relationship is frequently used in the discussion of hierarchical models in chapters 5 and 7.

Example 2.1. Suppose that $M = R^I$. Then P_M is the identity operator and (2.11) reduces to $\hat{\underline{m}} = \underline{n}$. Note that $\hat{\underline{\mu}} = \{\log n_i\}$ is well defined if and only if $n_i > 0$ for all $i \in I$. If $I = \{1\}$, then the result states that the maximum-likelihood estimate of the mean m of a Poisson random variable n is n.

Example 2.2. Suppose $M = \text{span}\,\{\underline{e}\}$. Then $\hat{\underline{\mu}} = c\underline{e}$ for some c and $\hat{\underline{m}} = (e^c)\underline{e}$. By (2.14),

$$((e^c)\underline{e},\underline{e}) = qe^c = (\underline{n},\underline{e}) = \sum_{i \in I} n_i. \tag{2.17}$$

Thus $e^c = \frac{1}{q}\sum_{i \in I} n_i$, the average of the observations, provided some $n_i > 0$. If for some $i \in I$, $n_i > 0$, $\underline{\hat{m}} = (\frac{1}{q}\sum_{i \in I} n_i)\underline{e}$.

Example 2.3. Suppose that $I = \overline{2} \times \overline{2}$ and M is the additive manifold. Then $M = \text{span}\,\{\underline{\nu}^{(k)}: k \in \overline{4}\}$, where the $\underline{\nu}^{(k)}$ are defined by (1.71), (1.72), (1.73), and (1.74). Thus $I_1 = \{<1,1>, <1,2>\}$, $I_2 = \{<2,1>, <2,2>\}$, $I_3 = \{<1,1>, <2,1>\}$, and $I_4 = \{<1,2>, <2,2>\}$, and (2.16) reduces to the conditions $\hat{m}_{i+} = n_{i+}$ for $i \in \overline{2}$ and $\hat{m}_{+j} = n_{+j}$ for $j \in \overline{2}$. As shown in Example 1.5, if $\hat{m}_{ij} = n_{i+}n_{+j}/n_{++}$, $n_{i+} > 0$ for $i \in \overline{2}$, and $n_{+j} > 0$ for $j \in \overline{2}$, then $\underline{\mu} \in M$, $\hat{m}_{i+} = n_{i+}$ for $i \in \overline{2}$, and $\hat{m}_{+j} = n_{+j}$ for $j \in \overline{2}$. Thus $\underline{\hat{m}} = \{n_{i+}n_{+j}/n_{++}\}$ if n_{i+} and n_{+j} are positive.

So far, no convenient conditions have been given for the existence of the maximum-likelihood estimate. In order to rectify this situation, the following theorem is useful:

THEOREM 2.2. *A necessary and sufficient condition that the maximum-likelihood estimate* $\underline{\hat{\mu}}$ *of* $\underline{\mu}$ *exist is that there exist* $\underline{\delta} \in M^{\perp}$ *such that* $n_i + \delta_i > 0$ *for every* $i \in I$.

Proof. To prove necessity, assume that $\underline{\hat{\mu}}$ satisfies equation (2.11). Then $\underline{m} - \underline{n} \in M^{\perp}$. In addition, $\underline{\hat{m}} - \underline{n} + \underline{n} = \underline{\hat{m}}$, where $\hat{m}_i > 0$ for each $i \in I$. Thus $\underline{\delta} = \underline{m} - \underline{n}$ has the desired properties.

In order to prove sufficiency, assume that there exists $\underline{\delta} \in M^{\perp}$ such that $n_i + \delta_i > 0$ for each $i \in I$. Suppose that

$$\hat{\ell}^{(p)}(\underline{n},\underline{\mu}) = \sum_{i \in I} (n_i\mu_i - e^{\mu_i}) = (\underline{n},\underline{\mu}) - \sum_{i \in I} e^{\mu_i}. \tag{2.18}$$

Then $\hat{\ell}^{(p)}(\underline{n},\underline{\mu})$ and $\ell(\underline{n},\underline{\mu})$ differ only by a constant. Since $\underline{\delta} \in M^{\perp}$, $(\underline{n},\underline{\mu}) = (\underline{n} + \underline{\delta},\underline{\mu})$ and

$$\hat{\ell}^{(p)}(\underline{n},\underline{\mu}) = \sum_{i \in I} [(n_i + \delta_i)\mu_i - e^{\mu_i}]. \tag{2.19}$$

Each summand is bounded above. Therefore, if any summand is small enough, then $\hat{\ell}^{(p)}(\underline{n},\underline{\mu}) < \hat{\ell}^{(p)}(\underline{n},\underline{0})$. For any $i \in I$, $n_i + \delta_i > 0$. Thus as $\mu_i \longrightarrow -\infty$, $(n_i + \delta_i)\mu_i - e^{\mu_i} \longrightarrow -\infty$. On the other hand, as $\mu_i \longrightarrow +\infty$, $(n_i + \delta_i)\mu_i - e^{\mu_i} \longrightarrow -\infty$. Suppose $A = \{\underline{\mu} \in M: \hat{\ell}^{(p)}(\underline{n},\underline{\mu}) \geq \hat{\ell}^{(p)}(\underline{n},\underline{0})\}$. Then A is bounded. Since $\hat{\ell}^{(p)}(\underline{n},\underline{\mu})$ is continuous in $\underline{\mu}$, A is closed. Therefore, $\hat{\ell}^{(p)}(\underline{n},\underline{\mu})$ has a finite maximum for some $\underline{\mu} \in A$. ||

The following corollary follows immediately:

COROLLARY 2.1. *If* $n_i > 0$ *for every* $i \in I$, *then the maximum likelihood estimate* $\hat{\underline{\mu}}$ *exists.*

Proof. Use $\underline{\delta} = 0$ and apply Theorem 2.2. ||

A conjugate condition to Theorem 2.2 is often useful:

THEOREM 2.3. *A necessary and sufficient condition that the maximum-likelihood estimate* $\hat{\underline{\mu}}$ *exist is that there not exist* $\underline{\mu} \in M$ *such that* $\underline{\mu} \neq \underline{0}$, $\mu_i \leq 0$ *for every* $i \in I$, *and* $(\underline{n},\underline{\mu}) = 0$.

Proof. Suppose that the maximum likelihood estimate of $\underline{\mu}$ exists. Then there exists $\underline{\delta} \in M^{\perp}$ such that $n_i + \delta_i > 0$ for each $i \in I$. If $\underline{\mu} \in M$, $(\underline{n},\underline{\mu}) = 0$, $\mu_i \leq 0$ for every $i \in I$, and $\underline{\mu} \neq \underline{0}$, then $(\underline{n} + \underline{\delta},\underline{\mu}) < 0$. Since $(\underline{n},\underline{\mu})$ and $(\underline{n} + \underline{\delta},\underline{\mu})$ are equal, a contradiction results. Thus no such $\underline{\mu}$ exists.

On the other hand, suppose that the maximum-likelihood estimate does not exist. Then there does not exist $\underline{\delta} \in M^{\perp}$ such that $n_i + \delta_i > 0$ for every $i \in I$. Let I_0 be the set of indices in I such that $n_i = 0$. Suppose $S = \{\underline{x} \in R^I: x_i > 0 \ \forall i \in I_0\}$. Then S and $M^{\perp}$ are disjoint convex sets. By the separating hyperplane theorem (Blackwell and Girshick 1954), there exists $\underline{\mu} \in R^I$, $\underline{\mu} \neq \underline{0}$, such that if $\underline{\nu} \in M^{\perp}$, $(\underline{\mu},\underline{\nu}) \geq 0$, and if $\underline{\nu} \in S$, $(\underline{\mu},\underline{\nu}) \leq 0$. Suppose $j \in I - I_0$. If $\underline{\nu} \in S$, then $\underline{\nu} + c\underline{\delta}^{(j)} \in S$ for any real-valued c. Thus $(\underline{\mu},\underline{\delta}^{(j)}) = \mu_j = 0$. Now suppose $j \in I_0$. Then if $\underline{\nu} \in S$, $\underline{\nu} + c\underline{\delta}^{(j)} \in S$ for all positive c. Thus $(\underline{\mu},\underline{\delta}^{(j)}) = \mu_j \leq 0$. It is now sufficient to show that $\underline{\mu} \in M$. This result follows since if $P_{M^{\perp}}$ is the orthogonal projection from R^I to $M^{\perp}$, then

$$-(\underline{\mu},P_{M^{\perp}}\underline{\mu}) = -\ ||P_{M^{\perp}}\underline{\mu}||^2 . \tag{2.20}$$

Unless $P_{M^{\perp}}\underline{\mu}$ is $\underline{0}$, there is a contradiction. Thus $\underline{\mu} \in M$. ||

If $\{\underline{\mu}^{(j)}: j \in \bar{s}\}$ spans M and each $\underline{\mu}^{(j)}$ satisfies (2.15), then Theorem 2.3 implies that $\hat{\underline{m}}$ can exist only if $\sum_{i \in I_j} n_i$ is positive for all $j \in \bar{s}$. Given (2.16), one may conclude that $\hat{\underline{m}}$ can exist only when the marginal totals to be fit are positive. As shown in Appendix B, the condition that all marginal totals to be fitted must be positive is not sufficient to ensure that $\hat{\underline{m}}$ exists. Procedures are discussed in this appendix for determining whether $\hat{\underline{m}}$ exists in cases in which some cell counts n_i are 0 but all marginal totals $\sum_{i \in I_j} n_i$ are positive.

THE MULTINOMIAL MODEL

The multinomial model is closely related to the Poisson model. In the maximum-likelihood estimation problem for the multinomial model, an element $\hat{\underline{\mu}}^{(m)}$ of $\tilde{M}$ is sought such that

$$\ell^{(m)}(\underline{n},\hat{\underline{\mu}}^{(m)}) = \sup_{\underline{\mu}\in\tilde{M}} \ell^{(m)}(\underline{n},\underline{\mu}), \tag{2.21}$$

where

$$\tilde{M} = \{\underline{\mu} \in M\colon \sum_{i\in I_k} e^{\mu_i} = \sum_{i\in I_k} n_i \;\forall k \in \overline{r}\}.$$

It is assumed that M has dimension greater than r. The fundamental result of this section is that if $\hat{\underline{\mu}}$ is the maximum-likelihood estimate of $\underline{\mu} \in M$ for the Poisson model, then $\hat{\underline{\mu}} = \hat{\underline{\mu}}^{(m)}$. This equation means that if one side exists, then the other side exists and the two sides are equal. This result is extremely useful since it implies that conditions for existence of maximum-likelihood estimates under Poisson sampling also apply to multinomial sampling. The result is important in both numerical and algebraic work since it permits use of the relatively simple Poisson log likelihood in estimation problems involving multinomial sampling. This point is discussed in chapter 3. Results of this section are generalizations of those derived by Birch (1963).

In order to examine maximum-likelihood estimation for the multinomial case, the function

$$\hat{\ell}^{(m)}(\underline{n},\underline{\mu}^*) = (\underline{n},\underline{\mu}^*) - \sum_{k=1}^{r} (\underline{n},\underline{\nu}^{(k)}) \log (\underline{m}(\underline{\mu}^*),\underline{\nu}^{(k)}) \tag{2.22}$$

defined for $\underline{\mu}^* \in M - N$ may be considered. The functions $\ell^{(m)}(\underline{n},\underline{\mu})$ and $\hat{\ell}^{(m)}(\underline{n},P_{M-N}\underline{\mu})$ differ by a constant if $\underline{\mu} \in \tilde{M}$. By (1.50), to every $\underline{\mu}^* \in M - N$ there corresponds a unique $\underline{\mu} \in \tilde{M}$. such that $P_{M-N}\underline{\mu} = \underline{\mu}^*$. One may write $\underline{\mu}$ as $\underline{w}(\underline{\mu}^*)$. If $\hat{\ell}^{(m)}(\underline{n},\underline{\mu}^*)$ has a maximum for $\underline{\mu}^* = \hat{\underline{\mu}}^*$, then $\hat{\ell}^{(m)}(\underline{n},\underline{\mu})$ has a maximum for $\hat{\underline{\mu}} = \underline{w}(\hat{\underline{\mu}}^*)$. If $\ell^{(m)}(\underline{n},\underline{\mu})$ has a maximum for $\underline{\mu} = \hat{\underline{\mu}}$, then $\hat{\ell}^{(m)}(\underline{n},\underline{\mu}^*)$ has a maximum for $\underline{\mu}^* = P_{M-N}\underline{\mu}$. Thus maximization of $\hat{\ell}^{(m)}(\underline{n},\underline{\mu})$ for $\underline{\mu} \in \tilde{M}$ is equivalent to maximization of $\hat{\ell}^{(m)}(\underline{n},\underline{\mu}^*)$ for $\underline{\mu}^* \in M - N$.

Whether or not a maximum-likelihood estimate $\hat{\underline{\mu}}^{(m)}$ exists, $\sup_{\underline{\mu}\in\tilde{M}} \ell^{(m)}(\underline{n},\underline{\mu})$ finite. This result follows because $\ell^{(m)}(\underline{n},\underline{\mu})$ and $\ell(\underline{n},\underline{\mu})$ differ by a constant if $\underline{\mu} \in M$. Since $\sup_{\underline{\mu}\in M} \ell(\underline{n},\underline{\mu}) < \infty$ and $\tilde{M} \subset M$, $\sup_{\underline{\mu}\in\tilde{M}} \ell^{(m)}(\underline{n},\underline{\mu}) < \infty$. To complete the proof, observe that $\ell^{(m)}(\underline{n},\underline{\mu})$ and $\hat{\ell}^{(m)}(\underline{n},P_{M-N}\underline{\mu})$ differ by a constant. As a consequence, $\sup_{\underline{\mu}^* \in M-N} \hat{\ell}(\underline{n},\underline{\mu}^*) < \infty$.

In order to examine the properties of $\hat{\underline{\mu}}^{(m)}$, the first and second differentials of $\hat{\ell}^{(m)}(\underline{n},\underline{\mu}^*)$ are needed. Since

$$\hat{\ell}^{(m)}(\underline{n},\underline{\mu}^* + \underline{\nu}) = \ell(\underline{n},\underline{\mu}^*) + (\underline{n},\underline{\nu}) - \sum_{k=1}^{r} \frac{(\underline{n},\underline{\nu}^{(k)})}{(\underline{m}(\underline{\mu}^*),\underline{\nu}^{(k)})} \sum_{i \in I_k} m_i(\underline{\mu}^*)\nu_i^{(k)}\nu_i + o(\underline{\nu}), \tag{2.23}$$

it follows that if $\underline{\nu} \in M - N$, then

$$d\hat{\ell}^{(m)}_{\underline{\mu}^*}(\underline{n},\underline{\nu}) = (\underline{\nu},\underline{n}) - \sum_{k=1}^{r} \frac{(\underline{n},\underline{\nu}^{(k)})}{(\underline{m}(\underline{\mu}^*),\underline{\nu}^{(k)})} \sum_{i \in I_k} m_i(\underline{\mu}^*)\nu_i^{(k)}\nu_i. \tag{2.24}$$

If $\overline{\underline{m}}(\underline{\mu}^*) = \{e^{w_i(\underline{\mu}^*)}\}$, then

$$d\hat{\ell}^{(m)}_{\underline{\mu}^*}(\underline{n},\underline{\nu}) = (\underline{\nu},\underline{n} - \overline{\underline{m}}(\underline{\mu}^*)). \tag{2.25}$$

In order to find the second differential $d^2\hat{\ell}^{(m)}_{\underline{\mu}^*}(\underline{n},\underline{\xi})(\underline{\nu})$, it is only necessary to note that

$$\begin{aligned} d\hat{\ell}^{(m)}_{\underline{\mu}^*+\underline{\xi}}(\underline{n},\underline{\nu}) &= d\hat{\ell}^{(m)}_{\underline{\mu}^*}(\underline{n},\underline{\nu}) \\ &\quad - \sum_{k=1}^{r} \Bigg[\frac{(\underline{n},\underline{\nu}^{(k)})}{(\underline{m}(\underline{\mu}^*),\underline{\nu}^{(k)})} \sum_{i \in I_k} \nu_i \xi_i m_i(\underline{\mu}^*) \\ &\quad - \Big(\sum_{i \in I_k} m_i(\underline{\mu}^*)\nu_i\Big)\Big(\sum_{i \in I_k} m_i(\underline{\mu}^*)\xi_i\Big)/(\underline{m}(\underline{\mu}^*),\underline{\nu}^{(k)}) \Bigg] \\ &\quad + o_{\underline{\xi}}(\underline{\nu}). \end{aligned} \tag{2.26}$$

Thus

$$d^2\hat{\ell}_{\underline{\mu}^*}(\underline{n},\underline{\xi})(\underline{\nu}) = -(\underline{\nu},\overline{D}(\underline{\mu}^*)\underline{\xi}) + \sum_{k=1}^{r} \frac{(\underline{\nu},\overline{D}(\underline{\mu}^*)\underline{\nu}^{(k)})(\underline{\xi},\overline{D}(\underline{\mu}^*)\underline{\nu}^{(k)})}{(\underline{\nu}^{(k)},\overline{D}(\underline{\mu}^*)\underline{\nu}^{(k)})}, \tag{2.27}$$

where $\overline{D}(\underline{\mu}^*)\{x_i\} = \{\overline{m}_i(\underline{\mu}^*)x_i\}$. If $\overline{P}_N(\underline{\mu}^*)$ is the orthogonal projection on N relative to the inner product $((\cdot,\cdot))$ defined by $((\underline{x},\underline{y})) = (\underline{x},\overline{D}(\underline{\mu}^*)\underline{y})$ for $\underline{x} \in R^I$ and $\underline{y} \in R^I$, then

(2.28) $$d^2\hat{\ell}^{(m)}_{\underline{\mu}^*}(\underline{n},\underline{\xi})(\underline{\nu}) = -(\underline{\nu},\overline{D}(\underline{\mu}^*)[I - \overline{P}_N(\underline{\mu}^*)]\underline{\xi})$$

$$= -(\overline{Q}_N(\underline{\mu}^*)\underline{\nu},\overline{D}(\underline{\mu}^*)\overline{Q}_N(\underline{\mu}^*)\underline{\xi}).$$

Here $\overline{Q}_N(\underline{\mu}^*) = I - \overline{P}_N(\underline{\mu}^*)$. Since $-(\overline{Q}_N(\underline{\mu}^*)\underline{\nu},\overline{D}(\underline{\mu}^*)\overline{Q}_N(\underline{\mu}^*)\underline{\nu}) \leq 0$ for $\underline{\nu} \in M - N$, $\ell^{(m)}(\underline{n},\underline{\mu}^*)$ is concave. If $-(\overline{Q}_N(\underline{\mu}^*)\underline{\nu},\overline{D}(\underline{\mu}^*)\overline{Q}_N(\underline{\mu}^*)\underline{\nu}) = 0$, then $\overline{Q}_N(\underline{\mu}^*)\underline{\nu} = 0$. Therefore, $\underline{\nu} \in N$. Since $\underline{\nu} \in M - N$, $\underline{\nu} = 0$. Thus $\hat{\ell}^{(m)}(\underline{n},\underline{\mu}^*)$ is strictly concave for $\underline{\mu}^* \in M - N$.

The fundamental result for multinomial models now follows:

THEOREM 2.4. *If* $\hat{\underline{\mu}}^{(m)}$ *is the maximum-likelihood estimate for a multinomial model for which* $\underline{\mu} \in M$ *and if* $\hat{\underline{\mu}}$ *is the corresponding estimate for a Poisson model for which* $\underline{\mu} \in M$, *then* $\hat{\underline{\mu}}^{(m)} = \hat{\underline{\mu}}$, *in the sense that when one side of the equation exists, then the other side exists and the two sides are equal.*

Proof. Suppose $\hat{\underline{\mu}}$ exists. Then for $\underline{\nu} \in M$,

(2.29) $$(\underline{\nu},\underline{n} - \hat{\underline{m}}) = 0.$$

Since $(\underline{n},\underline{\nu}^{(k)}) = (\hat{\underline{m}},\underline{\nu}^{(k)})$ for $k \in \overline{r}$, $\underline{\mu} \in \tilde{M}$. If $\underline{\mu}^* = P_{M-N}\hat{\underline{\mu}}$, then for any $\underline{\nu} \in M - N$,

(2.30) $$d\hat{\ell}^{(m)}_{\hat{\underline{\mu}}^*}(\underline{n},\underline{\nu}) = (\underline{\nu},\underline{n} - \hat{\underline{m}}) = 0.$$

Therefore, $\hat{\ell}^{(m)}(\underline{n},\underline{\mu}^*)$ has a critical point at $\hat{\underline{\mu}}^*$. Since $\hat{\ell}^{(m)}(\underline{n},\underline{\mu}^*)$ is strictly concave, this critical point, a maximum, is the only point $\underline{\mu}^*$ for which $d\hat{\ell}^{(m)}_{\underline{\mu}^*}(\underline{n},\underline{\nu})$ is 0 for all $\underline{\nu} \in M - N$. Thus $\hat{\underline{\mu}}^{(m)} = \underline{w}(\underline{\mu}^*) = \hat{\underline{\mu}}$.

On the other hand, suppose that $\hat{\underline{\mu}}^{(m)}$ exists. Then for $\underline{\nu} \in M - N$,

(2.31) $$(\underline{\nu},\underline{n} - \hat{\underline{m}}^{(m)}) = 0,$$

where $\hat{\underline{m}}^{(m)} = \{e^{\hat{\mu}_i^{(m)}}\}$. If $k \in \overline{r}$, then $(\underline{\nu}^{(k)},\hat{\underline{m}}^{(m)}) = (\underline{\nu}^{(k)},\underline{n})$. Thus for any $\underline{\nu} \in M$,

(2.32) $$(\underline{\nu},\underline{n} - \hat{\underline{m}}^{(m)}) = 0.$$

By Theorem 2.1, $\hat{\underline{\mu}} = \hat{\underline{\mu}}^{(m)}$. ||

Since Theorem 2.4 holds, the results concerning necessary and sufficient conditions for existence of maximum-likelihood estimates under Poisson sampling also apply to multinomial sampling.

THE CONDITIONAL POISSON MODEL

Maximum-likelihood estimation in the conditional Poisson case is somewhat more difficult than maximum-likelihood estimation in the Poisson or multinomial cases. However, the basic techniques employed in this case are analogous to those used for the other two models.

The log likelihood $\ell^{(c)}(\underline{n},\underline{\mu},\underline{c})$ is bounded above, as may be seen by noting that

$$(2.33)\qquad p(\underline{n},\underline{\mu},\underline{c}) = \left[1 + \sum_{\underline{\bar{n}}\in S(\underline{c})} \prod_{i\in I} \left(\frac{n_i!}{\bar{n}_i!}\right) \exp(\underline{\bar{n}} - \underline{n}, P_{M-N}\underline{\mu})\right]^{-1}$$

Suppose $\hat{\ell}^{(c)}(\underline{n},\underline{\mu},\underline{c})$ is the restriction of $\ell^{(c)}(\underline{n},\underline{\mu},\underline{c})$ to $\underline{\mu} \in M - N$. We suppose that $M - N \neq \{\underline{0}\}$. If $\underline{m}(\underline{\mu},\underline{c})$ satisfies

$$(2.34)\qquad \underline{m}(\underline{\mu},\underline{c}) = \sum_{\underline{n}\in S(\underline{c})} \underline{n}\, p(\underline{n},\underline{\mu},\underline{c}),$$

then the first differential $d\hat{\ell}_{\underline{\mu}}(\underline{n},\underline{\nu},\underline{c})$ satisfies

$$(2.35)\qquad d\hat{\ell}_{\underline{\mu}}^{(c)}(\underline{n},\underline{\nu},\underline{c}) = (\underline{\nu},\underline{n} - \underline{m}(\underline{\mu},\underline{c}))$$

for $\underline{\nu} \in M - N$. If $D(\underline{\mu},\underline{c})$ satisfies

$$(2.36)\qquad D(\underline{\mu},\underline{c}) = \sum_{\underline{n}\in S(\underline{c})} \{[\underline{n} - \underline{m}(\underline{\mu},\underline{c})] \otimes [\underline{n} - \underline{m}(\underline{\mu},\underline{c})]\} p(\underline{n},\underline{\mu},\underline{c}),$$

then the second differential $d^2\hat{\ell}_{\underline{\mu}}^{(c)}(\underline{n},\underline{\xi},\underline{c})(\underline{\nu})$ satisfies

$$(2.37)\qquad d^2\hat{\ell}_{\underline{\mu}}^{(c)}(\underline{n},\underline{\xi},\underline{c})(\underline{\nu}) = -(\underline{\nu},D(\underline{\mu},\underline{c})\underline{\xi}).$$

Derivations of (2.35) and (2.37) are quite similar to those for (2.4) and (2.9). Since $-(\underline{\nu},D(\underline{\mu},\underline{c})\underline{\nu}) \leq 0$ for any $\underline{\nu} \in M - N$, $\underline{\mu} \in M - N$, $\hat{\ell}^{(c)}(\underline{n},\underline{\mu},\underline{c})$ is concave.

Unlike the corresponding functions in the Poisson or multinomial models, $\hat{\ell}^{(c)}(\underline{n},\underline{\mu},\underline{c})$ need not be strictly concave. If $\hat{\ell}^{(c)}(\underline{n},\underline{\mu},\underline{c})$ is not strictly concave, there exists $\underline{\nu} \in M - N$ such that $(\underline{\nu},D(\underline{\mu},\underline{c})\underline{\nu}) = 0$. In this case, $(\underline{\bar{n}},\underline{\nu})$ must be constant for all $\underline{\bar{n}} \in S(\underline{c})$. Suppose that N_1 is the span of all $\underline{\nu} \in M - N$ such that $(\underline{\bar{n}},\underline{\nu})$ is constant for $\underline{\bar{n}} \in S(\underline{c})$. If $L = (M - N) - N_1$, then

$$(2.38)\qquad p(\underline{n},\underline{\mu},\underline{c}) = \left[1 + \sum_{\underline{\bar{n}}\in S(\underline{c})} \prod_{i\in I} \left(\frac{n_i!}{\bar{n}_i!}\right) \exp(\underline{\bar{n}} - \underline{n}, P_L\underline{\mu})\right]^{-1}$$

Thus $P_{M-N}\underline{\mu} - P_L\underline{\mu}$ cannot be estimated from the data. This problem arises since specification of $P_N\underline{n}$ implies specification of $P_{N-N_1}\underline{n}$. From now on N_1 is assumed to be $\{\underline{0}\}$. In this case, $\hat{\ell}^{(c)}(\underline{n},\underline{\mu},\underline{c})$ is strictly concave. Thus if a maximum-likelihood estimate $\hat{\underline{\mu}}^{(c)}$ of $P_{M-N}\underline{\mu}$ exists, the estimate is unique and is the only solution in $M - N$ of the equation

(2.39) $$(\underline{\nu},\underline{n} - \underline{m}(\underline{\mu},\underline{c})) = 0$$

for every $\underline{\nu} \in M - N$. Thus

(2.40) $$P_{M-N}\underline{m}(\hat{\underline{\mu}}^{(c)},\underline{c}) = P_{M-N}\underline{n}.$$

On the other hand, if (2.40) holds for some $\hat{\underline{\mu}}^{(c)} \in M - N$, then $\hat{\underline{\mu}}^{(c)}$ is the maximum-likelihood estimate of $P_{M-N}\underline{\mu}$.

The results just derived are rather similar to the results found in the multinomia and Poisson models. The new results are not easily applied, however, since computation of $\underline{m}(\underline{\mu},\underline{c})$ requires two summations. As pointed out in chapter 1, these summations involve many terms even in simple tables with all n_i small. In contrast, $\underline{m}(\underline{\mu})$ may be derived from $\underline{\mu}$ by exponentiation. Thus computation of the maximum-likelihood estimate in the conditional Poisson model is much more costly than in the Poisson or multinomial model.

In the general conditional Poisson model, if $\underline{\mu} \in M - N$, it need not be the case that $\{\log m_i(\underline{\mu},\underline{c})\} \in M$. Thus the estimate $\hat{\underline{\mu}}^{(c)}$ of $P_{M-N}\underline{\mu}$ need not coincide with the estimate $\hat{\underline{\mu}}$ based on $\underline{\mu} \in M$. Thus conditional Poisson estimation is quite distinct from Poisson estimation. In particular, necessary and sufficient conditions for the existence of estimates are different in the conditional Poisson case. In the conditional Poisson case, the following theorem applies:

THEOREM 2.5. *The maximum-likelihood estimate* $\hat{\underline{\mu}}^{(c)}$ *of* $P_{M-N}\underline{\mu}$ *exists if and only if the set* $S = \{\underline{\mu} \in M - N: (\bar{\underline{n}} - \underline{n},\underline{\mu}) \le 0 \ \forall \bar{\underline{n}} \in S(\underline{c})\}$ *contains only the zero vector.*

Proof. Suppose that $S \neq \{\underline{0}\}$ and $\hat{\underline{\mu}}^{(c)}$ exists. Suppose $\underline{\mu} \neq \underline{0}$ and $\underline{\mu} \in S$. Then by (2.33), $p(\underline{n},\hat{\underline{\mu}}^{(c)} + k\underline{\mu},\underline{c})$ is an increasing function of k. Since $(\bar{\underline{n}},\underline{\mu}) = (\underline{n},\underline{\mu})$ for all $\bar{\underline{n}} \in S(\underline{c})$ implies $\underline{\mu} \in M$, it follows that $p(\underline{n},\hat{\underline{\mu}}^{(c)} + k\underline{\mu},\underline{c})$ is strictly increasing. However, in this case, $\hat{\underline{\mu}}^{(c)}$ cannot be the maximum-likelihood estimate. Thus $\hat{\underline{\mu}}^{(c)}$ does not exist.

On the other hand, suppose that $S = \{\underline{0}\}$. By (2.33), there exists some $k > 0$

such that $p(\underline{n},\underline{\mu},\underline{c}) < p(\underline{n},\underline{0},\underline{c})$, unless $(\overline{n} - \underline{n},\underline{\mu}) \le k$ for every $\overline{n} \in S(\underline{c})$. If $T(k) = \{\underline{\mu} \in M - N: (\overline{n} - \underline{n},\underline{\mu}) \le k \; \forall \overline{n} \in S(\underline{c})\}$ then it is only necessary to show that $T(k)$ is bounded. If $T(k)$ is bounded, then $T(k)$ is compact and the maximum of $\hat{\ell}^{(c)}(\underline{n},\underline{\mu},\underline{c})$ is achieved for some $\underline{\mu} \in T(k)$.

Suppose now that $T(k)$ is unbounded. Then for any $x_j > 0$, $T(x_j)$ is unbounded. If $x_j \longrightarrow 0$ as $j \longrightarrow \infty$, then $S = \lim_{j\to\infty} T(x_j)$. If x_j is a decreasing sequence, then $T(x_j) \subset T(x_{j'})$ if $j > j'$. If $\underline{\mu} \in T(x)$ for $x > 0$, then for any y such that $0 < y < 1$, $y\underline{\mu} \in T(x)$. Thus a sequence $\{\underline{\mu}^{(j)}: j > 0\}$ may be selected so that $\|\underline{\mu}^{(j)}\| = 1$ for all $j > 0$ and $\underline{\mu}^{(j)} \in T(x_j)$. Since $\{\underline{\mu}^{(j)}: j > 0\}$ is a bounded sequence, there exists a limit point $\underline{\mu}$ for the sequence. For each j, $T(x_j)$ is closed, while for $j > j'$, $\underline{\mu}^{(j)} \in T(x_{j'})$. It follows that $\underline{\mu} \in T(x_j)$ for each j. Consequently, $\underline{\mu} \in S$. Since $\underline{\mu} \ne \underline{0}$, a contradiction results. Thus $T(k)$ must be bounded. Therefore, $\hat{\underline{\mu}}^{(c)}$ exists. ||

The conditions of the theorem can in some cases be readily verified. The following corollary provides one criterion:

COROLLARY 2.2. *Suppose* $\{\underline{\nu}^{(k)}: k \in \overline{q-r}\}$ *is a basis of* $N^{\perp}$ *such that* $\nu_i^{(k)}$ *is an integer for each* $i \in I$ *and* $k \in \overline{q-r}$. *Suppose* $|\nu_i^{(k)}| \le 1$ *for any* $i \in I$ *and* $k \in \overline{q-r}$. *If* $n_i > 0$ *for each* $i \in I$, *then the maximum-likelihood estimate* $\hat{\underline{\mu}}^{(c)}$ *exists for conditional Poisson sampling with* $P_N\underline{n}$ *fixed and* $\underline{\mu} \in M$.

Proof. If $k \in \overline{q-r}$, then $\underline{n} + \underline{\nu}^{(k)}$ and $\underline{n} - \underline{\nu}^{(k)}$ are in $S(P_N\underline{n})$. If $\underline{\mu} \in S$, then for each $k \in \overline{q-r}$, $(\underline{\mu},\underline{\nu}^{(k)}) \le 0$ and $-(\underline{\mu},\underline{\nu}^{(k)}) \le 0$. Thus $\underline{\mu} = \underline{0}$. By Theorem 2.5, the maximum-likelihood estimate $\hat{\underline{\mu}}^{(c)}$ exists. ||

The manifold M has no role in this corollary. The result may be strengthened by noting that if $\overline{n} \in S(P_N\underline{n})$ and $P_M\overline{n} = P_M\underline{n}$, then by Theorem 2.5 a maximum-likelihood estimate exists for $\overline{n}$ if and only if a maximum likelihood exists for $\underline{n}$. Thus if N has the basis specified in Corollary 2.2 and $\overline{n}_i > 0$ for $i \in I$, then a maximum-likelihood estimate $\underline{\mu}^{(c)}$ exists for the sample vector $\underline{n}$.

The complete log-mean vector $\underline{\mu}$ may be estimated from the data if $P_N\underline{m}$ is known. The following theorem may be employed:

THEOREM 2.6. *Suppose that for some* $\overline{\underline{\mu}} \in M$, $P_N\{e^{\overline{\mu}_i}\} = \underline{c}$. *Then if* $\underline{\mu}^{(1)} \in M - N$, *there exists a unique* $\underline{\mu}^{(2)} \in M$ *such that* $P_N\{\exp(\mu_i^{(1)} + \mu_i^{(2)})\} = \underline{c}$. *The function*

$$f(\underline{c},\underline{\mu},\underline{\mu}^{(1)}) = (\underline{c},\underline{\mu}) - \sum_{i\in I} e^{\mu_i^{(1)}} e^{\mu_i} \tag{2.41}$$

defined for $\underline{\mu} \in N$ *achieves a maximum for* $\underline{\mu} = \underline{\mu}^{(2)}$.

Proof. The function $f(\underline{c},\underline{\mu},\underline{\mu}^{(1)})$ is very similar in form to $\ell(\underline{n},\underline{\mu})$. By similar arguments to those used to find the first two differentials of $\ell(\underline{n},\underline{\mu})$, one finds that the first differential $df_{\underline{\mu}}(\underline{c},\underline{\nu},\underline{\mu}^{(1)})$ satisfies

(2.42) $$df_{\underline{\mu}}(\underline{c},\underline{\nu},\underline{\mu}^{(1)}) = (\underline{\nu},\underline{c} - \{\exp(\mu_i + \mu_i^{(1)})\}),$$

where $\underline{\nu} \in N$. The second differential $d^2f_{\underline{\mu}}(\underline{c},\underline{\xi},\underline{\mu}^{(1)})(\underline{\nu})$ satisfies

(2.43) $$d^2f_{\underline{\mu}}(\underline{c},\underline{\xi},\underline{\mu}^{(1)})(\underline{\nu}) = -\sum_{i\in I} \xi_i \nu_i e^{\mu_i+\mu_i^{(1)}}$$

Thus $f(\underline{c},\underline{\mu},\underline{\mu}^{(1)})$ is a strictly concave function of $\underline{\mu}$. The function has at most one maximum. If the maximum exists, it is attained when

(2.44) $$P_N\{\exp(\mu_i + \mu_i^{(1)})\} = P_N\underline{c} = \underline{c}.$$

Thus if $\underline{\mu}^{(2)}$ exists, it is unique and is the location of the maximum of $f(\underline{c},\underline{\mu},\underline{\mu}^{(1)})$.

To show that $\underline{\mu}^{(2)}$ exists, it suffices to show that a necessary and sufficient condition that $f(\underline{c},\underline{\mu},\underline{\mu}^{(1)})$ have a maximum is that there exist a $\underline{\delta} \in N^{\perp}$ such that $c_i + \delta_i > 0$ for all $i \in I$. If this result holds, then $f(\underline{c},\underline{\mu},\underline{\mu}^{(1)})$ has a maximum for all values of $\underline{\mu}^{(1)} \in M - N$ or for none of them. By assumption, $f(\underline{c},\underline{\mu},P_{M-N}\bar{\underline{\mu}})$ has a maximum. Thus $\underline{\mu}^{(2)}$ exists for any $\underline{\mu}^{(1)} \in M - N$. The desired necessary and sufficient conditions follow by a proof almost identical to the one used in Theorem 2.2.||

If $\hat{\underline{\mu}}^{(c)}$ is the maximum-likelihood estimate of $P_{M-N}\underline{\mu}$ and if $P_{M-N}\underline{m}$ is know, then Theorem 2.6 may be used to find a $\underline{\mu}^{(2)} \in N$ such that $P_N\{\exp(\mu_i^{(c)} + \mu_i^{(2)})\} = P_N\underline{m}$. In this case, $\hat{\underline{\mu}}^{(c)} + \underline{\mu}^{(2)}$ is the maximum-likelihood estimate of $\underline{\mu}$. This theorem is also of interest in chapter 9, where flats are considered rather than linear manifolds.

Chapter 3

NUMERICAL EVALUATION OF MAXIMUM-LIKELIHOOD ESTIMATES

Determination of maximum-likelihood estimates has received considerable attention in the Poisson and multinomial cases. Algorithms for various contingency table models have been suggested by Roy and Kastenbaum (1956), Darroch (1962), Bishop (1967), Kullback and Ireland (1968), and others. Among authors who have proposed algorithms for logit or multinomial logit models are Dyke and Patterson (1952), Finney (1971), and Bock (1968). In this chapter, the problem is examined in terms of conventional function maximization methods. Two algorithms are suggested. Both methods converge for any $\underline{n}$ and $\mathcal{M}$ for which the maximum-likelihood estimate exists. One algorithm, a modified version of the Newton-Raphson procedure, has a superior convergence rate, while the other method, a generalization of the Deming-Stephan algorithm, is generally easier to apply to complex models. Some of the numerical techniques used in the chapter are also discussed in Haberman (1971).

In this chapter, Poisson and multinomial models are considered. The general theory developed also applies to conditional Poisson models, but evaluátion of functions and partial derivatives is very difficult in the latter case. Unless otherwise specified, Poisson or multinomial sampling is assumed in this chapter.

In some designs, iterative procedures are unnecessary. For example, if I is $\overline{2} \times \overline{2}$ and $\mathcal{M}$ is the additive manifold defined by (1.7), then if $\langle i,j \rangle \in \overline{2} \times \overline{2}$,

$$\hat{m}_{ij} = \frac{n_{i+}n_{+j}}{n_{++}} , \tag{3.1}$$

provided $n_{i+} > 0$ for $i \in \overline{2}$ and $n_{+j} > 0$ for $j \in \overline{2}$. Many other examples exist of manifolds for factorial tables such that $\underline{\hat{m}}$ can be expressed in closed form. Such manifolds are discussed at length in chapters 5 and 7. In this chapter, it is assumed that no closed-form expression for $\underline{\hat{m}}$ is available. Thus an iterative solution is required.

The function maximization algorithms proposed in this section apply equally well to $\hat{\ell}^{(p)}(\underline{n},\underline{\mu})$, $\hat{\ell}^{(m)}(\underline{n},\underline{\mu})$, and $\hat{\ell}^{(c)}(\underline{n},\underline{\mu},\underline{c})$. In general, the algorithms proposed apply to any function f from a linear manifold M to the real line R such that a maximum is achieved for some $\underline{\mu}^* \in M$ and for any $\underline{\mu} \in M$, $d^2f_{\underline{\mu}}$ exists and is negative definite. Convergence results depend on the continuity of $d^2f_{\underline{\mu}}$ and on the existence and continuity of $d^3f_{\underline{\mu}}$, the third differential.

THE MODIFIED NEWTON-RAPHSON ALGORITHM

The first method considered is a modified version of the Newton-Raphson algorithm. In the proposed method, if $\underline{\mu}^{(t)}$ is an estimate of $\underline{\mu}^*$, $t \geq 0$, then a new estimate $\underline{\mu}^{(t+1)}$ is defined by

$$(3.2) \qquad \underline{\mu}^{(t+1)} = \underline{\mu}^{(t)} - \alpha^{(t)}(d^2f_{\underline{\mu}^{(t)}})^{-1}(df_{\underline{\mu}^{(t)}}) = \underline{\mu}^{(t)} + \alpha^{(t)}\underline{s}^{(t)},$$

where $\alpha^{(t)}$ is an estimate of the maximum of

$$(3.3) \qquad h^{(t)}(\alpha) = f(\underline{\mu}^{(t)} + \alpha\underline{s}^{(t)})$$

such that $\alpha^{(t)} > 0$ satisfies

$$(3.4) \qquad |df_{\underline{\mu}^{(t+1)}}(\underline{s}^{(t)})| \leq \frac{b}{\alpha^{(t)}}[f(\underline{\mu}^{(t+1)}) - f(\underline{\mu}^{(t)})] .$$

In (3.4), $0 < b < 1$. The multiplier $\alpha^{(t)}$ is chosen to be 1 if this value of $\alpha^{(t)}$ satisfies (3.4). If 1 is not an acceptable value of $\alpha^{(t)}$, then $\alpha^{(t)}$ may be found by the cubic interpolation method of Davidon (1959). The properties of the algorithm are discussed in Haberman (1971).

When $\alpha^{(t)} = 1$, the iteration described by (3.2) coincides with the classical Newton-Raphson iteration. Use of values of $\alpha^{(t)}$ other than 1 prevents divergence of the algorithm. Without some condition comparable to (3.4), it is possible that the function value $f(\underline{\mu}^{(t+1)})$ may be smaller than $f(\underline{\mu}^{(t)})$, so that $\underline{\mu}^{(t+1)}$ is a poorer estimate of $\underline{\mu}^*$ than $\underline{\mu}^{(t)}$ is. The object of the proposed algorithm is to retain the excellent behavior of the Newton-Raphson algorithm in the neighborhood of a solution and to ensure convergence from initial estimates $\underline{\mu}^{(0)}$ which are not close to $\underline{\mu}^*$. The following theorem shows that both aims are achieved.

THEOREM 3.1. *Suppose* $f(\underline{\mu})$ *has a maximum at* $\underline{\mu}^*$ *and* $d^2f_{\underline{\mu}}$ *is continuous in* $\underline{\mu}$.

a) For each $t > 0$ *such that* $\underline{\mu}^{(t)} \neq \underline{\mu}^*$, *there exists* $\alpha^{(t)} > 0$ *such that* (3.4) *is satisfied.*

b) Either for some $t > 0$, $\underline{\mu}^{(t)} = \underline{\mu}^*$, *or* $\underline{\mu}^{(t)} \longrightarrow \underline{\mu}^*$ *as* $t \longrightarrow \infty$.

c) For any $\underline{\mu}^{(0)} \in M$, *there exists a* t_0 *such that if* $t \geq t_0$, *then* $\alpha^{(t)} = 1$.

d) If $d^3f_{\underline{\mu}}$ *exists and is continuous at* $\underline{\mu}^*$ *and if* $\underline{\mu}^{(t)} \neq \underline{\mu}^*$ *for* $t \geq 0$, *then*

$$\limsup_{t \to \infty} \frac{\|\underline{\mu}^{(t+1)} - \underline{\mu}^*\|}{\|\underline{\mu}^{(t)} - \underline{\mu}^*\|^2} \leq \frac{1}{2} \|(d^2f_{\underline{\mu}^*})^{-1} \circ d^3f_{\underline{\mu}^*}\| . \tag{3.5}$$

Remarks. The symbol $\circ$ represents functional composition. The function $[d^2f_{\underline{\mu}^*}]^{-1} \circ d^3f_{\underline{\mu}^*}$ is a mapping from M to the space of linear transformations from M to M. If ℓ is a linear function from a linear manifold A to a linear manifold B, then $\|\ell\| = \sup_{\{\underline{\mu} \in B:\ \|\underline{\mu}\| = 1\}} \|\ell(\underline{\mu})\|$. Thus

$$\|[d^2f_{\underline{\mu}^*}]^{-1} \circ d^3f_{\underline{\mu}^*}\| = \sup_{\substack{\{\underline{\mu} \in M:\ \|\underline{\mu}\| = 1\} \\ \{\underline{\nu} \in M:\ \|\underline{\mu}\| = 1\}}} \|[d^2f_{\underline{\mu}^*}]^{-1} \circ d^3f_{\underline{\mu}^*}(\underline{\mu})(\underline{\nu})\| .$$

By (c), the algorithm reduces to the conventional Newton-Raphson algorithm when t is sufficiently large. The convergence property (3.5) is known as quadratic convergence.

Proof. See Appendix C. ||

The usefulness of the modified Newton-Raphson algorithm depends primarily on the ease with which $\underline{s}^{(t)}$ can be computed. If $\underline{s}^{(t)}$ is not difficult to compute, then the stability and high rate of convergence of the algorithm make it highly attractive. If $\underline{s}^{(t)}$ is difficult to compute, simpler methods must be sought which do not require this calculation.

If $f(\underline{\mu})$ is $\hat{\ell}^{(p)}(\underline{n},\underline{\mu})$, the kernel of the Poisson log likelihood, then $\underline{s}^{(t)}$ satisfies

$$\underline{s}^{(t)} = P_M^*(\underline{\mu}^{(t)})D^{-1}(\underline{\mu}^{(t)})[\underline{n} - \underline{m}(\underline{\mu}^{(t)})], \tag{3.6}$$

and (3.4) reduces to the condition

$$|(\underline{n} - \underline{m}(\underline{\mu}^{(t+1)}), \underline{s}^{(t)})| \leq \frac{b}{\alpha^{(t)}} [\hat{\ell}^{(p)}(\underline{n},\underline{\mu}^{(t+1)}) - \hat{\ell}^{(p)}(\underline{n},\underline{\mu}^{(t)})], \tag{3.7}$$

where, as in chapter 1, $D(\underline{\mu}^{(t)})\underline{x} = \{\exp(\mu_i^{(t)})x_i\}$ for $\underline{x} \in R^I$ and $P_M^*(\underline{\mu}^{(t)})$ is the orthogonal projection on M with respect to the inner product defined for $\underline{x} \in R^I$ and $\underline{y} \in R^I$ by

$$(\underline{x},\underline{y})^{(t)} = (\underline{x}, D(\underline{\mu}^{(t)})\underline{y}). \tag{3.8}$$

To verify that $\underline{s}^{(t)}$ satisfies (3.6), observe that if (3.6) holds, then for every $\underline{\nu} \in M$,

$$\begin{aligned} d^2\hat{\ell}^{(p)}_{\underline{\mu}^{(t)}}(\underline{n},\underline{s}^{(t)})(\underline{\nu}) &= -(\underline{\nu}, D(\underline{\mu}^{(t)})\underline{s}^{(t)}) \\ &= -(\underline{\nu}, D(\underline{\mu}^{(t)})P^*_M(\underline{\mu}^{(t)})D^{-1}(\underline{\mu}^{(t)})[\underline{n} - \underline{m}(\underline{\mu}^{(t)})]) \\ &= -(P^*_M(\underline{\mu}^{(t)})\underline{\nu}, D(\underline{\mu}^{(t)})D^{-1}(\underline{\mu}^{(t)})[\underline{n} - \underline{m}(\underline{\mu}^{(t)})]) \\ &= -(\underline{\nu}, \underline{n} - \underline{m}(\underline{\mu}^{(t)})) \\ &= -d\hat{\ell}^{(p)}_{\underline{\mu}^{(t)}}(\underline{n},\underline{\nu}). \end{aligned} \tag{3.9}$$

The third equation holds since $P^*_M(\underline{\mu}^{(t)})$ is orthogonal with respect to the inner product $(\cdot,\cdot)^{(t)}$.

An alternate expression for $\underline{s}^{(t)}$ may be derived if M is a linear transformaticn from R^p onto M with adjoint M^T (see Halmos 1958). Then by Kruskal (1968a),

$$\begin{aligned} \underline{s}^{(t)} &= [M(M^TD(\underline{\mu}^{(t)})M)^{-1}M^TD(\underline{\mu}^{(t)})]D^{-1}(\underline{\mu}^{(t)})[\underline{n} - \underline{m}(\underline{\mu}^{(t)})] \\ &= M(M^TD(\underline{\mu}^{(t)})M)^{-1}M^T[\underline{n} - \underline{m}(\underline{\mu}^{(t)})]. \end{aligned} \tag{3.10}$$

Evaluation of this expression may be facilitated by use of the modified Cholesky decomposition of $M^TD(\underline{\mu}^{(t)})M$ (see Wilkinson 1965).

A more direct way to compute $\underline{s}^{(t)}$ is by the modified Gram-Schmidt algorithm of Bjorck (1967a,1967b,1968). If $\{\underline{\nu}^{(k,1)}: k \in \overline{p}\}$ is a basis of M and $P^*_M(\underline{\mu}^{(t)})\underline{Y}^{(1)}$ is to be found, then the Bjorck algorithm includes p steps. At the beginning of step j, $j \in \overline{p}$, $\{\underline{\nu}^{(k,j)}: k \in \overline{p}\}$ is a basis of M such that $\{\underline{\nu}^{(k,j)}: k \in \overline{j}\}$ is orthogonal with respect to $(\cdot,\cdot)^{(t)}$ and $Y^{(j)} = [I - P^*_{M^{(j-1)}}(\underline{\mu}^{(t)})]Y^{(1)}$, where $M^{(j-1)} =$ span $\{\underline{\nu}^{(k)}: k \in \overline{j-1}\}$. At step j, $\{\underline{\nu}^{(k,j+1)}: k \in \overline{p}\}$ and $\underline{Y}^{(j+1)}$ are defined by the following equations:

$$\underline{\nu}^{(k,j+1)} = \underline{\nu}^{(k,j)} \ \forall k \in \overline{j}, \tag{3.11}$$

$$\underline{\nu}^{(k,j+1)} = \underline{\nu}^{(k,j)} - \frac{(\underline{\nu}^{(k,j)},\underline{\nu}^{(j,j)})^{(t)}}{(\underline{\nu}^{(j,j)},\underline{\nu}^{(j,j)})^{(t)}}\underline{\nu}^{(j,j)} \quad \forall k \in \overline{p} - \overline{j}, \tag{3.12}$$

$$\underline{Y}^{(j+1)} = \underline{Y}^{(j)} - \frac{(\underline{Y}^{(j)},\underline{\nu}^{(j,j)})^{(t)}}{(\underline{\nu}^{(j,j)},\underline{\nu}^{(j,j)})^{(t)}}\underline{\nu}^{(j,j)} . \tag{3.13}$$

At the end of step p, $\{\underline{\nu}^{(k,p)}: k \in \overline{p}\}$ is an orthogonal basis of M relative to $(\cdot,\cdot)^{(t)}$ and $Y^{(p+1)} = [I - P_M^*(\underline{\mu}^{(t)})]\underline{Y}^{(1)}$. The projection $P_M^*(\underline{\mu}^{(t)})\underline{Y}^{(1)}$ is then $\underline{Y}^{(1)} - \underline{Y}^{(p+1)}$. The algorithm is algebraically equivalent to the Gram-Schmidt method, but the Bjorck approach has superior numerical properties, particularly when pivoting strategies are used to order the sets $\{\underline{\nu}^{(k,j)}: k \in \overline{p}\}$.

The unconventional inner product $(\cdot,\cdot)^{(t)}$ may be eliminated by using vectors

$$\underline{\lambda}^{(k,j)} = \{[m_i(\underline{\mu}^{(t)})]^{\frac{1}{2}} \nu_i^{(k,j)}\}$$

and

$$\underline{z}^{(j)} = \{[m_i(\underline{\mu}^{(t)})]^{\frac{1}{2}} Y_i^{(j)}\}.$$

In this case,

$$\underline{\lambda}^{(k,j+1)} = \underline{\lambda}^{(k,j)} \quad \forall k \in \overline{j}, \tag{3.14}$$

$$\underline{\lambda}^{(k,j+1)} = \underline{\lambda}^{(k,j)} - \frac{(\underline{\lambda}^{(k,j)},\underline{\lambda}^{(j,j)})}{(\underline{\lambda}^{(j,j)},\underline{\lambda}^{(j,j)})}\underline{\lambda}^{(j,j)} \quad \forall k \in \overline{p} - \overline{j}, \tag{3.15}$$

$$\underline{z}^{(j+1)} = \underline{z}^{(j)} - \frac{(\underline{z}^{(j)},\underline{\lambda}^{(j,j)})}{(\underline{\lambda}^{(j,j)},\underline{\lambda}^{(j,j)})}\underline{\lambda}^{(j,j)} . \tag{3.16}$$

The projection $\underline{Y}^{(1)} - \underline{Y}^{(p+1)}$ is found by observing that $Y^{(p+1)} = \{[m_i(\underline{\mu}^{(t)})]^{\frac{1}{2}} z_i^{(p+1)}\}$.

Any reasonable general method for computation of projections $P_M^*(\underline{\mu}^{(t)})\underline{Y}$ will involve computational labor approximately proportional to p^2q, where p is the dimension of M and q is the dimension of R^I. As a result, the Newton-Raphson algorithm normally is most satisfactory if p is small.

Example 3.1. Goodman (1961) considers the 2 × 2 × 2 table shown in table 3.1.

TABLE 3.1

PAROLE VIOLATORS

	Number of Violators	Number of Nonviolators
Without a Previous Criminal Record:		
Lone Offenders	26	27
Group Offenders	28	93
With a Previous Criminal Record:		
Lone Offenders	21	26
Group Offenders	36	49

Here $I = \bar{2} \times \bar{2} \times \bar{2}$. If the index k corresponds to presence or absence of a criminal record, i corresponds to type of offender, and j corresponds to conduct on parole, then one may wish to determine whether evidence exists that the cross-product ratio $m_{111}m_{221}/m_{121}m_{211}$ is equal to the cross-product ratio $m_{112}m_{222}/m_{122}m_{212}$. If equality holds, $\underline{\mu} \in \{\bar{\underline{\mu}}\}^{\perp}$, where

$$\bar{\underline{\mu}} = \begin{array}{|cc|}\hline 1 & -1 \\ -1 & 1 \\ \hline\end{array} \quad \begin{array}{|cc|}\hline -1 & +1 \\ +1 & -1 \\ \hline\end{array} \tag{3.17}$$

The manifold $M = \{\bar{\underline{\mu}}\}^{\perp}$ consists of all $\underline{\mu}$ such that for some $\{a_{ij}\}$, $\{b_{ik}\}$, and $\{c_{jk}\}$,

$$\mu_{ijk} = a_{ij} + b_{ik} + c_{jk}. \tag{3.18}$$

This manifold is also considered in Appendix B. In analysis-of-variance terminology, it corresponds to a hypothesis of no three-factor interaction.

Use of the Newton-Raphson algorithm requires evaluation of $P_M^*(\underline{\mu}^{(t)})$. To compute this projection, let $R = \text{span}\,\{D^{-1}(\underline{\mu}^{(t)})\bar{\underline{\mu}}\}$. Observe that if $\underline{\mu} \in M$,

$$\begin{aligned}(\underline{\mu}, D(\underline{\mu}^{(t)})[D^{-1}(\underline{\mu}^{(t)})\bar{\underline{\mu}}]) \\ = (\underline{\mu}, \bar{\underline{\mu}}) \\ = 0.\end{aligned} \tag{3.19}$$

Thus R is the orthogonal complement of M relative to the inner product $(\cdot,\cdot)^{(t)}$, and

(3.20) $$P^*_M(\underline{\mu}^{(t)}) = I - P^*_R(\underline{\mu}^{(t)})$$

$$= I - (c^{(t)})^{-1}\{[D^{-1}(\underline{\mu}^{(t)})\overline{\underline{\mu}}] \bullet [D^{-1}(\underline{\mu}^{(t)})\underline{\mu}]\}D(\underline{\mu}^{(t)}),$$

where

(3.21) $$c^{(t)} = (\overline{\underline{\mu}}, D^{-1}(\underline{\mu}^{(t)})\overline{\underline{\mu}})$$

$$= \sum_{i=1}^{2}\sum_{j=1}^{2}\sum_{k=1}^{2} [1/m_{ijk}(\underline{\mu}^{(t)})].$$

It now follows that

(3.22) $$\underline{s}^{(t)} = -\underline{d}(\underline{\mu}^{(t)}) + (c^{(t)})^{-1}(\overline{\underline{\mu}}, \underline{d}(\underline{\mu}^{(t)}))D^{-1}(\underline{\mu}^{(t)})\overline{\underline{\mu}} ,$$

where

(3.23) $$\underline{d}(\underline{\mu}^{(t)}) = D^{-1}(\underline{\mu}^{(t)})[\underline{n} - \underline{m}(\underline{\mu}^{(t)})] .$$

If $\underline{m}^{(t)} = \underline{m}(\underline{\mu}^{(t)})$,

(3.24) $$\underline{d}(\underline{\mu}^{(t)}) = \{(n_{ijk} - m^{(t)}_{ijk})/m^{(t)}_{ijk}\},$$

(3.25) $$(\overline{\underline{\mu}}, d(\underline{\mu}^{(t)})) = \sum_{i=1}^{2}\sum_{j=1}^{2}\sum_{k=1}^{2} \overline{\mu}_{ijk}(n_{ijk} - m^{(t)}_{ijk})/m^{(t)}_{ijk} ,$$

(3.26) $$D^{-1}(\underline{\mu}^{(t)})\overline{\underline{\mu}} = \{\overline{\mu}_{ijk}/m^{(t)}_{ijk}\} .$$

Thus $\underline{s}^{(t)}$ is readily evaluated.

To employ the modified Newton-Raphson algorith, it is necessary to select a starting value $\underline{\mu}^{(0)}$. A crude method would be to note that $\{\log n_{ijk}\}$ has a range from 3 to 4.5. A very simple starting value might be $\underline{\mu}^{(0)} = 4\underline{e}$, where $\underline{e}$ is the unit vector. If this choice is made, then

(3.27) $\underline{s}^{(0)} =$

-0.65	-0.37		-0.49	-0.65
-0.36	0.58		-0.47	0.03

If $b = 0.9$, $\alpha^{(0)} = 1$ and

(3.28) $\underline{\mu}^{(1)} =$

3.35	3.62		3.51	3.35
3.64	4.58		3.53	4.03

The vector $\underline{s}^{(0)}$ is rather substantial, so a second iteration is needed. In this case,

(3.29) $$\underline{s}^{(1)} = \begin{array}{|cc|}\hline -0.23 & -0.17 \\ -0.16 & -0.08 \\ \hline\end{array} \quad \begin{array}{|cc|}\hline -0.25 & -0.23 \\ -0.07 & -0.05 \\ \hline\end{array},$$

$\alpha^{(1)} = 1$, and

(3.30) $$\underline{\mu}^{(2)} = \begin{array}{|cc|}\hline 3.11 & 3.46 \\ 3.49 & 4.49 \\ \hline\end{array} \quad \begin{array}{|cc|}\hline 3.26 & 3.11 \\ 3.46 & 3.98 \\ \hline\end{array}.$$

The step size $\underline{s}^{(1)}$ is still substantial, so further iterations are required. After two more iterations,

(3.31) $$\underline{s}^{(3)} = \begin{array}{|cc|}\hline -0.0005 & -0.0001 \\ -0.0001 & -0.0000 \\ \hline\end{array} \quad \begin{array}{|cc|}\hline -0.0007 & -0.0005 \\ 0.0000 & -0.0000 \\ \hline\end{array},$$

$\alpha^{(3)} = 1$, and

(3.32) $$\underline{\mu}^{(4)} = \begin{array}{|cc|}\hline 3.08 & 3.44 \\ 3.47 & 4.49 \\ \hline\end{array} \quad \begin{array}{|cc|}\hline 3.23 & 3.08 \\ 3.46 & 3.97 \\ \hline\end{array}.$$

At this point, it is apparent that a close approximation to $\hat{\underline{\mu}}$ has been achieved. In fact, $\underline{\mu}^{(3)}$ and $\underline{\mu}^{(4)}$ differ by negligible amounts.

It should be observed that

(3.33) $$\underline{m}^{(4)} = \begin{array}{|cc|}\hline 21.81 & 31.19 \\ 32.19 & 88.81 \\ \hline\end{array} \quad \begin{array}{|cc|}\hline 25.19 & 21.81 \\ 31.81 & 53.19 \\ \hline\end{array}$$

and

(3.34) $$\underline{n} - \underline{m}^{(4)} = \begin{array}{|cc|}\hline 4.19 & -4.19 \\ -4.19 & 4.19 \\ \hline\end{array} \quad \begin{array}{|cc|}\hline -4.19 & 4.19 \\ 4.19 & -4.19 \\ \hline\end{array}.$$

The residual vector $\underline{n} - \underline{m}^{(4)}$ is approximately 4.19 $\bar{\underline{\mu}}$. As shown in the next chapter, this vector is large enough to suggest that the original hypothesis that $\underline{\mu} \in M$ is untenable.

Convergence with the starting value $\underline{\mu}^{(0)} = 4\underline{e}$ is not very rapid. Better results may be obtained if $\underline{\mu}^{(0)} = P_M^*(\underline{\nu})\underline{\nu}$, where $\underline{\nu} = \{\log n_i\}$. The motivation for this choice is explained in chapter 4. In this case,

$$\underline{\mu}^{(1)} = \begin{array}{|cc|}\hline 3.08 & 3.44 \\ 3.47 & 4.49 \\ \hline\end{array} \quad \begin{array}{|cc|}\hline 3.23 & 3.08 \\ 3.46 & 3.97 \\ \hline\end{array} \tag{3.35}$$

This result illustrates the utility of a good starting value. In this example, $\underline{\mu}^{(1)}$ is as good an estimate of $\hat{\underline{\mu}}$ as $\underline{\mu}^{(3)}$ was when $\underline{\mu}^{(0)}$ was $4\underline{e}$.

Example 3.2. Muller and Mayhall (1971) consider the variation of prevalence of *torus mandibularis*, a protuberance in the jaw, among Eskimo tribes. The data are summarized in table 3.2. The prevalence of this condition clearly increases as age increases. Other relationships in the table are difficult to ascertain by visual inspection. As a preliminary step in the analysis of the table, one might suppose that the only dependence among the four classifying variables is a relationship between presence or absence and age. This relationship might be expected to be a linear one between the logit corresponding to presence or absence of the condition and the age of the Eskimo.

TABLE 3.2

PRESENCE OR ABSENCE OF *TORUS MANDIBULARIS*

Population	Sex	Presence or Absence	Age Group 1-10	11-20	21-30	31-40	41-50	51+
Igloolik	Male	Present	4	8	13	18	10	12
		Absent	44	32	21	5	0	1
	Female	Present	1	11	19	13	6	10
		Absent	42	17	17	5	4	2
Hall Beach	Male	Present	2	5	7	5	4	4
		Absent	17	10	6	2	2	1
	Female	Present	1	3	2	5	4	2
		Absent	12	16	6	2	0	0
Aleut	Male	Present	4	2	4	7	4	3
		Absent	6	13	3	3	5	3
	Female	Present	3	1	2	2	2	4
		Absent	10	7	12	5	2	1

If $p_{ijk\ell}$ is the probability that an Eskimo is in tribe i, has sex j, *torus* condition k, and age group ℓ, then one may suppose that

(3.36) $$\log(p_{ij1\ell}/p_{ij2\ell}) = \alpha + \beta\ell$$

and

(3.37) $$p_{ijk\ell} = p_{i+++}p_{+j++}p_{++k\ell}.$$

Here p_{i+++} is the marginal probability that an Eskimo is in tribe i. The probabilities p_{+j++} and $p_{++k\ell}$ are defined in a similar manner. Given these assumptions, the log mean $\mu_{ijk\ell}$ satisfies the equation

(3.38) $$\mu_{ijk\ell} = a_i + b_j + c_k + d_\ell + \beta\ell(k - 3/2)$$

for some $\{a_i\}$, $\{b_j\}$, $\{c_k\}$, $\{d_\ell\}$, and β. The corresponding linear manifold $\mathcal{M} = \{\underline{\mu}\colon \mu_{ijk\ell} = a_i + b_j + c_k + d_\ell + \beta\ell(k - 3/2)\}$ has dimension 11.

Given the excellent results obtained in Example 3.1 when $P^*_{\mathcal{M}}(\underline{\nu})\underline{\nu}$ was used as an initial estimate $\underline{\mu}^{(0)}$, a repetition of this procedure seems appropriate. Unfortunately, n_{1125}, n_{2225}, and n_{2226} are all zero. Consequently, $\underline{\nu}$ is not properly defined. A simple expedient which avoids this difficulty is to define $\nu_{ijk\ell}$ as $\log(\frac{1}{2})$ when $n_{ijk\ell} = 0$.

The vector $\underline{s}^{(t)}$ may be obtained by means of (3.10) and the modified Cholesky decomposition. For such a computation, a basis $\{\underline{\nu}^{(h)}\colon h \in \overline{p}\}$ must be obtained for $\mathcal{M}$, and the cross-products

(3.39) $$(\underline{\nu}^{(h)}, D(\underline{\mu}^{(t)})\underline{\nu}^{(g)}) = \sum_{i \in I} \nu_i^{(h)} m_i^{(t)} \nu_i^{(g)}$$

should be accumulated and, if possible, stored in double-precision arithmetic. The mapping M is defined for $\underline{x} \in R^p$ by

(3.40) $$M\underline{x} = \sum_{h=1}^{p} x_h \underline{\nu}^{(h)} .$$

The modified Cholesky decomposition is used to solve the equation

(3.41) $$[M^T D(\underline{\mu}^{(t)})M]\underline{x}^{(t)} = M^T(\underline{n} - \underline{m}^{(t)}),$$

where

(3.42) $$[M^T D(\underline{\mu}^{(t)})M]_{gh} = (\underline{\nu}^{(g)}, D(\underline{\mu}^{(t)})\underline{\nu}^{(h)})$$

and

(3.43) $$[M^T(\underline{n} - \underline{m}^{(t)})]_h = (\underline{\nu}^{(h)}, \underline{n} - \underline{m}^{(t)}) .$$

Given the solution of (3.41), it follows from (3.10) that

$$s^{(t)} = Mx^{(t)} = \sum_{h=1}^{p} x_h^{(t)} \underline{\nu}^{(h)} \tag{3.44}$$

In this example, a possible basis consists of the following vectors:

$$\underline{\nu}^{(h)} = \{\delta_{\ell h}: i \in \overline{3},\ j \in \overline{2},\ k \in \overline{2},\ \ell \in \overline{6}\},\ h \in \overline{6}, \tag{3.45}$$

$$\underline{\nu}^{(6+h)} = \{\delta_{ih}: i \in \overline{3},\ j \in \overline{2},\ h \in \overline{2},\ \ell \in \overline{6}\},\ h \in \overline{2}, \tag{3.46}$$

$$\underline{\nu}^{(9)} = \{2\delta_{j1} - 1: i \in \overline{3},\ j \in \overline{2},\ h \in \overline{2},\ \ell \in \overline{6}\}, \tag{3.47}$$

$$\underline{\nu}^{(10)} = \{2\delta_{k1} - 1: i \in \overline{3},\ j \in \overline{2},\ h \in \overline{2},\ \ell \in \overline{6}\}, \tag{3.48}$$

$$\underline{\nu}^{(11)} = \{(2\delta_{k1} - 1)\ell: i \in \overline{3},\ j \in \overline{2},\ h \in \overline{2},\ \ell \in \overline{6}\}, \tag{3.49}$$

where δ is the Kronecker delta.

If $\underline{\mu}^{(0)} = \underline{\nu}$, then the algorithm coincides with the classical Newton-Raphson procedure. Convergence is slower than in Example 1, but very few iterations are required to obtain a quite accurate estimate of $\hat{\underline{\mu}}$. The largest coordinate in magnitude for $\underline{s}^{(0)}$ is -0.43. The corresponding values for $\underline{s}^{(1)}$ and $\underline{s}^{(2)}$ are, respectively, 0.077 and -0.0018. All coordinates of $\underline{s}^{(4)}$ have magnitude less than 0.0001. The estimate $\underline{m}^{(4)}$ of $\hat{\underline{m}}$ is given in table 3.3. As shown in chapter 4, the model is not entirely satisfactory.

The limiting convergence rate may be estimated by examining $d^3\hat{\ell}^{(p)}_{\underline{\mu}^{(t)}}$. Elementary arguments show that

$$\begin{aligned} d^2\hat{\ell}^{(p)}_{\underline{\mu}+\underline{\nu}}(\underline{n},\underline{\xi})(\underline{n}) &= -\sum_{i\in I} \xi_i\, n_i \exp(\hat{\mu}_i + \nu_i) \\ &= -\sum_{i\in I} \xi_i n_i [e^{\hat{\mu}_i} + \nu_i e^{\hat{\mu}_i} + o(\nu_i)] \\ &= d^2\hat{\ell}^{(p)}_{\underline{\mu}}(\underline{n},\underline{\xi})(\underline{n}) - \sum_{i\in I} \xi_i n_i \nu_i e^{\hat{\mu}_i} + o_{\underline{\nu}}(\underline{\xi})(\underline{n}), \end{aligned} \tag{3.50}$$

where $\|o_{\underline{\nu}}\|/\|\underline{\nu}\| \longrightarrow 0$ as $\underline{\nu} \longrightarrow \underline{0}$. Thus

TABLE 3.3

MAXIMUM-LIKELIHOOD ESTIMATES
OF MEANS FOR ESKIMO GROUPS

Population		Presence or Absence	1-10	11-20	21-30	31-40	41-50	51+
Igloolik	Male	Present	5.73	9.30	14.16	13.42	10.24	11.75
		Absent	39.84	29.71	20.79	9.05	3.18	1.67
	Female	Present	4.96	8.05	12.26	11.61	8.87	10.17
		Absent	34.48	25.72	18.00	7.84	2.75	1.45
Hall Beach	Male	Present	2.15	3.48	5.31	5.03	3.84	4.40
		Absent	14.92	11.13	7.79	3.39	1.19	0.63
	Female	Present	1.86	3.02	4.59	4.35	3.32	3.81
		Absent	12.91	9.63	6.74	2.94	1.03	0.54
Aleut	Male	Present	1.97	3.19	4.86	4.60	3.51	4.03
		Absent	13.66	10.19	7.13	3.10	1.09	0.57
	Female	Present	1.70	2.76	4.20	3.98	3.04	3.49
		Absent	11.82	8.82	6.17	2.69	0.94	0.50

(Age Group spans columns 1-10 through 51+.)

(3.51) $$d^3\hat{\ell}^{(p)}_{\hat{\underline{\mu}}}(\underline{n},\underline{\nu})(\underline{\xi})(\underline{\eta}) = -\sum_{i\in I} \xi_i\eta_i\nu_i e^{\hat{\mu}_i} .$$

To find $(d^2f_{\hat{\underline{\mu}}})^{-1} \circ d^3f_{\hat{\underline{\mu}}}$ for $f(\underline{\mu}) = \hat{\ell}^{(p)}(\underline{n},\underline{\mu})$, observe that this expression is a mapping from M to the space T of linear transformations from M to M. If $\underline{\nu} \in M$, an element $A(\underline{\nu}) \in T$ is sought such that for all $\underline{\xi} \in M$ and $\underline{\eta} \in M$,

(3.52) $$-\sum_{i\in I} \xi_i\eta_i\nu_i e^{\hat{\mu}_i} = \sum_{i\in I} \xi_i[A(\underline{\nu})(\underline{\eta})]_i e^{\hat{\mu}_i}.$$

To find $A(\underline{\nu})$, observe that

(3.53) $$(\underline{\xi},D(\hat{\underline{\mu}})P_M^*(\hat{\underline{\mu}})(\underline{\nu} \# \underline{\eta}))$$

$$= (\underline{\xi},D(\hat{\underline{\mu}})(\underline{\nu} \# \underline{\eta}))$$

$$= \sum_{i\in I} \xi_i\eta_i\nu_i e^{\hat{\mu}_i} ,$$

where $\underline{\nu} \# \underline{\eta}$ is defined as in chapter 1. Thus

(3.54) $$A(\underline{\nu})(\underline{\eta}) = -P_M^*(\hat{\underline{\mu}})(\underline{\nu} \# \underline{\eta}) = -P_M^*(\hat{\underline{\mu}})\{\nu_i\eta_i\}.$$

To estimate $\|[d^2f_{\hat{\underline{\mu}}}]^{-1} \circ d^3f_{\hat{\underline{\mu}}}\|$, note that

(3.55) $$\|A(\underline{\nu})\| = \sup_{\{\underline{\eta}\in M: \|\underline{\eta}\|=1\}} \|P_M^*(\hat{\underline{\mu}})\{\nu_i\eta_i\}\|.$$

Since whenever $\|\underline{\nu}\| = 1$ and $\|\underline{\eta}\| = 1$, $\|\{\nu_i\eta_i\}\| \le 1$, it follows that

(3.56) $$\sup_{\{\underline{\nu}\in M: \|\underline{\nu}\|=1\}} \|A(\underline{\nu})\| = \sup_{\{\underline{\nu}\in M: \|\underline{\nu}\|=1\}} \sup_{\{\underline{\eta}\in M: \|\underline{\eta}\|=1\}} \|P_M^*(\hat{\underline{\mu}})\{\nu_i\eta_i\}\|$$

$$\le \sup_{\{\underline{\mu}\in R^I: \|\underline{\mu}\|=1\}} \|P_M^*(\hat{\underline{\mu}})\underline{\mu}\|.$$

Suppose now that $C = \min_{i\in I} e^{\hat{\mu}_i}$ and $D = \max_{i\in I} e^{\hat{\mu}_i}$. Then

(3.57) $$\begin{aligned} \|P_M^*(\hat{\underline{\mu}})\underline{\mu}\|^2 &= (P_M^*(\hat{\underline{\mu}})\underline{\mu}, P_M^*(\hat{\underline{\mu}})\underline{\mu}) \\ &\le \frac{1}{C}\,(P_M^*(\hat{\underline{\mu}})\underline{\mu} D(\hat{\underline{\mu}}) P_M^*(\hat{\underline{\mu}})\underline{\mu}) \\ &\le \frac{1}{C}\,(\underline{\mu}, D(\hat{\underline{\mu}})\underline{\mu}) \\ &\le \frac{D}{C}\,\|\underline{\mu}\|^2 . \end{aligned}$$

Therefore, $\|[d^2f_{\hat{\underline{\mu}}}]^{-1} \circ d^3f_{\hat{\underline{\mu}}}\| \le D/C$. Thus if $\underline{\mu}^{(t)} \ne \hat{\underline{\mu}}$ for any $t \ge 0$, then

(3.58) $$\limsup_{t\to\infty} \frac{\|\underline{\mu}^{(t+1)} - \hat{\underline{\mu}}\|}{\|\underline{\mu}^{(t)} - \hat{\underline{\mu}}\|^2} \le \tfrac{1}{2}\,(D/C)^{\frac{1}{2}} .$$

This formula suggests that convergence is fastest when the range of the elements of $\hat{\underline{\mu}}$ is smallest.

More precise limits are relatively difficult to obtain. The limits given can be rather generous, but if $\underline{e} \in M$,

(3.59) $$\frac{\|A(\underline{e})\underline{e}\|}{\|\underline{e}\|\,\|\underline{e}\|} = q^{-\frac{1}{2}}$$

where q is the number of elements of I. Thus the right hand side of (3.59) must be at least $\frac{1}{2}q^{-\frac{1}{2}}$.

If $f(\underline{\mu})$ is $\hat{\ell}^{(m)}(\underline{n},\underline{\mu})$ for $\underline{\mu} \in M - N$, where $\hat{\ell}^{(m)}(\underline{n},\underline{\mu})$ is defined as in (2.22) as the kernel of the log likelihood under multinomial sampling, then $\underline{s}^{(t)}$ satisfies

(3.60) $$\underline{s}^{(t)} = P_{M-N}[P^*_M(\underline{\bar{\mu}}^{(t)}) - P^*_N(\underline{\bar{\mu}}^{(t)})]D^{-1}(\underline{\bar{\mu}}^{(t)})[\underline{n} - \underline{\bar{m}}^{(t)}]$$
$$= P_{M-N}\, P^*_{R^{(t)}}(\underline{\bar{\mu}}^{(t)})D^{-1}(\underline{\bar{\mu}}^{(t)})[\underline{n} - \underline{\bar{m}}^{(t)}] ,$$

where $\underline{\bar{m}}^{(t)} = \underline{m}(\underline{\bar{\mu}}^{(t)})$,

(3.61) $$R^{(t)} = \{\underline{\mu}\in M\colon (\underline{\mu}, D(\underline{\bar{\mu}}^{(t)})\underline{\nu}) = 0 \ \forall \underline{\nu} \in N\} ,$$

and for each $i \in I_k$ and $k \in \bar{r}$,

(3.62) $$m_i(\underline{\bar{\mu}}^{(t)}) = \frac{(\underline{n}, \underline{\nu}^{(k)})}{(\underline{m}(\underline{\mu}^{(t)}), \underline{\nu}^{(k)})}\, m_i(\underline{\mu}^{(t)})$$
$$= \Big\{\sum_{i\in I_k} n_i \Big/ \Big[\sum_{i'\in I_k} m_{i'}(\underline{\mu}^{(t)})\Big]\Big\} m_i(\underline{\mu}^{(t)}).$$

Thus $\underline{m}(\underline{\bar{\mu}}^{(t)})$ is the mean vector such that $P_{M-N}\underline{\bar{\mu}}^{(t)} = \underline{\mu}^{(t)}$.

To show that $\underline{s}^{(t)}$ satisfies (3.60), note that for every $\underline{\nu} \in M - N$,

(3.63) $$d^2\hat{\ell}^{(m)}_{\underline{\bar{\mu}}^{(t)}}(\underline{n}, \underline{s}^{(t)})(\underline{\nu})$$

$$= -(\underline{\nu}, D(\underline{\bar{\mu}}^{(t)})[I - P^*_N(\underline{\bar{\mu}}^{(t)})]P_{M-N}[P^*_M(\underline{\bar{\mu}}^{(t)}) - P^*_N(\underline{\bar{\mu}}^{(t)})]\, D^{-1}(\underline{\bar{\mu}}^{(t)})]\underline{n} - \underline{\bar{m}}^{(t)}])$$

$$= -(\underline{\nu}, D(\underline{\bar{\mu}}^{(t)})[I - P^*_N(\underline{\bar{\mu}}^{(t)})][P^*_M(\underline{\bar{\mu}}^{(t)}) - P^*_N(\underline{\bar{\mu}}^{(t)})]\, D^{-1}(\underline{\bar{\mu}}^{(t)})[\underline{n} - \underline{\bar{m}}^{(t)}])$$

$$= -(\underline{\nu}, D(\underline{\bar{\mu}}^{(t)})[P^*_M(\underline{\bar{\mu}}^{(t)}) - P^*_N(\underline{\bar{\mu}}^{(t)})]D^{-1}(\underline{\bar{\mu}}^{(t)})[\underline{n} - \underline{\bar{m}}^{(t)}])$$

$$= -([P^*_M(\underline{\bar{\mu}}^{(t)}) - P^*_N(\underline{\bar{\mu}}^{(t)})]\underline{\nu}, \underline{n} - \underline{\bar{m}}^{(t)})$$

$$= -(\underline{\nu} - P^*_N(\underline{\bar{\mu}}^{(t)})\underline{\nu}, \underline{n} - \underline{\bar{m}}^{(t)})$$

$$= -(\underline{\nu}, \underline{n} - \underline{\bar{m}}^{(t)})$$

$$= -\, d\hat{\ell}^{(m)}_{\underline{\bar{\mu}}^{(t)}}(\underline{n}, \underline{\nu}).$$

In (3.63), the second equation is based on the observation that

$$(3.64)\qquad [I - P_N^*(\bar{\underline{\mu}}^{(t)})]P_{M-N}[P_M^*(\bar{\underline{\mu}}^{(t)}) - P_N^*(\bar{\underline{\mu}}^{(t)})]$$

$$= [I - P_N^*(\bar{\underline{\mu}}^{(t)})]P_M[P_M^*(\bar{\underline{\mu}}^{(t)}) - P_N^*(\bar{\underline{\mu}}^{(t)})]$$

$$- [I - P_N^*(\bar{\underline{\mu}}^{(t)})]P_N[P_M^*(\bar{\underline{\mu}}^{(t)}) - P_N^*(\bar{\underline{\mu}}^{(t)})]$$

$$= [I - P_N^*(\bar{\underline{\mu}}^{(t)})][P_M^*(\bar{\underline{\mu}}^{(t)}) - P_N^*(\bar{\underline{\mu}}^{(t)})] .$$

The last equation of (3.64) follows since the ranges of $P_M^*(\bar{\underline{\mu}}^{(t)})$ and $P_N^*(\bar{\underline{\mu}}^{(t)})$ are in M, while both I and $P_N^*(\bar{\underline{\mu}}^{(t)})$ leave any element of N unchanged. The second-to-last equation in (3.63) is a consequence of the restriction $P_N\underline{n} = P_N\bar{\underline{m}}^{(t)}$.

Computation of $\underline{s}^{(t)}$ is more difficult in the multinomial case than in the Poisson case since $R^{(t)}$ varies with each iteration and both P_{M-N} and $P^*_{R^{(t)}}(\bar{\underline{\mu}}^{(t)})$ must be found. However, if each multinomial sample consists of two categories, simplifications are possible. This situation is considered briefly in Example 3.3 of this chapter and more extensively in chapter 8.

Since Poisson and multinomial models have the same maximum-likelihood estimates, either $\hat{\ell}^{(p)}(\underline{n},\underline{\mu})$ or $\hat{\ell}^{(m)}(\underline{n},\underline{\mu})$ may be used in the same estimation problem. The function $\hat{\ell}^{(p)}(\underline{n},\underline{\mu})$ has the advantage of simplicity, while $\hat{\ell}^{(m)}(\underline{n},\underline{\mu})$ permits use of a lower-dimensional manifold. In the social-mobility tables examined in chapter 6, $\hat{\ell}^{(p)}(\underline{n},\underline{\mu})$ is used to find maximum-likelihood estimates. On the other hand, $\hat{\ell}^{(m)}(\underline{n},\underline{\mu})$ is used in the logit models of chapter 8 since $M - N$ and $R^{(t)}$ are generally of much smaller dimension than M.

Example 3.3. Maximum-likelihood estimates for logit models such as the one presented in Examples 1.6 and 1.10 are normally found by use of $\hat{\ell}^{(m)}(\underline{n},\underline{\mu})$. In this example, $M - N$ is spanned by

$$(3.65)\qquad \underline{x} = \begin{bmatrix} 1 & -1 \\ 1 & -1 \\ 1 & -1 \end{bmatrix}$$

and

$$\underline{y} = \begin{bmatrix} 1 & -1 \\ 0 & 0 \\ -1 & 1 \end{bmatrix}$$

The Gram-Schmidt algorithm may be used to find vectors $\underline{x}^{(t)}$ and $\underline{y}^{(t)}$ which span $R^{(t)}$ and satisfy $(\underline{x}^{(t)}, D(\underline{\bar{\mu}}^{(t)})\underline{y}^{(t)}) = 0$. If $N_i = \bar{m}_{i1}^{(t)} + \bar{m}_{i2}^{(t)} = n_{i1} + n_{i2}$ for $i \in \bar{3}$ and $\underline{\mu}^{(t)}$ is defined for $i \in \bar{3}$ as in Example 1.6, then one may let

(3.67)
$$\underline{x}^{(t)} = \underline{x} - \sum_{i=1}^{3} \frac{\bar{m}_{i1}^{(t)} - \bar{m}_{i2}^{(t)}}{\bar{m}_{i1}^{(t)} + \bar{m}_{i2}^{(t)}} \underline{\mu}^{(i)}$$

$$= 2 \begin{array}{|cc|} \hline \bar{m}_{i2}^{(t)}/N_1 & -\bar{m}_{11}^{(t)}/N_1 \\ \bar{m}_{22}^{(t)}/N_2 & -\bar{m}_{21}^{(t)}/N_1 \\ \bar{m}_{32}^{(t)}/N_3 & -\bar{m}_{31}^{(t)}/N_1 \\ \hline \end{array}$$

and

(3.68)
$$\underline{y}^{(t)} = \underline{y} - \frac{\bar{m}_{11}^{(t)} - \bar{m}_{12}^{(t)}}{\bar{m}_{11}^{(t)} + \bar{m}_{12}^{(t)}} \underline{\mu}^{(1)} + \frac{\bar{m}_{31}^{(t)} - \bar{m}_{32}^{(t)}}{\bar{m}_{31}^{(t)} + \bar{m}_{32}^{(t)}} \underline{\mu}^{(3)}$$

$$- [(\bar{m}_{11}^{(t)}\bar{m}_{12}^{(t)}/N_1 - \bar{m}_{31}^{(t)}\bar{m}_{32}^{(t)}/N_3)/(\sum_{i=1}^{3} \bar{m}_{i1}^{(t)}\bar{m}_{i2}^{(t)}/N_i)]\ \underline{x}^{(t)}$$

$$= 2 \begin{array}{|cc|} \hline \bar{m}_{12}^{(t)}/N_1 & -\bar{m}_{11}^{(t)}/N_1 \\ 0 & 0 \\ -\bar{m}_{32}^{(t)}/N_3 & \bar{m}_{31}^{(t)}/N_3 \\ \hline \end{array} \ -2c^{(t)} \begin{array}{|cc|} \hline \bar{m}_{12}^{(t)}/N_1 & -\bar{m}_{11}^{(t)}/N_1 \\ \bar{m}_{22}^{(t)}/N_2 & -\bar{m}_{21}^{(t)}/N_2 \\ \bar{m}_{32}^{(t)}/N_3 & -\bar{m}_{32}^{(t)}/N_3 \\ \hline \end{array}$$

where

(3.69)
$$w_i^{(t)} = \bar{m}_{i1}^{(t)}\bar{m}_{i2}^{(t)}/N_i$$

and

(3.70)
$$c^{(t)} = \frac{w_1^{(t)} - w_3^{(t)}}{w_1^{(t)} + w_2^{(t)} + w_3^{(t)}} .$$

Given $\underline{x}^{(t)}$ and $\underline{y}^{(t)}$, $P_{R(t)}^{*}(\underline{\bar{\mu}}^{(t)})D^{-1}(\underline{\bar{\mu}}^{(t)})[\underline{n} - \underline{\bar{m}}^{(t)}]$ may be written as

(3.71)
$$P_{R(t)}^{*}(\underline{\bar{\mu}}^{(t)})D^{-1}(\underline{\bar{\mu}}^{(t)})[\underline{n} - \underline{\bar{m}}^{(t)}]$$

$$= \frac{(\underline{x}^{(t)},\underline{n} - \underline{\bar{m}}^{(t)})}{(\underline{x}^{(t)},D(\underline{\bar{\mu}}^{(t)})\underline{x}^{(t)})}\underline{x}^{(t)} + \frac{(\underline{y}^{(t)},\underline{n} - \underline{\bar{m}}^{(t)})}{(\underline{y}^{(t)},D(\underline{\bar{\mu}}^{(t)})\underline{y}^{(t)})}\underline{y}^{(t)} .$$

Since

(3.72) $$P_{M-N}\underline{x}^{(t)} = \underline{x}$$

and

(3.73) $$P_{M-N}\underline{y}^{(t)} = \underline{y} - c^{(t)}\underline{x} ,$$

one has

(3.74) $$\underline{s}^{(t)} = \left[\frac{(\underline{x}^{(t)},\underline{n} - \underline{\bar{m}}^{(t)})}{(\underline{x}^{(t)},D(\underline{\bar{\mu}}^{(t)})\underline{x}^{(t)})} - c^{(t)}\frac{(\underline{y}^{(t)},\underline{n} - \underline{\bar{m}}^{(t)})}{(\underline{y}^{(t)},D(\underline{\bar{\mu}}^{(t)})\underline{y}^{(t)})}\right]\underline{x}$$

$$+ \frac{(\underline{y}^{(t)},\underline{n} - \underline{\bar{m}}^{(t)})}{(\underline{y}^{(t)},D(\underline{\bar{\mu}}^{(t)})\underline{y}^{(t)})}\underline{y} .$$

To obtain the inner products used in (3.74), it is useful to recall that $n_{i1} - \bar{m}_{i1}^{(t)} = -(n_{i2} - \bar{m}_{i2}^{(t)})$ for each $i \in \bar{3}$. Thus

(3.75) $$(\underline{x}^{(t)},\underline{n} - \underline{\bar{m}}^{(t)}) = 2(n_{1+} - \bar{m}_{1+}^{(t)}) ,$$

(3.76) $$(\underline{y}^{(t)},\underline{n} - \underline{\bar{m}}^{(t)}) = 2(n_{11} - \bar{m}_{11}^{(t)} - n_{31} + \bar{m}_{31}^{(t)}) - 2c^{(t)}(n_{1+} - \bar{m}_{1+}^{(t)}),$$

(3.77) $$(\underline{x}^{(t)},D(\underline{\bar{\mu}}^{(t)})\underline{x}^{(t)}) = 4(w_1^{(t)} + w_2^{(t)} + w_3^{(t)}),$$

and

(3.78) $$(\underline{y}^{(t)},D(\underline{\bar{\mu}}^{(t)})\underline{y}^{(t)}) = 4(w_1^{(t)} + w_3^{(t)}) - 4(w_1^{(t)} + w_2^{(t)} + w_3^{(t)})(c^{(t)})^2 .$$

An appropriate initial estimate is $\underline{\mu}^{(0)} = P_{M-N}P_M^*(\underline{\nu})\underline{\nu}$. Evaluation of this quantity is easier than might appear to be the case since

(3.79) $$P_{M-N}P_M^*(\underline{\nu})\underline{\nu} = P_{M-N}[P_N^*(\underline{\nu}) + P_R^*(\underline{\nu})]\underline{\nu}$$

$$= P_{M-N}P_R^*(\underline{\nu})\underline{\nu},$$

where $R = \{\underline{\mu} \in M: (\underline{\mu},D(\underline{\nu})\underline{x}) = 0 \ \forall \underline{x} \in N\}$.

The space R is spanned by $\{\underline{u},\underline{z}\}$, where

(3.80)
$$\underline{u} = 2\begin{bmatrix} n_{12}/N_1 & -n_{11}/N_1 \\ n_{22}/N_2 & -n_{21}/N_2 \\ n_{32}/N_3 & -n_{31}/N_3 \end{bmatrix},$$

(3.81)
$$\underline{z} = 2\begin{bmatrix} n_{12}/N_1 & -n_{11}/N_1 \\ 0 & 0 \\ -n_{32}/N_3 & n_{31}/N_3 \end{bmatrix} - 2c\begin{bmatrix} n_{12}/N_1 & -n_{11}/N_1 \\ n_{22}/N_2 & -n_{21}/N_2 \\ n_{32}/N_3 & -n_{31}/N_3 \end{bmatrix}$$

(3.82)
$$w_i = n_{i1}n_{12}/N_i,$$

and

(3.83)
$$c = \frac{w_1 - w_3}{w_1 + w_2 + w_3}.$$

Since

(3.84)
$$P_{M-N}\underline{u} = \begin{bmatrix} 1 & -1 \\ 1 & -1 \\ 1 & -1 \end{bmatrix}$$

and

$$P_{M-N}\underline{z} = \begin{bmatrix} 1 & -1 \\ 0 & 0 \\ -1 & 1 \end{bmatrix} - c\begin{bmatrix} 1 & -1 \\ 1 & -1 \\ 1 & -1 \end{bmatrix}$$

it follows that

(3.85)
$$(\underline{\mu},D(\underline{\nu})\underline{\nu}) = 2\sum_{i=1}^{3} w_i(\nu_{i1} - \nu_{i2}),$$

(3.86)
$$(\underline{\mu},D(\underline{\nu})\underline{\mu}) = 4(w_1 + w_2 + w_3),$$

(3.87)
$$(\underline{z},D(\underline{\nu})\underline{\nu}) = 2[w_1(\nu_{11} - \nu_{12}) - w_3(\nu_{31} - \nu_{32})] - c(\underline{\mu},D(\underline{\nu})\underline{\nu}),$$

and

(3.88)
$$(\underline{z},D(\underline{\nu})\underline{z}) = 4(w_1 + w_3) - 4c^2(w_1 + w_2 + w_3).$$

This formula is used by Berkson (1955). In this formula, empirical logit i is $(\nu_{i1} - \nu_{i2})$, and the estimated logit i is $2\mu_{i1}^{(0)}$. Using this expression for $\underline{\mu}^{(0)}$ with the data in table 1.3,

(3.89)
$$\underline{\mu}^{(0)} = \begin{array}{|rr|} -0.886 & 0.886 \\ -0.398 & 0.398 \\ 0.090 & -0.090 \end{array}\,,$$

(3.90)
$$\underline{\bar{m}}^{(0)} \quad \begin{array}{|rr|} 2.178 & 12.822 \\ 4.662 & 10.338 \\ 8.172 & 6.828 \end{array}\,,$$

and

(3.91)
$$\underline{s}^{(0)} = \begin{array}{|rr|} -0.002 & 0.002 \\ -0.001 & 0.001 \\ 0.000 & -0.000 \end{array}\,,$$

After iteration 1, one has

(3.92)
$$\underline{\mu}^{(1)} = \begin{array}{|rr|} -0.888 & 0.888 \\ -0.399 & 0.399 \\ 0.090 & -0.090 \end{array}$$

and

(3.93)
$$\underline{\bar{m}}^{(1)} = \begin{array}{|rr|} 2.172 & 12.828 \\ 4.656 & 10.344 \\ 8.172 & 6.828 \end{array}\,.$$

No element of $\underline{s}^{(1)}$ exceeds 2×10^{-6} in magnitude.

THE DEMING-STEPHAN ALGORITHM

An algorithm developed by Deming and Stephan (1940) and Bishop (1967) has often been used to find maximum-likelihood estimates for hierarchical models for factorial tables (see chapters 5 and 8). This algorithm is actually a special case of the cyclic ascent method of function maximization (see Zangwill 1969). The equivalence is demonstrated in chapter 5. The cyclic ascent method is generally inferior to the Newton-Raphson method in convergence rate, but the former method requires no matrix inversion or computation of projections.

The basic difference in the algorithms is the care used in selection of directions. In the Newton-Raphson method, considerable effort is made to find a direction $\underline{s}^{(t)}$ such that the ray $\{\underline{\mu}^{(t)} + \alpha\underline{s}^{(t)}: \alpha > 0\}$ passes near $\underline{\mu}^{*}$. In the cyclic ascent method, a series of fixed directions is used at each cycle. Less effort is expended in computation of directions, but the resulting directions are not as well chosen as in the case for the Newton-Raphson method.

In a cyclic ascent algorithm, a set of nonzero vectors $\{\underline{\eta}^{(k)}: k \in \overline{s}\}$ is selected so that span $\{\underline{\eta}^{(k)}: k \in \overline{s}\} = M$. It may be convenient to choose a set of vectors such that s exceeds the dimension of M. This situation is particularly common in the case of hierarchical analysis-of-variance models. At the start of iteration cycle t, $t \geq 0$, $\underline{\mu}^{(t,1)}$ is an estimate of $\underline{\mu}^*$. Each cycle has s steps. At step k, $k \in \overline{s}$, of cycle t, an $\alpha^{(t,k)}$ is selected so that

$$\underline{\mu}^{(t,k+1)} = \underline{\mu}^{(t,k)} + \alpha^{(t,k)}\underline{\eta}^{(k)} \tag{3.94}$$

and

$$|\alpha^{(t,k)} df_{\underline{\mu}^{(t,k+1)}}(\underline{\eta}^{(k)})| \leq b[f(\underline{\mu}^{(t,k+1)}) - f(\underline{\mu}^{(t,k)})], \tag{3.95}$$

where b is defined as in the modified Newton-Raphson algorithm. If $|df_{\underline{\mu}^{(t)}}(\underline{\eta}^{(k)})| > 0$, $\alpha^{(t,k)}$ must not equal 0. It should be noted that $\alpha^{(t,k)}$ may be positive, negative, or zero. Condition (3.95) can be satisfied for some $\alpha^{(t,k)}$ for the same reason that condition (3.4) may be satisfied for some $\alpha^{(t)} > 0$. In order to proceed from cycle t to cycle $t + 1$, one sets $\underline{\mu}^{(t+1,1)} = \underline{\mu}^{(t,s+1)}$. If a standard interpolation method is used to select $\alpha^{(t,k)}$ and if $h^{(t,k)}(\alpha) = f(\underline{\mu}^{(t,k)} + \alpha\underline{\eta}^{(k)})$ achieves a maximum at $\overline{\alpha}^{(t,k)}$, then (see Haberman 1971)

$$\alpha^{(t,k)} - \overline{\alpha}^{(t,k)} = o^{(t,k)}\|\underline{\mu}^{(t,k)} - \underline{\mu}^*\|^2 , \tag{3.96}$$

where $o^{(t,k)} \longrightarrow 0$ as $\|\underline{\mu}^{(t,k)} - \underline{\mu}^*\| \longrightarrow 0$. This result is useful in the following theorem:

THEOREM 3.2. *If* $f(\underline{\mu})$ *has a maximum at* $\underline{\mu}^*$ *and* $d^2f_{\underline{\mu}}$ *is continuous in* $\underline{\mu}$, *then* $\underline{\mu}^{(t,k)} \longrightarrow \underline{\mu}^*$ *as* $t \longrightarrow \infty$. *If* $\underline{\mu}^{(t,k)} \neq \underline{\mu}^*$ *for all* $k \in \overline{s}$ *and* $t \geq 0$, *then for some norm* $|||\cdot|||$,

$$\limsup_{t\to\infty} \frac{|||\underline{\mu}^{(t+1,1)} - \underline{\mu}^*|||}{|||\underline{\mu}^{(t,1)} - \underline{\mu}^*|||} < 1. \tag{3.97}$$

Proof. The proof is similar to the proof of part (b) of Theorem 3.1 (see Appendix C). Assume $\underline{\mu}^{(t,k)} \neq \underline{\mu}^*$ for $k \in \overline{s}$ and $t \geq 0$. Then $\{f(\underline{\mu}^{(t,1)})\}$ is a strictly increasing sequence such that $f(\underline{\mu}^{(t+1,1)}) - f(\underline{\mu}^{(t,1)})$ converges to 0. The set of s-tuples of the form $\{\alpha^{(t,k)}: k \in \bar{s}\}$ is bounded since $\{\underline{\mu}: f(\underline{\mu}) \geq f(\underline{\mu}^{(0,1)})\}$ is bounded. If $\underline{\mu}^{(t,1)}$ does not converge to $\underline{\mu}^*$, one may find a limit point $<\underline{\nu},\{\alpha^{(h)}: k \in \bar{s}\}>$ of the sequence $\{<\underline{\mu}^{(t,1)},\{\alpha^{(t,k)}: k \in \bar{s}\}>: t \geq 0\}$ such that $\underline{\nu} \neq \underline{\mu}^*$. By continuity and (3.95), if $\underline{\nu}^{(1)} = \underline{\nu}$ and

$$\underline{\nu}^{(k+1)} = \underline{\nu}^{(k)} + \alpha^{(k)}\underline{\eta}^{(k)} \tag{3.98}$$

for $k \in \bar{s}$, then

$$|\alpha^{(k)} df_{\underline{\nu}^{(k+1)}}(\underline{\eta}^{(k)})| \leq b[f(\underline{\nu}^{(k+1)}) - f(\underline{\nu}^{(k)})]. \tag{3.99}$$

Since $f(\underline{\mu}^{(t+1,1)}) - f(\underline{\mu}^{(t,1)}) \longrightarrow 0$ as $t \longrightarrow \infty$, $f(\underline{\nu}^{(k+1)}) - f(\underline{\nu}^{(k)}) = 0$ and

$$\alpha^{(k)} df_{\underline{\nu}^{(k+1)}}(\underline{\eta}^{(k)}) = 0. \tag{3.100}$$

By Taylor's theorem,

$$f(\underline{\nu}^{(k)}) = f(\underline{\nu}^{(k+1)}) + \frac{(\alpha^{(k)})^2}{2}[d^2 f_{\underline{\zeta}^{(k)}}(\underline{\eta}^{(k)})](\underline{\eta}^{(k)}), \tag{3.101}$$

where $\underline{\zeta}^{(k)}$ is on the line segment between $\underline{\nu}^{(k)}$ and $\underline{\nu}^{(k+1)}$. Since $d^2 f_{\underline{\zeta}^{(k)}}$ is negative definite, $\alpha^{(k)} = 0$.

To complete the convergence proof, note that if $\alpha^{(t,k)} \neq 0$, there exists $\beta^{(t,k)}$ between 0 and $\alpha^{(t,k)}$ such that

$$\frac{1}{\alpha^{(t,k)}}[f(\underline{\mu}^{(t+1,k)} - f(\underline{\mu}^{(t,k)})] = df_{\underline{\mu}^{(t,k)} + \beta^{(t,k)}\underline{\eta}^{(k)}}(\underline{\eta}^{(k)}). \tag{3.102}$$

If $\alpha^{(t,k)} = 0$, let $\beta^{(t,k)} = 0$. If $\{<\underline{\mu}^{(t,1)}, \{\alpha^{(t,k)}: k \in \bar{s}\}>: t \in K\}$ converges to $<\underline{\nu},\{\alpha^{(k)}: k \in \bar{s}\}>$, one may construct a subsequence with $J \subset K$ such that

$$\{<\underline{\mu}^{(t,1)},\{(\alpha^{(t,k)},\beta^{(t,k)}): k \in \bar{s}\}>: t \in J\}$$

converges to $<\underline{\nu},\{(\alpha^{(k)},\beta^{(k)}): k \in \bar{s}\}>$. Either $\alpha^{(t,k)} = 0$ for $t \in J$ sufficiently large or a sequence $\{\alpha^{(t,k)}: t \in H\}$ may be found such that all members of the sequence are nonzero and have the same sign. In the former case, $df_{\underline{\nu}^{(k)}}(\underline{\eta}^{(k)}) = 0$. In the latter case,

$$|df_{\underline{\nu}^{(k)}}(\underline{\eta}^{(k)})| \leq b[df_{\underline{\nu}^{(k)}}(\underline{\eta}^{(k)})]. \tag{3.103}$$

Thus in either case, $df_{\underline{\nu}^{(k)}}(\underline{\eta}^{(k)}) = 0$. Since $\underline{\nu}^{(k)} = \underline{\nu}$ for all $k \in \bar{s}$, it follows that $df_{\underline{\nu}}(\underline{\eta}^{(k)}) = 0$ for all $k \in \bar{s}$. Therefore, $\underline{\nu} = \underline{\mu}^*$ and $\underline{\mu}^{(t,1)} \longrightarrow \underline{\mu}^*$ as $t \longrightarrow \infty$. Since we have also shown that $\alpha^{(t,k)} \longrightarrow 0$ for $k \in \bar{s}$, $\underline{\mu}^{(t,k)} \longrightarrow \underline{\mu}^*$ as t if $k \in \bar{s}$.

To complete the proof, the inner product $(\cdot,\cdot)_f$ is employed, where, if $\underline{x} \in M$ and $\underline{y} \in M$, then

$$(\underline{x},\underline{y})_f = [d^2 f_{\underline{\mu}^*}(\underline{x})](\underline{y}). \tag{3.104}$$

Observe that

$$df_{\underline{\mu}^{(t,k)}}(\underline{\eta}^{(k)}) = d^2 f_{\bar{\bar{\underline{\mu}}}^{(t,k)}}(\underline{\mu}^{(t,k)} - \underline{\mu}^*)(\underline{\eta}^{(k)}), \tag{3.105}$$

where $\bar{\bar{\underline{\mu}}}^{(t,k)}$ is on the line segment between $\underline{\mu}^*$ and $\underline{\mu}^{(t,k)}$. As a consequence,

$$\bar{\alpha}^{(t,k)} = \frac{(\underline{\mu}^{(t,k)} - \underline{\mu}^*, \underline{\eta}^{(k)})_f}{(\underline{\eta}^{(k)}, \underline{\eta}^{(k)})_f} + \bar{o}^{(t,k)} \|\underline{\mu}^{(t,k)} - \underline{\mu}^*\|_f \tag{3.106}$$

where $\bar{o}^{(t,k)} \longrightarrow 0$ as $\|\underline{\mu}^{(t,k)} - \underline{\mu}^*\|_f \longrightarrow 0$. Given the assumption made on $\alpha^{(t,k)} - \bar{\alpha}^{(t,k)}$, it follows that

$$\underline{\mu}^{(t,k+1)} - \underline{\mu}^* = Q_f^{(k)}(\underline{\mu}^{(t,k)} - \underline{\mu}^*) + \underline{o}^{(t,k)}, \tag{3.107}$$

where $\|\underline{o}^{(t,k)}\|_f / \|\underline{\mu}^{(t,k)} - \underline{\mu}^*\|_f \longrightarrow 0$ as $\|\underline{\mu}^{(t,k)} - \underline{\mu}^*\|_f \longrightarrow 0$ and $Q_f^{(k)}$ is the projection of $R^{(k)}$ along span $\{\underline{\eta}^{(k)}\}$, where

$$R^{(k)} = \{\underline{\mu} \in M: (\underline{\mu}, \underline{\eta}^{(k)})_f = 0\}. \tag{3.108}$$

Thus

$$\underline{\mu}^{(t+1,1)} - \underline{\mu}^* = \prod_{k=1}^{s} Q_f^{(s-k)}(\underline{\mu}^{(t,1)} - \underline{\mu}^*) + \underline{o}^{(t)}, \tag{3.109}$$

where $\|\underline{o}^{(t)}\|_f / \|\underline{\mu}^{(t,1)} - \underline{\mu}^*\|_f \longrightarrow 0$ as $\|\underline{\mu}^{(t,0)} - \underline{\mu}^*\|_f \longrightarrow 0$. If $\underline{x} \in M$, let $\|\underline{x}\|_f^2 = (\underline{x},\underline{x})_f$; and if A is a transformation from M to M, let

$$\|A\|_f = \sup_{\{\underline{x}:\ \|\underline{x}\|_f = 1\}} \|A\underline{x}\|_f . \tag{3.110}$$

Then $\|\prod_{k=1} Q_f^{(s-k)}\|_f < 1$. In fact, if $\underline{x} \in M$, then $\|Q_f^{(k)}\underline{x}\| \le \|\underline{x}\|_f$. Equality only holds if $\underline{x} \in R^{(k)}$. If $\underline{x} \in R^{(k)}$ for $k \in \overline{s}$, then $\underline{x} = \underline{0}$. Thus $\| \prod_{k=1}^{s} Q_f^{(s-k)} \|_f < 1$.

Hence if $\underline{\mu}^{(t,k)} \neq \underline{\mu}^*$ for $t \geq 0$ and $k \in \overline{s}$, then

(3.11)
$$\limsup_{t \to \infty} \frac{\|\underline{\mu}^{(t+1,1)} - \underline{\mu}^*\|_f}{\|\underline{\mu}^{(t,1)} - \underline{\mu}^*\|_f} \leq \| \prod_{k=1}^{s} Q_f^{(s-k)} \|_f < 1. \|$$

If $f(\underline{\mu}) = \hat{\ell}^{(p)}(\underline{n},\underline{\nu})$, then the cyclic ascent method has special advantages, particularly if $n_i^{(k)}$ is 0 or 1 for each $i \in I$ and $k \in \overline{s}$. Observe that

(3.112)
$$(\underline{m}(\underline{\mu}^{(t,k)} + \overline{\alpha}^{(t,k)}\underline{n}^{(k)}, \underline{n}^{(k)}) = (\underline{n}, \underline{n}^{(k)}).$$

Thus selection of $\alpha^{(t,k)}$ corresponds to a marginal adjustment. In particular, if $n_i^{(k)}$ is 1 for $i \in I_0$ and 0 for $i \in I - I_0$, then

(3.113)
$$\exp(\overline{\alpha}^{(t,k)}) \sum_{i \in I_0} m_i(\underline{\mu}^{(t,k)}) = \sum_{i \in I_0} n_i.$$

Solving for $\exp(\overline{\alpha}^{(t,k)})$, one has

(3.114)
$$\exp(\overline{\alpha}^{(t,k)}) = \sum_{i \in I_0} n_i / \sum_{i \in I_0} m_i(\underline{\mu}^{(t,k)}) .$$

Since $\underline{n}^{(k)} \in M$, $\sum_{i \in I_0} n_i$ is positive if $\hat{\underline{\mu}}$ exists. If $\underline{m}^{(t,k)} = \underline{m}(\underline{\mu}^{(t,k)})$, then

(3.115)
$$\begin{aligned} m_i^{(t,k+1)} &= m_i^{(t,k)} \sum_{i \in I_0} n_i / \sum_{i \in I_0} m_i^{(t,k)} && \text{if } i \in I_0 , \\ &= m_i^{(t,k)} && \text{otherwise.} \end{aligned}$$

The change from $\underline{m}^{(t,k)}$ to $\underline{m}^{(t,k+1)}$ involves a proportional adjustment based on the marginal total $\sum_{i \in I_0} n_i$ and $\sum_{i \in I_0} m_i^{(t,k)}$. This adjustment process is called iterative proportional fitting (see Bishop 1967).

Example 3.4. The iterative proportional fitting algorithm may be applied to the table considered in Example 3.1. The manifold M is spanned by the 12 vectors

$$\{\underline{\nu}^{(w,x,y)}: w \in \overline{3}, x \in \overline{2}, y \in \overline{2}\} ,$$

where

(3.116)
$$\begin{aligned} \nu_{ijk}^{(1,x,y)} &= 1 \text{ if } i = x \text{ and } j = y, \\ &= 0 \text{ otherwise;} \end{aligned}$$

(3.117) $$\nu_{ijk}^{(2,x,y)} = 1 \quad \text{if} \quad i = x \quad \text{and} \quad k = y,$$
$$= 0 \quad \text{otherwise;}$$

(3.118) $$\nu_{ijk}^{(3,x,y)} = 1 \quad \text{if} \quad j = x \quad \text{and} \quad k = y,$$
$$= 0 \quad \text{otherwise.}$$

For instance,

(3.119) $$\underline{\nu}^{(1,1,1)} = \begin{bmatrix} 1 & 0 \\ 0 & 0 \end{bmatrix} \begin{bmatrix} 1 & 0 \\ 0 & 0 \end{bmatrix},$$

(3.120) $$\underline{\nu}^{(2,1,1)} = \begin{bmatrix} 1 & 1 \\ 0 & 0 \end{bmatrix} \begin{bmatrix} 0 & 0 \\ 0 & 0 \end{bmatrix},$$

(3.121) $$\underline{\nu}^{(3,1,1)} = \begin{bmatrix} 1 & 0 \\ 1 & 0 \end{bmatrix} \begin{bmatrix} 0 & 0 \\ 0 & 0 \end{bmatrix}.$$

If the vectors $\underline{\nu}^{(w,x,y)}$ are ordered first by w, then by x, and then by y, the algorithm reduces to the following steps:

(3.122) $$m_{ijk}^{(t,2)} = m_{ijk}^{(t,1)} n_{ij+}/m_{ij+}^{(t,1)} ,$$

(3.123) $$m_{ijk}^{(t,3)} = m_{ijk}^{(t,2)} n_{i+k}/m_{i+k}^{(t,2)} ,$$

(3.124) $$m_{ijk}^{(t,4)} = m_{ijk}^{(t,3)} n_{+jk}/m_{+jk}^{(t,3)} ,$$

(3.125) $$\underline{m}^{(t+1,1)} = \underline{m}^{(t,4)} .$$

This condensation is based on (3.115) and the disjointness of $I(w,1,1)$, $I(w,1,2)$, $I(w,2,1)$, and $I(w,1,2)$, where

(3.126) $$I(w,x,y) = \{(i,j,k): \nu_{ijk}^{(w,x,y)} = 1\}.$$

If $\underline{\mu}^{(0,1)} = 4\underline{e}$, then $\underline{\mu}^{(3,3)}$ is comparable in accuracy to the estimate $\underline{\mu}^{(3)}$ obtained with the Newton-Raphson algorithm when $\underline{\mu}^{(0)} = 4\underline{e}$. The simplest way to decide when to stop iterations is to consider $\delta^{(t)} = \max (\delta_1^{(t)},\delta_2^{(t)},\delta_3^{(t)})$, where

(3.127) $$\delta_1^{(t)} = \max_{i,j} (n_{ij+} - m_{ij+}^{(t,1)}),$$

(3.128) $$\delta_2^{(t)} = \max_{i,k} (n_{i+k} - m_{i+k}^{(t,2)}),$$

(3.129) $$\delta_3^{(t)} = \max_{j,k} (n_{+jk} - m_{+jk}^{(t,3)}).$$

When $\delta^{(t)}$ is small enough, say less than 0.1, iterations may cease. In this sample, $\delta^{(2)} = 0.39$ and $\delta^{(3)} = 0.02$.

The second starting value used in Example 3.1 would not normally be used with the present algorithm since a separate subroutine would be needed to compute projections. In the first example, such a subroutine is already present.

Example 3.5. The data examined in Example 3.2 may be fit to the model defined by (3.38) by use of the cyclic coordinate ascent method. The vectors $\{\underline{\eta}^{(h)}: h \in \overline{14}\}$ may be used to span M, where

(3.130) $$\underline{\eta}^{(h)} = \{\delta_{hi}: i \in \overline{3}, j \in \overline{2}, k \in \overline{2}, \ell \in \overline{6}\}, h \in \overline{3},$$

(3.131) $$\underline{\eta}^{(h+3)} = \{\delta_{hk}: i \in \overline{3}, j \in \overline{2}, k \in \overline{2}, \ell \in \overline{6}\}, h \in \overline{2},$$

(3.132) $$\underline{\eta}^{(h+5)} = \{\delta_{hk}: i \in \overline{3}, j \in \overline{2}, k \in \overline{2}, \ell \in \overline{6}\}, h \in \overline{2},$$

(3.133) $$\underline{\eta}^{(h+7)} = \{\delta_{h} : i \in \overline{3}, j \in \overline{2}, k \in \overline{2}, \ell \in \overline{6}\}, h \in \overline{6},$$

(3.134) $$\underline{\eta}^{(14)} = \{(2\delta_{1k} - 1)\ell: i \in \overline{3}, j \in \overline{2}, k \in \overline{2}, \ell \in \overline{6}\}.$$

The basic iteration cycle may be reduced to five steps to produce the following procedure:

(3.135) $$m_{ijk\ell}^{(t,2)} = m_{ijk\ell}^{(t,1)} n_{i+++}/m_{i+++}^{(t,1)} ,$$

(3.136) $$m_{ijk\ell}^{(t,3)} = m_{ijk\ell}^{(t,2)} n_{++k+}/m_{++k+}^{(t,2)} ,$$

(3.137) $$m_{ijk\ell}^{(t,4)} = m_{ijk\ell}^{(t,3)} n_{++k+}/m_{++k+}^{(t,3)} ,$$

(3.138) $$m_{ijk\ell}^{(t,5)} = m_{ijk\ell}^{(t,4)} n_{+++\ell}/m_{+++\ell}^{(t,4)} ,$$

(3.139) $$m_{ijk\ell}^{(t,6)} = m_{ijk\ell}^{(t,5)} (c^{(t)})^{\ell(2\delta_{1k}-1)} ,$$

where $c^{(t)}$ satisfies

$$|\log c^{(t)}| \, |\sum_{\ell=1}^{6} [n_{++1} (c^{(t)})^{\ell} - n_{++2} (c^{(t)})^{-\ell} - m_{++1}^{(t,6)}(c^{(t)})^{\ell} + m_{++2}^{(t,6)}(c^{(t)})^{-\ell}]| \le b[\hat{\ell}^{(p)}(\underline{n},\underline{\mu}^{(t,6)}) - \hat{\ell}^{(p)}(\underline{n},\underline{\mu}^{(t,5)})]. \tag{3.140}$$

It is reasonable to set $\underline{m}^{(0,1)} = \underline{e}$. After $\underline{m}^{(0,2)}$ has been determined, a rough estimate $\{\frac{1}{24} n_{i+++}\}$ of $\underline{m}$ is obtained. Convergence is much slower than for the Newton-Raphson method. If $b = 0.5$, the maximum difference between $m_{ijk\ell}^{(10,6)}$ and $m_{ijk\ell}$ is about 0.021. Thus convergence occurs, but the rate is relatively slow.

If $n_i^{(k)}$ is 1, 0, or -1 for each $i \in I$, then a simple expression for $\bar{\alpha}^{(t,k)}$ is still available. Suppose that

$$n_i^{(k)} = \begin{cases} 1 & \text{if } i \in I_0 , \\ -1 & \text{if } i \in I_1 , \\ 0 & \text{otherwise.} \end{cases} \tag{3.141}$$

Then (3.112) reduces to

$$\exp(\bar{\alpha}^{(t,k)}) \sum_{i\in I_0} m_i^{(t,k)} - \exp(-\bar{\alpha}^{(t,k)}) \sum_{i\in I_1} m_i^{(t,k)} = \sum_{i\in I_0} n_i - \sum_{i\in I_1} n_i . \tag{3.142}$$

An adjustment for the difference between two marginals is to be made. The equation reduces to a quadratic equation in which only the positive root is acceptable. It follows that

$$\exp(\bar{\alpha}^{(t,k)}) = \left\{ \sum_{i\in I_0} n_i - \sum_{i\in I_1} n_i + \left[\left(\sum_{i\in I_0} n_i - \sum_{i\in I_1} n_i \right)^2 + 4 \left(\sum_{i\in I_0} m_i^{(t,k)} \right) \left(\sum_{i\in I_0} m_i^{(t,k)} \right) \right]^{\frac{1}{2}} \right\} \Big/ \left(2 \sum_{i\in I_0} m_i^{(t,k)} \right). \tag{3.143}$$

If $h^{(t,k)} = \exp(\bar{\alpha}^{(t,k)})$, then

(3.144) $$m_i^{(t,k+1)} = m_i^{(t,k)} h^{(t,k)} \quad \text{if } i \in I_0 ,$$
$$= m_i^{(t,k)} / h^{(t,k)} \quad \text{if } i \in I_1 ,$$
$$= m_i^{(t,k)} \quad \text{otherwise} .$$

Example 3.5. The basis vectors $\{\underline{\mu}^{(j)}: j \in \overline{5}\}$ used in Example 1.6 may be replaced by the new basis $\{\underline{\eta}^{(j)}: j \in \overline{6}\}$, where

(3.145) $$\underline{\eta}^{(j)} = \underline{\mu}^{(j)}, \quad j \in \overline{3} ,$$

(3.146) $$\underline{\eta}^{(4)} = \begin{bmatrix} 1 & 0 \\ 1 & 0 \\ 1 & 0 \end{bmatrix} ,$$

(3.147) $$\underline{\eta}^{(5)} = \begin{bmatrix} 0 & 1 \\ 0 & 1 \\ 0 & 1 \end{bmatrix} ,$$

and

(3.148) $$\underline{\eta}^{(6)} = \underline{\mu}^{(5)} .$$

The basic iteration cycle may be reduced to the following three steps:

(3.149) $$m_{ij}^{(t,2)} = m_{ij}^{(t,1)} \, n_{i+}/m_{i+}^{(t,1)} ,$$

(3.150) $$m_{ij}^{(t,3)} = m_{ij}^{(t,2)} \, n_{+j}/m_{+j}^{(t,2)}$$

(3.151) $$\underline{m}^{(t,4)} = \begin{bmatrix} m_{11}^{(t,3)} h^{(t)} & m_{12}^{(t,3)}/h^{(t)} \\ m_{21}^{(t,3)} & m_{22}^{(t,3)} \\ m_{31}^{(t,3)}/h^{(t)} & m_{32}^{(t,3)} h^{(t)} \end{bmatrix}$$

(3.152) $$h^{(t)} = \Big\{ n_{11} + n_{32} - n_{12} - n_{31} + \Big[(n_{11} + n_{32} - n_{12} - n_{31})^2 + 4(m_{11}^{(t,3)} + m_{32}^{(t,3)})(m_{12}^{(t,3)} + m_{31}^{(t,3)}) \Big]^{\frac{1}{2}} \Big\} \Big/ \Big[2(m_{11}^{(t,3)} + m_{32}^{(t,3)}) \Big] .$$

If $\underline{m}^{(0,1)}$ is $\underline{e}$, then

(3.153)
$$\underline{m}^{(1,1)} = \begin{array}{|cc|} 3.39 & 14.77 \\ 5.00 & 10.00 \\ 7.39 & 6.77 \end{array}$$

and

(3.154)
$$\underline{m}^{(2,1)} = \begin{array}{|cc|} 2.51 & 13.33 \\ 4.80 & 10.21 \\ 8.04 & 6.85 \end{array}$$

Convergence to three decimal places occurs after six iterations. At this cycle,

(3.155)
$$\underline{m}^{(6,1)} = \begin{array}{|cc|} 2.19 & 12.84 \\ 4.66 & 10.34 \\ 8.17 & 6.83 \end{array}$$

Convergence is clearly much slower in this example than was the case with the Newton-Raphson method.

These simplifications are of considerable importance in the factorial tables considered in chapters 5 and 8. For some complete factorial tables, the cyclic accent algorithm converges to the maximum-likelihood estimate after one cycle. This situation is discussed in chapter 5.

If the cyclic ascent method does not lead to convergence after a single cycle, it is most useful when p is large, for the computational labor per cycle is proportional to pq rather than p^2q, the corresponding indicator of computational labor for the modified Newton-Raphson method. If p is large, the improved convergence properties of the Newton-Raphson method do not adequately compensate for the added computation per iteration. It is not clear precisely how large p should be for the cyclic ascent method to be preferable. Results of chapter 6 suggest that the Newton-Raphson method is satisfactory for manifolds of dimension as large as 28.

Chapter 4

ASYMPTOTIC PROPERTIES

Maximum-likelihood estimators generally have convenient asymptotic properties. The estimates considered in this paper are no exception. However, a few complications still exist. In the multinomial case, estimates are subject to nonlinear constraints which can obscure the relationship between Poisson and multinomial models. In the conditional Poisson case, since the maximum-likelihood estimates are very difficult to compute, the sampling properties of Poisson maximum-likelihood estimates are examined even in the conditional Poisson case. The development in the early part of this section will closely resemble that used in standard asymptotic theory; however, homogeneity properties rather than compactness properties are used in this chapter. This change is necessary since M is not compact.

In the first part of the chapter, the asymptotic distributions of the maximum-likelihood estimates $\hat{\underline{\mu}}$ and $\hat{\underline{m}}$ are obtained. These results are then employed to construct approximate confidence intervals and to find the asymptotic distribution of the log likelihood ratio and Pearson chi-square. These statistics are then used to test hypotheses. Since frequency tables are often complex, simultaneous confidence intervals and tests are desirable. Such procedures are devised in the last sections of this chapter.

In this chapter, we consider a sequence $\{\underline{n}^{(N)}: N \geq 1\}$ of random vectors with respective means $\{\underline{m}^{(N)}: N \geq 1\}$ and log means $\{\underline{\mu}^{(N)}: N \geq 1\}$. It is assumed that $\underline{\mu}^{(N)} \in M$ for $N \geq 1$, where $\underline{e} = \{1: i \in I\} \in M$, that $N^{-1}\,\underline{m}^{(N)} \longrightarrow \underline{m}^*$, and that $\underline{\mu}^* = \{\log m_i^*\} \in M$. If $i \in I$, these assumptions imply that $m_i^{(N)} > 0$ for $N \geq 1$ and $m_i^* > 0$. Sampling may be Poisson, multinomial, or conditional Poisson. For multinomial sampling, the vectors $\underline{\nu}^{(k)}$, $k \in \overline{r}$, are constant (see chapter 1). For conditional Poisson sampling, N is constant and included in M. It is assumed that N has a basis $\{\underline{\nu}^{(k)}: k \in \overline{r}\}$ such that $\nu_i^{(k)}$ is an integer if $i \in I$ and $k \in \overline{r}$. Sampling is assumed conditional on $P_N\underline{n} = P_N\underline{m}^{(N)}$.

In the Poisson case, the manifold $\mathcal{N}$ is defined to be $\{\underline{0}\}$. Given this convention, the results of chapter 1 show that for all three sampling methods,

(4.1) $$\frac{1}{N}\underline{n}^{(N)} \xrightarrow{P} \underline{m}^*$$

and

(4.2) $$N^{-\frac{1}{2}}(\underline{n}^{(N)} - \underline{m}^{(N)} \xrightarrow{\mathcal{D}} N(\underline{0}, D(\underline{\mu}^*)[I - P^*_{\mathcal{N}}(\underline{\mu}^*)]),$$

where $P^*_{\mathcal{N}}(\underline{\mu}^*)$ is an orthogonal projection from R^I to $\mathcal{N}$ with respect to the inner product $((\cdot,\cdot))$ such that if $\underline{x} \in R^I$ and $\underline{y} \in R^I$, then

(4.3) $$((\underline{x},\underline{y})) = (\underline{x}, D(\underline{\mu}^*)\underline{y}) .$$

Formulas (4.1) and (4.2) are used repeatedly in this chapter.

MAXIMUM-LIKELIHOOD ESTIMATION

In this section, the asymptotic properties of $\hat{\underline{\mu}}^{(N)}$ and $\hat{\underline{m}}^{(N)}$ are considered, where $\hat{\underline{\mu}}^{(N)}$ is the Poisson maximum-likelihood estimate of $\underline{\mu}^{(N)}$ and $\hat{\underline{m}}^{(N)}$ is the Poisson maximum-likelihood estimate of $\underline{m}^{(N)}$. Both estimates are based on the observation vector $\underline{n}^{(N)}$. Existence of $\hat{\underline{\mu}}^{(N)}$ and $\hat{\underline{m}}^{(N)}$ is not a problem since as $N \longrightarrow \infty$, $P\{n_i^{(N)} > 0 \ \forall i \in I\} \longrightarrow 1$. Thus as $N \longrightarrow \infty$, $P\{\hat{\underline{\mu}}^{(N)}$ exists$\} \longrightarrow 1$. Hence problems of existence of estimates do not affect asymptotic results.

As the problem is presently posed, $\|\underline{n}^{(N)}\| \longrightarrow \infty$ with probability 1 as $N \longrightarrow \infty$. In order to properly scale the problem for development of asymptotic results, let

(4.4) $$\bar{\underline{\mu}}^{(N)} = \hat{\underline{\mu}}^{(N)} - (\log N)\underline{e}.$$

Then

(4.5) $$\underline{m}(\bar{\underline{\mu}}^{(N)}) = \frac{1}{N}\underline{m}(\hat{\underline{\mu}}^{(N)}).$$

Since $\underline{e} \in \mathcal{M}$, $\bar{\underline{\mu}}^{(N)} \in \mathcal{M}$. Thus $\hat{\ell}^{(p)}(N^{-1}\underline{n}^{(N)}, \underline{\mu})$ has a maximum at $\bar{\underline{\mu}}^{(N)}$. Since $N^{-1}\underline{n}^{(N)} \xrightarrow{P} \underline{m}^*$, it is convenient to work with $\bar{\underline{\mu}}^{(N)}$ and $\underline{m}(\bar{\underline{\mu}}^{(N)})$ and then apply the results to $\hat{\underline{\mu}}^{(N)}$ and $\hat{\underline{m}}^{(N)}$.

Some motivation for use of $\bar{\underline{\mu}}^{(N)}$ and $\bar{\underline{m}}^{(N)}$ may be found by considering simple multinomial sampling in which r is 1 and $\underline{\nu}^{(1)} = \underline{e}$. Suppose that $(\underline{m}^{(N)}, \underline{e}) = N$. Then $\underline{n}^{(N)}$ is the vector of frequencies, while $N^{-1}\underline{n}^{(N)}$ is the vector of empirical probabilities. Thus $\underline{m}^{(N)}$ represents a vector of expected frequencies, and $N^{-1}\underline{m}^{(N)}$ represents a vector of cell probabilities. The vector $\underline{m}^*$ is also a vector of cell probabilities. The estimates $\bar{\underline{\mu}}^{(N)}$ and $\bar{\underline{m}}^{(N)}$ correspond to log-linear models in cell probabilities rather than cell expectations.

The basic asymptotic properties of $\hat{\underline{\mu}}^{(N)}$ and $\hat{\underline{m}}^{(N)}$ are given by the following theorem:

THEOREM 4.1. *The following relationships hold under the assumptions of this chapter as* $N \longrightarrow \infty$:

$$\hat{\underline{\mu}}^{(N)} - \underline{\mu}^{(N)} \xrightarrow{P} 0\ , \tag{4.6}$$

$$\frac{1}{N}\hat{\underline{m}}^{(N)} \xrightarrow{P} \underline{m}^*\ , \tag{4.7}$$

$$N^{\frac{1}{2}}(\hat{\underline{\mu}}^{(N)} - \underline{\mu}^{(N)}) \xrightarrow{\mathcal{D}} N(\underline{0},[P_M^*(\underline{\mu}^*) - P_N^*(\underline{\mu}^*)]D^{-1}(\underline{\mu}^*))\ , \tag{4.8}$$

$$N^{\frac{1}{2}}(\hat{\underline{m}}^{(N)} - \underline{m}^{(N)}) \xrightarrow{\mathcal{D}} N(\underline{0},D(\underline{\mu}^*)[P_M^*(\underline{\mu}^*) - P_N^*(\underline{\mu}^*)])\ . \tag{4.9}$$

Proof. The linear functional $d\hat{\ell}_{\underline{\mu}}^{(p)}(\underline{x},\underline{\nu})$ defined for $\underline{x} \in R^I$, $\underline{\mu} \in M$, and $\underline{\nu} \in M$ may be regarded as a function from $R^I \times M$ to M^*, the space of linear functions from M to R. Since $\underline{\mu}^* \in M$, $d\hat{\ell}_{\underline{\mu}^*}^{(p)}(\underline{m}^*,\underline{\nu}) = 0$ for all $\underline{\nu} \in M$. The second partial differential of $d\hat{\ell}_{\underline{\mu}}^{(p)}(\underline{x},\underline{\nu})$ is $d^2\hat{\ell}_{\underline{\mu}}^{(p)}$, where

$$d^2\hat{\ell}_{\underline{\mu}}^{(p)}(\underline{x},\underline{\nu})(\underline{\eta}) = -(\underline{\eta},D(\underline{\mu})\underline{\nu}) \tag{4.10}$$

for $\underline{\nu} \in M$ and $\underline{\eta} \in M$. This differential is continuous and invertible. By the implicit function theorem (see Loomis and Sternberg 1968), there exists an open ball $A \in R^I$ and an open ball $B \in M$ such that $\underline{m}^* \in A$, $\underline{\mu}^* \in B$, and there exists a differentiable function F from A to B such that if $\underline{x} \in A$, then $d\hat{\ell}_{F(\underline{x})}^{(p)}(\underline{x},\underline{\nu}) = 0$ for $\underline{\nu} \in M$. The differential of F at $\underline{y} \in A$ satisfies the equation

$$d^2\hat{\ell}_{F(\underline{y})}^{(p)}(\underline{y},dF_{\underline{y}}(\underline{x}))(\underline{\nu}) = (\underline{x},\underline{\nu}) \tag{4.11}$$

for every $\underline{\nu} \in M$. The linear function $(\underline{x},\underline{\nu})$ is the first partial differential of $d\hat{\ell}_{F(\underline{y})}^{(p)}(\underline{y},\underline{\nu})$ at $\underline{x}$ (see Loomis and Sternberg 1968). The differential $dF_{\underline{y}}$ is continuous for $\underline{y} \in A$. In particular,

$$dF_{\underline{m}^*}(\underline{x}) = P_M^*(\underline{\mu}^*)D^{-1}(\underline{\mu}^*)\underline{x} \tag{4.12}$$

for $\underline{x} \in R^I$. To verify (4.12), note that

(4.13) $$d^2\hat{\ell}^{(p)}_{\underline{\mu}^*}(\underline{m}^*, P^*_M(\underline{\mu}^*)D^{-1}(\underline{\mu}^*)\underline{x})(\underline{\nu}) = (\underline{\nu}, D(\underline{\mu}^*)P^*_M(\underline{\mu}^*)D^{-1}(\underline{\mu}^*)\underline{x}) = (\underline{\nu},\underline{x}),$$

provided $\underline{\nu} \in M$.

If $N^{-1}\underline{n}^{(N)} \in A$, then $\underline{\bar{\mu}}^{(N)} = F(N^{-1}\underline{n}^{(N)})$. This equation follows from the definition of F and the uniqueness of $\underline{\bar{\mu}}^{(N)}$. Since $N^{-1}\underline{n}^{(N)} \xrightarrow{P} \underline{m}^*$, the probability that $N^{-1}\underline{n}^{(N)} \in A$ approaches 1 as $N \longrightarrow \infty$. For N sufficiently large, $N^{-1}\underline{m}^{(N)} \in A$. If $N^{-1}\underline{n}^{(N)} \in A$, $N^{-1}\underline{m}^{(N)} \in A$, and $\underline{c} \in R^I$, then by Taylor's theorem,

(4.14) $$(\underline{c}, F(\tfrac{1}{N}\,\underline{n}^{(N)})) = (\underline{c}, F(\tfrac{1}{N}\,\underline{m}^{(N)})) + (\underline{c}, dF_{\underline{x}^{(N)}}(\tfrac{1}{N}\,\underline{n}^{(N)} - \tfrac{1}{N}\,\underline{m}^{(N)}))\ ,$$

where $\underline{x}^{(N)}$ is on the line segment joining $N^{-1}\underline{n}^{(N)}$ and $N^{-1}\underline{m}^{(N)}$. Since $F(N^{-1}\underline{m}^{(N)}) = \underline{\mu}^{(N)} - (\log N)\underline{e}$, it follows that if $N^{-1}\underline{n}^{(N)} \in A$ and $N^{-1}\underline{m}^{(N)} \in A$, then

(4.15) $$(\underline{c}, \underline{\hat{\mu}}^{(N)} - \underline{\mu}^{(N)}) = (\underline{c}, dF_{\underline{x}^{(N)}}(\tfrac{1}{N}\,\underline{n}^{(N)} - \tfrac{1}{N}\,\underline{m}^{(N)})).$$

Since $N^{-1}\underline{n}^{(N)} \xrightarrow{P} \underline{m}^*$ and $N^{-1}\underline{m}^{(N)} \longrightarrow \underline{m}^*$, it follows that $\underline{x}^{(N)} \xrightarrow{P} \underline{m}^*$, where $\underline{x}^{(N)}$ may be arbitrarily defined if $N^{-1}\underline{n}^{(N)}$ or $N^{-1}\underline{m}^{(N)}$ is not in A. Thus $dF_{\underline{x}^{(N)}} \xrightarrow{P} dF_{\underline{m}^*}$. Since (4.2) holds, it follows that

(4.16) $$N^{\frac{1}{2}}(\underline{c}, \underline{\hat{\mu}}^{(N)}\quad \underline{\mu}^{(N)}) - (\underline{c}, P^*_M(\underline{\mu}^*)D^{-1}(\underline{\mu}^*)N^{-\frac{1}{2}}(\underline{n}^{(N)} - \underline{m}^{(N)})) \xrightarrow{P} \underline{0}.$$

If $\underline{x} \in R^I$, then

(4.17) $$\begin{aligned}(\underline{c}, P^*_M(\underline{\mu}^*)D^{-1}(\underline{\mu}^*)\underline{x}) &= (D^{-1}(\underline{\mu}^*)\underline{c}, D(\underline{\mu}^*)P^*_M(\underline{\mu}^*)D^{-1}(\underline{\mu}^*)\underline{x}) \\ &= (P^*_M(\underline{\mu}^*)D^{-1}(\underline{\mu}^*)\underline{c}, \underline{x}).\end{aligned}$$

Thus

(4.18) $$\begin{aligned}N^{\frac{1}{2}}(\underline{c}, \underline{\hat{\mu}}^{(N)} - \underline{\mu}^{(N)}) &\xrightarrow{\mathcal{D}} N(\underline{0}, (P^*_M(\underline{\mu}^*)D^{-1}(\underline{\mu}^*)\underline{c}, D(\underline{\mu}^*)[I - P^*_N(\underline{\mu}^*)]P^*_M(\underline{\mu}^*)D^{-1}(\underline{\mu}^*)\underline{c})) \\ &= N(0, (\underline{c}, [P^*_M(\underline{\mu}^*) - P^*_N(\underline{\mu}^*)]D^{-1}(\underline{\mu}^*)\underline{c})).\end{aligned}$$

Since $\underline{c}$ is arbitrary, it follows by Rao (1965) that (4.8) holds. To prove (4.6), note that if $N\,(\underline{\hat{\mu}}^{(N)} - \underline{\mu}^{(N)})$ converges in distribution, then $\underline{\hat{\mu}}^{(N)} - \underline{\mu}^{(N)} \xrightarrow{P} 0$.

To complete the proof, observe that

(4.19) $$e^{\hat{\mu}_i^{(N)}} = e^{\mu_i^{(N)}}\ (1 + (\hat{\mu}_i^{(N)} - \mu_i^{(N)}) + o(\hat{\mu}_i^{(N)} - \mu_i^{(N)})),$$

and rearrangement of terms yields

(4.20) $$N^{\frac{1}{2}}(\underline{\hat{m}}^{(N)} - \underline{m}^{(N)}) = [\tfrac{1}{N} D(\underline{\mu}^{(N)})](N^{\frac{1}{2}}(\underline{\hat{\mu}}^{(N)} - \underline{\mu}^{(N)}) + N^{\frac{1}{2}} o(\underline{\hat{\mu}}^{(N)} - \underline{\mu}^{(N)})).$$

Now $N^{-1}D(\underline{\mu}^{(N)}) \longrightarrow D(\underline{\mu}^{*})$ and $\underline{\hat{\mu}}^{(N)} - \underline{\mu}^{(N)} \xrightarrow{P} \underline{0}$. Therefore,

(4.21) $$N^{\frac{1}{2}}(\underline{\hat{m}}^{(N)} - \underline{m}^{(N)}) - D(\underline{\mu}^{*})[N\,(\underline{\hat{\mu}}^{(N)} - \underline{\mu}^{(N)})] \xrightarrow{P} 0$$

and

(4.22) $$N^{-\frac{1}{2}}(\underline{\hat{m}}^{(N)} - \underline{m}^{(N)}) \xrightarrow{\mathcal{D}} N(\underline{0}, D(\underline{\mu}^{*})[P^{*}_{M}(\underline{\mu}^{*}) - P^{*}_{N}(\underline{\mu}^{*})]).$$

Formulas (4.9) and (4.22) coincide. Formula (4.7) follows immediately.||

Remark. If only multinomial sampling is considered, Theorem 4.1 can be proven, after some manipulation, by use of general theorems on asymptotic properties of maximum likelihood estimates (see Cramer 1946, Mitra 1958, and Rao 1965). The method of proof chosen for Theorem 4.1 permits simultaneous consideration of all sampling methods and exploits uniqueness properties which do not generally hold for parametric models considered by any of the authors named above.

If Poisson sampling is employed, then $P^{*}_{N}(\underline{\mu}^{*})$ vanishes. Thus $N^{-\frac{1}{2}}(\underline{\hat{\mu}}^{(N)} - \underline{\mu}^{(N)}) \xrightarrow{\mathcal{D}} N(\underline{0}, P^{*}_{M}(\underline{\mu}^{*})D^{-1}(\underline{\mu}^{*}))$ and $N^{-\frac{1}{2}}(\underline{\hat{m}}^{(N)} - \underline{m}^{(N)}) \xrightarrow{\mathcal{D}} N(\underline{0}, D(\underline{\mu}^{*})P^{*}_{M}(\underline{\mu}^{*}))$. If multinomial sampling is used, then $P^{*}_{N}(\underline{\mu}^{*})$ does not vanish. It satisfies

(4.23) $$P^{*}_{N}(\underline{\mu}^{*}) = \sum_{k=1}^{r} \frac{1}{(\underline{\nu}^{(k)}, D(\underline{\mu}^{*})\underline{\nu}^{(k)})} \underline{\nu}^{(k)} \bullet [D(\underline{\mu}^{*})\underline{\nu}^{(k)}].$$

Thus the asymptotic covariance operator for $N^{\frac{1}{2}}(\underline{\hat{\mu}}^{(N)} - \underline{\mu}^{(N)})$ is

(4.24) $$[P^{*}_{M}(\underline{\mu}^{*}) - P^{*}_{N}(\underline{\mu}^{*})]D^{-1}(\underline{\mu}^{*})$$

$$= P^{*}_{M}(\underline{\mu}^{*})D^{-1}(\underline{\mu}^{*}) - \sum_{k=1}^{r} \frac{1}{(\underline{\nu}^{(k)}, D(\underline{\mu}^{*})\underline{\nu}^{(k)})} \underline{\nu}^{(k)} \bullet \underline{\nu}^{(k)}.$$

Example 4.1. Consider the $2 \times 2 \times 2$ table of Example 3.1. Here $\mathcal{M} = \{\underline{\mu}: \mu_{ijk} = a_{ij} + b_{ik} + c_{jk}\}$ and

(4.25) $$P^{*}_{M}(\underline{\mu}^{*}) = I - c^{-1}\, \overline{\underline{\nu}} \bullet \overline{\underline{\mu}}\ ,$$

where

(4.26)
$$\underline{\bar{\mu}} = \boxed{\begin{array}{cc} 1 & -1 \\ -1 & 1 \end{array}} \quad \boxed{\begin{array}{cc} -1 & 1 \\ 1 & -1 \end{array}} ,$$

(4.27)
$$\underline{\bar{\nu}} = \boxed{\begin{array}{cc} 1/m^*_{111} & -1/m^*_{121} \\ -1/m^*_{211} & 1/m^*_{221} \end{array}} \quad \boxed{\begin{array}{cc} -1/m^*_{112} & 1/m^*_{122} \\ 1/m^*_{212} & -1/m^*_{222} \end{array}} ,$$

and

(4.28)
$$c = \sum_{i=1}^{2} \sum_{j=1}^{2} \sum_{k=1}^{2} 1/m^*_{ijk} .$$

If Poisson sampling is present and the model is correct, then $N^{\frac{1}{2}}(\underline{\hat{\mu}}^{(N)} - \underline{\mu}^{(N)})$ has asymptotic covariance

(4.29)
$$P^*_M(\underline{\mu}^*)D^{-1}(\underline{\mu}^*) = D^{-1}(\underline{\mu}^*) - c^{-1}\, \underline{\bar{\nu}} \bullet \underline{\bar{\nu}} .$$

Since

(4.30)
$$NP^*_M(\underline{\hat{\mu}}^{(N)})D^{-1}(\underline{\hat{\mu}}^{(N)}) \xrightarrow{P} P^*_M(\underline{\mu}^*)D^{-1}(\underline{\mu}^*) ,$$

one may estimate the asymptotic covariance of $\underline{\hat{\mu}}$ by

(4.31)
$$\ddagger(\underline{\hat{\mu}}) = D^{-1}(\underline{\hat{\mu}}) - \hat{c}^{-1}\, \underline{\hat{\nu}} \bullet \underline{\hat{\nu}} ,$$

where $\hat{c} = \sum_{i=1}^{2} \sum_{j=1}^{2} \sum_{k=1}^{2} 1/\hat{m}_{ijk}$ and

(4.32)
$$\underline{\hat{\nu}} = \boxed{\begin{array}{cc} 1/\hat{m}_{111} & -1/\hat{m}_{121} \\ -1/\hat{m}_{211} & 1/\hat{m}_{221} \end{array}} \quad \boxed{\begin{array}{cc} -1/\hat{m}_{112} & 1/\hat{m}_{122} \\ 1/\hat{m}_{212} & -1/\hat{m}_{222} \end{array}} .$$

Were the model in Example 3.1 correct, the estimated asymptotic covariance $\ddagger(\underline{\hat{\mu}})$ of $\underline{\hat{\mu}}$ would have the matrix

(4.33) $[\ddagger(\underline{\hat{\mu}})] =$

$$\begin{bmatrix}
0.0376 & 0.0056 & 0.0057 & -0.0020 & 0.0071 & -0.0056 & -0.0082 & 0.0034 \\
0.0056 & 0.0273 & -0.0039 & 0.0014 & -0.0048 & 0.0038 & 0.0056 & -0.0023 \\
0.0057 & -0.0039 & 0.0280 & 0.0014 & -0.0050 & 0.0039 & 0.0057 & -0.0024 \\
-0.0020 & 0.0014 & 0.0014 & 0.0108 & 0.0017 & -0.0014 & -0.0020 & 0.0008 \\
0.0071 & -0.0048 & -0.0050 & 0.0017 & 0.0335 & 0.0049 & 0.0071 & -0.0029 \\
-0.0056 & 0.0038 & 0.0039 & -0.0014 & 0.0049 & 0.0276 & -0.0056 & 0.0023 \\
-0.0082 & 0.0056 & 0.0057 & -0.0020 & 0.0071 & -0.0056 & 0.0376 & 0.0034 \\
0.0034 & -0.0023 & -0.0024 & 0.0008 & -0.0029 & 0.0023 & 0.0034 & 0.0174
\end{bmatrix}$$

The standard basis used in this matrix has the order $\{\underline{\delta}^{<1,1,1>}, \underline{\delta}^{<2,1,1>}, \underline{\delta}^{<1,2,1>}, \underline{\delta}^{<2,2,1>}, \underline{\delta}^{<1,1,2>}, \underline{\delta}^{<2,1,2>}, \underline{\delta}^{<1,2,2>}, \underline{\delta}^{<2,2,2>}\}$. Similar conventions are used with other factorial tables. Similarly, the asymptotic covariance for $N^{-\frac{1}{2}}(\hat{\underline{m}}^{(N)} - \underline{m}^{(N)})$ is

$$D(\underline{\mu}^*)P_M^*(\underline{\mu}^*) = D(\underline{\mu}^*) - c^{-1}\, \bar{\underline{\mu}} \otimes \bar{\underline{\mu}} \,. \tag{4.34}$$

The estimated asymptotic covariance of $\hat{\underline{m}}$ is then

$$\ddagger(\hat{\underline{m}}) = D(\hat{\underline{\mu}}) - \hat{c}^{-1}\, \bar{\underline{\mu}} \otimes \bar{\underline{\mu}} \,. \tag{4.35}$$

The corresponding covariance matrix is

$$[\ddagger(\hat{\underline{m}})] = \tag{4.36}$$

$$\begin{bmatrix}
17.90 & 3.91 & 3.91 & -3.91 & 3.91 & -3.91 & -3.91 & 3.91 \\
3.91 & 28.28 & -3.91 & 3.91 & -3.91 & 3.91 & 3.91 & -3.91 \\
3.91 & -3.91 & 27.28 & 3.91 & -3.91 & 3.91 & 3.91 & -3.91 \\
-3.91 & 3.91 & 3.91 & 84.90 & 3.91 & -3.91 & -3.91 & 3.91 \\
3.91 & -3.91 & -3.91 & 3.91 & 21.28 & 3.91 & 3.91 & -3.91 \\
-3.91 & 3.91 & 3.91 & -3.91 & 3.91 & 27.90 & -3.91 & 3.91 \\
-3.91 & 3.91 & 3.91 & -3.91 & 3.91 & -3.91 & 17.90 & 3.91 \\
3.91 & -3.91 & -3.91 & 3.91 & -3.91 & 3.91 & 3.91 & 49.28
\end{bmatrix}$$

If $\underline{c}$ is orthogonal to N, then

$$N^{\frac{1}{2}}[(\underline{c},\hat{\underline{\mu}}^{(N)}) - (\underline{c},\underline{\mu}^{(N)})] \xrightarrow{\mathcal{D}} N(\underline{0},(\underline{c},P_M^*(\underline{\mu}^*)D^{-1}(\underline{\mu}^*)\underline{c})). \tag{4.37}$$

This formula shows that the asymptotic distribution of $N^{\frac{1}{2}}[(\underline{c},\hat{\underline{\mu}}^{(N)}) - (\underline{c},\underline{\mu}^{(N)})]$ is independent of N, provided $\underline{c}$ and N are orthogonal. To verify (4.37), observe that

$$(\underline{c},P_N^*(\underline{\mu}^*)D^{-1}(\underline{\mu}^*)\underline{c}) = 0 \,. \tag{4.38}$$

Note also that if $\hat{\underline{\mu}}^{(N,k)}$ corresponds to the hypothesis that $\underline{\mu}^{(N)} \in M_k$ for $k \in \bar{2}$ and if $\underline{\mu}^{(N)} \in M_1 \subset M_2$ for all N, then $(\underline{c},P_{M_1}^*(\underline{\mu}^*)D^{-1}(\underline{\mu}^*)\underline{c})$ is no greater than $(\underline{c},P_{M_2}^*(\underline{\mu}^*)D^{-1}(\underline{\mu}^*)\underline{c})$. Thus $N^{\frac{1}{2}}[(\underline{c},\hat{\underline{\mu}}^{(N,1)}) - (\underline{c},\underline{\mu}^{(N)})]$ has an asymptotic variance no greater than the asymptotic variance of $N^{\frac{1}{2}}[(\underline{c},\hat{\underline{\mu}}^{(N,2)}) - (\underline{c},\underline{\mu}^{(N)})]$.

Example 4.2. In Example 4.1, if M were $R^{\bar{2}\times\bar{2}\times\bar{2}}$ rather than $\{\underline{\mu}: \mu_{ijk} = a_{ij} + b_{ik} + c_{jk}\}$, the asymptotic covariance of $N^{\frac{1}{2}}(\hat{\underline{\mu}}^{(N)} - \underline{\mu}^{(N)})$ would be $D^{-1}(\underline{\mu}^*)$. The asymptotic variance of $N^{\frac{1}{2}}(\hat{\mu}_{ijk}^{(N)} - \mu_{ijk}^{(N)})$ would then be $1/m_{ijk}^*$ rather than $1/m_{ijk}^* - (1/m_{ijk}^*)^2/c$, the asymptotic variance corresponding to the manifold for no three-factor interaction. If $M = \{\underline{\mu}: \mu_{ijk} = a_{ij} + b_{ik} + c_{jk}\}$ and the model is correct, the estimated asymptotic variance of $\hat{\mu}_{111}$ is 0.0376. If $M = R^{\bar{2}\times\bar{2}\times\bar{2}}$, the corresponding estimate is 0.0385. It should be noted that the estimated variance for the smaller manifold can exceed the estimated variance for the larger manifold since the maximum-likelihood estimates for the two manifolds need not coincide. For example, in both models the asymptotic covariance of $\hat{\mu}_{221}$ is 0.0108 to three significant figures.

To construct asymptotic confidence intervals for linear combinations $(\underline{c},\underline{\mu})$ of $\underline{\mu}$, where $P_M\underline{c} \notin N$, observe that

$$(4.39)\quad (\underline{c},[P_M^*(\underline{\mu}^*) - P_N^*(\underline{\mu}^*)]D^{-1}(\underline{\mu}^*)\underline{c}) = (P_M\underline{c},[P_M^*(\underline{\mu}^*) - P_N^*(\underline{\mu}^*)]D^{-1}(\underline{\mu}^*)P_M\underline{c}) > 0 ,$$

$$(4.40)\quad NP_N^*(\hat{\underline{\mu}}^{(N)})D^{-1}(\hat{\underline{\mu}}^{(N)}) \xrightarrow{P} P_N^*(\underline{\mu}^*)D^{-1}(\underline{\mu}^*) ,$$

and

$$(4.41)\quad NP_M^*(\hat{\underline{\mu}}^{(N)})D^{-1}(\hat{\underline{\mu}}^{(N)}) \xrightarrow{P} P_M^*(\underline{\mu}^*)D^{-1}(\underline{\mu}^*) .$$

Hence an approximate two-sided $(1-\alpha)$-level confidence interval is given by those values of $(\underline{c},\underline{\mu})$ such that

$$(4.42)\quad |(\underline{c},\underline{\mu}) - (\underline{c},\hat{\underline{\mu}})| \le \Phi^{(\alpha/2)} [(\underline{c},[P_M^*(\hat{\underline{\mu}}) - P_N^*(\hat{\underline{\mu}})]D^{-1}(\hat{\underline{\mu}})\underline{c})]^{\frac{1}{2}}.$$

If $\underline{c}$ is orthogonal to N, then (4.42) reduces to

$$(4.43)\quad |(\underline{c},\underline{\mu}) - (\underline{c},\hat{\underline{\mu}})| \le \Phi^{(\alpha/2)} (\underline{c},P_M^*(\hat{\underline{\mu}})D^{-1}(\hat{\underline{\mu}})\underline{c})^{\frac{1}{2}} .$$

As in all confidence intervals in this monograph, the use of strict inequality ($<$) rather than inequality ($\le$) is permissible whenever the asymptotic variance is positive. Superscripts have been omitted since a general approximation is given. The term $\Phi^{(\alpha/2)}$ is the upper $\alpha/2$-point of the standardized normal distribution. The asymptotically smallest confidence region is obtained by using the smallest manifold M known to contain $\underline{\mu}$.

These confidence intervals also correspond to approximate α-level tests. For example, an approximate level-α two-sided test of the null hypothesis $(\underline{c},\underline{\mu}) = 0$, where $\underline{c}$ is orthogonal to N, is to reject the null hypothesis whenever

$$(4.44)\quad |(\underline{c},\hat{\underline{\mu}})|/(\underline{c},P_M^*(\hat{\underline{\mu}}^*)D^{-1}(\hat{\underline{\mu}})\underline{c})^{\frac{1}{2}} > \Phi^{(\alpha/2)}$$

One-sided tests and confidence intervals may also be constructed.

Example 4.3. Suppose that $M = R^{\overline{2}\times\overline{2}}$ and $I = \overline{2} \times \overline{2}$. This example is a 2 x 2 table without any linear restrictions on $\underline{\mu}$. Suppose that

(4.45) $$\underline{c} = \begin{array}{|cc|} 1 & -1 \\ -1 & 1 \end{array} .$$

Then $P_M^*(\hat{\underline{\mu}})$ is I, the identity operator. If $n_{ij} > 0$ for $\langle i,j\rangle \in \bar{2} \times \bar{2}$, then by Theorem 2.1, $\hat{\underline{\mu}} = \{\log n_{ij}\}$. If $\underline{c}$ is orthogonal to N, then

$$\frac{(\underline{c},\hat{\underline{\mu}}) - (\underline{c},\underline{\mu})}{(1/n_{11} + 1/n_{12} + 1/n_{21} + 1/n_{22})^{\frac{1}{2}}}$$

is approximately normal for large enough m_{ij}, $\langle i,j\rangle \in \bar{2} \times \bar{2}$. An approximate confidence interval for the log cross-product ratio $r = \log (m_{11}m_{22}/m_{12}m_{21})$ is

(4.46) $$\left|r - \log \frac{n_{11}n_{22}}{n_{12}n_{21}}\right| \le \Phi^{(\alpha/2)} (1/n_{11} + 1/n_{12} + 1/n_{21} + 1/n_{22})^{\frac{1}{2}} .$$

This confidence interval is valid if Poisson sampling is used, if each row sum is fixed, if each column sum is fixed, or if both row and column sums are fixed (see Plackett 1962 and Goodman 1964).

In Example 1.2, the maximum-likelihood estimate $\hat{\underline{\mu}}$ for $M = R^{\bar{2}\times\bar{2}}$ is

$$\hat{\underline{\mu}} = \begin{array}{|cc|} 6.38 & 6.16 \\ 8.34 & 8.31 \end{array} .$$

The log cross-product ratio r has a maximum-likelihood estimate $\log[(588)(4061)/(4196)(473)] = 0.185$. One has

(4.48) $$(1/588 + 1/473 + 1/4196 + 1/4061)^{\frac{1}{2}} = 0.0656$$

and $\Phi^{(0.025)} = 1.96$, so a 95% confidence interval for r is $[0.056,0.313]$. This interval corresponds to the confidence interval $[1.058,1.368]$ for the cross-product ratio $m_{11}m_{22}/m_{12}m_{21}$. One may clearly conclude that sex and toxemia are related in a substantial manner, although the data do not permit a very accurate assessment of the magnitude of the association.

Example 4.4. In Example 4.2 the relationship between parole violation and type of offender is of interest. A reasonable way to examine these relationships is to consider the log cross-product ratios $\log (m_{111}m_{221}/m_{121}m_{211})$ and $\log (m_{112}m_{222}/m_{122}m_{212})$. These ratios correspond to the linear combinations $(\underline{\mu}^{(1)},\underline{\mu})$ and $(\underline{\mu}^{(2)},\underline{\mu})$, where

(4.49) $$\underline{\mu}^{(1)} = \boxed{\begin{matrix} 1 & -1 \\ -1 & 1 \end{matrix}} \quad \boxed{\begin{matrix} 0 & 0 \\ 0 & 0 \end{matrix}}$$

and

(4.50) $$\underline{\mu}^{(2)} \quad \boxed{\begin{matrix} 0 & 0 \\ 0 & 0 \end{matrix}} \quad \boxed{\begin{matrix} 1 & -1 \\ -1 & 1 \end{matrix}} .$$

If $M = R^{\overline{2}\times\overline{2}\times\overline{2}}$, then a confidence interval for $(\underline{\mu}^{(1)},\underline{\mu})$ is obtained by considering the 2×2 table consisting of offenders without a previous criminal record. The resulting interval is

(4.51) $$[r_1 - \Phi^{(\alpha/2)}c_1^{\frac{1}{2}}, r_1 + \Phi^{(\alpha/2)}c_1^{\frac{1}{2}}],$$

where

(4.52) $$r_1 = \log (n_{111}n_{221}/n_{121}n_{211})$$

$$= 1.205$$

and

(4.53) $$c_1 = \frac{1}{n_{111}} + \frac{1}{n_{121}} + \frac{1}{n_{211}} + \frac{1}{n_{221}}$$

$$= 0.112 .$$

Thus a 95% confidence interval for $\mu_{111} - \mu_{121} - \mu_{211} + \mu_{211}$ is [0.527,1.883]. By similar arguments, one obtains the 95% confidence interval [-0.623,0.813] for $\mu_{112} - \mu_{122} - \mu_{212} + \mu_{222}$.

If $\underline{\mu} \in M = \{\overline{\underline{\mu}}\}^{\perp}$, where $\overline{\underline{\mu}}$ is defined by (3.17), then $(\underline{\mu}^{(1)},\underline{\mu}) = (\underline{\mu}^{(2)},\underline{\mu})$. In this case, the common cross-product ratio $(\frac{1}{2}(\underline{\mu}^{(1)} + \underline{\mu}^{(2)}),\underline{\mu})$ has a 95% confidence interval

(4.54) $$[r_0 - 1.96\ c_0^{\frac{1}{2}}, r_0 + 1.96\ c_0^{\frac{1}{2}}]$$

$$= [0.164,1.150],$$

where

(4.55) $$r_0 = \tfrac{1}{2}(\underline{\mu}^{(1)} + \underline{\mu}^{(2)},\underline{\mu})$$

$$= 0.657$$

and

(4.56) $$c_0 = \frac{1}{4}(\underline{\mu}^{(1)} + \underline{\mu}^{(2)}, [D^{-1}(\hat{\underline{\mu}}) - \hat{c}^{-1}\, \hat{\underline{\nu}} \bullet \hat{\underline{\nu}}](\underline{\mu}^{(1)} + \underline{\mu}^{(2)}))$$

$$= \hat{c}\{1 - [\frac{1}{\hat{c}}(\frac{1}{\hat{m}_{111}} + \frac{1}{\hat{m}_{121}} + \frac{1}{\hat{m}_{211}} + \frac{1}{\hat{m}_{221}} - \frac{1}{\hat{m}_{112}} - \frac{1}{\hat{m}_{122}} - \frac{1}{\hat{m}_{212}} - \frac{1}{\hat{m}_{222}})]^2\}$$

$$\doteq 0.0634.$$

Here $\hat{c}$ and $\hat{\underline{\nu}}$ are defined as in Example 4.1. However, since the confidence intervals for the two individual cross product ratios have a relatively small intersection, the assumption that $\underline{\mu} \in M$ would appear to be dubious.

The hypothesis that $\underline{\mu} \in M$ may be tested by observing that the condition $\underline{\mu} \in M$ is equivalent to the conditions $(\underline{\mu}, \underline{\mu}^{(1)} - \underline{\mu}^{(2)}) = 0$ and $\underline{\mu} \in R^{\overline{2}\times\overline{2}\times\overline{2}}$. A two-sided test of this hypothesis is to reject the hypothesis that $\underline{\mu} \in M$ whenever

(4.57) $$|r_1 - r_2|/(c_1 + c_2)^{\frac{1}{2}} > \Phi^{(\alpha/2)},$$

where

(4.58) $$r_2 = \log(n_{112}n_{222}/n_{122}n_{212})$$

$$= 0.095,$$

(4.59) $$c_2 = \frac{1}{n_{112}} + \frac{1}{n_{222}} + \frac{1}{n_{122}} + \frac{1}{n_{212}}$$

$$= 0.134,$$

and r_1 and c_1 are defined by (4.52) and (4.53). Since

(4.60) $$|r_1 - r_2|/(c_1 + c_2)^{\frac{1}{2}} = 2.24,$$

the null hypothesis may be rejected at the 5% level. Other tests of this hypothesis are discussed in the next section.

Substantial simplifications are possible if $D(\underline{\mu})$ maps M into itself for each $\underline{\mu} \in M$. In this case, $P^*_M(\underline{\mu}) = P_M$, the conventional orthogonal projection of R^I on M (see Kruskal 1968a). If $\underline{c} \in M$, then the approximate confidence interval becomes

(4.61) $$|(\underline{c}, \hat{\underline{\mu}}) - (\underline{c}, \underline{\mu})| \leq \Phi^{(\alpha/2)}(c, D^{-1}(\hat{\underline{\mu}})\underline{c}) .$$

Unfortunately, if no two coordinates, μ_i and $\mu_{i'}$, are the same for distinct indices i and i' in I, then the conditions $D(\underline{\mu})(M) \subset M$ and $\underline{e} \in M$ imply that $M = R^I$. To prove this result, suppose $\mu_{i'} > \mu_i$ if $i \neq i'$. Then

(4.62) $$\{[1/\exp(\mu_{i'})]^n D(\underline{\mu})\}\underline{e} \longrightarrow \underline{\delta}^{(i')} ,$$

where $\delta_i^{(i')} = \delta_{ii'}$ for every $i \in I$. Since finite-dimensional linear manifolds are closed, the vector $\underline{\delta}^{(i')} \in M$. Now replace $\underline{e}$ by $\underline{e} - \underline{\delta}^{(i')}$ and proceed by induction. The final result is $\underline{\delta}^{(i)} \in M$ for every $i \in I$. The span of $\{\underline{\delta}^{(i)}: i \in I\}$ is R^I, so $M = R^I$. The case $M = R^I$ has been investigated by Goodman (1964) and Plackett (1962). Results for other situations have received much less attention.

Confidence intervals for linear combinations of $\underline{m}$ are generally not as useful as confidence intervals for linear combinations of $\underline{m}$. They can be obtained by use of $\ddagger(\hat{\underline{m}})$, but such intervals depend explicitly on the manifold N. The relevant asymptotic result is

(4.63) $$[(\underline{c},\hat{\underline{m}}^{(N)}) - (\underline{c},\underline{m}^{(N)})]/(\underline{c},D(\hat{\underline{\mu}}^{(N)})[P_M(\hat{\underline{\mu}}^{(N)}) - P_N^*(\hat{\underline{\mu}}^{(N)})]\underline{c})^{\frac{1}{2}} \xrightarrow{\mathcal{D}} N(0,1) .$$

The approximate confidence interval is given by the inequality

(4.64) $$|(\underline{c},\hat{\underline{m}}) - (\underline{c},\underline{m})| \le \Phi^{(\alpha/2)} (\underline{c},D(\hat{\underline{\mu}})[P_M^*(\hat{\underline{\mu}}) - P_N^*(\hat{\underline{\mu}})]\underline{c})^{\frac{1}{2}} .$$

The corresponding two-sided test of the hypothesis $(\underline{c},\underline{m}) = d$ is to reject this hypothesis if

(4.65) $$|(\underline{c},\hat{\underline{m}}) - d|/(\underline{c},D(\hat{\underline{\mu}})[P_M^*(\hat{\underline{\mu}}) - P_N^*(\hat{\underline{\mu}})]\underline{c})^{\frac{1}{2}} > \Phi^{(\alpha/2)} .$$

Example 4.5. Consider the logit model in Example 1.6. Suppose that the quantity to be estimated is the probability of death if the frog has received a log dose of 0.85. If one proceeds as in Example 3.3, one finds that

(4.66) $$D(\hat{\mu})[P_M^*(\hat{\mu}) - P_N^*(\hat{\mu})] = \frac{1}{a}\underline{y} \bullet \underline{y} + \frac{1}{d}\underline{z} \bullet \underline{z} ,$$

where

(4.67) $$\hat{w}_i = \hat{m}_{i1}\hat{m}_{i2}/N_i ,$$

(4.68) $$a = \hat{w}_1 + \hat{w}_2 + \hat{w}_3 ,$$

(4.69) $$\underline{y} = \begin{bmatrix} \hat{w}_1 & -\hat{w}_1 \\ \hat{w}_2 & -\hat{w}_2 \\ \hat{w}_3 & -\hat{w}_3 \end{bmatrix} ,$$

(4.70) $$b = (\hat{w}_1 - \hat{w}_3)/(\hat{w}_1 + \hat{w}_2 + \hat{w}_3) ,$$

(4.71) $$d = \hat{w}_1 + \hat{w}_3 - b^2(\hat{w}_1 + \hat{w}_2 + \hat{w}_3) ,$$

and

(4.72) $$\underline{z} = \begin{bmatrix} \hat{w}_1 & -\hat{w}_1 \\ 0 & 0 \\ -\hat{w}_3 & \hat{w}_3 \end{bmatrix} - b \begin{bmatrix} \hat{w}_1 & -\hat{w}_1 \\ \hat{w}_2 & -\hat{w}_2 \\ \hat{w}_3 & -\hat{w}_3 \end{bmatrix}$$

The linear combination of interest is $m_{21} = (\underline{c},\underline{m})$, where

(4.73) $$\underline{c} = \begin{bmatrix} 0 & 0 \\ 1 & 0 \\ 0 & 0 \end{bmatrix} .$$

Thus

(4.74) $$(\underline{c}, D(\hat{\underline{\mu}})[P_M^*(\hat{\underline{\mu}}) - P_N^*(\hat{\underline{\mu}})]\underline{c})$$

$$= \hat{w}_2^2/a + b^2\hat{w}_2^2/d$$

$$= \hat{w}_2^2[\frac{1}{a} + \frac{b^2}{d}]$$

$$= \frac{\hat{w}_2^2(\hat{w}_1 + \hat{w}_3)}{4\hat{w}_1\hat{w}_3 + \hat{w}_2(\hat{w}_1 + \hat{w}_3)}$$

$$= 1.26.$$

The 95% confidence interval for m_{21} is given by

(4.75) $$m_{21} \in \left[\hat{m}_{21} - 1.96\ \hat{w}_2 \left(\frac{1}{a} + \frac{b^2}{d}\right)^{\frac{1}{2}}, \hat{m}_{21} + 1.96\ \hat{w}_2 \left(\frac{1}{a} + \frac{b^2}{d}\right)^{\frac{1}{2}}\right] .$$

$$= [2.461, 6.863] .$$

The corresponding interval for p_{21} is [0.164,0.458]. This interval may be compared to the interval [0.172,0.481] found in Example 1.17 by use of exact nonrandomized intervals. Given the size of the uncertainty concerning p_{21}, the difference between the intervals is quite small.

In this example, a confidence interval for p_{21} could have been constructed from confidence intervals for $\mu_{21} - \mu_{22} = \log(p_{21}/p_{22})$. Although the interval based on the log odds is easily seen to be asymptotically equivalent to the interval based on a linear combination of $\underline{m}$, the two intervals are not identical for finite samples. The interval based on the log odds may be advantageous since the range of $\log(p_{21}/p_{22})$ is unrestricted, while the range of p_{21} is from 0 to 1.

To construct confidence intervals based on the log odds, one considers the vector $(\underline{g},\underline{\mu})$, where

(4.76)
$$\underline{g} = \begin{bmatrix} 0 & 0 \\ 1 & -1 \\ 0 & 0 \end{bmatrix} .$$

One has

(4.77)
$$\begin{aligned}(g,[P_M^*(\hat{\underline{\mu}}) - P_N^*(\hat{\underline{\mu}})]D^{-1}(\hat{\underline{\mu}})\underline{g}) &= (D^{-1}(\hat{\underline{\mu}})\underline{g},D(\hat{\underline{\mu}})[P_M^*(\hat{\underline{\mu}}) - P_N^*(\hat{\underline{\mu}})]D^{-1}(\hat{\underline{\mu}})\underline{g}) \\ &= \frac{1}{a}(D^{-1}(\hat{\underline{\mu}})\underline{g},\underline{y})^2 + \frac{1}{d}(D^{-1}(\hat{\underline{\mu}})\underline{g},\underline{z})^2 \\ &= 1/a + b^2/d \\ &= \frac{\hat{w}_1 + \hat{w}_3}{4\hat{w}_1\hat{w}_3 + \hat{w}_2(\hat{w}_1 + \hat{w}_3)} \\ &= 0.1224 .\end{aligned}$$

The 95% confidence interval for $\log(p_{21}/p_{22})$ is

(4.78)
$$[\hat{\mu}_{21} - \hat{\mu}_{22} - 1.96\ (0.1224)^{\frac{1}{2}},\ \hat{\mu}_{21} - \hat{\mu}_{22} + 1.96\ (0.1224)^{\frac{1}{2}}] = [-1.484,-0.112] .$$

The corresponding interval for p_{21} is

(4.79)
$$\left[\frac{e^{-1.484}}{1 + e^{-1.484}}, \frac{e^{-0.112}}{1 + e^{-0.112}}\right] = [0.185,0.472] .$$

This interval is also rather similar to the interval found in Example 1.17. In this example, the new interval is in fact more similar to the interval in Example 1.17 than is the old one. Although very little evidence exists concerning which approximate interval is in general to be preferred, the author's experience does suggest a modest preference for intervals based on log odds.

Although confidence intervals for linear combinations of $\underline{m}$ depend on N, confidence intervals for linear combinations of proportions do not have this problem. This remark is useful when the table $\underline{n}$ has been generated by observing independent random variables (or vectors) $X_t \in I$, $t \in \overline{T}$, where T is fixed or Poisson. The observation n_i is then the number of $t \in \overline{T}$ such that $X_t = i$. If $\mathcal{I} = \{I_k : k \in \overline{s}\}$ is a partition of I such that the distribution of X_t given $X_t \in I_k$ is independent of t and the number T_k of $X_t \in I_k$ is fixed or Poisson, then $\underline{n}$ is a Poisson or multinomial sample. In such a case, the vector $\underline{p}(\mathcal{I})$ of conditional probabilities

$$\{P\{X_t = \underline{i} | X_t \in I_k\} : \underline{i} \in I_k,\ k \in \overline{s}\} = \{m_i / \sum_{i \in I_k} m_i : \underline{i} \in I_k,\ k \in \overline{s}\}$$

is of interest. More generally, if $\mathcal{J} = \{J_\ell : \ell \in \overline{r}\}$ is a subpartition of $\mathcal{I}$, the vector

$$\underline{p}(\mathcal{I}) = \{P\{X_t = \underline{i} | X_t \in J_\ell\} : \underline{i} \in J_\ell,\ \ell \in \overline{r}\}$$

may be of interest.

Example 4.6. In table 1.1, the random vector $\underline{X}_t = \langle i,j \rangle$ if infant t is in group i and has sex j. If the sample is random, then $I_1 = \overline{2} \times \overline{2}$, $s = 1$, and $P\{\underline{X}_t = \langle i,j \rangle | X_t \in I_1\} = P\{\underline{X}_t = \langle i,j \rangle\}$ is independent of t. If T is fixed, a simple multinomial sample is present, while if T is Poisson, the sample is Poisson. If the number of toxemia cases and the number of controls is fixed and two random samples are taken, one for each group then $I_k = \{k\} \times \overline{2}$ for $k \in \overline{2}$ and

$$P\{\underline{X}_t = \langle i,j \rangle | \underline{X}_t \in I_1\} = P\{\underline{X}_t = \langle i,j \rangle | X_{t1} = k\}$$

is constant for each $t \in \overline{T}$. If $X_{t1} = i$, this probability is $P\{X_{\underline{t}} = \langle i,j \rangle | X_{t1} = i\}$; otherwise, the conditional probability is 0. Given any of these sampling schemes, one might wish to know the conditional probabilities given the group that the infant is male or female. The vector

$$\begin{aligned} \underline{p}(\mathcal{I}) &= \{P\{\underline{X}_t = \langle i,j \rangle | X_{t1} = i\}\} \\ &= \{P\{\underline{X}_t = \langle i,j \rangle | \underline{X}_t \in I_k\} : \langle i,j \rangle \in I_k,\ k \in \overline{2}\} \\ &= \{m_{ij} / \sum_{k=1}^{2} m_{ik} : \langle i,j \rangle \in \overline{2} \times \overline{2}\} = \{m_{ij}/m_{i+}\} \end{aligned} \tag{4.80}$$

gives these probabilities if $\mathcal{I}$ is defined as in the first sampling scheme.

Confidence intervals for linear combinations of $\underline{p}(\mathcal{I})$ are readily constructed if $\mathcal{N} \subset \text{span}\ \{\underline{\nu}(I) : I \in \mathcal{I}\}$, where $\underline{\nu}(I) = \{X_I(i) : i \in I\}$. In such a case,

(4.81)
$$(\underline{\hat{m}},\underline{\nu}(I)) = \sum_{i\in I} \hat{m}_i = \sum_{i\in I} n_i = (\underline{n},\underline{\nu}(I)).$$

Thus the maximum-likelihood estimate $\underline{\hat{p}}(\mathcal{I})$ of $\underline{p}(\mathcal{I})$ is

(4.82)
$$\{\hat{m}_i/\sum_{i'\in I} \hat{m}_{i'}: i \in I, I \in \mathcal{I}\} = \{\hat{m}_i/(\underline{n},\underline{\nu}(I)): i \in I, I \in \mathcal{I}\} .$$

The vector $\underline{\hat{\mu}}(\mathcal{I}) = \{\log \hat{p}_i(\mathcal{I})\}$ is then

(4.83)
$$\underline{\hat{\mu}}(\mathcal{I}) = \underline{\hat{\mu}} - \sum_{I\in\mathcal{I}} [\log (\underline{n},\underline{\nu}(I))]\underline{\nu}(I),$$

and the vector $\underline{\mu}(\mathcal{I}) = \{\log p_i(\mathcal{I})\}$ is

(4.84)
$$\underline{\mu}(\mathcal{I}) = \underline{\mu} - \sum_{I\in\mathcal{I}} [\log (\underline{m},\underline{\nu}(I))]\underline{\nu}(I).$$

Since

(4.85)
$$N^{\frac{1}{2}}\log[(\underline{n}^{(N)},\underline{\nu}(I))/(\underline{m}^{(N)},\underline{\nu}(I))]$$
$$= N^{\frac{1}{2}}[(\underline{n}^{(N)},\underline{\nu}(I)) - (\underline{m}^{(N)},\underline{\nu}(I))]/(\underline{m}^{(N)},\underline{\nu}(I)) + o^{(N)},$$

where $o^{(N)} \xrightarrow{P} 0$, $N^{\frac{1}{2}}[\underline{\hat{\mu}}^{(N)}(\mathcal{I}) - \underline{\mu}^{(N)}(\mathcal{I})]$ is asymptotically equivalent to

(4.86)
$$N^{\frac{1}{2}}[\underline{\hat{\mu}}^{(N)} - \underline{\mu}^{(N)} - \sum_{I\in\mathcal{I}} \frac{1}{(\underline{m}^{(N)},\underline{\nu}(I))} [\underline{\nu}(I) \otimes \underline{\nu}(I)](\underline{n}^{(N)} - \underline{m}^{(N)})$$
$$= [P^*_{\mathcal{M}}(\underline{\mu}^*) - P^*_{\mathcal{R}}(\underline{\mu}^*)]D^{-1}(\underline{\mu}^*)N^{\frac{1}{2}}(\underline{n}^{(N)} - \underline{m}^{(N)}) + o_1^{(N)} ,$$

where $o_1^{(N)} \xrightarrow{P} 0$ and $\mathcal{R} = \text{span } \{\underline{\nu}(I): I \in \mathcal{I}\}$. This equation follows from (4.16). One may now conclude that

(4.87)
$$N^{\frac{1}{2}}[\underline{\hat{\mu}}^{(N)}(\mathcal{I}) - \underline{\mu}^{(N)}(\mathcal{I})] \xrightarrow{\mathcal{D}}$$
$$N(\underline{0},[P^*_{\mathcal{M}}(\underline{\mu}^*) - P^*_{\mathcal{R}}(\underline{\mu}^*)]D^{-1}(\underline{\mu}^*)D(\underline{\mu}^*)[I - P^*_{\mathcal{N}}(\underline{\mu}^*)][P^*_{\mathcal{M}}(\underline{\mu}^*) - P^*_{\mathcal{R}}(\underline{\mu}^*)]D^{-1}(\underline{\mu}^*))$$
$$= N(\underline{0},[P^*_{\mathcal{M}}(\underline{\mu}^*) - P^*_{\mathcal{R}}(\underline{\mu}^*)]D^{-1}(\underline{\mu}^*)).$$

Since $\underline{\mu}^{(N)}(I) \longrightarrow \underline{\mu}^*(I)$, $\hat{\underline{\mu}}^{(N)}(I) \xrightarrow{P} \underline{\mu}^*(I)$; that is $\hat{\underline{\mu}}^{(N)}(I)$ is consistent. Furthermore, $\underline{p}^{(N)}(I) \longrightarrow \underline{p}^*(I)$, $\hat{\underline{p}}^{(N)} \xrightarrow{P} \underline{p}^*(I)$, and by the same argument as in (4.20),

(4.88)
$$N^{\frac{1}{2}}[\hat{\underline{p}}^{(N)}(I) - \underline{p}^{(N)}(I)] \xrightarrow{\mathcal{D}}$$

$$N(\underline{0}, D(\underline{\mu}^*(I))[P_M^*(\underline{\mu}^*) - P_R^*(\underline{\mu}^*)]D^{-1}(\underline{\mu}^*)D(\underline{\mu}^*(I))) .$$

Thus if $\underline{c} \in R^I$, the approximate level-$(1-\alpha)$ confidence interval for $(\underline{c},\hat{\underline{p}}(I) - \underline{p}(I))$ is given by all $(\underline{c},\underline{p}(I))$ such that

(4.89)
$$|(\underline{c},\underline{p}(I)) - (\underline{c},\hat{\underline{p}}(I))| \le \Phi^{(\alpha/2)}(\underline{c}, D(\hat{\underline{\mu}}(I))[P_M^*(\hat{\underline{\mu}}) - P_R^*(\hat{\underline{\mu}})]D^{-1}(\hat{\underline{\mu}})D(\hat{\underline{\mu}}(I))\underline{c})^{\frac{1}{2}} .$$

Similarly, the approximate level-$(1-\alpha)$ confidence interval for $(\underline{c},\underline{\mu}(I))$ consists of $(\underline{c},\underline{\mu}(I))$ such that

(4.90)
$$(\underline{c},\underline{\mu}(I)) - (\underline{c},\hat{\underline{\mu}}(I))| \le \Phi^{(\alpha/2)}(\underline{c},[P_M^*(\hat{\underline{\mu}}) - P_R^*(\hat{\underline{\mu}})]D^{-1}(\hat{\underline{\mu}})\underline{c})^{\frac{1}{2}} ,$$

provided $P_M\underline{c} \notin R$.

Example 4.7. In Example 4.6, if $M = R^{\overline{2}\times\overline{2}}$ and a 95% confidence interval is desired for the probability that a toxemia subject is male, then $I_k = \{k\} \times \overline{2}$ for $k \in \overline{2}$ and $R = \text{span}\,\{\underline{\nu}(I_k)\colon k \in \overline{2}\}$. The quantity to be estimated $p_{11}(I) = (\underline{p}(I),\underline{\delta}^{<1,1>})$, where $\underline{\delta}^{<1,1>} = \{\chi_{\{<1,1>\}}{<i,j>}\}$, has a maximum-likelihood estimate n_{11}/n_{1+}. Since $P_M^*(\hat{\underline{\mu}}) = I$, $\hat{\underline{p}}(I) = \{n_{ij}/n_{i+}\}$, and

(4.91)
$$P_R^*(\hat{\underline{\mu}})D^{-1}(\hat{\underline{\mu}}) = \sum_{k=1}^{2} \underline{\nu}(I_k) \otimes \underline{\nu}(I_k)/(\underline{n},\underline{\nu}(I_k)),$$

it follows that

(4.92)
$$(\underline{\delta}^{<1,1>}, D(\hat{\underline{\mu}}(I))[P_M^*(\hat{\underline{\mu}}) - P_R^*(\hat{\underline{\mu}})]D^{-1}(\hat{\underline{\mu}})D(\hat{\underline{\mu}}(I))\underline{\delta}^{<1,1>})$$

$$= (\underline{\delta}^{<1,1>}, D(\hat{\underline{\mu}}(I))D^{-1}(\hat{\underline{\mu}})D(\hat{\underline{\mu}}(I))\underline{\delta}^{<1,1>})$$

$$- \sum_{k=1}^{2} (\underline{\delta}^{<1,1>}, D(\hat{\underline{\mu}}(I))\underline{\nu}(I_k))^2/(\underline{n},\underline{\nu}(I_k))$$

$$= n_{11}/n_{1+}^2 - n_{11}^2/n_{1+}^3$$

$$= \frac{1}{n_{1+}} \left(\frac{n_{11}}{n_{1+}}\right) \left(\frac{n_{12}}{n_{1+}}\right) .$$

The confidence interval is then

$$(4.93)\qquad \left[\frac{n_{11}}{n_{1+}} - 1.96\left[\frac{1}{n_{1+}}\left(\frac{n_{11}}{n_{1+}}\right)\left(\frac{n_{12}}{n_{1+}}\right)\right]^{\frac{1}{2}},\ \frac{n_{11}}{n_{1+}} + 1.96\left[\frac{1}{n_{1+}}\left(\frac{n_{11}}{n_{1+}}\right)\left(\frac{n_{12}}{n_{1+}}\right)\right]^{\frac{1}{2}}\right] = [0.524, 0.584]\ .$$

If the observations are independent Poisson random variables or a simple multinomial sample, or if each group is an independent multinomial sample, the confidence interval is the same.

Asymptotic properties of $\hat{\underline{\mu}}$ have consequences that are useful for computation. In chapter 3, $P_M^*(\underline{\nu})\underline{\nu}$ was used as an estimate of $\hat{\underline{\mu}}$, where $\underline{\nu} = \{\log n_i\}$. The motivation for this selection can be seen by examination of (4.16). If the model is correct,

$$(4.94)\qquad \frac{1}{N}\,\underline{n}^{(N)} \longrightarrow \underline{m}^*\ .$$

Thus

$$(4.95)\qquad N^{\frac{1}{2}}(\hat{\underline{\mu}}^{(N)} - \underline{\mu}^{(N)}) - N^{\frac{1}{2}}P_M^*(\underline{\nu}^{(N)})D^{-1}(\underline{\nu}^{(N)})(\underline{n}^{(N)} - \underline{m}^{(N)}) \xrightarrow{P} 0,$$

where $\underline{\nu}^{(N)} = \{\log n_i^{(N)}\}$. Since

$$(4.96)\qquad \log\,(n_i^{(N)}/m_i^{(N)}) = \frac{(n_i^{(N)} - m_i^{(N)})}{m_i^{(N)}} + o\left(\frac{n_i^{(N)} - m_i^{(N)}}{m_i^{(N)}}\right)^2 ,$$

where $o(x)/|x| \longrightarrow -\frac{1}{2}$ as $x \longrightarrow 0$, it follows that

$$(4.97)\qquad \begin{aligned} & N^{\frac{1}{2}}(\hat{\underline{\mu}}^{(N)} - \underline{\mu}^{(N)}) - N^{\frac{1}{2}}P_M^*(\underline{\nu}^{(N)})(\underline{\nu}^{(N)} - \underline{\mu}^{(N)}) \\ &= N^{\frac{1}{2}}(\hat{\underline{\mu}}^{(N)} - \underline{\mu}^{(N)}) - N^{\frac{1}{2}}P_M^*(\underline{\nu}^{(N)})\underline{\nu}^{(N)} + N^{\frac{1}{2}}\underline{\mu}^{(N)} \\ &= N^{\frac{1}{2}}[\hat{\underline{\mu}}^{(N)} - P_M^*(\underline{\nu}^{(N)})\underline{\nu}^{(N)}] \\ &\xrightarrow{P} \underline{0}\ . \end{aligned}$$

Consequently, $\hat{\underline{\mu}}^{(N)}$ and $P_M^*(\underline{\nu}^{(N)})\underline{\nu}^{(N)}$ are asymptotically equivalent to order $N^{-\frac{1}{2}}$. Theorem 4.1 and (4.97) thus imply that

$$(4.98)\qquad N^{\frac{1}{2}}[P_M^*(\underline{\nu}^{(N)})\underline{\nu}^{(N)} - \underline{\mu}^{(N)}] \xrightarrow{\mathcal{D}} N(\underline{0},[P_M^*(\underline{\mu}^*) - P_N^*(\underline{\mu}^*)]D^{-1}(\underline{\mu}^*))\ .$$

If the maximum-likelihood estimate is obtained by use of $\hat{\ell}^{(m)}(\underline{n},\underline{\mu})$, then the initial estimate $P_{M-N}P_M^*(\underline{\nu})\underline{\nu}$ of $P_{M-N}\underline{\mu}$ satisfies the condition

$$(4.99)\qquad N^{\frac{1}{2}}[P_{M-N}\hat{\underline{\mu}}^{(N)} - P_{M-N}P_M^*(\underline{\nu}^{(N)})\underline{\nu}^{(N)}] \xrightarrow{P} \underline{0}\ .$$

Consequently, $P_{M-N}P_M^*(\underline{\nu})\underline{\nu}$ and $P_{M-N}\hat{\underline{\mu}}^{(N)}$ are asymptotically equivalent to order $N^{-\frac{1}{2}}$, and

$$N^{\frac{1}{2}}[P_{M-N}P_M^*(\underline{\nu}^{(N)})\underline{\nu}^{(N)})\underline{\mu}^{(N)} \xrightarrow{\mathcal{D}} \tag{4.100}$$

$$N(\underline{0}, P_{M-N}[P_M^*(\underline{\mu}^*) - P_N^*(\underline{\mu}^*)]D^{-1}(\underline{\mu}^*)P_{M-N}).$$

A sharper result may be obtained by use of a more complete asymptotic expansion. If F is defined as in the proof of Theorem 4.1, then

$$dF_{\underline{y}}(\underline{x}) = P_M^*(F(\underline{y}))D^{-1}(F(\underline{y}))\underline{x} \tag{4.101}$$

for each $\underline{x} \in R^I$. This result may be verified in the same manner as was used to confirm (4.12). The second differential is then

$$d^2F_{\underline{y}}(\underline{x})(\underline{z}) = P_M^*(F(\underline{y}))[P_M^*F(\underline{y}))D^{-1}(F(\underline{y}))\underline{x} \# P_M^*(F(\underline{y}))D^{-1}(F(\underline{y}))\underline{z}], \tag{4.102}$$

where $\underline{x} \# \underline{y} = \{x_i y_i\}$. To prove (4.102), note that since $d^3\hat{\ell}(p)$ is nonsingular, (4.11) implies that $d^2F_{\underline{y}}$ exists and satisfies

$$\begin{aligned} &[d^3\ell_{F(\underline{y})}(\underline{y}, dF_{\underline{y}}(\underline{x}))(\underline{\nu})](dF_{\underline{y}}(\underline{z})) \\ &+ d^2\ell_{F(\underline{y})}(\underline{y}, [d^2F_{\underline{y}}(\underline{x})(\underline{z})])(\underline{\nu}) \\ &= - \sum_{i\in I} m_i(F(\underline{y}))[dF_{\underline{y}}(\underline{x})]_i[dF_{\underline{y}}(\underline{z})]_i\nu_i \\ &\quad - \sum_{i\in I} m_i(F(\underline{y}))[d^2F_{\underline{y}}(\underline{x})(\underline{z})]_i\nu_i \end{aligned} \tag{4.103}$$

for all $\underline{x}$, $\underline{y}$, and $\underline{z}$ in R^I and $\underline{\nu} \in M$. Since $d^2F_{\underline{y}}(\underline{x})(\underline{z}) \in M$, (4.102) follows from (4.101). A Taylor expansion of $F(\underline{n}^{(N)})$ yields

$$\begin{aligned} \hat{\underline{\mu}}^{(N)} - \underline{\mu}^{(N)} &= P_M^*(\underline{\mu}^{(N)})D^{-1}(\underline{\mu}^{(N)})(\underline{n}^{(N)} - \underline{m}^{(N)}) \\ &- \tfrac{1}{2} P_M^*(\underline{\mu}^{(N)}) \left[P_M^*(\underline{\mu}^{(N)}) \left\{ \frac{n_i^{(N)} - m_i^{(N)}}{m_i^{(N)}} \right\} \# P_M^*(\underline{\mu}^{(N)}) \left\{ \frac{n_i^{(N)} - m_i^{(N)}}{m_i^{(N)}} \right\} \right] \\ &+ \underline{o}^{(N)}, \end{aligned} \tag{4.104}$$

where $N\underline{o}^{(N)} \xrightarrow{P} \underline{0}$. A similar expansion for $P_M^*(\underline{\nu}^{(N)})\underline{\nu}^{(N)}$ yields

$$(4.105)\qquad P_M^*(\underline{\nu}^{(N)})\underline{\nu}^{(N)} - \underline{\mu}^{(N)} = P_M^*(\underline{\mu}^{(N)})D^{-1}(\underline{\mu}^{(N)})(\underline{n}^{(N)} - \underline{m}^{(N)}) - P_M^*(\underline{\mu}^{(N)})\left\{\left[\frac{n_i^{(N)} - m_i^{(N)}}{m_i^{(N)}}\right] \# \left[P_M^*(\underline{\mu}^{(N)})\left(\frac{n_i^{(N)} - m_i^{(N)}}{m_i^{(N)}}\right) - \tfrac{1}{2}\left(\frac{n_i^{(N)} - m_i^{(N)}}{m_i^{(N)}}\right)\right]\right\} + \underline{\bar{o}}^{(N)} ,$$

where $N\underline{\bar{o}}^{(N)} \xrightarrow{P} \underline{0}$. Thus the difference $N[P_M^*(\underline{\nu}^{(N)})\underline{\nu}^{(N)} - \hat{\underline{\mu}}^{(N)}]$ is a random variable which converges in distribution to a finite distribution.

The convergence from the initial estimate $P_M^*(\underline{\nu})\underline{\nu}$ to $\hat{\underline{\mu}}$ is quite rapid if the Newton-Raphson algorithm is employed with $\hat{\ell}^{(p)}(\underline{n},\underline{\mu})$. By arguments very similar to those used in Appendix C to prove parts (c) and (d) of Theorem 3.1, it follows that for N sufficiently large

$$(4.106)\qquad P\{\|\underline{\mu}^{(N,1)} - \hat{\underline{\mu}}^{(N)}\| \le b(\varepsilon)\| P_M^*(\underline{\nu}^{(N)})\underline{\nu}^{(N)}\hat{\underline{\mu}}^{(N)}\|^2\} \longrightarrow 1,$$

where ε is an arbitrary positive number,

$$(4.107)\qquad b(\varepsilon) = \|d^2f_{\underline{\mu}^*}^{-1} \circ d^3f_{\underline{\mu}^*}\| + \varepsilon,$$

and $\underline{\mu}^{(N,t)}$ is the estimate of $\hat{\underline{\mu}}$ obtained after t iterations of the conditioned Newton-Raphson algorithm using $P_M^*(\underline{\nu}^{(N)})\underline{\nu}^{(N)}$ as an initial estimate. The result also applies to the classical Newton-Raphson algorithm. If

$$(4.108)\qquad \underline{r}^{(N,t)} = \underline{\mu}^{(N,t)} - \hat{\underline{\mu}}^{(N)} ,$$

then (4.97) implies that $N\underline{r}^{(N,0)} \xrightarrow{\mathcal{D}} \underline{r}^{(0)}$, where $\underline{r}^{(0)}$ is a random vector. From (4.108), it follows that $N^2\underline{r}^{(N,1)} \xrightarrow{\mathcal{D}} \underline{r}^{(1)}$, where $\underline{r}^{(1)}$ is a finite random vector. In general,

$$(4.109)\qquad P\{\|\underline{r}^{(N,t+1)}\| \le b(\varepsilon)\|\underline{r}^{(N,t)}\|^2\} \longrightarrow 1,$$

so a simple induction shows that $(N)^{2^t}\underline{r}^{(N,t)} \longrightarrow \underline{r}^{(t)}$, where $\underline{r}^{(t)}$ is a finite random vector. Similar results apply if computations are based on $\hat{\ell}^{(m)}$.

The question has been raised whether the estimates $P_M^*(\underline{\nu})\underline{\nu}$ or $P_{M-N}P_M^*(\underline{\nu})\underline{\nu}$ are as good as the maximum-likelihood estimates $\hat{\underline{\mu}}$ and $P_{M-N}\hat{\underline{\mu}}$. Articles by Berkson (1955) and Silverstone (1957) discuss this issue in a situation similar to that found in Example 1.6.

Since the estimates differ only by a term of order N^{-1}, the basic asymptotic properties given in Theorem 4.1 apply to both $P_M^*(\underline{\nu})\underline{\nu}$ and $\hat{\underline{\mu}}$. However, in small samples the two estimates may differ substantially. This problem arose in Example 3.2. In such cases, the maximum-likelihood estimate may be far more reasonable than the estimate $P_M^*(\underline{\nu})\underline{\nu}$.

Example 4.8. As in Example 2.2, suppose that $M = \text{span}\{\underline{e}\}$ and $\underline{\mu} = c\underline{e}$. Then $\hat{\underline{m}} = (\frac{1}{q}\Sigma_{i\in I}\, n_i)\underline{e} = \bar{n}.\underline{e}$ and $\hat{\underline{\mu}} = (\log \bar{n}.)\underline{e}$, provided $\bar{n}. > 0$. Even if $\bar{n}. = 0$, $\bar{n}.\underline{e}$ is the extended maximum-likelihood estimate of $\underline{m}$ (see Appendix B). The estimate $P_M^*(\underline{\nu})\underline{\nu}$ of $\underline{\mu}$ is $(\Sigma_{i\in I} n_i \log n_i/\Sigma_{i\in I} n_i)\underline{e}$, provided $n_i > 0$ for each $i \in I$. The corresponding estimate of $\underline{m}$ is

$$\underline{m}^+ = (\prod_{i\in I} n_i^{f_i})\underline{e} \ , \tag{4.110}$$

where

$$f_i = n_i/\sum_{i\in I} n_i \ . \tag{4.111}$$

If some but not all n_i are zero, then the estimates may still be defined. In the case of $P_M^*(\underline{\nu})\underline{\nu}$, one lets $0 \log 0$ be 0. If all n_i are zero, then $\underline{m}^+$ may be set to $\underline{0}$.

As a consequence of a standard inequality of information theory given in Rao (1965), $\Sigma_{i\in I} n_i \log n_i/\Sigma_{i\in I} n_i \geq \log \bar{n}.$, with equality if and only if all n_i are equal. As an extreme case, it should be noted that if one $n_i = a$ and all other n_i are 0, $P_M^*(\underline{\nu})\underline{\nu} = (\log a)\underline{e}$ and $\hat{\underline{\mu}} = [\log (a/q)]\underline{e}$. Thus the difference between the estimates may be quite large. The estimate $\underline{m}$ is a minimum-variance unbiased estimate with variance e^c/q. In contrast, the information inequality implies that $\underline{m}^+$ must be biased. The bias becomes quite serious as e^c becomes small. In fact, as e^c approaches 0,

$$\frac{1}{e^c} E(\prod_{i\in I} n_i^{f_i}) \longrightarrow \frac{1}{e^c}[qe^c\exp(-qe^c)] \longrightarrow q \ . \tag{4.112}$$

Thus $\underline{m}^+$ cannot be expected to be a satisfactory estimate when the common mean is small.

Since the moments of $\hat{\underline{\mu}}$ and $P_M^*(\underline{\nu})\underline{\nu}$ are not properly defined, small sample comparisons can be troublesome. However, it should be noted that whenever $P_M^*(\underline{\nu})\underline{\nu}$ is well defined, $\Sigma_{i\in I} n_i \log n_i/\Sigma_{i\in I} n_i \geq 0$. This result implies that $P_M^*(\underline{\nu})\underline{\nu}$ is less than satisfactory when $c < 0$. On the other hand, $\hat{\underline{\mu}}$ is less restricted, for $\log \bar{n}.$ may be as small as $-\log q$. If q is large, $\log \bar{n}.$ can provide sensible estimates of c even when c is rather small.

If attention is restricted to Fisher-consistent estimates, the maximum-likelihood estimates considered in this chapter are asymptotically efficient (see Kallianpur and Rao 1955). For the purposes of this chapter, a Fisher-consistent estimate $G(\underline{n})$ of a differentiable function $g(\underline{\mu})$ of the log-mean vector with domain in some finite-dimensional space R^J is a function which is differentiable in a neighborhood of $\underline{m}^*$ and which satisfies $G(\underline{m}(\underline{\mu})) = g(\underline{\mu})$ for all $\underline{\mu} \in M$. If N' is N for multinomial and conditional Poisson sampling and span $\{\underline{e}\}$ for Poisson sampling, it is assumed that g is a function of $P_{M-N'}\underline{\mu}$. Under this last assumption

$$G(\underline{m}(\underline{\mu} + c\underline{e})) = G(e^c\underline{m}(\underline{\mu})) = g(\underline{\mu}). \tag{4.113}$$

In particular,

$$G(\tfrac{1}{N}\underline{m}^{(N)}) = g(\underline{\mu}^{(N)}); \tag{4.114}$$

and as $N \to \infty$,

$$G(\tfrac{1}{N}\underline{m}^{(N)}) \to G(\underline{m}^*) = g(\underline{\mu}^*). \tag{4.115}$$

Thus,

$$g(\underline{\mu}^{(N)}) \to g(\underline{\mu}^*). \tag{4.116}$$

Given these results, it is appropriate to make the further assumption that $G(c\underline{n}) = G(\underline{n})$ for all c and $\underline{n}$. Thus G is a function of relative frequencies. The restriction that $G(\underline{m}(\underline{\mu})) = g(\underline{\mu})$ is essentially a requirement that the true parameter be obtained when complete information is available. It should be noted that $g(\hat{\underline{\mu}})$ and $g(P_M^*(\underline{\nu})\underline{\nu})$ are Fisher-consistent estimates of $g(\underline{\mu})$. The basic properties of Fisher-consistent estimates are summarized in the following theorem:

THEOREM 4.2. *If* $G(\underline{n})$ *is a Fisher-consistent estimate of* $g(\underline{\mu})$, *then*

$$G(\underline{n}^{(N)}) \xrightarrow{P} g(\underline{\mu}^*), \tag{4.117}$$

$$N^{\frac{1}{2}}(G(\underline{n}^{(N)}) - g(\underline{\mu}^{(N)})) \xrightarrow{\mathcal{D}} N(0, dG_{\underline{m}^*}D(\underline{\mu}^*)[I - P_N^*(\underline{\mu}^*)]dG_{\underline{m}^*}^T), \tag{4.118}$$

and for all $\underline{c} \in R^J$,

$$\begin{aligned}(\underline{c}, dG_{\underline{m}^*}D(\underline{\mu}^*)[I - P_N^*(\underline{\mu}^*]dG_{\underline{m}^*}^T(\underline{c})) \\ \geq (c, dg_{\underline{\mu}^*}[P_M^*(\underline{\mu}^*) - P_N^*(\underline{\mu}^*)]D^{-1}(\underline{\mu}^*)dg_{\underline{\mu}^*}^T(\underline{c})).\end{aligned} \tag{4.119}$$

Remark. It should be recalled that if A is a linear operator from R^I to R^J, A^T is the adjoint of A.

Proof. Since $N^{-1}\underline{n}^{(N)} \longrightarrow \underline{m}^*$,

$$G(\underline{n}^{(N)}) = G(\tfrac{1}{N}\, n^{(N)}) \xrightarrow{P} G(\underline{m}^*) = g(\underline{\mu}^*). \tag{4.120}$$

Since G is differentiable in a neighborhood of $\underline{m}^*$ and $N^{-1}m^{(N)} \longrightarrow \underline{m}^*$,

$$\begin{aligned} &N^{\frac{1}{2}}[G(\underline{n}^{(N)}) - g(\underline{\mu}^{(N)})] \\ &= N^{\frac{1}{2}}[G(\tfrac{1}{N}\,\underline{n}^{(N)}) - G(\tfrac{1}{N}\,\underline{m}^{(N)})] \\ &= dG_{\underline{m}^*}[N^{-\frac{1}{2}}(\underline{n}^{(N)} - \underline{m}^{(N)})] + N^{\frac{1}{2}}\underline{o}(\tfrac{1}{N}(\underline{n}^{(N)} - \underline{m}^{(N)})), \end{aligned} \tag{4.121}$$

where $\underline{o}(\underline{x})/\|\underline{x}\| \longrightarrow \underline{0}$ as $\underline{x} \longrightarrow \underline{0}$. Since $N^{-\frac{1}{2}}(\underline{n}^{(N)} - \underline{m}^{(N)}) \xrightarrow{\mathcal{D}} N(\underline{0}, D(\underline{\mu}^*)[I - P_N^*(\underline{\mu}^*)])$, (4.117) follows.

To complete the proof, observe that the equation $G(\underline{m}(\underline{\mu})) = g(\underline{\mu})$ if $\underline{\mu} \in M$ implies that

$$dG_{\underline{m}^*}D(\underline{\mu}^*)(\underline{\mu}) = dg_{\underline{\mu}^*}(\underline{\mu}) \tag{4.122}$$

for each $\underline{\mu} \in M$. Thus

$$\begin{aligned} &dG_{\underline{m}^*}D(\underline{\mu}^*)[I - P_N^*(\underline{\mu}^*)]dG_{\underline{m}^*}^T \\ &= dG_{\underline{m}^*}D(\underline{\mu}^*)[I - P_M^*(\underline{\mu}^*)]dG_{\underline{m}^*}^T \\ &+ [dG_{\underline{m}^*}D(\underline{\mu}^*)][P_M^*(\underline{\mu}^*) - P_N^*(\underline{\mu}^*)]D^{-1}(\underline{\mu}^*)[dG_{\underline{m}^*}D(\underline{\mu}^*)]^T \\ &= dG_{\underline{m}^*}D(\underline{\mu}^*)[I - P_M^*(\underline{\mu}^*)]dG_{\underline{m}^*}^T \\ &+ dg_{\underline{\mu}^*}[P_M^*(\underline{\mu}^*) - P_N^*(\underline{\mu}^*)]D^{-1}(\underline{\mu}^*)dg_{\underline{\mu}^*}^T . \end{aligned} \tag{4.123}$$

Since both terms on the right-hand side of (4.123) are non-negative definite, (4.119) follows.||

COROLLARY 4.1. *The maximum-likelihood estimate* $g(\hat{\underline{\mu}})$ *of* $g(\underline{\mu})$ *has minimum asymptotic covariance among Fisher-consistent estimates; that is, for each* $\underline{c} \in R^J$, $(\underline{c}, g(\hat{\underline{\mu}}))$ *has the smallest asymptotic variance of all Fisher-consistent estimates* $(\underline{c}, G(\underline{n}))$.

Remark. This corollary implies that $g(\hat{\underline{\mu}})$ is an asymptotically efficient estimate of $g(\underline{\mu})$.

Proof. It is sufficient to note that $(c, g(\hat{\underline{\mu}}))$ has asymptotic covariance

$$(\underline{c}, dg_{\underline{\mu}*}[P_M^*(\underline{\mu}^*) - P_N^*(\underline{\mu}^*)]D^{-1}(\underline{\mu}^*)dg_{\underline{\mu}*}^T(\underline{c})).\|$$

COROLLARY 4.2. *If* $G(\underline{n})$ *is Fisher-consistent for* $g(\underline{\mu})$ *and has the same asymptotic covariance as* $g(\hat{\underline{\mu}})$, *then*

$$N^{\frac{1}{2}}[G(\underline{n}^{(N)}) - g(\hat{\underline{\mu}}^{(N)})] \xrightarrow{P} \underline{0}. \tag{4.124}$$

Proof. Under the hypothesis of the corollary

$$dG_{\underline{m}*}D(\underline{\mu}^*)[I - P_M^*(\underline{\mu}^*)]dG_{\underline{m}*}^T = 0. \tag{4.125}$$

Thus $dG_{\underline{m}*}D(\underline{\mu}^*)(R) = \{\underline{0}\}$, where $R = D^{-1}(\underline{\mu}^*)(M^{\perp})$. Since $dG_{\underline{m}*}D(\underline{\mu}^*)(\underline{\mu}) = dg_{\underline{\mu}*}(\underline{\mu})$ if $\underline{\mu} \in M$, $dG_{\underline{\mu}*}D(\underline{\mu}^*)$ is now uniquely determined for all $\underline{\mu} \in R^I$. The operator $dg_{\underline{\mu}*}P_M^*(\underline{\mu}^*)D^{-1}(\underline{\mu}^*)$ satisfies the equations which define $dG_{\underline{m}*}$, so

$$dG_{\underline{m}*} = dg_{\underline{\mu}*}P_M^*(\underline{\mu}^*)D^{-1}(\underline{\mu}^*) \tag{4.126}$$

Since

$$N^{\frac{1}{2}}[g(\hat{\underline{\mu}}^{(N)}) - g(\underline{\mu}^{(N)})] \tag{4.127}$$

$$= dg_{\underline{\mu}*}P_M^*(\underline{\mu}^*)D^{-1}(\underline{\mu}^*)[N^{-\frac{1}{2}}(\underline{n}^{(N)} - \underline{m}^{(N)})] + N^{\frac{1}{2}}\underline{o}(\tfrac{1}{N}(\underline{n}^{(N)} - \underline{m}^{(N)})),$$

the corollary follows.||

These results provide some justification for use of maximum-likelihood estimates, for it has now been shown that maximum-likelihood estimates have minimal asymptotic covariances among Fisher-consistent estimates and Fisher-consistent estimates with this minimal asymptotic covariance are asymptotically equivalent to order $N^{-\frac{1}{2}}$ to maximum-likelihood estimates. These optimality properties are not unique to maximum-likelihood estimates; the estimate $P_M^*(\underline{\nu})\underline{\nu}$ of $\underline{\mu}$ is one estimate which has these same properties. Nonetheless, the results do suggest that use of maximum-likelihood estimates is a reasonable procedure. Investigations which have employed different criteria of asymptotic efficiency have found maximum-likelihood estimates superior to other competitors, although the practical consequences of these conclusions are quite unclear (see Rao 1963 and Bahadur 1967). This uncertainty reflects the more basic problem that relatively little is known about the accuracy of the asymptotic results in this section when they are applied to finite samples.

HYPOTHESIS TESTS

Hypothesis tests for frequency data are generally based on test statistics which have an asymptotic chi-square distribution under the null hypothesis. Several such test statistics exist; the principal ones are the Pearson chi-square (see Pearson 1900) and the log likelihood ratio (see Wilks 1938). The former statistic is probably the most familiar, but the log likelihood ratio has received increasing attention in recent years. In this section, three hypothesis testing situations are considered. The first of these tests the null hypothesis $H_0\colon \underline{\mu} = \underline{\mu}^{(0)} \in M$ against the alternative $H_A\colon \underline{\mu} \in M$. The second situation tests the null hypothesis $H_0\colon \underline{\mu} \in M_1 \subset M_2$ against the alternative $H_A\colon \underline{\mu} \in M_2$. The third situation involves a nested set of hypothesis $H_i\colon \underline{\mu} \in M_i$, where $M_1 \subset M_2 \subset \cdots \subset M_s$ and $M_i \neq M_j$ if $i \neq j$.

In the first testing situation, the approximate level-α test based on the likelihood ratio is to reject $H_0\colon \underline{\mu} = \underline{\mu}^{(0)} \in M$ and accept $H_A\colon \underline{\mu} \in M$ if and only if $-2\Delta(\underline{n},\hat{\underline{\mu}},\underline{\mu}^{(0)}) > \chi^2_{p-r}(\alpha)$, where $\chi^2_{p-r}(\alpha)$ is the upper α-point of the χ^2_{p-r} distribution and $\Delta(\underline{n},\hat{\underline{\mu}},\underline{\mu}^{(0)})$, the log likelihood ratio, satisfies

$$
\begin{aligned}
(4.128)\qquad \Delta(\underline{n},\hat{\underline{\mu}},\underline{\mu}^{(0)}) &= \ell(\underline{n},\underline{\mu}^{(0)}) - \ell(\underline{n},\hat{\underline{\mu}}) \\
&= \hat{\ell}^{(p)}(\underline{n},\underline{\mu}^{(0)}) - \hat{\ell}^{(p)}(\underline{n},\hat{\underline{\mu}}).
\end{aligned}
$$

This ratio may be employed with Poisson, multinomial, or conditional Poisson sampling. In the case of multinomial sampling, $\Delta(\underline{n},\hat{\underline{\mu}},\underline{\mu}^{(0)})$ is the correct likelihood ratio, for

$$
(4.129)\qquad \sum_{i\in I} \exp(\mu_i^{(0)}) = \sum_{i\in I} \exp(\hat{\mu}_i) = \sum_{i\in I} n_i
$$

implies that

$$
\begin{aligned}
(4.130)\qquad \Delta(\underline{n},\hat{\underline{\mu}},\underline{\mu}^{(0)}) &= (\underline{n},\underline{\mu}^{(0)}) - \sum_{i\in I} \exp(\mu_i^{(0)} - (\underline{n},\hat{\underline{\mu}}) + \sum_{i\in I} \exp(\hat{\mu}_i) \\
&= (\underline{n},\underline{\mu}^{(0)}) - (\underline{n},\hat{\underline{\mu}}) \\
&= \ell^{(m)}(\underline{n},\underline{\mu}^{(0)}) - \ell^{(m)}(\underline{n},\hat{\underline{\mu}}) \\
&= \hat{\ell}^{(m)}(\underline{n},P_{M-N}\underline{\mu}^{(0)}) - \hat{\ell}^{(m)}(\underline{n},P_{M-N}\hat{\underline{\mu}}).
\end{aligned}
$$

In the case of conditional Poisson sampling, $-2\Delta(\underline{n},\hat{\underline{\mu}},\underline{\mu}^{(0)})$ may still be used as a test criterion, even though it does not in general correspond to the true likelihood ratio.

An alternate test may be based on the Pearson chi-square statistic,

$$C(\hat{\underline{\mu}},\underline{\mu}^{(0)}) = (\hat{\underline{m}} - \underline{m}^{(0)}, D^{-1}(\underline{\mu}^{(0)})(\hat{\underline{m}} - \underline{m}^{(0)})) \tag{4.131}$$

$$= \sum_{i \in I} (\hat{m}_i - m_i^{(0)})^2 / m_i^{(0)} .$$

The approximate level-α test is to reject H_0 whenever

$$C(\hat{\underline{\mu}},\underline{\mu}^{(0)}) > \chi^2_{p-r}(\alpha) .$$

When $\hat{\underline{\mu}}$ is not defined, the extended maximum-likelihood estimates discussed in Appendix B may be used to define $\Delta(\underline{n},\hat{\underline{\mu}},\underline{\mu}^{(0)})$ and $C(\hat{\underline{\mu}},\underline{\mu}^{(0)})$. Other test statistics have been proposed, but they are less commonly used than either the Pearson chi-square or the log likelihood ratio.

To begin the analysis of these tests, their asymptotic behavior under H_0 must be considered. The basic results are summarized in Theorem 4.3.

THEOREM 4.3. *Consider a sequence of null hypotheses* H_0: $\underline{\mu}^{(N)} = \underline{\mu}^{(N,0)}$. *If these hypotheses are true, then* $-2\Delta(\underline{n}^{(N)},\hat{\underline{\mu}}^{(N)},\underline{\mu}^{(N,0)})$ *and* $C(\hat{\underline{\mu}}^{(N)},\underline{\mu}^{(N,0)})$ *are asymptotically equivalent; that is,*

$$-2\Delta(\underline{n}^{(N)},\hat{\underline{\mu}}^{(N)},\underline{\mu}^{(N,0)}) - C(\hat{\underline{\mu}}^{(N)},\underline{\mu}^{(N,0)}) \xrightarrow{P} 0, \tag{4.132}$$

and

$$\lim_{N\to\infty} P\{-2\Delta(\underline{n}^{(N)},\hat{\underline{\mu}}^{(N)},\underline{\mu}^{(N,0)}) > \chi^2_{p-r}(\alpha)\} \tag{4.133}$$

$$= \lim_{N\to\infty} P\{C(\hat{\underline{\mu}}^{(N)},\underline{\mu}^{(N,0)}) > \chi^2_{p-r}(\alpha)\}$$

$$= \alpha.$$

Proof. Suppose that $\Delta(\underline{n}^{(N)},\hat{\underline{\mu}}^{(N)},\underline{\mu}^{(N)})$ is regarded as a function of $\underline{\mu}^{(N)}$. Then $\Delta(\underline{n}^{(N)},\hat{\underline{\mu}}^{(N)},\underline{\mu}^{(N)}) = 0$ and $d\Delta_{\hat{\underline{\mu}}^{(N)}}(\underline{n}^{(N)},\underline{\mu}^{(N)},\underline{\nu}) = 0$ for every $\underline{\nu} \in M$. By Taylor's theorem, (2.4), and (2.9),

$$\Delta(\underline{n}^{(N)},\hat{\underline{\mu}}^{(N)},\underline{\mu}^{(N)}) = (\underline{n}^{(N)} - \hat{\underline{m}}^{(N)},\underline{\mu}^{(N)} - \hat{\underline{\mu}}^{(N)}) \tag{4.134}$$

$$- \frac{1}{2}(\hat{\underline{\mu}}^{(N)} - \underline{\mu}^{(N)}, D(\underline{\nu}^{(N)})(\hat{\underline{\mu}}^{(N)} - \underline{\mu}^{(N)}))$$

$$= - \frac{1}{2}(\hat{\underline{\mu}}^{(N)} - \underline{\mu}^{(N)}, D(\underline{\nu}^{(N)})(\hat{\underline{\mu}}^{(N)} - \underline{\mu}^{(N)})),$$

where $\underline{\nu}^{(N)}$ is on the line segment between $\underline{\mu}^{(N)}$ and $\hat{\underline{\mu}}^{(N)}$. Since $N^{-1}\hat{\underline{m}}^{(N)} \xrightarrow{P} \underline{m}^*$ and $N^{-1}\underline{m}^{(N)} \longrightarrow \underline{m}^*$, it follows that $N^{-1}D(\underline{\nu}^{(N)}) \xrightarrow{P} D(\underline{\mu}^*)$. To show the asymptotic equivalence of the two test statistics, observe that (4.20) and (4.134) imply that

$$(4.135)\qquad -2\Delta(\underline{n}^{(N)},\hat{\underline{\mu}}^{(N)},\underline{\mu}^{(N)}) = (N^{\frac{1}{2}}(\hat{\underline{\mu}}^{(N)} - \underline{\mu}^{(N)}),\tfrac{1}{N}D(\underline{\nu}^{(N)})N^{\frac{1}{2}}(\hat{\underline{\mu}}^{(N)} - \underline{\mu}^{(N)}))$$

$$= (\hat{\underline{m}}^{(N)} - \underline{m}^{(N)},D^{-1}(\underline{\mu}^{(N)})(\hat{\underline{m}}^{(N)} - \underline{m}^{(N)})) + o^{(N)},$$

where $o^{(N)} \xrightarrow{P} 0$. To complete the proof, observe that (4.16) implies that

$$(4.136)\qquad -2\Delta(\underline{n}^{(N)},\hat{\underline{\mu}}^{(N)},\underline{\mu}^{(N)}) - (P_M^*(\underline{\mu}^*)D^{-1}(\underline{\mu}^*)[N^{-\frac{1}{2}}(\underline{n}^{(N)} - \underline{m}^{(N)})],D(\underline{\mu}^*) P_M^*(\underline{\mu}^*)D^{-1}(\underline{\mu}^*)[N^{-\frac{1}{2}}(\underline{n}^{(N)} - \underline{m}^{(N)})]) \xrightarrow{P} 0.$$

If $\underline{x}^{(N)} = D^{-\frac{1}{2}}(\underline{\mu}^*)[N^{-\frac{1}{2}}(\underline{n}^{(N)} - \underline{m}^{(N)})]$ and $A_M(\underline{\mu}^*) = D^{\frac{1}{2}}(\underline{\mu}^*)P_M^*(\underline{\mu}^*)D^{-\frac{1}{2}}(\underline{\mu}^*)$, then

$$(4.137)\qquad (P_M^*(\underline{\mu}^*)D^{-1}(\underline{\mu}^*)[N^{-\frac{1}{2}}(\underline{n}^{(N)} - \underline{m}^{(N)})],D(\underline{\mu}^*)P_M^*(\underline{\mu}^*)D^{-1}(\underline{\mu}^*)[N^{-\frac{1}{2}}(\underline{n}^{(N)} - \underline{m}^{(N)})])$$

$$= (\underline{x}^{(N)},A_M(\underline{\mu}^*)\underline{x}^{(N)})$$

and

$$(4.138)\qquad \underline{x}^{(N)} \longrightarrow N(\underline{0},I - A_N(\underline{\mu}^*)).$$

The operator $A_M(\underline{\mu}^*)$ is the orthogonal projection from R^I to $D^{\frac{1}{2}}(\underline{\mu}^*)(M)$. This fact follows since the range of $A_M(\underline{\mu}^*)$ is $D^{\frac{1}{2}}(\underline{\mu}^*)(M)$, $A_M(\underline{\mu}^*)A_M(\underline{\mu}^*) = A_M(\underline{\mu}^*)$, and for each $\underline{x} \in R^I$ and $\underline{y} \in R^I$,

$$(4.139)\qquad (\underline{x},D^{\frac{1}{2}}(\underline{\mu}^*)P_M^*(\underline{\mu}^*)D^{-\frac{1}{2}}(\underline{\mu}^*)\underline{y})$$

$$= (D^{-\frac{1}{2}}(\underline{\mu}^*)\underline{x},D(\underline{\mu}^*)P_M^*(\underline{\mu}^*)D^{-\frac{1}{2}}(\underline{\mu}^*)\underline{y})$$

$$= (P_M^*(\underline{\mu}^*)D^{-\frac{1}{2}}(\underline{\mu}^*)\underline{x},D^{\frac{1}{2}}(\underline{\mu}^*)\underline{y})$$

$$= (D^{\frac{1}{2}}(\underline{\mu}^*)P_M^*(\underline{\mu}^*)D^{-\frac{1}{2}}(\underline{\mu}^*)\underline{x},\underline{y}).$$

Since $A_M(\underline{\mu}^*)$ is symmetric and idempotent, it follows from Halmos (1958) and $A_M(\underline{\mu}^*)$ is the orthogonal projection onto $D^{\frac{1}{2}}(\underline{\mu}^*)(M)$. If $\underline{x} \sim N(\underline{0},I)$, then

$$(4.140)\qquad \underline{x}^{(N)} \xrightarrow{\mathcal{D}} [I - A_N(\underline{\mu}^*)]\underline{x}$$

and

(4.141) $$(\underline{x}^{(N)}, A_M(\underline{\mu}^*)\underline{x}^{(N)}) \xrightarrow{\mathcal{D}} ([I - A_N(\underline{\mu}^*)]\underline{x}, A_M(\underline{\mu}^*)[I - A_N(\underline{\mu}^*)]\underline{x}).$$

Since $D^{\frac{1}{2}}(\underline{\mu}^*)(N) \subset D^{\frac{1}{2}}(\underline{\mu}^*)(M)$,

(4.142) $$(\underline{x}^{(N)}, A_M(\underline{\mu}^*)\underline{x}^{(N)}) \xrightarrow{\mathcal{D}} (\underline{x}, [A_M(\underline{\mu}^*) - A_N(\underline{\mu}^*)]\underline{x}).$$

By Rao (1965), (4.136), and (4.137),

(4.143) $$-2\Delta(\underline{n}^{(N)}, \hat{\underline{\mu}}^{(N)}, \underline{\mu}^{(N)}) \xrightarrow{\mathcal{D}} \chi^2_{p-r}.$$

By (4.143) and (4.135),

(4.144) $$C(\hat{\underline{\mu}}^{(N)}, \underline{\mu}^{(N)}) \xrightarrow{\mathcal{D}} \chi^2_{p-r}.$$

Since $\underline{\mu}^{(N)} = \underline{\mu}^{(N,0)}$, (4.133) now follows. ||

Theorem 4.2 justifies the statement that a test which rejects H_0 whenever $-2\Delta(\underline{n}, \hat{\underline{\mu}}, \underline{\mu}^{(0)}) > \chi^2_{p-r}(\alpha)$ has approximate level α. It is now necessary to consider whether the likelihood ratio test or the Pearson chi-square test has any virtues relative to other level-α tests. In this regard, two statements can be made. Both tests are consistent, and both tests have the same asymptotic power properties when contiguous alternatives are considered. If the alternative is fixed, the tests do not have the same asymptotic properties.

THEOREM 4.4. *Suppose that a sequence of null hypotheses* $H_0: \underline{\mu}^{(N)} = \underline{\mu}^{(N,0)} \in M$ *is given such that* $\underline{\mu}^{(N,0)} - (\log N)\underline{e} \longrightarrow \underline{\mu}^{(*,0)} \neq \underline{\mu}^*$. *Then*

(4.145) $$\frac{1}{N}[-2\Delta(\underline{n}^{(N)}, \hat{\underline{\mu}}^{(N)}, \underline{\mu}^{(N,0)}] \xrightarrow{P} -2\Delta(\underline{m}^*, \underline{\mu}^*, \underline{\mu}^{(*,0)}) > 0$$

and

(4.146) $$\frac{1}{N} C(\hat{\underline{\mu}}^{(N)}, \underline{\mu}^{(N,0)}) \xrightarrow{P} C(\underline{\mu}^*, \underline{\mu}^{(*,0)}) > 0.$$

Thus $P\{-2\Delta(\underline{n}^{(N)}, \hat{\underline{\mu}}^{(N)}, \underline{\mu}^{(N,0)}) > \chi^2_{p-r}(\alpha)\} \longrightarrow 1$ *and* $P\{C(\hat{\underline{\mu}}^{(N)}, \underline{\mu}^{(N,0)}) > \chi^2_{p-r}(\alpha)\} \longrightarrow 1$; *that is, both the likelihood ratio test and the Pearson chi-square test are consistent.*

Proof. Observe that

(4.147) $$\frac{1}{N}\Delta(\underline{n}^{(N)}, \hat{\underline{\mu}}^{(N)}, \underline{\mu}^{(N,0)})$$
$$= \frac{1}{N}\Delta(\underline{n}^{(N)}, \hat{\underline{\mu}}^{(N)}, \underline{\mu}^{(N)}) + \frac{1}{N}\Delta(\underline{n}^{(N)}, \underline{\mu}^{(N)}, \underline{\mu}^{(N,0)}) .$$

By (4.143),

$$\frac{1}{N}\,\Delta(\underline{n}^{(N)},\hat{\underline{\mu}}^{(N)},\underline{\mu}^{(N)}) \xrightarrow{P} 0. \tag{4.148}$$

Note now that

$$\frac{1}{N}\,\Delta(\underline{n}^{(N)},\underline{\mu}^{(N)},\underline{\mu}^{(N,0)}) \tag{4.149}$$

$$= \Delta(\frac{1}{N}\,\underline{n}^{(N)},\underline{\mu}^{(N)} - (\log N)\underline{e},\underline{\mu}^{(N,0)} - (\log N)\underline{e}) \xrightarrow{P} (\underline{m}^*,\underline{\mu}^*,\underline{\mu}^{(*,0)})$$

Since $\ell(\underline{m}^*,\underline{\mu}^*) > \ell(\underline{m}^*,\underline{\mu}^{(*,0)})$, (4.145) has been verified. To prove (4.146), $C(\hat{\underline{\mu}}^{(N)},\underline{\mu}^{(N,0)})$ is decomposed so that

$$C(\hat{\underline{\mu}}^{(N)},\underline{\mu}^{(N,0)}) = ([(\underline{m}^{(N)} - \underline{m}^{(N)}) + (\underline{m}^{(N)} - \underline{m}^{(N,0)})], \tag{4.150}$$

$$D^{-1}(\underline{\mu}^{(N,0)})[(\hat{\underline{m}}^{(N)} - \underline{m}^{(N)}) + (\underline{m}^{(N)} - \underline{m}^{(N,0)})])$$

$$= ([\hat{\underline{m}}^{(N)} - \underline{m}^{(N)}],D^{-1}(\underline{\mu}^{(N,0)})[\hat{\underline{m}}^{(N)} - \underline{m}^{(N)}])$$

$$+ 2([\hat{\underline{m}}^{(N)} - \underline{m}^{(N)}],D^{-1}(\underline{\mu}^{(N,0)})[\underline{m}^{(N)} - \underline{m}^{(N,0)}])$$

$$+ C(\underline{\mu}^{(N)},\underline{\mu}^{(N,0)}).$$

Since

$$\lim_{N\to\infty} \frac{1}{N}C(\underline{\mu}^{(N)},\underline{\mu}^{(N,0)}) = C(\underline{\mu}^*,\underline{\mu}^{(*,0)}) \tag{4.151}$$

and $C(\underline{\mu}^*,\underline{\mu}^{(*,0)}) > 0$ if $\underline{\mu}^* \neq \underline{\mu}^{(*,0)}$, Theorem 4.1 implies (4.146).||

Given the results of this theorem, there is a strong temptation to use $-2\Delta(\underline{m}^*,\underline{\mu}^*,\underline{\mu}^{(*,0)})$ and $C(\underline{\mu}^*,\underline{\mu}^{(*,0)})$ to compare the asymptotic efficiencies of the two tests. This procedure has, in fact, been proposed by Anderson and Goodman (1957) in a similar context. In a more general context, Bahadur (1967) has considered this possibility. The suggestion is that the likelihood ratio test is superior to the chi-square test against the given sequence of alternatives if $-2\Delta(\underline{m}^*,\underline{\mu}^*,\underline{\mu}^{(*,0)}) > C(\underline{\mu}^*,\underline{\mu}^{(*,0)})$. Since $-2\Delta(\underline{m}^*,\underline{\mu}^*,\underline{\mu}^{(*,0)})$ may or may not exceed $C(\underline{\mu}^*,\underline{\mu}^{(*,0)})$, this criterion does not lead to a clear decision as to which statistic is preferable. However, it is clear that the behaviors of the two tests do not coincide under the alternative hypothesis.

Limiting results concerning asymptotic power may be obtained by a method due to Pitman (see Noether 1955). Under the asymptotic sequences used in this argument, the likelihood ratio test and the Pearson chi-square test are asymptotically equivalent.

This result does not contradict Theorem 4.3 since the alternatives are contiguous in asymptotic power computations; in other words,

(4.152) $$\underline{\mu}^{(N)} - \underline{\mu}^{(N,0)} = N^{-\frac{1}{2}}\underline{c}^{(N)} ,$$

where $\underline{c}^{(N)} \longrightarrow \underline{c}^{*}$. Thus

$$\underline{\mu}^{(N,0)} - (\log N)\underline{e} \longrightarrow \underline{\mu}^{*} .$$

THEOREM 4.5. *Consider a sequence of null hypothesis* H_0: $\underline{\mu}^{(N)} = \underline{\mu}^{(N,0)}$, *where the true log means* $\underline{\mu}^{(N)}$ *satisfy* (4.152). *Then*

(4.153) $$\lim_{N\to\infty} P\{-2\Delta(\underline{n}^{(N)},\hat{\underline{\mu}}^{(N)},\underline{\mu}^{(N,0)}) > \chi^2_{p-r}(\alpha)\}$$

$$= \lim_{N\to\infty} P\{C(\underline{\mu}^{(N)},\underline{\mu}^{(N,0)}) > \chi^2_{p-r}(\alpha)\}$$

$$= P\{\chi'^2_{p-r,\delta^2} > \chi^2_{p-r}(\alpha)\} ,$$

where χ'^2_{p-r,δ^2} *has a noncentral chi-square distribution with* $p - r$ *degrees of freedom and noncentrality parameter* $\delta^2 = (\underline{c}^{*},D(\underline{\mu}^{*})\underline{c}^{*})$.

Remark. Conventions vary concerning the definition of the noncentrality parameter. In this theorem χ'^2_{p-r,δ^2} is the distribution of $\Sigma_{i=1}^{p-r}\xi_i^2$, where the ξ_i are independent random variables such that $\xi_1 \sim N(\delta,1)$ and $\xi_i \sim N(0,1)$ for $i > 1$.

Proof. The proof is very similar to the proof of Theorem 4.3. Instead of (4.134), one has

(4.154) $$\Delta(\underline{n}^{(N)},\hat{\underline{\mu}}^{(N)},\underline{\mu}^{(N,0)})$$

$$= -\frac{1}{2}(\hat{\underline{\mu}}^{(N)} - \underline{\mu}^{(N,0)},D(\underline{\nu}^{(N)})(\hat{\underline{\mu}}^{(N)} - \underline{\mu}^{(N,0)})),$$

where $\underline{\nu}^{(N)}$ is on the line segment between $\underline{\mu}^{(N)}$ and $\hat{\underline{\mu}}^{(N)}$. Since $N^{-1}\underline{m}^{(N,0)} \longrightarrow \underline{m}$ and $N^{-1}\hat{\underline{m}}^{(N)} \xrightarrow{P} \underline{m}^{*}$, $N^{-1}D(\underline{\nu}^{(N)}) \xrightarrow{P} D(\underline{\mu}^{*})$ and

(4.155) $$-2\Delta(\underline{n}^{(N)},\hat{\underline{\mu}}^{(N)},\underline{\mu}^{(N,0)})$$

$$= (\hat{\underline{m}}^{(N)} - \underline{m}^{(N,0)},D^{-1}(\underline{\mu}^{(N)})(\hat{\underline{m}}^{(N)} - \underline{m}^{(N,0)})) + o^{(N)} ,$$

where $o^{(N)} \xrightarrow{P} 0$. Thus $C(\hat{\underline{\mu}}^{(N)},\underline{\mu}^{(N,0)})$ and $-2\Delta(\underline{n}^{(N)},\hat{\underline{\mu}}^{(N)},\underline{\mu}^{(N,0)})$ are asymptotically equivalent, and (4.153) holds for $C(\hat{\underline{\mu}}^{(N)},\underline{\mu}^{(N,0)})$ if it holds for $-2\Delta(\underline{n}^{(N)},\hat{\underline{\mu}}^{(N)},\underline{\mu}^{(N,0)})$. To prove (4.153) for $-2\Delta(\underline{n}^{(N)},\hat{\underline{\mu}}^{(N)},\underline{\mu}^{(N,0)})$, observe that (4.16) implies that

(4.156)
$$-2\Delta(\underline{n}^{(N)},\hat{\underline{\mu}}^{(N)},\underline{\mu}^{(N)})$$
$$-(P_M^*(\underline{\mu}^*)D^{-1}(\underline{\mu}^*)N^{-\frac{1}{2}}(\underline{n}^{(N)} - \underline{m}^{(N)}) + \frac{1}{N}D(\underline{\mu}^{(N)})\underline{c}^{(N)}],$$
$$D(\underline{\mu}^*)P_M^*(\underline{\mu}^*)D^{-1}(\underline{\mu}^*)[N^{-\frac{1}{2}}(\underline{n}^{(N)} - \underline{m}^{(N)}) + \frac{1}{N}D(\underline{\mu}^{(N)})\underline{c}^{(N)}]) \xrightarrow{P} 0.$$

If $\underline{x}^{(N)} = D^{-\frac{1}{2}}(\underline{\mu}^*)[N^{-\frac{1}{2}}(\underline{n}^{(N)} - \underline{m}^{(N)})]$, then

(4.157)
$$-2\Delta(\underline{n}^{(N)},\hat{\underline{\mu}}^{(N)},\underline{\mu}^{(N)})$$
$$-([\underline{x}^{(N)} + D^{\frac{1}{2}}(\underline{\mu}^*)\underline{c}^*],A_M(\underline{\mu}^*)[\underline{x}^{(N)} + D^{\frac{1}{2}}(\underline{\mu}^*)\underline{c}^*]) \xrightarrow{P} 0.$$

For each N,

(4.158)
$$N^{-\frac{1}{2}}P_{\mathcal{N}}\underline{m}^{(N)} = N^{-\frac{1}{2}}P_{\mathcal{N}}\underline{m}^{(N,0)}$$
$$= N^{-\frac{1}{2}}P_{\mathcal{N}}\underline{m}^{(N)} + N^{-1}P_{\mathcal{N}}D(\underline{\mu}^{(N)})\underline{c}^{(N)} + \underline{o}^{(N)},$$

where $\underline{o}^{(N)} \longrightarrow \underline{0}$. Thus

(4.159)
$$D(\underline{\mu}^*)\underline{c}^* \in \mathcal{N}^{\perp}.$$

If $\underline{x}$ is defined as in (4.140), then

(4.160)
$$-2\Delta(\underline{n}^{(N)},\hat{\underline{\mu}}^{(N)},\underline{\mu}^{(N)}) \xrightarrow{\mathcal{D}} (\underline{x} + D^{\frac{1}{2}}(\underline{\mu}^*)\underline{c}^*,[A_M(\underline{\mu}^*) - A_{\mathcal{N}}(\underline{\mu}^*)][\underline{x} + D^{\frac{1}{2}}(\underline{\mu}^*)\underline{c}^*]).$$

Thus the asymptotic distribution of $-2\Delta(\underline{n}^{(N)},\hat{\underline{\mu}}^{(N)},\underline{\mu}^{(N)})$ is noncentral chi-square with $p - r$ degrees of freedom and noncentrality parameter

(4.161)
$$(D^{\frac{1}{2}}(\underline{\mu}^*)\underline{c}^*,[A_M(\underline{\mu}^*) - A_{\mathcal{N}}(\underline{\mu}^*)]D^{\frac{1}{2}}(\underline{\mu}^*)\underline{c}^*)$$
$$= (\underline{c}^*,D(\underline{\mu}^*)\underline{c}^*)$$
$$= \sum_{i\in I} m_i^*(c_i^*)^2 .$$

The proof of the theorem is now complete.||

Readers familiar with Cochran (1952) may recall an expression for the noncentrality parameter based on differences between means rather than between log means. The two formulations are essentially equivalent. If

$$\underline{m}^{(N)} = \underline{m}^{(N,0)} + N^{\frac{1}{2}}\underline{d}^{(N)} , \tag{4.162}$$

where $\underline{d}^{(N)} \longrightarrow \underline{d}^*$, then

$$\underline{\mu}^{(N)} = \underline{\mu}^{(N,0)} + N^{-\frac{1}{2}}\underline{c}^{(N)}, \tag{4.163}$$

where $\underline{c}^{(N)} \longrightarrow D^{-1}(\underline{\mu}^*)\underline{d}^*$. The noncentrality parameter is then $\sum_{i\in I}(d_i^*)^2/m_i^*$, a form which corresponds to the one in Cochran (1952).

Standard compilations of statistical tables generally do not include the noncentral chi-square distribution, but approximations due to Patnaik (1949) are available which permit computation of percentage points of χ'^2_{p-r,δ^2} by use of tables of chi-square. In addition, Haynam, Govindarajulu, and Leone (1970) have published detailed tables for the noncentral chi-square distribution.

Although Theorem 4.5 does not discriminate between $-2\Delta(\underline{n},\underline{\mu},\underline{\mu}^{(0)})$ and $C(\underline{\mu},\underline{\mu}^{(0)})$, it does imply that reduction in the dimension of M improves the power of the test, provided $\underline{\mu}$ remains in M. This follows since δ^2 in (4.153) does not depend on M, provided $\underline{\mu}^{(N)}$ and $\underline{\mu}^{(N,0)}$ are in M for each N, and since, as Perlman and Das Gupta (1974) have noted, $P\{\chi'^2_{p-r,\delta^2} > \chi^2_{p-r}(\alpha)\}$ increases as p decreases. Consequently, it is useful to make the alternate hypothesis as specific as possible. Similar remarks apply in hypothesis testing for linear models with known error variance.

Before considering some numerical examples which illustrate the results of this section, it is useful to present some expressions for $-2\Delta(\underline{n},\hat{\underline{\mu}},\underline{\mu}^{(0)})$ which may be employed for computational purposes. Under Poisson sampling, the likelihood ratio statistic $-2\Delta(\underline{n},\hat{\underline{\mu}},\underline{\mu}^{(0)})$ may be written in any of the following forms:

$$\begin{aligned} -2\Delta(\underline{n},\hat{\underline{\mu}},\underline{\mu}^{(0)}) &= -2[\sum_{i\in I} n_i\mu_i^{(0)} - \sum_{i\in I}\exp(\mu_i^{(0)}) - \sum_{i\in I} n_i\hat{\mu}_i + \sum_{i\in I}\exp(\hat{\mu}_i)] \\ &= 2\sum_{i\in I} n_i\log(\hat{m}_i/m_i^{(0)}) - 2\sum_{i\in I}\hat{m}_i + 2\sum_{i\in I} m_i^{(0)} \\ &= 2\sum_{i\in I}\hat{m}_i\log(m_i/m_i^{(0)}) - 2\sum_{i\in I}\hat{m}_i + 2\sum_{i\in I} m_i^{(0)} . \end{aligned} \tag{4.164}$$

The last form follows since $\underline{\mu}^{(0)}$ and $\hat{\underline{\mu}}$ are in M and $P_M\underline{n} = P_M\underline{m}$ (see Goodman 1970). Under multinomial or conditional Poisson sampling,

(4.165) $$\sum_{i\in I} m_i^{(0)} = \sum_{i\in I} m_i = \sum_{i\in I} n_i .$$

Thus

(4.166) $$-2\Delta(\underline{n},\hat{\underline{\mu}},\underline{\mu}^{(0)}) = 2 \sum_{i\in I} n_i \log(m_i/m_i^{(0)})$$

$$= 2 \sum_{i\in I} n_i(\hat{\underline{\mu}}_i - \mu_i^{(0)})$$

$$= 2[(\underline{n},\hat{\underline{\mu}}) - (\underline{n},\underline{\mu}^{(0)})]$$

$$= 2 \sum_{i\in I} m_i \log(m_i/m_i^{(0)}).$$

Example 4.9. Snedecor and Cochran (1967) report an experiment in which crosses between two types of maize are examined. Of 1301 plants observed, 773 are green, 231 are golden, 238 are green-striped, and 59 are golden-green-striped. Under the Mendelian theory of inheritance, the respective expected frequencies of these four characteristics are 1301 (9/16) = 731.9, 1301 (3/16) = 243.9, 1301 (3/16) = 243.9, and 1301 (1/16) = 81.3. The frequencies may be regarded as a simple multinomial vector in R^4. The null hypothesis is that $\underline{\mu} = \underline{\nu} = \langle \log 731.9, \log 243.9, \log 243.9, \log 81.3\rangle$, and the alternative hypothesis is the trival hypothesis that $\underline{\mu} \in R^4$. If the second expression in (4.166) is used for $-2\Delta(\underline{n},\hat{\underline{\mu}},\underline{\mu})$ and the fact that $\hat{\underline{m}} = \underline{n}$ is observed, then it follows immediately that

(4.167) $$-2\Delta(\underline{n},\hat{\underline{\mu}},\underline{\nu})$$

$$= 2[773 \log (\frac{773}{731.9}) + 231 \log (\frac{231}{243.9})$$

$$+ 238 \log (\frac{238}{243.9}) + 59 \log (\frac{59}{81.3})] = 10.08.$$

Under multinomial sampling, $p = 4$ and $r = 1$. Thus under the null hypothesis, the test statistic should have an approximate χ_3^2 distribution. Since a value of χ_3^2 greater than 10.08 occurs with probability less than 0.02, there is good reason to reject the null hypothesis. Snedecor and Cochran obtain a similar conclusion by using the conventional Pearson chi-square, which in this example is equal to 9.25. They attribute the deviation from the null hypothesis primarily to weakness of the golden-green-striped plants. It is worthwhile to note the magnitude of the weakness in the golden-green-striped plants that is likely to lead to a significant result. If all other types of plants occur in the proper proportions, then for some ε,

(4.168) $$\underline{m} = <731.9 + 3\varepsilon, 243.9 + \varepsilon, 243.9 + \varepsilon, 81.3 - 5\varepsilon>.$$

Using Cochran's expression for the noncentrality parameter,

(4.169) $$\delta^2 = 0.33\varepsilon^2.$$

Since the approximate power is 0.5 if $\delta^2 = 5.76$, an ε greater than 4.2 will lead to rejection of the null hypothesis with approximate probability 0.5 or greater. Thus if the golden-green-striped plants have a frequency no more than 3/4 the frequency expected under Mendelian theory, then the chi-square tests for samples of 1301 are likely to lead to acceptance of the alternative hypothesis.

In the second testing situation, the null hypothesis $H_0\colon \underline{\mu} \in M_1$ is tested against the alternative $H_A\colon \underline{\mu} \in M_2$, where $N \subset M_1 \subset M_2$, $M_1 \neq M_2$, and $\underline{e} \in M_1$. The likelihood ratio test rejects H_0 whenever $-2\Delta(\underline{n},\hat{\underline{\mu}}^{(2)},\hat{\underline{\mu}}^{(1)}) > \chi^2_{p_2-p_1}(\alpha)$, where for $k \in \overline{2}$, $\hat{\underline{\mu}}^{(k)}$ is the maximum-likelihood estimate of $\underline{\mu}$ under the hypothesis that $\underline{\mu} \in M_k$ and p_k is the dimension of M_k.

The likelihood ratio statistic $-2\Delta(\underline{n},\hat{\underline{\mu}}^{(2)},\underline{\mu}^{(1)})$ applies to both Poisson and multinomial sampling. In analogy to (4.130), one has

(4.170)
$$\begin{aligned}
\Delta(\underline{n},\hat{\underline{\mu}}^{(2)},\hat{\underline{\mu}}^{(1)}) &= \ell(\underline{n},\hat{\underline{\mu}}^{(1)}) - \ell(\underline{n},\hat{\underline{\mu}}^{(2)}) \\
&= \hat{\ell}^{(p)}(\underline{n},\hat{\underline{\mu}}^{(1)}) - \hat{\ell}^{(p)}(\underline{n},\hat{\underline{\mu}}^{(2)}) \\
&= (\underline{n},\hat{\underline{\mu}}^{(1)}) - \sum_{i\in I} \exp(\hat{\mu}_i) \\
&\quad - (\underline{n},\hat{\underline{\mu}}^{(2)}) - \sum_{i\in I} \exp(\hat{\mu}_i^{(2)}) \\
&= (\underline{n},\hat{\underline{\mu}}^{(1)}) - (\underline{n},\hat{\underline{\mu}}^{(2)}) \\
&= \ell^{(m)}(\underline{n},\hat{\underline{\mu}}^{(1)}) - \hat{\ell}^{(m)}(\underline{n},\hat{\underline{\mu}}^{(2)}) \\
&= \hat{\ell}^{(m)}(n,P_{M_1-N}\hat{\underline{\mu}}^{(1)}) - \hat{\ell}^{(m)}(\underline{n},P_{M_2-N}\hat{\underline{\mu}}^{(2)}).
\end{aligned}$$

Under conditional Poisson sampling, $-2\Delta(\underline{n},\hat{\underline{\mu}}^{(2)},\hat{\underline{\mu}}^{(1)})$ may still be employed, although $\hat{\underline{\mu}}^{(2)}$ and $\hat{\underline{\mu}}^{(1)}$ are not generally the maximum-likelihood estimates under conditional Poisson sampling.

The corresponding test based on the Pearson chi-square rejects H_0 whenever $C(\hat{\underline{\mu}}^{(2)},\hat{\underline{\mu}}^{(1)}) > \chi^2_{p_2-p_1}(\alpha)$. Here

(4.171) $$C(\hat{\underline{\mu}}^{(2)},\hat{\underline{\mu}}^{(1)}) = \sum_{i\in I} (\hat{m}_i^{(2)} - \hat{m}_i^{(1)})^2/\hat{m}_i^{(1)} ,$$

where $\hat{\underline{m}}^{(k)} = \underline{m}(\hat{\underline{\mu}}^{(k)})$ for $k \in \overline{2}$. This test may also be used under conditional Poisson sampling, although $\hat{\underline{m}}^{(1)}$ and $\hat{\underline{m}}^{(2)}$ are generally not the true maximum-likelihood estimates. Just as in the first testing situation, extended maximum-likelihood estimates may be used when maximum-likelihood estimates are not defined. In (4.171), the convention is used that $(\hat{m}_i^{(2)} - \hat{m}_i^{(1)})^2/\hat{m}_i^{(1)}$ is 0 when $\hat{m}_i^{(1)}$ and $\hat{m}_i^{(2)}$ are 0.

The analysis of this testing situation is analogous to that used in the previous case. Once again, discussion begins with asymptotic properties under H_0.

THEOREM 4.6. *Consider a sequence of null hypotheses* H_0: $\underline{\mu}^{(N)} \in M_1$ *and alternatives* H_A: $\underline{\mu}^{(N)} \in M_2$. *Suppose that* $\hat{\underline{\mu}}^{(N,k)}$ *is the maximum-likelihood estimate of* $\underline{\mu}^{(N)}$ *under the hypothesis that* $\underline{\mu}^{(N)} \in M_k$. *Then if* $\underline{\mu}^{(N)} \in M_1$ *for each* N, $-2\Delta(\underline{n}^{(N)},\hat{\underline{\mu}}^{(N,2)},\hat{\underline{\mu}}^{(N,1)})$ *and* $C(\hat{\underline{\mu}}^{(N,2)},\hat{\underline{\mu}}^{(N,1)})$ *are asymptotically equivalent and*

(4.172) $$\begin{aligned}&\lim_{N\to\infty} P\{-2\Delta(\underline{n}^{(N)},\hat{\underline{\mu}}^{(N,2)},\hat{\underline{\mu}}^{(N,1)}) > \chi^2_{p_2-p_1}(\alpha)\}\\ &= \lim_{N\to\infty} P\{C(\hat{\underline{\mu}}^{(N,2)},\hat{\underline{\mu}}^{(N,1)}) > \chi^2_{p_2-p_1}(\alpha)\}\\ &= \alpha.\end{aligned}$$

Proof. Observe that

(4.173) $$\Delta(\underline{n}^{(N)},\hat{\underline{\mu}}^{(N,2)},\hat{\underline{\mu}}^{(N,1)}) = \Delta(\underline{n}^{(N)},\hat{\underline{\mu}}^{(N,2)},\underline{\mu}^{(N)}) - \Delta(\underline{n}^{(N)},\hat{\underline{\mu}}^{(N,1)},\underline{\mu}^{(N)}).$$

By (4.136) and (4.137),

(4.174) $$-2\Delta(\underline{n}^{(N)},\hat{\underline{\mu}}^{(N,2)},\hat{\underline{\mu}}^{(N,1)}) - (\underline{x}^{(N)},[A_{M_2}(\underline{\mu}^*) - A_{M_1}(\underline{\mu}^*)]\underline{x}^{(N)}) \xrightarrow{P} 0,$$

where $\underline{x}^{(N)} = D^{-\frac{1}{2}}(\underline{\mu}^*)\ [N^{-\frac{1}{2}}(\underline{n}^{(N)} - \underline{m}^{(N)})]$. By (4.140),

(4.175) $$\begin{aligned}&(\underline{x}^{(N)},[A_{M_2}(\underline{\mu}^*) - A_{M_1}(\underline{\mu}^*)]\underline{x}^{(N)})\\ &\xrightarrow{\mathcal{D}} ([I - A_N(\underline{\mu}^*)]\underline{x},[A_{M_2}(\underline{\mu}^*) - A_{M_1}(\underline{\mu}^*)][I - A_N(\underline{\mu}^*)]\underline{x})\\ &= (\underline{x},[A_{M_2}(\underline{\mu}^*) - A_{M_1}(\underline{\mu}^*)]\underline{x}),\end{aligned}$$

where $\underline{x} \sim N(\underline{0},I)$. Since $A_{M_2}(\underline{\mu}^*)$ has rank $p_2 - p_1$, it follows from (4.174) and Rao (1965) that

$$(4.176)\qquad -2\Delta(\underline{n}^{(N)},\hat{\underline{\mu}}^{(N,2)},\hat{\underline{\mu}}^{(N,1)}) \longrightarrow \chi^2_{p_2-p_1}\ .$$

To complete the proof, it is only necessary to show that $C(\hat{\underline{\mu}}^{(N,2)},\hat{\underline{\mu}}^{(N,1)})$ and $-2\Delta(\underline{n}^{(N)},\hat{\underline{\mu}}^{(N,2)},\hat{\underline{\mu}}^{(N,1)})$ are asymptotically equivalent. By (4.16) and (4.21),

$$(4.177)\qquad N^{-\frac{1}{2}}[\hat{\underline{m}}^{(N,2)} - \hat{\underline{m}}^{(N,1)}] - D^{\frac{1}{2}}(\hat{\underline{\mu}}^*)[A_{M_2}(\hat{\underline{\mu}}^*) - A_{M_1}(\hat{\underline{\mu}}^*)]\underline{x}^{(N)} \xrightarrow{P} \underline{0}.$$

Since

$$(4.178)\qquad C(\hat{\underline{\mu}}^{(N,2)},\hat{\underline{\mu}}^{(N,1)}) = N^{-\frac{1}{2}}(\hat{\underline{m}}^{(N,2)} - \hat{\underline{m}}^{(N,1)}),ND^{-1}(\hat{\underline{\mu}}^{(N,1)})\ N^{-\frac{1}{2}}(\hat{\underline{m}}^{(N,2)} - \hat{\underline{m}}^{(N,1)}))$$

and $N^{-1}D(\hat{\underline{\mu}}^{(N,1)}) \xrightarrow{P} D(\underline{\mu}^*)$,

$$(4.179)\qquad C(\hat{\underline{\mu}}^{(N,2)},\hat{\underline{\mu}}^{(N,1)}) - (\underline{x}^{(N)},[A_{M_2}(\underline{\mu}^*) - A_{M_1}(\underline{\mu}^*]\underline{x}^{(N)}) \xrightarrow{P} 0.$$

By (4.174), $C(\hat{\underline{\mu}}^{(N,2)},\hat{\underline{\mu}}^{(N,1)})$ and $-2\Delta(\underline{n}^{(N)},\hat{\underline{\mu}}^{(N,2)},\hat{\underline{\mu}}^{(N,1)})$ are asymptotically equivalent, so

$$(4.180)\qquad C(\hat{\underline{\mu}}^{(N,2)},\hat{\underline{\mu}}^{(N,1)}) \longrightarrow \chi^2_{p_2-p_1}$$

and (4.172) holds.||

Under the alternative hypothesis, both tests are consistent and both tests have the same asymptotic power when contiguous alternatives are considered. Results are summarized by the following two theorems.

THEOREM 4.7. *Suppose that a sequence of hypothesis tests of* H_0: $\underline{\mu}^{(N)} \in M_1$ *against* H_A: $\underline{\mu}^{(N)} \in M_2$ *is given, where* M_1 *is a proper submanifold of* M_2. *Suppose that* $\underline{\mu}^{(N)} - (\log N)\underline{e} \longrightarrow \underline{\mu}^* \in M_2$, *where* $\underline{\mu}^* \notin M_1$. *Then*

$$(4.181)\qquad \frac{1}{N}[-2\Delta(\underline{n}^{(N)},\hat{\underline{\mu}}^{(N,2)},\hat{\underline{\mu}}^{(N,1)})] \xrightarrow{P} -2\Delta(\underline{m}^*,\underline{\mu}^*,\underline{\nu}^*) > 0.$$

where $\underline{\nu}^*$ *is the location of the maximum for* $\underline{\mu} \in M_1$ *of* $\ell(m^*,\underline{\mu})$. *In addition,*

$$(4.182)\qquad \frac{1}{N}\,C(\hat{\underline{\mu}}^{(N,2)},\hat{\underline{\mu}}^{(N,1)}) \xrightarrow{P} C(\underline{\mu}^*,\underline{\nu}^*) > 0.$$

Thus

$$(4.183)\qquad \begin{aligned} &\lim_{N\to\infty} P\{-2\Delta(\underline{n}^{(N)},\hat{\underline{\mu}}^{(N,2)},\hat{\underline{\mu}}^{(N,1)}) > \chi^2_{p_2-p_1}(\alpha)\} \\ &= \lim_{N\to\infty} P\{C(\hat{\underline{\mu}}^{(N,2)},\hat{\underline{\mu}}^{(N,1)}) > \chi^2_{p_2-p_1}(\alpha)\} \\ &= 1\ . \end{aligned}$$

Proof. Consider the decomposition of $\Delta(\underline{n}^{(N)},\hat{\underline{\mu}}^{(N,2)},\hat{\underline{\mu}}^{(N,1)})$ provided by (4.173). Since $-2\Delta(\underline{n}^{(N)},\hat{\underline{\mu}}^{(N,2)},\underline{\mu}^{(N)}) \xrightarrow{\mathcal{D}} \chi^2_{p_2-r}$,

$$\frac{1}{N}\Delta(\underline{n}^{(N)},\hat{\underline{\mu}}^{(N,2)},\hat{\underline{\mu}}^{(N,1)}) + \frac{1}{N}\Delta(\underline{n}^{(N)},\hat{\underline{\mu}}^{(N,1)},\underline{\mu}^{(N)}) \xrightarrow{P} 0. \tag{4.184}$$

The argument used to prove Theorem 4.1 may be used to show that $\hat{\underline{\mu}}^{(N,1)} - (\log N)\,\underline{e} \xrightarrow{P} \underline{\nu}^*$. Since

$$\begin{aligned}\frac{1}{N}\Delta(\underline{n}^{(N)},\hat{\underline{\mu}}^{(N,1)},\underline{\mu}^{(N)}) &= \Delta(\tfrac{1}{N}\,\underline{n}^{(N)},\hat{\underline{\mu}}^{(N,1)} - (\log N)\underline{e},\underline{\mu}^{(N)} - (\log N)\underline{e}) \\ &\xrightarrow{P} \Delta(\underline{m}^*,\underline{\nu}^*,\underline{\mu}^*),\end{aligned} \tag{4.185}$$

(4.184) implies (4.181). To prove (4.182), an argument may be used which is very similar to the argument used in (4.151). Given (4.181) and (4.182), (4.183) follows immediately.||

THEOREM 4.8. *Suppose that a sequence of hypothesis tests of* H_0: $\underline{\mu}^{(N)} \in M_1$ *against* H_A: $\underline{\mu}^{(N)} \in M_2$ *is given, where* M_1 *is a proper submanifold of* M_2. *Suppose that* $\underline{\mu}^{(N)} \notin M_1$, *but that* $\underline{\mu}^{(N)} - N^{-\frac{1}{2}}\underline{c}^{(N)} \in M_1$, *where* $\underline{c}^{(N)} \longrightarrow \underline{c}^*$. *If* $\underline{\mu}^{(N)} - (\log N)\underline{e} \longrightarrow \underline{\mu}^*$, *then*

$$\begin{aligned}&\lim_{N\to\infty} P\{-2\Delta(\underline{n}^{(N)},\hat{\underline{\mu}}^{(N,2)},\hat{\underline{\mu}}^{(N,1)}) > \chi^2_{p_2-p_1}(\alpha)\} \\ &= \lim_{N\to\infty} P\{C(\hat{\underline{\mu}}^{(N,2)},\hat{\underline{\mu}}^{(N,1)}) > \chi^2_{p_2-p_1}(\alpha)\} \\ &= P\{\chi'^2_{p_2-p_1,\delta^2} > \chi^2_{p-r}(\alpha)\},\end{aligned} \tag{4.186}$$

where $\delta^2 = (\underline{c}^*,D(\underline{\mu}^*)[P^*_{M_2}(\underline{\mu}^*) - P^*_{M_1}(\underline{\mu}^*)]\underline{c}^*)$.

Remark. The assumption that $\underline{\mu}^{(N)} \in M_2$ is not needed in this theorem. A situation in which both the null and alternative hypotheses are false often arises in practice, although standard analyses usually ignore the possibility. Under the assumptions of the theorem, $\delta^2 > 0$ whenever $P^*_{M_2}(\underline{\mu}^*)\underline{c}^* \neq P^*_{M_1}(\underline{\mu}^*)\underline{c}^*$. This condition is satisfied when $\underline{c}^* \in M_2$ but $\underline{c}^* \notin M_1$. It need not be satisfied if $\underline{c}^* \notin M_2$.

Proof. In analogy to (4.134), one now has

$$-2\Delta(\underline{n}^{(N)},\hat{\underline{\mu}}^{(N,2)},\hat{\underline{\mu}}^{(N,1)}) = (\hat{\underline{\mu}}^{(N,2)} - \hat{\underline{\mu}}^{(N,1)},D(\underline{\nu}^{(N)})(\hat{\underline{\mu}}^{(N,2)} - \hat{\underline{\mu}}^{(N,1)})), \tag{4.187}$$

where $\underline{\nu}^{(N)}$ is on the line segment between $\hat{\underline{\mu}}^{(N,1)}$ and $\hat{\underline{\mu}}^{(N,2)}$. Since

$\underline{\mu}^{(N)} - (\log N)\underline{e} \longrightarrow \underline{\mu}^* \in M_1$, (4.14) implies that if $F_j(\underline{n})$ is the maximum-likelihood estimate of $\underline{\mu} \in M_j$ for $j \in \overline{2}$ and for an observation $\underline{n}$,

$$N^{\frac{1}{2}}[\hat{\underline{\mu}}^{(N,1)} - F_1(\underline{m}^{(N)})] = P^*_{M_1}(\underline{\mu}^*)D^{-1}(\underline{\mu}^*)[N^{-\frac{1}{2}}(\underline{n}^{(N)} - \underline{m}^{(N)})] + \underline{o}^{(N)} \tag{4.188}$$

and

$$N^{\frac{1}{2}}[\hat{\underline{\mu}}^{(N,2)} - F_2(\underline{m}^{(N)})] = P^*_{M_2}(\underline{\mu}^*)D^{-1}(\underline{\mu}^*)[N^{-\frac{1}{2}}(\underline{n}^{(N)} - \underline{m}^{(N)})] + \underline{o}_1^{(N)}, \tag{4.189}$$

where $\underline{o}^{(N)}$ and $\underline{o}_1^{(N)}$ converge in probability to $\underline{0}$. In addition, if $j \in \overline{2}$, then

$$F_j(\underline{m}^{(N)}) = \underline{\mu}^{(N)} - N^{-\frac{1}{2}}\underline{c}^{(N)} + N^{-\frac{1}{2}}P^*_{M_j}(\underline{\mu}^*)\underline{c}^{(N)} + \underline{o}_2^{(N)}, \tag{4.190}$$

where $\underline{o}_2^{(N)} \longrightarrow \underline{0}$. It follows from (4.188), (4.189), and (4.190) that

$$N^{\frac{1}{2}}[\hat{\underline{\mu}}^{(N,2)} - \hat{\underline{\mu}}^{(N,1)}] = [P^*_{M_2}(\underline{\mu}^*) - P^*_{M_1}(\underline{\mu}^*)]\{D^{-1}(\underline{\mu}^*)[N^{-\frac{1}{2}}(\underline{n}^{(N)} - \underline{m}^{(N)})] + N^{-\frac{1}{2}}\underline{c}^{(N)}\} + \underline{o}_3^{(N)}, \tag{4.191}$$

where $\underline{o}_3^{(N)} \xrightarrow{P} \underline{0}$.

The statistics $-2\Delta(\underline{n}^{(N)},\hat{\underline{\mu}}^{(N,2)},\hat{\underline{\mu}}^{(N,1)})$ and $C(\hat{\underline{\mu}}^{(N,2)},\hat{\underline{\mu}}^{(N,1)})$ are asymptotically equivalent since $\hat{\underline{\mu}}^{(N,2)} - \hat{\underline{\mu}}^{(N,1)} \xrightarrow{P} \underline{0}$ and $N^{-1}D(\underline{\nu}^{(N)}) \xrightarrow{P} D(\underline{\mu}^*)$. By (4.187) and (4.191),

$$-2\Delta(\underline{n}^{(N)},\hat{\underline{\mu}}^{(N,2)},\hat{\underline{\mu}}^{(N,1)}) - (\hat{\underline{m}}^{(N,2)} - \hat{\underline{m}}^{(N,1)},D^{-1}(\hat{\underline{\mu}}^{(N,1)})(\hat{\underline{m}}^{(N,2)} - \hat{\underline{m}}^{(N,1)})) \xrightarrow{P} 0. \tag{4.192}$$

Thus it is sufficient to prove that the first limit in (4.186) has the desired value.

To complete the proof, observe that $-2\Delta(\underline{n}^{(N)},\hat{\underline{\mu}}^{(N,2)},\hat{\underline{\mu}}^{(N,1)})$ is asymptotically equivalent to $(\underline{x}^{(N)} + D^{\frac{1}{2}}(\underline{\mu}^*)\underline{c}^{(N)},[A_{M_2}(\underline{\mu}^*) - A_{M_1}(\underline{\mu}^*)][\underline{x}^{(N)} + D^{\frac{1}{2}}(\underline{\mu}^*)\underline{c}^{(N)}])$, where $\underline{x}^{(N)} = D^{-1}(\underline{\mu}^*)[N^{-\frac{1}{2}}(\underline{n}^{(N)} - \underline{m}^{(N)})]$. If $\underline{x} \sim N(\underline{0},I)$, then

$$\begin{aligned}(\underline{x}^{(N)} + D^{\frac{1}{2}}(\underline{\mu}^*)\underline{c}^{(N)},[A_{M_2}(\underline{\mu}^*) - A_{M_1}(\underline{\mu}^*)][\underline{x}^{(N)} + D^{\frac{1}{2}}(\underline{\mu}^*)\underline{c}^{(N)}])\\ \xrightarrow{\mathcal{D}} ([I - A_N(\underline{\mu}^*)]\underline{x} + D^{\frac{1}{2}}(\underline{\mu}^*)\underline{c}^*,[A_{M_2}(\underline{\mu}^*) - A_{M_1}(\underline{\mu}^*)]\{[I - A_N(\underline{\mu}^*)]\underline{x} + D^{\frac{1}{2}}(\underline{\mu}^*)\underline{c}^*\})\\ = (\underline{x} + D^{\frac{1}{2}}(\underline{\mu}^*)\underline{c}^*,[A_{M_2}(\underline{\mu}^*) - A_{M_1}(\underline{\mu}^*)][\underline{x} + D^{\frac{1}{2}}(\underline{\mu}^*)\underline{c}^*]).\end{aligned} \tag{4.193}$$

To verify (4.186), it is only necessary to note that the last term in (4.193) is distributed as $\chi'^2_{p_2-p_1,\delta^2}$, where

$$\begin{aligned}\delta^2 &= (D^{\frac{1}{2}}(\underline{\mu}^*)\underline{c}^*,[A_{M_2}(\underline{\mu}^*) - A_{M_1}(\underline{\mu}^*)]D^{\frac{1}{2}}(\underline{\mu}^*)\underline{c}^*)\\ &= (\underline{c}^*,D(\underline{\mu}^*)[P^*_{M_2}(\underline{\mu}^*) - P^*_{M_1}(\underline{\mu}^*)]\underline{c}^*).\|\end{aligned} \tag{4.194}$$

The noncentrality parameter in Theorem 4.8 may be written in several forms. For example, one has

(4.195)
$$\delta^2 = (\underline{c}^*, D(\underline{\mu}^*)\underline{c}^*) - (\underline{c}^*, D(\underline{\mu}^*)P^*_{M_1}(\underline{\mu}^*)\underline{c}^*)$$
$$= ([I - P^*_{M_1}(\underline{\mu}^*)]\underline{c}^*, D(\underline{\mu}^*)[I - P^*_{M_1}(\underline{\mu}^*)]\underline{c}^*).$$

The term $(\underline{c}^*, D(\underline{\mu}^*)\underline{c}^*)$ also appears in the noncentrality parameter for testing a simple null hypothesis H_0: $\underline{\mu} = \underline{\mu}^{(0)}$. The noncentrality parameter in this situation has an extra term since $\underline{\mu}^{(N)} - N^{-\frac{1}{2}}\underline{c}^{(N)}$ need not, in any sense, be the closest point in M_1 to $\underline{\mu}^{(N)}$. In the simple hypothesis testing problem, $(\underline{c}^*, D(\underline{\mu}^*)\underline{c}^*)$ is the limit of the distance from $\underline{\mu}^{(N)}$ to $\underline{\mu}^{(N,0)}$ with respect to the metric $(\cdot,\cdot)^{(N)}$, where

(4.196)
$$(\underline{x},\underline{y})^{(N)} = (\underline{x}, D(\underline{\mu}^{(N)})\underline{y}) .$$

In the present problem, δ^2 is the limit of the distance from $\underline{\mu}^{(N)}$ to M_1 with respect to $(\cdot,\cdot)^{(N)}$. By (4.190), if $\underline{\mu}^{(N)} \in M_2$, this noncentrality parameter is also the limit of $(\underline{\mu}^{(N)} - F_1(\underline{m}^{(N)}), D(\underline{\mu}^{(N)})(\underline{\mu}^{(N)} - F_1(\underline{m}^{(N)}))$ as $N \to \infty$. If $\underline{\bar{m}}^{(N)} = \underline{m}(F_1(\underline{m}^{(N)}))$, then δ^2 is also the limit of $\sum_{i\in I}(m_i^{(N)} - \bar{m}_i^{(N)})^2/\bar{m}_i^{(N)}$ as $N \to \infty$. This last expression is of special interest since it is the Pearson chi-square statistic for an observation $\underline{n}^{(N)} = \underline{m}^{(N)}$. No information appears to exist concerning which of these approximations for the noncentrality parameter is most useful in practice.

The likelihood ratio test statistic satisfies

(4.197)
$$-2\Delta(\underline{n},\underline{\hat{\mu}}^{(2)},\underline{\hat{\mu}}^{(1)}) = 2 \sum_{i\in I} n_i \log (\hat{m}_i^{(2)}/\hat{m}_i^{(1)})$$
$$= 2 \sum_{i\in I} \hat{m}_i^{(2)} \log (\hat{m}_i^{(2)}/\hat{m}_i^{(1)}).$$

The first equation follows since

(4.198)
$$\sum_{i\in I} \hat{m}_i^{(1)} = \sum_{i\in I} \hat{m}_i^{(2)} = \sum_{i\in I} n_i .$$

The second equation depends on the observation that $P_{M_2}\underline{n} = P_{M_2}\underline{\hat{m}}^{(2)}$ and $\underline{\hat{\mu}}^{(i)} \in M_2$ for $i \in \overline{2}$ (see Goodman 1970). It is occasionally useful to note that the Pearson statistic satisfies

(4.199)
$$C(\hat{\underline{\mu}}^{(2)},\hat{\underline{\mu}}^{(1)}) = \sum_{i\in I} (\hat{m}_i^{(2)} - \hat{m}_i^{(1)})^2/\hat{m}_i^{(1)} = \sum_{i\in I} (\hat{m}_i^{(2)})^2/\hat{m}_i^{(1)} - N,$$

where $N = \sum_{i\in I} n_i$. This result follows since $\underline{e} \in M_1 \subset M_2$. Thus

(4.200)
$$\sum_{i\in I} \hat{m}_i^{(2)} = \sum_{i\in I} \hat{m}_i^{(1)} = \sum_{i\in I} n_i .$$

Example 4.10. Suppose that k independent Poisson samples $\{n_i: i \in \overline{k}\}$ are given, and a test is required for the hypothesis that the samples are from the same population. Then one wishes to test the hypothesis $H_0: \underline{\mu} \in \text{span}\,\{\underline{e}\}$ against the alternative $H_A: \underline{\mu} \in R^k$. The maximum-likelihood estimate $\hat{\underline{m}}^{(1)}$ is $\overline{n}.\underline{e}$, while $\hat{\underline{m}}^{(2)}$ is $\underline{n}$. The Pearson chi-square in this case is $\frac{1}{\overline{n}.}\sum_{i=1}^k(n_i - \overline{n}_i)^2$, which is the test statistic for the variance test of Fisher, Thornton, and MacKenzie (1922); while the log likelihood ratio chi-square is $2\sum_{i=1}^k n_i \log(n_i/\overline{n}.)$. Both statistics have $k - 1$ degrees of freedom. Under the alternative hypothesis, the two statistics are approximately distributed as χ'^2_{k-1,δ_1^2}, where

(4.201)
$$\delta_1^2 = \sum_{i=1}^k m_i(\mu_i - \log \overline{m}.)^2.$$

Example 4.11. In Example 4.4, the hypothesis of no three-factor interaction was tested by examining the statistic $\log (n_{111}n_{221}/n_{121}n_{211}) - \log (n_{112}n_{222}/n_{122}n_{212})$. The hypothesis may also be tested by using a chi-square statistic. The null hypothesis $H_0: \underline{\mu} \in M$ is tested against $H_A: \underline{\mu} \in R^{\overline{2}\times\overline{2}\times\overline{2}}$. The resulting Pearson statistic of 4.49 differs only slightly from the log likelihood ratio chi-square of 4.47. Since M has dimension 7 and $R^{\overline{2}\times\overline{2}\times\overline{2}}$ has dimension 8, the number of degrees of freedom for the test is 1. Thus results are significant at the 5% level.

Example 4.12. One might wish to assess the adequacy of the model presented in Example 3.2 for presence of *torus mandibularis* in Eskimos. One approach to this problem is to test the null hypothesis that $\underline{\mu}$ satisfies (3.38) against the alternative that $\underline{\mu} \in R^{\overline{3}\times\overline{2}\times\overline{2}\times\overline{6}}$. It follows from tables 3.2 and 3.3 that the Pearson chi-square is 86.92 and the log likelihood ratio chi-square, $-2\Delta(\underline{n},\hat{\underline{\mu}}^{(2)},\hat{\underline{\mu}}^{(1)})$ is 81.36. The appropriate number of degrees of freedom is 3 x 2 x 2 x 6 - 11, or 61. Both statistics suggest that the fit is not fully satisfactory. A χ^2_{61} random variable exceeds 80.2 with probability 0.05 and exceeds 84.5 with probability 0.025.

A second approach to the problem is based on the general observation that four-factor interaction is usually not encountered. Thus one might consider the alternative hypothesis that $\underline{\mu} \in M_2$, where M_2 is the set of $\underline{\mu}$ for which $\{a_{ijk}\}$, $\{b_{ijk}\}$, $\{c_{ik\ell}\}$, and $\{d_{jk\ell}\}$ exist such that

(4.202) $$\mu_{ijk\ell} = a_{ijk} + b_{ijk} + c_{ik\ell} + d_{jk\ell}$$

for $\langle i,j,k,\ell\rangle \in \overline{3} \times \overline{2} \times \overline{2} \times \overline{6}$. In this case, M_2 has dimension 62, a reduction of 10 from the dimension of $R^{\overline{3}\times\overline{2}\times\overline{2}\times\overline{6}}$. Even if the four-factor interaction exists, some increase in power may occur if the interaction is small. The model specified in (4.202) is an example of the hierarchical models discussed in chapter 5, so the Deming-Stephan algorithm may be used to obtain the maximum-likelihood estimate $\underline{\hat{m}}^{(2)}$. Given the initial estimate $\underline{m}^{(0,1)} = \underline{\hat{m}}^{(1)}$, the maximum-likelihood estimate is obtained by use of the iteration cycle defined by

(4.203) $$m_{ijk\ell}^{(t,2)} = m_{ijk\ell}^{(t,1)} \frac{n_{ijk+}}{m_{ijk+}^{(t,1)}},$$

(4.204) $$m_{ijk\ell}^{(t,3)} = m_{ijk\ell}^{(t,2)} \frac{n_{ij+\ell}}{m_{ij+\ell}^{(t,2)}},$$

(4.205) $$m_{ijk\ell}^{(t,4)} = m_{ijk\ell}^{(t,3)} \frac{n_{i+k\ell}}{m_{i+k\ell}^{(t,3)}},$$

(4.206) $$m_{ijk\ell}^{(t,5)} = m_{ijk\ell}^{(t,4)} \frac{n_{+jk\ell}}{m_{+jk\ell}^{(t,4)}},$$

and

(4.207) $$\underline{m}^{(t+1,1)} = \underline{m}^{(t,5)}.$$

The resulting chi-square statistics are 65.4 for the Pearson chi-square and 59.8 for the likelihood ratio chi-square. Since the probability that χ_{51}^2 exceeds 59.2 is 0.20, and the probability that χ_{51}^2 exceeds 64.3 is 0.10, these results cast some doubt on the quality of the fit, but they lead to a much weaker conclusion than does the first result.

An initial explanation of the observed results may be obtained by observing that the likelihood ratio chi-square for H_0: $\underline{\mu} \in M_2$ and H_A: $\underline{\mu} \in R^{\overline{6}\times\overline{2}\times\overline{2}\times\overline{3}}$ is 21.6. Since the test statistic is based on 10 degrees of freedom, there does appear to be a four-factor interaction. Thus the assumption used in the second procedure may be doubtful.

On the other hand, the observed difficulties may reflect the relatively small amount of data present. The results concerning distributions are asymptotic; however, 541 subjects have been classified into some 72 different cells. In addition, three cells contain no subjects and six cells contain one subject. Thus the observed results may reflect difficulties in the application of the theory rather than problems involving the data. Therefore, there is reason to question the model proposed in Example 3.2, but the data do not permit a clear conclusion.

In practice, considerable uncertainty often exists concerning which manifolds can provide an adequate description of a contingency table. One method of approaching this problem is to consider a nested sequence of linear manifolds $\{M_i: i \in \overline{s}\}$, where M_i is a proper submanifold of M_{i+1} if $i \in \overline{s-1}$. The manifold M_i has dimension p_i, and the maximum-likelihood estimate of $\underline{\mu} \in M_i$ is $\hat{\underline{\mu}}^{(i)}$. It is assumed that $\underline{\mu} \in M_s$, $\underline{e} \in M_1$, and $N \subset M_1$.

Example 4.13. In Example 1.3, several hypotheses might be considered. Clearly, children with higher birth orders are more likely to have mothers with previous infant losses than are children with lower birth orders, but the relationship of type of children to birth order and type of mother is not clear. One might consider the manifolds M_1, M_2, M_3, and M_4, where

(4.208) $$M_1 = \{\underline{\mu} \in R^{\overline{3}\times\overline{2}\times\overline{2}}: \mu_{ijk} = a_{ik} + b_j\},$$

(4.209) $$M_2 = \{\underline{\mu} \in R^{\overline{3}\times\overline{2}\times\overline{2}}: \mu_{ijk} = a_{ik} + b_{ij}\},$$

(4.210) $$M_3 = \{\underline{\mu} \in R^{\overline{3}\times\overline{2}\times\overline{2}}: \mu_{ijk} = a_{ik} + b_{ij} + c_{jk}\},$$

and

(4.211) $$M_4 = R^{\overline{3}\times\overline{2}\times\overline{2}} .$$

Manifolds of this type are discussed at length in chapter 5. In this sequence, M_1 corresponds to the hypothesis that the type of child is independent of the birth order and the type of mother. The manifold M_2 corresponds to the hypothesis that the type of child and the type of mother are independent given the birth order, while M_3 corresponds to the hypothesis that birth order does not affect the association between type of child and type of mother. One may also describe M_3 as a hypothesis of no three-factor interaction. The manifold M_4 represents the trivial hypothesis that $\underline{\mu} \in R^{3\times2\times2}$. The manifolds are nested in the desired order. It is easily seen that $p_1 = 7$, $p_2 = 9$, $p_3 = 10$, and $p_4 = 12$.

By means of the techniques developed for the second hypothesis testing problem, any individual null hypothesis H_0: $\underline{\mu} \in M_i$ may be tested against any alternative H_A: $\underline{\mu} \in M_j$, where $i < j$. However, it is quite unreasonable to perform all $s(s-1)/2$ possible tests. More than one test of certain null hypotheses will be made, and the expected number of tests leading to rejection of a null hypothesis is $s(s-1)\alpha/2$ if all tests are made at level α.

A more reasonable procedure is to consider the $s - 1$ hypothesis tests with null hypotheses H_i: $\underline{\mu} \in M_i$ and alternatives H_{i+1}: $\underline{\mu} \in M_{i+1}$, where $i \in \overline{s-1}$. Only $s - 1$ tests are involved, and each null hypothesis is tested exactly once. This sequence of tests provides all information which can be obtained from an arbitrary test of H_0: $\underline{\mu} \in M_i$ against H_A: $\underline{\mu} \in M_j$, where $i < j$. If H_0 is false and H_A is true, then for some k, $i \le k < j$, $\underline{\mu} \notin M_k$ but $\underline{\mu} \in M_{k+1}$. Thus H_k is false and H_{k+1} is true. A test therefore exists for which the null hypothesis is false and the alternative is true. On the other hand, if H_0 is true, then all the hypotheses H_k, $i \le k < j$, are true. Each null hypothesis in the series of tests is thus true.

Another sense in which information is preserved by the sequence of tests chosen is based on a decomposition of the log likelihood ratio. One has

$$\Delta(\underline{n},\hat{\underline{\mu}}^{(j)},\hat{\underline{\mu}}^{(i)}) = \sum_{k=i}^{j-1} \Delta(\underline{n},\hat{\underline{\mu}}^{(k+1)},\hat{\underline{\mu}}^{(k)}). \tag{4.212}$$

Thus all log likelihood ratios can be expressed in terms of the $s - 1$ log likelihood ratios for tests of H_i against H_{i+1}. Since (4.212) only holds approximately for the Pearson chi-square, it is reasonable to confine attention in this problem to the log likelihood ratio chi-square.

Two procedures are now available. The first is based on one in Goodman (1969b). In this approach, the hypothesis H_i is tested at level α_i against H_{i+1}, where $1 - \prod_{i=1}^{s-1}(1 - \alpha_i) = \alpha$. Test i rejects H_i whenever $-2\Delta(n,\hat{\underline{\mu}}^{(i+1)},\hat{\underline{\mu}}^{(i)}) > \chi_{p_{i+1}-p_i}(\alpha_i)$. If k is the largest integer such that H_k has been rejected, then one may conclude that $\underline{\mu} \in M_k$ and therefore $\underline{\mu} \notin M_i$ for $i < k$. The approximate probability that this conclusion is false does not exceed α. A simple choice for α_i is $\alpha_i = 1 - (1 - \alpha)^{1/(s-1)}$ for each i.

To justify this procedure, consider the standard sequence $\{\underline{n}^{(N)}\}$ of contingency tables. If $\hat{\underline{\mu}}^{(N,i)}$ is the maximum-likelihood estimate of $\underline{\mu}^{(N)}$ if it is assumed that $\underline{\mu}^{(N)} \in M_i$, then for each i such that $\underline{\mu}^{(N)} \in M_i$ for all N, Theorem 4.3 implies that

(4.213) $$P\{-2\Delta(\underline{n}^{(N)},\hat{\underline{\mu}}^{(N,i+1)},\hat{\underline{\mu}}^{(N,i)}) > \chi^2_{p_{i+1}-p_i}(\alpha_i)\} \longrightarrow \alpha_i$$

By (4.174), (4.175), and Rao (1965), $-2\Delta(\underline{n}^{(N)},\hat{\underline{\mu}}^{(n,i+1)},\hat{\underline{\mu}}^{(N,i)})$ and $-2\Delta(\underline{n}^{(N)},\hat{\underline{\mu}}^{(N,j+1)},\hat{\underline{\mu}}^{(N,j)})$ are asymptotically independent if $i < j$ and $\underline{\mu}^{(N)} \in M_i$ for each N. This result follows since

(4.214) $$\begin{aligned}[A_{M_i}(\underline{\mu}^*) - A_{M_{i+1}}(\underline{\mu}^*)][A_{M_j}(\underline{\mu}^*) - A_{M_{j+1}}(\underline{\mu}^*)] &= A_{M_i}(\underline{\mu}^*) - A_{M_{i+1}}(\underline{\mu}^*) - A_{M_i}(\underline{\mu}^*) + A_{M_{i+1}}(\underline{\mu}^*)\\ &= 0 .\end{aligned}$$

Thus if k is the smallest integer such that $\underline{\mu}^{(N)} \in M_k$ for all N, then

(4.215) $$P\{\exists i \geq k \ni -2\Delta(\underline{n}^{(N)},\hat{\underline{\mu}}^{(N,i+1)},\hat{\underline{\mu}}^{(N,i)}) > \chi^2_{p_{i+1}-p_i}(\alpha_i)\} \longrightarrow 1 - \prod_{i=k}^{s-1} (1 - \alpha_i).$$

The limiting probability that any hypothesis H_i is falsely rejected is therefore no greater than $1 - \prod_{i=1}^{s-1} (1 - \alpha_i)$.

It is useful to note that

(4.216) $$1 - \prod_{i=1}^{s-1} (1 - \alpha_i) < \sum_{i=1}^{s-1} \alpha_i .$$

This result follows from the more general Bonferroni inequality (see Miller 1966) which states that the probability of occurrence of at least one of k events with probability α_i, $i \in \overline{k}$, is no greater than $\sum_{i=1}^{k} \alpha_i$. When the α_i are small, the two sides are nearly equal. Thus a simple way to choose α_i is to let $\alpha_i = \alpha/(s - 1)$ for each $i \in \overline{s-1}$.

The test procedure is consistent, and power calculations are possible. If $\underline{\mu}^{(N)} \in M_{k+1}$ for each N but $\underline{\mu}^* \notin M_k$, then Theorem 4.7 implies that $P\{-2\Delta(\underline{n}^{(N)},\hat{\underline{\mu}}^{(N,k+1)},\hat{\underline{\mu}}^{(N,k)}) > \chi^2_{p_{k+1}-p_k}(\alpha_k)\} \longrightarrow 1$. Thus the probability approaches 1 that all false hypotheses are rejected. This result should be carefully considered. It need not be the case that for all $i < k$, $P\{-2\Delta(\underline{n}^{(N)},\hat{\underline{\mu}}^{(N,i+1)},\hat{\underline{\mu}}^{(N,i)}) > \chi^2_{p_{i+1}-p_i}(\alpha_i)\} \longrightarrow 1$. Theorem 4.7 applies when the null hypothesis is false but the alternative is true. It does not provide information about cases when both hypotheses are false. Furthermore, the probability that some true hypothesis is rejected need not approach 0; instead the limit is $1 - \prod_{i=k+1}^{s-1} (1 - \alpha_i)$. If $\underline{\mu}^{(N)} \in M_{k+1}$ for each N, $\underline{\mu}^{(N)} \notin M_k$ for any N, $\underline{\mu}^{(N)} - N^{-\frac{1}{2}}\underline{c}^{(N)} \in M_k$ for each N, and $\underline{c}^{(N)} \longrightarrow \underline{c}^*$, then Theorem 4.8 implies that

$$P\{-2\Delta(\underline{n}^{(N)}, \hat{\underline{\mu}}^{(N,k+1)}, \hat{\underline{\mu}}^{(N,k)}) > \chi^2_{p_{k+1}-p_k}(\alpha_k)\} \tag{4.217}$$

$$\longrightarrow P\{\chi'^2_{p_{k+1}-p_k,\delta^2} > \chi^2_{p_{k+1}-p_k}(\alpha_k)\},$$

where $\delta^2 = (\underline{c}^*, D(\underline{\mu}^*)[P^*_{M_{k+1}}(\underline{\mu}^*) - P^*_{M_k}(\underline{\mu}^*)]\underline{c}^*)$. Thus the probability that all false hypothesis are rejected approaches $P\{\chi'^2_{p_{k+1}-p_k,\delta^2} > \chi^2_{p_{k+1}-p_k}(\alpha_k)\}$. If one wishes to find the probability that particular false hypotheses are rejected, then analysis becomes extremely complicated, for it is difficult to analyze the behavior of test statistics when both the null and alternative hypotheses are false.

Example 4.14. The procedure just advocated may be applied to the testing situation in Example 4.13. Since $s = 4$, one may take $\alpha_i = 0.03$ for $i \in \overline{3}$ and obtain an α of 0.087. The maximum-likelihood estimates $\hat{\underline{m}}^{(1)}$, $\hat{\underline{m}}^{(2)}$, and $\hat{\underline{m}}^{(4)}$ can be expressed in closed form. It is easily shown that for any $\langle i,j,k\rangle \in \overline{3} \times \overline{2} \times \overline{2}$,

$$\hat{m}^{(1)}_{ijk} = n_{i+k}n_{+j+}/n_{+++}, \tag{4.218}$$

$$\hat{m}^{(2)}_{ijk} = n_{i+k}n_{ij+}/n_{i++}, \tag{4.219}$$

and

$$\hat{m}^{(4)}_{ijk} = n_{ijk} \tag{4.220}$$

(see chapter 5). Although $\hat{\underline{m}}^{(3)}$ does not have an expression in closed form, it may be found by use of the iteration cycle in Example 3.4. The equations (3.122), (3.123), (3.124), and (3.125) still apply. Since $M_2 \subset M_3$, a reasonable value for $\underline{m}^{(0,1)}$ is $\hat{\underline{m}}^{(2)}$. The likelihood ratio chi-square statistics $-2\Delta(\underline{n}, \hat{\underline{\mu}}^{(2)}, \hat{\underline{\mu}}^{(1)})$, $-2\Delta(\underline{n}, \hat{\underline{\mu}}^{(3)}, \hat{\underline{\mu}}^{(2)})$, and $-2\Delta(\underline{n}, \hat{\underline{\mu}}^{(4)}, \hat{\underline{\mu}}^{(3)})$ are, respectively, 0.482, 2.301, and 0.853. The respective degrees of freedom are 2, 1, and 2. Since none of the statistics are significant at the 3% level, one may conclude that there is no evidence that $\underline{\mu}$ is not an element of M_1. In other words, no reason exists to suppose that the type of child is dependent on either the status of the mother or the birth order. This conclusion is not dependent on the choice of a relatively low significance level; it should be noted that none of the test statistics are significant at the 10% level. The argument presented here leads to a different conclusion from that reached by Snedecor and Cochran, who never consider the possibilities that $\underline{\mu} \in M_1$ or that $\underline{\mu} \in M_3$ but $\underline{\mu} \notin M_4$.

A second procedure may sometimes be used. This approach is related to work by Gabriel (1966,1969) and Goodman (1971a). In this method, one rejects any hypothesis H_i for which a $j > i$ exists such that $-2\Delta(\underline{n},\hat{\underline{\mu}}^{(j)},\hat{\underline{\mu}}^{(i)}) > \chi^2_{p_s-p_1}(\alpha)$. If k is the largest integer such that H_k has been rejected, one concludes that $\underline{\mu} \notin M_k$. The approximate probability that this conclusion is false does not exceed α.

The justification of this procedure is quite simple. If $\underline{\mu} \in M_k$, then $-2\Delta(\underline{n},\hat{\underline{\mu}}^{(j)},\hat{\underline{\mu}}^{(k)}) \leq -2\Delta(\underline{n},\hat{\underline{\mu}}^{(s)},\hat{\underline{\mu}}^{(k)})$ for any $j \in \bar{s} - \bar{k}$. Thus if $\underline{\mu}^{(N)} \in M_k$ for each N,

$$(4.221)\qquad P\{-2\Delta(\underline{n}^{(N)},\hat{\underline{\mu}}^{(N,j)},\hat{\underline{\mu}}^{(N,k)}) > \chi^2_{p_s-p_1}(\alpha)\ \forall j \in \bar{s}-\bar{k}\}$$

$$\longrightarrow P\{\chi^2_{p_s-p_k} > \chi^2_{p_s-p_1}(\alpha)\}$$

$$< \alpha.$$

The power of the procedure is readily determined. If $\underline{\mu}^{(N)}$, $\underline{c}^{(N)}$, and $\underline{c}^*$ are defined as in (4.217), then

$$(4.222)\qquad P\{-2\Delta(\underline{n}^{(N)},\hat{\underline{\mu}}^{(N,j)},\hat{\underline{\mu}}^{(N,k)}) > \chi^2_{p_s-p_1}(\alpha)\ \forall j \in \bar{s}-\bar{k}\}$$

$$\longrightarrow P\{\chi'^2_{p_s-p_k,\delta^2} > \chi^2_{p_s-p_1}(\alpha)\},$$

where

$$\delta^2 = ([I - P^*_{M_k}(\underline{\mu}^*)]\underline{c}^*, D(\underline{\mu}^*)[I - P^*_{M_k}(\underline{\mu}^*)]\underline{c}^*).$$

Example 4.15. This technique may be applied to the situation considered in Example 4.13. The results of Example 4.14 show that $-2\Delta(\underline{n},\hat{\underline{\mu}}^{(4)},\hat{\underline{\mu}}^{(1)}) < \chi^2_5$ (0.10), so once again no reason exists to suppose that $\underline{\mu}$ is not in M_1.

Sometimes the procedures of this section may be applied when the hypotheses are not perfectly nested. The following example is instructive in this regard.

Example 4.16. Goodman (1972a) considers a study by Wilner, Walkley, and Cook (1955) of the effect on racial attitudes of segregation or integration in public housing. In this study, 608 white women living in public housing projects were classified according to proximity to a Negro family, frequency of contacts with Negroes, favorableness of local norms toward Negroes, and favorableness of respondents' attitudes (sentiments) toward Negroes in general. The data are summarized in table 4.1.

TABLE 4.1

ATTITUDES TOWARD NEGROES
OF WHITE WOMEN
IN PUBLIC HOUSING PROJECTS

Proximity	Contact	Norms	Sentiment Favorable	Sentiment Unfavorable
Close	Frequent	Favorable	77	32
		Unfavorable	30	36
	Infrequent	Favorable	14	19
		Unfavorable	15	27
Distant	Frequent	Favorable	43	20
		Unfavorable	36	37
	Infrequent	Favorable	27	36
		Unfavorable	41	118

The model proposed by Goodman for these data assumes that

$$\mu_{ijk\ell} = a_{ij}^{PC} + a_{ik}^{PN} + a_{jk}^{CN} + a_{j\ell}^{CS} + a_{k\ell}^{NS} \tag{4.223}$$

for some numbers $\{a_{ij}^{PC}\}$, $\{a_{ik}^{PN}\}$, $\{a_{jk}^{CN}\}$, $\{a_{j\ell}^{CS}\}$, $\{a_{k\ell}^{NS}\}$, where the symbols P, C, N, and S respectively represent proximity, contact, norms, and sentiment. The model is based on Wilner's hypothesis that proximity affects contact and local norms, and these latter two variables affect sentiment. This hypothesis leads to the terms a_{ij}^{PC}, a_{ik}^{PN}, $a_{j\ell}^{CS}$, and $a_{k\ell}^{NS}$. It is also assumed that contact and local norms interact. This assumption leads to the term a_{jk}^{CN}.

The terms a_{ij}, a_{ik}, a_{jk}, $a_{j\ell}$, and $a_{k\ell}$ are not uniquely determined by $\underline{\mu}$. As explained in chapter 5, one might describe $\underline{\mu}$ by the unique parametrization

$$\mu_{ijk\ell} = \alpha + \alpha_i^P + \alpha_j^C + \alpha_k^N + \alpha_\ell^S + \alpha_{ij}^{PC} + \alpha_{ik}^{PN} + \alpha_{jk}^{CN} + \alpha_{j\ell}^{CS} + \alpha_{k\ell}^{NS} , \tag{4.224}$$

where

(4.225) $$\alpha_+^P = \alpha_+^C = \alpha_+^N = \alpha_+^S = \alpha_{i+}^{PC} = \alpha_{+j}^{PC}$$

$$= \alpha_{+k}^{PN} = \alpha_{i+}^{PN} = \alpha_{+k}^{CN} = \alpha_{j+}^{CN} = \alpha_{j+}^{CS} = \alpha_{+\ell}^{CS} = \alpha_{+\ell}^{NS} = \alpha_{k+}^{NS} = 0 \ .$$

This parametrization is probably more familiar to statisticians than the first one. In the terminology of analysis of variance, the model provides for all two-factor interactions except for that between proximity and sentiment.

A test of the proposed model involves two phases. In the first phase, it is necessary to determine whether the model fits the data. In the second phase, the possibility of simplifying the model is considered. In order to construct an appropriate test procedure, the following manifolds are defined:

(4.226) $$M_1 = \{\underline{\mu}\colon \mu_{ijk\ell} = a_{ij}^{PC} + a_{ik}^{PN} + a_{jk}^{CN} + a_{j\ell}^{CS} \ \forall \langle i,j,k,\ell\rangle \in \overline{2} \times \overline{2} \times \overline{2} \times \overline{2}\},$$

(4.227) $$M_2 = \{\underline{\mu}\colon \mu_{ijk\ell} = a_{ij}^{PC} + a_{ik}^{PN} + a_{jk}^{CN} + a_{k\ell}^{NS} \ \forall \langle i,j,k,\ell\rangle \in \overline{2} \times \overline{2} \times \overline{2} \times \overline{2}\},$$

(4.228) $$M_3 = \{\underline{\mu}\colon \mu_{ijk\ell} = a_{ij}^{PC} + a_{ik}^{PN} + a_{j\ell}^{CS} + a_{k\ell}^{NS} \ \forall \langle i,j,k,\ell\rangle \in \overline{2} \times \overline{2} \times \overline{2} \times \overline{2}\},$$

(4.229) $$M_4 = \{\underline{\mu}\colon \mu_{ijk\ell} = a_{ij}^{PC} + a_{jk}^{CN} + a_{j\ell}^{CS} + a_{k\ell}^{NS} \ \forall \langle i,j,k,\ell\rangle \in \overline{2} \times \overline{2} \times \overline{2} \times \overline{2}\},$$

(4.230) $$M_5 = \{\underline{\mu}\colon \mu_{ijk\ell} = a_{ik}^{PN} + a_{jk}^{CN} + a_{j\ell}^{CS} + a_{k\ell}^{NS} \ \forall \langle i,j,k,\ell\rangle \in \overline{2} \times \overline{2} \times \overline{2} \times \overline{2}\},$$

(4.231) $$M_6 = \{\underline{\mu}\colon \mu_{ijk\ell} = a_{ij}^{PC} + a_{ik}^{PN} + a_{jk}^{CN} + a_{j\ell}^{CS} + a_{k\ell}^{NS} \ \forall \langle i,j,k,\ell\rangle \in \overline{2} \times \overline{2} \times \overline{2} \times \overline{2}\},$$

(4.232) $$M_7 = R^{\overline{2}\times\overline{2}\times\overline{2}\times\overline{2}} \ .$$

The first test desired has the null hypothesis $H_0\colon \underline{\mu} \in M_6$ and the alternative $H_A\colon \underline{\mu} \in M_7$. The other five tests of interest have the null hypothesis $H_0\colon \underline{\mu} \in M_k$, $k \in \overline{5}$, and the alternative $H_A\colon \underline{\mu} \in M_6$. Each of these five tests considers the possibility that a particular two-factor interaction included in (4.224) may be omitted. For instance, if $\underline{\mu} \in M_1$, then the term $\alpha_{k\ell}^{NS}$ may be removed. The manifolds M_k, $k \in \overline{5}$, each have dimension 9, while M_6 has dimension 10 and M_7 has dimension 16. Thus $-2\Delta(\underline{n},\hat{\underline{\mu}}^{(7)},\hat{\underline{\mu}}^{(6)})$ has an approximate χ_6^2 distribution, and $-2\Delta(\underline{n},\hat{\underline{\mu}}^{(6)},\hat{\underline{\mu}}^{(k)})$ has an approximate χ_1^2

distribution for each $k \in \bar{5}$. The statistic $-2\Delta(\underline{n},\hat{\underline{\mu}}^{(7)},\hat{\underline{\mu}}^{(6)})$ is asymptotically independent of the remaining test statistics; however, $-2\Delta(\underline{n},\hat{\underline{\mu}}^{(6)},\hat{\underline{\mu}}^{(k)})$ and $-2\Delta(\underline{n},\hat{\underline{\mu}}^{(6)},\hat{\underline{\mu}}^{(k')})$ are not asymptotically independent if $1 \le k < k' \le 5$.

The hypotheses to be considered are not fully nested since $M_k \subset M_6 \subset M_7$ for each $k \in \bar{5}$, but none of the manifolds M_k, $k \in \bar{5}$, are included in one another. Thus the procedures for nested hypotheses cannot be directly applied. However, little real difficulty is involved. Suppose it is decided that if $-2\Delta(\underline{n},\hat{\underline{\mu}}^{(7)},\hat{\underline{\mu}}^{(6)}) > \chi^2_6(0.05)$, then sufficient evidence exists to conclude that $\underline{\mu} \notin M_6$, and that if $-2\Delta(\underline{n},\hat{\underline{\mu}}^{(7)},\hat{\underline{\mu}}^{(6)}) \le \chi^2_6(0.05)$ and $-2\Delta(\underline{n},\hat{\underline{\mu}}^{(6)},\hat{\underline{\mu}}^{(k)}) > \chi^2_1(0.01)$ for $k \in \bar{5}$, then sufficient evidence exists to conclude that $\underline{\mu} \notin M_k$. Then the Bonferroni inequality implies that the approximate probability that a hypothesis $\underline{\mu} \in M_k$, $k \in \bar{6}$, is falsely rejected does not exceed 0.10.

In this example, the likelihood ratio chi-square statistics suggest that the original model M_6 is an appropriate one for these data. One has $-2\Delta(\underline{n},\hat{\underline{\mu}}^{(7)},\hat{\underline{\mu}}^{(6)}) = 2.53$, so no evidence exists that $\underline{\mu}$ is not in M_6. In fact, the fit is unusually close. On the other hand, $-2\Delta(\underline{n},\hat{\underline{\mu}}^{(6)},\hat{\underline{\mu}}^{(1)}) = 21.69$, $-2\Delta(\underline{n},\hat{\underline{\mu}}^{(6)},\hat{\underline{\mu}}^{(2)}) = 31.78$, $-2\Delta(\underline{n},\hat{\underline{\mu}}^{(6)},\hat{\underline{\mu}}^{(3)}) = 9.84$, $-2\Delta(\underline{n},\hat{\underline{\mu}}^{(6)},\hat{\underline{\mu}}^{(4)}) = 13.95$, and $-2\Delta(\underline{n},\hat{\underline{\mu}}^{(6)},\hat{\underline{\mu}}^{(5)}) = 47.68$. Since the smallest of these numbers exceeds $\chi^2_1(0.002)$, one may conclude that $\underline{\mu} \notin M_k$ for any $k \in \bar{5}$. The logical implication of these conclusions is that the five interaction terms in (4.224) are both necessary and sufficient; in other words, the Wilner model appears to fit the data without employing an unnecessarily complex model. The evidence supporting this last conclusion is unusually strong considering the complexity of the model.

SIMULTANEOUS TESTING

When a complex table is analyzed, uncertainty concerning the appropriate model to consider is often so great that carefully constructed sequences of hypotheses tests such as those in Example 4.16 are not likely to lead to an adequate understanding of the data. The procedure considered in this section can sometimes offer an indication of what manifolds are likely to be useful in describing the behavior of the table. The approach adopted is a generalization of a proposal in Goodman (1970) for analysis of dichotomous variables.

In this section, the log-mean vector $\underline{\mu}$ is assumed to lie in a manifold M, which is the direct sum of s components M_t, $t \in \bar{s}$, with dimension p_t. In other words, $M = \bigoplus_{t=1}^{s} M_t$ and

(4.233) $$\underline{\mu} = \sum_{t=1}^{s} P^{(t)}\underline{\mu},$$

where $P^{(t)}\underline{\mu} \in M_t$. A procedure is desired which can be employed to determine which $P^{(t)}\underline{\mu}$ are not equal to $\underline{0}$.

Example 4.17. The study of problem children considered in Example 4.13 can be analyzed using the methods of this section. The manifold M in this case is $R^{\overline{3}x\overline{2}x\overline{2}}$. By use of methods developed in chapter 5, this manifold can be divided into five orthogonal components M_t, $t \in \overline{5}$, where

(4.234) $$M_1 = \{\underline{\mu} \in R^{\overline{3}x\overline{2}x\overline{2}}: \mu_{ijk} = u + a_i + b_j + c_k,\ a_+ = b_+ = c_+ = 0\ \forall\langle i,j,k\rangle \in \overline{3} \times \overline{2} \times \overline{2}\},$$

(4.235) $$M_2 = \{\underline{\mu} \in R^{\overline{3}x\overline{2}x\overline{2}}: \mu_{ijk} = d_{ij},\ d_{i+} = 0,\ d_{+j} = 0\ \forall\langle i,j,k\rangle \in \overline{3} \times \overline{2} \times \overline{2}\},$$

(4.236) $$M_3 = \{\underline{\mu} \in R^{\overline{3}x\overline{2}x\overline{2}}: \mu_{ijk} = e_{ik},\ e_{i+} = e_{+k} = 0\ \forall\langle i,j,k\rangle \in \overline{3} \times \overline{2} \times \overline{2}\},$$

(4.237) $$M_4 = \{\underline{\mu} \in R^{\overline{3}x\overline{2}x\overline{2}}: \mu_{ijk} = f_{jk},\ f_{j+} = f_{+k} = 0\ \forall\langle i,j,k\rangle \in \overline{3} \times \overline{2} \times \overline{2}\},$$

and

(4.238) $$M_5 = \{\underline{\mu} \in R^{\overline{3}x\overline{2}x\overline{2}}: \mu_{+jk} = \mu_{i+k} = \mu_{+jk} = 0\ \forall\langle i,j,k\rangle \in \overline{3} \times \overline{2} \times \overline{2}\}.$$

The manifold M_1 is the basic component of M. If $\underline{\mu} \in M_1$, then birth order, type of child, and type of mother are mutually independent. There is no reason to suspect that the component $P^{(1)}\underline{\mu}$ of $\underline{\mu}$ is $\underline{0}$. The manifold M_2 represents interaction between birth order and type of child, M_3 represents interaction between birth order and type of mother, and M_4 represents interaction between type of child and type of mother. The last manifold, M_5, represents interaction between the three variables in the study. Which components $P^{(t)}\underline{\mu}$, $1 < t \le 5$, are not zero determines which relationships exist between the variables in the study.

The procedure to be used is based on a chi-square statistic for testing the single null hypothesis that $P^{(t)}\underline{\mu} = \underline{0}$. To simplify the analysis, it is assumed that $\underline{e} \in M_1$, $N \subset M_1$, and $1 < t \le s$. This condition is met in Example 4.17 if the data come from a Poisson or simple multinomial sample. To construct an appropriate test, observe that if $\{\underline{n}^{(N)}\}$ is the standard sequence of random vectors which was defined at the beginning of this chapter and if $1 < t \le s$, then

$$N^{\frac{1}{2}}[P^{(t)}\underline{\hat{\mu}}^{(N)} - P^{(t)}\underline{\mu}^{(N)}] \xrightarrow{\mathcal{D}} N(\underline{0}, P^{(t)}[P_M^*(\underline{\mu}^*) - P_N^*(\underline{\mu}^*)]D^{-1}(\underline{\mu}^*)(P^{(t)})^T) \tag{4.239}$$
$$= N(\underline{0}, P^{(t)}P_M^*(\underline{\mu}^*)D^{-1}(\underline{\mu}^*)(P^{(t)})^T) ,$$

where $(P^{(t)})^T$ is the adjoint of the linear mapping $P^{(t)}$ from M to $M^{(t)}$. The last equation follows since $P^{(t)}(M_{t_1}) = \{\underline{0}\}$ for any $t \ne t_1$ and $N \subset M_1$.

It is now necessary to show that if

$$W_t(\underline{\mu}^*) = P^{(t)}P_M^*(\underline{\mu}^*)D^{-1}(\underline{\mu}^*)(P^{(t)})^T , \tag{4.240}$$

then $W_t(\underline{\mu}^*)$ is a nonsingular mapping from M_t onto M_t. To verify this statement, suppose that $W_t(\underline{\mu}^*)\underline{x} = \underline{0}$ for some $\underline{\mu} \in M_t$. Then

$$(\underline{x}, W_t(\underline{\mu}^*)\underline{x}) = (\underline{x}, P^{(t)}P_M^*(\underline{\mu}^*)D^{-1}(\underline{\mu}^*)(P^{(t)})^T\underline{x}) \tag{4.241}$$
$$= (D^{-1}(\underline{\mu}^*)(P^{(t)})^T\underline{x}, D(\underline{\mu}^*)P_M^*(\underline{\mu}^*)D^{-1}(\underline{\mu}^*)(P^{(t)})^T\underline{x})$$
$$= (P_M^*(\underline{\mu}^*)D^{-1}(\underline{\mu}^*)(P^{(t)})^T\underline{x}, D(\underline{\mu}^*)P_M^*(\underline{\mu}^*)D^{-1}(\underline{\mu}^*)(P^{(t)})^T\underline{x})$$
$$= 0 .$$

The third equation in (4.241) utilizes the fact that $P_M^*(\underline{\mu}^*)$ is orthogonal with respect to the inner product defined in (4.3). It now follows that

$$P_M^*(\underline{\mu}^*)D^{-1}(\underline{\mu}^*)(P^{(t)})^T\underline{x} = 0. \tag{4.242}$$

Since the null space of $P_M^*(\underline{\mu}^*)$ is $D^{-1}(\underline{\mu}^*)M^\perp$, $(P^{(t)})^T\underline{x} \in M^\perp$. Since $(P^{(t)})^T\underline{x} \in M$, $(P^{(t)})^T\underline{x} = \underline{0}$. Thus $W_t(\underline{\mu}^*)$ is nonsingular.

These observations lead to a test of an individual null hypothesis H_0: $P^{(t)}\underline{\mu} = \underline{0}$ against the alternative H_A: $P^{(t)}\underline{\mu} \in M_t$ in which H_0 is rejected whenever $(P^{(t)}\underline{\hat{\mu}}, W_t^{-1}(\underline{\hat{\mu}})P^{(t)}\underline{\hat{\mu}}) > \chi^2_{p_t}(\alpha)$. This test has approximate level α, as is shown in the following theorem.

THEOREM 4.9. *Consider the sequence of null hypotheses* H_0: $P^{(t)}\underline{\mu}^{(N)} = \underline{0}$ *and alternatives* H_A: $P^{(t)}\underline{\mu}^{(N)} \in M_t$, *where* $1 < t \le s$. *Then if* $P^{(t)}\underline{\mu}^{(N)} = \underline{0}$ *for each* N,

$$P\{(P^{(t)}\underline{\hat{\mu}}^{(N)}, W_t^{-1}(\underline{\hat{\mu}}^{(N)})P^{(t)}\underline{\hat{\mu}}^{(N)}) > \chi^2_{p_t}(\alpha)\} \longrightarrow \alpha. \tag{4.243}$$

Proof. Note that $NW_t(\hat{\underline{\mu}}^{(N)}) \xrightarrow{P} W_t(\underline{\mu}^*)$. By Rao (1965) and (4.239),

(4.244) $$(P^{(t)}\hat{\underline{\mu}}^{(N)}, W_t^{-1}(\hat{\underline{\mu}}^{(N)})P^{(t)}\hat{\underline{\mu}}^{(N)}) \longrightarrow \chi^2_{p_t} .$$

The theorem now follows.||

The test is consistent under the alternative hypothesis and has an easily computed asymptotic power. Results are summarized in Theorems 4.10 and 4.11.

THEOREM 4.10. *Consider the sequence of null hypotheses* $H_0: P^{(t)}\underline{\mu}^{(N)} = \underline{0}$ *and alternatives* $H_A: P^{(t)}\underline{\mu}^{(N)} \in M_t$, *where* $1 < t \le s$. *If* $P^{(t)}\underline{\mu}^* \ne \underline{0}$, *then*

(4.245) $$\frac{1}{N}(P^{(t)}\hat{\underline{\mu}}^{(N)}, W_t^{-1}(\hat{\underline{\mu}}^{(N)})P^{(t)}\hat{\underline{\mu}}^{(N)}) \xrightarrow{P} (P^{(t)}\underline{\mu}^*, W_t^{-1}(\underline{\mu}^*)P^{(t)}\underline{\mu}^*)$$

and

(4.246) $$P\{(P^{(t)}\hat{\underline{\mu}}^{(N)}, W_t^{-1}(\hat{\underline{\mu}}^{(N)})P^{(t)}\hat{\underline{\mu}}^{(N)}) > \chi^2_{p_t}(\alpha)\} \longrightarrow 1.$$

Proof. It is still the case that $NW_t(\hat{\underline{\mu}}^{(N)}) \xrightarrow{P} W_t(\underline{\mu}^*)$. Since $P^{(t)}(\hat{\underline{\mu}}^{(N)} - \underline{\mu}^{(N)}) \xrightarrow{P} \underline{0}$ and

(4.247) $$P^{(t)}(\underline{\mu}^{(N)} - \underline{\mu}^*) = P^{(t)}[\underline{\mu}^{(N)} - (\log N)\underline{e} - \underline{\mu}^*] \longrightarrow \underline{0} ,$$

it follows that $P^{(t)}\hat{\underline{\mu}}^{(N)} \xrightarrow{P} P^{(t)}\underline{\mu}^*$. The theorem now follows.

THEOREM 4.11. *Consider the sequence of null hypotheses* $H_0: P^{(t)}\underline{\mu}^{(N)} = \underline{0}$ *and alternatives* $H_A: P^{(t)}\underline{\mu} \in M_t$, *where* $1 < t \le s$. *If* $\underline{\mu}^{(N)} - (\log N)\underline{e} \longrightarrow \underline{\mu}^*$ *and* $N^{\frac{1}{2}}P^{(t)}\underline{\mu}^{(N)} \longrightarrow \underline{c}^*$, *then*

(4.248) $$P\{(P^{(t)}\hat{\underline{\mu}}^{(N)}, W_t^{-1}(\hat{\underline{\mu}}^{(N)})P^{(t)}\hat{\underline{\mu}}^{(N)}) > \chi^2_{p_t}(\alpha)\} \longrightarrow P\{\chi'^2_{p_t,\delta^2} > \chi^2_{p_t}(\alpha)\} ,$$

where $\delta^2 = (\underline{c}^*, W_t^{-1}(\underline{\mu}^*)\underline{c}^*)$.

Proof. Once again $NW_t(\hat{\underline{\mu}}^{(N)}) \xrightarrow{P} W_t(\underline{\mu}^*)$. Since

(4.249) $$N^{\frac{1}{2}}P^{(t)}(\hat{\underline{\mu}}^{(N)} - \underline{\mu}^*) \xrightarrow{D} N(\underline{c}^*, W_t(\underline{\mu}^*)),$$

(4.248) follows from Rao (1965).||

The simultaneous test procedure based on the test of the null hypothesis that $P^{(t)}\underline{\mu} = \underline{0}$ is constructed by selecting α_t so that $\sum_{t=2}^{s} \alpha_t = \alpha$. If the test for $P^{(t)}\underline{\mu}$ is performed at approximate level α_t for each $t > 1$, then the Bonferroni inequality implies that the approximate probability that a null hypothesis is falsely rejected does not exceed α. The fact that the tests are not asymptotically independent has no real consequences.

The procedure is easiest to apply when $W_t(\hat{\underline{\mu}})$ is readily computed for each $t > 1$. This situation occurs when $M = R^I$ or each linear manifold M_t, $t > 1$, has dimension 1. Computations are also simplified if the manifolds M_t, $t \in \bar{s}$, are mutually orthogonal. In the case considered by Goodman (1970), all these conditions are satisfied.

If $M = R^I$, then $P^*_M(\hat{\underline{\mu}})$ is the identity and

$$W_t(\hat{\underline{\mu}}) = P^{(t)}D^{-1}(\hat{\underline{\mu}})(P^{(t)})^T . \tag{4.250}$$

Since $P^{(t)}$ is normally easy to calculate, the only computational problem is solution for $\underline{x}^{(t)}$ of the equation

$$W_t(\hat{\underline{\mu}})\underline{x}^{(t)} = P^{(t)}\hat{\underline{\mu}} . \tag{4.251}$$

Given this solution,

$$(P^{(t)}\hat{\underline{\mu}}, W_t^{-1}(\hat{\underline{\mu}})P^{(t)}\hat{\underline{\mu}}) = (P^{(t)}\hat{\underline{\mu}}, \underline{x}^{(t)}) . \tag{4.252}$$

It should be noted that solution of (4.251) is particularly easy if M_t has dimension 1.

If the manifolds M_t, $t \in \bar{s}$, are orthogonal and $M = R^I$, then more attractive expressions are available for the test statistics. The mapping $P^{(t)}$ then satisfies the equation $P^{(t)}\underline{x} = P_{M_t}\underline{x}$ for all $\underline{x} \in R^I$. The only reason that $P^{(t)}$ is not said to be equal to P_{M_t} is that the range spaces of the two mappings are different (see Eaton 1969). It should be noted that $P^{(t)}$ is a mapping of R^I onto M_t, whereas P_{M_t} is a mapping of R^I into R^I which has range M_t. This difference implies a difference in the adjoints of the two transformations. One has $(P_{M_t})^T = P_{M_t}$, while $(P^{(t)})^T$ is the injection $I^{(t)}$ of M_t into R^I defined by $I^{(t)}\underline{x} = \underline{x}$ for each $\underline{x} \in M_t$. Given these results, $\underline{x}^{(t)} = D(\hat{\underline{\mu}})P^*_{B_t(\hat{\underline{\mu}})}(\hat{\underline{\mu}})\hat{\underline{\mu}}$, where $B_t(\hat{\underline{\mu}}) = D^{-1}(\hat{\underline{\mu}})(M_t)$, the image of M_t under the transformation $D^{-1}(\hat{\underline{\mu}})$. To verify this assertion, observe that $D(\hat{\underline{\mu}})P^*_{B_t(\hat{\underline{\mu}})}(\hat{\underline{\mu}})\hat{\underline{\mu}} \in D(\hat{\underline{\mu}})B_t(\hat{\underline{\mu}}) = M_t$ and

$$\begin{aligned} W_t(\hat{\underline{\mu}})D(\hat{\underline{\mu}})P^*_{B_t(\hat{\underline{\mu}})}(\hat{\underline{\mu}})\hat{\underline{\mu}} &= P^{(t)}D^{-1}(\hat{\underline{\mu}})I^{(t)}D(\hat{\underline{\mu}})P^*_{B_t(\hat{\underline{\mu}})}(\hat{\underline{\mu}})\hat{\underline{\mu}} \\ &= P^{(t)}D^{-1}(\hat{\underline{\mu}})D(\hat{\underline{\mu}})P^*_{B_t(\hat{\underline{\mu}})}(\hat{\underline{\mu}})\hat{\underline{\mu}} \\ &= P^{(t)}P^*_{B_t(\hat{\underline{\mu}})}(\hat{\underline{\mu}})\hat{\underline{\mu}} \\ &= P^{(t)}[I - P^*_{M_t^{\perp}}(\hat{\underline{\mu}})]\hat{\underline{\mu}} \\ &= P^{(t)}\hat{\underline{\mu}} . \end{aligned} \tag{4.253}$$

The second-to-last equation follows since the orthogonal complement of $B_t(\hat{\underline{\mu}})$ with respect to the inner product determined by $D(\hat{\underline{\mu}})$ is $M_t^{\perp}$. Given $\underline{x}^{(t)}$, (4.252) reduces to

(4.254)
$$(P^{(t)}\hat{\underline{\mu}}, W_t^{-1}(\hat{\underline{\mu}})P^{(t)}\hat{\underline{\mu}}) = (\hat{\underline{\mu}}, D(\hat{\underline{\mu}})P^*_{B_t(\hat{\underline{\mu}})}(\hat{\underline{\mu}})\hat{\underline{\mu}})$$
$$= (P^*_{B_t(\hat{\underline{\mu}})}(\hat{\underline{\mu}})\hat{\underline{\mu}}, D(\hat{\underline{\mu}})P^*_{B_t(\hat{\underline{\mu}})}(\hat{\underline{\mu}})\hat{\underline{\mu}}) .$$

If in addition M_t has dimension 1 and is equal to span $\{\underline{c}^{(t)}\}$, then

(4.255)
$$(P^{(t)}\hat{\underline{\mu}}, W_t^{-1}(\hat{\underline{\mu}})P^{(t)}\hat{\underline{\mu}}) = (\underline{c}^{(t)}, \hat{\underline{\mu}})^2/(\underline{c}^{(t)}, D^{-1}(\hat{\underline{\mu}})\underline{c}^{(t)}),$$

where

(4.256)
$$(\underline{c}^{(t)}, \hat{\underline{\mu}}) = \sum_{i\in I} c_i^{(t)} \log n_i$$

and

(4.257)
$$(\underline{c}^{(t)}, D^{-1}(\hat{\underline{\mu}})\, \underline{c}^{(t)}) = \sum_{i\in I} (c_i^{(t)})^2/n_i$$

(see Goodman 1970).

Example 4.18. Consider use of the proposed procedure in the situation described in Example 4.17. Since $M = R^{\overline{3}\times\overline{2}\times\overline{2}}$, $W_t(\hat{\underline{\mu}})$ is $P^{(t)}D^{-1}(\underline{\mu})(P^{(t)})^T$ and $\hat{\underline{\mu}} = \{\log n_{ijk}\}$. The manifolds M_t, $t \in \overline{5}$, are mutually orthogonal, so $P^{(t)}\underline{x} = P_{M_t}\underline{x}$ for each $\underline{x} \in M_t$ and $(P^{(t)})^T = I^{(t)}$.

To determine the appropriate test statistics, it is helpful to construct bases for the manifolds M_t, $1 < t \le 5$. The manifold M_2 is spanned by $\underline{w}^{(1)}$ and $\underline{w}^{(2)}$, where

(4.258)
$$\underline{w}^{(1)} = \begin{array}{|rr|} 1 & 1 \\ -1 & -1 \\ \hline -1 & -1 \\ 1 & 1 \\ \hline 0 & 0 \\ 0 & 0 \end{array}$$

and

(4.259)
$$\underline{w}^{(2)} = \begin{array}{|rr|} 0 & 0 \\ 0 & 0 \\ \hline 1 & 1 \\ -1 & -1 \\ \hline -1 & -1 \\ 1 & 1 \end{array}$$

The tabular presentation in these equations has the format used in table 1.2 to represent the original data. Similarly, M_3 is spanned by $\underline{x}^{(1)}$ and $\underline{x}^{(2)}$, where

$$\underline{x}^{(1)} = \begin{array}{|cc|} \hline 1 & -1 \\ 1 & -1 \\ \hline -1 & 1 \\ -1 & 1 \\ \hline 0 & 0 \\ 0 & 0 \\ \hline \end{array} \tag{4.260}$$

and

$$\underline{x}^{(2)} = \begin{array}{|cc|} \hline 0 & 0 \\ 0 & 0 \\ \hline 1 & 1 \\ -1 & -1 \\ \hline -1 & -1 \\ 1 & 1 \\ \hline \end{array} \tag{4.261}$$

The manifold M_4 is spanned by the single vector $\underline{y}^{(1)}$, where

$$\underline{y}^{(1)} = \begin{array}{|cc|} \hline 1 & -1 \\ -1 & 1 \\ \hline 1 & -1 \\ -1 & 1 \\ \hline 1 & -1 \\ -1 & 1 \\ \hline \end{array}\ , \tag{4.262}$$

and M_5 is spanned by $\underline{z}^{(1)}$ and $\underline{z}^{(2)}$, where

$$\underline{z}^{(1)} = \begin{array}{|cc|} \hline 1 & -1 \\ -1 & 1 \\ \hline -1 & 1 \\ 1 & -1 \\ \hline 0 & 0 \\ 0 & 0 \\ \hline \end{array} \tag{4.263}$$

and

(4.264)
$$\underline{z}^{(2)} = \left[\begin{array}{rr} 0 & 0 \\ 0 & 0 \\ \hline 1 & -1 \\ -1 & 1 \\ \hline -1 & 1 \\ 1 & -1 \end{array}\right] .$$

Since M_2, M_3, and M_5 all have dimension 2, similar computational formulas apply to the corresponding test statistics. Consequently, it is sufficient to consider M_2 in some detail. The manifold $B_2(\hat{\underline{\mu}})$ is spanned by $D^{-1}(\hat{\underline{\mu}})\underline{w}^{(1)}$ and $D^{-1}(\hat{\underline{\mu}})\underline{w}^{(2)}$, so the normal equations imply that

(4.265)
$$P^*_{B_2(\hat{\underline{\mu}})}(\hat{\underline{\mu}})\hat{\underline{\mu}} = aD^{-1}(\hat{\underline{\mu}})\underline{w}^{(1)} + bD^{-1}(\hat{\underline{\mu}})\underline{w}^{(2)} ,$$

where

(4.266)
$$a(\underline{w}^{(1)},D^{-1}(\hat{\underline{\mu}})\underline{w}^{(1)}) + b(\underline{w}^{(1)},D^{-1}(\hat{\underline{\mu}})\underline{w}^{(2)}) = (\underline{w}^{(1)},\hat{\underline{\mu}})$$

and

(4.267)
$$a(\underline{w}^{(1)},D^{-1}(\hat{\underline{\mu}})\underline{w}^{(2)}) + b(\underline{w}^{(2)},D^{-1}(\hat{\underline{\mu}})\underline{w}^{(2)}) = (\underline{w}^{(2)},\hat{\underline{\mu}}).$$

Elementary calculations show that

(4.268)
$$a = \frac{(\underline{w}^{(2)},D^{-1}(\hat{\underline{\mu}})\underline{w}^{(2)})(\underline{w}^{(1)},\hat{\underline{\mu}}) - (\underline{w}^{(1)},D^{-1}(\hat{\underline{\mu}})\underline{w}^{(2)})(\underline{w}^{(2)},\hat{\underline{\mu}})}{(\underline{w}^{(1)},D^{-1}(\hat{\underline{\mu}})\underline{w}^{(1)})(\underline{w}^{(2)},D^{-1}(\hat{\underline{\mu}})\underline{w}^{(2)}) - (\underline{w}^{(1)},D^{-1}(\hat{\underline{\mu}})\underline{w}^{(2)})^2}$$

and

(4.269)
$$b = \frac{(\underline{w}^{(1)},D^{-1}(\hat{\underline{\mu}})\underline{w}^{(1)})(\underline{w}^{(2)},\hat{\underline{\mu}}) - (\underline{w}^{(1)},D^{-1}(\hat{\underline{\mu}})\underline{w}^{(2)})(\underline{w}^{(1)},\hat{\underline{\mu}})}{(\underline{w}^{(1)},D^{-1}(\hat{\underline{\mu}})\underline{w}^{(1)})(\underline{w}^{(2)},D^{-1}(\hat{\underline{\mu}})\underline{w}^{(2)}) - (\underline{w}^{(1)},D^{-1}(\hat{\underline{\mu}})\underline{w}^{(2)})^2} .$$

It now follows that

(4.270)
$$(P^{(2)}\hat{\underline{\mu}},W_2^{-1}(\hat{\underline{\mu}})P^{(2)}\hat{\underline{\mu}})$$
$$= (\hat{\underline{\mu}},D(\hat{\underline{\mu}})P^*_{B_2(\hat{\underline{\mu}})}(\hat{\underline{\mu}})\hat{\underline{\mu}})$$
$$= a(\underline{w}^{(1)},\hat{\underline{\mu}}) + b(\underline{w}^{(2)},\hat{\underline{\mu}})$$
$$= [(\underline{w}^{(2)},D^{-1}(\hat{\underline{\mu}})\underline{w}^{(2)})(\underline{w}^{(1)},\hat{\underline{\mu}})^2 - 2(\underline{w}^{(1)},D^{-1}(\hat{\underline{\mu}})\underline{w}^{(2)})(\underline{w}^{(1)},\hat{\underline{\mu}})(\underline{w}^{(2)},\hat{\underline{\mu}})$$
$$+ (\underline{w}^{(1)},D^{-1}(\hat{\underline{\mu}})\underline{w}^{(2)})(\underline{w}^{(2)},\hat{\underline{\mu}})^2]/[(\underline{w}^{(1)},D^{-1}(\hat{\underline{\mu}})\underline{w}^{(1)})(\underline{w}^{(2)},D^{-1}(\hat{\underline{\mu}})\underline{w}^{(2)})$$
$$- (\underline{w}^{(1)},D^{-1}(\hat{\underline{\mu}})\underline{w}^{(2)})^2] .$$

After some algebraic manipulations, one finds that

(4.271) $(P^{(2)}\underline{\hat{\mu}}, W_2^{-1}(\underline{\hat{\mu}})P^{(2)}\underline{\hat{\mu}})$

$$= [g_1(h_2^{(2)} - h_3^{(2)})^2 + g_2(h_1^{(2)} - h_3^{(2)})^2 + g_3(h_1^{(2)} - h_2^{(2)})^2]/[g_1g_2 + g_1g_3 + g_2g_3]$$

$$= 0.679 ,$$

where for each $i \in \overline{3}$,

(4.272) $$g_i = \frac{1}{n_{i11}} + \frac{1}{n_{i12}} + \frac{1}{n_{i21}} + \frac{1}{n_{i22}}$$

and

(4.275) $$h_i^{(2)} = \log n_{i11} + \log n_{i12} - \log n_{i21} - \log n_{i22} .$$

Similarly,

(4.274) $(P^{(3)}\underline{\hat{\mu}}, W_3^{-1}(\underline{\hat{\mu}})P^{(3)}\underline{\hat{\mu}})$

$$= [g_1(h_2^{(3)} - h_3^{(3)})^2 + g_2(h_1^{(3)} - h_3^{(3)})^2 + g_3(h_1^{(3)} - h_2^{(3)})^2]/[g_1g_2 + g_1g_3 + g_2g_3]$$

$$= 22.61$$

and

(4.275) $(P^{(5)}\underline{\hat{\mu}}, W_5^{-1}(\underline{\hat{\mu}})P^{(5)}\underline{\hat{\mu}})$

$$= [g_1(h_2^{(5)} - h_3^{(5)})^2 + g_2(h_1^{(5)} - h_3^{(5)})^2 + g_3(h_1^{(5)} - h_2^{(5)})^2]/[g_1g_2 + g_1g_3 + g_2g_3]$$

$$= 0.849 ,$$

where for $i \in \overline{3}$,

(4.276) $$h_i^{(3)} = \log n_{i11} + \log n_{i21} - \log n_{i12} - \log n_{i22}$$

and

(4.277) $$h_i^{(5)} = \log n_{i11} - \log n_{i12} - \log n_{i21} + \log n_{i22}.$$

The statistics for manifolds of dimension 2 are simple expressions, but they have been found by a rather lengthy argument. In contrast, $(P^{(4)}\underline{\hat{\mu}}, W_4^{-1}(\underline{\hat{\mu}})P^{(4)}\underline{\hat{\mu}})$ can be expressed without difficulty by use of (4.255). One has

(4.278) $(P^{(4)}\underline{\hat{\mu}}, W_4^{-1}(\underline{\hat{\mu}})P^{(4)}\underline{\hat{\mu}})$

$$= (h_1^{(5)} + h_2^{(5)} + h_3^{(5)})^2/(g_1 + g_2 + g_3)$$

$$= 2.14.$$

If $\alpha = 0.10$ and $\alpha_t = \alpha/4$ for t such that $1 < t \leq 5$, then one may conclude that $P^{(3)}\underline{\mu} \neq \underline{0}$ but no evidence exists that $P^{(2)}\underline{\mu}$, $P^{(4)}\underline{\mu}$, or $P^{(5)}\underline{\mu}$ differs from $\underline{0}$. These results suggest that the only interaction among the variables is one between birth order and status of mother, an effect which is sufficiently obvious so that in Example 4.14 it was assumed to be present. The conclusions reached by this analysis are essentially the same as those reached in Example 4.14.

SIMULTANEOUS CONFIDENCE INTERVALS

Simultaneous confidence intervals are readily constructed for linear combinations of $\underline{\mu}$ or $\underline{\mu}(I)$, where $\underline{\mu} \in M$. Two methods are available which are suitable for use with frequency data. The first method, which has been considered in specific problems by Goodman (1964) and Reiersøl(1961), is based on the Scheffé (1959) method for obtaining simultaneous confidence intervals in analysis of variance. The second method, which has also been explored by Goodman (1964), uses the Bonferroni inequality to construct simultaneous confidence intervals.

To find simultaneous confidence intervals for $\underline{\mu}$ by the first method, one assumes that intervals are desired for all linear combinations $(\underline{c},\underline{\mu})$ of $\underline{\mu}$ for $\underline{c}$ in a linear manifold C orthogonal to N. The orthogonality condition is trivial in the Poisson case; otherwise, the condition reduces to the requirement that $(\underline{c},\underline{\nu}^{(k)}) = 0$ for all $k \in \overline{r}$ and $\underline{c} \in C$. To construct the intervals, define the manifold $\mathcal{D}(\hat{\underline{\mu}}) = P^*_M(\hat{\underline{\mu}})D^{-1}(\hat{\underline{\mu}})(C)$. If $c \in C$, then since $\underline{\mu} \in M$,

$$(\underline{c},\underline{\mu}) = (D^{-1}(\hat{\underline{\mu}})\underline{c},D(\hat{\underline{\mu}})\underline{\mu}) \tag{4.279}$$

$$= (D^{-1}(\hat{\underline{\mu}})\underline{c},D(\hat{\underline{\mu}})P^*_M(\hat{\underline{\mu}})\underline{\mu})$$

$$= (P^*_M(\hat{\underline{\mu}})D^{-1}(\hat{\underline{\mu}})\underline{c},D(\hat{\underline{\mu}})\underline{\mu}).$$

Thus to each linear combination $(\underline{c},\underline{\mu})$ where $\underline{c} \in C$, corresponds a linear combination $(\underline{d},D(\hat{\underline{\mu}})\underline{\mu})$, where $\underline{d} \in \mathcal{D}(\hat{\underline{\mu}})$. Similarly, each linear combination $(\underline{d},D(\hat{\underline{\mu}})\underline{\mu})$, where $\underline{d} \in \mathcal{D}(\hat{\underline{\mu}})$, corresponds to at least one linear combination $(\underline{c},\underline{\mu})$, where $\underline{c} \in C$.

If $d \in \mathcal{D}(\hat{\underline{\mu}})$, then

$$(\underline{d},D(\hat{\underline{\mu}})(\underline{\mu} - \hat{\underline{\mu}})) = (P^*_{\mathcal{D}(\hat{\underline{\mu}})}(\hat{\underline{\mu}})\underline{d},D(\hat{\underline{\mu}})(\underline{\mu} - \hat{\underline{\mu}})) \tag{4.280}$$

$$= (\underline{d},D(\hat{\underline{\mu}})P^*_{\mathcal{D}(\hat{\underline{\mu}})}(\hat{\underline{\mu}})(\underline{\mu} - \hat{\underline{\mu}})).$$

In (4.280), the facts that $\mathcal{D}(\hat{\underline{\mu}}) \subset M$ and $\mathcal{D}(\hat{\underline{\mu}})$ and N are orthogonal relative to the inner product defined by $D(\hat{\underline{\mu}})$ have been exploited. By Schwartz's inequality (see Halmos 1958),

$$(4.281) \qquad |(\underline{d},D(\hat{\underline{\mu}})(\underline{\mu} - \hat{\underline{\mu}}))| \le (\underline{d},D(\hat{\underline{\mu}})\underline{d})^{\frac{1}{2}} \, (\underline{\mu} - \hat{\underline{\mu}},D(\hat{\underline{\mu}})P^{*}_{\mathcal{D}(\hat{\underline{\mu}})}(\hat{\underline{\mu}})(\underline{\mu} - \hat{\underline{\mu}}))^{\frac{1}{2}} ,$$

with equality if $\underline{d} = P^{*}_{\mathcal{D}(\hat{\underline{\mu}})}(\underline{\mu} - \hat{\underline{\mu}})$. Thus

$$(4.282) \qquad P\{|(\underline{d},D(\hat{\underline{\mu}})(\underline{\mu} - \hat{\underline{\mu}}))| \le \chi_d(\alpha) \, (\underline{d},D(\hat{\underline{\mu}})\underline{d})^{\frac{1}{2}} \; \forall \underline{d} \in \mathcal{D}(\hat{\underline{\mu}})\}$$

$$= P\{(\underline{\mu} - \hat{\underline{\mu}},D(\hat{\underline{\mu}})P^{*}_{\mathcal{D}(\hat{\underline{\mu}})}(\hat{\underline{\mu}})(\underline{\mu} - \hat{\underline{\mu}}))^{\frac{1}{2}} \le \chi_d(\alpha)\},$$

where $\chi_d(\alpha) = (\chi^2_d(\alpha))^{\frac{1}{2}}$ and $\dim \mathcal{D}(\hat{\underline{\mu}}) = d$.

The dimension d of $P^{*}_{M}(\hat{\underline{\mu}})D^{-1}(\hat{\underline{\mu}})(C)$ is $\dim P_M(C)$, for $P^{*}_{M}(\hat{\underline{\mu}})D^{-1}(\hat{\underline{\mu}})(M^{\perp}) = \{\underline{0}\}$. Thus $P^{*}_{M}(\hat{\underline{\mu}})D^{-1}(\hat{\underline{\mu}})(C) = P^{*}_{M}(\hat{\underline{\mu}})D^{-1}(\hat{\underline{\mu}})P_M(C)$. To show that d has the desired value, it suffices to note that if $\underline{x} \in P_M(C)$ and $P^{*}_{M}(\hat{\underline{\mu}})D^{-1}(\hat{\underline{\mu}})\underline{x} = \underline{0}$, then $\underline{x} \in D^{-1}(\hat{\underline{\mu}})(M^{\perp})$. Therefore, $\underline{x}$ must be $\underline{0}$.

Since Theorem 4.1 implies that

$$(4.283) \qquad D^{\frac{1}{2}}(\hat{\underline{\mu}}^{(N)})P^{*}_{\mathcal{D}(\hat{\underline{\mu}}^{(N)})}(\hat{\underline{\mu}}^{(N)})(\underline{\mu}^{(N)} - \hat{\underline{\mu}}^{(N)}) \xrightarrow{\mathcal{D}}$$

$$N(\underline{0},D^{\frac{1}{2}}(\underline{\mu}^{*})P^{*}_{\mathcal{D}(\underline{\mu}^{*})}(\underline{\mu}^{*})[P^{*}_{M}(\underline{\mu}^{*}) - P^{*}_{N}(\underline{\mu}^{*})]D^{-1}(\underline{\mu}^{*})D(\underline{\mu}^{*})P^{*}_{\mathcal{D}(\underline{\mu}^{*})}(\underline{\mu}^{*})D^{-\frac{1}{2}}(\underline{\mu}^{*}))$$

$$= N(\underline{0},A_{\mathcal{D}(\underline{\mu}^{*})}(\underline{\mu}^{*})) ,$$

by Rao (1965),

$$(4.284) \qquad P\{(\underline{\mu}^{(N)} - \hat{\underline{\mu}}^{(N)},D(\hat{\underline{\mu}}^{(N)})P^{*}_{\mathcal{D}(\hat{\underline{\mu}}^{(N)})}(\hat{\underline{\mu}}^{(N)})(\underline{\mu}^{(N)} - \hat{\underline{\mu}}^{(N)})) \le \chi_{\alpha}(\alpha)\} \longrightarrow 1 - \alpha .$$

Thus the asymptotic level-$(1-\alpha)$ simultaneous confidence interval for any linear combination $(\underline{c},\underline{\mu})$, where $\underline{c} \in C$, consists of those $(\underline{c},\underline{\mu})$ for which

$$(4.285) \qquad |(\underline{c},\underline{\mu}) - (\underline{c},\hat{\underline{\mu}})| \le \chi_d(\alpha)(\underline{c},P^{*}_{M}(\hat{\underline{\mu}})D^{-1}(\hat{\underline{\mu}})\underline{c})^{\frac{1}{2}} .$$

Several remarks concerning (4.285) are in order. First, it should be noted that $(\underline{c},P^{*}_{M}(\hat{\underline{\mu}})D^{-1}(\hat{\underline{\mu}})\underline{c})$ is an estimate of the asymptotic covariance of $(\underline{c},\underline{\mu} - \hat{\underline{\mu}})$. Second, if $M = R^I$, then formulas are considerably simplified (see Goodman 1964). The simultaneous confidence interval becomes

(4.286) $$(\underline{c},\underline{\mu}) - (\underline{c},\underline{\hat{\mu}}) \le \chi_d(\alpha)\left(\sum_{i \in I} c_i^2/n_i\right)^{\frac{1}{2}} .$$

Third, simultaneous confidence intervals are inefficient if only a few intervals are of interest. In such a case, (4.43) is quite useful. Suppose that simultaneous intervals are required for $\{(\underline{c}^{(j)},\underline{\mu}): j \in k\}$, where $P_M\underline{c}^{(j)} \notin N$ for any $j \in \overline{k}$. Then one may select $\{\alpha_j: j \in \overline{k}\}$ so that all α_j are positive and $\sum_{j=1}^{k} \alpha_j = \alpha$. One may then use the simultaneous intervals

(4.287) $$|(\underline{c}^{(j)},\underline{\mu}) - (\underline{c}^{(j)},\underline{\hat{\mu}})| \le \Phi^{(\alpha_j/2)}(\underline{c}^{(j)},[P_M^*(\underline{\hat{\mu}}) - P_N^*(\underline{\hat{\mu}})]D^{-1}(\underline{\hat{\mu}})\underline{c}^{(j)})^{\frac{1}{2}} ,$$

which if $\underline{c}^{(j)}$ is orthogonal to N for $j \in \overline{k}$ reduce to the intervals

(4.288) $$|(\underline{c}^{(j)},\underline{\mu}) - (\underline{c}^{(j)},\underline{\hat{\mu}})| \le \Phi^{(\alpha_j/2)}(\underline{c}^{(j)},P_M^*(\underline{\hat{\mu}})D^{-1}(\underline{\hat{\mu}})\underline{c}^{(j)})^{\frac{1}{2}} .$$

If $M = R^I$ and $\alpha_j = \alpha/k$ for each $j \in \overline{k}$, then the intervals for $(\underline{c}^{(j)},\underline{\mu})$ satisfy the inequality

(4.289) $$|(\underline{c}^{(j)},\underline{\mu}) - (\underline{c}^{(j)},\underline{\hat{\mu}})| \le \Phi^{(\alpha/2k)}\left(\sum_{i \in I} c_i^2/n_i\right)^{\frac{1}{2}}$$

(see Goodman 1964). For no additional cost, one also obtains the intervals

(4.290) $$|(\underline{c},\underline{\mu}) - (\underline{c},\underline{\hat{\mu}})| \le \sum_{j=1}^{k} |s_j| \Phi^{(\alpha_j/2)}(\underline{c}^{(j)},P_M^*(\underline{\hat{\mu}})D^{-1}(\underline{\hat{\mu}})\underline{c}^{(j)})^{\frac{1}{2}} ,$$

where

(4.291) $$\underline{c} = \sum_{j=1}^{k} s_j\underline{c}^{(j)} .$$

This result follows since

(4.292) $$|(\underline{c},\underline{\mu}) - (\underline{c},\underline{\hat{\mu}})| \le \sum_{j=1}^{k} |s_j|\, |(\underline{c}^{(j)},\underline{\mu}) - (\underline{c}^{(j)},\underline{\hat{\mu}})| .$$

Thus if $C = \text{span}\{\underline{c}^{(j)}: j \in \overline{k}\}$, simultaneous confidence intervals are available for all $(\underline{c},\underline{\mu})$ such that $\underline{c} \in C$. If $k > d$, then $\{s_j: j \in \overline{k}\}$ may be selected so that the right-hand side of (4.290) is minimized.

The intervals based on (4.288) are shorter than those based on (4.285) if $\Phi^{(\alpha_j/2)} < \chi_d(\alpha)$ for each $j \in \overline{k}$. If each α_j is α/k, then this condition reduces to the requirement that $\Phi^{(\alpha/2k)}$ be less than $\chi_d(\alpha)$. Dunn (1961) has shown that for the customary values of α of 0.05 and 0.01, k must be much larger than d before this inequality is violated. If d is 2 and $\alpha = 0.05$, the inequality holds if $k \le 3$. If d is 5 and α is 0.05, the inequality is valid if $k \le 55$. For even moderately large d, the inequality holds for enormous values of k. For example, if $d = 10$, then $\Phi^{(0.05/2k)} < \chi_{10}(0.05)$ if k does not exceed about 2700. The inequalities on k are even less strict when $\alpha = 0.01$. The difference in the lengths of the intervals may be quite substantial. For example, if $k = 250$, $\Phi^{(0.05/2k)} = 3.72$. On the other hand, if $d = 10$, then $\chi_d(0.05) = 4.28$ and if $d = 30$, then $\chi_d(0.05) = 6.62$.

In the problems considered by Goodman (1964), the intervals based on $\Phi^{(\alpha/2k)}$ are clearly preferable to those based on $\chi_d(\alpha)$. This finding appears to be rather general, although when d is only 2 or 3, intervals based on $\chi_d(\alpha)$ sometimes may be worth some consideration.

It should also be noted that the arguments in this section also apply to simultaneous confidence intervals for linear combinations $(\underline{c},\underline{\mu}(I))$ of the vector $\underline{\mu}(I)$ of log conditional probabilities, where $\underline{c} \in C \subset R^{\perp}$, $R = \text{span}\{\underline{\nu}(I)\colon I \in \mathcal{I}\}$, and $\dim P_M(C) = d$. In this case, $\sum_{i\in I} c_i$ must be 0 for each $\underline{c} \in C$ and $I \in \mathcal{I}$. The Scheffé-type approximate level-$(1-\alpha)$ simultaneous confidence interval for $(\underline{c},\underline{\mu}(I))$, where $\underline{c} \in C$, consists of all $(\underline{c},\underline{\mu}(I))$ such that

$$|(\underline{c},\underline{\mu}(I)) - (\underline{c},\hat{\underline{\mu}}(I))| \le \chi_d(\alpha)(\underline{c},P_M^*(\hat{\underline{\mu}})D^{-1}(\hat{\underline{\mu}})\underline{c})^{\frac{1}{2}} . \tag{4.293}$$

The corresponding Bonferroni intervals are given by those $(\underline{c}^{(j)},\underline{\mu}(I))$ such that

$$|(\underline{c}^{(j)},\underline{\mu}(I)) - (\underline{c}^{(j)},\hat{\underline{\mu}}(I))| \le \Phi^{(\alpha_j/2)}(\underline{c}^{(j)},P_M^*(\hat{\underline{\mu}})D^{-1}(\hat{\underline{\mu}})\underline{c}^{(j)})^{\frac{1}{2}} \tag{4.294}$$

for $\underline{c}^{(j)} \in C$ and $j \in \overline{k}$, where $\sum_{j=1}^{k} \alpha_j = \alpha$.

If the assumption that C is orthogonal to R is dropped, then the Bonferroni intervals satisfy

$$|(\underline{c}^{(j)},\underline{\mu}(I)) - (\underline{c}^{(j)},\hat{\underline{\mu}}(I))| \le \Phi^{(\alpha_j/2)}(\underline{c}^{(j)},[P_M^*(\hat{\underline{\mu}}) - P_R^*(\hat{\underline{\mu}})]D^{-1}(\hat{\underline{\mu}})\underline{c}^{(j)})^{\frac{1}{2}} . \tag{4.295}$$

If desired, Bonferroni intervals can also be constructed for linear combinations $(\underline{c}^{(j)},\underline{m})$ or $(\underline{c}^{(j)},\underline{p}(I))$, where $j \in \overline{k}$, by use of (4.64) or (4.90).

Example 4.19. In some logit analyses, simultaneous confidence intervals are required for the response at any given log dosage. For instance, given the data in Example 1.6, one might wish to find simultaneous confidence intervals for the log odds $a + bt$ corresponding to a log dose t, where t is any real number. Here $a + bt$ is defined as in (1.18). Given these confidence intervals, one can then construct simultaneous confidence intervals for the probability of death $e^{a+bt}/(1 + e^{a+bt})$ given log dosage t. The problem is analogous to a regression problem examined by Working and Hotelling (1929).

Simultaneous confidence intervals may be constructed by observing that if $\underline{\mu}^{(4)}$ and $\underline{\mu}^{(5)}$ are defined respectively by (1.24) and (1.25), then

$$a + bt = \tfrac{1}{3}(\underline{\mu}^{(4)},\underline{\mu}) - 5(t - 0.85)(\underline{\mu}^{(5)},\underline{\mu}) . \tag{4.296}$$

If $\underline{c}(t)$ is $\frac{1}{3}\underline{\mu}^{(4)} - 5(t - 0.85)\underline{\mu}^{(5)}$, then simultaneous confidence intervals are desired for all linear combinations $(\underline{c}(t),\underline{\mu})$.

The set of all vectors $\underline{c}(t)$ such that t is real is a flat or affine space rather than a linear manifold, but it is not difficult to show that the problem of obtaining simultaneous confidence intervals for $(\underline{c}(t),\underline{\mu})$ for any t is equivalent to obtaining simultaneous confidence intervals for $(h\underline{c}(t),\underline{\mu})$ for any h and t (see Miller 1966). Since the set of all vectors $h\underline{c}(t)$ is the linear manifold $M - N = \text{span}\,\{\underline{\mu}^{(4)},\underline{\mu}^{(5)}\}$, the results of this section can be applied.

Computation of simultaneous confidence intervals for $a + bt = (\underline{c}(t),\underline{\mu})$ requires evaluation of $(\underline{c}(t),\hat{\underline{\mu}})$, the maximum-likelihood estimate of $(\underline{c}(t),\underline{\mu})$, and $(\underline{c}(t),P_M^*(\hat{\underline{\mu}})D^{-1}(\hat{\underline{\mu}})\underline{c}(t))$, the estimated asymptotic covariance of $(\underline{c}(t),\hat{\underline{\mu}})$. To find $(\underline{c}(t),\hat{\underline{\mu}})$, note that

$$\begin{aligned}(\underline{c}(t),\hat{\underline{\mu}}) &= (\underline{c}(t),P_{M-N}\hat{\underline{\mu}}) \\ &= \tfrac{1}{3}(\underline{\mu}^{(4)},P_{M-N}\hat{\underline{\mu}}) - 5(t - 0.85)(\underline{\mu}^{(5)},P_{M-N}\hat{\underline{\mu}}) .\end{aligned} \tag{4.297}$$

In Example 3.3, it is shown that

$$P_{M-N}\hat{\underline{\mu}} = \begin{array}{|rr|} -0.888 & 0.888 \\ -0.399 & 0.399 \\ 0.090 & -0.090 \end{array} . \tag{4.298}$$

Thus

$$(\underline{c}(t),\hat{\underline{\mu}}) = -0.798 + 9.78(t - 0.85) . \tag{4.299}$$

Evaluation of the estimated asymptotic covariance may be made by use of the results of Example 4.5. Using the notation of that example,

$$(4.300)\quad (\underline{c}(t), P_M^*(\hat{\underline{\mu}})D^{-1}(\hat{\underline{\mu}})\underline{c}(t))$$

$$= (\underline{c}(t), [P_M^*(\hat{\underline{\mu}}) - P_N^*(\hat{\underline{\mu}})]D^{-1}(\hat{\underline{\mu}})\underline{c}(t))$$

$$= (\underline{c}(t), D^{-1}(\hat{\underline{\mu}})y)^2/a + (\underline{c}(t), D^{-1}(\hat{\underline{\mu}})\underline{z})^2/d$$

$$= \frac{1}{a} + [b + 10(t - 0.85)]^2/d$$

$$= 0.114 + 0.193\,[10(t - 0.85) - 0.212]^2$$

$$= 0.114 + 19.3\,(t - 0.871)^2 .$$

Thus one may state that with approximate confidence 0.90 that for any real t

$$(4.301)\quad (\underline{c}(t), \underline{\mu}) \in [g(t), h(t)],$$

where

$$(4.302)\quad g(t) = -\,0.798 + 9.78(t - 0.85) - 2.15[.114 + 19.3(t - 0.871)^2]^{\frac{1}{2}}$$

and

$$(4.303)\quad h(t) = -\,0.798 + 9.78(t - 0.85) + 2.15[0.114 + 19.3(t - 0.871)^2]^{\frac{1}{2}} .$$

In these equations 2.15 is $\chi_2(0.10)$. This statement is equivalent to the assertion that with approximate confidence 0.90, for each log dosage t, the probability of death is in the interval $[(e^{g(t)}/(1 + e^{g(t)}), e^{h(t)}/(1 + e^{h(t)})]$.

Simultaneous confidence intervals for the observed log dosages 0.75, 0.85, and 0.95 are readily obtained. The intervals for p_{11}, p_{21}, and p_{31} are respectively [0.042,0.396], [0.175,0.488], and [0.300,0.773]. These intervals are so wide that one may clearly conclude that the data permit only a very rough assessment of the effect of digitalis on frogs. In this example, obtaining simultaneous confidence intervals for all possible t is not very wasteful, even if these three confidence intervals are the only ones desired, for $\Phi^{(0.1016)} = 2.13$. If more intervals are desired, then the method based on $\chi_2(0.10)$ is clearly preferable.

The simultaneous confidence intervals for $(\underline{c}(t), \underline{\mu})$ behave in the same manner as do simultaneous confidence intervals for a regression line (see Miller 1966). The narrowest interval corresponds to $t = 0.871$, a log dosage equal to the average of the log dosages t_i weighted by $\hat{m}_{i1}\hat{m}_{i2}/N_i$. The intervals widen as $|t - 0.871|$ increases in size, and for large enough $|t - 0.871|$, the length is approximately proportional to $|t - 0.871|$.

If the probability of death is not constant with respect to dosage, these simultaneous confidence intervals may also be employed to obtain simultaneous confidence regions for the log dosage t_p which results in a specified probability p of death. To find these regions, observe that

$$(4.304)\qquad (\underline{c}(t),\underline{\mu}) = \log\left(\frac{p}{1-p}\right),$$

and the probability that

$$(4.305)\qquad |(\underline{c}(t_p),\hat{\underline{\mu}}) - (\underline{c}(t_p),\underline{\mu})| \leq \chi_2(\alpha)(\underline{c}(t_p),P_M^*(\hat{\underline{\mu}})D^{-1}(\hat{\underline{\mu}})\underline{c}(t_p))^{\frac{1}{2}}$$

for all $p \in (0,1)$ is approximately $1 - \alpha$. The last result holds since t_p is a continuous monotone increasing function of p with range $(-\infty, \infty)$. The simultaneous 90% confidence region for t_p in this example consists of all t such that

$$(4.306)\qquad \begin{aligned} &- 0.798 + 9.78(t - 0.85) - \log\left(\frac{p}{1-p}\right) \\ &\leq 2.15[0.114 + 19.3(t - 0.871)^2]^{\frac{1}{2}} \end{aligned}$$

(see Miller 1966). In order to determine this set, it is necessary to square both sides of the inequality. The region for t_p then consists of t such that

$$(4.307)\qquad \begin{aligned} &[- 0.798 + 9.78(t - 0.85) - \log\left(\frac{p}{1-p}\right)]^2 \\ &\leq 4.605\,[0.114 + 19.3(t - 0.871)^2]\ . \end{aligned}$$

After some rearrangement of terms, one finds that the region consists of t for which

$$(4.308)\qquad \begin{aligned} &(t - 0.871)^2[(4.605)(19.3) - (9.78)^2] \\ &+ 2(9.78)[\log\left(\frac{p}{1-p}\right) + 0.798 - (9.78)(0.0212)] \\ &+ (4.605)(0.114) - [\log\left(\frac{p}{1-p}\right) + 0.798 - (9.78)(0.0212)]^2 \\ &= -6.79(t - 0.871)^2 + 2(9.78)[\log\left(\frac{p}{1-p}\right) + 0.591] \\ &+ 0.524 - [\log\left(\frac{p}{1-p}\right) + 0.591]^2 \end{aligned}$$

$$= -6.79\{t - 0.871 - \frac{9.78}{6.79}[\log(\frac{p}{1-p}) + 0.591]\}^2$$

$$+ 0.524 - (1 - (9.78)^2/6.79)[\log(\frac{p}{1-p}) + 0.591]^2$$

$$= -6.79[t - 1.72 - 1.44\log(\frac{p}{1-p})]^2 + 0.524 + 13.1[\log(\frac{p}{1-p}) + .591]^2$$

$$\geq 0.$$

Thus the confidence region is the interval $[t_1(p), t_2(p)]$, where

$$t_1(p) = 1.72 + 1.44\log(\frac{p}{1-p}) - \{0.0771 + 1.93[\log(\frac{p}{1-p}) + 0.591]^2\}^{\frac{1}{2}} \quad (4.309)$$

and

$$t_2(p) = 1.72 + 1.44\log(\frac{p}{1-p}) + \{0.0771 + 1.93[\log(\frac{p}{1-p}) + 0.591]^2\}^{\frac{1}{2}} \quad (4.310)$$

These confidence intervals are quite wide. For example, in order to assess the median lethal dose LD50, one notes that if $p = 0.50$, $t_1(p) = 0.854$ and $t_2(p) = 2.586$. The interval for t_p is shortest when $p = 0.356$. At this point, $t_1(p) = 0.592$ and $t_2(p) = 1.158$. Even here, the interval is reasonably wide. Once again, the lack of data causes difficulties.

Although the confidence regions for t_p found in this example are wide, they are at least bounded intervals. Such results need not in general occur. In problems similar to the one considered here, one may obtain regions which are unbounded on one or more sides or regions which consist of two intervals (see Miller 1966).

ANALYSIS OF RESIDUALS

In regression analysis and analysis of variance, examination of residuals forms an important part of good statistical practice (see Draper and Smith 1966). Such an examination may also have considerable value in analysis of frequency data. The residual analysis in the case of frequency data involves investigation of the vector $\underline{r} = D^{-\frac{1}{2}}(\hat{\underline{\mu}})(\underline{n} - \hat{\underline{m}}) = \{(n_i - \hat{m}_i)/\hat{m}_i\}$ of standardized residuals. This vector has an asymptotic distribution independent of the manifold N determined by the sampling technique used. In fact, if $\underline{\mu}^{(N)} \in M$ for all N and $\underline{r}^{(N)} = D^{-\frac{1}{2}}(\hat{\underline{\mu}}^{(N)})(\underline{n}^{(N)} - \hat{\underline{m}}^{(N)})$, then (4.16) and (4.20) imply that

$$\underline{r}^{(N)} \xrightarrow{\mathcal{D}} N(\underline{0}, I - A_M(\underline{\mu}^*)). \quad (4.311)$$

Thus a residual r_i, $i \in I$, is approximately distributed as $N(0,c_i)$, where $c_i \leq 1$. Since $c_i^{(N)} = (\underline{\delta}^{(i)},[I - A_M(\underline{\hat{\mu}}^{(N)})]\underline{\delta}^{(i)}) \xrightarrow{P} (\underline{\delta}^{(i)},[I - A_M(\underline{\mu}^*)]\underline{\delta}^{(i)})$, where $\underline{\delta}^{(i)}$ is the ith standard basis vector (see chapter 1), the sequence of residuals $\{\underline{r}^{(N)}\}$ has the property that $r_i^{(N)}/(c_i^{(N)})^{\frac{1}{2}} \xrightarrow{\mathcal{D}} N(0,1)$ for each $i \in I$. Thus the adjusted residual $s_i = r_i/(c_i)^{\frac{1}{2}}$, $i \in I$, is approximately distributed as $N(0,1)$, where $c_i = (\underline{\delta}^{(i)},[I - A_M(\underline{\hat{\mu}})]\underline{\delta}^{(i)})$.

The definition of $\underline{r}$ as $\{(n_i - \hat{m}_i)/\hat{m}_i\}^{\frac{1}{2}}$ is to some extent arbitrary. Other asymptotically equivalent definitions include $\{2(n_i^{\frac{1}{2}} - \hat{m}_i^{\frac{1}{2}})\}$ and $\{n_i^{\frac{1}{2}} + (n_i + 1)^{\frac{1}{2}} - (4\hat{m}_i + 1)^{\frac{1}{2}}\}$, the vector of Freeman-Tukey deviates (see Freeman and Tukey 1950). Analyses based on other choices of residuals have been considered by Cox and Snell (1968). The choice of $\underline{r}$ made here is based on simplicity. No clear evidence exists that other choices are better for use with general log-linear models.

Systematic deviations of the adjusted residuals from the expected $N(0,1)$ distribution can be used to isolate inadequacies in the model when they exist. Such analyses are complicated by correlations among residuals and by the restraint that by Theorem 2.1, $\underline{r}$ must be orthogonal to the image of M under $D(\underline{\hat{\mu}})$; however, in many cases these problems are relatively minor (see Anscombe and Tukey 1963). In some problems, computation of the terms c_i, $i \in I$, is relatively tedious. In such cases, the standardized residuals can be rather informative, but analysis is less precise than with adjusted residuals. Specific methods for analysis of residuals depend on the structure of the table. Draper and Smith (1966) suggest a variety of possible graphical and analytic techniques which may be used in regression analysis. Similar techniques may be appropriate in analysis of frequency data. Further details are provided by Anscombe and Tukey (1963).

Example 4.20. Yates (1948) considers a study which investigates the relationship between quality of school children's homework and the conditions under which it is carried out. The data are summarized in table 4.2. In this table, the index set I is $\overline{3} \times \overline{5}$. If teacher's rating and homework condition are independent, then

$$m_{ij} = m_{i+}m_{+j}/m_{++} . \tag{4.312}$$

Just as in Example 1.4, this condition is equivalent to the hypothesis that $\underline{\mu}$ can be written as

$$\mu_{ij} = a + b_i + c_j , \tag{4.313}$$

TABLE 4.2

RELATION BETWEEN TEACHER'S RATING AND HOMEWORK CONDITIONS

Teacher's Rating	Homework Conditions				
	A	B	C	D	E
A	141	67	114	79	39
B	131	66	143	72	35
C	36	14	38	28	16

where

(4.314)
$$\sum_{i=1}^{3} b_i = \sum_{j=1}^{5} c_j$$
$$= 0 \;.$$

The set of $\underline{\mu}$ such that (4.313) is satisfied for some a, $\{b_i\}$, and $\{c_j\}$ is a linear manifold M. As shown in chapter 5, M is a hierarchical manifold with dimension $(3 - 1) + (5 - 1) + 1 = 7$ which is spanned by the vectors $\{\underline{\nu}(\{1\},i): i \in \overline{3}\}$ and $\{\underline{\nu}(\{2\},j): j \in \overline{5}\}$, where for $i' \in \overline{3}$, $i \in \overline{3}$, $j' \in \overline{5}$, and $j \in \overline{5}$,

(4.315)
$$\nu_{ij}(\{1\},i') = \delta_{ii'}$$

and

(4.316)
$$\nu_{ij}(\{2\},j') = \delta_{jj'} \;.$$

The maximum-likelihood estimate $\hat{\underline{m}}$ is $\{n_{i+}n_{+j}/n_{++}\}$, and the operator $I - A_M(\hat{\underline{\mu}}^*)$ satisfies

(4.317)
$$I - A_M(\hat{\underline{\mu}}) =$$
$$I - \sum_{i=1}^{3} \frac{1}{n_{i+}} [D^{\frac{1}{2}}(\hat{\underline{\mu}})\underline{\nu}(\{1\},i)] \otimes [D^{\frac{1}{2}}(\hat{\underline{\mu}})\underline{\nu}(\{1\},i)]$$
$$- \sum_{j=1}^{5} \frac{1}{n_{+j}} [D^{\frac{1}{2}}(\hat{\underline{\mu}})\underline{\nu}(\{2\},j)] \otimes [D^{\frac{1}{2}}(\hat{\underline{\mu}})\underline{\nu}(\{2\},j)]$$
$$+ \frac{1}{n_{++}} [D^{\frac{1}{2}}(\hat{\underline{\mu}})\underline{e}] \otimes [D^{\frac{1}{2}}(\hat{\underline{\mu}})\underline{e}] \;.$$

Thus if $\langle i,j\rangle \in \overline{3} \times \overline{5}$, then

(4.318)
$$c_{ij} = 1 - \frac{1}{n_{i+}}\left(\frac{n_{i+}n_{+j}}{n_{++}}\right) - \frac{1}{n_{+j}}\left(\frac{n_{i+}n_{+j}}{n_{++}}\right) + \frac{1}{n_{+j}}\left(\frac{n_{i+}n_{+j}}{n_{++}}\right)$$
$$= 1 - \frac{n_{+j}}{n_{++}} - \frac{n_{i+}}{n_{++}} + \frac{n_{i+}}{n_{++}}\frac{n_{+j}}{n_{++}}$$
$$= \left(1 - \frac{n_{i+}}{n_{++}}\right)\left(1 - \frac{n_{+j}}{n_{++}}\right) .$$

The maximum-likelihood estimate $\hat{\underline{m}}$ then satisfies

(4.319) $\hat{\underline{m}}$ =

133.0	63.5	127.4	77.3	38.9
135.1	64.5	129.4	78.5	39.5
39.9	19.0	38.2	23.2	11.7

.

The standardized residual vector $\underline{r}$ is then

(4.320) $\underline{r}$ =

0.694	0.443	-1.185	0.194	0.022
-0.354	0.189	1.195	-0.736	-0.713
-0.617	-1.155	-0.035	0.999	1.272

,

and the adjusted residual vector is

(4.321) $\underline{s}$ =

1.103	0.635	-1.866	0.284	0.031
-0.565	0.272	1.892	-1.082	-0.997
-0.792	-1.339	-0.044	1.180	1.427

.

The analysis begins by considering the test for goodness of fit which uses the null hypothesis H_0: $\underline{\mu} \in M$ and the alternative H_A: $\underline{\mu} \in R^{\overline{3}\times\overline{5}}$. The Pearson chi-square statistic thus satisfies

(4.322)
$$C(\underline{\nu},\hat{\underline{\mu}}) = \sum_{i=1}^{3}\sum_{j=1}^{5} (n_{ij} - n_{i+}n_{+j}/n_{++})^2/(n_{i+}n_{+j}/n_{++})$$
$$= 9.09,$$

where $\underline{\nu} = \{\log n_i\}$. The likelihood ratio chi-square statistic is

(4.323)
$$-2\Delta(\underline{n},\underline{\nu},\hat{\underline{\mu}}) = 2\sum_{i=1}^{3}\sum_{j=1}^{5} n_{ij}\log(n_{ij}n_{++}/n_{i+}n_{+j})$$
$$= 9.04.$$

Since $R^{\overline{3x5}}$ has dimension 15 and M has dimension 7, the degrees of freedom for the test statistics is 8. Since $\chi_8^2(0.30) = 9.52$, these statistics do not suggest the existence of any deviations from the null hypothesis. Nonetheless, it may be the case that a small relationship may exist between teacher's rating and homework conditions, but the sample is not large enough for the tests to have much power. The behavior of the residuals may be used to investigate this possibility.

The initial steps in the analysis of the residuals can be applied to any set of residuals, no matter what the structure of the table may be. One begins by searching for unusually large residuals. Even if the chi-square statistics are not large, such residuals still suggest inadequacies in the model and they give an indication of which observations n_{ij} are poorly explained by the model. In this example, the largest observed value of $|s_{ij}|$ is 1.892, which is not unusually large for the magnitude of a standard normal deviate. A second general procedure, the normal plot, may be used to detect more subtle peculiarities in the residuals. In this technique, which is discussed by Tukey (1962) in some detail, the adjusted residuals s_{ij} are ordered and then plotted on normal probability paper. The kth smallest adjusted residual of the $q = 15$ adjusted residuals in the table is assigned to the probability coordinate $(3k - 1)/(3q + 1)$. Alternative possibilities are $(k - \frac{1}{2})/q$ and $k/(q + 1)$. Such a plot is shown in figure 4.1. In the figure, the dashed line represents percentiles for the standard normal distribution. The residuals tend to be slightly larger than expected, but this plot does not suggest any unusual behavior of the data. Thus gross analyses of the residuals provide no evidence of any inadequacies in the model.

Other analyses depend upon the specific structure of the table. It is interesting to note that the largest residual occurs at the center of the table; more children have rating B and homework condition C than expected on the basis of independence. The result is not statistically significant at the 5% level, even if one ignores the fact that the appropriate test is being made after the data have been examined; however, some tendency to use the middle ratings could conceivably exist. The adjusted residuals s_{11} and s_{35} are positive and s_{31} is negative. This result faintly suggests that better conditions for homework are positively related to better teacher ratings, although the small positive value of s_{15} does little to support this hypothesis.

If one is persistent, the possibility of a positive relationship may be investigated by introducing a linear-by-linear term into the model (see Tukey 1962 and chapter 5). The

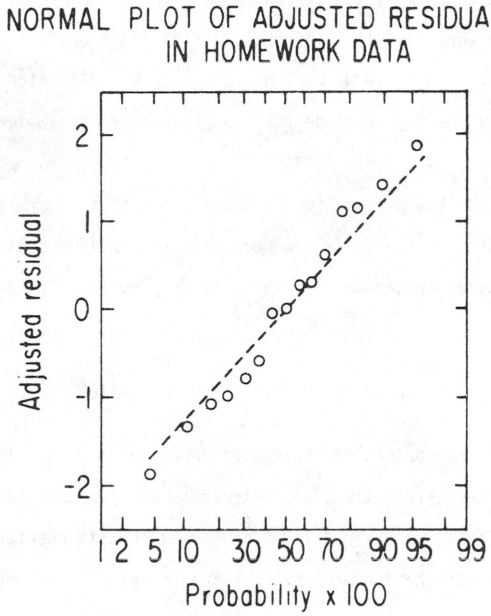

Figure 4.1.

linear manifold M^* is now considered, where M^* is the direct sum of M and span $\{\underline{z}\}$, and where

(4.324)
$$\underline{z} = \begin{array}{|ccccc|} 2 & 1 & 0 & -1 & -2 \\ 0 & 0 & 0 & 0 & 0 \\ -2 & -1 & 0 & 1 & 2 \end{array}$$

If

(4.325)
$$\mu_{ij} = a + b_i + c_j + dz_{ij},$$

where

(4.326)
$$\sum_{i=1}^{3} b_i = \sum_{j=1}^{5} c_j$$
$$= 0$$

and d is positive, then a positive relationship exists between homework conditions and teacher ratings.

The maximum-likelihood estimates corresponding to M^* may be found by the Newton-

Raphson algorithm by methods very similar to those used in Example 3.2. In this example, the basic vectors used were $\{\underline{\nu}(\{1\},i), i \in \overline{3}\}$, $\{\underline{\nu}(\{2\},j), j \in \overline{4}\}$, and $\underline{z}$. The likelihood ratio chi-square for $H_0: \underline{\mu} \in M$ and $H_A: \underline{\mu} \in M^*$ is 2.33, which is not significant at the 10% level. Thus one may conclude that no evidence exists which would justify rejection of the model.

At this point, the basic tools for estimation and testing are available for use with general log-linear models. It is now necessary to consider specific classes of models which are important in the analysis of frequency data. The next four chapters are devoted to this task.

ACCURACY OF ASYMPTOTIC APPROXIMATIONS

In this chapter, approximations have been developed for distributions of maximum-likelihood estimates, test statistics, and residuals, and approximate tests and confidence intervals have been created; however, the methods used in this chapter do not provide any indication of how accurate these approximations are for particular mean vectors $\underline{m}$. The statistician who wishes to use these methods clearly should have this information, but it is far from clear how this need can be satisfied. Very little is known about the accuracy of the approximations commonly used in contingency table analysis, and rectifying the situation appears to be an arduous task. Nevertheless, some knowledge concerning special cases does exist, and some tentative recommendations can be made. These recommendations are likely to be refined as practical experience with log-linear models increases and as more Monte Carlo studies are made, but a statistician who follows these suggestions will probably not be led too much astray.

The first tentative recommendation is that approximations considered in this chapter are generally adequate if $m_i \geq 25$ for all $i \in I$. This recommendation is mainly important when confidence intervals are constructed, residuals are analyzed, or asymptotic covariances are estimated. In many cases in which the dimension of M is much less than the dimension of R^I, some m_i may be much less than 25. Nevertheless, extreme caution should be exercised when the sum of the m_i does not exceed 25.

The second tentative recommendation is that the chi-square approximation for the level and power of the statistical tests proposed in this chapter should be adequate whenever $m_i \geq 5$ for all $i \in I$. If the test involves more than one degree of freedom, some of the m_i may be less than 5; however, serious problems may arise in some cases if some m_i are less than 1.

These recommendations are based on slender evidence. The approximation of the distribution of a Poisson random variable n_1 with mean m_1 by the normal distribution is fairly satisfactory if $m_1 \geq 25$, and the corresponding approximation for a binomial random variable n_1 with sample size N and probability p is fairly satisfactory if $m_1 = Np \geq 25$ and $m_2 = N(1 - p) \geq 25$. These results may be verified empirically and by reference to asymptotic expansions (see Feller 1966). Examination of more complex sampling procedures is exceedingly difficult, as may be seen by inspection of Yarnold (1970).

The rule which permits some m_i less than 25 when the dimension of M is small but $\sum_{i\in I} m_i \geq 25$ is based on the observation that if Poisson sampling is used and $\underline{\mu} \in \text{span}\{\underline{e}\}$, then $\hat{\underline{m}} = \bar{n}.\underline{e}$, where $\bar{n}. = q^{-1} \sum_{i\in I} n_i$ and I has q elements. Since $\sum_{i\in I} n_i$ has a Poisson distribution with mean qm_{i*} for an arbitrary $i* \in I$, the normal approximation for $\hat{\underline{m}}$ is fairly adequate if $qm_{i*} = \sum_{i\in I} m_i \geq 25$.

The observations concerning chi-square tests are based on Cochran's (1954) recommendations for the Pearson chi-square test of independence for an $r \times c$ contingency table. He recommends that all m_i exceed 1 and at least 80% exceed 5. This rule has been used extensively for other testing situations, and it generally appears to be conservative. Simple special cases have been explained by Lewontin and Felsenstein (1965), Good, Gover, and Mitchell (1970), Yarnold (1970), and Odoroff (1970), among others. In all of these studies, the requirement that $m_i \geq 5$ for $i \in I$ is found to be a conservative one. The minimum value of m_i permitted varies considerably from study to study, depending on the null and alternative hypotheses considered. The most conservative requirement is made by Odoroff in his study of tests for $2 \times 2 \times 2$ and $3 \times 2 \times 2$ tables with no three-factor interaction. He recommends that all m_i be at least 4.

It may appear strange that the values of m_i required for chi-square tests appear to be much smaller than those required for other purposes. The apparent explanation is that errors associated with the levels of chi-square tests primarily reflect the discreteness of the distribution of $\underline{n}$, whereas deviations of the distributions of $\hat{\underline{\mu}}$, $\hat{\underline{m}}$, $\underline{r}$, and $\underline{s}$ from their asymptotic distributions also reflect the skewness of the distribution of $\underline{n}$.

Just as in the case of approximate chi-square tests, the difference between the nominal and actual levels of approximate confidence intervals also tends to be relatively small, but approximate confidence intervals can still be somewhat unsatisfactory when m_i does not exceed 25. The basic problem is illustrated by the following example due to Schaffer (1971).

Example 4.21. Suppose $I = \{1,2\}$ and n_1 is binomial with sample size $N = 100$ and probability p. An approximate 95% confidence interval for p is

$$\left[n_1/N - 1.96\left[\left(\frac{n_1}{N}\right)\left(\frac{n_2}{N}\right)/N\right]^{\frac{1}{2}},\ n_1/N + 1.96\left[\left(\frac{n_1}{N}\right)\left(\frac{n_2}{N}\right)/N\right]^{\frac{1}{2}}\right].$$

The probability p is included in this interval if

$$g = \frac{N}{N+Z^2}\{Np + Z^2/2 - Z[Np(1-p) + Z^2/4]^{\frac{1}{2}}\} < n_1 < h \tag{4.327}$$

$$= \frac{N}{N+Z^2}\{Np + Z^2/2 + Z[Np(1-p) + Z^2/4]^{\frac{1}{2}}\} ,$$

where $Z = 1.96$ (see Cramér 1946). If $p = 0.2$, the probability that $g < n_1 < h$ is 0.933, which may be compared to the nominal value of 0.950. This discrepancy is noticeable but probably acceptable in size for most purposes. However, the probability that $n_1 \le g$ is 0.047 and the probability that $n_1 \ge h$ is 0.020. Since both nominal probabilities are 0.025, the confidence interval is not very satisfactory if even tails are considered to be desirable. Schaffer (1971) explains the difficulty by showing that the difference between the nominal and actual value of $P\{g \le n_1 \le h\}$ primarily reflects the discreteness of the binomial distribution, while the difference between the nominal and actual value of $P\{n_1 < g\}$ or $P\{n_1 > h\}$ reflects both the discreteness and the skewness of the distribution of n_1.

Since so little is really known about the accuracy of the approximations of this chapter, it is not surprising that little is known about how to improve the approximations. Some efforts associated with estimation of linear functionals of $\underline{\mu}$ when $\underline{n}$ is multinomial are discussed by Goodman (1966), Gart and Zweifel (1967), and Gart (1970), among others. These studies have generally emphasized construction of estimates with reduced bias for the trivial model $\underline{\mu} \in R^I$; whether similar estimates have value in other cases is unclear.

Chapter 5

COMPLETE FACTORIAL TABLES

INTRODUCTION

The simplest contingency table models are based on complete factorial analysis of variance models. In these models, the index set I is $\prod_{j=1}^{d}\bar{r}_j$, the Cartesian product of the d sets $\bar{r}_j$, $j \in \bar{d}$, where $r_j \geq 1$ represents possible values assumed by a discrete variable. The models make no use of ordinal relations among categories represented by sets $\bar{r}_j$, $j \in \bar{d}$. In this sense, they resemble analysis of variance models which do not consider trend effects.

Example 5.1. In Example 1.5, $I = \bar{2} \times \bar{2}$. Thus $\bar{r}_1 = \bar{r}_2 = \bar{2}$. The group the infant belongs to is represented by $\bar{r}_1$, where 1 is for toxemia and 2 is for control. The sex of the infant is represented by $\bar{r}_2$, where 1 is for male and 2 is for female. In the model suggested by (1.8),

$$\mu_{ij} = a + b_i + c_j, \tag{5.1}$$

where $i \in \bar{2}$, $j \in \bar{2}$, and

$$\sum_{i=1}^{2} b_i = \sum_{j=1}^{2} c_j = 0. \tag{5.2}$$

In analysis-of-variance terminology, this model for μ_{ij} is the additive model for a 2 x 2 table.

Example 5.2. In Example 3.2, the index set $I = \bar{3} \times \bar{2} \times \bar{2} \times \bar{6}$. Thus $d = 4$, $\bar{r}_1 = \bar{3}$, $\bar{r}_2 = \bar{r}_3 = \bar{2}$, and $\bar{r}_4 = \bar{6}$. In this example, $\bar{r}_1$ represents tribe; $\bar{r}_2$, sex; $\bar{r}_3$, presence or absence of *torus*; and $\bar{r}_4$, age group. The model suggested by (3.38) is not an elementary analysis-of-variance model since it exploits the ordering of age groups. Such models are not considered until the end of this chapter. On the other hand, one might let

(5.3) $$\mu_{ijk\ell} = a_i + b_j + c_{k\ell}$$

for some $\{a_i\}$, $\{b_j\}$, and $\{c_{k\ell}\}$. Such a model corresponds to an analysis-of-variance model for a four-way table in which only main effects and the interaction between the third and fourth variables are present. This correspondence may be clearer if a unique parametrization is provided for $\mu_{ijk\ell}$. Any $\underline{\mu}$ which satisfies (5.3) for all $\langle i,j,k,\ell\rangle \in \overline{3} \times \overline{2} \times \overline{2} \times \overline{6}$ must also satisfy an equation

(5.4) $$\mu_{ijk\ell} = \alpha + \beta_i + \gamma_j + \delta_k + \varepsilon_\ell + \eta_k ,$$

where

(5.5) $$\beta_+ = \gamma_+ = \delta_+ = \varepsilon_+ = \eta_{+\ell} = \eta_{k+} = 0 .$$

In an analysis of variance β_i, γ_j, δ_k, and ε_ℓ are main effects and $\eta_{k\ell}$ is the interaction between the third and fourth variables.

In a complete factorial table, $n_{\underline{i}}$ represents the number of times the independent random vectors $\underline{X}_t$ defined on I have value $\underline{i}$, where $t \in \overline{N}$. The random vectors $\underline{X}_t$ may arise from three basic sampling methods. If N is a Poisson random variable and the $\underline{X}_t$ are identically distributed, then the $n_{\underline{i}}$ are independent Poisson random variables. If N is a constant and the $\underline{X}_t$ are identically distributed, then $\underline{n}$ has a multinomial distribution. The last possibility is somewhat more complicated. A set $G \subset \overline{d}$ is chosen so that the conditional distribution of $\{X_{tj}: j \in \overline{d} - G\}$ given $X_{tj}: j \in G$ is independent of t. If $\underline{\overline{i}} \in \prod_{j \in G} \overline{r}_j$, then $N_{\underline{\overline{i}}}$ t's are selected so that $\{X_{tj}: j \in G\} = \{\overline{i}_j: j \in G\}$. In this case $\underline{n}$ consists of a collection of independent multinomial samples.

Example 5.3. Example 5.1 can be used to illustrate the various sampling methods considered. Poisson sampling is discussed in Example 1.8. In this example, infant t is described by a random vector $\langle X_{t1}, X_{t2}\rangle$, where X_{t1} is 1 if the infant is in the toxemia group and 2 otherwise, and X_{t2} is 1 if the infant is male or 2 if the infant is female. The number N of infants studied is a Poisson random variable. In Example 1.9, several possibilities are contemplated. If a random sample of 10,000 infants is taken, then N is constant and the vectors $\underline{X}_t$ are distributed as in Poisson sampling. If 2,000 toxemia babies and 8,000 controls are classified by sex, then $G = \{1\}$ and the distribution of sex, X_{t2}, depends on t only through the group, X_{t1}. The two independent multinomial samples have sizes $N_1 = 2{,}000$ and $N_2 = 8{,}000$.

Log-linear models have been developed for factorial tables by Birch (1963), Bishop (1967), Goodman (1970), and others. The models which they have considered are generally known as hierarchical models. They correspond to familiar models used in analysis of variance for factorial tables. These models are remarkably well suited for use with the iterative proportional fitting algorithm associated with Deming and Stephan, and some of them have closed-form maximum-likelihood estimates; consequently, they have received considerable attention.

Rigorous analysis of the properties of these models has generally been avoided due to the complex nature of the linear manifolds encountered in such analyses. Bishop (1970) and Goodman (1970) have proposed conditions for existence of closed-form maximum-likelihood estimates which are satisfactory when $d \le 4$; however, these conditions do not apply to all hierarchical models for which $d > 4$. More recently, Goodman (1971b) has considered a constructive procedure which for any d provides closed-form estimates whenever they exist. His approach is closely related to the one adopted in this chapter, although the recursive definitions used in this chapter may at first sight appear to have little relationship to the formulas in Goodman (1971b). The approach adopted in Goodman (1971b) has the advantage that it is more intuitive, while the techniques used here permit more detailed analyses of properties of models with closed-form maximum-likelihood estimates. Analysis of closed-form solutions has also been made in terms of the behavior of the Deming-Stephan algorithm. It has been observed (see Bishop 1967) that this converges to the maximum likelihood estimate of $\underline{m}$ after one cycle if $\underline{m}$ has a closed-form maximum-likelihood estimate. In this chapter, it is demonstrated that this observation depends on d. If the unit vector is used as a starting value, the algorithm converges in one cycle whenever $d \le 6$ and a closed-form estimate exists. This property does not necessarily hold if $d > 6$. If an arbitrary starting value is used, the algorithm converges in one cycle whenever $d \le 4$ and a closed-form estimate exists. Convergence in one cycle need not occur if $d > 4$. These conclusions are reached by use of direct products of simple linear manifolds defined on R^{r_j}, where $j \in \overline{d}$. These direct products are also used to suggest a simple modification of the Deming-Stephan procedure for use with nonhierarchical models. This modification removes the computational problems associated with such models, although it does not solve problems of interpretation. Since results depend on the use of direct products, it is necessary to examine these manifolds in detail.

DIRECT PRODUCTS

Direct products are closely related to tensor products, Kronecker products, and outer products (see Halmos 1958 and Eaton 1970). For the purposes of this paper, a direct product may be defined by considering an index set I which is a Cartesian product of sets I_j, where $j \in \overline{d}$. Thus $I = \Pi_{j=1}^{d} I_j$. If $\underline{\mu}^{(j)} \in R^{I_j}$ for each $j \in \overline{d}$, then the direct product $\otimes_{j=1}^{d} \underline{\mu}^{(j)}$ is the element $\underline{\mu}$ of R^I such that

$$\mu_{i_1 \ldots i_d} = \prod_{j=1}^{d} \mu_{i_j}^{(j)} \tag{5.6}$$

for every $i_j \in I_j$ and for every $j \in \overline{d}$. The operation $\otimes$ is a multiliner mapping from $\Pi_{j=1}^{d} R^{I_j}$ to R^I (see Loomis and Sternberg 1968). If M_j is a manifold in R^{I_j}, then the direct product $\otimes_{j=1}^{d} M_j$ is the manifold spanned by all vectors $\underline{\mu} \in R^I$ such that $\underline{\mu} = \otimes_{j=1}^{d} \underline{\mu}^{(j)}$ for some $\underline{\mu}^{(j)} \in M_j$, where $j \in \overline{d}$.

Example 5.4. Consider the index set $I = \overline{2} \times \overline{2}$ of Example 5.1. The set of M such that (5.1) and (5.2) hold may be described in various ways in terms of sums of direct products of linear manifolds in R^2. To do so, suppose that $\underline{\mu}^{(0)} = \langle 1,1 \rangle$ and $\underline{\mu}^{(1)} = \langle 1,-1 \rangle$. Then

$$\underline{\mu}^{(0)} \otimes \underline{\mu}^{(0)} = \begin{bmatrix} 1 & 1 \\ 1 & 1 \end{bmatrix}, \tag{5.7}$$

$$\underline{\mu}^{(0)} \otimes \underline{\mu}^{(1)} = \begin{bmatrix} 1 & -1 \\ 1 & -1 \end{bmatrix}, \tag{5.8}$$

$$\underline{\mu}^{(1)} \otimes \underline{\mu}^{(0)} = \begin{bmatrix} 1 & 1 \\ -1 & -1 \end{bmatrix}, \tag{5.9}$$

and

$$\underline{\mu}^{(1)} \otimes \underline{\mu}^{(1)} = \begin{bmatrix} 1 & -1 \\ -1 & 1 \end{bmatrix}. \tag{5.10}$$

If (5.1) and (5.2) hold, then

$$\underline{\mu} = a\underline{\mu}^{(0)} \otimes \underline{\mu}^{(0)} + b_1\underline{\mu}^{(1)} \otimes \underline{\mu}^{(0)} + c_1\underline{\mu}^{(0)} \otimes \underline{\mu}^{(1)}. \tag{5.11}$$

If $M_0 = \text{span}\,\{\underline{\mu}^{(0)}\}$ and $M_1 = \text{span}\,\{\underline{\mu}^{(1)}\}$, then (5.11) implies that $\underline{\mu}$ is in the sum of the linear manifolds $M_i \otimes M_j = \text{span}\,\{\underline{\mu}^{(i)} \otimes \underline{\mu}^{(j)}\}$, where $\langle i,j\rangle \in \overline{2} \times \overline{2} - \{\langle 2,2\rangle\}$. Conversely, if $\underline{\mu}$ satisfies (5.11), then (5.1) and (5.2) are satisfied if $b_2 = -b_1$ and $c_2 = -c_1$. Thus the set M of $\underline{\mu}$ such that (5.1) and (5.2) hold if the linear manifold $(M_0 \otimes M_0) + (M_1 \otimes M_0) + (M_0 \otimes M_1)$. Since span $\{\underline{\mu}^{(0)},\underline{\mu}^{(1)}\} = R^2$, (5.11) implies that the condition $\underline{\mu} \in M$ is equivalent to the condition $\underline{\mu} \in (R^2 \otimes M_0) + (M_0 \otimes M_1)$. On the other hand, since $R^2 = \text{span}\,\{\langle 1,0\rangle,\langle 0,1\rangle\}$, one has the alternative parametrization

(5.12) $$\mu_{ij} = b_i' + c_j\ ,$$

where $c_1 + c_2 = 0$.

A number of important results follow from the definitions. These are summarized in the following lemmas:

LEMMA 5.1. *Suppose* $\{\underline{\mu}^{(k_j,j)} : k_j \in \overline{p}_j\}$ *is a basis of* M_j *for* $j \in \overline{d}$. *Suppose* $S = \{\otimes_{j=1}^{d}\underline{\mu}^{(k_j,j)} : k_j \in \overline{p}_j\ \forall j \in \overline{d}\}$. *Then* S *is a basis for* $\otimes_{j=1}^{d}M_j$, *and* $\otimes_{j=1}^{d}M_j$ *has dimension* $\prod_{j=1}^{d}p_j$.

Remark. This proof is based on a similar result in Halmos (1958).

Proof. If $\underline{\mu}^{(j)} \in M_j$ for every $j \in \overline{d}$, then $\otimes_{j=1}^{d}\mu^{(j)}$ is a linear combination of vectors in S. Thus S spans $\otimes_{j=1}^{d}M_j$. To prove independence, we show that if $f \le d$, then

(5.13) $$\sum\left\{a_{\underline{k}} \bigotimes_{j=1}^{f} \underline{\mu}^{(k_j,j)} : \underline{k} \in \prod_{j=1}^{f} I_j\right\} = \underline{0}$$

implies $a_{\underline{k}} = 0$ for every $k \in \prod_{j=1}^{d}I_j$. Here $\underline{k} = \{k_j\colon j \in \overline{f}\}$. This statement clearly holds if $f = 1$. Suppose that the statement holds if $f \le f' < d$. By induction, it is sufficient to prove that the statement holds if $f = f' + 1$. Now if $f = f' + 1$, and if $k_{f'+1} \in I_{f'+1}$, then

(5.14) $$\sum\left\{a_{\underline{k}} \bigotimes_{j=1}^{f'} \underline{\mu}^{(k_j,j)} : \underline{k} \in \left(\prod_{j=1}^{f'} I_j\right) \times \{k_{f'+1}\}\right\} = \underline{0}.$$

By the induction hypothesis, $a_{\underline{k}} = 0$ for every $\underline{k} \in \prod_{j=1}^{f'+1}I_j$. Thus S is independent, and $\otimes_{j=1}^{d}M_j$ has dimension $\prod_{j=1}^{d}p_j$, the number of elements of S.||

Example 5.5. If $R^2 \otimes M_0$ is defined as in Example 5.4, then $\{\langle 1,0\rangle,\langle 0,1\rangle\}$ is a basis of R^2 and $\{\langle 1,1\rangle\}$ is a basis of M_0. The set S consists of the vectors

(5.15)
$$\langle 1,0\rangle \otimes \langle 1,1\rangle = \begin{array}{|cc|} 1 & 1 \\ 0 & 0 \end{array}$$

and

(5.16)
$$\langle 0,1\rangle \otimes \langle 1,1\rangle = \begin{array}{|cc|} 0 & 0 \\ 1 & 1 \end{array}$$

These two vectors are a basis of $R^2 \otimes M_0$, and this manifold has dimension $2 \times 1 = 2$. Since $\underline{\mu}^{(0)} \otimes \underline{\mu}^{(1)}$ is not contained in $R^2 \otimes M_0$, M has dimension 3.

Example 5.6. The space R^{I_j} has dimension equal to the number p_j of elements of I_j. Thus $\otimes_{j=1}^{d} R^{I_j}$ has dimension $\prod_{j=1}^{d} p_j$, which is the number of elements of I. Therefore, $R^I = \otimes_{j=1}^{d} R^{I_j}$.

LEMMA 5.2. *If* $(.,.)_J$ *is the conventional inner product on* R^J *and if for each* $j \in \overline{d}$, $\underline{\mu}^{(j)} \in R^{I_j}$ *and* $\underline{\nu}^{(j)} \in R^{I_j}$, *then*

(5.17)
$$\left(\bigotimes_{j=1}^{d} \underline{\mu}^{(j)}, \bigotimes_{j=1}^{d} \underline{\nu}^{(j)}\right)_I = \prod_{j=1}^{d} (\underline{\mu}^{(j)}, \underline{\nu}^{(j)})_{I_j}$$

Proof. Observe that

(5.18)
$$\left(\bigotimes_{j=1}^{d} \underline{\mu}^{(j)}, \bigotimes_{j=1}^{d} \underline{\nu}^{(j)}\right)_I = \sum_{\underline{i} \in I} \prod_{j=1}^{d} \mu_{i_j}^{(j)} \prod_{j=1}^{d} \nu_{i_j}^{(j)}$$

$$= \prod_{j=1}^{d} \sum_{i_j \in I_j} \mu_{i_j}^{(j)} \nu_{i_j}^{(j)}$$

$$= \prod_{j=1}^{d} (\underline{\mu}^{(j)}, \underline{\nu}^{(j)})_{I_j} . \;\|$$

Example 5.7. In Example 5.4, the vectors $\underline{\mu}^{(i)} \otimes \underline{\mu}^{(j)}$ and $\underline{\mu}^{(i')} \otimes \underline{\mu}^{(j')}$ are orthogonal if $i \neq i'$ or $j \neq j'$. This follows since

(5.19)
$$(\underline{\mu}^{(i)} \otimes \underline{\mu}^{(j)}, \underline{\mu}^{(i')} \otimes \underline{\mu}^{(j')})_{\overline{2}\times\overline{2}} = (\underline{\mu}^{(i)}, \underline{\mu}^{(i')})_2 (\underline{\mu}^{(j)}, \underline{\mu}^{(j')})_2$$

and

(5.20)
$$(\underline{\mu}^{(0)}, \underline{\mu}^{(1)})_2 = 0.$$

Thus (5.11) provides a decomposition of $\underline{\mu}$ into orthogonal components.

LEMMA 5.3. *Suppose that* $M_{j'}$ *is the direct sum of* $M_{j'}^{(1)}$ *and* $M_{j'}^{(2)}$. *Suppose that*

$M = \otimes_{j=1}^{d} M_j$ *and for* $k \in \overline{2}$, $M^{(k)} = \otimes_{j=1}^{d} M_j^{(k)}$, *where* $M_j^{(k)} = M_j$ *for* $k \in \overline{2}$ *and* $j \in \overline{d} - \{j'\}$. *Then* M *is the direct sum of* $M^{(1)}$ *and* $M^{(2)}$.

Proof. Suppose that $\underline{\mu}^{(j)} \in M_j$ for each $j \in \overline{d}$. Suppose that $\underline{\mu}^{(j')} = \underline{\mu}^{(j',1)} + \underline{\mu}^{(j',2)}$, where $\underline{\mu}^{(j',k)} \in M_j^{(k)}$ for $k \in \overline{2}$. Let $\underline{\mu}^{(j,k)} = \underline{\mu}^{(j)}$ if $k \in \overline{2}$ and $j \in \overline{d} - \{j'\}$. Then by multilinearity,

$$\bigotimes_{j=1}^{d} \underline{\mu}^{(j)} = \bigotimes_{j=1}^{d} \underline{\mu}^{(j,1)} + \bigotimes_{j=1}^{d} \underline{\mu}^{(j,2)} . \tag{5.21}$$

Thus $M = M^{(1)} + M^{(2)}$, where M has dimension $\prod_{j=1}^{d} p_j$. If $M_{j'}^{(k)}$ has dimension $p_{j'}^{(k)}$ for $k \in \overline{2}$, then $M^{(k)}$ has dimension $p_{j'}^{(k)} \prod\{p_j: j \in \overline{d}, j \neq j'\}$. Now

$$p_{j'}^{(1)} \prod\{p_j: j \in \overline{d}, j \neq j'\} + p_{j'}^{(2)} \prod\{p_j: j \in \overline{d}, j \neq j'\} = \prod_{j=1}^{d} p_j. \tag{5.22}$$

Therefore, M is the direct sum of $M^{(1)}$ and $M^{(2)}$. ||

Example 5.8. Suppose $M_1 \subset R^{I_1}$, $M_2 \subset R^{I_1}$, $M_3 \subset R^{I_2}$, $M_4 \subset R^{I_2}$, $M_1 \cap M_2 = \{\underline{0}\}$, and $M_3 \cap M_4 = \{\underline{0}\}$. Then

$$\begin{aligned} &(M_1 \oplus M_2) \otimes (M_3 \oplus M_4) \\ &= (M_1 \oplus M_2) \otimes M_3 \oplus (M_1 + M_2) \otimes M_4 \\ &= (M_1 \otimes M_2) \oplus (M_1 \otimes M_4) \oplus (M_2 \otimes M_3) \oplus (M_2 \otimes M_4). \end{aligned} \tag{5.23}$$

The symbol $\oplus$ represents direct summation.

In the case of the 2 x 2 table considered in Examples 5.1 and 5.4, since $R^2 = M_0 \oplus M_1$,

$$R^{\overline{2}\times\overline{2}} = (M_0 \otimes M_0) \oplus (M_1 \otimes M_0) \oplus (M_0 \otimes M_1) \oplus (M_1 \otimes M_1). \tag{5.24}$$

Thus any $\underline{\mu} \in R^{\overline{2}\times\overline{2}}$ may be uniquely written as

$$\mu_{ij} = a + b_i + c_j + d_{ij}, \tag{5.25}$$

where (5.2) holds and $d_{11} = d_{22} = -d_{12} = -d_{21}$. The condition that (5.1) holds is equivalent to the condition that $d_{11} = 0$.

In Example 5.4, M_0 and M_1 are orthogonal, so the decomposition in (5.24) is a decomposition into orthogonal linear manifolds.

LEMMA 5.4. *Using the notation of* Lemma 5.3, *suppose that* $M_{j'}^{(1)}$ *and* $M_{j'}^{(2)}$ *are orthogonal. Then* $M^{(1)}$ *and* $M^{(2)}$ *are orthogonal.*

Proof. Suppose $\underline{\mu}^{(j)} \in M_j$ if $j \in \overline{d} - \{j'\}$ and $\underline{\mu}^{(j')} \in M_{j'}^{(1)}$. Suppose that $\underline{\nu}^{(j)} \in M_j$ if $j \in \overline{d} - \{j'\}$ and $\underline{\nu}^{(j')} \in M_{j'}^{(2)}$. Then by (5.17),

$$\left(\bigotimes_{j=1}^{d} \underline{\mu}^{(j)}, \bigotimes_{j=1}^{d} \underline{\nu}^{(j)}\right)_I = \prod_{j=1}^{d} (\underline{\mu}^{(j)}, \underline{\nu}^{(j)})_{I_j} = 0.$$

Since $M^{(1)}$ is generated by products such as $\otimes_{j=1}^{d} \underline{\mu}^{(j)}$, and $M^{(2)}$ is generated by products such as $\otimes_{j=1}^{d} \underline{\nu}^{(j)}$, the linear manifolds $M^{(1)}$ and $M^{(2)}$ are orthogonal.||

Example 5.9. Suppose that M_1, M_2, M_3, and M_4 are defined as in (5.23), except that M_1 and M_2 are orthogonal and M_3 and M_4 are orthogonal. Then

$$(M_1 \oplus M_2) \otimes (M_3 \oplus M_4) \tag{5.26}$$

$$= (M_1 \otimes M_3) \oplus (M_1 \otimes M_4) \oplus (M_2 \otimes M_3) \oplus (M_2 \otimes M_4),$$

where $\oplus$ represents direct summation of orthogonal manifolds.

LEMMA 5.5. *Suppose* $M = \otimes_{j=1}^{d} M_j$. *Suppose that* T *is the set of* $\underline{\mu}$ *such that if* $k \in \overline{d}$ *and* $\underline{i}^{(k)} \in \prod\{I_j: j \in \overline{d}, j \neq k\}$ *then* $\{\mu_{\underline{i}}: i_k \in I_k$ *and* $i_j = i_j^{(k)}\ \forall j \in \overline{d}, j \neq k\} \in M_k$. *Then* $M = T$.

Remark. To understand this lemma better, consider the case $M = M_1 \otimes M_2$. If $\underline{\mu} \in M$, $k \in I_2$, then $\{\mu_{jk}: j \in I_1\} \in M_1$. If $j \in I_1$, then $\{\mu_{jk}: k \in I_2\} \in M_2$. In particular, if $I_1 = I_2 = \overline{2}$ and $M_1 = M_2 = \text{span}\{\underline{t}\}$, where $t_1 = 1$ and $t_2 = -1$, then

$$\mu_{11} + \mu_{12} = \mu_{21} + \mu_{22} = \mu_{11} + \mu_{21} = \mu_{12} + \mu_{22} = 0. \tag{5.27}$$

Thus M corresponds to the interaction term for a two-way analysis of variance and the lemma can be used to relate results of this section to more conventional expositions.

Proof. Suppose $\underline{\mu}^{(j)} \in M_j$ for each $j \in \overline{d}$. Then if $\underline{\mu} = \otimes_{j=1}^{d} \underline{\mu}^{(j)}$, $k \in \overline{d}$, and $\underline{i}^{(k)} \in \prod\{I_j: j \in \overline{d}, j \neq k\}$,

$$\{\mu_{\underline{i}}: i_k \in I_k \text{ and } i_j = i_j^{(k)}\ \forall j \in \overline{d}, j \neq k\} \tag{5.28}$$

$$= \prod\{\mu_{i_j^{(k)}}: j \in \overline{d}, j \neq k\}\, \underline{\mu}^{(k)} \in M_k.$$

Therefore $M \subset T$.

To prove that $T \subset M$, we show that $M^{\perp} \subset T^{\perp}$. Observe that

$$R^I = \bigotimes_{j=1}^{d} (M_j \oplus M_j). \tag{5.29}$$

Thus by Lemmas 5.3 and 5.4,

$$M^{\perp} = \operatorname{span}\{\underline{\mu}: \underline{\mu} = \bigotimes_{j=1}^{d} \underline{\mu}^{(j)}, \underline{\mu}^{(j)} \in M_j \text{ if } j \in B \text{ and } \underline{\mu}^{(j)} \in M_j^{\perp} \text{ if } j \in \overline{d} - B, \text{ where } B \neq \overline{d}, B \subset \overline{d}\}. \tag{5.30}$$

Suppose that $B \neq \overline{d}$, $B \subset \overline{d}$, and $k \in \overline{d} - B$. Suppose $\mu^{(j)} \in M_j$ for all $j \in B$, and $\underline{\mu}^{(j)} \in M_j^{\perp}$ for all $j \in \overline{d} - B$. Then if $\underline{\nu} \in T$,

$$\begin{aligned}(\bigotimes_{j=1}^{d} \underline{\mu}^{(j)}, \underline{\nu})_I &= \sum\left\{\sum_{i_k \in I_k}\left[\prod\left\{\mu^{(j)}_{i^{(k)}_j}: j \in \overline{d}, j \neq k\right\}\right]\mu^{(k)}_{i_k}\nu_{\underline{i}^{(k)}|i_k} : \underline{i}^{(k)} \in \prod\{I_j: j \in \overline{d}, j \neq k\}\right\} \\ &= \sum\left\{\left[\prod_{j \in \overline{d}-\{k\}}\left\{\mu^{(j)}_{i^{(k)}_j} : j \in \overline{d}, j \neq k\right\}\right]\sum_{i_k \in I_k}\mu^{(k)}_{i_k}\nu_{\underline{i}^{(k)}|i_k} : \underline{i}^{(k)} \in \prod\{I_j: j \in \overline{d}, j \neq k\}\right\} = 0,\end{aligned} \tag{5.31}$$

where $\underline{i}^{(k)}|i_k$ is the element $\underline{h}$ of I such that $h_k = i_k$ and for $j \in \overline{d} - \{k\}$, $h_j = i^{(k)}_j$. As a consequence, $\bigotimes_{j=1}^{d}\underline{\mu}^{(j)} \in T^{\perp}$. Since $M^{\perp}$ is spanned by vectors such as $\bigotimes_{j=1}^{d}\underline{\mu}^{(j)}$, the proof of the lemma is complete. ||

Example 5.10. The decomposition of $R^{\overline{2}\times\overline{2}}$ into orthogonal components considered in the preceding examples may be generalized to other two-way tables with index sets $I_1 \times I_2$. For example, the space $R^{\overline{3}\times\overline{4}} = R^3 \otimes R^4$ may be decomposed into the four orthogonal manifolds $\operatorname{span}\{\underline{e}^{(3)}\} \otimes \operatorname{span}\{\underline{e}^{(4)}\}$, $\operatorname{span}\{\underline{e}^{(3)}\} \otimes \{\underline{e}^{(4)}\}^{\perp}$, $\{\underline{e}^{(3)}\}^{\perp} \otimes \operatorname{span}\{\underline{e}^{(4)}\}$, and $\{\underline{e}^{(3)}\}^{\perp} \otimes \{\underline{e}^{(4)}\}^{\perp}$, where $\underline{e}^{(k)}$ is the unit vector for the space R^k. If $\underline{\mu} \in \operatorname{span}\{\underline{e}^{(3)}\} \otimes \operatorname{span}\{\underline{e}^{(4)}\}$, then $\{\mu_{i_1 i_2}: i_1 \in \overline{3}\} \in \operatorname{span}\{\underline{e}^{(3)}\}$ for any $i_2 \in \overline{4}$. Thus the value of $\mu_{i_1 i_2}$ does not depend on i_1. Since $\{\mu_{i_1 i_2}: i_2 \in \overline{4}\} \in \operatorname{span}\{\underline{e}^{(4)}\}$, the value of $\mu_{i_1 i_2}$ also does not depend on i_2. Thus for some α, $\mu_{i_1 i_2} = \alpha$ if $i_1 \in \overline{3}$ and $i_2 \in \overline{4}$. If $\underline{\mu} \in \operatorname{span}\{\underline{e}^{(3)}\} \otimes \{\underline{e}^{(4)}\}^{\perp}$, then $\{\mu_{i_1 i_2}: i_1 \in \overline{3}\} \in \operatorname{span}\{\underline{e}^{(3)}\}$ for each $i_2 \in \overline{4}$ and $\{\mu_{i_1 i_2}: i_2 \in \overline{4}\} \in \{\underline{e}^{(4)}\}^{\perp}$ for each $i_1 \in \overline{3}$. Thus $\mu_{i_1 i_2}$ is independent of i_1; in other words, for some $\underline{\gamma} = \{\gamma_{i_2}: i_2 \in \overline{4}\}$, $\mu_{i_1 i_2} = \gamma_{i_2}$ for any $i_1 \in \overline{3}$ and $i_2 \in \overline{4}$. The vector $\underline{\gamma}$ must be an element of $\{\underline{e}^{(4)}\}^{\perp}$, so $\gamma_+ = 0$. Similarly if $\underline{\mu} \in \{\underline{e}^{(3)}\}^{\perp} \otimes \operatorname{span}\{\underline{e}^{(4)}\}$, then for some $\underline{\beta} \in R^3$, $\mu_{i_1 i_2} = \beta_{i_1}$ for $i_1 \in \overline{3}$ and $i_2 \in \overline{4}$ and $\beta_+ = 0$. If $\underline{\mu} \in \{\underline{e}^{(3)}\}^{\perp} \otimes \{\underline{e}^{(4)}\}^{\perp}$, then $\{\mu_{i_1 i_2}: i_1 \in \overline{3}\} \in \{\underline{e}^{(3)}\}^{\perp}$ for $i_2 \in \overline{4}$

and $\{\mu_{i_1 i_2}: i_2 \in \overline{4}\} \in \{\underline{e}^{(4)}\}^{\perp}$ for $i_1 \in \overline{3}$. Thus $\mu_{i_1 +} = 0$ for $i_1 \in \overline{3}$ and $\mu_{+i_2} = 0$ for $i_2 \in \overline{4}$. One may now write an arbitrary element $\underline{\mu} \in R^{\overline{3}\times\overline{4}}$ as

$$\mu_{i_1 i_2} = \alpha + \beta_{i_1} + \gamma_{i_2} + \delta_{i_1 i_2}, \tag{5.32}$$

where

$$\beta_+ = \gamma_+ = \delta_{i_1 +} = \delta_{+ i_2} = 0. \tag{5.33}$$

Equivalently, one may write $\underline{\mu}$ as

$$\underline{\mu} = \alpha \underline{e}^{(3)} \otimes \underline{e}^{(4)} + \underline{\beta} \otimes \underline{e}^{(4)} + \underline{e}^{(3)} \otimes \underline{\gamma} + \underline{\delta}, \tag{5.34}$$

where $\alpha\underline{e}^{(3)} \otimes \underline{e}^{(4)} \in \text{span}\,\{\underline{e}^{(3)}\} \otimes \text{span}\,\{\underline{e}^{(4)}\}$, $\underline{\beta} \otimes \underline{e}^{(4)} \in \{\underline{e}^{(3)}\}^{\perp} \otimes \text{span}\,\{\underline{e}^{(4)}\}$, $\underline{e}^{(3)} \otimes \underline{\gamma} \in \text{span}\,\{\underline{e}^{(3)}\} \otimes \{\underline{e}^{(4)}\}^{\perp}$, and $\underline{\delta} \in \{\underline{e}^{(3)}\}^{\perp} \otimes \{\underline{e}^{(4)}\}^{\perp}$.

These lemmas, or results similar to them, have presumably been proven before; however, it appears difficult to find published references for proofs other than the one for Lemma 5.1. Consequently, the proofs have been included here. These results facilitate the examination of hierarchical models presented in the next section.

HIERARCHICAL MODELS

Given these lemmas, it is possible to examine analysis-of-variance models in detail. In simple models for factorial tables, R^{r_j} is decomposed into $M_0^{(j)}$ and $M_1^{(j)}$, where $M_0^{(j)} = \text{span}\,\{\underline{e}^{(r_j)}\}$ and $M_1^{(j)} = (M_0^{(j)})^{\perp}$. Here $\underline{e}^{(r_j)} = \{1: i \in \overline{r}_j\}$. Direct sums of the form

$$= \bigoplus_{g=1}^{h} \bigotimes_{j=1}^{d} M^{(j)}_{\chi_{B_g}(j)} = \bigoplus_{g=1}^{h} M_{B_g} \tag{5.35}$$

are considered, where $B_g \subset \overline{d}$ for every $g \in \overline{h}$. The function $\chi_{B_g}(j)$ is the indicator of B_g. That the summands are actually orthogonal follows from Lemma 5.4.

Example 5.11. To clarify the concepts presented in this exposition, suppose that $I = \overline{2} \times \overline{2}$. Consider the case in which $h = 4$ and $B_1 = \phi$, $B_2 = \{1\}$, $B_3 = \{2\}$, and $B_4 = \{1,2\}$. Then $M_\phi = \text{span}\,\{\underline{e}^{(2)} \otimes \underline{e}^{(2)}\}$ is the space of vectors $\underline{\mu}$ such that $\mu_{11} = \mu_{12} = \mu_{21} = \mu_{22}$. This manifold corresponds to the grand mean of analysis of variance. By Lemma 5.5, $M_{\{1\}} = \{\underline{e}^{(2)}\}^{\perp} \otimes \text{span}\,\{\underline{e}^{(2)}\}$ is the set of vectors $\underline{\mu}$ such that for some β_1 and β_2, $\mu_{11} = \mu_{12} = \beta_1$, $\mu_{21} = \mu_{22} = \beta_2$, and $\beta_1 + \beta_2 = 0$. Thus $M_{\{1\}}$ corresponds to the row effect. Similarly, $M_{\{2\}} = \text{span}\,\{\underline{e}^{(2)}\} \circledast \{\underline{e}^{(2)}\}^{\perp}$ corresponds to the column effect. The manifold $M_{\{1,2\}} = \{\underline{e}^{(2)}\}^{\perp} \circledast \{\underline{e}^{(2)}\}^{\perp}$ is the set of $\underline{\mu}$ such that $\mu_{11} + \mu_{12} = \mu_{21} + \mu_{22} = \mu_{12} + \mu_{22} = \mu_{11} + \mu_{21} = 0$. This manifold corresponds to the interaction effect. By Lemmas 5.3 and 5.4,

$$R^I = (\text{span}\,\{\underline{e}^{(2)}\} \oplus \{\underline{e}^{(2)}\}^{\perp}) \circledast (\text{span}\,\{\underline{e}^{(2)}\} \oplus \{\underline{e}^{(2)}\}^{\perp})$$
$$= M_{\phi} \oplus M_{\{1\}} \oplus M_{\{2\}} \oplus M_{\{1,2\}} . \tag{5.36}$$

Since span $\{\underline{e}^{(2)}\}$ and $\{\underline{e}^{(2)}\}^{\perp}$ both have dimension 1, M_B has dimension 1 if $B \subset \overline{2}$.

Given the theory of direct products, it is immediately clear that M_B has dimension $\prod_{j \in B}(r_j - 1)$, where a null product is 1. To construct a basis for M_B, observe that $\{\underline{e}^{(r)}\}^{\perp}$ has the basis $\{\underline{\nu}^{(r,j)}: j \in \overline{r} - \overline{1}\}$, where if $i \in \overline{r}$, then

$$\nu_i^{(r,j)} = \begin{cases} 1, & i = j , \\ -1, & i = j + 1 , \\ 0, & \text{otherwise} . \end{cases} \tag{5.37}$$

A basis for $\circledast_{j=1}^{d} M^{(j)}_{X_B(j)}$ may now be constructed from direct products of vectors of the form $\underline{e}^{(r)}$ and $\underline{\nu}^{(r,j)}$. This basis will be written as $\mathcal{B}(B)$.

If M is defined by (5.35), then M has the basis $\bigcup_{g=1}^{h} \mathcal{B}(B_g)$. Thus M has dimension $\sum_{g=1}^{h} \prod_{j \in B_g}(r_j - 1)$. If $\underline{\mu} \in M$, then $\underline{\mu}$ may be uniquely expressed as

$$\underline{\mu} = \sum_{g=1}^{h} \underline{\mu}^{B_g} , \tag{5.38}$$

where $\underline{\mu}^{B_g} \in M_{B_g}$ for every $g \in \overline{h}$.

Example 5.12. If $I = \overline{r} \times \overline{s}$, then a simple additive manifold consists of all $\underline{\mu}$ such that if $i \in \overline{r}$ and $j \in \overline{s}$, then

$$\mu_{ij} = \alpha + \beta_i + \gamma_j, \tag{5.39}$$

where

$$\sum_{i=1}^{r} \beta_i = \sum_{j=1}^{s} \gamma_j = 0. \tag{5.40}$$

Using the notation of (5.38), one has $\mu_{ij}^{\phi} = \alpha$, $\mu_{ij}^{\{1\}} = \beta_i$, and $\mu_{ij}^{\{2\}} = \gamma_j$. The manifold M_{ϕ} has dimension 1, $M_{\{1\}}$ has dimension $r - 1$, and $M_{\{2\}}$ has dimension $s - 1$. Thus

$M_\phi \oplus M_{\{1\}} \oplus M_{\{2\}}$ has dimension $r + s - 1$.

If $r = 3$ and $s = 4$, then $\underline{e}^{(3)} \otimes \underline{e}^{(4)}$ is a basis for M_ϕ. The vectors $\underline{\nu}^{(3,1)} \otimes \underline{e}^{(4)}$ and $\underline{\nu}^{(3,2)} \otimes \underline{e}^{(4)}$ form a basis for $M_{\{1\}}$, where

(5.41) $$\underline{\nu}^{(3,1)} \otimes \underline{e}^{(4)} = \begin{array}{|cccc|} \hline 1 & 1 & 1 & 1 \\ -1 & -1 & -1 & -1 \\ 0 & 0 & 0 & 0 \\ \hline \end{array}$$

and

(5.42) $$\underline{\nu}^{(3,2)} \otimes \underline{e}^{(4)} = \begin{array}{|cccc|} \hline 0 & 0 & 0 & 0 \\ 1 & 1 & 1 & 1 \\ -1 & -1 & -1 & -1 \\ \hline \end{array} .$$

The vectors $\underline{e}^{(3)} \otimes \underline{\nu}^{(4,1)}$, $\underline{e}^{(3)} \otimes \underline{\nu}^{(4.2)}$, and $\underline{e}^{(3)} \otimes \underline{\nu}^{(4,3)}$ are a basis for $M_{\{2\}}$. Here

(5.43) $$\underline{e}^{(3)} \otimes \underline{\nu}^{(4,1)} = \begin{array}{|cccc|} \hline 1 & -1 & 0 & 0 \\ 1 & -1 & 0 & 0 \\ 1 & -1 & 0 & 0 \\ \hline \end{array} ,$$

(5.44) $$\underline{e}^{(3)} \otimes \underline{\nu}^{(4,2)} = \begin{array}{|cccc|} \hline 0 & 1 & -1 & 0 \\ 0 & 1 & -1 & 0 \\ 0 & 1 & -1 & 0 \\ \hline \end{array} ,$$

and

(5.45) $$\underline{e}^{(3)} \otimes \underline{\nu}^{(4,3)} = \begin{array}{|cccc|} \hline 0 & 0 & 1 & -1 \\ 0 & 0 & 1 & -1 \\ 0 & 0 & 1 & -1 \\ \hline \end{array} .$$

The space M is then spanned by the six independent vectors $\underline{e}^{(3)} \otimes \underline{e}^{(4)}$, $\underline{\nu}^{(3,1)} \otimes \underline{e}^{(4)}$, $\underline{\nu}^{(3,2)} \otimes \underline{e}^{(4)}$, $\underline{e}^{(3)} \otimes \underline{\nu}^{(4,1)}$, $\underline{e}^{(3)} \otimes \underline{\nu}^{(4,2)}$, and $\underline{e}^{(3)} \otimes \underline{\nu}^{(4,3)}$.

Example 5.13. If $I = \overline{r} \times \overline{s} \times \overline{t}$, then a common manifold consists of all $\underline{\mu}$ such that if $i \in \overline{r}$, $j \in \overline{s}$, and $k \in \overline{t}$,

(5.46) $$\mu_{ijk} = \alpha + \beta_i + \gamma_j + \delta_k + \varepsilon_{ik} + \lambda_{jk},$$

where

(5.47) $$\sum_{i=1}^{r} \beta_i = \sum_{j=1}^{s} \gamma_j = \sum_{k=1}^{t} \delta_k = \sum_{i=1}^{r} \varepsilon_{ik} = \sum_{k=1}^{t} \varepsilon_{ik} = \sum_{j=1}^{s} \lambda_{jk} = \sum_{k=1}^{t} \lambda_{jk} = 0.$$

In this case, $\mu_{ijk}^{\phi} = \alpha$, $\mu_{ijk}^{\{1\}} = \beta_i$, $\mu_{ijk}^{\{2\}} = \gamma_j$, $\mu_{ijk}^{\{3\}} = \delta_k$, $\mu_{ijk}^{\{1,3\}} = \varepsilon_{ik}$, and $\mu_{ijk}^{\{2,3\}} = \lambda_{jk}$. The manifold corresponding to (5.46) has dimension

(5.48) $$\begin{aligned} 1 + (r - 1) + (s - 1) + (t - 1) + (r - 1)(t - 1) + (s - 1)(t - 1) \\ = rt + st - t \\ = (r + s - 1)t. \end{aligned}$$

In analysis-of-variance models, it is especially convenient to employ hierarchical models. To examine this concept, we consider the manifold M defined by (5.35). A set B_g is hierarchical (relative to M) if every subset of B_g is an element of $H = \{B_g\colon g \in \bar{h}\}$. The linear manifold M is a hierarchical manifold if for every $g \in \bar{h}$, B_g is hierarchical. The class H is called a hierarchical class if M is hierarchical.

To each hierarchical class corresponds a subclass E such that if $g \in \bar{h}$, then there exists an $E \in E$ such that $B_g \subset E$ and such that if $E \subset B_g$ for some $g \in \bar{h}$, then $E = B_g$. This subclass is the generating class of H. This terminology is reasonable since the class $H(E)$ of subsets of elements of E is a hierarchical class. For each $g \in \bar{h}$, $B_g \in H(E)$, so $H \subset H(E)$. If $E \in H(E)$, then E is a subset of an element of H, so $E \in H$. Thus $H = H(E)$.

Any nonempty class E of subsets of $\bar{d}$ such that $E \in E$, $E' \in E$, and $E \subset E'$ implies $E = E'$ is called a generating class. The hierarchical class $H(E)$ of subsets of elements of E is called the span of E. Clearly any generating class determines a linear manifold, namely, the manifold for which $\{B_g\colon g \in \bar{h}\} = H(E)$. This manifold is the hierarchical manifold generated by E. It is written $M(E)$. If the index set I is not clear from context, the manifold will be written $M(I,E)$.

Example 5.14. Consider the manifold $M = M_{\phi} \oplus M_{\{1\}} \oplus M_{\{2\}}$ which was defined in Example 5.12. The class $H = \{\phi,\{1\},\{2\}\}$, and each set in H is hierarchical. Thus H and M are hierarchical. Neither $\{1\}$ or $\{2\}$ is contained in other elements of H, but $\phi \subset \{1\}$ and $\phi \subset \{2\}$. Thus $E = \{\{1\},\{2\}\}$ is the generating class of M. If M were equal to $M_{\{1\}} \oplus M_{\{2\}}$, it would not be hierarchical; for ϕ, a subset of both $\{1\}$ and $\{2\}$, would not be in H.

Hierarchical models can be described in simpler terms than models which are not hierarchical. To examine this situation, let B be a hierarchical set relative to M and let

$$N_B = \odot\{M_{B'}: B' \subset B\} \tag{5.49}$$

Clearly $N_B \subset M$. If M is a hierarchical manifold generated by E, then

$$M \subset \sum_{B \in E} N_B \ . \tag{5.50}$$

Therefore

$$M = \sum_{B \in E} N_B \ . \tag{5.51}$$

Now define $N_1^{(j)} = R^{r_j}$ and $N_0^{(j)} = \text{span}\,\{\underline{e}^{(r_j)}\}$. A simple induction based on Lemma 5.3 shows that

$$N_B = \bigotimes_{j=1}^{d} N^{(j)}_{\chi_B(j)} \ . \tag{5.52}$$

Therefore, if M is hierarchical,

$$M = \sum_{B \in E} \bigotimes_{j=1}^{d} N^{(j)}_{\chi_B(j)} \ . \tag{5.53}$$

By Lemma 5.5, N_B consists of all $\underline{\mu}$ such that for some $\underline{u}^B \in \prod_{j \in B} R^{r_j}$, $\mu_{\underline{i}} = u^B_{\{i_j:\ j \in B\}}$ for each $\underline{i} \in I$. If M is hierarchical, then M consists of those $\underline{\mu}$ such that for some vectors $\underline{u}^B \in \prod_{j \in B} R^{r_j}$, $B \in E$, one has

$$\mu_{\underline{i}} = \sum_{B \in E} u^B_{\{i_j:\ j \in B\}} \tag{5.54}$$

for all $\underline{i} \in I$.

Example 5.15. By (5.51) and (5.52), $M(\{\overline{d}\}) = \otimes_{j=1}^{d} R^{r_j} = R^I$.

Example 5.16. As in Example 5.14, consider the manifold $M = M_\phi \odot M_{\{1\}} \odot M_{\{2\}}$. Then $N_{\{1\}} = M_\phi \odot M_{\{1\}}$ and $N_{\{2\}} = M_\phi \odot M_{\{2\}}$. Thus

$$\begin{aligned} N_{\{1\}} &= \text{span}\,\{\underline{e}^{(r)}\} \otimes \text{span}\,\{\underline{e}^{(s)}\} \quad \{\underline{e}^{(r)}\}^{\perp} \otimes \text{span}\,\{\underline{e}^{(s)}\} \\ &= R^r \otimes \text{span}\,\{\underline{e}^{(s)}\} \end{aligned} \tag{5.55}$$

and

$$\begin{aligned} N_{\{2\}} &= \text{span}\,\{\underline{e}^{(r)}\} \otimes \text{span}\,\{\underline{e}^{(s)}\} \quad \text{span}\,\{\underline{e}^{(r)}\} \otimes \{\underline{e}^{(s)}\}^{\perp} \\ &= \text{span}\,\{\underline{e}^{(r)}\} \otimes R^s \ . \end{aligned} \tag{5.56}$$

One may then write M as $N_{\{1\}} + N_{\{2\}}$. In other words, if $\underline{\mu} \in M$, then

(5.57) $$\underline{\mu} = \underline{a} \otimes \underline{e}^{(s)} + \underline{e}^{(r)} \otimes \underline{b} ,$$

where $\underline{a} \in R^r$ and $\underline{b} \in R^s$. If coordinates are used, one may write

(5.58) $$\mu_{ij} = a_i + b_j$$

for each $\langle i,j \rangle \in \bar{r} \times \bar{s}$. This parametric form is not usually encountered since $\underline{a}$ and $\underline{b}$ are not uniquely determined by $\underline{\mu}$, but the expression does have the advantage of simplicity of form.

Example 5.17. Consider the manifold M defined in Example 5.13. This manifold is hierarchical, with $H = \{\phi,\{1\},\{2\},\{3\},\{1,3\},\{2,3\}\}$ and $E = \{\{1,3\},\{2,3\}\}$. The spaces $N_{\{1,3\}}$ and $N_{\{2,3\}}$ satisfy the relationships

(5.59) $$\begin{aligned} N_{\{1,3\}} &= \text{span}\,\{\underline{e}^{(r)}\} \otimes \text{span}\,\{\underline{e}^{(s)}\} \otimes \text{span}\,\{\underline{e}^{(t)}\} \oplus \{\underline{e}^{(r)}\}^{\perp} \otimes \text{span}\,\{\underline{e}^{(s)}\} \otimes \text{span}\,\{\underline{e}^{(t)}\} \\ &\oplus \text{span}\,\{\underline{e}^{(r)}\} \otimes \text{span}\,\{\underline{e}^{(s)}\} \otimes \{\underline{e}^{(t)}\}^{\perp} \oplus \{\underline{e}^{(r)}\}^{\perp} \otimes \text{span}\,\{\underline{e}^{(s)}\} \otimes \{\underline{e}^{(t)}\}^{\perp} \\ &= R^r \otimes \text{span}\,\{\underline{e}^{(s)}\} \otimes R^t \end{aligned}$$

and

(5.60) $$\begin{aligned} N_{\{2,3\}} &= \text{span}\,\{\underline{e}^{(r)}\} \otimes \text{span}\,\{\underline{e}^{(s)}\} \otimes \text{span}\,\{\underline{e}^{(t)}\} \oplus \text{span}\,\{\underline{e}^{(r)}\} \otimes \{\underline{e}^{(s)}\}^{\perp} \otimes \text{span}\,\{\underline{e}^{(t)}\} \\ &\oplus \text{span}\,\{\underline{e}^{(r)}\} \otimes \text{span}\,\{\underline{e}^{(s)}\} \otimes \{e^{(t)}\}^{\perp} \oplus \text{span}\,\{\underline{e}^{(r)}\} \otimes \{\underline{e}^{(s)}\}^{\perp} \otimes \{\underline{e}^{(t)}\}^{\perp} \\ &= \text{span}\,\{\underline{e}^{(r)}\} \otimes R^s \otimes R^t . \end{aligned}$$

Thus

(5.61) $$M = R^r \otimes \text{span}\,\{\underline{e}^{(s)}\} \otimes R^t + \text{span}\,\{\underline{e}^{(r)}\} \otimes R^s \otimes R^t .$$

If $\underline{\mu} \in M$, then for some $\underline{a} \in R^r \otimes R^t$ and $\underline{b} \in R^s \otimes R^t$,

(5.62) $$\mu_{ijk} = a_{ik} + b_{jk}$$

for all $\langle i,j,k \rangle \in \bar{r} \times \bar{s} \times \bar{t}$. Note that (5.62) is a much simpler expression than (5.46). The fact that $\underline{a}$ and $\underline{b}$ are not uniquely determined does not prevent use of equations such as (5.62) to provide simple descriptions of manifolds.

If one wishes to determine whether one hierarchical manifold $M(E_1)$ is contained in another hierarchical manifold $M(E_2)$, it is only necessary to determine whether each set $E_1 \in \mathcal{E}_1$ is contained in some set $E_2 \in \mathcal{E}_2$. The relationship $M(\mathcal{E}_1) \subset M(\mathcal{E}_2)$ holds if and only if this condition is satisfied. That the condition is sufficient follows from the observation that $N_{E_1} \subset N_{E_2}$ if $E_1 \subset E_2$. Necessity follows since if some $E \in \mathcal{E}_1$ is not included in any set in $\mathcal{E}_2$, then E is not in $H(\mathcal{E}_2)$ and M_E is orthogonal to $M(\mathcal{E}_2)$. Thus $M(\mathcal{E}_1)$, which includes M_E, cannot be contained in $M(\mathcal{E}_2)$.

Example 5.18. Suppose that $I = \overline{r} \times \overline{s} \times \overline{t}$, $\mathcal{E}_1 = \{\{1\},\{2\},\{3\}\}$, and $\mathcal{E}_2 = \{\{1,2\},\{1,3\}\}$. Since $\{1\} \subset \{1,2\}$, $\{2\} \subset \{1,2\}$, and $\{3\} \subset \{1,3\}$, the manifold $M(\mathcal{E}_1)$ is contained in $M(\mathcal{E}_2)$. Thus if $\underline{\mu}$ satisfies the equation

$$\mu_{ijk} = a_i + b_j + c_k$$

for each $\langle i,j,k\rangle \in \overline{r} \times \overline{s} \times \overline{t}$, then $\underline{\mu} \in M(\mathcal{E}_2)$.

A simple set of spanning vectors may be found for any hierarchical model. This feature is useful in determination of closed-form maximum-likelihood estimates and in use of the Deming-Stephan algorithm.

To find this set of spanning vectors, observe that if $\underline{\delta}(r,k) \in R^r$ is defined as $\delta_i(r,k) = \delta_{ik}$, the Kronecker delta, then $\{\underline{\delta}(r,k): k \in \overline{r}\}$ is an orthogonal basis of R^r. If $j \in \overline{d}$, then $N_0^{(j)}$ is clearly spanned by $\underline{e}^{(r_j)}$. Thus if $B \in \mathcal{E}$, N_B is spanned by an orthogonal set of vectors with all elements either zero or one. The spanning vectors of all N_B such that $B \in \mathcal{E}$ also span M. In order to explicitly write down the spanning vectors, we make the following definitions:

DEFINITION 5.1. *If* $B \neq \phi$ *and* $B \subset \overline{d}$, *then* $I(B) = \prod_{j \in B} \overline{r}_j$. *If* $B = \phi$, *then* $I(B) = \{\alpha\}$, *where* α *is a special symbol.*

DEFINITION 5.2. *If* $B \neq \phi$ *and* $A \subset \overline{d}$, *then* $\pi_B^A: I(A) \longrightarrow I(B)$ *is defined for* $\underline{i} = \{i_j: j \in A\} \in I(A)$ *by* $\pi_B^A \underline{i} = \{i_j: j \in B\}$. *If* $B = \phi$, *then* $\pi_B^A \underline{i} = \alpha$. *The mapping* π_B^A *is called the projection from* $I(A)$ *onto* $I(B)$. *If* $A = \overline{d}$, *then* π_B^A *is written* π_B.

DEFINITION 5.3. *If* $B \subset \overline{d}$ *and* $\overline{\underline{i}} \in I(B)$, *then* $\underline{\nu}(B,\overline{\underline{i}}) \in R^I$ *is defined for* $\underline{i} \in I$ *by*

$$\nu_{\underline{i}}(B,\overline{\underline{i}}) = 1, \quad \underline{i} \in \pi_B^{-1}\overline{\underline{i}} , \tag{5.63}$$

$$= 0, \quad \underline{i} \notin \pi_B^{-1}\overline{\underline{i}} .$$

Remark. This definition means that $\nu_{\underline{i}}(B,\overline{\underline{i}})$ is 1 if $i_j = \overline{i}_j$ for every $j \in B$.

Example 5.19. Suppose that $I = \overline{3} \times \overline{4}$. Then $I(\{1\}) = \overline{3}$ and $\pi_{\{1\}}\langle i,j\rangle = i$. Then vector $\underline{\nu}(\{1\},1)$ satisfies

(5.64)
$$\underline{\nu}(\{1\},1) = \begin{array}{|cccc|} \hline 1 & 1 & 1 & 1 \\ 0 & 0 & 0 & 0 \\ 0 & 0 & 0 & 0 \\ \hline \end{array} .$$

Similarly, $I(\{2\}) = \overline{4}$, $\pi_{\{2\}}\langle i,j\rangle = j$, and

(5.65)
$$\underline{\nu}(\{2\},1) = \begin{array}{|cccc|} \hline 1 & 0 & 0 & 0 \\ 1 & 0 & 0 & 0 \\ 1 & 0 & 0 & 0 \\ \hline \end{array} .$$

The set $I(\phi) = \{\alpha\}$, $\pi_\phi\langle i,j\rangle = \alpha$, and

(5.66)
$$\underline{\nu}(\phi,\alpha) = \begin{array}{|cccc|} \hline 1 & 1 & 1 & 1 \\ 1 & 1 & 1 & 1 \\ 1 & 1 & 1 & 1 \\ \hline \end{array} .$$

At the other extreme, $I(\{1,2\}) = I = \overline{3} \times \overline{4}$, $\pi_{\{1,2\}}\langle i,j\rangle = \langle i,j\rangle$, and

(5.67)
$$\underline{\nu}(\{1,2\},\langle 1,1\rangle) = \begin{array}{|cccc|} \hline 1 & 0 & 0 & 0 \\ 0 & 0 & 0 & 0 \\ 0 & 0 & 0 & 0 \\ \hline \end{array} .$$

Given these definitions, it follows that M is spanned by C, where $C = \{\underline{\nu}(B,\underline{\overline{i}}): \underline{\overline{i}} \in I(E),\ E \in E\}$. This set of generators permits several simplifications. A complete minimal sufficient statistic for any probability model considered is $S(\underline{n})$, where $S(\underline{n}) = \{(\underline{n},\underline{\nu}(B,\underline{\overline{i}})): \underline{\overline{i}} \in I(E),\ E \in E\}$. It should be noted that $(\underline{n},\underline{\nu}(E,\underline{\overline{i}}))$ satisfies

(5.68)
$$(\underline{n},\underline{\nu}(E,\underline{\overline{i}})) = \sum\{n_{\underline{i}}: \underline{i} \in \pi_E^{-1}\underline{i}\}.$$

Thus $(\underline{n},\underline{\nu}(E,\underline{\overline{i}}))$ is the marginal total corresponding to E and $\underline{\overline{i}}$. This total will be written as $n^E_{\underline{\overline{i}}}$, and the symbol $\underline{n}^E$ will represent $\{n^E_{\underline{\overline{i}}}: \underline{\overline{i}} \in I(E)\}$, the vector of E-marginal totals of $\underline{n}$. Thus $S(\underline{n})$ is equivalent to $\{\underline{n}^E: E \in E\}$.

Example 5.20. Suppose that $I = \overline{3} \times \overline{4}$ and M is defined as in Example 5.12. Then $C = \{\underline{\nu}(\{1\},i): i \in \overline{3}\} \cup \{\underline{\nu}(\{2\},j): j \in 4\}$ and

(5.69)
$$S(\underline{n}) = \{\underline{n}^{\{1\}}, \underline{n}^{\{2\}}\}$$
$$= \{n_1^{\{1\}}, n_2^{\{1\}}, n_3^{\{1\}}, n_1^{\{2\}}, n_2^{\{2\}}, n_3^{\{2\}}, n_4^{\{2\}}\}$$
$$= \{n_{1+}, n_{2+}, n_{3+}, n_{+1}, n_{+2}, n_{+3}, n_{+4}\}.$$

It is useful to note that

(5.70)
$$(\underline{n}, \underline{\nu}(\{1\}, i)) = \sum\{n_{i'j}: \langle i',j\rangle \in \overline{3} \times \overline{4},\ i' = i\}$$
$$= \sum_{j=1}^{4} n_{ij}$$
$$= n_{i+}\ .$$

A similar result holds for $(\underline{n}, \underline{\nu}(\{2\}, j))$.

Example 5.21. In Example 5.13,

$$C = \{\underline{\nu}(\{1,3\}, \langle i,k\rangle): \langle i,k\rangle \in r \times \overline{t}\}$$
$$\cup\ \{\underline{\nu}(\{2,3\}, \langle j,k\rangle): \langle j,k\rangle \in \overline{s} \times \overline{t}\}.$$

These results show that a necessary condition for existence of a Poisson or multinomial maximum-likelihood estimate is that $n_{\underline{i}}^{E} > 0$ for $\underline{i} \in I(E)$ and all $E \in \mathcal{E}$. That this condition is not sufficient is shown by the case in which M is defined by (B.1) and $\underline{n}$ is defined by (B.10). If it exists, the maximum-likelihood estimate $\hat{\underline{m}}(\underline{n}, \mathcal{E})$ or $\hat{\underline{m}}(\underline{n}, I, \mathcal{E})$ of $\underline{m}$ satisfies the condition $\hat{\underline{m}}^{E}(\underline{n}, \mathcal{E}) = \underline{n}^{E}$ for each $E \in \mathcal{E}$, where $\hat{\underline{m}}^{E}(\underline{n}, \mathcal{E})$ is $\{(\hat{\underline{m}}(\underline{n}, \mathcal{E}), \underline{\nu}(E, \underline{i})): \underline{i} \in I(E)\}$. In other words, the maximum-likelihood estimate has the same E-marginal totals as the data for each $E \in \mathcal{E}$.

It is useful to note that if $F \subset E$, then $\underline{n}^{F}$ is determined by $\underline{n}^{E}$. To show this result, suppose that $S_{F\underline{i}}^{E} = \{\underline{j} \in I(E): j_k = i_k\ \forall k \in F\}$, where $\underline{i} \in I(F)$. Then

(5.71)
$$\underline{\nu}(F, \underline{i}) = \sum_{\underline{j} \in S_{F\underline{i}}^{E}} \underline{\nu}(E, \underline{j})\ .$$

Consequently, if $F \in H(E)$ and $S(\underline{n})$ is known, then $\underline{n}^{F}$ is known. In addition, if $\underline{i} \in I(F)$ and if for some $\underline{j} \in S_{F\underline{i}}^{F}$, $n_{\underline{j}}^{E} > 0$, then $n_{\underline{i}}^{F} > 0$.

Example 5.22. If $I = \overline{r} \times \overline{s} \times \overline{t}$, then

(5.72)
$$S_{\{1\}}^{\{1,2\}} i = \{\langle i',j\rangle \in \overline{r} \times \overline{s}: i' = i\}$$
$$= \{\langle i,j\rangle: j \in \overline{s}\}$$

and

$$\underline{\nu}(\{1\},i) = \sum_{j=1}^{s} \{\underline{\nu}(\{1,2\},<i,j>\}. \tag{5.73}$$

Thus

$$n_i^{\{1\}} = \sum_{j=1}^{s} n_{ij}^{\{1,2\}} \quad . \tag{5.74}$$

Equivalently, one may say that

$$n_{i++} = \sum_{j=1}^{s} n_{ij+} \quad . \tag{5.75}$$

Hierarchical manifolds remain unchanged if the decomposition of R^{r_j} is changed for $j \in \overline{d}$. If $\underline{c}^{(j)}$ is not orthogonal to $\underline{e}^{(r_j)}$, then $R^{r_j} = \text{span}\ \{\underline{e}^{(r_j)}\} \oplus \{\underline{c}^{(j)}\}^{\perp}$. Suppose that $\overline{M}_0^{(j)} = \text{span}\ \{\underline{e}^{(r_1)}\}$ and $\overline{M}_1^{(j)} = \{\underline{c}^{(j)}\}^{\perp}$. Then

$$\sum_{\{B':\ B' \sqsubseteq B\}} \bigoplus_{j=1}^{d} \overline{M}^{(j)}_{\chi_{B'}(j)} = \bigoplus_{j=1}^{d} N^{(j)}_{\chi_B(j)} = N_B. \tag{5.76}$$

The proofs of (5.52) and (5.76) are identical. If $\overline{M}$ is defined by

$$\overline{M} = \sum_{g=1}^{h} \bigoplus_{j=1}^{d} \overline{M}^{(j)}_{\chi_{B'}(j)} \quad , \tag{5.77}$$

then

$$\overline{M} = \sum_{B \in E} N_B \quad . \tag{5.78}$$

This result follows in the same manner as (5.51).

Example 5.23. In the r x s table considered in (5.39), this equivalence states that

$$\{\underline{\mu}:\ \mu_{ij} = \alpha + \beta_i + \gamma_j,\ \sum_{i=1}^{r} \beta_i = \sum_{j=1}^{s} \gamma_j = 0\} \tag{5.79}$$

$$= \{\underline{\mu}:\ \mu_{ij} = \alpha' + \beta_i' + \gamma_j',\ \sum_{i=1}^{r} w_i\beta_i' = \sum_{j=1}^{s} v_j\gamma_j' = 0\} \ ,$$

where $\sum_{i=1}^{r} w_i \neq 0$ and $\sum_{j=1}^{s} v_j \neq 0$. This result was demonstrated by Scheffé (1959) under the assumption that $w_i \geq 0$ for $i \in \overline{r}$ and $v_j \geq 0$ for $j \in \overline{s}$, where $w_i \neq 0$ for some $i \in \overline{r}$ and $v_j \neq 0$ for some $j \in \overline{s}$. The present result generalizes Scheffé's bservation to all hierarchical manifolds.

This invariance of hierarchical models under different decompositions of R^{r_j} for $j \in \overline{d}$ may be used to obtain alternative bases for M. For example, if $\underline{c}^{(j)} = \underline{\delta}(r_j,r_j)$, then $[\underline{c}^{(j)}]^{\perp} = \text{span}\ \{\underline{\delta}(r_j,k):\ k \in \overline{r_j - 1}\}$. Thus (5.77) implies that M has the basis $\{\underline{\nu}(B,\underline{I}):\ \underline{I} \in \prod_{j \in B}(\overline{r_j - 1}),\ B \in H(E)\}$.

Example 5.24. In Example 5.23, the additive manifold defined by (5.79) has the basis $\{\underline{\nu}(\phi,\alpha)\} \cup \{\underline{\nu}(\{1\},i): i \in \overline{r-1}\} \cup \{\underline{\nu}(\{2\},j): j \in \overline{c-1}\}$.

Another convenient feature of hierarchical models is associated with multinomial sampling. If $B \in H(E)$ and $\{n_{\underline{i}}: \underline{i} \in \pi_B^{-1}\underline{\bar{i}}\}$ is an independent multinomial sample for each $\underline{\bar{i}} \in I(B)$, then the maximum-likelihood estimates for Poisson and multinomial sampling coincide. In fact, if $\underline{\bar{i}} \in I(B)$, then $\underline{\nu}(B,\bar{i}) \in H(E)$. For example, if multinomial sampling fixes $n^{\{1,2\}}_{i_1 i_2}$ for each $i_1 \in \bar{r}_1$ and $i_2 \in \bar{r}_2$ and $E = \{\{1,2,3\},\{1,2,4\},\{2,5\}\}$, then the maximum-likelihood estimates are the same under the Poisson and multinomial models. On the other hand, if a model is not hierarchical, then the maximum-likelihood estimates coincide only if B is included in a hierarchical set. Thus if $H = H(E),\{\{1\},\{1,2\}\}$ is not hierarchical, and the equivalence of maximum-likelihood estimates does not hold.

CLOSED-FORM MAXIMUM-LIKELIHOOD ESTIMATES

Hierarchical models frequently are associated with closed-form expressions for Poisson maximum-likelihood estimates. Models with this property are attractive since iterative procedures are not needed for computation of maximum-likelihood estimates and since such models may be interpreted in terms of probabilistic concepts such as independence, conditional independence, and equiprobability (see Goodman 1970). The basic result of this section is that manifolds with decomposable generating classes have closed-form maximum-likelihood estimates which satisfy (5.118), where decomposability is defined as follows:

DEFINITION 5.4. *A generating class* E *is decomposable if* E *either consists of one set or is the union of two disjoint decomposable classes* E_1 *and* E_2 *such that there exists* $E_1 \in E_1$ *and* $E_2 \in E_2$ *such that*

$$[\cup(E_1)] \cap [\cup(E_2)] = E_1 \cap E_2 \,. \tag{5.80}$$

Remark. The classes E_1 and E_2 are disjoint if they contain no common sets. The symbol $\cup(E)$ represents the union of all sets included in E.

Example 5.25. If $E = \{\{1,2\},\{1,3\}\}$, then one may let $E_1 = \{\{1,2\}\}$, $E_2 = \{\{1,3\}\}$, $E_1 = \{1,2\}$, and $E_2 = \{1,3\}$. Since E_1 and E_2 both consist of a single set, they are decomposable. By (5.80), E is decomposable. This argument is quite general; it applies to any generating class consisting of two sets.

Example 5.26. There exist generating classes containing three sets which are not decomposable. If $E = \{\{1,2\},\{1,3\},\{2,3\}\}$, then any one set in E is contained in the union of the other two sets. For example, if $E_1 = \{\{1,2\}\}$ and $E_2 = \{\{1,3\},\{2,3\}\}$, then $[U(E_1)] \cup [U(E_2)] = \{1,2\}$, which is equal to neither $\{1,2\} \cap \{1,3\}$ nor $\{1,2\} \cap \{2,3\}$. The same argument applies to any other choice of E_1 and E_2.

This definition is useful since, as shown in Lemmas 5.7 and 5.9, generating classes consisting of single sets correspond to closed-form maximum likelihood estimates and (5.80) ensures that $\hat{\underline{m}}(\underline{n},E)$ may be expressed in terms of $\hat{\underline{m}}(\underline{n}^A,I(A),E_1)$ and $\hat{\underline{m}}(\underline{n}^B,I(B),E_2)$, where $A = U(E_1)$ and $B = U(E_2)$. Given these results, induction may be used to demonstrate that $\hat{\underline{m}}(\underline{n},E)$ may be expressed in closed form if E is decomposable.

LEMMA 5.6. *If* $A = U(E)$, $D = \bar{d} - A$, $\underline{\mu} \in M(I,E)$, *and* $\underline{m} = \{e^{\mu_{\underline{i}}}\}$, *then for each* $\underline{i} \in I$,

$$m_{\underline{i}} = m^A_{\pi_A \underline{i}} / \prod_{j \in D} r_j \,, \tag{5.81}$$

and $\{\log m^A_{\bar{\underline{i}}} : \bar{\underline{i}} \in I(A)\} \in M(I(A),E)$. *Conversely, if* $\{\log m^A_{\bar{\underline{i}}} : \bar{\underline{i}} \in I(A)\} \in M(I(A),E)$ *and* (5.81) *holds for each* $\underline{i} \in I$, *then* $\underline{\mu} \in M(I,E)$.

Remark. In (5.81), a null product is 1.

Proof. If $\underline{\mu} \in M(I,E)$, then for some $\{\underline{u}^E \in R^{I(E)} : E \in E\}$,

$$\mu_{\underline{i}} = \sum_{E \in E} u^E_{\pi_E \underline{i}} \,. \tag{5.82}$$

If $\underline{i} \in \pi_A^{-1} \bar{\underline{i}}$ for some $\bar{\underline{i}} \in I(A)$, then as an immediate consequence of Definition 5.2, $\pi_E \underline{i} = \pi_E^A \bar{\underline{i}}$. Thus for any $\underline{i} \in I$,

$$m_{\underline{i}} = \exp\Big(\sum_{E \in E} u^E_{\pi_E \underline{i}}\Big) \,, \tag{5.83}$$

and for any $\bar{\underline{i}} \in I(A)$,

$$m^A_{\bar{\underline{i}}} = \sum_{\underline{i} \in \pi_A^{-1} \bar{\underline{i}}} m_{\underline{i}} \tag{5.84}$$

$$= \Big(\prod_{j \in D} r_j\Big) \exp\Big(\sum_{E \in E} u^E_{\pi^A_E \bar{\underline{i}}}\Big) \,.$$

If $\underline{i} \in \pi_A^{-1} \bar{\underline{i}}$, then $m_{\underline{i}}$ satisfies (5.81). Since

(5.85)
$$\log m^A_{\bar{i}} = \log(\prod_{j\in D} r_j) + \sum_{E\in E} u^E_{\pi^A_E \bar{i}} ,$$

$\{\log m^A_{\bar{i}}: \bar{i} \in I(A)\} \in M(I(A),E)$.

Conversely, if $\{\log m^A_{\bar{i}}: \bar{i} \in I(A)\} \in M(I(A),E)$, then for some $\{\underline{u}^E: E \in E\}$,

(5.86)
$$m^A_{\bar{i}} = \exp\left(\sum_{E\in E} u^E_{\pi^A_E \bar{i}}\right).$$

By (5.81), for every $\underline{i} \in I$

(5.87)
$$\mu_{\underline{i}} = \sum_{E\in E} u^E_{\pi_E \underline{i}} - \log(\prod_{j\in D} r_j),$$

so $\underline{\mu} \in M(I,E)$.||

Remark. If $D = \phi$, the lemma is trivial. Otherwise, as Goodman (1970) has noted, (5.81) is equivalent to the statement that the random vectors $\underline{X}_t$, $t \in \bar{N}$, from which $\underline{n}$ is generated are such that any possible value of $\{X_{tj}: j \in D\}$ is equally probable given $\{X_{tj}: j \in A\}$.

LEMMA 5.7. *If* $A = U(E)$ *and* $D = \bar{d} - A$, *then for each* $\underline{i} \in I$,

(5.88)
$$\hat{m}_{\underline{i}}(\underline{n},I,E) = \hat{m}_{\pi_A \underline{i}}(\underline{n}^A,I(A),E)/\prod_{j\in D} r_j ,$$

in the sense that the two sides of (5.88) *are equal when* $\underline{\hat{m}}(\underline{n},I,E)$ *exists and* $\underline{\hat{m}}(\underline{n},I,E)$ *exists if and only if* $\underline{\hat{m}}(\underline{n}^A,I(A),E)$ *exists.*

Proof. By Lemma 5.6, if $\underline{\hat{m}}(\underline{n},I,E)$ exists, then $\{\log \hat{m}^A_{\bar{i}}(\underline{n},I,E): \bar{i} \in I(A)\} \in M(I(A),E)$. Since $\underline{\hat{m}}^E = \underline{n}^E$ for each $E \in E$ and $E \in A$ for all $E \in E$, $\underline{\hat{m}}^A(\underline{n},I,E)$ satisfies the conditions for the maximum-likelihood estimate $\underline{\hat{m}}(\underline{n}^A,I(A),E)$. Thus (5.81) implies that (5.84) holds.

On the other hand, if $\underline{\hat{m}}(\underline{n}^A,I(A),E)$ exists, then by Lemma 5.6, $\{\log \bar{m}_{\underline{i}}\} = \{\log [m_{\pi_A \underline{i}}(\underline{n}^A,I(A),E)/\prod_{j\in D} r_j]: \underline{i} \in I\} \in M(I,E)$ and $\underline{\bar{m}}^A = \underline{\hat{m}}(\underline{n}^A,I(A),E)$. If $E \in E$, then $\underline{\bar{m}}^E = \underline{\hat{m}}^E(\underline{n}^A,I(A),E) = \underline{n}^E$, where $\underline{\hat{m}}^E(\underline{n}^A,I(A),E)$ is the vector of E-marginal totals of $\underline{\hat{m}}(\underline{n}^A,I(A),E)$. Consequently, $\underline{\bar{m}} = \underline{\hat{m}}(\underline{n},I,E)$ and (5.84) holds in this case.||

Example 5.27. If $E = \{E\}$ and $D = \bar{d} - E$, then $M(I(E),E) = R^{I(E)}$ (see Example 5.15). By Example 2.1 and Lemma 5.7, $\underline{\hat{m}}(\underline{n},I,E)$ exists if and only if $n^E_{\bar{i}} > 0$ for every $\bar{i} \in I(E)$. If $\underline{\hat{m}}(\underline{n},I,E)$ exists, then

(5.89)
$$\hat{m}_{\underline{i}}(\underline{n},I,E) = n^{E}_{\pi_E \underline{i}} / \prod_{j \in D} r_j .$$

For instance, if one believed that the sex ratio was 1 for both the toxemia and control groups in Example 1.2, then one would assume that for some $\underline{b} \in R^2$,

(5.90)
$$\mu_{ij} = b_i$$

for $\langle i,j \rangle \in \overline{2} \times \overline{2}$. By (5.54), this assumption is equivalent to the hypothesis that $\underline{\mu} \in M(\{1\})$, and by (5.87), $\hat{\underline{m}}$ satisfies

(5.91)
$$\hat{m}_{ij} = n_{i+}/2$$

if $\langle i,j \rangle \in \overline{2} \times \overline{2}$.

LEMMA 5.8. *If* E_1 *and* E_2 *are disjoint generating classes such that for some* $E_1 \in E_1$ *and* $E_2 \in E_2$, (5.80) *is satisfied, and if* $\underline{\mu} \in M(I,E)$ *and* $\underline{m} = \{e^{\mu_{\underline{i}}}\}$, *where* $E = E_1 \cup E_2$, *then*

(5.92)
$$m_{\underline{i}} = \frac{m^{A}_{\pi_A \underline{i}} m^{B}_{\pi_B \underline{i}}}{m^{C}_{\pi_C \underline{i}}} \prod_{j \in D} \frac{1}{r_j}$$

for all $\underline{i} \in I$, *where* $A = \cup(E_1)$, $B = \cup(E_2)$, $C = E_1 \cap E_2 = A \cap B$, $D = \overline{d} - (A \cup B)$, $\{\log m^{A}_{\underline{i}}: \underline{i} \in I(A)\} \in M(I(A),E_1)$ *and* $\{\log m^{B}_{\underline{i}}: \underline{i} \in I(B)\} \in M(I(B),E_2)$. *Conversely, if* $\underline{a} \in M(I(A),E_1)$, $\underline{b} \in M(I(B),E_2)$, *for each* $\underline{i} \in I(C)$,

(5.93)
$$\sum\{\exp(a_{\underline{j}}): \underline{j} \in (\pi^{A}_{C})^{-1}\underline{i}\}$$
$$= \sum\{\exp(b_{\underline{k}}): \underline{k} \in (\pi^{B}_{C})^{-1}\underline{i}\}$$
$$= c_{\underline{i}} ,$$

and for each $\underline{i} \in I$,

(5.94)
$$m_{\underline{i}} = \frac{\exp(a_{\pi_A \underline{i}}) \exp(b_{\pi_B \underline{i}})}{\exp(c_{\pi_C \underline{i}})} \prod_{j \in D} \frac{1}{r_j} ,$$

then $\underline{\mu} \in M(I,E)$, $\underline{m}^A = \{\exp(a_{\underline{i}}): \underline{i} \in I(A)\}$, $\underline{m}^B = \{\exp(b_{\underline{i}}): \underline{i} \in I(B)\}$, *and* $\underline{m}^C = \{\exp(c_{\underline{i}}): \underline{i} \in I(C)\}$. *In particular, if* (5.82) *holds for all* $\underline{i} \in I$,

$\{\log m^A_{\bar{\underline{i}}}: \bar{\underline{i}} \in I(A)\} \in M(I(A),E_1)$, *and* $\{\log m^B_{\bar{\underline{i}}}: \bar{\underline{i}} \in I(B)\} \in M(I(B),E_2)$, *then* $\underline{\mu} \in M(I,E)$.

Proof. If $\underline{\mu} \in M(I,E)$, then for some $\{\underline{u}^E \in R^{I(E)}: E \in E\}$,

$$\mu_{\underline{i}} = \sum_{E \in E} u^E_{\pi_E \underline{i}} = \sum_{E \in E_1} u^E_{\pi_E \underline{i}} + \sum_{E \in E_2} u^E_{\pi_E \underline{i}} \tag{5.95}$$

for all $\underline{i} \in I$. Thus

$$m_{\underline{i}} = \exp\Big(\sum_{E \in E_1} u^E_{\pi_E \underline{i}}\Big) \exp\Big(\sum_{E \in E_2} u^E_{\pi_E \underline{i}}\Big) . \tag{5.96}$$

If $\underline{i} \in \pi_A^{-1} \bar{\underline{i}}$ for some $\bar{\underline{i}} \in I(A)$, then $\pi_E \underline{i} = \pi^A_E \bar{\underline{i}}$, for any $E \in E_1$, so

$$m^A_{\bar{\underline{i}}} = \sum_{\underline{i} \in \pi_A^{-1} \bar{\underline{i}}} \exp\Big(\sum_{E \in E_1} u^E_{\pi_E \underline{i}}\Big) \exp\Big(\sum_{E \in E_2} u^E_{\pi_E \underline{i}}\Big) = \exp\Big(\sum_{E \in E_1} u^E_{\pi^A_E \bar{\underline{i}}}\Big) \sum_{\underline{i} \in \pi_A^{-1} \bar{\underline{i}}} \exp\Big(\sum_{E \in E_2} u^E_{\pi_E \underline{i}}\Big) . \tag{5.97}$$

Since $\{\underline{i} \in \pi_A^{-1} \bar{\underline{i}}\} = \{\underline{i}:$ for some $\bar{\underline{j}} \in I(F)$, $\underline{i} \in \pi_F^{-1} \bar{\underline{j}}$ and $\pi^F_A \bar{\underline{j}} = \bar{\underline{i}}\}$, where $F = A \cup B$, Lemma 5.6 implies that

$$m^A_{\bar{\underline{i}}} = \exp\Big(\sum_{E \in E_2} u^E_{\pi^A_E \bar{\underline{i}}}\Big) \Sigma \Big\{ \sum_{\underline{i} \in \pi_F^{-1} \bar{\underline{j}}} \exp\Big(\sum_{E \in E_2} u^E_{\pi_E \underline{i}}\Big): \bar{\underline{j}} \in (\pi^F_A)^{-1} \bar{\underline{i}}\Big\} = \exp\Big(\sum_{E \in E_1} u^E_{\pi^A_E \bar{\underline{i}}}\Big) \Sigma \Big\{\exp\Big(\sum_{E \in E_2} u^E_{\pi^F_E \bar{\underline{j}}}\Big): \bar{\underline{j}} \in (\pi^F_A)^{-1} \bar{\underline{i}}\Big\} \prod_{j \in D} r_j . \tag{5.98}$$

Since $E \subset B$ if $E \in E_2$, $\pi^F_E \bar{\underline{j}} = \pi^B_E \pi^F_B \bar{\underline{j}}$. The projection π^F_B, when restricted to $(\pi^F_A)^{-1} \bar{\underline{i}}$, is a one-to-one mapping onto $(\pi^B_C)^{-1} \pi^A_C \bar{\underline{i}}$, so

$$m^A_{\bar{\underline{i}}} = \exp\Big(\sum_{E \in E_1} u^E_{\pi^A_E \bar{\underline{i}}}\Big) \Big[\sum \Big\{\exp\Big(\sum_{E \in E_2} u^E_{\pi^B_E \bar{\underline{j}}}\Big): \bar{\underline{j}} \in (\pi^B_C)^{-1} \pi^A_C \bar{\underline{i}}\Big\}\Big] \prod_{j \in D} r_j . \tag{5.99}$$

Similarly, if $\bar{\underline{i}} \in I(B)$, then

$$m^B_{\bar{\underline{i}}} = \exp\Big(\sum_{E \in E_2} u^E_{\pi^B_E \bar{\underline{i}}}\Big) \Big[\sum \Big\{\exp\Big(\sum_{E \in E_1} u^E_{\pi^A_E \bar{\underline{j}}}\Big): \bar{\underline{j}} \in (\pi^A_C)^{-1} \pi^B_C \bar{\underline{i}}\Big\}\Big] \prod_{j \in D} r_j . \tag{5.100}$$

Since for each $\bar{\underline{i}} \in I(C)$,

(5.101)
$$m^C_{\underline{i}} = \sum\{m^B_{\underline{j}}: \underline{j} \in (\pi^B_C)^{-1}\underline{i}\},$$

it follows from (5.100 that

(5.102)
$$m^C_{\underline{i}} = [\sum_{\underline{j}\in(\pi^B_C)^{-1}\underline{i}} \exp(\sum_{E\in E_2} u^E_{\pi^B_E\underline{j}})][\sum_{\underline{k}\in(\pi^A_C)^{-1}\underline{i}} \exp(\sum_{E\in E_1} u^E_{\pi^A_E\underline{k}})] \prod_{j\in D} r_j .$$

For any $\underline{i} \in I$, $\pi^B_C\pi_B\underline{i} = \pi^A_C\pi_A\underline{i} = \pi_C\underline{i}$; therefore, (5.99), (5.100), and (5.102) imply (5.94).

To show that $\{\log m^A_{\underline{i}}: \overline{i} \in I(A)\} \in M(I(A,E)$, it is only necessary to note that for some $\underline{a}^C \in R^{I(C)}$, $\underline{m}^A$ satisfies $\log m^A_{\underline{i}} = \sum_{E\in E_1} u^E_{\pi^A_E\overline{i}} + a^C_{\pi^A_C\overline{i}}$ for all $\overline{i} \in I(A)$. Since $C \subset E_1 \in E_1$, the vector $\{a^C_{\pi^A_C\overline{i}}: \overline{i} \in I(A)\} \in M(I(A),E_1)$, and therefore, $\{\log m^A_{\overline{i}}: \overline{i} \in I(A)\} \in M(I(A),E_1)$. The same argument can also be used to demonstrate that $\{\log m^B_{\overline{i}}: \overline{i} \in I(B)\} \in M(I(B),E_2)$.

To prove the converse, suppose $\underline{a} \in M(I(A),E_1)$, $\underline{b} \in M(I(B),E_2)$, and both (5.95) and (5.96) are satisfied. Then if $\overline{i} \in I(A)$,

(5.103)
$$m^A_{\overline{i}} = \frac{\exp(a_{\overline{i}})}{\exp(c_{\pi^A_C\overline{i}})} (\prod_{j\in D} \frac{1}{r_j}) \sum_{\underline{i}\in\pi_A^{-1}\overline{i}} \exp(b_{\pi_B\underline{i}}).$$

By the argument used in (5.98) and (5.99),

(5.104)
$$m^A_{\overline{i}} = \frac{\exp(a_{\overline{i}})}{\exp(c_{\pi^A_C\overline{i}})} \sum\{\exp(b_{\underline{j}}): \underline{j} \in (\pi^B_C)^{-1}\pi^A_C\overline{i}\} = \exp(a_{\overline{i}}).$$

Similarly, if $\overline{i} \in I(B)$, then $m^B_{\overline{i}} = \exp(b_{\overline{i}})$. Therefore, (5.94) is satisfied for all $\underline{i} \in I$. By Lemma 5.6, $\{\log m^A_{\pi_A\underline{i}}/\prod_{j\in\overline{d}-A} r_j\} \in M(I,E_1)$, $\{\log m^B_{\pi_B\underline{i}}/\prod_{j\in\overline{d}-B} r_j\} \in M(I,E_2)$, and $\{\log m^C_{\pi_C\underline{i}}/\prod_{j\in\overline{d}-C} r_j\} \in M(I,\{C\})$. If (5.94) holds for all $\underline{i} \in I$, then $\underline{\mu}$ is the sum of these vectors. Since $M(I,E_1)$, $M(I,E_2)$, and $M(I,\{C\})$ are all contained in $M(I,E)$, $\underline{\mu} \in M(I,E)$. ||

Remark. The interpretation of (5.94) provided by Goodman (1970) is that the vectors $\underline{X}_t$, $t \in \overline{N}$, from which $\underline{n}$ is generated are such that $\{X_{tj}: j \in A - C\}$ and $\{X_{tj}: j \in B - C\}$ are conditionally independent given $\{X_{tj}: j \in C\}$ and if $D \neq \phi$, each value of $\{X_{tj}: j \in D\}$ is equally probable given any value of $\{X_{tj}: j \in A \cup B\}$. If

$C = \Phi$, the conditional independence statement may be replaced by the statement that $\{X_{tj}: j \in A\}$ and $\{X_{tj}: j \in B\}$ are independent.

Example 5.28. If the variables represented by the rows and columns of an r x c contingency table are independent, then if $\langle i,j\rangle \in \overline{r} \times \overline{s}$,

$$m_{ij} = \frac{m_{i+}m_{+j}}{m_{++}} \tag{5.105}$$

Since no assumptions are made concerning the marginal totals m_{i+} and m_{+j}, one has the model $\{\log m_{i+}\} \in M(\overline{r},\{\{1\}\})$ and $\{\log m_{+j}\} \in M(\overline{s},\{\{2\}\})$. By the preceding lemma, the condition that (5.105) holds for $\langle i,j\rangle \in \overline{r} \times \overline{s}$ is equivalent to the assertion that $\underline{\mu} \in M(\{\{1\},\{2\}\})$. This manifold, which has already been discussed in Example 5.12, is the additive manifold for a two-way table. This result corresponds to the observation in Example 1.5 that the additive model for $\underline{\mu}$ in a 2 x 2 table was equivalent to the model of independence between sex and toxemia or control status.

Example 5.29. Two of the models considered in Example 4.13 for the 3 x 2 x 2 table given in Example 1.3 may be constructed by use of Lemma 5.8. If type of mother and type of child are independent given the birth order, then

$$m_{ijk} = \frac{m_{ij+}m_{i+k}}{m_{i++}} \tag{5.106}$$

for all $\langle i,j,k\rangle \in \overline{3} \times \overline{2} \times \overline{2}$. If no further restrictions are made on the marginal totals, then the lemma implies that the model of (5.106) is equivalent to the model $\underline{\mu} \in M(\{\{1,2\},\{1,3\}\})$. If $\underline{\mu} \in M(\{\{1,2\},\{1,3\}\})$, then for some $\underline{a} \in R^{\overline{3}\times\overline{2}}$ and $\underline{b} \in R^{\overline{3}\times\overline{2}}$,

$$\mu_{ijk} = a_{ij} + b_{ik} \tag{5.107}$$

for all $\langle i,j,k\rangle \in \overline{3} \times \overline{2} \times \overline{2}$. Thus $M(\{\{1,2\},\{1,3\}\})$ is the manifold M_2 of Example 4.13. The model M_1 in that example is $M(\{\{1,3\},\{2\}\})$. The lemma shows that $\underline{\mu} \in M(\{\{1,3\},\{2\}\})$ if and only if

$$m_{ijk} = \frac{m_{i+k}m_{+j+}}{m_{+++}} \tag{5.108}$$

for $\langle i,j,k\rangle \in \overline{3} \times \overline{2} \times \overline{2}$. Thus $\underline{\mu} \in M(\{\{1,3\},\{2\}\})$ if and only if type of child is independent of birth order and type of mother.

LEMMA 5.9. *If* $\mathcal{E}_1$ *and* $\mathcal{E}_2$ *are disjoint generating classes such that for some* $E_1 \in \mathcal{E}_1$ *and* $E_2 \in \mathcal{E}_2$, (5.80) *is satisfied, then* $\underline{\hat{m}}(\underline{n},I,\mathcal{E})$ *exists if and only if both*

$\hat{\underline{m}}(\underline{n}^A, I(A), E_1)$ *and* $\hat{\underline{m}}(\underline{n}^B, I(B), E_2)$ *exist. If* $\hat{\underline{m}}(\underline{n}^A, I, E)$ *exists, then for any* $\underline{i} \in I$,

$$(5.109) \qquad \hat{m}_{\underline{i}}(\underline{n}, I, E) = \frac{\hat{m}_{\pi_A \underline{i}}(\underline{n}^A, I(A), E_1)\hat{m}_{\pi_B \underline{i}}(\underline{n}^B, I(B), E_2)}{n^C_{\pi_C \underline{i}}} \prod_{j \in D} \frac{1}{r_j},$$

where $A = U(E_1)$, $B = U(E_2)$, $C = A \cap B$, *and* $D = \bar{d} - (A \cup B)$.

Proof. If $\hat{\underline{m}}(\underline{n}, I, E)$ exists, then $\hat{\underline{m}}^C(\underline{n}, I, E) = \underline{n}^C$, $\{\log m^A_{\underline{i}}(\underline{n}, I, E)\colon \underline{i} \in I(A)\} \in M(I(A), E_1)$, and $\{\log m^B_{\underline{i}}(\underline{n}, I, E)\colon \underline{i} \in I(B)\} \in M(I(B), E_2)$. If $E \in E_1$, then $\underline{m}^E(\underline{n}, I, E) = \underline{n}^E$, so $\hat{\underline{m}}^A(\underline{n}, I, E)$ satisfies all conditions for $\hat{\underline{m}}(\underline{n}^A, I(A), E_1)$. Thus $\hat{\underline{m}}(\underline{n}^A, I(A), E_1) = \hat{\underline{m}}^A(\underline{n}, I, E)$. Similarly, $\hat{\underline{m}}(\underline{n}^B, I(B), E_2) = \hat{\underline{m}}^B(\underline{n}, I, E)$. These results, together with Lemma 5.8, imply that (5.109) is satisfied.

On the other hand, if both $\hat{\underline{m}}(\underline{n}^A, I(A), E_1)$ and $\hat{\underline{m}}(\underline{n}^B, I(B), E_2)$ exist, then $\hat{\underline{m}}^C(\underline{n}^A, I(A), E_1) = \hat{\underline{m}}^C(\underline{n}^B, I(B), E_2) = \underline{n}^C$.

If $\bar{m}_{\underline{i}}$ is the right-hand side of (5.109) and $\bar{\mu}_{\underline{i}} = \log \bar{m}_{\underline{i}}$, then as a consequence of Lemma 5.8, $\bar{\underline{\mu}} \in M(I, E)$, $\bar{\underline{m}}^A = \hat{\underline{m}}(\underline{n}^A, I(A), E_1)$, and $\bar{\underline{m}}^B = \underline{m}(\underline{n}^B, I(B), E_2)$. If $E \in E_1$, $\underline{m}^E = \hat{\underline{m}}^E(\underline{n}^A, I(A), E_1) = \underline{n}^E$; and if $E \in E_2$, $\bar{\underline{m}}^E = \hat{\underline{m}}^E(\underline{n}^B, I(B), E_2) = \underline{n}^E$. Therefore, $\bar{\underline{m}} = \underline{m}(n, I, E)$.||

Example 5.30. Consider the models in Example 5.29. If $E = \{\{1,2\},\{1,3\}\}$, then $\hat{\underline{m}}(\underline{n}^{\{1,2\}}, I(\{1,2\}), \{\{1,2\}\})$ exists if and only if $n^{\{1,2\}}_{ij} = n_{ij+} > 0$ for each $\langle i,j\rangle \in \bar{3} \times \bar{2}$ and $\hat{\underline{m}}(\underline{n}^{\{1,3\}}, I(\{1,3\}), \{\{1,3\}\})$ exists if and only if $n^{\{1,3\}}_{ik} = n_{i+k} > 0$ for each $\langle i,k\rangle \in \bar{3} \times \bar{2}$. Thus $\hat{\underline{m}}(\underline{n}, I, E)$ exists if and only if $n_{ij+} > 0$ for $\langle i,j\rangle \in \bar{3} \times \bar{2}$ and $n_{i+k} > 0$ for $\langle i,k\rangle \in \bar{3} \times \bar{2}$. If $\hat{\underline{m}}(\underline{n}, I, E)$ exists, then $\hat{\underline{m}}(\underline{n}^{\{1,2\}}, I(\{1,2\}, \{\{1,2\}\}) = \underline{n}^{\{1,2\}}$, $\hat{\underline{m}}(\underline{n}^{\{1,3\}}, I(\{1,3\}, \{\{1,3\}\}) = \underline{n}^{\{1,3\}}$, and

$$(5.110) \qquad \hat{m}_{ijk}(\underline{n}, I, E) = \frac{n_{ij+}n_{i+k}}{n_{i++}}$$

for $\langle i,j,k\rangle \in \bar{3} \times \bar{2} \times \bar{2}$. If $E = \{\{1,3\},\{2\}\}$, then $\hat{\underline{m}}(\underline{n}^{\{2\}}, I(\{2\}), \{\{2\}\})$ exists if and only if $n^{\{2\}}_j = n_{+j+} > 0$ for $j \in \bar{2}$. Thus $\hat{\underline{m}}(\underline{n}, I, E)$ exists if and only if $n_{i+k} > 0$ for $\langle i,k\rangle \in \bar{3} \times \bar{2}$ and $n_{+j+} > 0$ for $j \in \bar{2}$. If $\hat{\underline{m}}(\underline{n}, I, E)$ exists, then

$$(5.111) \qquad \hat{m}_{ijk}(\underline{n}, I, E) = \frac{n_{i+k}n_{+j+}}{n_{+++}}$$

for all $\langle i,j,k\rangle \in \bar{3} \times \bar{2} \times \bar{2}$.

Example 5.31. These lemmas may be used several times in succession. For example, if $d = 4$ and $E = \{\{1,2\},\{1,3\},\{3,4\}\}$, then $E = E_1 \cup E_2$, where $E_1 = \{\{1,2\},\{1,3\}\}$ and $E_2 = \{\{3,4\}\}$. Since $[U(E_1)] \cap [U(E_2)] = \{3\}$, which is the intersection of $\{1,3\}$

and $\{3,4\}$, the conditions of Lemmas 5.8 and 5.9 are satisfied. Using the results of Examples 5.28 and 5.29,

(5.112)
$$m_{i_1i_2i_3i_4} = \frac{m_{i_1i_2i_3+}\ m_{++i_3i_4}}{m_{++i_3+}}$$
$$= \frac{m_{i_1i_2++}m_{i_1+i_3+}m_{++i_3i_4}}{m_{i_1+++}m_{++i_3+}}\ ;$$

and if $\hat{\underline{m}}(\underline{n},I,E)$ exists, then

(5.113)
$$\hat{m}_{i_1i_2i_3i_4}(\underline{n},I,E)$$
$$= \hat{m}_{i_1i_2i_3}(\underline{n}^{\{1,2,3\}},I(\{1,2,3\}),E_1)\ \hat{m}_{i_3i_4}(\underline{n}^{\{3,4\}},I(\{3,4\}),E_2)/n^{\{3\}}_{i_3}$$
$$= \frac{n_{i_1i_2++}n_{i_1+i_3+}n_{++i_3i_4}}{n_{i_1+++}n_{++i_3+}}\ .$$

The maximum-likelihood estimate exists if and only if all elements of $\underline{n}^{\{1,2\}}$, $\underline{n}^{\{1,3\}}$, and $\underline{n}^{\{1,4\}}$ are positive. Reference to Lemma 5.8 also shows that the assumption that $\underline{\mu} \in M$ is equivalent to the hypothesis that the variables $\{X_{tj}: j \in \overline{4}\}$ are such that $\{X_{t1},X_{t2}\}$ and X_{t4} are conditionally independent given X_{t3} and X_{t2} and X_{t3} are conditionally independent given X_{t2}.

A relatively straightforward induction may now be used to show that a closed-form maximum-likelihood estimate exists for $\underline{\mu} \in M(E)$ if E is decomposable. In order to derive a general formula for this estimate, the following definitions are useful.

DEFINITION 5.5. *The intersection class* $F(E)$ *generated by* E *is the class of pairwise intersections of distinct elements of* E, *i.e.*,

(5.114)
$$F(E) = \{E \cap E' : E \in E,\ E' \in E,\ E \neq E'\}.$$

Example 5.32. If E consists of a single element E, then $F(E)$ is empty.

Example 5.33. If $E = \{\{1,2,3\},\{1,2,4\},\{2,5\}\}$, then $F(E) = \{\{1,2\},\{2\}\}$.

DEFINITION 5.6. *If* $F \subset \overline{d}$ *the raw replication number* $c(F,E)$ *is the number of sets in* E *which contain* F.

Example 5.34. In Example 5.33, $c(\{1,2\},E) = 2$ and $c(\{2\},E) = 3$.

DEFINITION 5.7. *If* $F \in F(E)$, *the adjusted replication number* $d(F,E)$ *satisfies the equation*

(5.115) $$d(F,E) = c(F,E) - 1 - \sum_{F' \in \mathcal{F}(F,E)} d(F',E),$$

where $\mathcal{F}(F,E)$ *is the subclass of* $F(E)$ *consisting of proper supersets of* F, *i.e.*,

(5.116) $$\mathcal{F}(F,E) = \{F' \in F(E): F \subset F', F' \neq F\}.$$

Remark. The sets of $F(E)$ are partially ordered by inclusion, so $d(F,E)$ is well defined.

Example 5.35. In Example 5.33, $F(\{1,2\},E) = \phi$ and $F(\{2\},E) = \{\{1,2\}\}$. Thus $d(\{1,2\},E) = 2 - 1 = 1$ and $d(\{2\},E) = 3 - 1 - 1 = 1$.

Example 5.36. To illustrate these definitions, suppose that d is 5 and E is $\{\{1,2\},\{2,3\},\{4,5\}\}$. Then $\{\{1,2\}\}$ and $\{\{2,3\}\}$ are decomposable, for each class contains a single set. Since $[\cup\{\{1,2\}\}] \cap [\cup\{\{2,3\}\}] = \{1,2\} \cap \{2,3\} = \{2\}$, $\{\{1,2\},\{2,3\}\}$ is decomposable. Now $\cup\{\{1,2\},\{2,3\}\} = \{1,2,3\}$, $\cup\{\{4,5\}\} = \{4,5\}$, and $\{1,2,3\} \cap \{4,5\} = \phi$. Since $\{1,2\} \cap \{4,5\} = \phi$, $\{\{1,2\},\{2,3\},\{4,5\}\}$ is decomposable. The class $F(E) = \{\{2\},\phi\}$. Since $\{2\} \subset \{1,2\}$ and $\{2\} \subset \{2,3\}$, $c(\{2\},E) = 2$. Since ϕ is included in each set in E, $c(\phi,E) = 3$. No set in $F(E)$ contains $\{2\}$ as a proper subset, so $d(\{2\},E) = 2 - 1 = 1$. The only set in $F(E)$ which contains ϕ as a proper subset is $\{2\}$. Thus

(5.117) $$d(\phi,E) = c(\phi,E) - 1 - d(\{2\},E) = 3 - 1 - 1 = 1.$$

Since $\cup(E) = \{1,2,3,4,5\} = \overline{5}$, the set $D(E) = \phi$.

Given these definitions, we now have the following theorem:

THEOREM 5.1. *If* E *is a decomposable generating class, then the maximum-likelihood estimate* $\hat{\underline{m}}(\underline{n},E)$ *of* $\underline{m}$ *corresponding to* $\underline{n}$ *and* $M(E)$ *exists if and only if* $n^E_{\underline{\overline{i}}} > 0$ *for each* $\underline{\overline{i}} \in I(E)$ *and each* $E \in E$. *If* $\hat{\underline{m}}(\underline{n},E)$ *exists, then for each* $\underline{i} \in I$,

(5.118) $$\hat{m}_{\underline{i}}(\underline{n},E) = \frac{\left(\prod_{E \in E} n^E_{\pi_E \underline{i}}\right)\left[\prod_{j \in D(E)} \frac{1}{r_j}\right]}{\prod_{F \in F(E)} (n^F_{\pi_F \underline{i}})^{d(F,E)}}$$

Remarks. In this theorem, Poisson or multinomial sampling is assumed. A null product is 1.

Proof. The proof is by induction. Suppose that $E = \{E\}$. Then $F(E) = \phi$ and $D(E) = \overline{d} - E$. Thus the theorem reduces to Lemma 5.7.

Now assume that the theorem holds for all decomposable generating classes properly included in E. Suppose that E_1 and E_2 are disjoint decomposable generating classes such that $E = E_1 \cup E_2$ and there exist $E_1 \in E_1$ and $E_2 \in E_2$ such that (5.118) holds.

As a first step, the relationship between functions of E and functions of E_1 and E_2 must be considered. The hierarchical class $H(E)$ generated by E is the union of $H(E_1)$ and $H(E_2)$. If $F \in F(E)$, then

(5.119) $$c(F,E) = c(F,E_1) + c(F,E_2).$$

Suppose now that $F(F,E)$ is empty. Then

(5.120) $$d(F,E) = c(F,E_1) + c(F,E_2) - 1.$$

Given this condition, three possibilities exist: $F \in H(E_1) - H(E_2)$, $F \in H(E_2) - H(E_1)$, and $F \in H(E_1) \cap H(E_2)$. If $F \in H(E_1) - H(E_2)$, then $c(F,E_2) = 0$ and

(5.121) $$d(F,E) = d(F,E_1) = c(F,E_1) - 1.$$

Similarly, if $F \in H(E_2) - H(E_1)$, then

(5.122) $$d(F,E) = d(F,E_2) = c(F,E_2) - 1.$$

If $F \in H(E_1) \cap H(E_2)$, then $F = E_1 \cap E_2$. In this case, $F(F,E_1)$ and $F(F,E_2)$ are disjoint. Thus

(5.123) $$\begin{aligned} d(F,E) &= c(F,E_1) + c(F,E_2) - 1 \\ &= [c(F,E_1) - 1] + [c(F,E_2) - 1] + 1 \\ &= d(F,E_1) + d(F,E_2) + 1. \end{aligned}$$

Now assume that $F(F,E)$ is not empty. Once again, there are three possibilities. If $F \in H(E_1) - H(E_2)$, then $d(F,E)$ mmay be found by induction. Suppose that $d(F',E) = d(F',E_1)$ if $F' \in F(F,E)$. Observe that $F(F,E) \subset H(E_1) - H(E_2)$. This statement holds if $F(F,E)$ is empty, and sets are partially ordered by inclusion. Thus it suffices to show that under the given assumption, $d(F,E) = d(F,E_1)$. Since $c(F,E) = c(F,E_1)$ and $F(F,E) = F(F,E_1)$, the desired result is an immediate consequence of the definition of $d(F,E)$. Thus $d(F,E) = d(F,E_1)$ whenever $F \in H(E_1) - H(E_2)$. Similarly, $d(F,E) = d(F,E_2)$ whenever $F \in H(E_2) - H(E_1)$. Suppose now that $F \in H(E_2) \cap H(E_1)$. Then $F = E_1 \cap E_2$ or $F \subset E_1 \cap E_2$, $F \neq E_1 \cap E_2$. If $F = E_1 \cap E_2$, then $F(F,E)$ is the union of $F(F,E_1)$ and

$\mathcal{F}(F,E_2)$, where $\mathcal{F}(F,E_1)$ and $\mathcal{F}(F,E_2)$ are disjoint. Then since $\mathcal{F}(F,E_1) \subset \mathcal{H}(E_1) - \mathcal{H}(E_2)$ and $\mathcal{F}(F,E_2) \subset \mathcal{H}(E_2) - \mathcal{H}(E_1)$,

$$(5.124) \qquad d(F,\mathcal{E}) = c(F,\mathcal{E}_1) + c(F,\mathcal{E}_2) - 1 - \sum_{F' \in \mathcal{F}(F,\mathcal{E}_1)} d(F',\mathcal{E}_1) - \sum_{F' \in \mathcal{F}(F,\mathcal{E}_2)} d(F',\mathcal{E}_2)$$

$$= d(F,\mathcal{E}_1) + d(F,\mathcal{E}_2) + 1.$$

Now suppose that $F \subset E_1 \cap E_2$, $F \neq E_1 \cap E_2$. Assume that if $F' \in \mathcal{F}(F,\mathcal{E})$ and $F' \neq E_1 \cap E_2$, $F' \subset E_1 \cap E_2$, then $d(F',\mathcal{E}) = d(F',\mathcal{E}_1) + d(F',\mathcal{E}_2)$. Observe that $\mathcal{F}(F,\mathcal{E})$ is the union of the following disjoint classes: $\{E_1 \cap E_2\}$, $\mathcal{F}(F,\mathcal{E}) \cap [\mathcal{H}(\mathcal{E}_1) - \mathcal{H}(\mathcal{E}_2)]$, $\mathcal{F}(F,\mathcal{E}) \cap [\mathcal{H}(\mathcal{E}_2) - \mathcal{H}(\mathcal{E}_1)]$, and $\mathcal{F}(F,\mathcal{E}) \cap \mathcal{H}(\mathcal{E}_1) \cap \mathcal{H}(\mathcal{E}_2) - \{E_1 \cap E_2\}$. It follows from (5.119), (5.121), (5.122), (5.123), (5.124), and the definition of $d(F,\mathcal{E})$ that

$$(5.125) \qquad d(F,\mathcal{E}) = d(F,\mathcal{E}_1) + d(F,\mathcal{E}_2).$$

Since the subsets in $\mathcal{H}(\mathcal{E}_1) \cap \mathcal{H}(\mathcal{E}_2) \cap \mathcal{F}(\mathcal{E})$ are partially ordered by inclusion, (5.125) holds for $F \in \mathcal{F}(\mathcal{E}) \cap \mathcal{H}(\mathcal{E}_1) \cap \mathcal{H}(\mathcal{E}_2)$ if $F \neq E_1 \cap E_2$.

If $\hat{\underline{m}}(\underline{n},\mathcal{E})$ exists, then by Lemma 5.9 and the induction hypothesis,

$$(5.126) \qquad \hat{m}_{\underline{i}}(\underline{n},\mathcal{E}) = \frac{\hat{m}_{\pi_A \underline{i}}(\underline{n}^A, I(A), \mathcal{E}_1)\,\hat{m}_{\pi_B \underline{i}}(\underline{n}^B, I(B), \mathcal{E}_2)}{n^C_{\pi_C \underline{i}} \prod_{j \in D(\mathcal{E})} r_j}$$

$$= \frac{\prod_{E \in \mathcal{E}_1} n^E_{\pi_E \underline{i}}}{\prod_{F \in \mathcal{F}(\mathcal{E}_1)} (n^F_{\pi_F \underline{i}})^{d(F,\mathcal{E}_1)}} \; \frac{\prod_{E \in \mathcal{E}_2} n^E_{\pi_E \underline{i}}}{\prod_{F \in \mathcal{F}(\mathcal{E}_2)} (n^F_{\pi_F \underline{i}})^{d(F,\mathcal{E}_2)}}$$

$$/[n^C_{\pi_C \underline{i}} \prod_{j \in D(\mathcal{E})} r_j]$$

$$= [\prod_{E \in \mathcal{E}} n^E_{\pi_E \underline{i}} / \prod_{F \in \mathcal{F}(\mathcal{E})} n^F_{\pi_F \underline{i}}] \prod_{j \in D(\mathcal{E})} \frac{1}{r_j},$$

where $A = \cup(\mathcal{E}_1)$, $B = \cup(\mathcal{E}_2)$, and $C = A \cap B$. Since $\hat{\underline{m}}(\underline{n},\mathcal{E})$ exists if and only if $\hat{\underline{m}}(\underline{n}^A, I(A), \mathcal{E}_1)$ and $\hat{\underline{m}}(\underline{n}^B, I(B), \mathcal{E}_2)$ exist, Lemma 5.9 and the induction hypothesis imply that $\hat{\underline{m}}(\underline{n},\mathcal{E})$ exists if and only if $n^E_{\underline{i}} > 0$ for all $\underline{i} \in I(E)$ and $E \in \mathcal{E}$. ||

It should be noted that the right-hand side of (5.118) is well defined whenever $n^F_{\underline{i}} > 0$ for all $\underline{i} \in I(F)$ and $F \in \mathcal{F}(\mathcal{E})$. In such a case, the marginal restraints on

$\hat{m}_{\underline{i}}(\underline{n},E)$ are satisfied, even if for some $\underline{i} \in I$, $\hat{m}_{\underline{i}}(\underline{n},E) = 0$. This feature is used in chapter 7 when closed-form estimates are considered for incomplete tables. The estimate $\underline{\hat{m}}(n,E)$ is thus an extended maximum likelihood estimate (see Appendix B).

Example 5.37. Consider the decomposable generating class E such that $E = \{\{1,2\}, \{2,3\}, \{4,5\}\}$ and $d = 5$. If $N = n_{\alpha}^{\phi} = (\underline{n},\underline{e})$, then

$$\hat{m}_{i_1 i_2 i_3 i_4 i_5}(\underline{n},E) = n_{i_1 i_2}^{\{1,2\}} n_{i_2 i_3}^{\{2,3\}} n_{i_4 i_5}^{\{4,5\}} / n_{i_2}^{\{2\}} N . \tag{5.127}$$

This equation follows from Theorem 5.1 and from Example 5.36.

The following corollaries provide results for a large number of common situations.

COROLLARY 5.1. *Suppose that* $F(E)$ *contains a single element* F. *Then* E *is decomposable and if* $\underline{\hat{m}}(\underline{n},E)$ *exists, then for each* $\underline{i} \in I$,

$$\hat{m}_{\underline{i}}(\underline{n},E) = \frac{\left(\prod_{E \in E} n_{\pi_E \underline{i}}^{E}\right) \prod_{j \in D(E)} \frac{1}{r_j}}{\left(n_{\pi_F \underline{i}}^{F}\right)^{k-1}} \tag{5.128}$$

where E *has* k *elements.*

Proof. Suppose all proper nonempty subclasses of E are decomposable. This assumption is valid if $k = 1$. If $E_1 \cup E_2 = E'$, where $E' \not\subset E$, $E_1 \cap E_2 = \phi$, and neither E_1 nor E_2 is empty, then E_1 and E_2 are decomposable. If $E_1 \in E_1$ and $E_2 \in E_2$, then $[\cup(E_1)] \cap [\cup(E_2)] = E_1 \cap E_2 = F$. Thus E' is decomposable. By induction, E is decomposable. Since $d(F,E) = k - 1$, (5.128) follows from (5.118).||

Example 5.38. If $E = \{\{1,2\}, \{2,3\}\}$ and $d = 3$, then

$$\hat{m}_{i_1 i_2 i_3}(\underline{n},E) = n_{i_1 i_2}^{\{1,2\}} n_{i_2 i_3}^{\{2,3\}} / n_{i_2}^{\{2\}} . \tag{5.129}$$

COROLLARY 5.2. *Suppose that* $F(E) = \{F_1, F_2\}$, *where* $F_1 \subset F_2$. *Suppose* E *has* k *elements, of which* k' *contain* F_2. *Then* E *is decomposable and if* $\underline{\hat{m}}(\underline{n},E)$ *exists, for each* $i \in I$, $\hat{m}_{\underline{i}}(\underline{n},E)$ *satisfies*

$$\hat{m}_{\underline{i}}(\underline{n},E) = \frac{\left(\prod_{E \in E} n_{\pi_E \underline{i}}^{E}\right)\left[\prod_{j \in D(E)} \frac{1}{r_j}\right]}{\left(n_{\pi_{F_1} \underline{i}}^{F_1}\right)^{k-k'} \left(n_{\pi_{F_2} \underline{i}}^{F_2}\right)^{k'-1}} . \tag{5.130}$$

Proof. Suppose that $\mathcal{E}_1 = \{E \in \mathcal{E}: F_2 \subset E\}$ and $\mathcal{E}_2 = \mathcal{E} - \mathcal{E}_1$. Since $F_1 \in F(\mathcal{E})$, $\mathcal{E}_2$ is not empty. In addition, $F(\mathcal{E}_1) = \{F_2\}$ and $F(\mathcal{E}_2) = \{F_1\}$. Thus $\mathcal{E}_1$ and $\mathcal{E}_2$ are disjoint decomposable generating classes. If $E_1 \in \mathcal{E}_1$ and $E_2 \in \mathcal{E}_2$, then $E_1 \cap E_2 = F_1$. Consequently, $[U(\mathcal{E}_1)] \cap [U(\mathcal{E}_2)] = E_1 \cap E_2$. Hence $\mathcal{E}$ is decomposable. Since $\mathcal{E}$ has k' elements containing F_2, $d(F_2,\mathcal{E}) = k' - 1$. Since $\mathcal{E}$ has k elements containing F_1, $d(F_1,\mathcal{E}) = (k - 1) - (k' - 1) = k - k'$. Equation (5.130) follows from (5.118).||

Example 5.39. If $\mathcal{E} = \{\{1,2\}, \{2,3\}, \{4,5\}\}$, then $F(\mathcal{E}) = \{\{2\},\phi\}$. The maximum-likelihood estimate of $\underline{m}$, if it exists, satisfies (5.127).

COROLLARY 5.3. *Suppose* $F(\mathcal{E}) = \{\phi,F_1,F_2\}$, *where* F_1 *and* F_2 *are disjoint non-empty sets. Then* $\mathcal{E}$ *is decomposable. If* $\hat{\underline{m}}(\underline{n},\mathcal{E})$ *exists, then for each* $\underline{i} \in I$,

$$\hat{m}_{\underline{i}}(\underline{n},\mathcal{E}) = \frac{\left(\prod_{E\in\mathcal{E}} n^{E}_{\pi_E \underline{i}}\right) \prod_{j\in D(\mathcal{E})} \frac{1}{r_j}}{(n^{F_1}_{\pi_{F_1}\underline{i}})^{k_1-1} (n^{F_2}_{\pi_{F_2}\underline{i}})^{k_2-1} N^{k-k_1-k_2+1}}, \tag{5.131}$$

where if $j \in \overline{2}$, k_j *of the* k *elements of* $\mathcal{E}$ *contain* F_j.

Remark. In (5.31), N is defined as in (5.127).

Proof. Let $\mathcal{E}_1 = \{E \in \mathcal{E}: F_2 \subset E\}$ and let $\mathcal{E}_2 = \mathcal{E} - \mathcal{E}_1$. Then $F(\mathcal{E}_1) = \{F_2\}$ and $F(\mathcal{E}_2) \subset \{\phi,F_1\}$. By Corollaries 5.1 and 5.2, $\mathcal{E}_1$ and $\mathcal{E}_2$ are disjoint decomposable generating classes. If $E_1 \in \mathcal{E}_1$ and $E_2 \in \mathcal{E}_2$, then $E_1 \cap E_2$ is F_1 or ϕ. Thus $[U(\mathcal{E}_1)] \cap [U(\mathcal{E}_2)]$ is F_1 or ϕ. In either case, $\mathcal{E}$ is decomposable. Observe now that $d(F_1,\mathcal{E}) = k_1 - 1$, $d(F_2,\mathcal{E}) = k_2 - 1$, and $d(\phi,\mathcal{E}) = k - k_1 - k_2 + 1$. These results imply that (5.131) holds if $\hat{\underline{m}}(\underline{n},\mathcal{E})$ exists.||

Example 5.40. Suppose that $d = 4$ and $\mathcal{E} = \{\{1,2\}, \{2,3\}, \{3,4\}\}$. Then

$$\hat{m}_{\underline{i}}(\underline{n},\mathcal{E}) = n^{\{1,2\}}_{i_1 i_2} n^{\{2,3\}}_{i_2 i_3} n^{\{3,4\}}_{i_3 i_4} / n^{\{2\}}_{i_2} n^{\{3,4\}}_{i_3}, \tag{5.132}$$

provided $\hat{\underline{m}}(\underline{n},\mathcal{E})$ exists.

COROLLARY 5.4. *Suppose that* $F(\mathcal{E}) = \{\phi,F_1,F_2\}$, *where* F_1 *is not empty and* $F_1 \subset F_2$. *Then* $\mathcal{E}$ *is decomposable. If* k_1, k_2, *and* k *are defined as in* Corollary 5.3, *then if* $\hat{\underline{m}}(\underline{n},\mathcal{E})$ *exists and* $\underline{i} \in I$,

$$\hat{m}_{\underline{i}}(\underline{n},\mathcal{E}) = \frac{\left(\prod_{E\in\mathcal{E}} n^{E}_{\pi_E \underline{i}}\right) \prod_{j\in D(\mathcal{E})} \frac{1}{r_j}}{(n^{F_1}_{\pi_{F_1}\underline{i}})^{k_1-k_2} (n^{F_2}_{\pi_{F_2}\underline{i}})^{k_2-1} N^{k-k_1}}. \tag{5.133}$$

Proof. To prove that $\mathcal{E}$ is decomposable, it is sufficient to apply the argument used in Corollary 5.3. To verify that (5.133) holds, observe that $d(F_2,\mathcal{E}) = k_2 - 1$, $d(F_1,\mathcal{E}) = k_1 - k_2$, and $d(\phi,\mathcal{E}) = k - k_1$. ||

Example 5.41. Suppose $\mathcal{E} = \{\{1,2,3\}, \{1,2,4\}, \{2,5\}, \{6\}\}$. Then $F(\mathcal{E}) = \{\{1,2\},\{2\},\phi\}$; and if it exists,

$$(5.134) \qquad \hat{m}_{i_1i_2i_3i_4i_5i_6}(\underline{n},\mathcal{E}) = \frac{n^{\{1,2,3\}}_{i_1i_2i_3}\, n^{\{1,2,4\}}_{i_1i_2i_4}\, n^{\{2,5\}}_{i_2i_5}\, n^{\{6\}}_{i_6}}{n^{\{1,2\}}_{i_1i_2}\, n^{\{2\}}_{i_2} N} .$$

Two omissions require explanation. Consider the case $F(\mathcal{E}) = \{F_1,F_2\}$, where $F_1 \cap F_2 \neq \phi$ and neither set is included in the other one. This case has not been considered since it is vacuous. Suppose that $F(\mathcal{E})$ has the proposed form and $E_1 \cap E_2 = F_1$, where E_1 and E_2 are sets in $\mathcal{E}$. If $E_1 \cap E = F_1$ for every $E \in \mathcal{E} - \{E_1\}$, then $F_1 \subset F_2$. This contradiction implies that for some $E_3 \in \mathcal{E} - \{E_1\}$, $E_1 \cap E_3 = F_2$. Without loss of generality, suppose that $E_2 \cap E_3 = F_1$. Then $F_1 \subset E_3$ and $F_1 \subset E_1$. Therefore, $F_1 \subset F_2$. Since $F_1 \not\subset F_2$, no $\mathcal{E}$ exists such that $F(\mathcal{E}) = \{F_1,F_2\}$. Now suppose that $F(\mathcal{E}) = \{\phi,F_1,F_2\}$, where F_1 and F_2 are defined as before. This case is also impossible. Once again, select sets E_1 and E_2 in $\mathcal{E}$ such that $E_1 \cap E_2 = F_1$. Let $\bar{\mathcal{E}}$ be the subclass of $\mathcal{E}$ consisting of sets not disjoint from E_1. If $F_2 \subset E$, then $E \in \bar{\mathcal{E}}$. If for all $E \in \bar{\mathcal{E}}$, $E_1 \cap E = F_1$, then $F_1 \subset F_2$. Since $F_1 \not\subset F_2$, there exists an $E_3 \in \mathcal{E} - \{E_1\}$ such that $E_1 \cap E_3 = F_2$. Either $E_2 \cap E_3 = \phi$, $E_2 \subset E_3 = F_1$, or $E_2 \cap E_3 = F_2$. If $E_2 \cap E_3 = \phi$, then F_1 and F_2 are disjoint. Since $F_1 \cap F_2 \neq \phi$, $E_2 \cap E_3 = F_1$ or $E_2 \cap E_3 = F_2$. Just as in the case $F(\mathcal{E}) = \{F_1,F_2\}$, neither of these conditions is possible. Thus $F(\mathcal{E})$ cannot equal $\{\phi,F_1,F_2\}$.

These corollaries and examples correspond to results in Goodman (1970), Bishop (1967,1970), and Birch (1963). In these papers, results were derived on a case-by-case basis rather than by use of a general theorem such as Theorem 5.1.

Theorem 5.1 does not provide closed-form maximum-likelihood estimates for all generating classes $\mathcal{E}$. The simplest example of a generating class which is not decomposable is $\{\{1,2\}, \{1,3\}, \{2,3\}\}$. No decomposition of the class is possible since each set is contained in the union of the other two sets (see Example 5.26 and Darroch 1962).

A simple algorithm exists which permits decomposability to be determined. In order to justify use of the algorithm, the following three lemmas are needed:

LEMMA 5.10. *Suppose that* $\mathcal{E}$ *is a decomposable generating class. For any* $E \in \mathcal{E}$, *the sets of* $\mathcal{E}$ *may be ordered so that* $\mathcal{E} = \{E_k: k \in \overline{s}\}$, $E_1 = E$, *and for each* $r \in \overline{s-1}$, *there exists a* $k_r \in \overline{r}$ *such that*

$$(\bigcup_{k=1}^{r} E_k) \cap E_{r+1} = E_{k_r} \cap E_{r+1}. \tag{5.135}$$

Remark. Note that $\bigcup_{k=1}^{r} E_k = \bigcup\{E_k: k \in \overline{r}\}$.

Proof. The proof is by induction. The result is trivial if $\mathcal{E}$ has one element. Now suppose that $\mathcal{E} = \mathcal{E}_1 \cup \mathcal{E}_2$, where $\mathcal{E}_1$ and $\mathcal{E}_2$ are disjoint decomposable generating classes such that there exist $E' \in \mathcal{E}_1$ and $E'' \in \mathcal{E}_2$ for which

$$[\bigcup(\mathcal{E}_1)] \cap [\bigcup(\mathcal{E}_2)] = E' \cap E'' . \tag{5.136}$$

Without loss of generality, assume that $E \in \mathcal{E}_1$. Suppose that the lemma applies to all subclasses of $\mathcal{E}$. Then $\mathcal{E}_1 = \{G_k: k \in \overline{t}\}$, where $G_1 = E$, $t < s$, and for each $r \in \overline{t-1}$, there exists some $k_r \in \overline{r}$ such that

$$(\bigcup_{k=1}^{r} G_k) \cap G_{r+1} = G_{k_r} \cap G_{r+1} . \tag{5.137}$$

In addition, $\mathcal{E}_2 = \{G_k: k \in \overline{s} - \overline{t}\}$, where $G_{t+1} = E''$ and for each $r \in \overline{s-1} - \overline{t}$, there exists some $k_r \in \overline{r} - \overline{t}$ such that

$$(\bigcup_{k=t+1}^{r} G_k) \cap G_{r+1} = G_{k_r} \cap G_{r+1} . \tag{5.138}$$

Observe that

$$(\bigcup_{k=1}^{t} G_k) \cap G_{t+1} = E' \cap E'' \tag{5.139}$$

and note that if $r > t + 1$, then

$$\begin{aligned}(\bigcup_{k=1}^{r} G_k) \cap G_{r+1} &= (G_{k_r} \cap G_{r+1}) \cup (E'' \cap G_{r+1}) \\ &= G_{k_r} \cap G_{r+1} .\end{aligned} \tag{5.140}$$

The last equation holds since

$$E'' \cap G_{r+1} \subset (\bigcup_{k=1}^{r} G_k) \cap G_{r+1} = G_{k_r} \cap G_{r+1} . \tag{5.141}$$

The ordering $\mathcal{E} = \{G_k: k \in \overline{s}\}$ satisfies all the conditions of the lemma to be proven.||

Example 5.42. Suppose that $\mathcal{E} = \{E_k: k \in \overline{4}\}$, where $E_1 = \{1,2,3\}$, $E_2 = \{1,2,4\}$, $E_3 = \{2,3,5\}$, and $E_4 = \{1,3,6\}$. Then $k_1 = 1$, $k_2 = 1$, and $k_3 = 1$. One has

$$E_1 \cap E_2 = \{1,2,3\} \cap \{1,2,4\}, \tag{5.142}$$

$$\begin{aligned}(E_1 \cup E_2) \cap E_3 &= (\{1,2,3\} \cup \{1,2,4\}) \cap \{2,3,5\} \\ &= \{2,3\} \\ &= \{1,2,3\} \cap \{2,3,5\},\end{aligned} \tag{5.143}$$

and

$$\begin{aligned}(E_1 \cup E_2 \cup E_3) \cap E_4 &= (\{1,2,3\} \cup \{1,2,4\} \cup \{2,3,5\}) \cap \{1,3,6\} \\ &= \{1,3\} \\ &= \{1,2,3\} \cap \{1,3,6\}.\end{aligned} \tag{5.144}$$

LEMMA 5.11. *Suppose that* $\mathcal{E}$ *is a decomposable generating class such that for some* $E \in \mathcal{E}$ *and* $E' \in \mathcal{E} - \{E\}$,

$$E \cap E' = E \cap [\cup(\mathcal{E} - \{E\})]. \tag{5.145}$$

Then $\mathcal{E} - \{E\}$ *is decomposable.*

Proof. By Lemma 5.10, there exists an ordering of $\mathcal{E}$ so that $\mathcal{E} = \{E_k: k \in \overline{s}\}$, $E_1 = E'$, and for each $r \in \overline{s-1}$, there exists k_r such that

$$E_{r+1} \cap \left(\bigcup_{k=1}^{r} E_k\right) = E_{r+1} \cap E_{k_r}. \tag{5.146}$$

Suppose that $E_t = E$. Clearly $\{E_k: k \in \overline{t-1}\}$ is decomposable. Suppose that $\{E_k: k \in \overline{r}\} - \{E\}$ is decomposable, where $t \le r < s$. If $E_{k_r} \ne E$, then (5.146) implies that $\{E_k: k \in \overline{r+1}\} - E$ is decomposable. If $E_{k_r} = E$, then observe that

$$E_{r+1} \cap E' \subset E_{r+1} \cap \left(\bigcup_{k=1}^{r} E_k\right) = E_{r+1} \cap E \subset E' \cap E. \tag{5.147}$$

Thus

$$E_{r+1} \cap E' = E_{r+1} \cap \left(\bigcup_{k=1}^{r} E_k\right). \tag{5.148}$$

Hence $\{E_k: k \in \overline{r+1}\} - \{E\}$ is decomposable. By induction, $\mathcal{E} - \{E\}$ is decomposable.||

Example 5.43. Suppose $\mathcal{E}$ is defined as in Example 5.42. Then since

$$\{1,2,4\} \cap \{1,2,3\} = \{1,2,4\} \cap (\{1,2,3\} \cup \{2,3,5\} \cup \{1,3,6\}), \tag{5.149}$$

$\{\{1,2,3\},\{2,3,5\},\{1,3,6\}\}$ is decomposable.

LEMMA 5.12. *Suppose* $U(E)$ *has* d' *elements. Suppose the largest set of* E *has* d^* *elements. If* E *has more than* $d' - d^* + 1$ *sets, it is not decomposable.*

Proof. Suppose E is decomposable and $\{E_k: k \in \overline{s}\}$ is an ordering of E such that (5.135) holds for $r \in \overline{s-1}$ and E_1 has d^* elements. If $r \in \overline{s-1}$, then $E_{r+1} - \cup_{k=1}^{r} E_k \neq \phi$. Thus $U(E)$ has at least $s - 1 + d^*$ elements. Since $s - 1 + d^*$ exceeds d', a contradiction results.||

Example 5.44. Consider the generating class $E = \{\{1,2\},\{1,3\},\{2,3\}\}$. Then $U(E) = \{1,2,3\}$, $d' = 3$, and $d^* = 2$. Since E has more than $3 - 2 + 1$ sets, it cannot be decomposable.

These lemmas demonstrate that hierarchical models have a simpler structure than the one suggested by the original definition. A generating class E is decomposable if and only if $E = \{E_k: k \in \overline{s}\}$, where (5.135) is satisfied for each $r \in \overline{s-1}$ by some $k_r \in \overline{r}$. A simple algorithm is now available for determining whether a given generating class E is decomposable. If $s \leq 2$, E is always decomposable, so it is only necessary to consider the case $s > 2$. Define $E^{(0)} = E$. Assume that r is 0 or is in $\overline{s-3}$. Suppose that $E^{(r)}$ has been found and no decision has been made concerning the decomposability of E. Suppose that $U(E^{(r)})$ has d_r elements and the largest set in $E^{(r)}$ has b_r elements. Note that $E^{(r)}$ has $s - r$ sets.

a) If $s - r > d_r - b_r + 1$, then E is not decomposable.

b) If there exists $E_r \in E^{(r)}$ and $E_r' \in E^{(r)} - \{E_r\}$ such that

$$E_r \cap E_r' = E_r \cap [U(E^{(r)} - \{E_r\})], \tag{5.150}$$

then let $E^{(r+1)} = E^{(r)} - \{E_r\}$. If $r = s - 3$, then E is decomposable.

c) If (5.150) is not satisfied for any two distinct elements E_r and E_r' contained in $E^{(r)}$, then E is not decomposable.

To show that the algorithm provides a valid test of decomposability, suppose that E is decomposable. Then $E^{(0)}$ is decomposable. Suppose $E^{(t)}$ is decomposable if $0 \leq t - r < s - 3$. Then by Lemma 5.11, $E^{(r+1)}$ is decomposable. By induction, $E^{(s-3)}$ is decomposable. The correct conclusion is therefore made.

Suppose now that E is not decomposable. Suppose that for each $r \leq s - 3$, an $E_r \in E^{(r)}$ and an $E_r' \in E^{(r)} - E_r$ exist so that (5.150) is satisfied. Then $E^{(s-3)} - \{E_{s-3}\}$ has only two elements. It is therefore decomposable. By (5.150), $E^{(s-3)}$ is decomposable. A simple induction now shows that $E^{(0)}$ is decomposable. Since

$E^{(0)} = E$, a contradiction results. Therefore, there exists an $r \in \overline{s-3} \cup \{0\}$ such that either $s - r > d_r - b_r + 1$ or (5.150) does not hold for any $E_r \in E^{(r)}$ and $E_r' \in E^{(r)} - \{E_r\}$.

Example 5.45. Consider $E = E^{(0)} = \{\{1,2\},\{2,3\},\{3,4\},\{1,5\}\}$. Then $b_0 = 2$ and $d_0 = 5$. We have $s = 4$. Then $4 - 0 \le 5 - 2 + 1$. In addition,

$$\{1,5\} \cap \{1,2\} = \{1,5\} \cap (\{1,2\} \cup \{2,3\} \cup \{3,4\}). \tag{5.151}$$

Thus $E_0 = \{1,5\}$, $E_0' = \{1,2\}$, and $E^{(1)} = \{\{1,2\},\{2,3\},\{3,4\}\}$. Now $d_1 = 4$ and $b_1 = 2$. Then $4 - 1 \le 4 - 2 + 1$. Observe that

$$\{3,4\} \cap \{2,3\} = \{3,4\} \cap (\{2,3\} \cup \{1,2\}). \tag{5.152}$$

Thus possible values of E_1 and E_1' are $\{3,4\}$ and $\{2,3\}$, respectively. Since $s - 3 = 1$, E is decomposable.

Exhaustive enumerations of hierarchical models for $d \le 4$ have been provided by Goodman (1970) and by Bishop (1970). These enumerations specify which models have closed-form maximum-likelihood estimates. If $d < 3$, all hierarchical models have closed-form estimates. If $d = 3$, the only hierarcical model without a closed-form estimate has the generating class $\{\{1,2\},\{2,3\},\{1,3\}\}$. If $d = 4$, there are 27 classes of hierarchical models, of which 17 correspond to decomposable generating classes. In this enumeration, two models belong to the same class if the corresponding generating classes E_1 and E_2 satisfy

$$E_2 = \sigma(E_1) = \{\sigma(E): E \in E\}, \tag{5.153}$$

where σ is a permutation of $\overline{d}$. Enumerations are not available if $d > 4$ since the number of possible hierarchical models becomes enormous.

A partial converse may be obtained for Theorem 5.1. Suppose that $E = \{E_k: k \in \overline{s}\}$, where $s > 1$. Let

$$F_k = E_k \cap \left(\bigcup_{j=1}^{k-1} E_j\right) \tag{5.154}$$

for each $k \in \overline{s-1}$. Suppose that

$$m_{\underline{i}}^*(\underline{n}) = \frac{1}{\prod_{j \in D(E)} r_j} n^{E_1}_{\pi_{E_1}\underline{i}} \prod_{k=2}^{s} \left(n^{E_k}_{\pi_{E_k}\underline{i}} / n^{F_k}_{\pi_{F_k}\underline{i}}\right), \tag{5.155}$$

where $\underline{i} \in I$. If E is decomposable and the ordering of E is such that for $r \in \overline{s-1}$

there exists $k \in \overline{r}$ such that (5.135) holds, then whenever $n^E_{\underline{i}} > 0$ for all $\underline{i} \in I(E)$ and $E \in \mathcal{E}$, $\hat{\underline{m}}(\underline{n},\mathcal{E}) = \underline{m}^*(\underline{n})$. This result is easily verified by use of Lemmas 5.7 and 5.9. Thus the maximum-likelihood estimate $\hat{\underline{m}}(\underline{n},\mathcal{E})$ given by (5.118) can always be expressed so that it satisfies (5.155). The converse to this statement is proven in the following theorem.

THEOREM 5.2. *Suppose that* $\hat{\underline{m}}(\underline{n},\mathcal{E}) = \underline{m}^*(\underline{n})$ *whenever* $n^E_{\underline{i}} > 0$ *for all* $\underline{i} \in I(E)$ *and* $E \in \mathcal{E}$. *Then* $\mathcal{E}$ *is decomposable.*

Proof. This result may be proven by induction on the number of elements in $\mathcal{E}$. If $\mathcal{E}$ has two elements, then $\mathcal{E}$ must be decomposable. In general, suppose the result has been established for all generating classes with no more than $s - 1 \geq 2$ elements. If $A = \cup_{k=1}^{s-1} E_k$ and $\underline{i} \in I(A)$, then Lemma 5.8 implies

$$\hat{m}^A_{\underline{i}}(\underline{n},\mathcal{E}) = n^{E_1}_{\pi^A_{E_1}\underline{i}} \prod_{k=1}^{s-1} \left(n^{E_k}_{\pi^A_{E_k}\underline{i}} \Big/ n^{F_k}_{\pi^A_{F_k}\underline{i}} \right) \tag{5.156}$$

if $n^E_{\underline{i}} > 0$ for all $\underline{i} \in I(E)$ and $E \in \mathcal{E}$. If $\mathcal{E}' = \{E_k : k \in \overline{s-1}\}$, then $\{\log \hat{m}^A_{\underline{i}}(\underline{n},\mathcal{E}) : \underline{i} \in I(A)\} \in M(I(A),\mathcal{E}')$ and $\hat{\underline{m}}^E(\underline{n},\mathcal{E}) = \underline{n}^E$ for all $E \in \mathcal{E}'$. Thus $\hat{\underline{m}}(\underline{n}^A, I(A), \mathcal{E}') = \hat{\underline{m}}^A(\underline{n},\mathcal{E})$ and

$$\hat{m}_{\underline{i}}(\underline{n},\mathcal{E}) = \frac{\hat{m}_{\pi_A\underline{i}}(\underline{n}^A, I(A), \mathcal{E}')\, n_{\pi_{E_s}\underline{i}}}{[\prod_{j\in D(\mathcal{E})} r_j]\, n^{F_s}_{\pi_{E_s}\underline{i}}} \tag{5.157}$$

for all $\underline{i} \in I$. In particular, if $\underline{a} \in R^{I(A)}$, $a^E_{\underline{i}} > 0$ for all $\underline{i} \in I(E)$ and $E \in \mathcal{E}'$, $a_{\underline{i}} > 0$ for $\underline{i} \in I(A)$, and $\underline{x} = \{a_{\pi_A\underline{i}} / \prod_{j\in D(\mathcal{E}')} r_j : \underline{i} \in I\}$, then $\hat{\underline{m}}(\underline{a}, I(A), \mathcal{E}') = \underline{m}^A(\underline{x},\mathcal{E})$. By (5.156) and the induction hypothesis, $\mathcal{E}'$ is decomposable.

If $\underline{\mu} \in M(\mathcal{E})$, then $\hat{\underline{m}}(\underline{m}(\underline{\mu}),\mathcal{E}) = \underline{m}(\underline{\mu})$, $\hat{\underline{m}}(\underline{m}^A(\underline{\mu}), I(A), \mathcal{E}') = \underline{m}^A(\underline{\mu})$, and

$$m_{\underline{i}}(\underline{\mu}) = \frac{m^A_{\pi_A\underline{i}}(\underline{\mu})\, m^{E_s}_{\pi_{E_s}\underline{i}}(\underline{\mu})}{[\prod_{j\in D(\mathcal{E})} r_j]\, n^{F_s}_{\pi_{F_s}\underline{i}}(\underline{\mu})} \tag{5.158}$$

for every $\underline{i} \in I$. If $f(\underline{\mu}) = \langle \underline{m}^A(\underline{\mu}), \underline{m}^{E_s}(\underline{\mu}) \rangle$ for all $\underline{\mu} \in M(\mathcal{E})$, then f is a continuous mapping with range $T = \{\langle \underline{m}^A(\underline{\mu}), \underline{m}^{E_s}(\underline{\mu}) \rangle : \underline{\mu} \in M(\mathcal{E})\}$. By (5.158), the inverse of this mapping is also continuous. Thus $M(\mathcal{E})$ and T are homeomorphic. By Hurewicz and Wallman (1941), $M(\mathcal{E})$ and T have the same dimension.

The dimension of $M(E)$ may be found by use of a standard result in Halmos (1958). Since $M(E) = M(E') + M(\{E_s\})$,

$$\dim M(E) = \dim M(E') + \dim M(\{E_s\}) - \dim [M(E') \cap M(\{E_s\})] \tag{5.159}$$

$$= \dim M(E') + \prod_{j\in E_s} r_j - \dim [M(E') \cap M(\{E_s\})].$$

To find the dimension of T, observe that if $S = \{\underline{m}^A(\underline{E}): \underline{\mu} \in M(E)\}$, then $S = \{\underline{m}(\underline{E}): \underline{\mu} \in M(I(A),E')\}$. Since S is homeomorphic with $M(I(A),E')$, which has the dimension of $M(E')$, S has the dimension of $M(E')$. Given $\underline{m}^A(\underline{E})$, $\{m^{E_s}_{\pi_{F_s}^{E_s}\underline{i}} : \underline{i} \in I(E_s)\}$ may be any solution $\underline{a}$ of the equations

$$\sum\{a_{\underline{i}} : \underline{i} \in S^{E_s}_{F_s \underline{j}}\} = 1, \tag{5.160}$$

where $\underline{j} \in I(F_s)$, such that $a_{\underline{i}} > 0$ for all $\underline{i} \in I(E_s)$. The set U of such solutions has dimension $(\prod_{j\in F_s} r_j)(\prod_{j\in E_s - F_s} r_j - 1)$. Since T is homeomorphic to the Cartesian product $S \times U$, the dimension of T is $\dim(E') + \prod_{j\in E_s} r_j - \prod_{j\in F_s} r_j$.

The dimensions of T and $M(E)$ are equal if and only if $\dim[M(E') \cap (\{E_s\})] = \prod_{j\in F_s} r_j$. Since $M(E') \subset M(\{A\})$ and $M(\{A\}) \cap M(\{E_s\}) = M(\{F_s\})$, which has dimension $\prod_{j\in F_s} r_j$, $M(E') \cap M(\{E_s\}) = M(\{F_s\})$. Equality can only hold if for some $E' \in E'$, $E' \cap E_s = F_s$. If this condition is satisfied, then E is decomposable. Thus the induction hypothesis holds if E has s elements. By induction, the theorem holds for all generating classes.||

The estimate specified by (5.155) is a Markov estimate (see Anderson and Goodman 1957). It corresponds to the maximum-likelihood estimate of $\underline{m}$ given that

$$m_{\underline{i}} = (m^{E_1}_{\pi_{E_1}\underline{i}} / \prod_{j\in D(E)} r_j) \prod_{k=2}^{2} (m^{E_k}_{\pi_{E_k}\underline{i}} / m^{F_k}_{\pi_{F_k}\underline{i}}) \tag{5.161}$$

for $\underline{i} \in I$. The assumption that $\underline{m}$ satisfies (5.161) is easily seen to be equivalent to the hypothesis that in a table based on a sample of N discrete random vectors $\{\underline{X}_t: t \in \bar{N}$ for each $t \in \bar{N}$ and $r \in \bar{s} - \bar{1}$, $\{X_{tj}: j \in E_r - F_r\}$ and $\{X_{tj}: j \in \cup_{k=1}^{r-1} E_k - F_r\}$ are conditionally independent given $\{X_{tj}: j \in F_r\}$ and each value of $\{X_{tj}: j \in D(E)\}$ is equally probable given any value of $\{X_{tj}: j \in U(E)\}$. Goodman (1970) observed that the Markov and maximum-likelihood estimates are the same when the dimension of $M(E)$ is the same as the dimension of the set of $\underline{\mu} \in R^I$ such that (5.161) is satisfied. As shown in Theorem 5.2, this criterion implies that E is decomposable. On the other hand, Lemmas 5.6, 5.8, and 5.10 imply that if E is decomposable and the sets of E are ordered so that (5.135) holds, then (5.161) is satisfied. Thus the model $\underline{\mu} \in M(E)$ is equivalent to the hypothesis that for $t \in \overline{N}$ and $r \in \overline{S} - 1$, $\{X_{tj}: j \in E_r - F_r\}$ and $\{X_{tj}: j \in \cup_{k=1}^{r-1} E_k - F_r\}$ are conditionally independent given $\{X_{tj}: j \in F_r\}$ and each value of $\{X_{tj}: j \in D(E)\}$ is equally probable given any value of $\{X_{tj}: j \in M(E)\}$. If the sets of E are ordered so that (5.135) does not hold, then the Markov model is more restrictive than the corresponding log-linear model. In this sense, a model $\underline{\mu} \in U(E)$ in which E is not decomposable cannot be described by use of a series of hypotheses of independence, conditional independence, and equiprobability.

Example 5.46. Suppose that $d = 4$ and $E = \{\{1,2\},\{1,3\},\{2,3,4\}\}$. The Markov estimate satisfies

(5.162) $$m^*_{i_1i_2i_3i_4}(\underline{n}) = n^{\{1,2\}}_{i_1i_2} n^{\{1,3\}}_{i_1i_3} n^{\{2,3,4\}}_{i_2i_3i_4} / n^{\{1\}}_{i_1} n^{\{2,3\}}_{i_2i_3}$$

It corresponds to the hypotheses that X_{t1} and X_{t3} are conditionally independent given X_{t2} and that X_{t1} and X_{t4} are conditionally independent given $\langle X_{t2}, X_{t3}\rangle$. The estimate is not the maximum-likelihood estimate since the set of $\underline{\mu} \in R^I$ which satisfy (5.161) has dimension

(5.163) $$r_1r_2 + r_1(r_3 - 1) + r_2r_3(r_4 - 1) = r_1r_2 + r_1r_3 + r_2r_3r_4 - r_1 - r_2r_3,$$

while $M(E)$ has dimension

(5.164) $$r_1r_2 + r_1r_3 - r_1 + r_2r_3r_4 - (r_2 + r_3) = r_1r_2 + r_1r_3 + r_2r_3r_4 - r_1 - r_2 - r_3.$$

Thus the Markov model is more restrictive than the hypothesis that $\underline{\mu} \in M(E)$. No other permutation of the sets of E results in a Markov estimate which corresponds to the maximum-likelihood estimate, for E is not decomposable.

Computation of likelihood ratio and Pearson chi-square statistics is greatly simplified when the null and alternative hypotheses correspond to decomposable generating classes. If E is a decomposable generating class, then a simple induction based on (5.159) shows that

(5.165) $$\dim M(E) = \sum_{E\in E} \prod_{j\in E} r_j - \sum_{F\in F(E)} d(F,E) \prod_{j\in F} r_j.$$

If $H_0\colon \underline{\mu} \in M(E_1)$ and $H_A\colon \underline{\mu} \in M(E_2)$ are the null and alternative hypotheses, then (5.108) implies that

(5.166) $$-2\Delta(\underline{n},\hat{\underline{\mu}}(\underline{n},E_2),\hat{\underline{\mu}}(\underline{n},E_1)) = 2\Big[\sum_{E\in E_2} \sum_{\underline{i}\in \underline{I}(E)} n_{\underline{i}}^{E} \log n_{\underline{i}}^{E}$$

$$- \sum_{F\in F(E_2)} \sum_{\underline{i}\in \underline{I}(F)} n_{\underline{i}}^{F} \log n_{\underline{i}}^{F} - n_{\alpha}^{\phi} \log(\prod\{r_j\colon j \in D(E_1) - D(E_2)\})$$

$$- \sum_{E\in E_1} \sum_{\underline{i}\in \underline{I}(E)} n_{\underline{i}}^{E} \log n_{\underline{i}}^{E} + \sum_{F\in F(E_1)} \sum_{\underline{i}\in \underline{I}(F)} n_{\underline{i}}^{F} \log n_{\underline{i}}^{F}\Big].$$

This formula is rather useful if computations are done on a calculator or by hand. Tables of $n \log n$ for n up to 999 are given by Kullback (1959), who also provides a number of examples of likelihood ratios expressed as in (5.165). The formula often involves subtractions of quantities which are nearly equal, so considerable care is required to ensure numerical accuracy; however, the reduction in the number of calculations and the elimination of all multiplications except for those involving

$$n_{\alpha}^{\phi} \log (\prod\{r_j\colon j \in D(E_1) - D(E_2)\})$$

often more than compensates for this difficulty.

Example 5.47. In Example 4.13, a test is made in which $I = \overline{3} \times \overline{2} \times \overline{2}$, $E_1 = \{\{1,3\},\{2\}\}$, and $E_2 = \{\{1,2\},\{1,3\}\}$ (see also Example 5.29). Thus $F(E_1) = \{\phi\}$, $d(\phi,E_1) = 1$, $F(E_2) = \{\{1\}\}$, and $d(\{1\},E_2) = 1$. By (5.166)

(5.167) $$-2\Delta(\underline{n},\hat{\underline{\mu}}(\underline{n},E_2),\hat{\underline{\mu}}(\underline{n},E_1))$$

$$= 2\Big(\sum_{i_1=1}^{3} \sum_{i_2=1}^{2} n_{i_1i_2+} \log n_{i_1i_2+}$$

$$+ \sum_{i_1=1}^{3} \sum_{i_3=1}^{2} n_{i_1+i_3} \log n_{i_1+i_3} - \sum_{i_1=1} n_{i_1++} \log n_{i_1++}$$

$$- \sum_{i_1=1}^{3} \sum_{i_3=1}^{2} n_{i_1+i_3} \log n_{i_1+i_3} - \sum_{i_2=1}^{2} n_{+i_2+} \log n_{+i_2+} + n_{+++} \log n_{+++}\Big)$$

$$= 2\Big(\sum_{i_1=1}^{3} \sum_{i_2=1}^{2} n_{i_1i_2+} \log n_{i_1i_2+} + n_{+++} \log n_{+++}$$

$$\sum_{i_1=1}^{3} n_{i_1++} \log n_{i_1++} - \sum_{i_2=1}^{2} n_{+i_2+} \log n_{+i_2+})$$

$$= 2(471.747 + 266.169 + 281.714 + 176.118 + 190.699 + 133.604$$

$$+ 2153.463 - 848.590 - 534.195 - 383.074 - 1173.820 - 733.594)$$

$$= 0.482.$$

Observe that computations require the use of six or seven significant figures during intermediate steps, but only 11 additions or subtractions and 12 table references are needed.

The degrees of freedom for the test may be found by noting that $M(E_1)$ has dimension $(3)(2) + 2 - (1)(1) = 7$ and $M(E_2)$ has dimension $(3)(2) + (3)(2) - (1)(3) = 9$. Thus there are $9 - 7 = 2$ degrees of freedom.

When the Pearson chi-square statistic $C(\hat{\underline{\mu}}(\underline{n},E_2),\hat{\underline{\mu}}(\underline{n},E_1))$ is employed and $\hat{\underline{m}}(\underline{n},E_1)$ and $\hat{\underline{m}}(\underline{n},E_2)$ are not explicitly required, efficient computations depend on the order of summations. The technique was originally developed by Leslie (1951), who proposed the formula

$$n_{++}(\sum_{i=1}^{r} \frac{1}{n_{i+}} \sum_{j=1}^{c} n_{ij}^2/n_{+j} - 1)$$

for the Pearson chi-square test for independence in an $r \times c$ table. Example 5.48 illustrates efficient calculation in a slightly more complex case.

Example 5.48. Under the circumstances of Example 5.47, (4.199) implies that

(5.168)
$$C(\hat{\underline{\mu}}(\underline{n},E_2),\hat{\underline{\mu}}(\underline{n},E_1))$$

$$= \sum_{i_1=1}^{3} \sum_{i_2=1}^{2} \sum_{i_3=1}^{2} (n_{i_1i_2+}n_{i_1+i_3}/n_{i_1++})^2(n_{i_1+i_3}n_{+i_2+}/n_{+++}) - n_{+++}$$

$$= n_{+++}[\sum_{i_1=1}^{3} \sum_{i_2=1}^{2} \sum_{i_3=1}^{2} (n_{i_1+i_3}n_{i_1i_2+}^2/n_{i_1++}^2n_{+i_2+}) - 1]$$

$$= n_{+++}(\sum_{i_1=1}^{3} \sum_{i_2=1}^{2} n_{i_1i_2+}^2/n_{i_1++}n_{+i_2+} - 1)$$

$$= n_{+++}(\sum_{i_1=1}^{3} \frac{1}{n_{i_1++}} \sum_{i_2=1}^{2} n_{i_1i_2+}^2/n_{+i_2+} - 1)$$

$$= 365[(1/166)(102^2/218 + 64^2/147) + (1/113)(67^2/218 + 46^2/147)$$

$$+ (1/86)(49^2/218 + 37^2/47) - 1]$$

$$= 0.478.$$

Once again, care must be taken to ensure numerical accuracy. Given tables of squares and reciprocals, 12 table references, seven additions or subtractions, and 10 multiplications are required. Thus in this example, the computational labor required to find the Pearson chi-square exceeds that required for the likelihood ratio chi-square.

THE DEMING-STEPHAN ALGORITHM

The iterative proportional-fitting procedure mentioned in chapter 3 may be applied to estimation problems involving hierarchical models. Each vector $\underline{\nu}(E,\underline{\bar{i}})$, where $E \in \mathcal{E}$ and $\underline{\bar{i}} \in I(E)$, has elements which are either 0 or 1. If $\underline{\bar{i}} \neq \underline{\bar{j}}$, then $\pi_E^{-1}\underline{\bar{i}}$ is disjoint from $\pi_E^{-1}\underline{\bar{j}}$. If $\mathcal{E} = \{E_k: k \in \bar{s}\}$ and if $\underline{m}^{(t,1)}$ is an estimate of $\hat{\underline{m}}$, then the algorithm consists of an s-step cycle such that for $k \in \bar{s}$ and $\underline{i} \in I$,

$$m_{\underline{i}}^{(t,k+1)} = \frac{m_{\underline{i}}^{(t,k)} n_{\pi_{E_k}\underline{i}}^{E_k}}{(\underline{m}^{(t,k)}, \underline{\nu}(E_k, \pi_{E_k}\underline{i}))} \tag{5.169}$$

$$= m_{\underline{i}}^{(t,k)}\, n_{\pi_{E_k}\underline{i}}^{E_k} / [m^{(t,k)}]_{\pi_{E_k}\underline{i}}^{E_k} .$$

Since individual steps in a cycle consist of proportional adjustments of the fitted estimates $\underline{m}^{(t,k)}$ so that the E_k-marginals $[\underline{m}^{(t+1,k)}]^{E_k} = \{[m^{(t+1,k)}]_{\underline{\bar{i}}}^{E_k}: \underline{\bar{i}} \in I(E_k)\}$ for the new fitted estimates are equal to the E_k-marginals $\underline{n}^{E_k}$ of the data, the algorithm is often described as iterative proportional fitting. It is associated with Deming and Stephan (1940) and Bishop (1967). A Fortran IV algorithm by Haberman (1972) is available which performs iterative proportional fitting.

Example 5.49. Example 3.4 provides a routine example of use of the Deming-Stephan algorithm. In this example, $\mathcal{E} = \{\{1,2\},\{1,3\},\{2,3\}\}$. The steps suggested by (5.169) are described by (3.122), (3.123) and (3.124).

Example 5.50. In Example 4.12, the model specified by (4.202) corresponds to the manifold $\mathcal{M}(\mathcal{E})$, where $\mathcal{E} = \{\{1,2,3\},\{1,2,4\},\{1,3,4\},\{2,3,4\}\}$. The steps in the Deming-Stephan algorithm are described by (4.203), (4.204), (4.205), (4.206), and (4.207).

If $\mathcal{E}$ is decomposable, the Deming-Stephan algorithm may converge to the maximum-likelihood estimate after a single cycle. For some ordering of E, this convergence property holds no matter what $\underline{m}^{(1,1)}$ is. If $\underline{m}^{(1,1)} = \underline{e}$ and $d \leq 6$, convergence in one cycle occurs for any ordering of E, provided only that E is decomposable. These properties make the algorithm very attractive for use with hierarchical models.

If E is decomposable, then E can be ordered so that the Deming-Stephan algorithm converges in one cycle. In fact, the following theorem applies:

THEOREM 5.3. *Suppose* E *is decomposable and* $\hat{\underline{m}}(n,E)$ *exists. Then there exists an ordering* $E = \{E_k : k \in \overline{s}\}$ *such that if* $\{\log m_{\underline{i}}^{(1,1)}\} \in M(E)$ *and* $\underline{m}^{(1,k)}$ *is defined by* (5.169), *then* $\underline{m}^{(1,s+1)} = \hat{\underline{m}}(\underline{n},E)$.

Proof. Suppose that $\{E_k : k \in \overline{s}\}$ satisfies (5.135) for each $r \in \overline{s-1}$. Suppose $F_{r+1} = E_{k_r} \cap E_{r+1}$. Since $\hat{\underline{m}}(\underline{m}^{(1,k)},E) = \underline{m}^{(1,k)}$, $m_{\underline{i}}^{(1,k)}$ satisfies

(5.170)
$$m_{\underline{i}}^{(1,k)} = [m^{(1,k)}]^{E_1}_{\pi_{E_1}\underline{i}} \prod_{r=2}^{s} \{[m^{(1,k)}]^{E_r}_{\pi_{E_r}\underline{i}}/[m^{(1,k)}]^{F_r}_{\pi_{F_r}\underline{i}}\} \prod_{j\in D(E)} \frac{1}{r_j} .$$

Consider the hypothesis that

(5.171)
$$m_{\underline{i}}^{(1,r)} = n^{E_1}_{\pi_{E_1}\underline{i}} \prod_{j=2}^{r-1} (n^{E_j}_{\pi_{E_j}\underline{i}}/n^{F_j}_{\pi_{F_j}\underline{i}}) \prod_{j=r}^{s} \{[m^{(1,r)}]^{E_j}_{\pi_{E_j}\underline{i}}/[m^{(1,r)}]^{F_j}_{\pi_{F_j}\underline{i}}\} \prod_{j\in D(E)} \frac{1}{r_j}$$

$$= \hat{m}_{\pi_{E_1}\underline{i}}(\underline{n}^{A^{(r-1)}}, I(A^{(r-1)}), E^{(r-1)}) \prod_{j=r}^{s} \{[m^{(1,r)}]^{E_j}_{\pi_{E_j}\underline{i}}/[m^{(1,r)}]^{F_j}_{\pi_{F_j}\underline{i}}\} \prod_{j\in D(E)} \frac{1}{r_j} ,$$

where $E^{(r)} = \{E_k : k \in \overline{r}\}$ and $A^{(r)} = U(E^{(r)})$. This assumption clearly holds if $r = 2$. Suppose that it holds for some r such that $2 \leq r \leq s$. By successive applications of Lemma 5.8, $[\underline{m}^{(1,r)}]^{A^{(r-1)}} = \hat{\underline{m}}(\underline{n}^{A^{(r-1)}}, I(A^{(r-1)}), E^{(r-1)})$ and $[\underline{m}^{(1,r)}]^{E_k} = \underline{n}^{E_k}$ if $k \in \overline{r-1}$. Since $F_r \subset E_{k_r}$, for all $\underline{i} \in I(F_r)$

(5.172)
$$[m^{(1,r)}]^{F_r}_{\underline{i}} = n^{F_r}_{\underline{i}} .$$

By (5.169)

(5.173)
$$m_{\underline{i}}^{(1,r+1)} = n^{E_1}_{\pi_{E_1}\underline{i}} \prod_{j=2}^{r} (n^{E_j}_{\pi_{E_j}\underline{i}}/n^{F_j}_{\pi_{F_j}\underline{i}}) \prod_{j=r+1}^{s} \{[m^{(1,r+1)}]^{E_j}_{\pi_{E_j}\underline{i}}/[m^{(1,r+1)}]^{F_j}_{\pi_{F_j}\underline{i}}\} \prod_{j\in D(E)} \frac{1}{r_j} .$$

By induction,

(5.174)
$$m_{\underline{i}}^{(1,s+1)} = n^{E_1}_{\pi_{E_1}\underline{i}} \prod_{r=2}^{2} [n^{E_r}_{\pi_{E_r}\underline{i}}/n^{F_r}_{\pi_{F_r}\underline{i}}] \prod_{j\in D(E)} \frac{1}{r_j}$$

$$= \hat{m}_{\underline{i}}(\underline{n},E). ||$$

TOTAL DECOMPOSABILITY

The Deming-Stephan algorithm converges in a single cycle under more general conditions than those suggested by Theorem 5.3. Results depend on restrictions on $\underline{m}^{(1,1)}$ or E. We first consider the case in which $\underline{m}^{(1,1)}$ is $\underline{e}$ and E is totally decomposable. A generating class E is totally decomposable if E and all of its nonempty subclasses are decomposable. The following preliminary results are needed:

DEFINITION 5.8. *The restriction of* E *to the set* $A \subset \overline{d}$ *is the generating class*

$$E(A) = \{E \cap A\colon E \in E \text{ and } \forall E' \in E,\ E \cap A \subset E' \cap A \text{ implies } E \cap A = E' \cap A\}. \tag{5.175}$$

LEMMA 5.13. *If* E *is totally decomposable and* $A \subset \overline{d}$, *then* $E(A)$ *is totally decomposable.*

Proof. Assume the lemma is true for all totally decomposable generating classes with fewer elements than E. This assumption is trivial if E has 1 element. If $E(A)$ has fewer elements than E, then there exists a generating class $\overline{E} \subset E$ such that $E(A) = \overline{E}(A)$ and $\overline{E} \neq E$. Since $\overline{E} \subset E$, $\overline{E}$ must be totally decomposable. By assumption, $E(A) = \overline{E}(A)$ is totally decomposable. On the other hand, if $E(A)$ has the same number of elements as E and if $E = E' \cup \{E\}$, where $E \notin E'$ and for some $E' \in E'$

$$E \cap E' = E \cap [\cup(E')], \tag{5.176}$$

then $E(A) = E'(A) \cup \{E \cap A\}$ and

$$(E \cap A) \cap (E' \cap A) = (E \cap A) \cap [\cup(E'(A))]. \tag{5.177}$$

Since $E' \cap A \in E'(A)$, $E(A)$ is decomposable. If $\overline{E}$ is a proper subclass of $E(A)$, then $\overline{E} = E'(A)$ for some $E' \subset E$ such that $E' \neq E$. By assumption, $\overline{E}$ is decomposable. Thus $E(A)$ is totally decomposable. By induction, the lemma applies to all totally decomposable E. ||

LEMMA 5.14. *Suppose* E *is decomposable and* $E \in E$. *If* E *has at least two elements and* $\hat{\underline{m}}(\underline{n}, E - \{E\})$ *exists, then for each* $\underline{i} \in I$,

$$\hat{m}^{E}_{\pi_E \underline{i}}(\underline{n}, E - \{E\}) = \hat{m}_{\underline{i}}(\underline{n}, (E - \{E\})(E)) \prod_{j \in \overline{d} - E} r_j\ . \tag{5.178}$$

Proof. By Lemma 5.10, $E = \{E_k\colon k \in \overline{s}\}$, where $E_1 = E$ and for each $r \in \overline{s-1}$ there exists $k_r \in \overline{r}$ such that

(5.179)
$$E_{r+1} \cap E_{k_r} = E_{r+1} \cap (\bigcup_{k=1}^{r} E_k).$$

Suppose $A^{(r)} = \cup_{k=1}^{r} E_k$. The proof is by induction on r, where the induction hypothesis is

(5.180)
$$\hat{m}^{A^{(r)}}_{\pi_{A^{(r)}}\underline{i}}(\underline{n},E - \{E\}) = \hat{m}_{\underline{i}}(\underline{n},(E - \{E\})(A^{(r)})) \prod_{j\in\bar{d}-A^{(r)}} r_j$$

for all $\underline{i} \in I$. If $r = s$, the hypothesis is trivial. Suppose the hypothesis holds for $r \geq r' > 1$. Observe that (5.71) implies that

(5.181)
$$m^{A^{(r'-1)}}_{\pi_{A^{(r'-1)}}\underline{i}}(\underline{n},E - \{E\}) = m^{A^{(r'-1)}}_{\pi_{A^{(r'-1)}}\underline{i}}(\underline{n},(E - \{E\})(A^{(r')})).$$

If $F \in (E - \{E\})(A^{(r'-1)})$, then $F \subset A^{(r'-1)}$. By (5.71) and Lemma 5.6, if $\underline{\bar{i}} \in I(F)$ and the right hand side of (5.181) is $m_{\underline{i}}^{(r')}$, then

(5.182)
$$[m^{(r')}]^F_{\underline{\bar{i}}} = m^F_{\underline{i}}(\underline{n},E - \{E\})[\prod_{j\in\bar{d}-A^{(r'-1)}} r_j] = n^F_{\underline{\bar{i}}}[\prod_{j\in\bar{d}-A^{(r'-1)}} r_j].$$

Observe now that

(5.183)
$$\underline{m}(\underline{n},(E - \{E\})(A^{(r')})) = \underline{m}(\underline{y}) \# \underline{m}(\underline{z}),$$

where $\underline{y} \in M((E - \{E\})(A^{(r'-1)}))$ and $\underline{z} \in M(\{E_{r'}\})$. As in chapter 1, if $\underline{x} \in R^I$ and $\underline{y} \in R^I$, $\underline{x} \# \underline{y} = \{x_i y_i\}$. Thus

(5.184)
$$m^{A^{(r'-1)}}_{\pi_{A^{(r'-1)}}\underline{i}}(\underline{n},(E - \{E\})(A^{(r')})) = m_{\underline{i}}(\underline{y}) m^{A^{(r'-1)}}_{\pi_{A^{(r'-1)}}\underline{i}}(\underline{z}).$$

Note that $\{\log [m^{A^{(r'-1)}}_{\pi_{A^{(r'-1)}}\underline{i}}(\underline{z})]\}$ is an element of $M(\{E_{r'} \cap E_{k_{r'-1}}\})$, which is a submanifold of $M((E - \{E\})(A^{(r'-1)}))$. Consequently, $\{\log m_{\underline{i}}^{(r')}\} \in M((E - \{E\})(A^{(r'-1)}))$. This result and (5.182) show that

(5.185)
$$\underline{m}^{(r')} = (\prod_{j\in\bar{d}-A^{(r'-1)}} r_j)\hat{\underline{m}}(\underline{n},(E - \{E\})(A^{(r'-1)})).$$

This equation is equivalent to (5.180). By induction, the hypothesis is true if $r \geq 1$. If $r = 1$, (5.180) and (5.178) are equivalent.

Example 5.51. Suppose $E = \{2,3\}$, $E = \{\{1,2\},\{2,3\},\{3,4\}\}$, and $d = 4$. Then $E' = E - \{E\} = \{\{1,2\},\{3,4\}\}$ and

(5.186) $$\hat{m}_{i_1 i_2 i_3 i_4}(\underline{n},E') = n_{i_1 i_2}^{\{1,2\}} n_{i_3 i_4}^{\{3,4\}} / n_{\alpha}^{\phi} .$$

Thus

(5.187) $$\hat{m}_{+i_2 i_3 +}(\underline{n},E') = n_{i_2}^{\{2\}} n_{i_3}^{\{3\}} / n_{\alpha}^{\phi} .$$

Since $E'' = (E - \{E\})(E) = \{\{2\},\{3\}\}$,

(5.183) $$m_{i_1 i_2 i_3 i_4}(\underline{n},E'') = n_{i_2}^{\{2\}} n_{i_3}^{\{3\}} / n_{\alpha}^{\phi} r_1 r_4 .$$

Thus (5.178) is satisfied.

The following theorem may now be proven:

THEOREM 5.4. *If* E *is totally decomposable,* $\hat{\underline{m}}(\underline{n},E)$ *exists, and* $\underline{m}^{(1,1)} = \underline{e}$, *then no matter how* E *is ordered,* $\underline{m}^{(1,s+1)} = \hat{\underline{m}}(\underline{n},E)$.

Proof. Suppose $E = \{E_k : k \in \overline{s}\}$ and $E^{(r)} = \{E_k : k \in \overline{r}\}$ for each $r \in \overline{s}$. The proof is by induction, where the induction hypothesis is that $\underline{m}^{(1,r+1)} = \hat{\underline{m}}(\underline{n},E^{(r)})$. The hypothesis clearly holds when r is 1. Assume that the hypothesis holds for $r < s$. By Lemma 5.14,

(5.189) $$m_{\underline{i}}^{(1,r+2)} = \frac{\hat{m}_{\underline{i}}(\underline{n},E^{(r)}) n^{E_{r+1}}_{\pi_{E_{r+1}} \underline{i}}}{\hat{m}_{\underline{i}}(\underline{n},E^{(r)}(E_{r+1})) \prod_{j \in \overline{d}-E} r_j} .$$

Suppose now that $E_1 = E^{(r)}$, $E_2 = E^{(r+1)}$, and $E_0 = E^{(r)}(E_{r+1})$. The proof reduces to a demonstration of the following results:

a) If $F \in E_0$, $d(F,E_2) = d(F,E_1) + 1$.

b) If $F \in F(E_2) \cap F(E_0)$, $d(F,E_2) = d(F,E_1) - d(F,E_0)$.

c) If $F \in F(E_2) - [F(E_0) \cup E_0]$, $d(F,E_2) = d(F,E_1)$.

d) If $F \in F(E_0) - F(E_2)$, $d(F,E_0) = 0$.

To prove these assertions, assume that they hold for all $F' \in F(E_0) \cup F(E_2)$ such that $F \subset F'$ and $F \neq F'$. Let

(5.190) $$F_1 = \{F' \in F(E_2) : F \subset F', F \neq F', \text{ and } F' \in F(E_0)\},$$

(5.191) $$F_2 = \{F' \in F(E_2) : F \subset F', F \neq F', \text{ and } F' \in E_0\},$$

and

(5.192) $$F_3 = \{F' \in F(E_2) : F \subset F', F \neq F', \text{ and } F' \notin F(E_0) \cup E_0\}.$$

Then

(5.193) $$d(F,E_2) = c(F,E_2) - 1 - \sum_{F' \in F_1} d(F',E_2) - \sum_{F' \in F_2} d(F',E_2) - \sum_{F' \in F_3} d(F',E_2).$$

If $F \in E_0$, then $F_1 = F_2 = \phi$, $F(F,E_2) = F(F,E_1)$, and $c(F,E_2) = c(F,E_1) + 1$. Thus $d(F,E_2) = d(F,E_1) + 1$. If $F \in F(E_2) \cap F(E_0)$, then $c(F,E_2) = c(F,E_1) + 1$ and

(5.194) $$d(F,E_2) = c(F,E_1) + 1 - 1 - \sum_{F' \in F_1} d(F',E_1) - c(F,E_0) - \sum_{F' \in F_2} d(F',E_1)$$
$$+ \sum_{F' \in F_2} d(F',E_0) - \sum_{F' \in F_3} d(F',E_1)$$
$$= d(F,E_1) - d(F,E_0).$$

If $F \in F(E_2) - [F(E_0) \cup E_0]$, then either $F \not\subset E_{r+1}$ or $F \subset E_{r+1}$. If $F \not\subset E_{r+1}$, then $F_1 = F_2 = \phi$ and $c(F,E_2) = c(F,E_1)$. Thus $d(F,E_2) = d(F,E_1)$. Now suppose $F \subset E_{r+1}$. In this case, $c(F,E_2) = c(F,E_1) + 1$ and

(5.195) $$d(F,E_2) = d(F,E_1) - c(F,E_0) + 1 + \sum_{F' \in F_2} d(F',E_0)$$
$$= d(F,E_1).$$

To verify the second equality, observe that if $E_3 = \{E \in E_0: F \subset E\}$, then E_3 is totally decomposable. If $F' \in F_2$, then $F' \in F(E_3)$. Thus $d(F',E_0) = d(F',E_3)$, $F_2 = F(E_3)$, and $c(F,E_3) = c(F,E_0)$. We have

(5.196) $$\sum_{F' \in F(E_3)} d(F',E_3) = c(F,E_3) - 1 ,$$

so the second equality in (5.195) follows.

Suppose next that $F \in F(E_0) - F(E_2)$. Then

(5.197) $$d(F,E_0) = c(F,E_0) - 1 - \sum_{F' \in F_2} [d(F',E_1) - d(F',E_2)].$$

Let $E_4 = \{E \in E_1: F \subset E\}$ and $E_5 = \{E \in E_2: F \subset E\}$. Then $d(F',E_1) = d(F',E_4)$ and $d(F',E_2) = d(F',E_5)$ if $F' \in E_2$. In addition, $c(F,E_2) = c(F,E_1) + 1$. Observe now that

(5.198) $$c(F,E_4) - 1 - \sum_{F' \in F(F,E_4)} d(F,E_4)$$
$$= c(F,E_5) - 1 - \sum_{F' \in F(F,E_5)} d(F,E_5)$$
$$= 0.$$

Note that $c(F,E_5) = c(F,E_2)$ and $c(F,E_4) = c(F,E_1)$. Thus

$$d(F,E_0) = c(F,E_0) - 1 + 1 - \sum_{F' \in E_1} [d(F',E_1) - d(F',E_2)] \tag{5.199}$$

$$= 0.$$

Since F satisfies (a), (b), (c), or (d), the theorem follows by induction.||

Example 5.52. This theorem may be illustrated by considering the generating class $E = \{\{1,2\},\{2,3\},\{3,4\}\}$ investigated in Example 5.51. If the elements of E are ordered as given, then

$$m^{(1,1)}_{i_1i_2i_3i_4} = 1, \tag{5.200}$$

$$m^{(1,2)}_{i_1i_2i_3i_4} = n^{\{1,2\}}_{i_1i_2}/r_3r_4 , \tag{5.201}$$

$$m^{(1,3)}_{i_1i_2i_3i_4} = \frac{n^{\{1,2\}}_{i_1i_2} n^{\{2,3\}}_{i_2i_3}}{n^{\{2\}}_{i_2}}, \tag{5.202}$$

and

$$m^{(1,4)}_{i_1i_2i_3i_4} = \frac{n^{\{1,2\}}_{i_1i_2} n^{\{2,3\}}_{i_2i_3} n^{\{3,4\}}_{i_3i_4}}{n^{\{2\}}_{i_2} n^{\{3\}}_{i_3}} \tag{5.203}$$

If the order is changed so that $E_1 = \{1,2\}$, $E_2 = \{3,4\}$, and $E_3 = \{2,3\}$, then

$$m^{(1,1)}_{i_1i_2i_3i_4} = 1, \tag{5.204}$$

$$m^{(1,2)}_{i_1i_2i_3i_4} = n^{\{1,2\}}_{i_1i_2}/r_3r_4, \tag{5.205}$$

$$m^{(1,3)}_{i_1i_2i_3i_4} = \frac{n^{\{1,2\}}_{i_1i_2} n^{\{3,4\}}_{i_3i_4}}{n^{\phi}_{\alpha}} , \tag{5.206}$$

and

$$m^{(1,4)}_{i_1i_2i_3i_4} = \frac{n^{\{1,2\}}_{i_1i_2} n^{\{3,4\}}_{i_3i_4}}{n^{\phi}_{\alpha}} \frac{n^{\{2,3\}}_{i_2i_3}}{n^{\{2\}}_{i_2} n^{\{3\}}_{i_3}/n^{\phi}_{\alpha}} \tag{5.207}$$

$$= \frac{n^{\{1,2\}}_{i_1i_2} n^{\{2,3\}}_{i_2i_3} n^{\{3,4\}}_{i_3i_4}}{n^{\{2\}}_{i_2} n^{\{3\}}_{i_3}} .$$

Similar results hold for other permutations of the elements of E.

The theorem just proven is more general than may be evident, for whenever $d \le 5$, any decomposable generating class is totally decomposable. To prove this result, suppose

E is decomposable and $\bar{E}$ is a generating class contained in E which is not decomposable. Without loss of generality, one may choose $\bar{E}$ so that any generating class strictly included in $\bar{E}$ is decomposable. Suppose $d \leq 5$ and let $E = \{E_k: k \in \bar{s}\}$, where for each $r \in \overline{s-1}$ there exists $k_r \in \bar{r}$ such that (5.135) holds. Suppose t is the largest index such that $E_t \in \bar{E}$. Then $E_t - \bigcup_{k=1}^{t-1} E_k \neq \phi$. In addition, at least two elements E' and E'' must exist such that $\{E',E''\} \subset \{E_k: k \in \overline{t-1}\}$, $E_t \cap E' \not\subset E_t \cap E''$, and $E_t \cap E'' \not\subset E_t \cap E'$. Otherwise, $\bar{E}$ is decomposable. Since E is decomposable, there exists a set $E^* \in \{E_k: k \in \overline{t-1}\} - \bar{E}$ such that

$$E^* \cap E_t \supset (E_t \cap E') \cup (E_t \cap E''). \tag{5.208}$$

Now $s \geq t \geq 4$ and E^* must have at least three elements. By Lemma 5.12, E is not decomposable, a contradiction.

When $d = 6$, a decomposable generating class exists which is not totally decomposable. By the argument of the preceding paragraph, any such class must contain four sets, the largest of which has three elements. Suppose $E_4 = \{1,2,3\}$. Then $E' \cap E_4$ and $E'' \cap E_4$ must be disjoint singletons. Suppose $E' \cap E_4 = \{1\}$ and $E'' \cap E_4 = \{2\}$. Now $E^* \supset \{1,2\}$. Suppose $E^* = \{1,2,4\}$. If $E_3 = E^*$, then (5.135) is not satisfied by any $k_2 \in \bar{2}$. Assume $E' = E_3$. Now E'' must include $\{5\}$ or $\{6\}$; otherwise $E'' \subset E^*$. Assume $\{5\} \subset E''$. In order for $E_3 - (E_1 \cup E_2)$ to be nonempty, it is then necessary for $\{6\}$ to be contained in E' and for $\{6\}$ and E'' to be disjoint. If $\{5\} \subset E'$, then (5.135) is not satisfied by any $k_2 \in \bar{2}$. In order for $\{E',E'',E^*\}$ not to be decomposable, it must be the case that $E' = \{1,4,6\}$ and $E'' = \{2,4,5\}$. Except for decomposable classes which differ only by permutations of $\bar{6}$, the only decomposable class which is not totally decomposable is $\{\{1,2,4\},\{1,2,3\},\{2,4,5\},\{1,4,6\}\}$. In this case

$$\hat{m}_{\underline{i}}(\underline{n},E) = \frac{n_{i_1 i_2 i_4}^{\{1,2,4\}} n_{i_1 i_2 i_3}^{\{1,2,3\}} n_{i_2 i_4 i_5}^{\{2,4,5\}} n_{i_1 i_4 i_6}^{\{1,4,6\}}}{n_{i_1 i_2}^{\{1,2\}} n_{i_2 i_4}^{\{2,4\}} n_{i_1 i_4}^{\{1,4\}}}. \tag{5.209}$$

Even though this generating class is not totally decomposable, the conclusion of Theorem 5.4 remains valid. In summary, we have the following results.

THEOREM 5.5. *Suppose* E *is decomposable and* $U(E)$ *has no more than six elements. If* $\hat{\underline{m}}(\underline{n},E)$ *exists and* $\underline{m}^{(1,1)} = \underline{e}$, *then no matter how* E *is ordered* $\hat{\underline{m}}^{(1,s+1)} = \underline{m}(\underline{n},E)$.

This theorem is the strongest possible theorem of its kind, for $E = \{\{1,2,4\},\{2,3,5\},\{1,3,6\},\{5,7\},\{1,2,3\}\}$ is a decomposable generating class such that

$U(E) = \bar{7}$. This class is not totally decomposable, and convergence need not occur until the second step of the second cycle if E has the listed ordering.

If the starting value $\underline{m}^{(1,1)}$ is not $\underline{e}$, then convergence in one cycle may not occur even if E is a totally decomposable generating class. An example is the class {{3,4},{1,2},{4,5},{2,3}}. On the other hand, if every member of $F(E)$ is contained in a single set $E \in E$, then convergence in one cycle occurs for any ordering of E and any permissible starting value. In fact, suppose that $E_t = E$. If $r \in \overline{t-1}$, then

$$m_{\underline{i}}^{(1,r+1)} = \left[\prod_{k=1}^{r} n_{\pi_{E_k}\underline{i}}^{E_k}\right] m_{\underline{i}}(\underline{y}^{(r)}) , \tag{5.210}$$

where $\underline{y}^{(r)} \in M(\{E_k: k \in \bar{s} - \bar{r}\})$. This statement is trivial if $r = 0$. Suppose it holds for r. Let $\underline{y}^{(r)} = \underline{z}^{(r)} + \underline{w}^{(r)}$, where $\underline{z}^{(r)} \in M(\{E_{r+1}\})$ and $\underline{w}^{(r)} \in M(\{E_k: k \in \bar{s} - \overline{r+1}\})$. If $r = s - 1$, then $\underline{w}^{(r)} = \underline{0}$. By Lemma 5.14, $\{(\underline{m}^{(1,r+1)},\underline{\nu}(E_{r+1},\pi_{E_{r+1}}\underline{i}))\}$ is equal to $\underline{m}(\underline{z}^{(r)}) \# \underline{m}(\underline{x}^{(r)})$, where $\underline{x}^{(r)} \in M((E - \{E_{r+1}\})(E_{r+1})) \subset M(\{E\})$. By (5.169), (5.210) holds for $r + 1$ with $\underline{y}^{(r+1)} = \underline{w}^{(r)} - \underline{x}^{(r)}$. By induction the result holds for $\underline{m}^{(1,t)}$. Elementary calculations show that $\underline{m}^{(1,t+1)}$ satisfies $[\underline{m}^{(1,t+1)}]^{E_k} = \underline{n}^{E_k}$ for $k \in \bar{t}$. The proof of Theorem 5.2 now applies to $r > t + 1$. Thus convergence occurs at the end of the first cycle.

This result applies to any decomposable generating class with no more than three elements, for if $E_3 \cap E_1 = (E_3 \cap E_2) \cup (E_3 \cap E_1)$, then $E_3 \cap E_1 \subset E_1$, $E_3 \cap E_2 \subset E_1$, and $E_1 \cap E_2 \subset E_1$. If a generating class has more than three elements, then the conditions required in the previous paragraph need not hold. The class {{3,4},{1,2},{4,5},{2,3}} is one such example.

Failure to converge in one cycle does not preclude convergence in two cycles. In fact, no decomposable class is known for which convergence does not occur within two cycles.

NONHIERARCHICAL MODELS

Nonhierarchical models do not have spanning vectors consisting of zeros and ones, but the Deming-Stephan algorithm is readily adapted to these models.

As shown by (5.37) and the subsequent discussion, each analysis-of-variance model, whether or not it is hierarchical, has a basis consisting of vectors $\underline{\nu}$ of the form

$$\begin{aligned} \nu_{\underline{i}} &= 1, \quad \underline{i} \in I_1 , \\ &= -1, \quad \underline{i} \in I_2 , \\ &= 0, \quad \underline{i} \in I - (I_1 \cup I_2). \end{aligned} \tag{5.211}$$

Use of cyclic ascent with such spanning vectors is discussed in chapter 3.

Example 5.53. Consider the $r \times c$ table for which

$$\mu_{ij} = \alpha + \beta_i + \gamma_{ij} , \tag{5.212}$$

where

$$\sum_{i=1}^{r} \beta_i = \sum_{i=1}^{r} \gamma_{ij} = \sum_{j=1}^{c} \gamma_{ij} = 0. \tag{5.213}$$

The corresponding linear manifold M is spanned by $\{\underline{\nu}^{(k)}: k \in \overline{r}\} \cup \{\underline{\eta}^{(k,\ell)}: k \in \overline{r-1}, \ell \in \overline{c-1}\}$, where for each $k \in \overline{r}$, $i \in \overline{r}$, and $j \in \overline{c}$,

$$\nu_{ij}^{(k)} = \delta_{ik} ; \tag{5.214}$$

and for each $k \in \overline{r}$, $i \in \overline{r}$, $j \in \overline{c}$, and $\ell \in \overline{c}$,

$$\begin{aligned} \eta_{ij}^{(k,\ell)} &= 1 \text{ if } i = k, \quad j = \ell , \\ &= -1 \text{ if } i = k+1, \quad j = \ell , \\ &= -1 \text{ if } i = k, \quad j = \ell + 1 , \\ &= 1 \text{ if } i = k+1, \quad j = \ell + 1 , \\ &= 0 \text{ otherwise.} \end{aligned} \tag{5.215}$$

Here δ_{ik} is the Kronecker delta. If $\underline{m}(t,1)$ is an estimate of $\hat{\underline{m}}$, then one may define $\underline{m}^{(t,2)}$ by

$$m_{ij}^{(t,2)} = n_{i+} m_{ij}^{(1)} / m_{i+}^{(1)} , \tag{5.216}$$

where conventional summation notation is used. If $g = (k-1)r + \ell$, then $\underline{m}^{(t,g+1)}$ may be defined by

$$\begin{aligned} m_{ij}^{(t,g+1)} &= h^{(t,g)} m_{ij}^{(t,g)} && \text{if } i = k \text{ and } j = \ell \\ & && \text{or if } i = k+1 \text{ and } j = \ell + 1, \\ &= \frac{1}{h^{(t,g)}} m_{ij}^{(t,g)} && \text{if } i = k \text{ and } j = \ell + 1 \\ & && \text{or if } i = k+1 \text{ and } j = \ell , \\ &= m_{ij}^{(t,g)} && \text{otherwise ,} \end{aligned}$$

where

$$\Delta_k = n_k - n_{(k+1)\ell} - n_{k(\ell+1)} + n_{(k+1)(\ell+1)} \tag{5.218}$$

and

(5.219) $$h^{(t,g)} = \frac{\Delta_k^2 + [\Delta_k^2 + 4(m_{k\ell}^{(t,g)} + m_{(k+1)(\ell+1)}^{(t,g)})(m_{(k+1)\ell}^{(t,g)} + m_{k(\ell+1)}^{(t,g)})]^{1/2}}{m_{k\ell}^{(t,g)} + m_{(k+1)(\ell+1)}^{(t,g)}}$$

Thus computational problems involving nonhierarchical models are only slightly more difficult than those for hierarchical ones. As in conventional analysis of variance, interpretation of parameters in nonhierarchical models appears difficult; consequently, the usefulness of nonhierarchical models is not clear.

CALCULATION OF COMPONENTS

In order to examine the interrelationships which exist among the variables represented by a factorial table, it is useful to examine the components $\hat{\underline{\mu}}^{B_g} = P_{M_{B_g}} \hat{\underline{\mu}}$ of the maximum-likelihood estimate $\hat{\underline{\mu}}$ corresponding to the hypothesis $\underline{\mu} \in M$, where

(5.220) $$M = \bigodot_{g=1}^{h} M_{B_g}$$

and

(5.221) $$M_{B_g} = \bigotimes_{g=1}^{d} M^{(j)}_{\chi_{B_g}(j)} .$$

These components provide estimates of the vectors $P_{M_{B_g}} \underline{\mu} = \{v^{B_g}_{\pi_{B_g}\underline{i}}\}$, where $\underline{v}^{B_g} \in R^{I(B_g)}$ is the B_g-interaction vector. This vector is a linear function of $\underline{\mu}$ which satisfies the restrictions

(5.222) $$\Sigma\{v^{B_g}_{\underline{\bar{i}}}: \bar{i}_k = \bar{i}_k^{(j)} \ \forall k \in B_g - \{j\},\ i_j \in \bar{r}_j\} = 0$$

for each $\underline{\bar{i}}^{(j)} \in \prod_{k \in B_g - \{j\}} \bar{r}_k$ and $j \in B_g$. Similarly, $\hat{\underline{\mu}}^{B_g} = \{\hat{v}^{B_g}_{\pi_{B_g}\underline{i}}\}$, where $\hat{\underline{v}}^{B_g} \in R^{I(B_g)}$ is an estimate of $\underline{v}^{B_g}$ which satisfies the same linear restrictions as $\underline{v}^{B_g}$ and is a linear function of $\hat{\underline{\mu}}$. Thus $\underline{\mu}$ and $\hat{\underline{\mu}}$ respectively satisfy

(5.223) $$\mu_{\underline{i}} = \sum_{g=1}^{h} v^{B_g}_{\pi_{B_g}\underline{i}}$$

and

(5.224) $$\hat{\mu}_{\underline{i}} = \sum_{g=1}^{h} \hat{v}^{B_g}_{\pi_{B_g}\underline{i}} ,$$

where $\underline{i} \in I$.

Example 5.54. In the integration study of Example 4.16, a model was selected but no assessment was made of the magnitudes of the interactions investigated. To make such an assessment, it should be noted that the model M_6 chosen for the data is the hierarchical model $M(E)$, where $E = \{\{1,2\},\{1,3\},\{2,3\},\{2,4\},\{3,4\}\}$. The hierarchical class $H(E)$ consists of the sets ϕ, $\{1\}$, $\{2\}$, $\{3\}$, $\{4\}$, $\{1,2\}$, $\{1,3\}$, $\{2,3\}$, $\{2,4\}$, and $\{3,4\}$, and

(5.225)
$$M = \bigodot_{B \in H(E)} M_B .$$

If $\underline{\mu} \in M$, then

(5.226)
$$\mu_{i_1 i_2 i_3 i_4} = v^{\phi} + v^{\{1\}}_{i_1} + v^{\{2\}}_{i_2} + v^{\{3\}}_{i_3} + v^{\{4\}}_{i_4} + v^{\{1,2\}}_{i_1 i_2} + v^{\{1,3\}}_{i_1 i_3} + v^{\{2,3\}}_{i_2 i_3} + v^{\{2,4\}}_{i_2 i_4} + v^{\{3,4\}}_{i_3 i_4} ,$$

where for each $k \in \overline{4}$

(5.227)
$$v^{\{k\}}_{+} = 0$$

and for each $\{j,k\} \in H(E)$,

(5.228)
$$v^{\{j,k\}}_{+i_k} = v^{\{j,k\}}_{i_j +} = 0,$$

where $i_j \in \overline{2}$ and $i_k \in \overline{2}$ (see (4.224)). The vector $P_{M_B}\underline{\mu}$, where $B \in H(E)$, is equal to $\{v^B_{\pi_B \underline{i}} : \underline{i} \in \overline{2} \times \overline{2} \times \overline{2} \times \overline{2}\}$. For instance, $P_{M_{\{1\}}}\underline{\mu} = \{v^{1}_{i_1} : \langle i_1, i_2, i_3, i_4 \rangle \in \overline{2} \times \overline{2} \times \overline{2} \times \overline{2}\}$.

In this model, the vector $\underline{v}^{\{1,2\}}$ describes the interaction between proximity and norms. Similar interpretations apply to other terms $\underline{v}^B$, where $B \in H(E)$. Since all variables have two possible values, each manifold M_B has dimension 1. Thus $P_{M_B}\underline{\mu}$ is completely determined by $v^B_{\pi_B\langle 1,1,1,1\rangle}$. In fact, if $\underline{\nu}^{(2,1)}$ is defined as in (5.37), $\underline{f}^{(0)} = \underline{e}^{(2)}$, and $\underline{f}^{(1)} = \underline{\nu}^{(2,1)}$, then

(5.229)
$$P_{M_B}\underline{\mu} = v^B_{\pi_B\langle 1,1,1,1\rangle} \bigotimes_{j=1}^{d} \underline{f}^{(\chi_B(j))} .$$

For example,

(5.230)
$$P_{M_{\{1,2\}}}\underline{\mu} = v^{\{1,2\}}_{11} \langle 1,-1\rangle \otimes \langle 1,-1\rangle \otimes \langle 1,1\rangle \otimes \langle 1,1\rangle .$$

Thus the behavior of the model is effectively described by a determination of

$\{v^B_{\pi_B<1,1,1,1>}: B \in H(E)\}$. This vector is determined if $\{P_{M_B}\underline{\mu}: B \in H(E)\}$ is known. Similar remarks apply to the maximum-likelihood estimates $\hat{\underline{\mu}}^{B_g}$ and $\hat{\underline{v}}^{B_g}$.

A relatively simple algorithm is available for computation of $\hat{\underline{\mu}}^{B_g}$ and $\hat{\underline{v}}^{B_g}$ for all $g \in \overline{h}$. The algorithm requires that the sets B_g, $g \in \overline{h}$, be ordered so that if $g < g'$, then B_g contains no more elements than $B_{g'}$. Given this condition, the algorithm consists of h basic steps. Before step 1, $\hat{\underline{\mu}}^{(0)}$ is set equal to $\hat{\underline{\mu}}$. At step $g \in \overline{h}$,

$$\hat{v}^{B_g}_{\underline{\bar{i}}} = \Big(\prod_{j \in d-B_g} \frac{1}{r_j}\Big) \sum_{\underline{i} \in \pi^{-1}_{B_g}\underline{\bar{i}}} \hat{\mu}^{(g-1)}_{\underline{i}} \tag{5.231}$$

for $\underline{\bar{i}} \in I(B_g)$, $\hat{\underline{\mu}}^{B_g} = \{\hat{v}^{B_g}_{\pi_{B_g}\underline{i}}\}$, and

$$\hat{\underline{\mu}}^{(g)} = \hat{\underline{\mu}}^{(g-1)} - \hat{\underline{\mu}}^{B_g}. \tag{5.232}$$

The algorithm may be explained by observing that $\hat{v}^{B_g}_{\underline{\bar{i}}}$ is the average of those $\hat{\mu}^{(g-1)}_{\underline{i}}$ such that $\pi_{B_g}\underline{i} = \underline{\bar{i}}$. This average may be written as

$$\hat{v}^{B_g}_{\underline{\bar{i}}} = \frac{(\hat{\underline{\mu}}^{(g-1)}, \underline{\nu}(B_g, \underline{\bar{i}}))}{\|\underline{\nu}(B_g, \underline{\bar{i}})\|^2}. \tag{5.233}$$

Thus the algorithm asserts that

$$\begin{aligned} \hat{\underline{\mu}}^{B_g} &= P_{N_{B_g}} \hat{\underline{\mu}}^{(g-1)} \\ &= \Sigma\{P_{M_B}\hat{\underline{\mu}}^{(g-1)}: B \subset B_g\}. \end{aligned} \tag{5.234}$$

Given the ordering which has been imposed on the sets B_g, it is sufficient to show that

$$\hat{\underline{\mu}}^{(g-1)} = \sum_{g'=g}^{h} P_{M_{B_{g'}}} \hat{\underline{\mu}} \tag{5.235}$$

if $g \in \overline{h}$, for

$$\Sigma\{P_{M_B} \sum_{g'=g}^{h} P_{M_{B_{g'}}} \hat{\underline{\mu}}: B \subset B_g\} = P_{M_{B_g}} \hat{\underline{\mu}}. \tag{5.236}$$

If $g = 1$, then (5.235) follows from the definition of M. If (5.235) holds for $g_0 < h$, then (5.232) implies that (5.235) holds for $g_0 + 1$. By induction, (5.235) holds for all $g \in \overline{h}$. Thus (5.231) holds for each $g \in \overline{h}$.

The algorithm presented here is a convenient general algorithm. However, in many specific problems it is more efficient to employ the Yates algorithm (see Cochran and Cox 1954) or the generalized Yates algorithm (see Good 1958) in order to recover the vectors $\hat{\underline{\mu}}^{B_g}$. These algorithms are easiest to apply if $r_j \le 3$ for each $j \in \overline{d}$.

Example 5.55. In order to apply the proposed algorithm to the study considered in Example 5.54, it is first necessary to obtain $\hat{\underline{\mu}}$. For this step, the Deming-Stephan algorithm may be employed with the unit vector as a starting value. The iteration cycle used is given by the following equations:

(5.237) $$m_{ijk\ell}^{(t,2)} = m_{ijk\ell}^{(t,1)} \frac{n_{ij++}}{m_{ij++}^{(t,1)}} ,$$

(5.238) $$m_{ijk\ell}^{(t,3)} = m_{ijk\ell}^{(t,2)} \frac{n_{i+k+}}{m_{i+k+}^{(t,2)}} ,$$

(5.239) $$m_{ijk\ell}^{(t,4)} = m_{ijk\ell}^{(t,3)} \frac{n_{+jk+}}{m_{+jk+}^{(t,3)}} ,$$

(5.240) $$m_{ijk\ell}^{(t,5)} = m_{ijk\ell}^{(t,4)} \frac{n_{+j+\ell}}{m_{+j+\ell}^{(t,4)}} ,$$

(5.241) $$m_{ijk\ell}^{(t,6)} = m_{ijk\ell}^{(t,5)} \frac{n_{++k\ell}}{m_{++k\ell}^{(t,5)}} ,$$

and

(5.242) $$\underline{m}^{(t+1,1)} = \underline{m}^{(t,6)} .$$

During the fifth iteration, $\Delta^{(t)}$ is 0.06, where $\Delta^{(t)}$ is the maximum difference between the observed and fitted marginal totals used in the algorithm. The maximum-likelihood estimates $\hat{\underline{m}}$ and $\hat{\underline{\mu}}$ are given in table 5.1, together with the data $\underline{n}$.

To find $\{\hat{\underline{\mu}}^B : B \in H(E)\}$, one orders $H(E)$ as in Example 5.54 and uses the algorithm defined by (5.231) and (5.232). The initial steps are as follows:

(5.243) $$\hat{v}_{\alpha}^{\phi} = \hat{\mu}_{....}^{(0)} ,$$

(5.244) $$\hat{\underline{\mu}}^{\phi} = \{\hat{v}_{\alpha}^{\phi} : \langle i,j,k,\ell\rangle \in \overline{2} \times \overline{2} \times \overline{2} \times \overline{2}\} ,$$

(5.245) $$\hat{\underline{\mu}}^{(1)} = \hat{\underline{\mu}}^{(0)} - \hat{\underline{\mu}}^{\phi} ,$$

TABLE 5.1

MAXIMUM-LIKELIHOOD ESTIMATES FOR RACIAL ATTITUDES STUDY[a]

			Sentiment	
Proximity	Contact	Norms	Favorable	Unfavorable
Close	Frequent	Favorable	77 74.8 4.31	32 34.5 3.54
		Unfavorable	30 32.3 3.47	36 33.4 3.51
	Infrequent	Favorable	14 14.7 2.69	19 18.0 2.89
		Unfavorable	15 11.3 2.42	27 31.0 3.43
Distant	Frequent	Favorable	43 42.9 3.76	20 19.8 2.99
		Unfavorable	36 36.0 3.58	37 37.3 3.62
	Infrequent	Favorable	27 28.5 3.35	36 34.8 3.55
		Unfavorable	41 42.4 3.75	118 116.3 4.76

[a] First line is observation $n_{ijk\ell}$, second line is maximum-likelihood estimate $\hat{m}_{ijk\ell}$, and third line is maximum-likelihood estimate $\hat{\mu}_{ijk\ell}$.

(5.246) $$\hat{v}_i^{\{1\}} = \hat{\mu}_{i...}^{(1)} ,$$

(5.247) $$\hat{\underline{\mu}}^{\{1\}} = \{\hat{v}_i^{\{1\}}: \langle i,j,k,\ell \rangle \in \overline{2} \times \overline{2} \times \overline{2} \times \overline{2}\},$$

and

(5.248) $$\hat{\underline{\mu}}^{(2)} = \hat{\underline{\mu}}^{(1)} - \hat{\underline{\mu}}^{\{1\}},$$

where the dots indicate that an average has been taken. For example,

(5.249) $$\hat{\mu}_{i...}^{(1)} = \frac{1}{2} \sum_{\ell=1}^{2} \frac{1}{2}[\sum_{k=1}^{2} \frac{1}{2}(\sum_{j=1}^{2} \hat{\mu}_{ijk\ell})]$$

$$= \frac{1}{8} \sum_{j=1}^{2} \sum_{k=1}^{2} \sum_{\ell=1}^{2} \hat{\mu}_{ijk\ell}.$$

Results are given in table 5.2 in terms of $\{\hat{v}^{B}_{\pi_B<1,1,1,1>}: B \in H(E)\}$. The term $\hat{v}^{\phi}_{\alpha}$ is omitted since it only reflects the sampling size. As observed in Example 5.54, this information is sufficient to completely describe $\hat{\underline{\mu}}$.

TABLE 5.2

ESTIMATED INTERACTIONS
IN RACIAL ATTITUDES STUDY

Variable Combination	Set Representation	Interaction
Proximity	{1}	-0.192
Contact	{2}	0.122
Norms	{3}	-0.092
Sentiment	{4}	-0.058
Proximity x contact	{1,2}	0.304
Proximity x norms	{1,3}	0.166
Contact x norms	{2,3}	0.144
Contact x sentiment	{2,4}	0.243
Norms x sentiment	{3,4}	0.202

In this example, the two-factor interactions are of greatest interest. To see how these terms may be interpreted, it is useful to consider the proximity-by-contact interaction. If $k \in \overline{2}$ and $\ell \in \overline{2}$, then by (5.226),

(5.250) $$\frac{1}{4}(\hat{\mu}_{11k\ell} - \hat{\mu}_{12k\ell} - \hat{\mu}_{21k\ell} + \hat{\mu}_{22k\ell}) = 0.304.$$

The estimated log odds $\log(\hat{m}_{11k\ell}/\hat{m}_{12k\ell})$ for contact given close proximity, norms k, and sentiments ℓ thus exceed by 1.22 the estimated log odds $\log(\hat{m}_{21k\ell}/\hat{m}_{22k\ell})$ for contact given distant proximity, norms k, and sentiments ℓ. Therefore, the estimated odds $\hat{m}_{11k\ell}/\hat{m}_{12k\ell}$ are 3.37 times as great as the odds $\hat{m}_{21k\ell}/\hat{m}_{22k\ell}$. Similar interpretations apply to the other two-factor interactions.

ASYMPTOTIC PROPERTIES

Several examples have been given in chapter 4 of asymptotic distributions, confidence intervals, and hypothesis tests based on the asymptotic properties of hierarchical models. Examples 4.1, 4.2, 4.3, 4.4, 4.6, 4.7, 4.11, 4.13, 4.14, 4.15, 4.16, 4.17, 4.18, and 4.20 all involve hierarchical models for factorial tables. The only new consideration in this chapter involves procedures for computing the projection $P_M^*(\hat{\underline{\mu}})$ and other quantities related to the covariance structure of the maximum likelihood estimates.

In general, asymptotic covariances are relatively difficult to compute for hierarchical models. The basic procedure is illustrated by Example 5.56.

Example 5.56. In order to obtain the asymptotic covariance matrix for the estimated interactions $\{\hat{\nu}^B_{\pi_B<1,1,1>}: B \in H(E)\}$ for the data in Example 5.55, one observes that if M is a linear mapping from R^{10} onto M such that

(5.251)
$$M\underline{x} = \sum_{g=1}^{h} x_g \underline{\nu}(B_g, \pi_{B_g}<1,1,1,1>),$$

where the sets B_g are defined as in Example 5.55, then

(5.252)
$$\hat{\underline{\mu}} = M\hat{\underline{b}},$$

where $\hat{\underline{b}} = \{\hat{\nu}^{B_g}_{\pi_{B_g}<1,1,1,1>}: g \in \overline{h}\}$. By Kruskal (1968a), the operator $P_M^*(\hat{\underline{\mu}})$ satisfies

(5.253)
$$P_M^*(\hat{\underline{\mu}}) = M(M^T D(\hat{\underline{\mu}})M)^{-1} M^T D(\hat{\underline{\mu}}).$$

Thus the estimated asymptotic covariance of $\hat{\underline{b}}$ satisfies

(5.254)
$$M^{-1}[P_M^*(\hat{\underline{\mu}}) - P_N^*(\hat{\underline{\mu}})]D^{-1}(\hat{\underline{\mu}})(M^{-1})^T$$
$$= [M^T D(\hat{\underline{\mu}})M]^{-1} - M^{-1}P_N^*(\hat{\underline{\mu}})D^{-1}(\hat{\underline{\mu}})(M^{-1})^T.$$

The second term on the right-hand side of (5.253) may be ignored if $N = \{\underline{0}\}$ or if $N = \text{span}\ \{\underline{e}\}$ and $\hat{\nu}^{\phi}_{\alpha}$ is not of interest. The second condition follows since if $N = \text{span}\ \{\underline{e}\}$, then

(5.255)
$$M^{-1}P_N^*(\hat{\underline{\mu}})D^{-1}(\hat{\underline{\mu}})(M^{-1})^T$$
$$= M^{-1}[\underline{e} \otimes D(\hat{\underline{\mu}})\underline{e}]D^{-1}(\hat{\underline{\mu}})(M^{-1})^T/(\underline{e},D(\hat{\underline{\mu}})\underline{e})$$
$$= \underline{\delta}^{(1)} \otimes \underline{\delta}^{(1)}/(\underline{e},D(\hat{\underline{\mu}})\underline{e}),$$

where

(5.256)
$$\delta^{(1)}_{ijk\ell} = 1 \text{ if } i = j = k = \ell = 1,$$
$$= 0 \text{ otherwise.}$$

The asymptotic covariances desired can thus be computed by inversion of $M^T D(\hat{\underline{\mu}})M$. This task may be accomplished by noting that under the standard basis for R^{10},

$$[M^T D(\hat{\underline{\mu}})M]_{gh} = (\underline{\nu}(B_g, \pi_{B_g}\langle 1,1,1,1\rangle), D(\hat{\underline{\mu}})\underline{\nu}(B_h, \pi_{B_h}\langle 1,1,1,1\rangle)) \tag{5.257}$$

and $[(M^T D(\hat{\underline{\mu}})M)^{-1}]_{gh}$ is the asymptotic covariance of $\hat{v}^{B_g}_{\pi_{B_g}}\langle 1,1,1,1\rangle$ and $\hat{v}^{B_h}_{\pi_{B_h}}\langle 1,1,1,1\rangle$. Results are summarized in table 5.3. The letters P, C, N, and S stand respectively for proximity, contact, norms, and sentiment. A code such as PN represents the proximity-by-norms interaction.

TABLE 5.3

ASYMPTOTIC COVARIANCES OF INTERACTIONS IN RACIAL ATTITUDES STUDY

	P	C	N	S	PC	PN	CN	CS	NS
P	0.0020	-0.0006	-0.0003	0.0000	-0.0003	-0.0001	-0.0000	-0.0000	0.0000
C	-0.0006	0.0021	-0.0003	-0.0004	0.0004	-0.0001	0.0002	0.0001	-0.0001
N	-0.0003	-0.0003	0.0019	-0.0003	-0.0000	-0.0003	-0.0002	0.0000	0.0001
S	0.0000	-0.0004	-0.0003	0.0019	-0.0000	0.0000	-0.0000	-0.0001	0.0002
PC	-0.0003	0.0004	-0.0000	-0.0000	0.0020	-0.0003	-0.0002	-0.0000	0.0000
PN	-0.0001	-0.0001	0.0003	0.0000	-0.0003	0.0020	0.0005	0.0000	0.0000
CN	-0.0000	0.0002	0.0002	-0.0000	-0.0002	-0.0005	0.0021	-0.0003	-0.0004
CS	-0.0000	0.0001	0.0000	-0.0001	-0.0000	0.0000	-0.0003	0.0019	-0.0003
NS	0.0000	-0.0001	0.0001	0.0002	0.0000	-0.0000	-0.0004	-0.0003	0.0019

The estimated asymptotic standard deviations of the interactions have a narrow range; the smallest is 0.044 and the largest is 0.046. It should be noted that in this example, Goodman (1972a) obtains an estimate of 0.046 for each asymptotic standard deviation by use of the easily computed approximation $(\underline{\nu}(B_g, \pi_{B_g}\langle 1,1,1,1\rangle), D^{-1}(\hat{\underline{\mu}})\underline{\nu}(B_g, \pi_{B_g}\langle 1,1,1,1\rangle))^{\frac{1}{2}}$ for each $g \in \bar{h}$. This approximation has rather general applications and is easily computed. It normally overestimates the asymptotic standard deviation, but the error may be relatively small in problems such as this one.

Once $[M^T D(\hat{\underline{\mu}})M]^{-1}$ has been computed, such operators as $P^*_M(\hat{\underline{\mu}})D^{-1}(\hat{\underline{\mu}})$ and $A_M(\hat{\underline{\mu}})$ are readily determined. In this example, there is relatively little need for these operators since the fit of the model to the data is so close that an analysis of residuals appears to be unnecessary. If the computations are performed, it is found that the largest magnitude of an adjusted residual is only 1.36.

If a hierarchical manifold M is decomposable, then computation of $P_M^*(\hat{\underline{\mu}})$ becomes an unusually simple task. The following lemma provides the basis for the calculations.

LEMMA 5.14. *As in Lemma 5.8, suppose that* $E = E_1 \cup E_2$, *where* E_1 *and* E_2 *are disjoint generating classes such that for some* $E_1 \in E_1$ *and* $E_2 \in E_2$,

$$[U(E_1)] \cap [U(E_2)] = E_1 \cap E_2. \quad (5.258)$$

If $\underline{\mu} \in M(E)$, $A = U(E_1)$, $B = U(E_2)$, $C = A \cap B$, *and for any subset* E *of* $\overline{d}$, $\overline{\underline{\mu}}^E = \{\log [m^E_{\pi_E \underline{i}} / \prod_{j \in \overline{d}-E} r_j] : \underline{i} \in I\}$, *then*

$$P^*_{M(E)}(\underline{\mu})D^{-1}(\underline{\mu}) = P^*_{M(E_1)}(\overline{\underline{\mu}}^A)D^{-1}(\overline{\underline{\mu}}^A) + P^*_{M(E_2)}(\overline{\underline{\mu}}^B)D^{-1}(\overline{\underline{\mu}}^B) - P^*_{M(\{C\})}(\overline{\underline{\mu}}^C). \quad (5.259)$$

Proof. The first phase of the proof is a demonstration that

$$P^*_{M(E)}(\underline{\mu}) = P^*_{M(E_1)}(\underline{\mu}) + P^*_{M(E_2)}(\underline{\mu}) - P^*_{M(\{C\})}(\underline{\mu}). \quad (5.260)$$

The second phase is a proof that $P^*_{M(E_1)}(\overline{\underline{\mu}}^A) = P^*_{M(E_1)}(\underline{\mu})D^{-1}(\underline{\mu})$. The same argument shows that $P^*_{M(E_2)}(\overline{\underline{\mu}}^B)D^{-1}(\overline{\underline{\mu}}^B) = P^*_{M(E_2)}(\underline{\mu})D^{-1}(\underline{\mu})$ and $P^*_{M(\{C\})}(\overline{\underline{\mu}}^C)D^{-1}(\overline{\underline{\mu}}^C) = P^*_{M(\{C\})}(\underline{\mu})D^{-1}(\underline{\mu})$. Given these results, (5.259) follows immediately.

To verify (5.260), it is necessary to show that if $\underline{x} \in M(E_2)$ and $\underline{x} \in D^{-1}(\underline{\mu})[M(\{C\})]^{\perp}$, then $\underline{x} \in D^{-1}(\underline{\mu})[M(E_1)]^{\perp}$. Such a result implies that the orthogonal complement of $M(\{C\})$ relative to $M(E_2)$ and the inner product defined by $D(\underline{\mu})$ is orthogonal to $M(E_1)$ with respect to the same inner product. The result then follows from results in Halmos (1958) concerning combinations of projections.

Since $\{\underline{\nu}(E,\overline{\underline{i}}): \overline{\underline{i}} \in I(E), E \in E_1\}$ spans $M(E_1)$, it is only necessary to show that if $\overline{\underline{i}} \in I(E)$ and $E \in E_1$, then

$$(\underline{x}, D(\underline{\mu})\underline{\nu}(E,\overline{\underline{i}})) = 0. \quad (5.261)$$

Since $\underline{x} \in M(E_2)$, it satisfies an equation of the form

$$x_{\underline{i}} = \sum_{E' \in E_2} u^{E'}_{\pi_{E'}\underline{i}} . \quad (5.262)$$

If $\underline{m} = \{\exp(\mu_{\underline{i}})\}$, then

$$(\underline{x}, D(\underline{\mu})\underline{\nu}(E,\overline{\underline{i}})) \quad (5.263)$$

$$= \Sigma \{m_{\underline{i}} \sum_{E' \in E_2} u^{E'}_{\pi_{E'}\underline{i}} : \underline{i} \in \pi_E^{-1}\overline{\underline{i}}\}$$

$$= \Big(\prod_{j\in D} \frac{1}{r_j}\Big)\Sigma\Big\{\big(m^A_{\pi_A \underline{i}}\, m^B_{\pi_B \underline{i}} / m^C_{\pi_C \underline{i}}\big) \sum_{E' \in E_2} u^{E'}_{\pi_{E'} \underline{i}} : \underline{i} \in \pi_E^{-1} \underline{\bar{i}}\Big\} ,$$

where $D = \bar{d} - (A \cup B)$. If $G = E \cup B$, then $\pi_E^{-1}\underline{\bar i} = \cup\{\pi_G^{-1}\underline{\bar j} : \underline{\bar j} \in (\pi_E^G)^{-1}\underline{\bar i}\}$ and

(5.264) $$(\underline{x}, D(\underline{\mu})\underline{\nu}(E,\underline{\bar i}))$$

$$= \Big(\prod_{j\in D}\frac{1}{r_j}\Big) \Sigma\Big\{\big(m^B_{\pi_B^G \underline{\bar j}}/m^C_{\pi_C^G\underline{\bar j}}\big) \sum_{E'\in E_2} u^{E'}_{\pi^G_{E'}\underline{\bar j}} \sum_{\underline{i}\in\pi_G^{-1}\underline{\bar j}} m^A_{\pi_A \underline{i}} : \underline{\bar j}\in(\pi^G_E)^{-1}\underline{\bar i}\Big\} .$$

If $H = G \cap A$, then $H = C \cup E$ and

(5.265) $$\sum_{\underline{i}\in\pi_G^{-1}\underline{j}} m^A_{\pi_A\underline{i}}$$

$$= \Big(\prod_{j\in D} r_j\Big)\Sigma\big\{m^A_{\underline{\bar i}} : \underline{\bar i}\in(\pi^A_H)^{-1}\pi^G_H\underline{\bar j}\big\}$$

$$= \Big(\prod_{j\in D} r_j\Big) m^H_{\pi^G_H\underline{\bar j}} .$$

Thus

(5.266) $$(\underline{x}, D(\underline{\mu})\underline{\nu}(E,\underline{\bar i}))$$

$$= \Sigma\Big\{\big(m^B_{\pi^G_B\underline{\bar j}}\, m^H_{\pi^G_H\underline{\bar j}}/m^C_{\pi^G_C\underline{\bar j}}\big) \sum_{E'\in E_2} u^{E'}_{\pi^G_{E'}\underline{\bar j}} : \underline{\bar j}\in(\pi^G_E)^{-1}\underline{\bar i}\Big\} .$$

Since $(\pi^G_E)^{-1}\underline{\bar i} = \cup\{(\pi^G_H)^{-1}\underline{\bar k} : \underline{\bar k}\in(\pi^H_E)^{-1}\underline{\bar i}\}$,

(5.267) $$(\underline{x}, D(\underline{\mu})\underline{\nu}(E,\underline{\bar i}))$$

$$= \Sigma\Big\{\big(m^H_{\underline{\bar k}}/m^C_{\pi^H_C\underline{\bar k}}\big)\, \Sigma\Big\{m^B_{\pi^G_B\underline{\bar j}} \sum_{E'\in E_2} u^{E'}_{\pi^G_{E'}\underline{\bar j}} : \underline{\bar j}\in(\pi^G_H)^{-1}\underline{\bar k}\Big\} : \underline{\bar k}\in(\pi^H_E)^{-1}\underline{\bar i}\Big\}.$$

Observe that $\pi^G_{E'}\underline{\bar j} = \pi^B_{E'}\pi^G_B\underline{\bar j}$ if $\underline{\bar j}\in I(G)$ and $\pi^G_B\underline{\bar j}$ determines $\underline{\bar j}$ if $\underline{\bar j}\in(\pi^G_H)^{-1}\underline{\bar k}$. Therefore, if $\underline{k}\in I(H)$, then

(5.268) $$\{\pi^G_B\underline{\bar j} : \underline{\bar j}\in(\pi^G_H)^{-1}\underline{\bar k}\} = \{\underline{\bar h} : \underline{\bar h}\in(\pi^B_C)^{-1}\pi^H_C\underline{\bar k}\} ,$$

and (5.262) implies that

(5.269)
$$\Sigma \{m^B_{\pi^G_B \underline{\bar{j}}} \sum_{E' \in E_2} u^{E'}_{\pi^G_{E'} \underline{\bar{j}}} : \underline{\bar{j}} \in (\pi^G_H)^{-1} \underline{k}\}$$

$$= \Sigma \{m^B_{\underline{\bar{h}}} \sum_{E' \in E_2} u^{E'}_{\pi^B_{E'} \underline{\bar{h}}} : \underline{\bar{h}} \in (\pi^B_C)^{-1} \pi^H_C \underline{k}\}$$

$$\Sigma \{[\sum_{E' \in E_2} u^{E'}_{\pi^B_{E'} \underline{\bar{h}}}] \sum_{\underline{i} \in \pi_B^{-1} \underline{\bar{h}}} m_{\underline{i}} : \underline{\bar{h}} \in (\pi^B_C)^{-1} \pi^H_C \underline{k}\}$$

$$= \Sigma \{ \sum_{\underline{i} \in \pi_B^{-1} \underline{\bar{h}}} m_{\underline{i}} x_{\underline{i}} : \underline{\bar{h}} \in (\pi^B_C)^{-1} \pi^H_C \underline{k}\}$$

$$= \Sigma \{m_{\underline{i}} x_{\underline{i}} : \underline{i} \in \pi_C^{-1} (\pi^H_C \underline{k})\}$$

$$= (\underline{x}, D(\underline{\mu}) \underline{\nu}(C, \pi^H_C \underline{k}))$$

$$= 0.$$

The last equation follows since $\underline{x} \in D^{-1}(\underline{\mu})[M(\{C\})]^{\perp}$. By (5.267) and (5.269),

(5.270)
$$(\underline{x}, D(\underline{\mu}) \underline{\nu}(E, \underline{\bar{i}})) = 0.$$

Thus $\underline{x} \in D^{-1}(\underline{\mu})[M(E_1)]^{\perp}$ and (5.259) holds.

To prove that $P^*_{M(E_1)}(\underline{\bar{\mu}}^A) D^{-1}(\underline{\bar{\mu}}^A)$ and $P^*_{M(E_1)}(\underline{\mu}) D^{-1}(\underline{\mu})$ are equal, suppose that M is a linear mapping from R^{p_1} onto $M(E_1)$, where p_1 is the dimension of $M(E_1)$. Then

(5.271)
$$P^*_{M(E_1)}(\underline{\mu}^A) D^{-1}(\underline{\mu}^A) = M[M^T D(\underline{\bar{\mu}}^A) M]^{-1} M^T$$

and

(5.272)
$$P^*_{M(E_1)}(\underline{\mu}) D^{-1}(\underline{\mu}) = M[M^T D(\underline{\mu}) M]^{-1} M^T.$$

Thus it suffices to show that

(5.273)
$$M^T D(\underline{\bar{\mu}}^A) M = M^T D(\underline{\mu}) M.$$

To verify (5.273), note that this equation holds if for any $\underline{a}$ and $\underline{b}$ in R^{p_1},

(5.273)
$$(\underline{a}, M^T D(\underline{\bar{\mu}}^A) M \underline{b})_{p_1} = (\underline{a}, M^T D(\underline{\mu}) M \underline{b})_{p_1}.$$

Here $(\cdot,\cdot)_{p_1}$ is the standard inner product for R^{p_1}. This equation is equivalent to the equation

(5.275) $$(M\underline{a}, D(\underline{\bar{\mu}}^A)M\underline{b}) = (M\underline{a}, D(\underline{\mu})M\underline{b}).$$

Thus (5.273) holds if for each $\underline{x}$ and $\underline{y}$ in $M(E_1)$,

(5.276) $$(\underline{x}, D(\underline{\bar{\mu}}^A)\underline{y}) = (\underline{x}, D(\underline{\mu})\underline{y}).$$

Since $M(E_1) \subset M(\{A\})$, $\underline{u}$ and $\underline{v}$ in $R^{I(A)}$ exist such that $\underline{x} = \{u_{\pi_A \underline{i}}\}$ and $\underline{y} = \{v_{\pi_A \underline{i}}\}$. Thus

(5.277)
$$\begin{aligned}
&(\underline{x}, D(\underline{\bar{\mu}}^A)\underline{y}) \\
&= \sum_{\underline{i} \in I} u_{\pi_A \underline{i}} v_{\pi_A \underline{i}} m^A_{\pi_A \underline{i}} / \sum_{j \in \bar{d}-A} r_j \\
&= \sum_{\underline{\bar{i}} \in \bar{I}(A)} \sum_{\underline{i} \in \pi_A^{-1} \underline{\bar{i}}} u_{\underline{\bar{i}}} v_{\underline{\bar{i}}} m^A_{\underline{\bar{i}}} / \sum_{j \in \bar{d}-A} r_j \\
&= \sum_{\underline{\bar{i}} \in \bar{I}(A)} u_{\underline{\bar{i}}} v_{\underline{\bar{i}}} m^A_{\underline{\bar{i}}} \\
&= \sum_{\underline{\bar{i}} \in \bar{I}(A)} \sum_{\underline{i} \in \pi_A^{-1} \underline{\bar{i}}} u_{\pi_A \underline{i}} v_{\pi_A \underline{i}} m_{\underline{i}} \\
&= \sum_{\underline{i} \in I} u_{\pi_A \underline{i}} v_{\pi_A \underline{i}} m_{\underline{i}} \\
&= (\underline{x}, D(\underline{\mu})\underline{y}).
\end{aligned}$$

Therefore, $P^*_{M(E_1)}(\underline{\mu})D^{-1}(\underline{\mu}) = P^*_{M(E_1)}(\underline{\bar{\mu}}^A)D^{-1}(\underline{\bar{\mu}}^A)$. Both phases of the proof are now completed.||

The induction procedure used to derive (5.108) may be used to prove the following theorem.

THEOREM 5.6. *If* E *is decomposable, then*

(5.278)
$$\begin{aligned}
&P^*_{M(E)}(\underline{\mu})D^{-1}(\underline{\mu}) \\
&= \sum_{E \in \mathcal{E}} P^*_{M(\{E\})}(\underline{\bar{\mu}}^E)D^{-1}(\underline{\bar{\mu}}^E) \\
&- \sum_{F \in \bar{F}(E)} d(F,E) P^*_{M(\{F\})}(\underline{\bar{\mu}}^F)D^{-1}(\underline{\bar{\mu}}^F) \\
&= \sum_{E \in \mathcal{E}} \sum_{\underline{\bar{i}} \in \bar{I}(E)} \underline{\nu}(E,\underline{\bar{i}}) \otimes \underline{\nu}(E,\underline{\bar{i}})/m^E_{\underline{\bar{i}}} \\
&- \sum_{F \in \bar{F}(E)} d(F,E) \sum_{\underline{\bar{i}} \in \bar{I}(F)} \underline{\nu}(F,\underline{\bar{i}}) \otimes \underline{\nu}(F,\underline{\bar{i}})/m^F_{\underline{\bar{i}}} .
\end{aligned}$$

Proof. The proof of the first equation involves the same induction argument used in Theorem 5.1. The second equation follows since if $G \subset \bar{d}$, then $\{\underline{\nu}(G,\underline{i}): \underline{i} \in I(G)\}$ is an orthogonal basis of $M(\{G\})$ with respect to the inner product defined by $D(\underline{\bar{\mu}}^G)$ and

$$(5.279) \qquad (\underline{\nu}(G,\underline{i}),D(\underline{\bar{\mu}}^G)\underline{\nu}(G,\underline{i})) = \sum_{\underline{i}\in\pi_G^{-1}\underline{i}} m^G_{\pi_G\underline{i}} \Big/ \sum_{j\in\bar{d}-G} r_j = m^G_{\underline{i}}$$

if $\underline{i} \in I(G)$. ||

COROLLARY 5.5. *If* E *is decomposable, the estimated asymptotic covariance* $P^*_{M(E)}(\hat{\underline{\mu}})D^{-1}(\hat{\underline{\mu}})$ *of* $\hat{\underline{\mu}}$ *satisfies*

$$(5.280) \qquad P^*_{M(E)}(\hat{\underline{\mu}})D^{-1}(\hat{\underline{\mu}}) = \sum_{E\in E}\sum_{\underline{i}\in I(E)} \underline{\nu}(E,\underline{i}) \otimes \underline{\nu}(E,\underline{i})/n^E_{\underline{i}} - \sum_{F\in F(E)} d(F,E) \sum_{\underline{i}\in I(F)} \underline{\nu}(F,\underline{i}) \otimes \underline{\nu}(F,\underline{i})/n^F_{\underline{i}} .$$

Proof. The corollary follows from Theorem 5.6 since $\hat{m}^E_{\underline{i}} = n^E_{\underline{i}}$ if $E \in E$ and $\underline{i} \in I(E)$ and $\hat{m}^F_{\underline{i}} = n^F_{\underline{i}}$ if $F \in F(E)$ and $\underline{i} \in I(F)$. ||

Example 5.57. Consider the 3 x 5 table in Example 4.20. In this case, $E = \{\{1\},\{2\}\}$ and $I = \bar{3} \times \bar{5}$. Thus

$$(5.281) \qquad P^*_{M(E)}(\hat{\underline{\mu}})D^{-1}(\hat{\underline{\mu}}) = \sum_{i=1}^{3} \underline{\nu}(\{1\},i) \otimes \underline{\nu}(\{1\},i)/n_{i+} + \sum_{j=1}^{5} \underline{\nu}(\{2\},j) \otimes \underline{\nu}(\{2\},j)/n_{+j} - \underline{\nu}(\phi,\alpha) \otimes \nu(\phi,\alpha)/n_{++}.$$

Comparison with (4.317) is facilitated by noting that $\underline{\nu}(\phi,\alpha) = \underline{e}$ and

$$(5.282) \qquad A_{M(E)}(\hat{\underline{\mu}}) = D^{\frac{1}{2}}(\hat{\underline{\mu}})P^*_{M(E)}(\hat{\underline{\mu}})D^{-\frac{1}{2}}(\hat{\underline{\mu}}).$$

ORDERED CLASSIFICATIONS

The models examined in this chapter make no use of any natural ordering of the classifications corresponding to the variables represented by $\bar{r}_j$, where $j \in \bar{d}$. This situation can be remedied by considering more complex decompositions of R^{r_j} than the one into span $\{\underline{e}^{(r_j)}\}$ and $\{\underline{e}^{(r_j)}\}^{\perp}$. For example, linear trend effects can be examined for variables $\{X_{tj}: t \in \bar{N}\}$ by considering the decomposition

$$R^{r_j} = \text{span}\ \{\underline{e}^{(r_j)}\} \oplus \text{span}\ \{\underline{z}^{(j)}\} \oplus \{\underline{e}^{(r_j)}, \underline{z}^{(j)}\}^{\perp}, \tag{5.283}$$

where $(\underline{e}^{(r_j)}, \underline{z}^{(j)}) = 0$; i.e.,

$$\sum_{i=1}^{r_j} z_i^{(j)} = 0. \tag{5.284}$$

The elements of $\underline{z}^{(j)}$ may correspond to observed quantities such as log dosages, or they may be scores assigned to ordinal classifications.

Example 5.58. In Example 1.6, a logit analysis problem is considered in which $I = 3 \times 2$. The first variable is log dose and the second is outcome. The decomposition

$$R^3 = \text{span}\ \{\underline{e}^{(3)}\} \oplus \text{span}\ \{\underline{z}^{(1)}\} \oplus \{\underline{e}^{(3)}, \underline{z}^{(1)}\}^{\perp} \tag{5.285}$$

is employed, where $z_i^{(1)}$ is $10(t_i - 0.85)$, t_i is the log dose, and 0.85 is the average log dose. Since the second variable has only two values, no special decomposition is possible.

Example 5.59. In Example 3.2, the incidence of *torus mandibularis* among Eskimo tribes is considered. The resulting table has the index set $\bar{3} \times \bar{2} \times \bar{2} \times \bar{6}$. The first variable, the tribe of the Eskimo is nominal, so a special decompositon is inappropriate. The second and third variables, sex and presence or absence, have only two values, so a special decomposition is impossible. The last variable, age group, clearly is an ordered classification. Each age group includes a 10-year span of ages except the last group, which includes all ages greater than 50. In this case, the scores $t_1^{(4)} = -5$, $t_2^{(4)} = -3$, $t_3^{(4)} = -1$, $t_4^{(4)} = 1$, $t_5^{(4)} = 3$, and $t_6^{(4)} = 5$ may be employed to reflect the basically even spacing.

Example 5.60. In Example 4.20, the 3 x 5 table involves two ordinal classifications. The teachers' ratings may be assigned the scores +1, 0, and -1, and the homework conditions may be given the scores 2, 1, 0, -1, and -2.

Given these special decompositions, one may construct new linear manifolds which are the direct sums of hierarchical manifolds and special manifolds based on the special decompositions. Maximum-likelihood estimates are generally computed by use of the conditioned Newton-Raphson algorithm. The procedures employed are illustrated by the following examples.

Example 5.61. In the logit model of Examples 1.6 and 5.45 the linear manifold is the direct sum of $M(\{\{1\},\{2\}\})$ and span $\{\underline{z}^{(1)}\} \otimes$ span $\{<1,-1>\}$ = span $\{\underline{z}^{(1)} \otimes <1,-1>\}$. The dimension of $M(\{\{1\},\{2\}\})$ is 4, so M has dimension 5. As pointed out in Example 3.3, the maximum-likelihood estimate $\hat{\underline{m}}$ is found most readily by maximization of $\hat{\ell}^{(m)}(\underline{n},\underline{\mu})$, where $N = M(\{\{1\}\})$. This model has been discussed already in Examples 3.3, 3.6, 4.5, and 4.19. Further discussion of models of this type is found in chapter 8.

Example 5.62. The manifold M considered in Examples 3.2 and 5.59 for presence or absence of *torus mandibularis* among Eskimo tribes is the direct sum of $M(\{\{1\},\{2\},\{3\},\{4\}\})$ and span $\{\underline{e}^{(3)}\} \otimes$ span $\{\underline{e}^{(2)}\} \otimes \{e^{(2)}\}^{\perp} \otimes$ span $\{\underline{z}^{(4)}\}$ = span $\{\underline{e}^{(3)} \otimes \underline{e}^{(2)} \otimes <1,-1> \otimes \underline{z}^{(4)}\}$. The model assumes that the only relationship between the variables in the study is a tendency for the probability of *torus mandibularis* to increase with increasing age. This model is also discussed in Examples 3.6 and 4.12.

Example 5.63. In Example 4.20, one method of examining residuals involved use of a linear-by-linear term. Using the notation of Example 5.60, the manifold considered is $M(\{\{1\},\{2\}\}) \oplus$ span $\{\underline{z}^{(1)} \otimes \underline{z}^{(2)}\}$. This linear manifold is used to detect a tendency for better homework conditions to lead to better teacher ratings.

Numerous special models can be constructed besides the ones considered in this section. Space limitations preclude examination of all possibilities, but it is worthwhile to consider in some detail one example of an unconventional model. Such a study is made in the next chapter through an exploration of classical social-mobility tables.

Chapter 6

SOCIAL-MOBILITY TABLES

Social-mobility tables have received substantial attention in both statistical and sociological literature (see Goodman 1965 and 1969a). They present a major example of tables in which considerable structure exists but in which simple hierarchical hypotheses are inappropriate. In this paper, a simple method is developed for analysis of these tables. The method is applied to the classical British and Danish mobility tables developed respectively by Glass (1954) and Svalastoga (1959).

POSSIBLE MODELS

In the social-mobility tables analyzed in this paper, the social statuses of father and son are compared. Social status is defined in terms of occupational group, with these groups ordered in terms of status. Five or seven groups are typical divisions in the studies employed in this paper. The resulting table is a square contingency table.

Two effects are likely to be important in such a table. Inheritance of status is somewhat different from status transition. Therefore, the diagonal elements of the table may require special treatment. Transitions between similar status categories are more common than transitions between dissimilar categories; therefore, some means must be found to adjust for the size of the transition.

Log-linear models provide a convenient solution to the problem of model selection. Assume that the N subjects and their fathers can have status categories 1, 2, ..., r. Let the frequency of father's status category i and son's status category j be n_{ij}. Then the expected value of n_{ij} is m_{ij} and $\mu_{ij} = \log m_{ij}$. Assume that simple multinomial sampling has been employed to obtain the data. Then a reasonable model for the data is

(6.1) $$\mu_{ij} = \alpha + \beta_i + \gamma_j - |\eta_i - \eta_j| + \delta_{ij}\,\varepsilon_i\ ,$$

where δ_{ij} is the Kronecker delta and

(6.2) $$\sum_{i=1}^{r} \beta_i = \sum_{j=1}^{r} \gamma_j = 0.$$

To understand the nature of this model, consider the effect of setting $\eta_i = 0$ and $\varepsilon_i = 0$ for $i \in \overline{r}$. Then the model is the ordinary independence model for two-way tables. This model is not appropriate since status of father and status of son are not independent. To make the model more realistic, the other two terms are added. The first added term measures distance between categories. Category i is said to lie at position η_i. Thus categories i and j are separated by a distance $|\eta_i - \eta_j|$. The second added term is used to account for status inheritance. This term is only nonzero when father and son have the same status. If ε_i is positive, fathers of status i are more likely to have sons of status i than would be the case if only a distance term were present. It is entirely possible for ε_i to be negative. In this case, there is status disinheritance. If $\delta_{ij}\,\varepsilon_i$ is present in the model but $|\eta_i - \eta_j|$ is always 0, then the model may be treated by the methods of chapter 7. Such models have been considered by Goodman (1965, 1969a). They have proved quite useful for coarse tables, but they are less successful when applied to 7×7 or 5×5 tables. Thus the distance terms do appear to be needed.

The model will be employed in this paper in two forms. In the first form the simplifying assumption is made that adjacent categories have constant distance between them; i.e., $\eta_i - \eta_{i+1}$ is constant. In this case, the model becomes

(6.3) $$\mu_{ij} = \alpha + \beta_i + \gamma_j - c|i - j| + \delta_{ij}\,\varepsilon_i\ ,$$

where all parameters except c are defined as in equation (6.1). The assumption in this model is not likely to be strictly correct, but it may be an adequate approximation. An inspection of this model shows that the manifold M corresponding to (6.3) has dimension $3r = 1 + (r - 1) + (r - 1) + 1 + r$.

The second form of the model assumes that if $i < j$,

(6.4) $$|\eta_i - \eta_j| = \sum_{k=i}^{j-1} \lambda_k\ .$$

This assumption is correct if the ordering of statuses is correct. The model then becomes

(6.5)
$$\mu_{ij} = \alpha + \beta_i + \gamma_j - \sum_{k=1}^{j-1} \lambda_k \quad \text{if } i < j ,$$
$$= \alpha + \beta_i + \gamma_j - \sum_{k=j}^{i-1} \lambda_k \quad \text{if } i > j ,$$
$$= \alpha + \beta_i + \gamma_j + \varepsilon_i \quad \text{if } i = j ,$$

where β_i and γ_j satisfy (6.2). To uniquely define the parameters, the restrictions $\lambda_1 = \lambda_2$ and $\lambda_{r-2} = \lambda_{r-1}$ are imposed. In fact, suppose $\alpha = 2/r$, $\beta_i = -1/r$ if $i > 1$, $\beta_1 = (r - 1)/r$, $\gamma_j = -1/r$ if $j > 1$, $\gamma_j = (r - 1)/r$, $\lambda_1 = -1$, $\lambda_k = 0$ if $k > 1$, and $\varepsilon_i = 0$ if $i \in \overline{r}$. Then μ_{ij} is 2 if $i = j = 1$ and 0 otherwise. This vector can also be obtained by setting every parameter to 0 except ε_1. Thus the first restriction is needed. A similar argument shows that the restriction $\lambda_{r-2} = \lambda_{r-1}$ is also necessary. If M^+ is the manifold of $\underline{\mu}$ satisfying (6.5), then M^+ has dimension $4r - 4 = 1 + (r - 1) + (r - 1) + (r - 1) + (r - 2)$. Note that $\lambda_k = c$ for $k \in \overline{r - 1}$, then $\underline{\mu} \in M$. Thus $M \subset M^+$.

THE BRITISH TABLE

The two models were applied to the 7 x 7 British mobility table developed by the Glass study. Results are given in tables 6.1, 6.2, 6.3, and 6.4. Computation of the maximum-likelihood estimates was based on the modified Newton-Raphson method discussed in chapter 3. The chi-square tests compare the fitted model with the trivial model $\underline{\mu} \in R^{\overline{7}x\overline{7}}$. Since $n_{61} = n_{71} = 0$, the maximum-likelihood estimate $\hat{\underline{\mu}}$ does not exist for the latter model; however, the supremum of the likelihood may be found by use of the extended maximum-likelihood estimate discussed in Appendix B.

Both models provide rather acceptable fits, although the second model is appreciably better. The difference, a chi-square of 6.809 on 3 degrees of freedom, is nearly significant at the 5% level. Few substantial differences between the fit exist, although the results of the second fit do suggest that some variations may exist in the distances between adjacent statuses.

In neither model is it possible to remove the diagonal effects. This fact should be clear by inspection of tables 6.1 and 6.3. In the first model, removal of the diagonal effects increases chi-square by 212.534 and only increases the degrees of freedom by 7. In the second model, the increase of chi-square is 38.030 on 5 degrees of freedom.

TABLE 6.1

BRITISH SOCIAL MOBILITY: FIXED DISTANCES[a]

Father's Occupation	Son's Occupation 1	2	3	4	5	6	7
1	50.00	19.00	26.00	8.00	18.00	6.00	2.00
	50.00	18.34	19.63	11.41	21.36	4.95	3.31
	0.00	0.66	6.37	-3.41	-3.36	1.05	-1.31
	0.00	0.15	1.44	-1.01	-0.73	0.47	-0.72
2	16.00	40.00	34.00	18.00	31.00	8.00	3.00
	12.05	40.00	31.69	18.42	34.49	8.00	5.35
	3.95	0.00	2.31	-0.42	-3.49	0.00	-2.35
	1.14	0.00	0.41	-0.10	-0.59	0.00	-1.01
3	12.00	35.00	65.00	66.00	123.00	23.00	21.00
	13.98	34.37	65.00	64.41	120.58	27.97	18.69
	-1.98	0.63	0.00	1.59	2.42	-4.97	2.31
	-0.53	0.11	0.00	0.20	0.22	-0.94	0.53
4	11.00	20.00	58.00	110.00	223.00	64.00	32.00
	8.61	21.16	68.19	110.00	223.55	51.85	34.65
	2.39	-1.16	-10.19	-0.00	-0.55	12.15	-2.65
	0.82	-0.25	-1.23	-0.00	-0.04	1.69	-0.45
5	14.00	36.00	114.00	185.00	714.00	258.00	189.00
	14.34	35.24	113.58	198.89	714.00	260.12	173.83
	-0.34	0.76	0.42	-13.89	-0.00	-2.12	15.17
	-0.09	0.13	0.04	-0.99	-0.00	-0.13	1.15
6	0.00	6.00	19.00	40.00	179.00	143.00	71.00
	2.25	5.53	17.83	31.21	176.01	143.00	82.17
	-2.25	0.47	1.17	8.79	2.99	0.00	-11.17
	-1.50	0.20	0.28	1.57	0.23	0.00	-1.23
7	0.00	3.00	14.00	32.00	141.00	91.00	106.00
	1.78	4.37	14.08	24.65	139.01	97.11	106.00
	-1.78	-1.37	-0.08	7.35	1.99	-6.11	0.00
	-1.33	-0.65	-0.02	1.48	0.17	-0.62	0.00

-2 * log likelihood ratio = 31.404

Degrees of freedom of chi-square = 28

[a]First line is observation n_{ij}, second line is fitted value $\hat{m}_{ij}$, third line is raw residual $n_{ij} - \hat{m}_{ij}$, and fourth line is standardized residual $(n_{ij} - \hat{m}_{ij})(\hat{m}_{ij})^{-1/2}$.

TABLE 6.2

PARAMETER ESTIMATES FOR BRITISH FIXED-DISTANCE MODEL

Name	Value	Standard Deviation
β_1	-0.604	0.104
β_2	-0.677	0.087
β_3	0.024	0.059
β_4	0.090	0.053
β_5	1.151	0.047
β_6	-0.149	0.060
β_7	0.166	0.060
γ_1	-0.012	0.123
γ_2	-0.664	0.085
γ_3	-0.045	0.061
γ_4	-0.036	0.057
γ_5	1.143	0.049
γ_6	0.233	0.054
γ_7	0.381	0.084
c	0.551	0.029
ε_1	0.799	0.254
ε_2	0.301	0.220
ε_3	-0.533	0.165
ε_4	-0.082	0.128
ε_5	-0.452	0.085
ε_6	0.151	0.119
ε_7	-0.612	0.152

TABLE 6.3

BRITISH SOCIAL MOBILITY: VARIABLE DISTANCES[a]

Father's Occupation	Son's Occupation 1	2	3	4	5	6	7
1	50.00	19.00	26.00	8.00	18.00	6.00	2.00
	50.00	21.07	20.77	10.11	19.06	4.78	3.22
	0.00	-2.07	5.23	-2.11	-1.06	1.22	-1.22
	0.00	-0.45	1.15	-0.66	-0.24	0.56	-0.68
2	16.00	40.00	34.00	18.00	31.00	8.00	3.00
	13.93	40.00	34.44	16.76	31.60	7.93	5.34
	2.07	0.00	-0.44	1.24	-0.60	0.07	-2.34
	0.55	0.00	-0.07	0.30	-0.11	0.03	-1.01
3	12.00	35.00	65.00	66.00	123.00	23.00	21.00
	14.77	37.02	65.00	62.06	117.01	29.35	19.78
	-2.77	-2.02	0.00	3.94	5.99	-6.35	1.22
	-0.72	-0.33	0.00	0.50	0.55	-1.17	0.27
4	11.00	20.00	58.00	110.00	223.00	64.00	32.00
	7.58	19.01	65.48	110.00	222.49	55.82	37.62
	3.42	0.99	-7.48	0.00	0.51	8.18	-5.62
	1.24	0.23	-0.92	0.00	0.03	1.10	-0.92
5	14.00	36.00	114.00	185.00	714.00	258.00	189.00
	12.77	32.02	110.29	198.76	714.00	264.15	178.02
	1.23	3.98	3.71	-13.76	0.00	-6.15	10.98
	0.34	0.70	0.35	-0.98	0.00	-0.38	0.82
6	0.00	6.00	19.00	40.00	179.00	143.00	71.00
	2.19	5.48	18.89	34.05	180.37	143.00	74.02
	-2.19	0.52	0.11	5.95	-1.37	0.00	-3.02
	-1.48	0.22	0.02	1.02	-0.10	0.00	-0.35
7	0.00	3.00	14.00	32.00	141.00	91.00	106.00
	1.75	4.39	15.13	27.27	144.47	87.98	106.00
	-1.75	-1.39	-1.13	4.73	-3.47	3.02	0.00
	-1.32	-0.66	-0.29	0.91	-0.29	0.32	0.00

-2 * log likelihood ratio = 24.595

Degrees of freedom of chi-square = 25

[a]First line of entry is observation n_{ij}, second line is estimate $\hat{m}_{ij}$, third line is raw residual $n_{ij} - \hat{m}_{ij}$, and fourth line is standardized residual $(n_{ij} - \hat{m}_{ij})(\hat{m}_{ij})^{-1/2}$.

TABLE 6.4

PARAMETER ESTIMATES FOR BRITISH VARIABLE-DISTANCE MODEL

Name	Value	Standard Deviation
β_1	-0.478	0.165
β_2	-0.598	0.101
β_3	0.086	0.080
β_4	0.074	0.068
β_5	1.112	0.059
β_6	-0.209	0.069
β_7	0.012	0.092
γ_1	-0.882	0.178
γ_2	-0.589	0.097
γ_3	0.022	0.081
γ_4	0.043	0.071
γ_5	1.108	0.060
γ_6	0.168	0.064
γ_7	0.217	0.094
δ_1	0.626	0.109
δ_2	0.626	0.109
δ_3	0.655	0.071
δ_4	0.516	0.055
δ_5	0.443	0.056
δ_6	0.443	0.056
ε_1	0.532	0.400
ε_2	0.136	0.263
ε_3	-0.674	0.180
ε_4	-0.070	0.137
ε_5	-0.388	0.088
ε_6	0.264	0.131
ε_7	-0.306	0.208

Detection of systematic effects in the diagonal terms seems difficult in both models, but the use of linear trend models in mobility tables seems quite promising. It should be noted that the trend effects all differ significantly from zero in the two models.

The analysis which has been made is based on the assumption that the asymptotic theory provides an adequate approximation to the distributions actually present. Although two cells are zero, the preponderance of cells contain large counts. Consequently, the asymptotic approximation is probably acceptable. A rigorous demonstration of this conclusion would require a time-consuming Monte Carlo study.

THE DANISH TABLE

To confirm the results derived for the 7×7 British table, the 5×5 Danish table was examined. This table, which was developed by Svalastoga and his co-workers, is difficult to compare with the British table since the occupation divisions in the two tables have no simple relationship to each other. Results are summarized in tables 6.5 through 6.8.

Both models give reasonable fits, although the corresponding models in the British case are a bit more successful. The difference in effectiveness between the fixed- and variable-distance models is quite limited, as may be seen by examination of the difference in chi-square for the two models. This limited difference is reflected in the small variability of δ_i for $i \in \overline{4}$. Thus the categories do appear to be nearly equally spaced. The Danish table does have one feature not present in the British table. In either model, each term ε_i is negative. An examination of the standard deviations suggests that almost all these terms are in fact negative for their respective models. This result suggests a tendency for status inheritance not to occur, in the sense that father and son are less likely to have the same status than would be expected on the basis of the zero distance between the two statuses.

This last conclusion appears somewhat unusual. One would expect a tendency for sons to retain their fathers' occupations. A possible reason for the result is that the term for status inheritance reflects not only status inheritance but also the fact that each status group is composed on individuals with varying statuses. The classification into five or seven groups simply combines individuals with similar statuses. Therefore, the average distance between individuals in the same status group is greater than zero. Thus negative values of ε_i are to be expected. If class i includes statuses within a

TABLE 6.5

DANISH SOCIAL MOBILITY: FIXED DISTANCES[a]

Father's Occupation	Son's Occupation 1	2	3	4	5
1	18.00	17.00	16.00	4.00	2.00
	18.00	15.19	13.55	7.33	2.93
	0.00	1.81	2.45	-3.33	-0.93
	0.00	0.46	0.67	-1.23	-0.54
2	24.00	105.00	109.00	59.00	21.00
	27.63	105.00	105.48	57.06	22.84
	-3.63	0.00	3.52	1.94	-1.84
	-0.69	0.00	0.34	0.26	-0.38
3	23.00	84.00	289.00	217.00	95.00
	20.71	88.62	289.00	221.15	88.52
	2.29	-4.62	0.00	-4.15	6.48
	0.50	-0.49	0.00	-0.28	0.69
4	8.00	49.00	175.00	348.00	196.00
	9.12	39.04	180.12	348.00	201.71
	-1.12	9.96	-5.12	0.00	-3.71
	-0.37	1.59	-0.38	0.00	-0.26
5	6.00	8.00	69.00	201.00	246.00
	3.54	15.14	69.86	195.46	246.00
	2.46	-7.14	-0.86	5.54	0.00
	1.31	-1.84	-0.10	0.40	0.00

-2 * log likelihood ratio = 13.004

Degrees of freedom of chi-square = 10

[a]Entries are arranged as in table 6.1.

TABLE 6.6

PARAMETER ESTIMATES FOR DANISH FIXED-DISTANCE MODEL

Name	Value	Standard Deviation
β_1	-1.280	0.135
β_2	-0.049	0.070
β_3	0.484	0.060
β_4	0.486	0.068
β_5	0.360	0.066
γ_1	-0.994	0.109
γ_2	-0.362	0.074
γ_3	0.345	0.059
γ_4	0.552	0.062
γ_5	0.458	0.091
c	0.822	0.055
ε_1	-0.020	0.343
ε_2	-0.119	0.175
ε_3	-0.347	0.125
ε_4	-0.370	0.109
ε_5	-0.498	0.158

TABLE 6.7

DANISH SOCIAL MOBILITY: VARIABLES DISTANCES[a]

Father's Occupation	Son's Occupation 1	2	3	4	5
1	18.00	17.00	16.00	4.00	2.00
	18.00	14.49	14.04	7.49	2.98
	-0.00	2.51	1.96	-3.49	-0.98
	-0.00	0.66	0.52	-1.28	-0.57
2	24.00	105.00	109.00	59.00	21.00
	26.51	105.00	106.81	56.99	22.69
	-2.51	0.00	2.19	2.01	-1.69
	-0.49	0.00	0.21	0.27	-0.35
3	23.00	84.00	289.00	217.00	95.00
	21.54	89.61	289.00	220.19	87.66
	1.46	-5.61	0.00	-3.19	7.34
	0.31	-0.59	0.00	-0.21	0.78
4	8.00	49.00	175.00	348.00	198.00
	9.35	38.89	179.09	348.00	202.67
	-1.35	10.11	-4.09	0.00	-4.67
	-0.44	1.62	-0.31	0.00	-0.33
5	6.00	8.00	69.00	201.00	246.00
	3.61	15.00	69.07	196.33	246.00
	2.39	-7.00	-0.07	4.67	0.00
	1.26	-1.81	-0.01	0.33	0.00

-2 * log likelihood ratio = 12.797

Degrees of freedom of chi-square = 9

[a]Entries are arranged as in table 6.1.

TABLE 6.8

PARAMETER ESTIMATES FOR DANISH VARIABLE-DISTANCE MODEL

Name	Value	Standard Deviation
β_1	-1.321	0.162
β_2	-0.891	0.083
β_3	0.501	0.071
β_4	0.503	0.078
β_5	0.387	0.088
γ_1	-1.032	0.138
γ_2	-0.386	0.091
γ_3	0.367	0.070
γ_4	0.570	0.073
γ_5	0.486	0.086
δ_1	0.780	0.108
δ_2	0.780	0.108
δ_3	0.836	0.064
δ_4	0.836	0.064
ε_1	0.083	0.414
ε_2	-0.049	0.233
ε_3	-0.356	0.126
ε_4	-0.380	0.111
ε_5	-0.526	0.170

range of 1 distance unit and the statuses of individuals in this class are uniformly distributed, then the average distance between individuals in the same class is 1/3. Thus ε_i of about -0.3 in the Danish table and -0.2 in the British table might occur even if no status inheritance or disinheritance exists. Therefore, whether status inheritance exists at all is unclear in the Danish table. A fully satisfactory correction for variations within categories does not seem available, for a uniform distribution is not likely for very high or low categories. The same problem applies to the British data, but in this case there are large positive values of ε_i present which presumably reflect real status inheritance. There are also large negative values of ε_i which presumably reflect status disinheritance. Even these conclusions must be presented cautiously since it has been arbitrarily assumed that $\lambda_1 = \lambda_2$ and $\lambda_5 = \lambda_6$.

Variation of status within status categories affects off-diagonal as well as diagonal terms; however, in the off-diagonal case the effect is much smaller. The average distance between the status of an individual in one group and the status of an individual in the second group is now equal to the distance between the average statuses of the two groups. Nonetheless, the variation of status within groups is a problem if status categories are too inclusive. An example occurs in the British table. It is difficult to compare a 5 x 5 table and a 7 x 7 table. Consequently, the British table has often been represented in a 5 x 5 form (see Goodman 1969a). In this table, categories 2 and 3 and categories 6 and 7 of the original are combined. When the two models are applied to the new table, the results are considerably less satisfactory than the results obtained using the original table. In fact, the fixed-distance model has a chi-square statistic of 26.3 on 10 degrees of freedom, while the variable-distance model has a chi-square statistic of 15.4 on 9 degrees of freedom. This problem makes table comparison even more difficult.

Thus the models proposed in this section do appear rather effective in describing social-mobility tables, although they do not provide a clear indication of the behavior of status inheritance. More complex models for these tables can be produced which result in more satisfactory descriptions of the results. A detailed investigation of these models is provided by Goodman (1972b). His study includes the models presented in this chapter, although the presentation in terms of a multiplicative scale may mildly obscure this relationahip. The data are insufficient to provide definitive information concerning which of many possible models gives an accurate description of social mobility, but they do provide a good illustration of the use of special linear manifolds.

Chapter 7

INCOMPLETE CONTINGENCY TABLES

In some factorial tables, certain cross-classifications are either impossible, not observable, or exceptional in some other respect. In such cases, the methods developed in chapter 5 for complete factorial tables cannot be applied. However, alternative procedures for incomplete tables are available which are based on models for complete factorial tables but take account of the special features of these tables. These techniques have been studied by Goodman (1968), Bishop and Fienberg (1969), Fienberg (1970 and 1971), Mantel (1970), and Wagner (1970). Except for Fienberg (1971), all these investigations have been basically concerned with incomplete $r \times c$ tables. The present chapter considers general incomplete tables involving linear manifolds generated from the hierarchical manifolds of chapter 5. Results for $r \times c$ tables concerning algorithms, closed-form maximum-likelihood estimates, existence of maximum-likelihood estimates, and dimensionality are extended to more complex tables, and new results are derived concerning asymptotic properties of maximum-likelihood estimates.

PRELIMINARY RESULTS

In an incomplete contingency table model, the index set I is a subset of I^*, where $I^* = \Pi_{j=1}^{d} \bar{r}_j$, the index set for a complete factorial table. The vector of observations $\underline{n} = \{n_{\underline{i}}: \underline{i} \in I\}$ has mean $\underline{m} = \{m_{\underline{i}}: \underline{i} \in I\}$, and the log-mean vector $\underline{\mu} = \{\log m_{\underline{i}}: \underline{i} \in I\}$ is such that for some $\underline{\mu}^* \in M^*$, a linear manifold in R^{I^*}, $\mu_{\underline{i}} = \mu^*_{\underline{i}}$ for each $\underline{i} \in I$. In other words $\underline{\mu} = \rho\underline{\mu}^*$, where $\rho: R^{I^*} \longrightarrow R^I$ is the linear mapping such that $\rho\{x_{\underline{i}}: \underline{i} \in I^*\} = \{x_{\underline{i}}: \underline{i} \in I\}$, and $\underline{\mu} \in \rho M^*$, the image of M^* under ρ.

Example 7.1. Novitski and Sandler (1957) compiled the data presented in table 7.1. They wished to determine the relative frequencies of different kinds of sperm produced by male *D. melanogaster* carrying the translocation between the X and fourth chromosome known as $T(1,4)B^S$ (Translocation (1,4) Bar of Stone). The male sperm may be classified into four groups, AB, A'B, AB', and A'B', which represent two homologues. In the first homologue, the letter A denotes the translocation segment carrying the distal end of the X chromosome. If this segment is not present, then the fourth chromosome, which is

TABLE 7.1

NUMBER OF PROGENY FROM MATING TRANSLOCATION-BEARING MALES TO ATTACHED-X FEMALES

Type of Female	Fourth Chromosome	Male Gamete Type			
		AB	AB'	A'B	A'B'
Y	Marked	847	Lethal	1349	591
	Unmarked	566	Lethal	891	438
B	Marked	Lethal	196	655	273
	Unmarked	Lethal	150	632	275

denoted by A', must be present. In the second homologue, either B or B' is present, where B is the segment of the translocation carrying the base of the X chromosome and B' is the Y chromosome. In addition to these groupings, males may be classified in the experiment according to whether the fourth chromosome is marked or unmarked, and the males carrying the translocation are mated with attached-X females which carry either a Y chromosome or section B of the translocation. Thus one may construct a $2 \times 2 \times 2 \times 2$ table from the data.

The methods of chapter 5 cannot be used in this table since the combination of a male gamete of class AB' and a female gamete with a Y chromosome and the combination of a male gamete of class AB and a female gamete with the translocation segment are lethal or semilethal. Therefore, the index set I considered in this problem is $\overline{2} \times \overline{2} \times \overline{2} \times \overline{2} - \{\langle 1,2,1,1\rangle, \langle 1,2,2,1\rangle, \langle 1,1,1,2\rangle, \langle 1,1,2,2\rangle\}$, where the order of the variables in the table is first homologue, second homologue, fourth chromosome, and type of female.

If all variables are independent, then the observable variable combinations satisfy the relationship $\mu_{ijk\ell} = \mu^*_{ijk\ell} = a_i + b_j + c_k + d_\ell$ for each $\langle i,j,k,\ell\rangle \in I$. Here $\underline{\mu}^* \in M(I^*,E)$, $I^* = \overline{2} \times \overline{2} \times \overline{2} \times \overline{2}$, and $E = \{\{1\},\{2\},\{3\},\{4\}\}$. A model satisfying this relationship is called a quasi-independence model. This term is used since the model is consistent with the assumption of independence, but it is possible for dependence between the variables to exist without changing the relationship $\mu_{ijk\ell} = \mu^*_{ijk\ell}$ for $\langle i,j,k,\ell\rangle \in I$. In fact, $\mu_{ijk\ell} = \mu^*_{ijk\ell} + \lambda_{ijk\ell}$ for all $\langle i,j,k,\ell\rangle \in I$ for any $\underline{\lambda} \in R^{I^*}$ such that $\lambda_{ijk\ell} = 0$ for all $\langle i,j,k,\ell\rangle \in I$.

Example 7.2. Harris (1910) gathered the data shown in table 7.2 while investigating *Staphylea*. The combinations marked by dashes are impossible due to geometrical considerations. Thus $I^* = \overline{4} \times \overline{9}$ and $I = (\{1,4\} \times \{1,4,7,9\}) \cup (\{2,3\} \times \{2,3,5,6,8\})$. Locular composition and the coefficient of radial symmetry are essentially unrelated if for each $j \in J$, given any locular composition i such that $\langle i,j\rangle \in I$, the probability of coefficient j is constant. In such a case, $\{a_i\}$ and $\{b_j\}$ can be chosen so that $m_{ij} = a_i b_j$ for each $\langle i,j\rangle \in I$. Thus for each $\langle i,j\rangle \in I$

$$\mu_{ij} = \log a_i + \log b_j \quad . \tag{7.1}$$

Since $\underline{\mu}^* \in M(\{\{1\},\{2\}\})$ if

$$\mu^*_{ij} = \log a_i + \log b_j \tag{7.2}$$

for $\langle i,j\rangle \in \overline{4} \times \overline{9}$, it follows that $\underline{\mu} = \rho\underline{\mu}^*$ and $\underline{\mu} \in \rho M(\{\{1\},\{2\}\})$. Conversely, if $\underline{\mu} \in \rho M(\{\{1\},\{2\}\})$, then $\{a_i\}$ and $\{b_j\}$ exist such that $m_{ij} = a_i b_j$ for all $\langle i,j\rangle \in I$. As Goodman (1968) points out, the model proposed for the relationship between locular composition and coefficient of asymmetry is a quasi-independent model.

TABLE 7.2

RADIAL ASYMMETRY AND LOCULAR COMPOSITION IN STAPHYLEA (SERIES A)

Locular Composition	Coefficient of Radial Symmetry								
	0.00	0.47	0.82	0.94	1.23	1.41	1.63	1.70	1.89
3 even 0 odd	462	-	-	130	-	-	2	-	1
2 even 1 odd	-	614	138	-	21	14	-	1	-
1 even 2 odd	-	443	95	-	22	8	-	5	-
0 even 3 odd	103	-	-	35	-	-	1	-	0

Since incomplete tables are analyzed by use of linear manifolds for complete tables, procedures must be devised which relate different spaces R^{I_1} and R^{I_2}, where $I_2 \subset I_1$. For this purpose, the projection $\rho^{I_1}_{I_2}: R^{I_1} \longrightarrow R^{I_2}$ and the injection $\tau^{I_1}_{I_2}: R^{I_2} \longrightarrow R^{I_1}$ are quite useful. Here $\rho^{I_1}_{I_2}\{x_{\underline{i}}: \underline{i} \in I_1\} = \{x_{\underline{i}}: \underline{i} \in I_2\}$ and $\tau^{I_1}_{I_2}\{x_{\underline{i}}: \underline{i} \in I_2\} = \{y_{\underline{i}}: \underline{i} \in I_1\}$, where $y_{\underline{i}} = x_{\underline{i}}$ if $\underline{i} \in I_2$ and $y_{\underline{i}} = 0$ if $\underline{i} \in I_1 - I_2$. For brevity in notation, if $I_1 = I^*$, the superscript I_1 is not used for $\rho^{I_1}_{I_2}$ or $\tau^{I_1}_{I_2}$; and if $I_2 = I$, the superscript I_2 is omitted. This usage is consistent with the original definition of ρ.

The basic properties of these operators are summarized by Lemma 7.1.

LEMMA 7.1. *Suppose that* $I_3 \subset I_2 \subset I_1 \subset I^*$ *and* $\{J_p: p \in \overline{s}\}$ *is a partition of some subset* J *of* I^*. *Then*

(7.3) $$\rho_{I_3}^{I_2} \rho_{I_2}^{I_1} = \rho_{I_3}^{I_1} ,$$

(7.4) $$\tau_{I_2}^{I_1} \tau_{I_3}^{I_2} = \tau_{I_3}^{I_1} ,$$

(7.5) $$\rho_{I_2}^{I_1} \tau_{I_3}^{I_1} = \tau_{I_3}^{I_2} ,$$

and

(7.6) $$\sum_{p=1}^{s} \tau_{J_p}^{J} \rho_{J_p}^{J} = I ,$$

the identity operator of R^J. *The transpose* $(\rho_{I_2}^{I_1})^T$ *of* $\rho_{I_2}^{I_1}$ *is* $\tau_{I_2}^{I_1}$, *and the transpose* $(\tau_{I_2}^{I_1})^T$ *of* $\tau_{I_2}^{I_1}$ *is* $\rho_{I_2}^{I_1}$.

Remark. In (7.5), it should be noted that if $I_2 = I_3$, then $\tau_{I_3}^{I_2}$ is the identity operator on R^{I_2}.

Proof. These equations follow immediately from the definitions. If $\underline{x} \in R^{I_1}$, then

(7.7) $$\begin{aligned} \rho_{I_3}^{I_2} \rho_{I_2}^{I_1} \underline{x} &= \rho_{I_3}^{I_2}\{x_{\underline{i}}: \underline{i} \in I_2\} \\ &= \{x_{\underline{i}}: i \in I_3\} \\ &= \rho_{I_3}^{I_1} \underline{x} . \end{aligned}$$

Thus (7.3) follows.

If $\underline{y} \in R^{I_3}$, then

(7.8) $$\begin{aligned} \tau_{I_2}^{I_1} \tau_{I_3}^{I_2} \underline{y} &= \tau_{I_2}^{I_1} \underline{z} \\ &= \underline{w} , \end{aligned}$$

where $z_{\underline{i}} = y_{\underline{i}}$ if $\underline{i} \in I_3$, and $z_{\underline{i}} = 0$ if $\underline{i} \in I_2 - I_3$, $w_{\underline{i}} = z_{\underline{i}} = y_{\underline{i}}$ if $\underline{i} \in I_3$, $w_{\underline{i}} = z_{\underline{i}} = 0$ if $\underline{i} \in I_2 - I_3$, and $w_{\underline{i}} = 0$ if $\underline{i} \in I_1 - I_2$. Thus $w_{\underline{i}} = y_{\underline{i}}$ if $\underline{i} \in I_3$ and $w_{\underline{i}} = 0$ if $\underline{i} \in I_1 - I_3$. In other words, $\underline{w} = \tau_{I_3}^{\tilde{I}_1} \underline{z}$. Therefore, (7.4) must hold. Equation (7.5) follows since $\tau_{I_3}^{I_1} \underline{y} = \underline{v}$, where $v_{\underline{i}} = y_{\underline{i}}$ if $\underline{i} \in I_3$ and $v_{\underline{i}} = 0$ if $\underline{i} \in I_1 - I_3$. If $\underline{u} = \rho_{I_2}^{I_1} \underline{v}$, then $u_{\underline{i}} = y_{\underline{i}}$ if $\underline{i} \in I_3$ and $u_{\underline{i}} = v_{\underline{i}} = 0$ if

$\underline{i} \in (I_1 - I_3) \cap I_2 = I_2 - I_3$. Thus $\underline{u} = \tau_{I_3}^{I_2} \underline{y}$.

To prove (7.6), let $\underline{z} \in R^J$. If χ_{J_p} is the characteristic function of J_p for each $p \in \bar{s}$, then $\tau_{J_p}^{J} \rho_{J_p}^{J} \underline{z} = \{\chi_{J_p}(\underline{i}) z_{\underline{i}} : \underline{i} \in J\}$. Since for each $\underline{i} \in I$, exactly one $\chi_{J_p}(\underline{i})$ is 1, it follows that

(7.9)
$$\sum_{p=1}^{s} \tau_{J_p}^{J} \rho_{J_p}^{J} \underline{z} = \{\sum_{p=1}^{s} \chi_{J_p}(\underline{i}) z_{\underline{i}} : \underline{i} \in J\} = \underline{z}.$$

The results on transposes follow since if $\underline{x} \in R^{I_1}$ and $\underline{y} \in R^{I_2}$, then

(7.10)
$$(\underline{x}, \tau_{I_2}^{I_1} \underline{y})_{I_1} = \sum_{\underline{i} \in I_2} x_{\underline{i}} y_{\underline{i}} = (\rho_{I_2}^{I_1} \underline{x}, \underline{y})_{I_2} \; . \; \|$$

Example 7.3. In Example 7.2, the index set I may be partitioned into the two components $I_1 = \{1,4\} \times \{1,4,7,9\}$ and $I_2 = \{2,3\} \times \{2,3,5,6,8\}$. The vector $\rho_{I_1}^{I} \underline{n}$ is the subtable which consists of feasible observations corresponding to a locular composition of 3 even and 0 odd or 0 even and 3 odd. If $\underline{\mu} \in \rho M(\{\{1\},\{2\}\})$, then $\underline{\mu} = \rho \underline{\mu}^*$ for some $\underline{\mu}^* \in M(\{\{1\},\{2\}\})$ and $\rho_{I_1}^{I} \underline{\mu}$, the log-mean vector of $\rho_{I_1}^{I} \underline{n}$, is equal to $\rho_{I_1} \underline{\mu}^*$. Hence $\rho_{I_1}^{I} \underline{\mu} \in \rho_{I_1} M(\{\{1\},\{2\}\})$. Since I_1 is the Cartesian product of $\{1,4\}$ and $\{1,4,7,9\}$, $\rho_{I_1} M(\{\{1\},\{2\}\})$ is the ordinary additive manifold $M(I_1,\{\{1\},\{2\}\})$. In other words, the variables represented by the rows and columns of this subtable are independent. Similarly, $\rho_{I_2}^{I} \underline{\mu}$ the log-mean vector for $\rho_{I_2}^{I} \underline{n}$, is an element of $M(I_2,\{\{1\},\{2\}\})$, and the variables represented by the rows and columns of this subtable are independent.

The subtables may be used to generate the full observation vector $\underline{n}$ since

(7.11)
$$\tau_{I_1}^{I} (\rho_{I_1}^{I} \underline{n}) + \tau_{I_2}^{I} (\rho_{I_2}^{I} \underline{n}) = \underline{n}.$$

As shown later, it will be possible to analyze table 7.2 by considering each subtable separately and then combining the results found by this approach in order to make inferences concerning the main table.

In the linear manifolds ρM^* considered in this chapter, M^* is generally one of the analysis of variance models considered in chapter 5. Thus

(7.12)
$$M^* = \bigoplus_{g=1}^{h} M_{B_g},$$

where $B_g \subset \bar{d}$ for $g \in \bar{h}$ and if $B \subset \bar{d}$, then

(7.13)
$$M_B = \bigotimes_{j=1}^{d} M^{(j)}_{\chi_B(j)},$$

where χ_B is the characteristic function of B, $M_0^{(j)} = \text{span}\,\{\underline{e}^{(r_j)}\}$, and $M_1^{(j)} = \{\underline{e}^{(r_j)}\}^{\perp}$. Since ρ is linear,

(7.14)
$$\rho M^* = \sum_{g=1}^{h} \cdot \rho M_{B_g}.$$

In (7.14), the summation symbol $\sum$ is used since the manifolds $\rho M_{B_g}, g \in \bar{h}$, need not be orthogonal or disjoint. Thus the decomposition of $\underline{\mu} \in \rho M^*$ into components $\rho\underline{\mu}^{B_g} \in \rho M_{B_g}$ such that

(7.15)
$$\underline{\mu} = \sum_{g=1}^{h} \rho\underline{\mu}^{B_g}$$

need not be unique. This problem is discussed in more detail when computation of components is examined.

Example 7.4. Consider the table already examined in Examples 7.2 and 7.3. If $\underline{\mu} \in \rho M(\{\{1\},\{2\}\})$, then for all $\langle i,j\rangle \in I$,

(7.16)
$$\mu_{ij} = \alpha + \beta_i + \gamma_j,$$

where $\beta_+ = \gamma_+ = 0$. The vector $\underline{\mu}^{\phi} = \{\alpha: \langle i,j\rangle \in \bar{4} \times \bar{9}\} \in M_{\phi}$, $\underline{\mu}^{\{1\}} = \{\beta_i: \langle i,j\rangle \in \bar{4} \times \bar{9}\} \in M_{\{1\}}$ and $\underline{\mu}^{\{2\}} = \{\alpha_j: \langle i,j\rangle \in \bar{4} \times \bar{9}\} \in M_{\{2\}}$. Thus

(7.17)
$$\underline{\mu} = \rho\underline{\mu}^{\phi} + \rho\underline{\mu}^{\{1\}} + \rho\underline{\mu}^{\{2\}}.$$

Unlike the case of complete $\bar{4} \times \bar{9}$ tables, α, $\{\beta_i\}$, and $\{\gamma_j\}$ are not uniquely determined by the stated conditions. If $\alpha' = \alpha - \delta/9$, $\beta_i' = \beta_i + \delta$ if $i = 1$ or 4, $\beta_i' = \beta_i - \delta$ if $i = 2$ or 3, $\gamma_j' = \gamma_i - 10\delta/9$ if $j = 1, 4, 7,$ or 9, and $\gamma_j' = \gamma_j + 8\delta/9$ if $j = 2, 3, 5, 6,$ or 8, then $\beta_+' = 0$, $\gamma_+' = 0$, and

(7.18)
$$\mu_{ij} = \alpha' + \beta_i' + \gamma_j'.$$

Thus the decomposition into components is not unique.

Since the decomposition given in (7.14) is not necessarily a direct summation of linear manifolds, determination of the dimension of ρM^* may be much more difficult than determination of the dimension of M^*. This problem is of considerable importance since it involves the number of degrees of freedom used in chi-square statistics. In addition, proper determination of dimension is important in numerical calculations involving estimated asymptotic covariances and components of $\hat{\underline{\mu}}$.

A completely general procedure for finding the dimension of ρM^* may be constructed by use of an algorithm developed by Borosh and Fraenkel (1966). In this approach, one observes that if $\{\underline{\mu}^{(k)}: k \in \overline{p}\}$ is the basis of M^* constructed in chapter 5 by use of (5.37), then $\rho M^* = \text{span}\ \{\rho\underline{\mu}^{(k)}: k \in \overline{p}\}$. Since each element of $\underline{\mu}^{(k)}$, where $k \in \overline{p}$, is either 0, 1, or -1, each element of $\rho\underline{\mu}^{(k)}$ is 0, 1, or -1. Since 0, 1, and -1 are all integers, it is possible to find the dimension of ρM^* by use of arithmetic operations which only involve addition and multiplication of integers. Thus errors due to rounding can be avoided.

The basic algorithm used for computation of the dimension is Gaussian elimination. In this algorithm, one supposes that $\underline{\lambda}^{(k,0)} = \rho\underline{\mu}^{(k)}$ for each $k \in \overline{p}$, $r_0 = 0$, and $W_0 = \phi$. If $t \in \overline{p}$ and $\{\lambda^{(k,t-1)}: k \in \overline{p}\}$, r_{t-1}, W_{t-1}, and $\{\underline{i}^{(s)}: s \in W_{t-1}\}$ have been computed, then $\{\underline{\lambda}^{(k,t)}: k \in \overline{p}\}$ is defined by selecting an index $\underline{i}^{(t)} \in I - \{\underline{i}^{(s)}: s \in W_{t-1}\}$ such that $c^{(t)} = \lambda^{(t,t-1)}_{\underline{i}^{(t)}} \neq 0$. If such an index does not exist, $\underline{\lambda}^{(k,t)} = \underline{\lambda}^{(k,t-1)}$ for all $k \in \overline{p}$, $r_t = r_{t-1}$, and $W_t = W_{t-1}$. If $\underline{i}^{(t)}$ is found, then $r_r = r_{t-1} + 1$, $W_t = W_{t-1} \cup \{t\}$, $\underline{\lambda}^{(k,t)} = \underline{\lambda}^{(k,t-1)}$ if $d^{(t,k)} = 0$ or $k \leq t$, and

$$\underline{\lambda}^{(k,t)} = c^{(t)}\underline{\lambda}^{(k,t-1)} - d^{(t,k)}\underline{\lambda}^{(t,t-1)} \tag{7.19}$$

if $k > t$ and $d^{(t,k)} \neq 0$, where $d^{(t,k)} = \lambda^{(k,t-1)}_{\underline{i}^{(t)}}$. The index $\underline{i}^{(t)}$ is then said to have pivot number t. One concludes that span $\{\underline{\lambda}^{(k,0)}: k \in \overline{t}\}$ has dimension r_t. Therefore, ρM^*, which is span $\{\underline{\lambda}^{(k,0)}: k \in \overline{p}\}$, has dimension r_p.

This algorithm is a familiar one. The only feature which is slightly unconventional is the form of (7.19). Normally $\underline{\lambda}^{(k,t)}$ is defined as $\underline{\lambda}^{(k,t-1)} - d^{(t,k)}\underline{\lambda}^{(t,t-1)}/c^{(t)}$, but this form generally results in fractions rather than integers. The formula used in this algorithm avoids fractions at the possible cost of using very large integers. As shown in Example 7.6, such integers can become excessively large for use with a digital computer. In order to modify the basic procedure to avoid this difficulty, it is important to review its properties with some care.

The important feature of the algorithm is that it systematically creates vector elements which are 0. In fact, $\underline{\lambda}^{(k,t)} = \underline{0}$ if $k \in \overline{t} - W_t$ and $\lambda^{(k,t)}_{\underline{i}^{(s)}} = 0$ if $k > s$ and $s \in W_t$. This claim is easily proven by induction. The hypothesis is trivial if $t = 0$. If it holds for $t < p$, then $\underline{i}^{(t+1)}$ does or does not exist. In the former case, the result follows for $t + 1$ from (7.18). In the latter case, the result for $t + 1$ follows since $\underline{\lambda}^{(k,t+1)} = \underline{\lambda}^{(k,t)}$ for all $k \in \overline{p}$ and $W_{t+1} = W_t$.

If $V_t = \{\underline{i}^{(s)}: s \in W_t\}$ and $M(V_t,W_t)$ is the $r_t \times r_t$ matrix with elements $\{\lambda^{(s,t)}_{\underline{i}}: \underline{i} \in V_t, s \in W_t\}$, then $M(V_t,W_t)$ is triangular and the determinant det $M(V_t,W_t)$ is $\prod_{s \in W_t} \lambda^{(s,t)}_{\underline{i}^{(s)}}$ (see Birkhoff and MacLane 1941). Since $\lambda^{(s,t)}_{\underline{i}^{(s)}} \neq 0$ for any $s \in W_t$, the determinant is not 0. Thus the vectors $\{\underline{\lambda}^{(s,t)}: s \in W_t\}$ must be independent. Since $\underline{\lambda}^{(s,t)} = \underline{0}$ if $s \in \overline{t} - W_t$, span $\{\underline{\lambda}^{(s,t)}: s \in \overline{t}\}$ has dimension r_t. The transformations given by (7.18) are invertible, so span $\{\underline{\lambda}^{(s,0)}: s \in \overline{t}\}$ also has dimension r_t. Thus the dimension of $\rho M^* =$ span $\{\underline{\lambda}^{(s,0)}: s \in \overline{p}\}$ is r_p.

The modification proposed by Borosh and Fraenkel involves computation of (7.18) by use of modular arithmetic on the field of integers modulo some very large prime number p_1. If no term $\lambda^{(t,t-1)}_{\underline{i}^{(t)}} \neq 0$ in the original algorithm is a multiple of p_1, then the new set of vectors $\overline{\underline{\lambda}}^{(k,t)}$ satisfy $\overline{\lambda}^{(k,t)}_{\underline{i}} = \lambda^{(k,t)}_{\underline{i}}$ mod p_1 and the new determinant $\overline{M}(V_t,W_t)$ corresponding to $M(V_t,W_t)$ has the value $\prod_{s \in W_t} \lambda^{(s,t)}_{\underline{i}^{(s)}}$ mod p_1, which is not 0 since by assumption $\overline{\lambda}^{(s,t)}_{\underline{i}^{(s)}} \neq 0$. Thus the dimension of ρM^* computed by modular arithmetic is equal to the true dimension of ρM^*.

A very small risk exists that some term $\lambda^{(t,t-1)}_{\underline{i}^{(t)}}$ is a multiple of p_1. If one wishes to guard against this possibility, it is sufficient to note that ρM^* has rank r_p if det $M(V,W) = 0$ whenever $V \subset I$ and $W \subset \overline{p}$ both have $r > r_p$ elements, and if for some $V \subset I$ and $W \subset \overline{p}$ such that V and W both have r_p elements, det $M(V,W) \neq 0$ (see Birkhoff and MacLane 1941). It is always the case that det $\overline{M}(V,W) =$ det $M(V,W)$ mod p_1, so that dimension computed by use of modular arithmetic cannot exceed r_p and it is less than r_p only if det $M(V,W)$ is a multiple of p_1 whenever V and W both have r_p elements. By the Hadamard inequality (see Courant and Hilbert 1953),

(7.20)
$$|\det M(V,W)|^2 \le \prod_{\underline{i}\in V} [\sum_{k\in W} (\lambda_{\underline{i}}^{(k,0)})^2]$$
$$\le \prod_{\underline{i}\in V} [\sum_{k=1}^{p} (\lambda_{\underline{i}}^{(k,0)})^2]$$
$$\le \prod_{\underline{i}\in S} [\sum_{k=1}^{p} (\lambda_{\underline{i}}^{(k,0)})^2]$$

and

$$|\det M(V,W)|^2 \le \prod_{k\in W} [\sum_{\underline{i}\in V} (\lambda_{\underline{i}}^{(k,0)})^2]$$
$$\le \prod_{k\in T} \| \underline{\lambda}^{(k,0)} \|^2$$

where $T = \{k \in \overline{p}: \underline{\lambda}^{(k,0)} \ne \underline{0}\}$ and S is the set of indices $\underline{i} \in I$ consisting of the indices corresponding to the p largest values of $\sum_{k=1}^{p} (\lambda_{\underline{i}}^{(k,0)})^2$ which are not 0. If p_1^2 exceeds $\prod_{\underline{i}\in S} [\sum_{k=1}^{p} (\lambda_{\underline{i}}^{(k,0)})^2]$ or $\prod_{k\in T} \| \underline{\lambda}^{(k,0)} \|^2$, then $\det \overline{M}(V,W) = 0$ implies $\det M(V,W) = 0$. Thus the dimension computed by modular arithmetic is the true dimension.

If a suitable prime p_1 is not available, then a set of primes $\{p_j: j \in \overline{h}\}$ may be chosen so that $\prod_{j=1}^{h} p_j^2$ exceeds one of the two bounds. For each $j \in \overline{h}$, the rank is then computed by use of modular arithmetic based on the integers modulo p_j. The largest rank found is then r_p. This result follows since if $\det M(V,W) = 0 \bmod p_j$ for each $j \in \overline{h}$, then the Chinese remainder theorem implies that $\det M(V,W) = 0 \bmod \prod_{j=1}^{h} p_j$ (see Grosswald 1966). By the Hadamard inequality, $\det M(V,W)$ must then be 0. Therefore some $j \in \overline{h}$ $V \subset I$, and $W \subset \overline{p}$ must exist such that V and W have r_p elements and $\det M(V,W) \ne 0 \bmod p_j$. In this case, the rank computed by use of p_j must be the true rank.

Example 7.5. Example 7.1 provides a simple illustration of use of the basic algorithm for determination of dimension. In that example, $I = \overline{2} \times \overline{2} \times \overline{2} \times \overline{2} - \{\langle 1,2,1,1\rangle, \langle 1,2,2,1\rangle, \langle 1,1,1,2\rangle, \langle 1,1,2,2\rangle\}$ and $M^* = M(E)$, where $E = \{\{1\},\{2\},\{3\},\{4\}\}$. If one expects that interactions may exist between the variables in Example 7.1, one might also consider the manifold $\rho M(E')$, where $E' = \{\{1,2\},\{1,3\},\{1,4\},\{2,3\},\{2,4\},\{3,4\}\}$. To find the dimensions of $\rho M(E)$ and $\rho M(E')$, one notes that $H(E) = \{\phi,\{1\},\{2\},\{3\},\{4\}\}$ and $H(E') = H(E) \cup E'$. It follows from chapter 5 that $\rho M(E) = \text{span } \{\underline{\lambda}^{(k,0)}: k \in \overline{5}\}$ and $\rho M(E') = \text{span } \{\underline{\lambda}^{(k,0)}: k \in \overline{11}\}$, where the elements of $\{\underline{\lambda}^{(k,0)}: k \in \overline{11}\}$ are given in table 7.3. The resulting vectors $\{\underline{\lambda}^{(k,5)}: k \in \overline{11}\}$ and $\{\underline{\lambda}^{(k,11)}: k \in \overline{11}\}$ are given in tables 7.4 and 7.5. One may conclude that $\rho M(E)$ has dimension 5 and $\rho M(E')$ has dimension 10.

Example 7.6. The problem of excessively large integers can arise even in tables of rather modest size. If $E = \{\{1,2\},\{1,3\},\{2,3\}\}$, $I^* = \overline{3} \times \overline{3} \times \overline{3}$, and I consists of those elements $<i,j,k>$ of I^* such that at least one of i, j, and k is 2, then $\rho M(E) = \text{span}\{\underline{\lambda}^{(k,0)}: k \in \overline{19}\}$, where this set of vectors is given in table 7.6. Since an IBM 7094 was used for computations, a rule was adopted that the basic algorithm with regular integer arithmetic was not acceptable if an integer larger than $2^{18} - 1 = 262{,}143$ was encountered during an iteration. In this example, the algorithm was judged to have failed when it was found that $\lambda_{213}^{(12,7)} = 1{,}259{,}712$.

In order to properly compute the dimension, modular arithmetic must be used. To determine how many primes are necessary to ensure a correct answer, the bounds given in (7.20) and (7.21) must be computed. In both cases, one finds that the product of the primes chosen should be at least $(14)^3(10)^6(19)^{1/2}$, which is approximately 1.20×10^{10}. For this purpose it suffices to select the primes 254,039 and 254,047 from Kavan's (1937) table of decompositions into prime factors. If the prime 254,039 is used, one obtains the vectors $\{\overline{\underline{\lambda}}^{(k,19)}: k \in \overline{19}\}$ shown in table 7.7. Since the dimension obtained with this prime is 19, which is the maximum possible dimension of the span of a set of 19 vectors, one may conclude that $\rho M(E)$ has dimension 19 without use of a second prime.

These examples show that computation of dimension is always feasible; however, the sort of calculations involved are hardly suitable for the back of an envelope. Therefore, there is good reason to seek computational rules which are simple but apply only to limited classes of models. Some of these rules are discussed in the next section. For now, it is sufficient to observe that a simple rule can be used in many tables to prove that $\dim \rho M(E) = \dim M(E)$ if $E \neq \overline{d}$. This rule is that $\dim \rho M(E) = \dim M(E)$ if for some $\underline{i}^{(0)} \in I$, every $\underline{i} \in I^*$ such that $i_j = i_j^{(0)}$ for some $j \in \overline{d}$ is in I.

To verify this rule, note that if $\underline{i} \in I^* - I$, $\underline{i} \in \prod_{j=1}^{d}(\overline{r}_j - \{i_j^{(0)}\})$ and $\rho\underline{\nu}(\overline{d},\underline{i}) = \underline{0}$. To use (5.76) and (5.77), let $\underline{c}^{(j)} = \underline{\delta}(r_j, i_j^{(0)})$ for each $j \in \overline{d}$. If $I^* - I$ has w elements, then $\rho\overline{M}_{\overline{d}} = \rho \bigotimes_{j=1}^{d} M_j^{(2)} = \text{span}\{\rho\underline{\nu}(\overline{d},\underline{i}): \underline{i} \in I^*\} = \text{span}\{\rho\underline{\nu}(\overline{d},\underline{i}): \underline{i} \in I\}$ has dimension $\prod_{j=1}^{d}(r_j - 1) - w$. If $E^* = \{\overline{d} - \{j\}: j \in \overline{d}\}$, then $H(E^*) = \{B \subset \overline{d}: B \neq \overline{d}\}$ and by (5.76) and (5.77), $R^{I^*} = M(E^*) \oplus \overline{M}_{\overline{d}}$. Thus

TABLE 7.3

ELEMENTS $\lambda^{(k,0)}_{i_1 i_2 i_3 i_4}$ OF SPANNING VECTORS IN EXAMPLE 7.4

	Vector Number										
Index	1	2	3	4	5	6	7	8	9	10	11
<1,1,1,1>	1	1	1	1	1	1	1	1	1	1	1
<1,1,1,2>	-	-	-	-	-	-	-	-	-	-	-
<1,1,2,1>	1	1	1	-1	1	1	-1	1	-1	1	-1
<1,1,2,2>	-	-	-	-	-	-	-	-	-	-	-
<1,2,1,1>	-	-	-	-	-	-	-	-	-	-	-
<1,2,1,2>	1	1	-1	1	-1	-1	1	-1	-1	1	-1
<1,2,2,1>	-	-	-	-	-	-	-	-	-	-	-
<1,2,2,2>	1	1	-1	-1	-1	-1	-1	-1	1	1	1
<2,1,1,1>	1	-1	1	1	1	-1	-1	-1	1	1	1
<2,1,1,2>	1	-1	1	1	-1	-1	-1	1	1	-1	-1
<2,1,2,1>	1	-1	1	-1	1	-1	1	-1	-1	1	-1
<2,1,2,2>	1	-1	1	-1	-1	-1	1	1	-1	-1	1
<2,2,1,1>	1	-1	-1	1	1	1	-1	-1	-1	-1	1
<2,2,1,2>	1	-1	-1	1	-1	1	-1	1	-1	1	-1
<2,2,2,1>	1	-1	1	-1	1	1	1	-1	1	-1	-1
<2,2,2,2>	1	-1	1	-1	-1	1	1	1	1	1	1

TABLE 7.4

ELEMENTS $\lambda^{(k,5)}_{i_1 i_2 i_3 i_4}$ OF SPANNING VECTORS AFTER 5 ITERATIONS

Index	Pivot Number	Vector Number 1	2	3	4	5	6	7	8	9	10	11
<1,1,1,1>	1	1	0	0	0	0	0	0	0	0	0	0
<1,1,1,2>		-	-	-	-	-	-	-	-	-	-	-
<1,1,2,1>	4	1	0	0	-2	0	0	0	0	0	0	0
<1,1,2,2>		-	-	-	-	-	-	-	-	-	-	-
<1,2,1,1>		-	-	-	-	-	-	-	-	-	-	-
<1,2,1,2>	3	1	0	-2	0	0	0	0	0	0	0	0
<1,2,2,1>		-	-	-	-	-	-	-	-	-	-	-
<1,2,2,2>		1	0	-2	-2	0	0	0	0	16	0	64
<2,1,1,1>	2	1	-2	0	0	0	0	0	0	0	0	0
<2,1,1,2>	5	1	-2	0	0	4	0	0	0	0	0	0
<2,1,2,1>		1	-2	0	-2	0	0	16	0	0	0	0
<2,1,2,2>		1	-2	0	-2	4	0	16	0	0	0	64
<2,2,1,1>		1	-2	-2	0	-4	16	0	64	0	-16	0
<2,2,1,2>		1	-2	-2	0	0	16	0	64	0	0	0
<2,2,2,1>		1	-2	-2	-2	-4	16	16	64	16	-16	0
<2,2,2,2>		1	-2	-2	-2	0	16	16	64	16	0	64

TABLE 7.5

ELEMENTS $\lambda^{(k,11)}_{i_1 i_2 i_3 i_4}$ OF SPANNING VECTORS AFTER 11 ITERATIONS

Index	Pivot Number	Vector Number										
		1	2	3	4	5	6	7	8	9	10	11
<1,1,1,1>	1	1	0	0	0	0	0	0	0	0	0	0
<1,1,1,2>		-	-	-	-	-	-	-	-	-	-	-
<1,1,2,1>	4	1	0	0	-2	0	0	0	0	0	0	0
<1,1,2,2>		-	-	-	-	-	-	-	-	-	-	-
<1,2,1,1>		-	-	-	-	-	-	-	-	-	-	-
<1,2,1,2>	3	1	0	-2	0	0	0	0	0	0	0	0
<1,2,2,1>		-	-	-	-	-	-	-	-	-	-	-
<1,2,2,2>	9	1	0	-2	-2	0	0	0	0	16	0	0
<2,1,1,1>	2	1	-2	0	0	0	0	0	0	0	0	0
<2,1,1,2>	5	1	-2	0	0	4	0	0	0	0	0	0
<2,1,2,1>	7	1	-2	0	-2	0	0	16	0	0	0	0
<2,1,2,2>	11	1	-2	0	-2	4	0	16	0	0	0	1024
<2,2,1,1>	6	1	-2	-2	0	-4	16	0	0	0	0	0
<2,2,1,2>	10	1	-2	-2	0	0	16	0	0	0	256	0
<2,2,2,1>		1	-2	-2	-2	-4	16	16	0	16	0	-1024
<2,2,2,2>		1	-2	-2	-2	0	16	16	0	16	256	0

TABLE 7.6

SPANNING VECTORS $\underline{\lambda}^{(k,0)}$ FOR EXAMPLE 7.5

	Vector Number																		
Index	1	2	3	4	5	6	7	8	9	10	11	12	13	14	15	16	17	18	19
<1,1,1>	-	-	-	-	-	-	-	-	-	-	-	-	-	-	-	-	-	-	-
<1,1,2>	1	1	0	1	0	-1	1	1	0	0	0	-1	0	1	0	-1	0	1	0
<1,1,3>	-	-	-	-	-	-	-	-	-	-	-	-	-	-	-	-	-	-	-
<1,2,1>	1	1	0	-1	1	1	0	-1	0	1	0	1	0	0	0	-1	1	0	0
<1,2,2>	1	1	0	-1	1	-1	1	-1	0	1	0	-1	0	1	0	1	-1	-1	1
<1,2,3>	1	1	0	-1	1	0	-1	-1	0	1	0	0	0	-1	0	0	0	1	-1
<1,3,1>	-	-	-	-	-	-	-	-	-	-	-	-	-	-	-	-	-	-	-
<1,3,2>	1	1	0	0	-1	-1	1	0	0	-1	0	-1	0	1	0	0	1	0	-1
<1,3,3>	-	-	-	-	-	-	-	-	-	-	-	-	-	-	-	-	-	-	-
<2,1,1>	1	-1	1	1	0	1	0	-1	1	0	0	-1	1	0	0	1	0	0	0
<2,1,2>	1	-1	1	1	0	-1	1	-1	1	0	0	1	-1	-1	1	-1	0	1	0
<2,1,3>	1	-1	1	1	0	0	-1	-1	1	0	0	0	0	1	-1	0	0	-1	0
<2,2,1>	1	-1	1	-1	1	1	0	1	-1	-1	1	-1	1	0	0	1	1	0	0
<2,2,2>	1	-1	1	-1	1	-1	1	1	-1	-1	1	1	-1	-1	1	-1	-1	-1	1
<2,2,3>	1	-1	1	-1	1	0	-1	1	-1	-1	1	0	0	1	-1	0	0	1	-1
<2,3,1>	1	-1	1	0	-1	1	0	0	0	1	-1	-1	1	0	0	0	-1	0	0
<2,3,2>	1	-1	1	0	-1	-1	1	0	0	1	-1	1	-1	-1	1	0	1	0	-1
<2,3,3>	1	-1	1	0	-1	0	-1	0	0	1	-1	0	0	1	-1	0	0	0	1
<3,1,1>	-	-	-	-	-	-	-	-	-	-	-	-	-	-	-	-	-	-	-
<3,1,2>	1	0	1	1	0	-1	1	0	-1	0	0	0	1	0	-1	-1	0	1	0
<3,1,3>	-	-	-	-	-	-	-	-	-	-	-	-	-	-	-	-	-	-	-
<3,2,1>	1	0	-1	-1	1	1	0	0	1	0	-1	0	-1	0	0	-1	1	0	0
<3,2,2>	1	0	-1	-1	1	-1	1	0	1	0	-1	0	1	0	-1	1	-1	-1	1
<3,2,3>	1	0	-1	-1	1	0	-1	0	1	0	-1	0	0	0	1	0	0	1	-1
<3,3,1>	-	-	-	-	-	-	-	-	-	-	-	-	-	-	-	-	-	-	-
<3,3,2>	1	0	-1	0	-1	-1	1	0	0	0	1	0	1	0	-1	0	1	0	-1
<3,3,3>	-	-	-	-	-	-	-	-	-	-	-	-	-	-	-	-	-	-	-

TABLE 7.7

ELEMENTS $\overline{\lambda}^{(k,19)}_{i_1 i_2 i_3}$ OF SPANNING VECTORS MODULO 254,039

OBTAINED AFTER FINAL ITERATION

Index	Pivot Number	Vector Number										
		1	2	3	4	5	6	7	8	9	10	11
<1,1,1>		-	-	-	-	-	-	-	-	-	-	-
<1,1,2>	1	1	0	0	0	0	0	0	0	0	0	0
<1,1,3>		-	-	-	-	-	-	-	-	-	-	-
<1,2,1>	6	1	0	0	-2	0	36	0	0	0	0	0
<1,2,2>	13	1	0	0	-2	0	-36	3888	0	0	0	0
<1,2,3>	4	1	0	0	-2	0	0	0	0	0	0	0
<1,3,1>		-	-	-	-	-	-	-	-	-	-	-
<1,3,2>	5	1	0	0	-1	3	0	0	0	0	0	0
<1,3,3>		-	-	-	-	-	-	-	-	-	-	-
<2,1,1>	2	1	-2	0	0	0	0	0	0	0	0	0
<2,1,2>	7	1	-2	0	0	0	-72	3888	0	0	0	0
<2,1,3>	16	1	-2	0	0	0	-36	0	0	0	0	0
<2,2,1>	9	1	-2	0	-2	0	-36	3888	16	0	0	0
<2,2,2>	17	1	-2	0	-2	0	-108	7776	16	0	0	0
<2,2,3>	19	1	-2	0	-2	0	-72	3888	16	0	0	0
<2,3,1>	11	1	-2	0	-1	3	0	0	8	0	-288	0
<2,3,2>	18	1	-2	0	-1	3	-72	3888	8	0	-288	0
<2,3,3>	13	1	-2	0	-1	3	-36	0	8	0	-288	0
<3,1,1>		-	-	-	-	-	-	-	-	-	-	-
<3,1,2>	3	1	-1	3	0	0	0	0	0	0	0	0
<3,1,3>		-	-	-	-	-	-	-	-	-	-	-
<3,2,1>	9	1	-1	3	-2	0	36	0	8	-288	0	0
<3,2,2>	14	1	-1	3	-2	0	-36	3888	8	-288	0	0
<3,2,3>	15	1	-1	3	-2	0	0	0	8	-288	0	0
<3,3,1>		-	-	-	-	-	-	-	-	-	-	-
<3,3,2>	11	1	-1	3	-1	3	0	0	4	-144	-144	191555
<3,3,3>		-	-	-	-	-	-	-	-	-	-	-

TABLE 7.7 *Continued*

Index	Pivot Number	Vector Number 12	13	14	15	16	17	18	19
<1,1,1>		-	-	-	-	-	-	-	-
<1,1,2>	1	0	0	0	0	0	0	0	0
<1,1,3>		-	-	-	-	-	-	-	-
<1,2,1>	6	0	0	0	0	0	0	0	0
<1,2,2>	13	-202046	-37915	0	0	0	0	0	0
<1,2,3>	4	0	0	0	0	0	0	0	0
<1,3,1>		-	-	-	-	-	-	-	-
<1,3,2>	5	0	0	0	0	0	0	0	0
<1,3,3>		-	-	-	-	-	-	-	-
<2,1,1>	2	0	0	0	0	0	0	0	0
<2,1,2>	7	0	0	0	0	0	0	0	0
<2,1,3>	16	101023	0	0	0	240259	0	0	0
<2,2,1>	9	0	0	0	0	0	0	0	0
<2,2,2>	17	0	0	0	0	-3234	184152	0	0
<2,2,3>	19	-153016	52838	58214	-170869	160215	60370	134165	-4254
<2,3,1>	11	0	0	0	0	0	0	0	0
<2,3,2>	18	0	0	0	0	-36009	-141390	-129541	0
<2,3,3>	13	101023	0	0	0	0	0	0	0
<3,1,1>		-	-	-	-	-	-	-	-
<3,1,2>	3	0	0	0	0	0	0	0	0
<3,1,3>		-	-	-	-	-	-	-	-
<3,2,1>	9	0	0	0	0	0	0	0	0
<3,2,2>	14	-101023	80815	103752	0	0	0	0	0
<3,2,3>	15	-76508	3841	182003	0	0	0	0	0
<3,3,1>		-	-	-	-	-	-	-	-
<3,3,2>	11	0	0	0	-110594	0	0	0	0
<3,3,3>		-	-	-	-	-	-	-	-

(7.22)
$$\dim \rho R^{I^*} = \prod_{j=1}^{d} r_j - w$$
$$\le \dim \rho M(E^*) + \dim \rho \bar{M}_{\bar{d}}$$
$$= \dim \rho M(E^*) + \prod_{j=1}^{d} (r_j - 1) - w.$$

Consequently,

(7.23)
$$\dim R^I = \prod_{j=1}^{d} r_j$$
$$\le \dim \rho M(E^*) + \dim \bar{M}_{\bar{d}}$$
$$\le \dim M(E^*) + \dim \bar{M}_{\bar{d}}$$
$$= \dim R^I.$$

Therefore, $\dim \rho M(E^*) = \dim M(E^*)$. In other words, ρ if restricted to $M(E^*)$ is an isomorphism. If $E \neq \bar{d}$, then $M(E) \subset M(E^*)$. Thus the restriction of ρ to $M(E)$ is an isomorphism, and $\dim \rho M(E) = \dim M(E)$.

Example 7.7. The labor of finding the dimension of $\rho M(E)$ in Example 7.6 can be eliminated by observing that $\underline{i}^{(0)} = \langle 2,2,2\rangle$ satisfies the conditions of the preceding paragraph. Thus $\dim \rho M(E) = \dim M(E) = \dim R^{\bar{3}\times\bar{3}\times\bar{3}} - \dim M_{\bar{3}} = 27 - 2 \times 2 \times 2 = 19$.

Hierarchical models for incomplete tables have some of the basic properties of hierarchical models for complete tables. The manifold $\rho M(E)$ satisfies

(7.24)
$$\rho M(E) = \sum_{E \in E} \rho N_E ,$$

so any element $\underline{\mu}$ of $M(E)$ can be written as

(7.25)
$$\mu_{\underline{i}} = \sum_{E \in E} u^E_{\pi_E \underline{i}} ,$$

where $\underline{u}^E \in R^{I^*(E)}$ for each $E \in E$, $I^*(E) = \prod_{j \in E} \bar{r}_j$, and $\underline{i} \in I$. Here π_E is defined as in chapter 5. Since $M(E) = \text{span } \{\underline{\nu}(E,\bar{\underline{i}}): \bar{\underline{i}} \in I^*(E), E \in E\}$, $\rho M(E)$ is spanned by $\{\rho\underline{\nu}(E,\bar{\underline{i}}): \bar{\underline{i}} \in I^*(E), E \in E\}$. If $\bar{\underline{i}} \notin \pi_E I$, then $\rho\underline{\nu}(E,\bar{\underline{i}}) = \underline{0}$, so $\rho M(E) = \text{span } \{\rho\underline{\nu}(E,\bar{\underline{i}}): \bar{\underline{i}} \in I(E), E \in E\}$, and the maximum-likelihood estimate $\hat{\underline{m}}$ must satisfy the condition $\hat{\underline{m}}^E(I) = \underline{n}^E(I)$ for all $E \in E$, where if $\bar{\underline{i}} \in I(E) = \pi_E I$,

(7.26)
$$\hat{m}^{E}_{\underline{\bar{i}}}(I) = \Sigma \{\hat{m}_{\underline{i}} : \underline{i} \in I \cap \pi_E^{-1}\underline{\bar{i}}\}$$

and

(7.27)
$$n^{E}_{\underline{\bar{i}}}(I) = \Sigma \{n_{\underline{i}} : \underline{i} \in I \cap \pi_E^{-1}\underline{\bar{i}}\}.$$

In other words, the E-marginal totals of $\underline{\hat{m}}$ and $\underline{n}$ must be equal, where summations for these marginal totals are restricted to indices in I. Conditions for complete tables correspond to the special case in which $I = I^*$. Clearly a necessary condition for the existence of $\underline{\hat{m}}$ is that $n^{E}_{\underline{\bar{i}}}(I) > 0$ whenever $\underline{\bar{i}} \in I^*(E)$ and $E \in \mathcal{E}$. Sufficient conditions are discussed in a later section

Example 7.8. In table 7.1, the simplest proposed model is that $\underline{\mu} \in \rho M(\mathcal{E})$, where $\mathcal{E} = \{\{1\},\{2\},\{3\},\{4\}\}$. In this case,

(7.28)
$$\rho M(\mathcal{E}) = \rho N_{\{1\}} + \rho N_{\{2\}} + \rho N_{\{3\}} + \rho N_{\{4\}}$$

and $\underline{\mu}$ can be written

(7.29)
$$\mu_{i_1 i_2 i_3 i_4} = u^{\{1\}}_{i_1} + u^{\{2\}}_{i_2} + u^{\{3\}}_{i_3} + u^{\{4\}}_{i_4} .$$

The maximum-likelihood estimate $\underline{\hat{m}}$ satisfies the conditions $\hat{m}_{1+++} = n_{1+++}$, $\hat{m}_{2+++} = n_{2+++}$, $\hat{m}_{+1++} = n_{+1++}$, $\hat{m}_{+2++} = n_{+2++}$, $\hat{m}_{++1+} = n_{++1+}$, $\hat{m}_{++2+} = n_{++2+}$, $\hat{m}_{+++1} = n_{+++1}$, and $\hat{m}_{+++2} = n_{+++2}$, where the summations are understood to be only over those indices which are in I. This estimate can only exist if all 8 marginal totals of $\underline{n}$ are positive.

SEPARABLE TABLES

Sometimes analysis of an incomplete table by means of a hierarchical model is facilitated by dividing the table into subtables which may be analyzed independently. Such tables have been considered by Goodman (1968) in the case of incomplete r x c tables under the quasi-independence model $\underline{\mu} \in \rho M(\{\{1\},\{2\}\})$ and by Fienberg (1971) in the general case. The classical example of such a table is table 7.2, which is examined in the following example. Historical background concerning analysis of this table is provided by Goodman (1968).

Example 7.9. In table 7.2, the assumption that $\underline{\mu} \in \rho M(\mathcal{E})$, where $\mathcal{E} = \{\{1\},\{2\}\}$, is equivalent to the hypothesis that for some $\underline{u}^{\{1\}} \in R^4$ and $\underline{u}^{\{2\}} \in R^9$,

$$\mu_{ij} = u_i^{\{1\}} + u_j^{\{2\}} \tag{7.30}$$

for each $\langle i,j\rangle \in I$. Since $I = I_1 \cup I_2$, where $I_1 = \{1,4\} \times \{1,4,7,9\}$ and $I_2 = \{2,3\} \times \{2,3,5,6,8\}$, the hypothesis that for some $\underline{u}^{\{1\}} \in R^4$ and $\underline{u}^{\{4\}} \in R^9$, (7.30) holds for all $\langle i,j\rangle \in I$ is equivalent to the statement that for some $\{u_1^{\{1\}}, u_4^{\{1\}}\} \in R^{\{1,4\}}$, and $\{u_1^{\{2\}}, u_4^{\{2\}}, u_7^{\{2\}}, u_9^{\{2\}}\} \in R^{\{1,4,7,9\}}$, (7.30) holds for $\langle i,j\rangle \in \{1,4\} \times \{1,4,7,9\}$, and for some $\{u_2^{\{1\}}, u_3^{\{1\}}\} \in R^{\{2,3\}}$ and $\{u_2^{\{2\}}, u_3^{\{2\}}, u_5^{\{2\}}, u_6^{\{2\}}, u_8^{\{2\}}\} \in R^{\{2,3,5,6,8\}}$, (7.30) holds for each $\langle i,j\rangle \in \{2,3\} \times \{2,3,5,6,8\}$; that is, the original hypothesis is equivalent to the assumption that $\rho_{I_k}^{I}\underline{\mu} \in \rho_{I_k}M(E)$ for $k \in \overline{2}$. Given $\rho_{I_k}^{I}\underline{\mu}$ for $k \in \overline{2}$, Lemma 7.1 implies that

$$\underline{\mu} = \tau_{I_1}^{I}(\rho_{I_1}^{I}\underline{\mu}) + \tau_{I_2}^{I}(\rho_{I_2}^{I}\underline{\mu}). \tag{7.31}$$

Thus the mapping f from $\rho M(E)$ to $\rho_{I_1}M(E) \times \rho_{I_2}M(E)$ defined by $f\underline{\mu} = \langle \rho_{I_1}^{I}\underline{\mu}, \rho_{I_2}^{I}\underline{\mu}\rangle$ is an invertible linear mapping. As shown in Example 7.2, $\rho_{I_k}M(E) = M(I_k,E)$, so $\rho_{I_1}M(E)$ has dimension $(2 - 1)(4 - 1) = 3$ and $\rho_{I_2}M(E)$ has dimension $(2 - 1)(5 - 1) = 4$. Thus $\rho M(E)$ has dimension 7.

The maximum-likelihood estimate $\underline{\hat{m}}$ satisfies the conditions $\hat{m}_{i+}(I) = n_{i+}(I)$ for $i \in \overline{4}$ and $\hat{m}_{+j}(I) = n_{+j}(I)$ for $j \in \overline{9}$. If $i \in \{1,4\}$ and $j \in \{1,4,6,8\}$, then $\hat{m}_{i+}(I) = \hat{m}_{i+}(I_1) = n_{i+}(I_1)$ and $\hat{m}_{+j}(I) = \hat{m}_{+j}(I_1) = n_{+j}$. Since $\rho_{I_1}\underline{\hat{\mu}} \in M(I_1,E)$,

$$\hat{m}_{ij} = \frac{n_{i+}(I_1)n_{+j}(I_1)}{n_{++}(I_1)} . \tag{7.32}$$

Similarly, if $i \in \{2,3\}$ and $j \in \{2,3,5,6,8\}$, then $\hat{m}_{i+}(I) = \hat{m}_{i+}(I_2) = n_{i+}(I_2)$, $\hat{m}_{+j}(I) = \hat{m}_{+j}(I_2) = n_{+j}(I_2)$, and

$$\hat{m}_{ij} = \frac{n_{i+}(I_2)n_{+j}(I_2)}{n_{++}(I_2)} . \tag{7.33}$$

Thus the maximum-likelihood estimate for $\underline{m}$ has been found by determining the maximum-likelihood estimates for the 2 x 4 table $\rho_{I_1}\underline{n} = \{n_{ij}: \langle i,j\rangle \in I_1\}$ and for the 2 x 5 table $\rho_{I_2}\underline{n} = \{n_{ij}: \langle i,j\rangle \in I_2\}$.

Analysis of the data by means of asymptotic theory also exploits the decomposition of $\underline{n}$ into $\rho_{I_1}\underline{n}$ and $\rho_{I_2}\underline{n}$. The Pearson chi-square statistic C for $H_0: \underline{\mu} \in \rho M(E)$ and [illegible] R^I is given by

(7.34)
$$C = \Sigma \left\{\frac{[n_{ij} - n_{i+}(I_1)n_{+j}(I_1)/n_{++}(I_1)]^2}{n_{i+}(I_1)n_{+j}(I_1)/n_{++}(I_1)} : \langle i,j\rangle \in I_1\right\}$$
$$+ \Sigma \left\{\frac{[n_{ij} - n_{i+}(I_2)n_{+j}(I_2)/n_{++}(I_2)]^2}{n_{i+}(I_2)n_{+j}(I_2)/n_{++}(I_2)} : \langle i,j\rangle \in I_2\right\}$$
$$= C_1 + C_2,$$

where C_k is the corresponding Pearson chi-square for H_0: $\rho_{I_k}\underline{\mu} \in M(I_k,E)$ and H_A: $\underline{\mu} \in R^{I_k}$. Similarly the likelihood ratio chi-square corresponding to C is the sum of the likelihood ratio chi-square statistics corresponding to C_1 and C_2.

An analysis of the residuals $\underline{n} - \hat{\underline{m}}$ may be performed by considering the two sub-tables separately. In each case, the approach used in Example 4.20 may be applied. Thus

(7.35)
$$c_{ij} = [1 - n_{i+}(I_k)/n_{++}(I_k)][1 - n_{+j}(I_k)/n_{++}(I_k)]$$

if $\langle i,j\rangle \in I_k$ and $k \in \overline{2}$.

Given these remarks, an analysis comparable to that made in Example 4.20 may be undertaken. The basic results are summarized in table 7.8. One may conclude from this analysis that little reason exists to reject the hypothesis that locular composition and radial asymmetry are quasi-independent. The Pearson chi-square for the full table is 7.49, while the likelihood ratio chi-square is 7.75. It is only worthwhile to consider adjusted residuals s_{ij} such that $i \le 2$ and $\langle i,j\rangle \in I$ since $s_{ij} + s_{(4-i)j} = 0$ if $\langle i,j\rangle \in I$. This equation follows since if $\langle i,j\rangle \in I_k$,

(7.36)
$$\hat{m}_{ij}c_{ij} = \frac{n_{i+}n_{+j}}{n_{++}(I_k)}[1 - n_{i+}/n_{++}(I_k)][1 - n_{+j}/n_{++}(I_k)]$$
$$= \frac{n_{i+}n_{(4-i)+}}{n_{++}(I_k)} \frac{n_{+j}}{n_{++}(I_k)}[1 - n_{+j}/n_{++}(I_k)]$$

and

(7.37)
$$n_{ij} - \hat{m}_{ij} = -(n_{(4-i)j} - \hat{m}_{(4-i)j}).$$

Of these adjusted residuals, the largest in magnitude is s_{28}, which is -2.05. This adjusted residual is not excessively large and corresponds to a very small observed count $n_{28} = 1$.

TABLE 7.8

MAXIMUM-LIKELIHOOD ESTIMATES FOR STAPHYLEA DATA[a]

Locular Composition	Coefficient of Radial Symmetry								
	0.00	0.47	0.82	0.94	1.25	1.41	1.63	1.70	1.89
3 even 0 odd	462	-	-	130	-	-	2	-	1
	458.0	-	-	133.8	-	-	2.4	-	0.8
	0.894	-	-	-0.847	-	-	-0.638	-	0.484
2 even 1 odd	-	614	138	-	21	14	-	1	-
	-	620	134.9	-	24.9	12.7	-	3.5	-
	-	0.265	0.451	-	-1.223	0.550	-	-2.05	-
1 even 2 odd	-	443	95	-	22	8	-	5	-
	-	445.0	98.1	-	18.1	9.26	-	2.5	-
	-	-0.265	-0.451	-	1.223	-0.550	-	2.05	-
0 even 3 odd	103	-	-	35	-	-	1	-	0
	107.0	-	-	31.2	-	-	0.6	-	0.2
	-0.894	-	-	0.847	-	-	0.638	-	-0.484

[a]First line in each entry is observation n_{ij}, second line is maximum-likelihood estimate $\hat{m}_{ij}$, and third line is adjusted residual s_{ij}.

The results in the preceding paragraph are slightly different from those in Goodman (1968) since the seventh and ninth columns of the table have not been combined to yield a single column in which the two feasible cells both have positive counts. This combination reduces the likelihood ratio chi-square and the Pearson chi-square, and the number of degrees of freedom is 6 instead of 7. Thus no change in conclusions occurs in this example if the columns are pooled. Pooling has the advantage that it can improve the accuracy of the asymptotic approximations used for testing hypothesis. A possible disadvantage is that if $\mu_{17} - \mu_{47} - \mu_{19} + \mu_{49}$ is not 0, some loss in power may occur.

The procedure employed in the preceding example may be generalized for use with other hierarchical models for incomplete tables. The basic tool required is the following definition:

DEFINITION 7.1. *The relation* $\underline{i} \underset{E}{\sim} \underline{i}'$ *holds if there exists a sequence* $\{\underline{i}^{(k)}: k \in \overline{\ell}\} \subset I$ *such that* $\underline{i}^{(1)} = \underline{i}$, $\underline{i}^{(\ell)} = \underline{i}'$, *and for each* $k \in \overline{\ell - 1}$ *there exists an* $E_k \in E$ *for which* $\pi_{E_k}\underline{i}^{(k)} = \pi_{E_k}\underline{i}^{(k+1)}$. *If* E *is clear from the context, then the notation* $\underline{i} \sim \underline{i}'$ *is used.*

Remark. As in chapter 5, $\pi_E\underline{i}^{(k)} = \pi_E\underline{i}^{(k+1)}$ if $i_j^{(k)} = i_j^{(k+1)}$ for each $j \in E$. The relation $\underset{E}{\sim}$ is easily seen to be an equivalence relationship. Therefore, this relationship may be used to partition I into equivalence classes $\{I_k: k \in \bar{s}\}$ such that the sets $\{I_k(E), k \in \bar{s}\}$ are a partition of $I(E)$ for each $E \in \mathcal{E}$. Here $I_k(E) = \pi_E I_k$. These sets must be mutually disjoint since if $\underline{i} \in I_k(E) \cap I_{k'}(E)$, where $k \neq k'$ and $E \in \mathcal{E}$, then $\underline{i} \in I_k$ and $\underline{i}' \in I_{k'}$ exist such that $\pi_E \underline{i} = \pi_E \underline{i}'$. Thus $\underline{i} \underset{\mathcal{E}}{\sim} \underline{i}'$, which is impossible since equivalence classes are disjoint. If $s = 1$, then $\underline{n} = \{n_{\underline{i}}: \underline{i} \in I\}$ is said to be an inseparable table, and the index set I is said to be inseparable. If $s > 1$, then $\underline{n}$ and I are separable. The terms $\mathcal{E}$-separable and $\mathcal{E}$-inseparable are used if $\mathcal{E}$ is not clear from the context. Thus the decomposition of $\underline{n}$ into subtables $\{n_{\underline{i}}: \underline{i} \in I_k\}$, where $k \in \bar{s}$, is a decomposition of the table $\underline{n}$ into inseparable subtables.

The equivalence classes may be determined by straightforward procedures. One first notes that each element $\underline{i}$ of I is contained in a set $J = \prod_{j=1}^{d} A_j$, where $A_j \subset \bar{r}_j$ fo each $j \in \bar{d}$, $J \subset I$, and A_j consists of a single element if $j \in \cap(\mathcal{E})$. Such a set is $\prod_{j=1}^{d} \{i_j\}$. If

(7.38) $$\mathcal{K} = \{J \subset I: J = \prod_{j=1}^{d} A_j,\ A_j \subset \bar{r}_j\ \forall j \in \bar{d},\ \exists i_j \in \bar{r}_j \ni A_j = \{i_j\}\ \forall j \in \cap(\mathcal{E})\},$$

then $I = \cup(\mathcal{K})$.

If

(7.39) $$\mathcal{J} = \{J \in \mathcal{K}: \nexists J' \in \mathcal{K} \ni J' \neq J \text{ and } J \subset J'\},$$

then $I = \cup(\mathcal{J})$. The sets $J \in \mathcal{J}$ may be described as the maximal hyperblocks of I. The following lemmas show the significance of this decomposition.

LEMMA 7.2. *Suppose* $J = \prod_{j=1}^{d} A_j$, *where* $A_j \subset \bar{r}_j$ *for all* $j \in \bar{d}$, *and for each* $j \in \cap(\mathcal{E})$ *there exists* $i_j \in \bar{r}_j$ *such that* $A_j = \{i_j\}$. *Then* J *is inseparable.*

Proof. If $\underline{i}$ and $\underline{i}'$ are in J, then the sequence $\{\underline{i}^{(k)}: k \in \overline{d+1}\}$ may be constructed, where $\underline{i}^{(1)} = \underline{i}$, $i_j^{(k+1)} = i_j^{(k)}$ if $j \in \bar{d}$, $k \in \bar{d}$, and $j \neq k$, and $i_k^{(k+1)} = i_k'$ if $k \in \bar{d}$. Given this sequence, $\underline{i}^{(d+1)} = \underline{i}'$. If $k \in \cap(\mathcal{E})$, then $\underline{i}^{(k+1)} = \underline{i}^{(k)}$ and for any $E \in \mathcal{E}$, $\pi_E \underline{i}^{(k+1)} = \pi_E \underline{i}^{(k)}$. If $k \notin \cap(\mathcal{E})$, then $E_k \in \mathcal{E}$ exists such that $k \in E_k$ and $\pi_{E_k} \underline{i}^{(k+1)} = \pi_{E_k} \underline{i}^{(k)}$. Thus $\underline{i} \sim \underline{i}'$. Since all elements of J are equivalent, J is inseparable.||

LEMMA 7.3. *If* $I = J_1 \cup J_2$, *where* J_1 *and* J_2 *are inseparable, then* I *is inseparable if and only if for some* $E \in \mathcal{E}$, $J_1(E) \cap J_2(E) \neq \phi$.

Proof. If I is inseparable, then $\underline{i} \sim \underline{i}'$ if $\underline{i} \in J_1$ and $\underline{i}' \in J_2$. A sequence

$\{\underline{i}^{(k)}: k \in \overline{\ell}\}$ must exist such that $\underline{i}^{(1)} = \underline{i}$, $\underline{i}' = \underline{i}^{(\ell)}$, and for each $k \in \overline{\ell - 1}$, $\pi_{E_k}\underline{i}^{(k+1)} = \pi_{E_k}\underline{i}^{(k)}$ for some $E_k \in E$. There must exist a $k \in \overline{\ell - 1}$, such that $\underline{i}^{(k)} \in J_1$ and $\underline{i}^{(k+1)} \in J_2$. Therefore $J_1(E) \cap J_2(E) \neq \phi$. Conversely, if $J_1(E) \cap J_2(E) \neq \phi$ for some $E \in E$, then $\underline{i}^{(1)} \in J_1$ and $\underline{i}^{(2)} \in J_2$ exist such that $\underline{i}^{(1)} \sim \underline{i}^{(2)}$. If $\underline{i}$ and $\underline{i}'$ are both in J_k for some $k \in \overline{2}$, then $\underline{i} \sim \underline{i}'$ since J_k is inseparable. If $\underline{i} \in J_1$ and $\underline{i}' \in J_2$, then $\underline{i} \sim \underline{i}^{(1)}$ and $\underline{i}' \sim \underline{i}^{(2)}$. By transitivity, $\underline{i} \sim \underline{i}'$. Thus I is inseparable.||

COROLLARY 7.1. *If* $I = J_1 \cup J_2$, *where* $J_1 \cap J_2 \neq \phi$ *and* J_1 *and* J_2 *are inseparable, then* I *is inseparable.*

Proof. This result follows from Lemma 7.3 since $J_1(E) \cap J_2(E) \neq \phi$ if $E \in E$.||

LEMMA 7.4. *If* $\underline{i} \in I$, $\underline{i}' \in I$, *and for some* $j \in \cap(E)$, $i_j \neq i'_j$, *then* $\underline{i} \not\sim \underline{i}'$.

Proof. If $\underline{i} \underset{E}{\sim} \underline{i}'$, then a sequence $\{\underline{i}^{(k)}: k \in \overline{\ell}\}$ exists such that $\underline{i}^{(1)} = \underline{i}$, $\underline{i}^{(\ell)} = \underline{i}'$, and for $k \in \overline{\ell - 1}$, $\pi_E\underline{i}^{(k+1)} = \pi_E\underline{i}^{(k)}$ for some $E \in E$. Since $j \in \cap(E)$, $i_j^{(k+1)} = i_j^{(k)}$ for each $k \in \overline{\ell - 1}$. Thus $i'_j = i_j$, a contradiction.||

These lemmas show that it is only necessary to examine sets $J \in J$ to determine the equivalence classes $\{I_k: k \in \overline{s}\}$.

Example 7.10. As in Example 7.8, suppose that the model $\underline{\mu} \in \rho(M(E))$ is used to analyze table 7.2, where $E = \{\{1\},\{2\}\}$. Then $\cap(E) = \phi$ and the elements of J are $I_1 = \{1,4\} \times \{1,4,7,9\}$ and $I_2 = \{2,3\} \times \{2,3,5,6,8\}$. By Lemma 7.2, I_1 and I_2 are inseparable. Since $I_1(\{k\}) \cap I_2(\{k\}) = \phi$ if $k \in \overline{2}$, Lemma 7.3 implies that $I = I_1 \cup I_2$ is separable. The equivalence classes are then I_1 and I_2.

Example 7.11. So far, the models $\underline{\mu} \in \rho M(E)$ and $\underline{\mu} \in \rho M(E')$ have been examined for use with the Novitski and Sandler data in table 7.1, where $E = \{\{1\},\{2\},\{3\},\{4\}\}$ and $E' = \{\{1,2\},\{1,3\},\{1,4\},\{2,3\},\{2,4\},\{3,4\}\}$. Since the elements of J are $J_1 = \overline{2} \times \{1\} \times \overline{2} \times \{1\}$, $J_2 = \overline{2} \times \{2\} \times \overline{2} \times \{2\}$, and $J_3 = \{2\} \times \overline{2} \times \overline{2} \times \overline{2}$, where $J_1 \cap J_3$ and $J_2 \cap J_3 \neq \phi$, Lemma 7.2 and Corollary 7.1 imply that I and $\underline{n}$ are E-inseparable.

The same argument can be used to show $\underline{n}$ is E'-inseparable, but it is easier to note that since $E \subset E'$, $\underline{i} \underset{E'}{\sim} \underline{i}'$ if $\underline{i} \underset{E}{\sim} \underline{i}'$. Thus the equivalence classes corresponding to E are a subpartition of the equivalence classes corresponding to E'. Since only one equivalence class corresponds to E, only one such class corresponds to E'. In other words, E' is inseparable.

Given the equivalence classes $\{I_k: k \in \bar{s}\}$ for a linear manifold $\rho M(E)$, one may define a linear mapping f from $\rho M(E)$ to $\prod_{k=1}^{s} \rho_{I_k} M(E)$, the Cartesian product of the manifolds $\rho_{I_k} M(E)$, so that $f\underline{\mu} = \{\rho_{I_k}\underline{\mu}: k \in \bar{s}\}$. To show that f is onto, it is only necessary to note that if $\underline{\mu}^{(k)} \in \rho_{I_k} M(E)$ for each $k \in \bar{s}$, then vectors $\{\bar{u}^E_{\bar{\underline{i}}}: \bar{\underline{i}} \in I_k(E)\} \in R^{I_k(E)}$, where $E \in E$, can be found so that for each $\underline{i} \in I_k$,

$$\mu^{(k)}_{\underline{i}} = \sum_{E \in E} \bar{u}^E_{\pi_E \underline{i}} . \tag{7.40}$$

If $\underline{\mu} = \sum_{k=1}^{s} \tau^I_{I_k} \underline{\mu}^{(k)}$, then

$$\mu_{\underline{i}} = \sum_{E \in E} u^E_{\pi_E \underline{i}} \tag{7.41}$$

for each $\underline{i} \in I$, where $\underline{u}^E \in R^{I(E)}$ is defined by $u^E_{\bar{\underline{i}}} = \bar{u}^E_{\bar{\underline{i}}}$ if $\bar{\underline{i}} \in I_k^{(E)}$ and $k \in \bar{s}$ and $u^E_{\bar{\underline{i}}} = 0$ if $\bar{\underline{i}} \in I(E) - \cup_{k=1}^{s} I_k(E)$. Thus $\underline{\mu} \in \rho M(E)$. If $\rho^I_{I_k}\underline{\mu} = \underline{\mu}^{(k)}$ for each $k \in \bar{s}$, then Lemma 7.1 implies that

$$\underline{\mu} = \sum_{k=1}^{s} \tau^I_{I_k} \rho^I_{I_k} \underline{\mu} \tag{7.42}$$

$$= \sum_{k=1}^{s} \tau^I_{I_k} \underline{\mu}^{(k)} .$$

Thus f is invertible. Therefore, $\rho M(E)$ and $\prod_{k=1}^{s} \rho_{I_k} M(E)$ are isomorphic vector spaces, and the dimension of $\rho M(E)$ satisfies

$$\dim \rho M(E) = \sum_{k=1}^{s} \dim \rho_{I_k} M(E) . \tag{7.43}$$

As in Example 7.8, the maximum-likelihood estimate $\hat{\underline{m}}(\underline{n},I,E)$ of $\underline{m}$ can be expressed in terms of the maximum-likelihood estimates $\hat{\underline{m}}(\rho^I_{I_k}\underline{n},I_k,E)$, where $k \in \bar{s}$. The basic result is summarized by the following theorem.

THEOREM 7.1. *If* $\{I_k: k \in \bar{s}\}$ *is the partition of* I *into equivalence classes determined by* $\tilde{E}$, *then* $\hat{\underline{m}}(\underline{n},I,E)$ *exists if and only if* $\hat{\underline{m}}(\rho^I_{I_k}\underline{n},I_k,E)$ *exists for each* $k \in \bar{s}$, *and*

$$\hat{\underline{m}}(\underline{n},I,E) = \sum_{k=1}^{s} \tau^I_{I_k} \hat{\underline{m}}(\rho^I_{I_k}\underline{n},I_k,E) \tag{7.44}$$

if $\hat{\underline{m}}(\underline{n},I,E)$ *exists.*

Remark. An equivalent formulation for (7.44) is the statement that $\hat{m}_{\underline{i}}(\underline{n},I,E) = \hat{m}_{\underline{i}}(\rho^{I}_{I_k}\underline{n},I_k,E)$ if $\underline{i} \in I_k$ and $k \in \bar{s}$.

Proof. If $\underline{\bar{I}} \in I_k(E)$ for some $k \in \bar{s}$ and $E \in E$, then Definition 7.1 implies that $I \cap \pi_E^{-1}\underline{\bar{I}} = I_k \cap \pi_E^{-1}\underline{\bar{I}}$. Therefore, given $k \in \bar{s}$, $n^E_{\underline{\bar{i}}}(I) = n^E_{\underline{\bar{i}}}(I_k) = [\rho_{I_k}\underline{n}]^E_{\underline{\bar{i}}}(I_k)$ for each $\underline{\bar{I}} \in I_k(E)$ and $E \in E$. If $\hat{\underline{m}}(\underline{n},I,E)$ exists, then $\rho_{I_k}\hat{\underline{\mu}}(\underline{n},I,E) \in \rho_{I_k}M(E)$, where $\hat{\underline{\mu}}(\underline{n},I,E) = \{\log \hat{m}_{\underline{i}}(\underline{n},I,E)\}$, and $\hat{m}^E_{\underline{\bar{i}}}(\underline{n},I,E)\ (I) = \hat{m}^E_{\underline{\bar{i}}}(\underline{n},I,E)\ (I_k) = n^E_{\underline{\bar{i}}}(I_k)$ for each $\underline{\bar{I}} \in I_k(E)$ and $E \in E$. Thus $\rho^I_{I_k}\hat{\underline{m}} = \{\hat{m}^E_{\underline{\bar{i}}}: \underline{i} \in I_k\}$ satisfies the conditions for $\hat{\underline{m}}(\rho^I_{I_k}\underline{n},I_k,E)$. Since maximum-likelihood estimates are unique if they exist, $\rho^I_{I_k}\hat{\underline{m}} = \hat{\underline{m}}(\rho^I_{I_k}\underline{n},I_k,E)$ for each $k \in \bar{s}$. Thus $\hat{\underline{m}}(\rho^I_{I_k}\underline{n},I_k,E)$ exists, and by Lemma 7.1,

$$\hat{\underline{m}}(\underline{n},I,E) = \sum_{k=1}^{s} \tau^I_{I_k}\rho^I_{I_k}\hat{\underline{m}}(\underline{n},I,E) \tag{7.45}$$

$$= \sum_{k=1}^{s} \tau^I_{I_k}\hat{\underline{m}}(\rho^I_{I_k}\underline{n},I_k,E).$$

On the other hand, if $\hat{\underline{m}}(\rho^I_{I_k}\underline{n},I_k,E)$ exists for each $k \in \bar{s}$, then $\hat{\underline{\mu}}(\rho^I_{I_k}\underline{n},I_k,E) \in \rho_{I_k}M(E)$ for each $k \in \bar{s}$ and

$$\underline{\mu} = \sum_{k=1}^{s} \tau^I_{I_k}\hat{\underline{\mu}}(\rho^I_{I_k}\underline{n},I_k,E) \in \rho M(E). \tag{7.46}$$

If $\underline{\bar{I}} \in I_k(E)$, $E \in E$, and $k \in \bar{s}$, and $\underline{m} = \{\exp(\mu_{\underline{i}})\}$, then

$$m^E_{\underline{\bar{i}}}(I) = m^E_{\underline{\bar{i}}}(I_k) \tag{7.47}$$

$$= \hat{m}^E_{\underline{\bar{i}}}(\rho^I_{I_k}\underline{n},I_k,E)\ (I_k)$$

$$= n^E_{\underline{\bar{i}}}(I_k)$$

$$= n^E_{\underline{\bar{i}}}(I).$$

Since $\underline{m}$ satisfies the conditions for $\hat{\underline{m}}(\underline{n},I,E)$, $\hat{\underline{m}}(\underline{n},I,E) = \underline{m}$. Therefore $\hat{\underline{m}}(\underline{n},I,E)$ exists. ||

Example 7.12. Suppose that $I = \bar{3} \times \bar{3} \times \bar{3}$ and I consists of the indices $\langle i_1,i_2,i_3\rangle \in I$ such that the number of i_j, $j \in \bar{3}$, which are equal to 3 is not 1. Thus $\underline{n}$ may be written as

(7.48) $$\underline{n} = \begin{bmatrix} n_{111} & n_{121} & - \\ n_{211} & n_{221} & - \\ - & - & n_{331} \end{bmatrix} \begin{bmatrix} n_{112} & n_{122} & - \\ n_{212} & n_{222} & \\ - & - & n_{332} \end{bmatrix} \begin{bmatrix} - & - & n_{133} \\ - & - & n_{233} \\ n_{313} & n_{323} & n_{333} \end{bmatrix}.$$

If $E = \{\{1,2\},\{1,3\},\{2,3\}\}$, then $\underline{n}$ is E-separable with $I_1 = \overline{2} \times \overline{2} \times \overline{2}$ and $I_2 = \{\langle 3,3,1\rangle,\langle 3,3,2\rangle,\langle 1,3,3\rangle,\langle 2,3,3\rangle,\langle 3,1,3\rangle,\langle 3,2,3\rangle,\langle 3,3,3\rangle\}$. Thus $\underline{\hat{m}}(\underline{n},I,E)$ may be found by considering $\underline{\hat{m}}(\rho^{I}_{I_1}\underline{n},I_1,E)$ and $\underline{\hat{m}}(\rho^{I}_{I_2}\underline{n},I_2,E)$. Since $\{n_{i_1i_2i_3}: \langle i_1,i_2,i_3\rangle \in I_1\}$ is a complete factorial table, the Deming-Stephan algorithm discussed in chapter 5 may be used to find $\underline{\hat{m}}(\rho^{I}_{I_1}\underline{n},I_1,E)$. No calculations are required to compute $\underline{\hat{m}}(\rho^{I}_{I_2}\underline{n},I_2,E)$, for $\rho_{I_2}M(E) = R^{I_2}$. To verify this assertion, it suffices to show that $\rho_{I_2}M(E)$ has dimension 7. This result follows since each coordinate of $\rho_{I_2}\underline{\nu}(\{g\},h)$, where $h \in \overline{2}$ and $g \in \overline{3}$, is 0 except for the coordinate corresponding to the index $\langle i_1,i_2,i_3\rangle$, where $i_g = h$ and $i_j = 3$ if $j \in \overline{3} - \{g\}$. Since the vector $\underline{e}^{I_2} = \{1: \underline{i} \in I_2\} \in \rho_{I_2}M(E)$, and $\underline{e}^{I_2}$ is not in span $\{\rho_{I_2}\underline{\nu}(\{g\},h): g \in \overline{3}, h \in \overline{2}\}$, it follows that $\rho_{I_2}M(E)$ has dimension greater than or equal to 7. Since R^{I_2} has dimension 7, $\rho_{I_2}M(E) = R^{I_2}$. By Example 2.1, $\hat{m}_{i_1i_2i_3}(\underline{n},I,E) = \hat{m}_{i_1i_2i_3}(\rho^{I}_{I_2}\underline{n},I_2,E) = n_{i_1i_2i_3}$ for $\langle i_1,i_2,i_3\rangle \in I_2$, provided $n_{i_1i_2i_3} > 0$ for each $\langle i_1,i_2,i_3\rangle \in I_2$.

If $E = \{\{1,3\},\{2,3\}\}$, then $\underline{n}$ remains E-separable, but the number of equivalence classes is larger. One has $I_1 = \overline{2} \times \overline{2} \times \{1\}$, $I_2 = \{\langle 3,3,1\rangle\}$, $I_3 = 2 \times 2 \times \{2\}$, $I_4 = \{\langle 3,3,2\rangle\}$, and $I_5 = \{\langle 1,3,3\rangle,\langle 2,3,3\rangle,\langle 3,1,3\rangle,\langle 3,2,3\rangle,\langle 3,3,3\rangle\}$. Each maximum-likelihood estimate $\underline{\hat{m}}(\rho^{I}_{I_k}\underline{n},I_k,E)$, $k \in \overline{5}$, can be written down in closed form if it exists. Thus if $\langle i_1,i_2\rangle \in \overline{2} \times \overline{2}$, then

(7.49) $$\hat{m}_{i_1i_21}(\underline{n},I,E) = \hat{m}_{i_1i_21}(\rho^{I}_{I_1}\underline{n},I_1,E) = \frac{n_{i_1+1}n_{+i_21}}{n_{++1}(I_1)}$$

and

(7.50) $$\hat{m}_{i_1i_22}(\underline{n},I,E) = \hat{m}_{i_1i_22}(\rho^{I}_{I_3}\underline{n},I_3,E) = \frac{n_{i_1+2}n_{+i_22}}{n_{++2}(I_3)}.$$

It is easily shown that $\rho_{I_2}M(E) = R^{I_2}$, $\rho_{I_4}M(E) = R^{I_4}$, and $\rho_{I_5}M(E) = R^{I_5}$. Thus

$\underline{\hat{m}}(\rho_{I_k}\underline{n}, I_k, E) = \rho_{I_k}\underline{n}$ for each $k \in \{2,4,5\}$ and

(7.51) $$\hat{m}_{i_1 i_2 i_3}(\underline{n}, I, E) = n_{i_1 i_2 i_3}$$

for each $\langle i_1, i_2, i_3\rangle \in I_2 \cup I_4 \cup I_5$. A necessary and sufficient condition that $\underline{\hat{m}}(\underline{n}, I, E)$ exists is then that $n_{i_1 + i_3} > 0$ and $n_{+ i_2 i_3} > 0$ for $i_1 \in \overline{2}$, $i_2 \in \overline{2}$, and $i_3 \in \overline{2}$ and $n_{i_1 i_2 i_3} > 0$ for $\langle i_1, i_2, i_3\rangle \in I_2 \cup I_4 \cup I_5$.

In separable tables, estimation of asymptotic covariances may be facilitated by noting that for any $\underline{\mu} \in R^I$

(7.52) $$P^*_{\rho_I M(E)}(\underline{\mu}) = \sum_{k=1}^{s} \tau^I_{I_k} P^*_{\rho_{I_k} M(E)}(\rho^I_{I_k}\underline{\mu})\rho^I_{I_k} .$$

Verification of this result depends on the following lemma.

LEMMA 7.5. *If* $\{I_k : k \in \overline{s}\}$ *are the equivalence classes determined by* $\tilde{E}$, *then*

(7.53) $$\rho_I M(E) = \bigoplus_{k=1}^{s} \tau^I_{I_k} \rho_{I_k} M(E).$$

The manifolds $\tau^I_{I_k} \rho_{I_k} M(E)$, $k \in \overline{s}$, *are mutually orthogonal with respect to any inner product* $((\cdot,\cdot))$ *such that for* $\underline{x}$ *and* $\underline{y}$ *in* R^I,

(7.54) $$((\underline{x},\underline{y})) = (\underline{x}, D(\underline{\mu})\underline{y}),$$

where $\underline{\mu} \in R^I$.

Proof. By (7.42) any $\underline{\mu} \in \rho_I M(E)$ satisfies

(7.55) $$\underline{\mu} = \sum_{k=1}^{s} \tau^I_{I_k} \rho^I_{I_k} \underline{\mu},$$

where $\tau^I_{I_k} \rho^I_{I_k} \underline{\mu} \in \tau^I_{I_k} \rho_{I_k} M(E)$. Thus

(7.56) $$\rho_I M(E) \subset \sum_{k=1}^{s} \tau^I_{I_k} \rho^I_{I_k} M(E).$$

Since $\rho_I M(E)$ is isomorphic with $\prod_{k=1}^{s} \rho_{I_k} M(E)$, (7.53) follows. The second half of the lemma follows since if $k \neq k'$, $\underline{x} \in \tau^I_{I_k} \rho_{I_k} M(E)$, and $\underline{y} \in \tau^I_{I_{k'}} \rho_{I_{k'}} M(E)$, then $x_{\underline{i}} = 0$ for $\underline{i} \in I - I_k$ and $y_{\underline{i}} = 0$ for $\underline{i} \in I - I_{k'}$. Since $(I - I_k) \cup (I - I_{k'}) = I$,

(7.57) $$(\underline{x}, D(\underline{\mu})\underline{y}) = \sum_{\underline{i} \in I} x_{\underline{i}} y_{\underline{i}} \exp \mu_{\underline{i}} = 0.$$

Thus the manifolds $\tau^I_{I_k}\rho_{I_k}M(E)$, $k \in \bar{s}$, are mutually orthogonal with respect to any inner product defined by (7.54).||

Given this lemma, it follows that if $\underline{\mu} \in R^I$, then

$$P^*_{\tau^I_{I_k}\rho_{I_k}M(E)}(\underline{\mu}) = \tau^I_{I_k} P^*_{\rho_{I_k}M(E)}(\rho^I_{I_k}\underline{\mu})\rho^I_{I_k} . \tag{7.58}$$

To prove this result, one observes that if $\underline{x} \in R^I$,

$$\begin{aligned} \rho^I_{I_k} D(\underline{\mu})\underline{x} &= \{\exp(\mu_{\underline{i}})x_{\underline{i}} : \underline{i} \in I_k\} \\ &= D(\rho^I_{I_k}\underline{\mu})\rho^I_{I_k}\underline{x}; \end{aligned} \tag{7.59}$$

that is, $\rho^I_{I_k} D(\underline{\mu}) = D(\rho^I_{I_k}\underline{\mu})\rho^I_{I_k}$. One now notes that

$$\begin{aligned} &\tau^I_{I_k} P^*_{\rho_{I_k}M(E)}(\rho^I_{I_k}\underline{\mu})\rho^I_{I_k}\tau^I_{I_k} P^*_{\rho_{I_k}M(E)}(\rho^I_{I_k}\underline{\mu})\rho^I_{I_k} \\ &= \tau^I_{I_k}[P^*_{\rho_{I_k}M(E)}(\rho^I_{I_k}\underline{\mu})]^2 \rho^I_{I_k} \\ &= \tau^I_{I_k} P^*_{\rho_{I_k}M(E)}(\rho^I_{I_k}\underline{\mu}) \rho^I_{I_k} \end{aligned} \tag{7.60}$$

and for each $\underline{x}$ and $\underline{y} \in R^I$,

$$\begin{aligned} &(\underline{x}, D(\underline{\mu})\tau^I_{I_k} P^*_{\rho_{I_k}M(E)}(\rho^I_{I_k}\underline{\mu})\rho^I_{I_k}\underline{y}) \\ &= (\rho^I_{I_k} D(\underline{\mu})\underline{x}, P^*_{\rho_{I_k}M(E)}(\rho^I_{I_k}\underline{\mu})\rho^I_{I_k}\underline{y})_{I_k} \\ &= (D(\rho^I_{I_k}\underline{\mu})\rho^I_{I_k}\underline{x}, P^*_{\rho_{I_k}M(E)}(\rho^I_{I_k}\underline{\mu})\rho^I_{I_k}\underline{y})_{I_k} \\ &= (\rho^I_{I_k}\underline{x}, D(\rho^I_{I_k}\underline{\mu})P^*_{\rho_{I_k}M(E)}(\rho^I_{I_k}\underline{\mu})\rho^I_{I_k}\underline{y})_{I_k} \\ &= (P^*_{\rho_{I_k}M(E)}(\rho^I_{I_k}\underline{\mu})\rho^I_{I_k}\underline{x}, D(\rho^I_{I_k}\underline{\mu})\rho^I_{I_k}\underline{y})_{I_k} \\ &= (P^*_{\rho_{I_k}M(E)}(\rho^I_{I_k}\underline{\mu})\rho^I_{I_k}\underline{x}, \rho^I_{I_k} D(\underline{\mu})\underline{y})_{I_k} \\ &= (\tau^I_{I_k} P^*_{\rho_{I_k}M(E)}(\rho^I_{I_k}\underline{\mu})\rho^I_{I_k}\underline{x}, D(\underline{\mu})\underline{y}). \end{aligned} \tag{7.61}$$

Thus the right-hand side of (7.58) is idempotent and symmetric with respect to the inner product defined by (7.54). Since the right-hand side has range $\tau^I_{I_k}\rho^I_{I_k}M(E)$, the two sides of (7.58) are equal.

Given (7.52) and (7.58), the asymptotic covariance of $\underline{\hat{\mu}}$ satisfies

(7.62)
$$P^*_{\rho_I M(E)}(\underline{\mu})D^{-1}(\underline{\mu}) - P^*_N(\underline{\mu})D^{-1}(\underline{\mu})$$
$$= \sum_{k=1}^{s} \tau^I_{I_k}[P^*_{\rho_{I_k}M(E)}(\rho^I_{I_k}\underline{\mu})D^{-1}(\rho^I_{I_k}\underline{\mu})]\rho^I_{I_k} - P^*_N(\underline{\mu})D^{-1}(\underline{\mu}).$$

If $\underline{c}$ is orthogonal to N, the asymptotic variance of $(\underline{c},\underline{\hat{\mu}})$ is

(7.63)
$$(\underline{c}, \sum_{k=1}^{s} \tau^I_{I_k}[P^*_{\rho_{I_k}M(E)}(\rho^I_{I_k}\underline{\mu})D^{-1}(\rho^I_{I_k}\underline{\mu})]\rho^I_{I_k}\underline{c})$$
$$= \sum_{k=1}^{s} (\rho^I_{I_k}\underline{c}, P^*_{\rho_{I_k}M(E)}(\rho^I_{I_k}\underline{\mu})D^{-1}(\rho^I_{I_k}\underline{\mu})\rho^I_{I_k}\underline{c});$$

and if in addition $\underline{c} = \tau^I_{I_k}\underline{d}$, then the asymptotic variance of $(\underline{c},\underline{\hat{\mu}}) = (\underline{d},\rho^I_{I_k}\underline{\hat{\mu}})$ is $(\underline{d},P^*_{\rho_{I_k}M(E)}(\rho^I_{I_k}\underline{\mu})D^{-1}(\rho^I_{I_k}\underline{\mu})\underline{d})$, which is the asymptotic variance obtained if only $\rho^I_{I_k}\underline{n}$ is considered.

Example 7.13. Suppose that table 7.2 was compiled by use of simple multinomial sampling. In this case, $N = \text{span}\,\{\underline{e}\}$. If the model $\underline{\mu} \in \rho_I M(E)$ is assumed valid, where $E = \{\{1\},\{2\}\}$, then one might wish to estimate the odds m_{1j}/m_{4j} that given the coefficient of radial symmetry corresponding to $j \in \{1,4,7,9\}$, the locular composition is 3 even 0 odd rather than 0 even 3 odd. Since $\underline{\mu} \in \rho_I M(E)$, for each $j \in \{1,4,7,9\}$

(7.64)
$$\log m_{1j}/m_{4j} = \mu_{1j} - \mu_{2j}$$
$$= \frac{1}{4}(\mu_{1+} - \mu_{2+})$$
$$= \frac{1}{4}(\underline{c},\underline{\mu}),$$

where

(7.65)
$$\underline{c} = \frac{1}{4}\,\rho[\underline{\nu}(\{1\},1) - \underline{\nu}(\{1\},4)].$$

The vector $\underline{c}$ is orthogonal to $\underline{e}$ and

(7.66)
$$\underline{c} = \tau^I_{I_1}\underline{d},$$

where

(7.67) $$\underline{d} = \frac{1}{4}\rho_{I_1}[\underline{\nu}(\{1\},1) - \underline{\nu}(\{1\},4)].$$

Since $\rho^{I}_{I_1}\underline{n}$ is a complete table, the estimated asymptotic covariance of $(\underline{c},\hat{\underline{\mu}})$ is

(7.68) $$(d,P^{*}_{\rho_{I_1}M(E)}(\rho^{I}_{I_1}\hat{\underline{\mu}})D^{-1}(\rho^{I}_{I_1}\hat{\underline{\mu}})\underline{d})$$

$$= (\underline{d},P^{*}_{M(I_1,E)}(\rho^{I}_{I_1}\hat{\underline{\mu}})D^{-1}(\rho^{I}_{I_1}\hat{\underline{\mu}})\underline{d})$$

$$= (\underline{d},[\sum_{i=1}^{2}\rho_{I_1}\underline{\nu}(\{1\},i) \circledast \rho_{I_1}\underline{\nu}(\{1\},i)/n_{i+}]\underline{d})$$

$$+ (\underline{d},[\Sigma\ \{\rho_{I_1}\underline{\nu}(\{2\},j) \circledast \rho_{I_1}\underline{\nu}(\{2\},j)/n_{+j}]): j \in \{1,4,7,9\}\}]\underline{d})$$

$$- (\underline{d},[\underline{e}^{I_1} \circledast \underline{e}^{I_1}/n_{++}(I_1)]\underline{d})$$

$$= \frac{1}{16}[16/n_{1+} + 16/n_{4+}]$$

$$= \frac{1}{n_{1+}} + \frac{1}{n_{4+}} .$$

Since for $j \in \{1,4,7,9\}$,

(7.69) $$(\underline{c},\hat{\underline{\mu}}) = \log \hat{m}_{1j}/\hat{m}_{4j}$$

$$= \log (n_{1+}/n_{4+})$$

$$= 4.28 ,$$

an approximate 95% confidence interval for $\log m_{1j}/m_{4j}$ is $[\log (n_{1+}/n_{4+}) - 1.96\ (1/n_{1+} + 1/n_{4+})^{1/2},\ \log (n_{1+}/n_{4+}) + 1.96\ (1/n_{1+} + 1/n_{4+})^{1/2}]$, which in this example is [1.26,1.65]. The corresponding interval for m_{1j}/m_{4j} is [3.52,5.20]. The notable feature of these confidence intervals is that they have been obtained without any reference to the table $\rho_{I_2}\underline{n}$ corresponding to locular compositions 2 even 1 odd and 1 even 2 odd.

In an analysis of residuals, the coefficient $c_{\underline{i}}$ used to obtain the adjusted residuals $s_{\underline{i}} = [(n_{\underline{i}} - \hat{m}_{\underline{i}})/\hat{m}_{\underline{i}}^{1/2}]/c_{\underline{i}}^{1/2}$ depends only on the subtable $\rho_{I_k}\underline{n}$, where $\underline{i} \in I_k$. This result follows since

(7.70) $$c_{\underline{i}} = (\underline{\delta}^{(\underline{i})},[I - A_{\rho_I M(E)}(\underline{\hat{\mu}})]\underline{\delta}^{(\underline{i})})$$

$$= (\underline{\delta}^{(\underline{i})},I\underline{\delta}^{(\underline{i})}) - \sum_{k'=1}^{s} (\underline{\delta}^{(\underline{i})},\tau^{I}_{I_k} A_{\rho_{I_{k'}} M(E)}(\rho^{I}_{I_{k'}}\underline{\hat{\mu}})\rho^{I}_{I_{k'}}\underline{\delta}^{(\underline{i})})$$

$$= (\rho^{I}_{I_k}\underline{\delta}^{(\underline{i})},[I - A_{\rho_{I_{k'}} M(E)}(\rho^{I}_{I_k}\underline{\hat{\mu}})]\rho^{I}_{I_k}\underline{\delta}^{(\underline{i})}).$$

This expression for $c_{\underline{i}}$ is precisely the expression obtained if adjusted residuals are found for the table $\rho^{I}_{I_k}\underline{n}$ and the manifold $\rho_{I_k} M(E)$. Example 7.9 illustrates the calculations used to find $\{c_{\underline{i}}: \underline{i} \in I\}$ when $\underline{n}$ is separable.

Statistics for hypothesis tests may also be decomposed into components corresponding to the inseparable tables $\rho^{I}_{I_k}\underline{n}$, where $k \in \overline{s}$. In this case, the null hypothesis H_0: $\underline{\mu} \in \rho_I M(E_1)$ and the alternative hypothesis H_A: $\underline{\mu} \in \rho_I M(E_2)$ where $M(E) \subset M(E')$, must have the property that the relation $\underset{E_1}{\sim}$ implies $\underset{E_2}{\sim}$. Then the equivalence classes $\{J_\ell: \ell \in \overline{t}\}$ corresponding to E_2 are a subpartition of the equivalence classes $\{I_k: k \in \overline{s}\}$ corresponding to E_1. In this case, if $\underline{i} \in J_\ell \subset I_k$, $\hat{m}_{\underline{i}}(\underline{n},I,E_2) = \hat{m}_{\underline{i}}(\rho^{I}_{J_\ell}\underline{n},J_\ell,E_2)$ $= \hat{m}_{\underline{i}}(\rho^{I}_{I_k}\underline{n},I_k,E_2)$. One may now write the likelihood ratio chi-square as

(7.71) $$-2\Delta(\underline{n},\underline{\hat{\mu}}(\underline{n},I,E_2),\underline{\hat{\mu}}(\underline{n},I,E_1))$$

$$= 2 \sum_{\underline{i} \in I} n_{\underline{i}} \log [(\hat{m}_{\underline{i}}(\underline{n},I,E_2)/\hat{m}_{\underline{i}}(\underline{n},I,E_1)]$$

$$= \sum_{k=1}^{s} 2 \sum_{\underline{i} \in I_k} n_{\underline{i}} \log [(\hat{m}_{\underline{i}}(\rho^{I}_{I_k}\underline{n},I_k,E_2)/\hat{m}_{\underline{i}}(\rho^{I}_{I_k}\underline{n},I_k,E_1)]$$

$$= \sum_{k=1}^{s} [-2\Delta(\rho^{I}_{I_k}\underline{n},\underline{\hat{\mu}}(\rho^{I}_{I_k}\underline{n},I_k,E_2),\underline{\hat{\mu}}(\rho^{I}_{I_k}\underline{n},I_k,E_1))],$$

where for each $k \in \overline{s}$ the summand $-2\Delta(\rho^{I}_{I_k}\underline{n},\underline{\hat{\mu}}(\rho^{I}_{I_k}\underline{n},I_k,E_2),\underline{\hat{\mu}}(\rho^{I}_{I_k}\underline{n},I_k,E_1))$ is the likelihood ratio chi-square for the test of H_0: $\rho^{I}_{I_k}\underline{\mu} \in \rho_{I_k} M(E_1)$ against H_A: $\rho^{I}_{I_k}\underline{\mu} \in \rho_{I_k} M(E_2)$. Thus the test is reduced to s separate tests for the E-inseparable subtables $\rho^{I}_{I_k}\underline{n}$ where $k \in \overline{s}$.

The decomposition corresponds to the observation that the condition $\underline{\mu} \in \rho_I M(E_h)$ is equivalent to the conditions $\rho^{I}_{I_k}\underline{\mu} \in \rho_{I_k} M(E_h)$ for each $k \in \overline{s}$. Under the null hypothesis, summand k in the decomposition has an asymptotic chi-square distribution with $\dim \rho_{I_k} M(E_2) - \dim \rho_{I_k} M(E_1)$ degrees of freedom, and the summands are asymptotically independent. The first assertion follows since the hypothesis that $\rho^{I}_{I_k}\underline{\mu} \in \rho_{I_k} M(E_h)$ is equivalent to the hypothesis that $\underline{\mu} \in (\rho^{I}_{I_k})^{-1}\rho_{I_k} M(E_h)$ if $h \in \overline{2}$. Thus

$$N \subset M(E_1) \subset (\rho^{I}_{I_k})^{-1}\rho_{I_k} M(E_1) \subset (\rho^{I}_{I_k})^{-1}\rho_{I_k} M(E_2). \tag{7.72}$$

Since any element $\underline{\mu} \in (\rho^{I}_{I_k})^{-1}\rho_{I_k} M(E_h)$ has a unique expression of the form

$$\underline{\mu} = \rho^{I}_{I_k}\underline{\mu}^{(1)} + \tau^{I}_{I-I_k}\underline{\mu}^{(2)} , \tag{7.73}$$

where $\underline{\mu}^{(1)} \in \rho_{I_k} M(E_h)$ and $\underline{\mu}^{(2)} \in R^{I-I_k}$, it follows that

$$(\rho^{I}_{I_k})^{-1}\rho_{I_k} M(E_h) = \tau^{I}_{I_k}\rho_{I_k} M(E_h) \oplus \tau^{I}_{I-I_k} R^{I-I_k} . \tag{7.74}$$

Since $\tau^{I}_{I_k}$ and $\tau^{I}_{I-I_k}$ are one-to-one mappings, the number of degrees of freedom is

$$\begin{aligned} &[\dim \rho_{I_k} M(E_2) + \dim R^{I-I_k}] \\ &- [\dim \rho_{I_k} M(E_1) + \dim R^{I-I_k}] \\ &= \dim \rho_{I_k} M(E_2) - \dim \rho_{I_k} M(E_1). \end{aligned} \tag{7.75}$$

The second assertion follows since $\tau^{I}_{I_k}\rho_{I_k} M(E_h)$ and $\tau^{I}_{I-I_k} R^{I-I_k}$ are orthogonal with respect to any inner product $((\cdot,\cdot))$ satisfying (7.54). Thus if $M_{hk} = (\rho^{I}_{I_k})^{-1}\rho_{I_k} M(E_h)$, then (7.52) implies that

$$A_{M_{2k}}(\underline{\mu}) - A_{M_{1k}}(\underline{\mu}) = \tau^{I}_{I_k}[A_{\rho_{I_k} M(E_2)}(\rho^{I}_{I_k}\underline{\mu}) - A_{\rho_{I_k} M(E_1)}(\rho^{I}_{I_k}\underline{\mu})]\rho^{I}_{I_k} . \tag{7.76}$$

By (4.174), (4.175), and Rao (1965), the summands are asymptotically independent if for $k \neq k'$,

$$[A_{M_{2k}}(\underline{\mu}) - A_{M_{1k}}(\underline{\mu})][A_{M_{2k'}}(\underline{\mu}) - A_{M_{1k'}}(\underline{\mu})] = 0 . \tag{7.77}$$

This result follows from (7.76) since $\rho^{I}_{I_k}\tau^{I}_{I_{k'}} = 0$.

A similar decomposition is available if the Pearson chi-square is employed. In this case,

(7.78)
$$C(\hat{\underline{\mu}}(\underline{n},I,E_2),\hat{\underline{\mu}}(\underline{n},I,E_1))$$

$$= \sum_{k=1}^{s} C(\hat{\underline{\mu}}(\rho^I_{I_k}\underline{n},I_k,E_2),\hat{\underline{\mu}}(\rho^I_{I_k}\underline{n},I_k,E_1)),$$

where the summand $C(\hat{\underline{\mu}}(\rho^I_{I_k}\underline{n},I_k,E_2),\hat{\underline{\mu}}(\rho^I_{I_k}\underline{n},I_k,E_1))$ is asymptotically equivalent under the null hypothesis to $-2\Delta(\rho^I_{I_k}\underline{n},\hat{\underline{\mu}}(\rho^I_{I_k}\underline{n},I_k,E_2),\hat{\underline{\mu}}(\rho^I_{I_k}\underline{n},I_k,E_1))$. Thus the summand $C(\hat{\underline{\mu}}(\rho^I_{I_k}\underline{n},I_k,E_2)),\hat{\underline{\mu}}(\rho^I_{I_k}\underline{n},I_k,E_1))$, which corresponds to the test of H_0: $\rho^I_{I_k}\underline{\mu} \in \rho_{I_k}M(E_1)$ against H_A: $\rho^I_{I_k}\underline{\mu} \in \rho_{I_k}M(E_2)$, has an asymptotic chi-square distribution with $\dim \rho_{I_k}M(E_2) - \dim \rho_{I_k}M(E_1)$ degrees of freedom. Once again, different summands are asymptotically independent.

It should be noted that the most common alternative hypothesis is the trivial hypothesis that $\underline{\mu} \in R^I = \rho_I M(\overline{d})$. If $E_2 = \{\overline{d}\}$, then $\underline{i} \sim_{E_2} \underline{i}'$ implies that $\underline{i} = \underline{i}'$. Therefore, $\underline{i} \sim_{E_1} \underline{i}'$ implies that $\underline{i} \sim_{E_2} \underline{i}'$ for any generating class E_1. Thus the basic condition for the decomposition is always satisfied in this case. It should also be noted that when Poisson sampling is employed, the summands in the decompositions are not only asymptotically independent but also exactly independent.

Example 7.14. Since complete tables are special cases of incomplete tables, the decompositions provided by (7.70) and (7.77) may be applied to the data in table 1.2 concerning mothers with previous infant loss. In Example 4.13, one of the models considered was $M(\{\{1,2\},\{1,3\}\})$. Since $I = \overline{3} \times \overline{2} \times \overline{2}$, the table is separable, and the equivalence classes $\{I_k: k \in \overline{3}\}$ satisfy the relationship $I_k = \{k\} \times \overline{2} \times \overline{2}$.

If the null hypothesis is H_0: $\underline{\mu} \in M(\{\{1,2\},\{1,3\}\}$ and the alternative hypothesis is H_A: $\underline{\mu} \in R^I$, then the likelihood ratio chi-square for the complete table satisfies

(7.79)
$$2\sum_{k=1}^{3}\sum_{i=1}^{2}\sum_{j=1}^{2} n_{ijk}\log(n_{ijk}n_{i++}/n_{ij+}n_{i+k})$$

$$= 3.15.$$

The corresponding Pearson chi-square is

(7.80)
$$\sum_{k=1}^{3}\sum_{i=1}^{2}\sum_{j=1}^{2}(n_{ijk} - n_{ij+}n_{1+k}/n_{i++})^2/(n_{ij+}n_{i+k}/n_{i++})$$

$$= 3.13.$$

Since there are 3 degrees of freedom, these results indicate that no reason exists to reject the null hypothesis. Nonetheless, the component chi-square terms $2\sum_{i=1}^{2}\sum_{j=1}^{2} n_{ijk}$ $\log(n_{ijk}n_{i++}/n_{ij+}n_{i+k})$ and $\sum_{i=1}^{2}\sum_{j=1}^{2}(n_{ijk} - n_{ij+}n_{i+k}/n_{i++})^2/n_{ij+}n_{i+k}/n_{i++})$ corresponding to $\rho_{I_k}\underline{n}$ may still be used to detect possible irregularities in the data which are not suggested by the chi-square statistics for the complete table. As shown in table 7.9, the chi-square statistics for birth orders 5 or greater are almost significant at the 10% level, while the other components are quite small. These results suggest that, given birth order of at least 5, type of child and type of mother may not be independent; however, since three components have been examined and no special reason existed before the analysis to believe that children with birth order 5 or greater might have any special properties, the suggestion can only be regarded as tentative.

TABLE 7.9

COMPONENTS OF X^2 FOR BIRTH ORDER DATA

Birth Order	Likelihood Ratio X^2	Pearson X^2
2	0.43	0.42
3-4	0.19	0.19
5	2.53	2.52

Separability was originally introduced by Goodman (1968) for use with quasi-independence models for incomplete $r \times c$ tables. In this case, $I^* = \bar{r} \times \bar{c}$ and $E = \{\{1\},\{2\}\}$. The equivalence classes I_k, $k \in \bar{s}$, satisfy

(7.81) $$I_k = I \cap [I_k(\{1\}) \times I_k(\{2\})]$$

and

(7.82) $$\dim \rho M(E) = \sum_{k=1}^{s} \dim \rho_{I_k} M(E)$$

$$= \sum_{k=1}^{s} (r_k + c_k - 1)$$

$$= a + b - s,$$

where $I_k(\{1\})$, a subset of $\bar{r}$, has r_k elements; $I_k(\{2\})$, a subset of $\bar{c}$, has c_k elements; $I(\{1\})$ has a elements, and $I(\{2\})$ has b elements. Thus computation of the dimension of $\rho M(E)$ is very easy in this case.

Verification of (7.81) and (7.82) is relatively straightforward. To show that I_k is included in $J_k = I \cap [I_k(\{1\}) \times I_k(\{2\})]$, suppose that $\langle i,j\rangle \in I_k$. Then $i \in I_k(\{1\})$ and $j \in I_k(\{2\})$. Consequently, $\langle i,j\rangle \in J_k$ and $I_k \subset J_k$. On the other hand, if $\langle i,j\rangle \in J_k$, then for some $j' \in I_k(\{2\}), \langle i,j'\rangle \in I_k$. Since $\langle i,j\rangle \underset{E}{\sim} \langle i,j'\rangle, \langle i,j\rangle \in I_k$. Thus (7.81) follows.

To prove (7.82), one notes that by Halmos (1958), for each $k \in \overline{s}$,

$$\text{(7.83)} \qquad \dim \rho_{I_k} M(E) = \dim \rho_{I_k} N_{\{1\}} + \dim \rho_{I_k} N_{\{2\}}$$

$$- \dim [\rho_{I_k} N_{\{1\}} \cap \rho_{I_k} N_{\{2\}}].$$

Since $\{\underline{v}(\{1\},i): i \in I_k(\{1\})$ is a basis of $\rho_{I_k} N_{\{1\}}$, $\dim \rho_{I_k} N_{\{1\}} = r_k$. Similarly, $\dim \rho_{I_k} N_{\{1\}} = c_k$. That (7.82) holds follows since by Lemma 7.6, the fact that $\{n_{\underline{i}}: \underline{i} \in I_k\}$ is inseparable implies that $\dim (\rho_{I_k} N_{\{1\}} \cap \rho_{I_k} N_{\{2\}}) = 1$.

LEMMA 7.6. *The dimension of* $\cap_{E \in E} \rho_I N_E$ *is the number of equivalence classes of* I *determined by* $\underset{E}{\sim}$.

Proof. Suppose $\underline{\mu} \in \cap_{E \in E} \rho_I N_E$. If $\underline{i} \underset{E}{\sim} \underline{i}'$, there exists a sequence $\{\underline{i}^{(k)}: k \in \overline{\ell}\} \subset I$ such that $\underline{i}^{(1)} = \underline{i}$, $\underline{i}^{(\ell)} = \underline{i}'$, and for each $k \in \overline{\ell - 1}$, there exists E_k such that $\pi_{E_k} \underline{i}^{(k)} = \pi_{E_k} \underline{i}^{(k+1)}$. Since $\underline{\mu} \in \rho_I N_{E_k}$, $\mu_{\underline{i}^{(k)}} = \mu_{\underline{i}^{(k+1)}}$. Therefore $\mu_{\underline{i}} = \mu_{\underline{i}'}$. In other words, $\mu_{\underline{i}}$ is constant for $\underline{i}$ in an equivalence class I_k, $k \in \overline{s}$.

On the other hand, if $\mu_{\underline{i}} = a_k$ for each $\underline{i} \in I_k$ and $k \in \overline{s}$, then $\underline{\mu} \in \cap_{E \in E} \rho_I N_E$. Since $\{a_k: k \in \overline{s}\}$ is arbitrary, $\dim (\cap_{E \in E} \rho_I N_E) = s.$ ||

Example 7.15. Consider the 5 x 6 table in which

(7.84) $\underline{n} =$

n_{11}	-	n_{13}	-	n_{15}	n_{16}
n_{21}	n_{22}	n_{23}	-	-	-
-	-	-	n_{34}	-	-
n_{41}	-	-	-	n_{45}	n_{46}
n_{51}	n_{52}	-	-	n_{55}	-

This table is separable if $E = \{\{1\},\{2\}\}$. One has $s = 2$,

(7.85)
$$\rho^I_{I_1}\underline{n} = \begin{array}{|cccccc|} n_{11} & - & n_{13} & - & n_{15} & n_{16} \\ n_{21} & n_{22} & n_{23} & - & - & - \\ - & - & - & - & - & - \\ n_{41} & - & - & - & n_{45} & n_{46} \\ n_{51} & n_{52} & - & - & n_{55} & - \end{array}$$

and

(7.86)
$$\rho^I_{I_2}\underline{n} = \begin{array}{|cccccc|} - & - & - & - & - & - \\ - & - & - & - & - & - \\ - & - & - & n_{43} & - & - \\ - & - & - & - & - & - \\ - & - & - & - & - & - \end{array}$$

Thus $r_1 = 4$, $c_1 = 5$, $r_2 = 1$, and $c_2 = 1$. The dimension of $\rho M(E)$ is then 9.

As Goodman (1968) points out, a two-way table is inseparable if and only if its dimension is $a + b - 1$. In other words, a is the number of rows containing observations and b is the corresponding number of columns. This observation is an immediate consequence of (7.82). It is equivalent to the observation that $\underline{n}$ is inseparable if and only if $\underline{\mu}$ has a unique parametrization

(7.87)
$$\mu_{ij} = u^{\phi} + u_i^{\{1\}} + u_j^{\{2\}}$$

for $\langle i,j\rangle \in I$, where $\underline{u}^{\{k\}} \in R^{I(\{k\})}$ and $u_+^{\{k\}} = 0$ for $k = 1$ or 2.

The special relationship between separability and dimension which is found in the case of two-way tables also exists in higher-way tables in which E has two elements E_1 and E_2. In such a case, one has

(7.88)
$$\dim \rho_I M(E) = \dim \rho_I N_{E_1} + \dim \rho_I N_{E_2} - \dim (\rho_I N_{E_1} \cap \rho_I N_{E_2}) = a + b - s,$$

where a is the number of elements of $I(E_1)$, b is the number of elements of $I(E_2)$, and s is the number of equivalence classes determined by $\tilde{E}$.

Example 7.16. If $\underline{n}$ is defined by (7.48) and $E = \{\{1,2\},\{1,3\}\}$, then $a = 9$, $b = 9$, and $s = 5$. Thus the dimension of $\rho M(E)$ is 13.

If E has three elements E_1, E_2, and E_3, then separability can be used only for finding an upper bound for the dimension of $\rho M(E)$. One has

$$\begin{aligned}(7.89)\qquad \dim \rho M(E) &= \dim \rho N_{E_1} + \dim \rho N_{E_2} - \dim (\rho N_{E_1} \cap \rho N_{E_2}) \\ &\quad + \dim \rho N_{E_3} - \dim [(\rho N_{E_1} + \rho N_{E_2}) \cap \rho N_{E_3}] \\ &\le \dim \rho N_{E_1} + \dim \rho N_{E_2} + \dim \rho N_{E_3} \\ &\quad - \dim (\rho N_{E_1} \cap \rho N_{E_2}) - \dim (\rho N_{E_1} \cap \rho N_{E_3}) \\ &\quad - \dim (\rho N_{E_2} \cap \rho N_{E_3}) + \dim (\rho N_{E_1} \cap \rho N_{E_2} \cap \rho N_{E_3}).\end{aligned}$$

where the inequality follows since

$$\begin{aligned}(7.90)\qquad & (\rho N_{E_1} \cap \rho N_{E_3}) + (\rho N_{E_2} \cap \rho N_{E_3}) \\ & \subset (\rho N_{E_1} + \rho N_{E_2}) \cap \rho N_{E_3}.\end{aligned}$$

Example 7.17. If $\underline{n}$ is defined by (7.48) and $E = \{\{1,2\},\{1,3\},\{2,3\}\}$, then $\dim \rho N_{\{1,2\}}$, $\dim \rho N_{\{1,3\}}$ and $\dim \rho N_{\{2,3\}}$ are all 9, $\rho N_{\{1,2\}} \cap \rho N_{\{1,3\}}$, $\rho N_{\{1,2\}} \cap \rho N_{\{2,3\}}$, and $\rho N_{\{1,3\}} \cap \rho N_{\{2,3\}}$ all have dimension 5, and $\rho N_{\{1,2\}} \cap \rho N_{\{1,3\}} \cap \rho N_{\{2,3\}}$ has dimension 2. Thus the upper bound for $\dim \rho M(E)$ is 14, which, by Example 7.12, is the dimension of $\rho M(E)$.

Example 7.18. The inequality in (7.89) may sometimes be a strict inequality. If

$$(7.91)\qquad \underline{n} = \begin{array}{|cc|}\hline - & n_{121} \\ n_{211} & n_{221} \\ \hline\end{array} \quad \begin{array}{|cc|}\hline n_{112} & n_{122} \\ n_{212} & - \\ \hline\end{array}$$

and $E = \{\{1,2\},\{1,3\},\{2,3\}\}$, then since I has 6 elements, $\rho M(E)$ has dimension no greater than 6. However, the bound given by (7.89) is 7 in this example.

EXISTENCE OF MAXIMUM-LIKELIHOOD ESTIMATES

The methods of Appendix B may be employed to determine whether the maximum-likelihood estimate $\hat{\underline{m}}$ exists. A few features of incomplete tables may facilitate this determination. First, Theorem 7.1 implies that it is only necessary to consider inseparable tables. Second, if $E = \{E_1,E_2\}$, $\underline{n}$ is inseparable, $J = \{\underline{i} \in I: n_{\underline{i}} > 0\}$, $\rho_J^I\underline{n}$ is inseparable, and $I(E_K) = J(E_K)$ for $k \in \overline{2}$, then Corollary B.3 and (7.88) imply that the maximum-likelihood estimate $\hat{\underline{m}}$ exists. If $E_1 = \{1\}$, $E_2 = \{2\}$, and $I^* = \overline{r} \times \overline{c}$, then this statement is equivalent to the theorem of Fienberg (1970) that the maximum-likelihood estimate $\hat{\underline{m}}$ for a quasi-independence model of an incomplete $r \times c$ table exists if $\rho_J^I\underline{n}$ is inseparable and all marginal totals n_{i+}, $i \in I(\{1\})$, and n_{+j}, $j \in I(\{2\})$, are positive.

Example 7.19. Suppose $E = \{\{1\},\{2\}\}$, $\underline{n}$ satisfies (7.84), and n_{51} and n_{22} are the only elements of $\underline{n}$ which are 0. The maximum-likelihood estimate for $\hat{\underline{m}}$ exists if and only if the maximum-likelihood estimates corresponding to $\rho_{I_1}^I\underline{n}$ and $\rho_{I_2}^I\underline{n}$ exist. The estimate $\hat{\underline{m}}(\rho_{I_2}^I\underline{n},I_2,E)$ exists since $n_{34} > 0$. The estimate $\hat{\underline{m}}(\rho_{I_1}^I\underline{n},I_1,E)$ exists since if $J_1 = \{\langle i,j\rangle \in I_1: n_{ij} > 0\}$, then $I_1(\{1\}) = J_1(\{1\}) = \overline{5} - \{3\}$, $I_1(\{2\}) = J_1(\{2\}) = \overline{6} - \{4\}$, and both I_1 and J_1 are inseparable.

Example 7.20. The maximum-likelihood estimate $\hat{\underline{m}}$ may exist when $\underline{n}$ is inseparable and $\rho_J^I\underline{n}$ is separable. This situation arises if $n_{11} > 0$, $n_{22} > 0$, and

$$\underline{n} = \begin{array}{|cc|} n_{11} & 0 \\ 0 & n_{22} \end{array} \;. \tag{7.92}$$

It should, however, be noted that $\hat{\underline{m}}$ does not exist if

$$\underline{n} = \begin{array}{|cc|} n_{11} & - \\ 0 & n_{22} \end{array} \;. \tag{7.93}$$

This result follows from Corollary (B.3) since (7.77) implies that $\dim \rho_I M(E) = 3$ and $\dim \rho_J M(E) = 2$.

Example 7.21. If

$$\underline{n} = \begin{array}{|ccc|} n_{111} & - & - \\ n_{211} & n_{221} & - \\ n_{311} & n_{321} & n_{331} \end{array} \quad \begin{array}{|ccc|} - & - & - \\ - & n_{222} & - \\ - & n_{322} & n_{331} \end{array} \quad \begin{array}{|ccc|} - & - & - \\ - & - & - \\ - & - & n_{333} \end{array} \;, \tag{7.94}$$

$E = \{\{1,3\},\{2,3\}\}$, and the only element of $\underline{n}$ equal to 0 is n_{211}, then the maximum-likelihood estimate exists. In this case, $I_k = I \cap \overline{3} \times \overline{3} \times \{k\}$ for $k \in \overline{3}$. If $J_k = \{\langle i_1,i_2,i_3\rangle \in I_k : n_{i_1 i_2 i_3} > 0\}$, then for each $k \in \overline{3}$, $\rho^I_{I_k}\underline{n}$ and $\rho^I_{J_k}\underline{n}$ are inseparable, $I_k(\{1,3\}) = J_k(\{1,3\})$, and $I_k(\{2,3\}) = J_k(\{2,3\})$. Thus $\hat{\underline{m}}(\rho^I_{I_k}\underline{n}, I_k, E)$ exists for each $k \in \overline{3}$, and Theorem 7.1 implies that $\hat{\underline{m}}(\underline{n},I,E)$ exists.

On the other hand, if n_{211} and n_{311} are 0, then $\rho^I_{J_1}\underline{n}$ is separable. Thus it is possible that $\hat{\underline{m}}(\underline{n},I,E)$ does not exist, even though all marginal totals corresponding to $\{1,3\}$ and $\{2,3\}$ are positive.

To show that $\hat{\underline{m}}(\underline{n},I,E)$ does not exist, one notes that

$$\underline{\mu} = \begin{bmatrix} 0 & - & - \\ -1 & 0 & - \\ -1 & 0 & 0 \end{bmatrix} \quad \begin{bmatrix} - & - & - \\ - & 0 & - \\ - & 0 & 0 \end{bmatrix} \quad \begin{bmatrix} - & - & - \\ - & - & - \\ - & - & 0 \end{bmatrix} \tag{7.95}$$

is an element of $\rho_I M(E)$.

When E contains more than two elements, special techniques are of little help. One may proceed in such cases as in Examples B.1 and B.2, or the Borosh and Fraenkel (1966) algorithm can be employed to determine if $\dim \rho M(E)$ and $\dim \rho_J M(E)$ are equal. If equality holds, Corollary B.3 implies that $\hat{\underline{m}}(\underline{n},I,E)$ exists.

CLOSED-FORM MAXIMUM-LIKELIHOOD ESTIMATES

In complete tables, closed-form maximum-likelihood estimates $\hat{\underline{m}}(\underline{n},I,E)$ are available when E is decomposable. In incomplete tables, further conditions must be imposed on I in order to obtain closed-form estimates. Goodman (1968) and Bishop and Fienberg (1969) have considered conditions which permit construction of closed-form estimates when $I^* = \overline{r} \times \overline{c}$ and $E = \{\{1\},\{2\}\}$; however, conditions for higher-way tables have not been examined in the literature. The condition proposed in this section for the existence of closed-form estimates is that the generating class E be decomposable and that the table $\underline{n}$ be reducible relative to E, where reducibility is defined in Definition 7.2. In the quasi-independence models for incomplete two-way tables considered by Goodman (1968) and Bishop and Fienberg (1969), the table $\underline{n}$ is shown to be reducible if the class J of maximal hyperblocks is decomposable. In models for higher-way tables, reducibility involves further restrictions on J.

The definitions, theorems, and proofs in this section are all quite difficult. Consequently, many readers may prefer to omit much of this section. In reading Definition 7.2, it is helpful to keep in mind the observation that $\underline{n}$ is reducible relative to $\{\{1\},\{2\}\}$ if

(7.96)
$$\underline{n} = \begin{array}{|ccc|} n_{11} & n_{12} & - \\ n_{21} & n_{22} & n_{23} \\ n_{31} & n_{32} & n_{33} \end{array}$$

or

(7.97)
$$\underline{n} = \begin{array}{|ccc|} n_{11} & n_{12} & - \\ n_{21} & n_{22} & n_{23} \\ - & - & n_{33} \end{array} ,$$

but $\underline{n}$ is not reducible if

(7.98)
$$\underline{n} = \begin{array}{|ccc|} - & n_{12} & n_{13} \\ n_{21} & - & n_{23} \\ n_{31} & n_{32} & - \end{array} .$$

DEFINITION 7.2. *An index set* I *or a table* $\{n_{\underline{i}} : \underline{i} \in I\}$ *is reducible relative to a decomposable generating class* E *if the class* J *of maximal hyperblocks defined by* (7.38) *and* (7.39) *is such that*

(7.99)
$$\tau_J^I \rho_J N_F \subset \rho M(E)$$

for all $J \in J$ *and* $F \in F(E)$ *for which* $d(F,E) > 0$, *and an ordering* $\{J_k : k \in \overline{\ell}\}$ *of* J *exists such that if* $H_k = \bigcup_{J=1}^{k-1} J_j$ *for* $k \in \overline{\ell + 1} - \overline{1}$ *and* $G_k = J_k \cap H_k$ *for* $k \in \overline{\ell} - \overline{1}$, *then for each* $k \in \overline{\ell} - \overline{1}$ *there exists* $h_k \in \overline{k - 1}$ *such that* $G_k = J_{h_k} \cap J_k$,

(7.100)
$$\tau_{G_k}^I \rho_{G_k} N_F \subset \rho M(E)$$

for each $F \in F(E)$ *such that* $d(F,E) > 0$, *and*

(7.101)
$$\pi_E^{-1} K_k(E) \cap H_{k+1} = \pi_E^{-1} K_k(E) \cap J_k ,$$

where $K_k = J_k - G_k$.

Remarks. The class $F(E)$ is defined as in Definition 5.5. The condition of the definition imply that J is a decomposable generating class.

Example 7.22. If I is the index set of a complete table, E is decomposable, and $\cap(E) = \phi$, then I is reducible. In this case, $\ell = 1$ and $J_1 = \Pi_{j=1}^{d}\overline{r}_j = I$. Condition (7.99) is trivial and all other conditions are vacuous.

If $\cap(E) \neq \phi$, then I is still reducible. In this case, J contains disjoint sets of the form $\Pi_{j=1}^{d}A_j$, where $A_j = \overline{r}_j$ if $j \notin \cap(E)$ and $A_j = \{i_j\}$ for some $i_j \in \overline{r}_j$ if $j \in \cap(E)$. Any ordering of the sets of J results in $\ell = \Pi_{j\in\cap(E)}r_j$ sets $\{J_k: k \in \overline{\ell}\}$ such that $K_k = J_k$ and $G_k = \phi$ for $k \in \overline{\ell} - \overline{1}$. Condition (7.100) is trivial since $\tau_{\phi}^{I}\rho_{\phi}N_F = \{\underline{0}\}$ if $F \in F(E)$. By Lemmas 7.2 and 7.5, if $F \in F(E)$, then

$$\tau_{J}^{I}\rho_{J}N_F \subset \tau_{J}^{I}\rho_{J}M(E) \subset \rho M(E). \tag{7.102}$$

Thus (7.99) holds. Lemma 7.2 also implies (7.101).

Example 7.23. In table 7.10, initial and final disability ratings are compared in 121 patients hospitalized due to strokes. Since a patient never leaves with a lower rating than the one he had on arrival, the table must be analyzed as an incomplete table with $I = \{\langle i,j\rangle \in \overline{5} \times \overline{5}: i + j \leq 6\}$. Bishop and Fienberg (1969) consider a quasi-independence model for this table. Given this model, $E = \{\{1\},\{2\}\}$ is decomposable and I is reducible. To demonstrate this result, let

$$J_k = \overline{k} \times \overline{6 - k} \tag{7.103}$$

for each $k \in \overline{5}$. Then for each $k \in \overline{6} - \overline{1}$

$$H_k = \{\langle i,j\rangle \in \overline{k - 1} \times \overline{5}: i + j \leq 6\}; \tag{7.104}$$

and for each $k \in \overline{5} - \overline{1}$

$$\begin{aligned} G_k &= \overline{k - 1} \times \overline{6 - k}. \\ &= J_k \cap J_{k-1}. \end{aligned} \tag{7.105}$$

Since $F(E) = \{\phi\}$ and

$$\tau_{G_k}^{I}\rho_{G_k}N_{\phi} = \text{span}\ \{\sum_{i=1}^{k-1} \rho\underline{v}(\{1\},i) - \sum_{j=6-k+1}^{5} \rho\underline{v}(\{2\},j)\}, \tag{7.106}$$

(7.99) holds for each $k \in \overline{5} - \overline{1}$. Similarly, (7.100) holds for each $k \in \overline{5} - \overline{1}$ since

$$\tau_{J_k}^{I}\rho_{J_k}N_{\phi} = \text{span}\ \{\sum_{i=1}^{k} \rho\underline{v}(\{1\},i) - \sum_{j=6-k+1}^{5} \rho\underline{v}(\{2\},j)\}. \tag{7.107}$$

TABLE 7.10

INITIAL AND FINAL RATINGS OF STROKE PATIENTS

	Final State				
Initial State	A	B	C	D	E
E	11	23	12	15	8
D	9	10	4	1	-
C	6	4	4	-	-
B	4	5	-	-	-
A	5	-	-	-	-

Since $K_k = \{k\} \times \overline{6-k}$ for $k \in \overline{5} - \overline{1}$, $K_k(\{1\}) = \{k\}$ and $K_k(\{2\}) = \overline{6-k}$. Thus

$$\pi_{\{1\}}K_k(\{1\}) \cap H_{k+1} = \pi_{\{1\}}K_k(\{1\}) \cap K_k = \{k\} \times \overline{6-k}$$

and

$$\pi_{\{2\}}K_k(\{2\}) \cap H_{k+1} = \pi_{\{2\}}K_k(\{2\}) \cap J_k = \overline{k} \times \overline{6-k}.$$

Consequently, I is reducible.

Example 7.24. If $E = \{\{1,2\},\{2,3\},\{3,4\}\}$ and $I = \overline{2} \times [\overline{2} \times \overline{2} - \overline{1} \times \overline{1}] \times \overline{2}$, then E is decomposable and I is reducible. In this example, $I = J_1 \cup J_2$, where $J_1 = \overline{2} \times \overline{2} \times \{2\} \times \overline{2}$ and $J_2 = \overline{2} \times \{2\} \times \overline{2} \times \overline{2}$. Thus $H_2 = \overline{2} \times \overline{2} \times \{2\} \times \overline{2}$, $G_2 = \overline{2} \times \{2\} \times \{2\} \times \overline{2} = J_1 \cap J_2$, and $K_2 = \overline{2} \times \{2\} \times \{1\} \times \overline{2}$.

To verify that (7.99) and (7.100) hold, observe that $F(E) = \{\{2\},\{3\},\phi\}$, $d(\{2\},E) = d(\{3\},E) = 1$ and $d(\phi,E) = 0$. Symmetry considerations show that only $\{2\}$ need be examined. Since $\rho_{J_2}N_{\{2\}} = \text{span}\ \{\rho_{J_2}\underline{\nu}(\{2\},2)\}$, $\tau^I_{J_2}\rho_{J_2}N_{\{2\}} = \text{span}\ \{\rho\underline{\nu}(\{2\},2)\}$, which is included in $\rho M(E)$. Therefore (7.100) holds for $k = 2$. Similarly, $\rho_{G_2}N_{\{2\}} = \text{span}\ \{\rho_{G_2}\underline{\nu}(\{2\},2)\}$. Since $\rho_{G_2}\underline{\nu}(\{2\},2) = \rho_{G_2}\underline{\nu}(\{2,3\},\langle 2,2\rangle)$, $\tau^I_{G_2}\rho_{G_2}N_{\{2\}} = \text{span}\ \{\rho\underline{\nu}(\{2,3\},\langle 2,2\rangle)\}$, which is included in $\rho M(E)$. Thus (7.99) also holds.

Since $K_2(\{1,2\}) = \overline{2} \times \{2\}$, $K_2(\{2,3\}) = \{2\} \times \{1\}$, and $K_2(\{3,4\}) = \{1\} \times \overline{2}$,

$$\pi_{\{1,2\}}K_2(\{1,2\}) \cap I = \pi_{\{1,2\}}K_2(\{1,2\}) = \overline{2} \times \{2\} \times \overline{2} \times \overline{2},$$

$$\pi_{\{2,3\}}K_2(\{2,3\}) \cap I = \pi_{\{2,3\}}K_2(\{2,3\}) = \overline{2} \times \{2\} \times \{1\} \times \overline{2},$$

and

$$\pi_{\{3,4\}}K_2(\{3,4\}) \cap I = \pi_{\{3,4\}}K_2(\{3,4\}) = \overline{2} \times \{2\} \times \{1\} \times \overline{2}.$$

Therefore, I is E-reducible.

Example 7.25. If $\mathcal{E}$ consists of a single element E, then $F(\mathcal{E}) = \phi$, and (7.99) and (7.100) are trivial. By (7.38) and (7.39), if $J \in \mathcal{J}$, then $J \subset \pi_E^{-1}\underline{\bar{i}} \cap I$ for some $\underline{\bar{i}} \in I(E)$. If $J_{k_1} \in \mathcal{J}$ and $J_{k_2} \in \mathcal{J}$ are both in $\pi_E^{-1}\underline{\bar{i}} \cap I$ and $k_1 < k_2$, then (7.101) implies that $J_{k_1} \subset J_{k_2}$, a contradiction. Thus each $J \in \mathcal{J}$ satisfies $J = \pi_E^{-1}\underline{\bar{i}} \cap I$ for some $\underline{\bar{i}} \in I(E)$. The elements of $\mathcal{J}$ are disjoint, and Lemma 7.5 implies that $\tau_J^I \rho_J M(\mathcal{E}) \subset M(\mathcal{E})$ if $J \in \mathcal{J}$.

Example 7.26. Goodman (1965, 1968, 1969) has considered a quasi-independence model for analysis of 3 x 3 social-mobility tables in which diagonal cells are not present. Thus

$$(7.109)\qquad \underline{n} = \begin{array}{|ccc|} - & n_{12} & n_{13} \\ n_{21} & - & n_{23} \\ n_{31} & n_{32} & - \end{array}\ ,$$

$\mathcal{E} = \{\{1\},\{2\}\}$, and $I = \bar{3} \times \bar{3} - \{<1,1>,<2,2>,<3,3>\}$. The elements of $\mathcal{J}$ are $\{<1,2>,<1,3>\}$, $\{<2,1>,<2,3>\}$, $\{<3,1>,<3,2>\}$, $\{<2,1>,<3,1>\}$, $\{<1,2>,<3,2>\}$, and $\{<1,3>,<2,3>\}$. Since $\cup(\mathcal{J})$ has six elements and $\mathcal{J}$ has six sets, none of which has more than two elements, Lemma 5.12 implies that $\mathcal{J}$ is not decomposable. Therefore, $\underline{n}$ is not reducible.

If I is reducible, then a closed-form expression for $\hat{\underline{m}}(\underline{n},I,\mathcal{E})$ is available. Theorem 7.2 provides the procedure required to determine such an expression.

THEOREM 7.2. *Suppose that* $\mathcal{E}$ *is decomposable and* I *is reducible relative to* $\mathcal{E}$. *If* j_k, J_k, H_k, *and* K_k *are defined as in Definition 7.2, then the maximum-likelihood estimate* $\hat{\underline{m}}(\underline{n},I,\mathcal{E})$ *exists if and only if* $n^E_{\underline{\bar{i}}}(I) > 0$ *for all* $\underline{\bar{i}} \in I(E)$ *and* $E \in \mathcal{E}$ *and* $n^F_{\underline{\bar{i}}}(G_k) > 0$ *for all* $\underline{\bar{i}} \in G_k(F)$, $F \in F(\mathcal{E})$, *such that* $d(F,\mathcal{E}) > 0$ *and* $k \in \bar{\ell} - \bar{1}$. *If* $\hat{\underline{m}}(\underline{n},I,\mathcal{E})$ *exists, then* $\hat{\underline{m}}(\underline{n},I,\mathcal{E}) = \underline{m}^{(0)}$, *where* $\{\underline{m}^{(k)}: k \in \bar{\ell}\}$ *satisfies the relationships* $\underline{m}^{(\ell)} = \underline{n}$,

$$(7.110)\qquad m_{\underline{i}}^{(k-1)} = m_{\underline{i}}^{(k)}$$

for all $\underline{i} \in I - J_k$, *and*

$$(7.111)\qquad m_{\underline{i}}^{(k-1)} = \hat{m}_{\underline{i}}(\rho^I_{J_k}\underline{m}^{(k)}, J_k, \mathcal{E})$$

$$= \frac{\prod_{E\in\mathcal{E}} [m^{(k)}]^E_{\pi_E\underline{i}}(J_k)}{\prod_{F\in F(\mathcal{E})} \{[m^{(k)}]^F_{\pi_F\underline{i}}(J_k)\}^{d(F,\mathcal{E})}} \prod_{j\in D(E)} \frac{1}{r_{jk}}$$

for all $\underline{i} \in J_k$, *where for each* $k \in \bar{\ell}$, $J_k = \prod_{j=1}^{d} A_{jk}$, *and for each* $j \in \bar{d}$, $A_{jk} \subset \bar{r}_j$ *has* r_{jk} *elements.*

If $K_1 = J_1$ *and for some* $k \in \bar{\ell}$, $\underline{i} \in K_k$, *then*

(7.112) $\hat{m}_{\underline{i}}(\underline{n}, I, \mathcal{E})$

$$= \frac{\prod_{E \in \mathcal{E}} n^{E}_{\pi_E \underline{i}}(I)}{\prod_{F \in \mathcal{F}(\mathcal{E})} [n^{F}_{\pi_F \underline{i}}(J_k)]^{d(F,\mathcal{E})}} \left\{ \prod_{k' \in T(\underline{i})} \prod_{F \in \mathcal{F}(\mathcal{E})} [n^{F}_{\pi_F \underline{i}}(G_{k'}) / n^{F}_{\pi_F \underline{i}}(J_{k'})]^{d(F,\mathcal{E})} \right\} \prod_{j \in D(\mathcal{E})} \frac{1}{r_{jk}}$$

$$= \frac{\prod_{E \in \mathcal{E}} n^{E}_{\pi_E \underline{i}}(I)}{\prod_{F \in \mathcal{F}(\mathcal{E})} \left\{ \prod_{J \in \mathcal{J}} [n^{F}_{\pi_F \underline{i}}(J)]^{\chi_J(\underline{i})} \Big/ \prod_{G \in \mathcal{F}(\mathcal{J})} [n^{F}_{\pi_F \underline{i}}(G)]^{\chi_G(\underline{i}) d(G,\mathcal{J})} \right\}^{d(F,\mathcal{E})}} \prod_{j \in D(\mathcal{E})} \frac{1}{r_{jk}},$$

where $T(\underline{i}) = \{k' \in \bar{\ell}: \underline{i} \in J_{k'}\}$.

Remarks. In (7.111), $\hat{\underline{m}}(\rho^{I}_{J_k} \underline{m}^{(k)}, J_k, \mathcal{E})$ may be an extended maximum-likelihood estimate (see Appendix B and chapter 4). The condition $n^{F}_{\underline{i}}(G_k) > 0$ for $\underline{i} \in G_k(F)$ is vacuous if $G_k = \phi$ since $G_k(F)$ is then ϕ. The theorem remains valid if $\mathcal{J}$ satisfies all conditions in Definition 7.2 but $\mathcal{J}$ is not the class of maximal hyperblocks, provided $\mathcal{J}$ is a class of hyperblocks with union I.

Proof. If for some $\underline{i} \in I(E)$ and $E \in \mathcal{E}$, $n^{E}_{\underline{i}}(I) = (\underline{n}, \rho\underline{\nu}(E, \underline{i})) = 0$, then since $-\rho\underline{\nu}(E,\underline{i}) \in \rho M(\mathcal{E})$, $-\rho\underline{\nu}(E,\underline{i}) \neq \underline{0}$, and all elements of this vector are nonpositive, Theorem 2.3 implies that the maximum-likelihood estimate does not exist. Similarly, if for some $\underline{i} \in G_k(F)$, $F \in \mathcal{F}(\mathcal{E})$, $d(F,\mathcal{E}) > 0$, and $k \in \bar{\ell} - T$, $n^{F}_{\underline{i}}(J_k) = (\underline{n}, \tau^{I}_{G_k} \rho_{G_k} \underline{\nu}(F,\underline{i})) = 0$, then since $-\tau^{I}_{G_k} \rho_{G_k} \underline{\nu}(F,\underline{i})$ is a nonzero vector with nonpositive elements which is an element of $\tau^{I}_{G_k} \rho_{G_k} N_F$, a submanifold of $\rho M(\mathcal{E})$, Theorem 2.3 implies that the maximum-likelihood estimate does not exist. Thus the conditions are necessary.

On the other hand, if $n^{E}_{\underline{i}}(I) > 0$ for each $\underline{i} \in I(E)$ and $E \in \mathcal{E}$ and $n^{F}_{\underline{i}}(G_k) > 0$ for each $\underline{i} \in G_k(F)$, $F \in \mathcal{F}(\mathcal{E})$ such that $d(F,\mathcal{E}) > 0$, and $k \in \bar{\ell} - T$, then $n^{F}_{\underline{i}}(J_k) > 0$ for each $\underline{i} \in G_k(F)$, $F \in \mathcal{F}(\mathcal{E})$ such that $d(F,\mathcal{E}) > 0$, and $k \in \bar{\ell}$, and a simple induction shows that for each $k \in \bar{\ell} \cup \{0\}$, $[m^{(k)}]^{E}_{\underline{i}}(I) = n^{E}_{\underline{i}}(I)$ for any $\underline{i} \in I(E)$ and $E \in \mathcal{E}$; while for each $F \in \mathcal{F}(\mathcal{E})$ such that $d(F,\mathcal{E}) > 0$, $[m^{(k)}]^{F}_{\underline{i}}(G_{k'}) = n^{F}_{\underline{i}}(G_{k'}) > 0$ for each $\underline{i} \in G_{k'}(F)$ and $k' \in \bar{\ell} - T$, and $[m^{(k)}]^{F}_{\underline{i}}(J_{k'}) = n^{F}_{\underline{i}}(J_{k'}) > 0$ for $\underline{i} \in J_{k'}(F)$ and $k' \in \bar{\ell}$. The induction hypothesis clearly holds if $k = \ell$. If it holds for some $k > 0$, then (7.110) and (7.111) imply that for each $\underline{i} \in I(E)$ and $E \in \mathcal{E}$,

$$[m^{(k-1)}]^E_{\underline{i}}(I - J_k) = [m^{(k)}]^E_{\underline{i}}(I - J_k) \tag{7.113}$$

and

$$[m^{(k-1)}]^E_{\underline{i}}(J_k) = [m^{(k)}]^E_{\underline{i}}(J_k). \tag{7.114}$$

Thus

$$[m^{(k-1)}]^G_{\underline{i}}(I) = [m^{(k)}]^E_{\underline{i}}(I) = n^E_{\underline{i}}(I). \tag{7.115}$$

Since $\rho M(E) = \text{span}\,\{\rho\underline{\nu}(E,\underline{I}): \underline{I} \in I(E),\ E \in \mathcal{E}\}$, $P_{\rho M(E)}\underline{m}^{(k-1)} = P_{\rho M(E)}\underline{n}$. Furthermore, since $\tau^I_{G_{k'}}\rho_{G_{k'}}\underline{\nu}(F,\underline{I}) \in \rho M(E)$ if $\underline{I} \in G_{k'}(F)$, $F \in F(E)$, $d(F,E) > 0$, and $k' \in \bar{\ell} - \bar{T}$, $[m^{(k-1)}]^F_{\underline{i}}(G_{k'}) = [m^{(k)}]^F_{\underline{i}}(G_{k'}) = n^F_{\underline{i}}(G_{k'})$. A similar argument applies to $[m^{(k)}]^F_{\underline{i}}(J_{k'})$. Thus the induction hypothesis holds for $k - 1$. Therefore the hypothesis holds for all $k \in \bar{\ell} \cup \{0\}$ and $\underline{m}^{(0)}$ satisfies all marginal restraints on $\hat{\underline{m}}(\underline{n},I,E)$.

To show that $\hat{\underline{m}}(\underline{n},I,E) = \underline{m}^{(0)}$, it is now sufficient to demonstrate that $\underline{\mu}^{(0)} = \{\log m^{(0)}_{\underline{i}}\} \in \rho M(E)$. To do so, observe that $I = \bigcup^{\ell}_{k=1} K_k$. If $\underline{i} \in K_k$ for some $k \in \bar{\ell}$, then $m^{(k')}_{\underline{i}} = m^{(k-1)}_{\underline{i}}$ for any $k' < k$. Since $[m^{(1)}]^F_{\underline{i}}(J_k) = n^F_{\underline{i}}(J_k)$ if $i \in J_k(F)$ and $F \in F(E)$ and $\pi_E K_k(E) \cap H_{k+1} = \pi_E K_k(E) \cap J_k$ if $E \in \mathcal{E}$, it follows that

$$m^{(1)}_{\underline{i}} = \frac{\prod_{E\in\mathcal{E}} [m^{(k)}]^E_{\pi_E\underline{i}}(H_{k+1})}{\prod_{F\in F(E)} [n^F_{\pi_F\underline{i}}(J_k)]^{d(F,E)}} \prod_{j\in D(E)} \frac{1}{r_{jk}}\ . \tag{7.116}$$

If $k' > k$, then (7.111) implies that $\{\log m^{(k'-1)}_{\underline{i}}: \underline{i} \in J_{k'}\} \in M(J_{k'},E)$ and $\{\log m^{(k'-1)}_{\underline{i}}: \underline{i} \in G_{k'}\} \in M(G_{k'},E)$. Therefore, if $\underline{i} \in K_k \cap J_{k'}$, then

$$m^{(k'-1)}_{\underline{i}} = \frac{\prod_{E\in\mathcal{E}} [m^{(k')}]^E_{\pi_E\underline{i}}(J_{k'})}{\prod_{F\in F(E)} [n^F_{\pi_F\underline{i}}(J_{k'})]^{d(F,E)}} \prod_{j\in D(E)} \frac{1}{r_{jk'}} \tag{7.117}$$

$$= \frac{\prod_{E\in\mathcal{E}} [m^{(k'-1)}]^E_{\pi_E\underline{i}}(G_{k'})}{\prod_{F\in F(E)} [n^F_{\pi_F\underline{i}}(G_{k'})]^{d(F,E)}} \prod_{j\in D(E)} \frac{1}{r_{jk'}}\ .$$

To verify (7.117), note that if $\underline{i} \in K_k \cap J_{k'}$, then $\underline{i} \in G_{k'}$. By Example 7.25, E must contain more than one element. Thus $F(E)$ is not empty, and (7.100) implies that $G_{k'} = \prod_{j=1}^{d} B_{jk}$, where $B_{jk} \subset A_{jk}$ and $B_{jk} = A_{jk}$ if $j \in D(E)$. Otherwise, $\underline{\mu} \in \rho M(E)$ would exist such that $\mu_{\underline{i}}$ depended on indices i_j, where $j \in D(E)$. If $\underline{i} \in \pi_E^{-1} K_{k'}(E) \cap J_{k'}$, then $[m^{(k')}]^E_{\pi_E \underline{i}}(J_{k'}) = [m^{(k')}]^E_{\pi_E \underline{i}}(H_{k'+1})$ and $[m^{(k'-1)}]^E_{\pi_E \underline{i}}(G_{k'}) = [m^{(k'-1)}]^E_{\pi_E \underline{i}}(G_{k'})$. Otherwise, $[m^{(k'-1)}]^E_{\pi_E \underline{i}}(G_{k'}) = [m^{(k')}]^E_{\pi_E \underline{i}}(J_{k'})$ and $[m^{(k'-1)}]^E_{\pi_E \underline{i}}(H_{k'}) = [m^{(k')}]^E_{\pi_E \underline{i}}(H_{k'+1})$. Consequently,

(7.118)
$$\prod_{E \in \mathcal{E}} [m^{(k'-1)}]^E_{\pi_E \underline{i}}(H_{k'})$$
$$= [\prod_{E \in \mathcal{E}} [m^{(k')}]^E_{\pi_E \underline{i}}(H_{k'+1})] \{\prod_{F \in F(\mathcal{E})} [n^F_{\pi_F \underline{i}}(G_{k'})/n^F_{\pi_F \underline{i}}(J_{k'})]^{d(F,\mathcal{E})}\}.$$

A simple induction shows that

(7.119)
$$\prod_{E \in \mathcal{E}} [m^{(k)}]^E_{\pi_E \underline{i}}(H_{k+1})$$
$$= [\prod_{E \in \mathcal{E}} n^E_{\pi_E \underline{i}}(I)] \prod_{k' \in T(\underline{i})} \{\prod_{F \in F(\mathcal{E})} [n^F_{\pi_F \underline{i}}(G_{k'})/n^F_{\pi_F \underline{i}}(J_{k'})]^{d(F,\mathcal{E})}\}.$$

Thus (7.116) implies that

(7.120)
$$m_{\underline{i}}^{(0)} = \frac{\prod_{E \in \mathcal{E}} n^E_{\pi_E \underline{i}}(I)}{\prod_{F \in F(\mathcal{E})} [n^F_{\pi_F \underline{i}}(J_k)]^{d(F,\mathcal{E})}}$$
$$\times \prod_{k' \in T(\underline{i})} \{\prod_{F \in F(\mathcal{E})} [n^F_{\pi_F \underline{i}}(G_{k'})/n^F_{\pi_F \underline{i}}(J_{k'})]^{d(F,\mathcal{E})}\} \prod_{j \in D(\mathcal{E})} \frac{1}{r_{jk}} .$$

Thus

(7.121)
$$\{\log m_{\underline{i}}^{(0)} : \underline{i} \in I\}$$
$$= \sum_{E \in \mathcal{E}} \{\log [n^E_{\pi_E \underline{i}}(I)] : \underline{i} \in I\}$$
$$+ \sum_{k'=1}^{\ell} (\log \prod_{j \in D(\mathcal{E})} r_{jk'}) \tau^I_{G_k} \rho_{G_{k'}} \{1 : \underline{i} \in I\}$$
$$- \sum_{k'=1}^{\ell} (\log \prod_{j \in D(\mathcal{E})} r_{jk'}) \tau^I_{J_{k'}} \rho_{J_{k'}} \{1 : \underline{i} \in I\}$$

$$- \sum_{F \in F(E)} d(F,E) \{ \sum_{k'=1} [\tau^I_{J_{k'}} \{\log [n^F_{\pi_F \underline{i}}(J_{k'})]: \underline{i} \in J_{k'}\}$$

$$- \tau^I_{G_{k'}} \{\log [n^F_{\pi_F \underline{i}}(G_{k'})]: \underline{i} \in G_{k'}\}]\} .$$

By (7.99) and (7.100), $\{\log m^{(0)}_{\underline{i}}: \underline{i} \in I\} \in \rho M(E)$ if $F(E)$ is not empty. If $F(E)$ is empty, the same conclusion is a consequence of Example 7.25. The last equation of (7.112) follows since $d(G,J)$ is the number of $k \in \overline{\ell} - \overline{T}$ such that $G = G_k$. ||

Example 7.27. In Example 7.23, the maximum-likelihood estimate exists if and only if $n_{i+}(I) > 0$ for $i \in \overline{5}$, if $n_{+j}(I) > 0$ for $j \in \overline{5}$, and $n_{++}(\overline{k - 1} \times \overline{6 - k}) = \sum_{i=1}^{k-1} \sum_{j=1}^{6-k} n_{ij} > 0$ for $k \in \overline{5} - \overline{1}$. If these conditions are satisfied, as they are in table 7.10, then

(7.122) $$m^{(k-1)}_{ij} = m^{(k)}_{ij}$$

if $i > k$ or $j > 6 - k$ and

(7.123) $$m^{(k-1)}_{ij} = [m^{(k)}_{i+}(\overline{k} \times \overline{6 - k})][m^{(k)}_{+j}(\overline{k} \times \overline{6 - k})]/m^{(k)}_{++}(\overline{k} \times \overline{6 - k})$$

$$= (\sum_{j=1}^{6-k} m^{(k)}_{ij}) (\sum_{i=1}^{k} m^{(k)}_{ij}) / \sum_{i=1}^{k} \sum_{j=1}^{6-k} m^{(k)}_{ij}$$

if $i \in \overline{k}$ and $j \in \overline{6 - k}$. This algorithm coincides with that of Bishop and Fienberg. Since $\underline{m}^{(5)} = \underline{m}^{(4)}$ and $\underline{m}^{(1)} = \underline{m}^{(0)}$, only $\underline{m}^{(3)}$, $\underline{m}^{(2)}$, and $\underline{m}^{(1)}$ must be found. One has

(7.124) $\underline{m}^{(3)} =$

13.92	20.08	12	15	8
7.92	11.08	4	1	-
4.17	5.83	4	-	-
3.75	5.25	-	-	-
5	-	-	-	-

,

(7.125) $\underline{m}^{(2)} =$

14.55	20.37	11.08	15	8
7.27	10.18	5.54	1	-
4.43	6.20	3.37	-	-
3.75	5.25	-	-	-
5	-	-	-	-

,

and

(7.126) $\underline{m}^{(1)}$

15.66	21.92	11.94	11.48	8
6.16	8.63	4.69	4.52	-
4.43	6.20	3.37	-	-
3.75	5.25	-	-	-
5	-	-	-	-

If (7.112) is used to find $\hat{m}(\underline{n},I,E)$, then a formula due to Goodman (1968) is obtained. Since $T\langle i,j\rangle = \{k: i < k \leq 6 - j\}$,

$$(7.127) \qquad \hat{m}_{ij}(\underline{n},I,E) = \frac{n_{i+}(I)n_{+j}(I)}{n_{++}(\overline{i} \times \overline{6-i})} \prod_{k=i+1}^{6-j} \left[\frac{n_{++}(\overline{k-1} \times \overline{6-k})}{n_{++}(\overline{k} \times \overline{6-k})}\right]$$

$$= \frac{\left[\sum_{j'=1}^{6-i} n_{ij'}\right]\left[\sum_{i'=1}^{6-j} n_{i'j}\right]}{\sum_{i'=1}^{i} \sum_{j'=1}^{6-i} n_{i'j'}} \prod_{k=i+1}^{6-j} \left[\sum_{i'=1}^{k-1} \sum_{j'=1}^{6-k} n_{i'j'} \Big/ \sum_{i'=1}^{k} \sum_{j'=1}^{6-k} n_{i'j'}\right].$$

The formula in Goodman (1968) is expressed somewhat differently, but the expression given there is equivalent to (7.127). As an example of the use of this formula, consider $\hat{m}_{32}(\underline{n},I,E)$. In this case, $6 - i = 3$ and $i + 1 = 6 - j = 4$. Thus $\sum_{j'=1}^{3} n_{ij'} = 14$, $\sum_{i'=1}^{4} n_{i'j} = 42$, $\sum_{i'=1}^{3} \sum_{j'=1}^{3} n_{i'j'} = 83$, $\sum_{i'=1}^{3} \sum_{j'=1}^{2} n_{i'j'} = 63$, and $\sum_{i'=1}^{4} \sum_{j'=1}^{2} n_{i'j'} = 72$. Therefore,

$$(7.128) \qquad \hat{m}_{32}(\underline{n},I,E) = \frac{(14)(42)}{83}\left(\frac{63}{72}\right)$$

$$= 6.20.$$

Example 7.28. In Example 7.24, the maximum-likelihood estimate exists if and only if $n_{i_1i_2++}(I) > 0$ for $\langle i_1,i_2\rangle \in \overline{2} \times \overline{2}$, $n_{+i_2i_3+}(I) > 0$ for $\langle i_2,i_3\rangle \in \overline{2} \times \overline{2} - \overline{1} \times \overline{1}$, and $n_{++i_3i_4}(I) > 0$ for $\langle i_3,i_4\rangle \in \overline{2} \times \overline{2}$. It should be noted that $n_{+2++}(G_2) = n_{++3+}(G_2) = n_{+23+}(I)$, so that the conditions related to the F-marginal totals for $F \in F(E)$ hold automatically if the conditions on the E-marginal totals are satisfied for all $E \in E$. If $\hat{m}(\underline{n},I,E)$ exists, then (7.110) and (7.111) imply that if $i_1 \in \overline{2}$, $i_3 \in \overline{2}$, and $i_4 \in \overline{2}$, then

(7.129)
$$m^{(1)}_{i_12i_3i_4} = \frac{n_{i_12++}(J_2)\, n_{+2i_3+}(J_2)\, n_{++i_3i_4}(J_2)}{n_{+2++}(J_2)\, n_{++i_3+}(J_2)}$$
$$= \frac{\left(\sum_{k=1}^{2}\sum_{\ell=1}^{2} n_{i_12k\ell}\right)\left(\sum_{i=1}^{2}\sum_{\ell=1}^{2} n_{i2i_3\ell}\right)\left(\sum_{i=1}^{2} n_{i2i_3i_4}\right)}{\left(\sum_{i=1}^{2}\sum_{k=1}^{2}\sum_{\ell=1}^{2} n_{i2k\ell}\right)\left(\sum_{i=1}^{2}\sum_{\ell=1}^{2} n_{i2i_3\ell}\right)}$$
$$= \frac{\left(\sum_{k=1}^{2}\sum_{\ell=1}^{2} n_{i_12k\ell}\right)\left(\sum_{i=1}^{2} n_{i2i_3i_4}\right)}{\sum_{i=1}^{2}\sum_{k=1}^{2}\sum_{\ell=1}^{2} n_{i2k\ell}} .$$

If $i_1 \in \overline{2}$ and $i_4 \in \overline{2}$, then $m^{(1)}_{i_1+2i_4} = n_{i_112i_4}$. Similarly, $m^{(0)}_{i_121i_4} = m^{(1)}_{i_121i_4}$ if $i_1 \in \overline{2}$ and $i_4 \in \overline{2}$, while

(7.130)
$$m^{(0)}_{i_1i_22i_4} = \frac{\left(\sum_{i=1}^{2}\sum_{j=1}^{2} m^{(1)}_{ij2i_4}\right)\left(\sum_{\ell=1}^{2} m^{(1)}_{i_1i_22\ell}\right)}{\sum_{i=1}^{2}\sum_{j=1}^{2}\sum_{\ell=1}^{2} m^{(1)}_{ij2\ell}}$$

if $i_1 \in \overline{2}$, $i_2 \in \overline{2}$, and $i_4 \in \overline{2}$. Some simplification is possible since $\sum_{i=1}^{2}\sum_{j=1}^{2}\sum_{\ell=1}^{2} m^{(1)}_{ij2\ell} = \sum_{i=1}^{2}\sum_{j=1}^{2}\sum_{\ell=1}^{2} n_{ij2\ell}$, $\sum_{i=1}^{2}\sum_{j=1}^{2} m^{(1)}_{ij2i_4} = \sum_{i=1}^{2}\sum_{j=1}^{2} n_{ij2i_4}$ for $i_4 \in \overline{2}$, $\sum_{\ell=1}^{2} m^{(1)}_{i_112\ell} = \sum_{\ell=1}^{2} n_{i_112\ell}$ for $i_1 \in \overline{2}$, and

(7.131)
$$\sum_{\ell=1}^{2} m^{(1)}_{i_122\ell} = \frac{\left(\sum_{k=1}^{2}\sum_{\ell=1}^{2} n_{i_12k\ell}\right)\left(\sum_{i=1}^{2}\sum_{\ell=1}^{2} n_{i22\ell}\right)}{\sum_{i=1}^{2}\sum_{k=1}^{2}\sum_{\ell=1}^{2} n_{i2k\ell}}$$

for $i_1 \in \overline{2}$. Thus for $i_1 \in \overline{2}$ and $i_4 \in \overline{2}$,

(7.132)
$$\hat{m}_{i_121i_4}(\underline{n},I,E) = \frac{\left(\sum_{k=1}^{2}\sum_{\ell=1}^{2} n_{i_12k\ell}\right)\left(\sum_{i=1}^{2} n_{i21i_4}\right)}{\sum_{i=1}^{2}\sum_{k=1}^{2}\sum_{\ell=1}^{2} n_{i2k\ell}} ,$$

(7.133)
$$\hat{m}_{i_122i_4}(\underline{n},I,E) = \frac{\left(\sum_{k=1}^{2}\sum_{\ell=1}^{2} n_{i_12k\ell}\right)\left(\sum_{i=1}^{2}\sum_{\ell=1}^{2} n_{i22\ell}\right)\left(\sum_{i=1}^{2}\sum_{j=1}^{2} n_{ij2i_4}\right)}{\left(\sum_{i=1}^{2}\sum_{j=1}^{2}\sum_{\ell=1}^{2} n_{ij2\ell}\right)\left(\sum_{i=1}^{2}\sum_{k=1}^{2}\sum_{\ell=1}^{2} n_{i2k\ell}\right)} ,$$

and

$$(7.134)\qquad \hat{m}_{i_1 1 2 i_4}(\underline{n},I,E) = \frac{\left(\sum_{i=1}^{2}\sum_{j=1}^{2} n_{ij2i_4}\right)\left(\sum_{\ell=1}^{2} n_{i_1 22\ell}\right)}{\sum_{i=1}^{2}\sum_{j=1}^{2}\sum_{\ell=1}^{2} n_{ij2\ell}}$$

These formulas can be derived from (7.112) by noting that $T\langle i_1,i_2,i_3,i_4\rangle = \phi$ if $i_2 \neq i$ and $T\langle i_1,2,2,i_4\rangle = \{2\}$ if $i_1 \in \overline{2}$ and $i_4 \in \overline{2}$. Thus (7.132) and (7.134) are derived as in (7.129). To derive (7.133), one observes that $n_{++2+}(G_2) = n_{++2+}(J_2)$ and $d(\phi,E) = 0$. Therefore,

$$(7.135)\qquad \hat{m}_{i_1 22 i_4}(\underline{n},I,E) = \hat{m}_{i_1 22 i_4}(\rho^I_{J_2}\underline{n},J_2,E)\,\frac{n_{+2++}(G_2)}{n_{+2++}(J_2)}$$

$$= \frac{\left(\sum_{i=1}^{2}\sum_{j=1}^{2} n_{ij2i_4}\right)\left(\sum_{\ell=1}^{2} n_{i_1 22\ell}\right)}{\sum_{i=1}^{2}\sum_{j=1}^{2}\sum_{\ell=1}^{2} n_{ij2\ell}} \quad \frac{\left(\sum_{i=1}^{2}\sum_{\ell=1}^{2} n_{i22\ell}\right)}{\sum_{i=1}^{2}\sum_{k=1}^{2}\sum_{\ell=1}^{2} n_{i2k\ell}} .$$

A number of other examples of closed-form estimates are given in Goodman (1968) for quasi-independence models of incomplete two-way tables. In such tables, I is reducible if and only if J is decomposable. The necessity of this condition follows immediately from Definition 7.2. That the condition is sufficient is a consequence of the following lemmas.

LEMMA 7.7. *Suppose* $E = \{\{1\},\{2\}\}$, $I \subset \overline{r} \times \overline{c}$, *and* J *is decomposable. If* $J = \{J_k : k \in \overline{\ell}\}$, *where for each* $k \in \overline{\ell} - \overline{1}$, *there exists* $h_k \in \overline{k-1}$ *such that*

$$(7.136)\qquad J_k \cap \left(\bigcup_{j=1}^{k-1} J_j\right) = J_k \cap J_{h_k}$$

$$= G_k ,$$

then for each $k \in \overline{\ell} - \overline{1}$, *either*

$$\pi^{-1}_{\{1\}}K_k(\{1\}) \cap \left(\bigcup_{j=1}^{k} J_j\right) = K_k$$

and

$$\pi^{-1}_{\{2\}}K_k(\{2\}) \cap \left(\bigcup_{j=1}^{k} J_j\right) = J_k$$

or

$$\pi^{-1}_{\{1\}}K_k(\{1\}) \cap \left(\bigcup_{j=1}^{k} J_j\right) = J_k$$

and

$$\pi^{-1}_{\{2\}}K_k(\{2\}) \cap \left(\bigcup_{j=1}^{k} J_j\right) = K_k ,$$

where

$$K_k = J_k - J_k \cap J_{h_k} .$$

Proof. Suppose $\langle i_1,i_2\rangle \in K_k$. If $\langle i_1,i_2'\rangle \in \cup_{j=1}^{k-1} J_j$, then the set $A = \{\langle i_1,i_2\rangle,\langle i_1,i_2'\rangle\} = \{i_1\} \times \{i_2,i_2'\} \in K$. Thus a smallest $k' \in \overline{\ell}$ exists such that $\{\langle i_1,i_2\rangle,\langle i_1,i_2'\rangle\} \in J_{k'}$. If $k' > k$, then

(7.137)
$$A \subset J_{k'} \cap \left(\bigcup_{j=1}^{k'-1} J_j\right) = J_{k'} \cap J_{h_k} .$$

Thus $A \subset J_{h_{k'}}$ and $h_{k'} < k'$, a contradiction. Therefore, $k' \leq k$. Since $\langle i_1,i_2\rangle \notin \cup_{j=1}^{k-1} J_j$, $k' = k$ and $A \subset J_k$. Consequently, $\pi_{\{1\}}^{-1}K_k(\{1\}) \cap (\cup_{j=1}^{k} J_j) \subset J_k$. Similarly, $\pi_{\{2\}}^{-1}K_k(\{2\}) \cap (\cup_{j=1}^{k} J_j) \subset J_k$.

If $J_k = A_{1k} \times A_{2k}$, where $A_{1k} \subset \overline{r}$ and $A_{2k} \subset \overline{c}$, then $G_k = B_{1k} \times B_{2k}$, where $B_{jk} \subset A_{jk}$ for $j \in \overline{2}$ and either $B_{1k} \neq A_{1k}$ or $B_{2k} \neq A_{2k}$. Without loss of generality, suppose that $B_{1k} \neq A_{1k}$. Then $(A_{1k} - B_{1k}) \times A_{2k} \subset K_k$ and

(7.138)
$$\begin{aligned}\pi_{\{2\}}^{-1}K_k(\{2\}) \cap \left(\bigcup_{j=1}^{k} J_j\right) &= (\overline{r} \times A_{2k}) \cap \left(\bigcup_{j=1}^{k} J_j\right)\\ &\supset (\overline{r} \times A_{2k}) \cap J_k\\ &= (\overline{r} \times A_{2k}) \cap (A_{1k} \times A_{2k})\\ &= A_{1k} \times A_{2k}\\ &= J_k .\end{aligned}$$

Therefore, $\pi_{\{2\}}^{-1}K_k(\{2\}) \cap (\cup_{j=1}^{k} J_j) = J_k$.

Consider the set $B_{1k} \times (A_{2k} \cup A_{2h_k})$. Since

(7.139)
$$\begin{aligned}B_{1k} \times (A_{2k} \cup A_{2h_k}) = (B_{1k} \times A_{2k}) \cup (B_{1k} \times A_{2h_k}) &\subset (A_{1h} \times A_{2k}) \cup (A_{1h_k} \times A_{2h_k})\\ &= J_k \cup J_{h_k} ,\end{aligned}$$

$B_{1k} \times (A_{2k} \cup A_{2h_k}) \subset I$. Thus $B_{1k} \times (A_{2k} \cup A_{2h_k}) \in K$. Let k' be the smallest index in $\overline{\ell}$ such that $B_{1k} \times (A_{2k} \cup A_{2h_k}) \in J_{k'}$. If $k' > k$, then

(7.140)
$$B_{1k} \times (A_{2k} \cup A_{2h_k}) \subset J_{k'} \cap (J_k \cup J_{h_k}) \subset J_{k'} \cap \left(\bigcup_{j=1}^{k'-1} J_j\right) = J_{k'} \cap J_{h_{k'}},$$

and $B_{1k} \times (A_{2k} \cup A_{2h_k}) \subset J_{h_{k'}}$, where $h_{k'} < k'$. This contradiction implies that $k' \leq k$. If $k' < k$, then

$$(7.141) \qquad J_k \cap \left(\bigcup_{j=1}^{k-1} J_j\right) \supset J_k \cap [B_{1k} \times (A_{2k} \cup A_{2h_k})]$$

$$= B_{1k} \times A_{2k}.$$

In this case, $B_{1k} \times A_{2k} \subset G_k$ and thus $B_{2k} = A_{2k}$. If $k' = k$, then $B_{1k} \times (A_{2k} \cup A_{2h_k}) \subset J_k$ and $A_{2h_k} \subset A_{2k}$. In this case, if $i_1 \in A_{1h_k}$ but $i_1 \notin A_{1k}$ and if $i_2 \in A_{2h_k}$, then $\langle i_1, i_2 \rangle \in J_{h_k}$, $\langle i_1, i_2 \rangle \notin J_k$, and

$$(7.142) \qquad \langle i_1, i_2 \rangle \in \pi^{-1}_{\{2\}} K_k(\{2\}) \cap \left(\bigcup_{j=1}^{k} J_j\right)$$

$$= \bar{r} \times A_{2k} \cap \left(\bigcup_{j=1}^{k} J_j\right),$$

a contradiction. Thus $A_{1h_k} \subset A_{1k}$ and $J_{h_k} \subset J_k$, a further contradiction. Thus $k' < k$ and $B_{2k} = A_{2k}$. In this case

$$(7.143) \qquad \pi^{-1}_{\{1\}} K_k(\{1\}) \cap \left(\bigcup_{j=1}^{k} J_j\right) = (A_{1k} - B_{1k}) \times A_{2k}$$

$$= K_k .$$

A similar argument shows that if $B_{1k} = A_{1k}$, then $\pi^{-1}_{\{1\}} K_k(\{1\}) \cap (\bigcup_{j=1}^{k} J_j) = K_k$ and $\pi^{-1}_{\{2\}} K_k(\{2\}) \cap (\bigcup_{j=1}^{k} J_j) = J_k$.||

LEMMA 7.8. *Under the hypotheses of* Lemma 7.7, *if* $J = A_1 \times A_2 \in \mathcal{J}$, $J^* = A_1^* \times A_2^* \in \mathcal{J}$, $J \neq J^*$, *and* $J \cap J^* \neq \phi$, *then either* $A_1 \subset A_1^*$ *and* $A_2^* \subset A_2^*$ *or* $A_1^* \subset A_1$ *and* $A_2 \subset A_2^*$.

Proof. Without loss of generality, suppose that $J_{k_1} = J$, $J_{k_2} = J^*$, and $k_1 > k_2$. Then

$$(7.144) \qquad J_{k_1} \cap \left(\bigcup_{j=1}^{k-1} J_j\right) = J_{k_1} \cap J_{h_{k_1}}$$

$$= G_{k_1}.$$

Either $B_{1k_1} \neq A_{1k_1}$ or $B_{2k_1} \neq A_{2k}$. Suppose that $B_{1k_1} \neq A_{1k_1}$. Then the set $(A_{1k} \cup A_{1k_2}) \times (A_{2k_1} \cap A_{2k_2})$ is included in $J_{k_1} \cup J_{k_2}$. This result follows in the same manner as (7.139). If k' is the smallest k' such that $(A_{1k_1} \cup A_{1k_2}) \times (A_{2k_1} \cap A_{2k_2}) \subset J_{k'}$, then the argument of (7.140) shows that $k' \leq k_1$. If $k' = k_1$, then

(7.145) $$J_{k_1} \cap (\bigcup_{j=1}^{k-1} J_j) \supset J_k \cap (A_{1k_1} \cup A_{1k_2}) \times (A_{2k_1} \cap A_{2k_2})$$

$$= A_{1k_1} \times (A_{2k_1} \cap A_{2k_2}).$$

Therefore, $B_{1k_1} = A_{1k_2}$, a contradiction. Thus $k' = k_1$ and $A_{1k_2} \subset A_{1k_1}$. Since

(7.146) $$A_{1k_2} \times (A_{2k_1} \cup A_{2k_2}) \subset (A_{1k_1} \times A_{2k_1}) \cup (A_{1k_2} \times A_{2k_2})$$

$$= J_{k1} \cup J_{k2},$$

$J_{k_2} \in \mathcal{J}$ only if $A_{2k_1} \subset A_{2k_2}$. A similar argument shows that if $B_{2k_1} \neq A_{2k_1}$, then $A_{1k_1} \subset A_{1k_1}$ and A_{2k_1} and $A_{2k_2} \subset A_{2k_2}$. ||

LEMMA 7.9. *Under the hypotheses of* Lemma 7.7, $\tau^I_{J_k} \rho_{J_k} N_\phi \subset \rho M(E)$ *for each* $k \in \bar{\ell}$ *and* $\tau^I_{G_k} \rho_{G_k} N_\phi \subset \rho M(E)$ *for each* $k \in \bar{\ell} - \bar{T}$.

Proof. The proof is by induction on ℓ. The induction hypothesis is that for any decomposable class $\mathcal{J}$ with $\ell \leq \ell_0$ elements, the vector $\tau^I_{J_k} \rho_{J_k} \underline{e} = \{\chi_{J_k}(\langle i_1, i_2\rangle)\}$ can be written

(7.147) $$\chi_{J_k}(\langle i_1, i_2\rangle) = \sum_{k'=1}^{\ell} a_{k'k}\, \chi_{C_{1k'}}(i_1) + \sum_{k'=1}^{\ell} b_{k'k}\, \chi_{C_{2k'}}(i_2)$$

for each $k \in \bar{\ell}$ and $\langle i_1, i_2\rangle \in I$, where $K_1 = J_1$ and $K_k = C_{1k} \times C_{2k}$ for each $k \in \bar{\ell}$ and $\tau^I_{G_k} \rho_{G_k} \underline{e} = \{\chi_{G_k}(\langle i_1, i_2\rangle)\}$ satisfies

(7.148) $$\chi_{G_k}(\langle i_1, i_2\rangle) = \sum_{k'=1}^{\ell} c_{k'k}\, \chi_{C_{1k'}}(i_1) + \sum_{k'=1}^{\ell} d_{k'k}\, \chi_{C_{2k'}}(i_2)$$

if $k \in \bar{\ell} - \bar{T}$ and $\langle i_1, i_2\rangle \in I$. Since $\tau^I_{J_k} \rho_{J_k} N_\phi = \text{span}\, \{\tau^I_{J_k} \rho_{J_k} \underline{e}\}$ and $\tau^I_{G_k} \rho_{G_k} N_\phi = \text{span}\, \{\tau^I_{G_k} \rho_{G_k} \underline{e}\}$, these hypotheses imply the conclusion of the lemmas.

The induction hypothesis is trivial if $\ell = 1$ since $\bar{\ell} - \bar{T}$ is vacuous and $\chi_{J_1}(\langle i_1, i_2\rangle) = \chi_{C_{11}}(i_1) = 1$ if $\langle i_1, i_2\rangle \in J_1 = C_{11} \times C_{21}$. If the hypothesis holds for $\mathcal{J}$ with $\ell \leq \ell_0$ elements and $\mathcal{J}$ has $\ell_0 + 1$ elements, then for each $k \in \bar{\ell}_0$ and $\langle i_1, i_2\rangle \in \bigcup_{j=1}^{\ell_0} J_j$, (7.147) holds for $\ell = \ell_0$, and for each $k \in \bar{\ell}_0 - \bar{T}$ and

$\langle i_1,i_2\rangle \in \bigcup_{j=1}^{\ell_0} J_j$, (7.148) holds for $0 = \ell_0$. Suppose without loss of generality that $C_{1(\ell_0+1)} \neq A_{1(\ell_0+1)}$. Then if $J_{\ell_0+1} \cap J_k \neq \phi$ for $k \in \bar{\ell}_0$, Lemma 7.8 implies that $A_{2(\ell_0+1)} \subset A_{2k}$. If $J_{\ell_0+1} \cap K_k \neq \phi$, then $A_{2(\ell_0+1)} \subset C_{2k}$. If $T_{\ell_0+1} = k \in \bar{\ell}_0$: $A_{2(\ell_0+1)} \subset C_{2k}$, $b_{(\ell_0+1)k} = 0$,

(7.149) $$a_{(\ell_0+1)k} = -\sum_{k' \in T_{\ell_0+1}} b_{k'k} ,$$

$d_{(\ell_0+1)k} = 0$, and

(7.150) $$c_{(\ell_0+1)k} = -\sum_{k' \in T_{\ell_0+1}} d_{k'k} ,$$

then (7.147) holds for $k \in \bar{\ell}_0$ and $\langle i_1,i_2\rangle \in I$ and (7.148) holds for $k \in \bar{\ell}_0 - \bar{T}$ and $\langle i_1,i_2\rangle \in I$. If $k = \ell_0 + 1$, then one may let $a_{k'k} = b_{k'k} = c_{k'k} = d_{k'k}$ if $k' \in \bar{\ell}$, $a_{kk} = 0$, $b_{kk} = 1$, $c_{kk} = -1$, and $d_{kk} = 1$. It follows from Lemma 7.7 that (7.147) and (7.148) hold for $k = \ell_0 + 1$. Thus the induction hypothesis holds for all ℓ.||

The following theorem follows immediately from these lemmas and Definition 7.2.

THEOREM 7.3. *Given the generating class* $E = \{\{1\},\{2\}\}$, $I \subset \bar{r} \times \bar{c}$ *is reducible if and only if* J *is decomposable. If* J *is decomposable, the maximum-likelihood estimate* $\hat{m}(\underline{n},I,E)$ *exists if and only if* $n_{i+}(I) > 0$ *for* $i \in I(\{1\})$, $n_{+j}(I) > 0$ *for* $j \in I(\{2\})$, *and* $n_{++}(G) > 0$ *for* $G \in F(J)$ *such that* $d(G,J) > 0$. *If* $\hat{m}(\underline{n},I,E)$ *exists, then for all* $\langle i,j\rangle \in I$,

(7.151) $$\hat{m}_{ij}(\underline{n},I,E) = n_{i+}(I)n_{+j}(I)/\{\prod_{j \in J} n_{++}(J)]^{\chi_J(i,j)} / \prod_{G \in F(J)} [n_{++}(G)]^{\chi_G(i,j)d(G,J)}\}.$$

Example 7.29. Goodman (1968) considers tables in which $\underline{n}$ has the form

(7.152) $$\underline{n} = \begin{array}{|ccc|} - & \underline{x} & \underline{v} \\ & & \\ \underline{w} & \underline{z} & - \end{array}$$

In this table, $\underline{x} = \{x_{ij}\}$, $\underline{z} = \{z_{ij}\}$, $\underline{v} = \{v_{ij}\}$, and $\underline{w} = \{w_{ij}\}$ are $r_1 \times c_2$, $r_2 \times c_2$ $r_1 \times c_3$, and $r_2 \times c_1$ arrays, where $r_1 + r_2 = r$ and $c_1 + c_2 + c_3 = c$. Thus if $E = \{\{1\},\{2\}\}$, $J = \{(\bar{r} - \bar{r}_1) \times \overline{c_1 + c_2}, \bar{r} \times (\overline{c_1 + c_2} - \bar{c}_1), \bar{r}_1 \times (\bar{c} - \bar{c}_1)\}$. This class is decomposable, with $F(J) = \{\phi, \bar{r}_1 \times (\overline{c_1 + c_2} - \bar{c}_1), \bar{r}_2 \times (\overline{c_1 + c_2} - \bar{c}_1)\}$, $d(\phi,J) = 0$, and $d(\bar{r}_1 \times (\overline{c_1 + c_2} - \bar{c}_1),J) = d(\bar{r}_2 \times (\overline{c_1 + c_2} - \bar{c}_1),J) = 1$. Thus if

(7.153)
$$\hat{\underline{m}}(\underline{n},I,E) = \begin{array}{|ccc|} - & \hat{\underline{x}} & \hat{\underline{v}} \\ & & \\ \hat{\underline{w}} & \hat{\underline{z}} & - \end{array} ,$$

then

(7.154)
$$\hat{v}_{ij} = \frac{(x_{i+} + v_{i+})\, v_{+j}}{x_{++} + v_{++}} ,$$

(7.155)
$$\hat{w}_{ij} = \frac{(w_{i+} + z_{i+})\, w_{+j}}{w_{++} + z_{++}} ,$$

(7.156)
$$\hat{x}_{ij} = \frac{(x_{i+} + v_{i+})(x_{+j} + z_{+j})x_{++}}{(x_{++} + v_{++})(x_{++} + z_{++})} ,$$

and

(7.157)
$$\hat{z}_{ij} = \frac{(w_{i+} + z_{i+})(x_{+j} + z_{+j})z_{++}}{(w_{++} + z_{++})(x_{++} + z_{++})} .$$

Theorem 7.3 may be generalized without difficulty to the case in which $E = \{E_1,E_2\}$ and for $k \in \overline{2}$, $E_k \cup \{j_k\} = \overline{d}$ for some $j_k \in \overline{d}$. Lemmas corresponding to Lemmas 7.7, 7.8, and 7.9 can be proven with only minor modifications in the previous arguments. The following theorem summarizes these results.

THEOREM 7.4. *Given a generating class* $E = \{E_1,E_2\}$ *such that* $E_1 \cup \{j_1\} = E_2 \cup \{j_2\} = \overline{d}$, $I \subset \prod_{j=1}^{d} \overline{r}_j$, *and* $F = E_1 \cap E_2$, *then* I *is reducible if and only if* J *is decomposable. If* J *is decomposable, the maximum-likelihood estimate* $\hat{\underline{m}}(\underline{n},I,E)$ *exists if and only if* $n_{\overline{i}}^{E_k}(I) > 0$ *for* $\overline{i} \in I(E_k)$ *and* $k \in \overline{2}$ *and* $n_{\overline{i}}^{F}(G) > 0$ *for* $\overline{i} \in G(F)$ *and* G *such that* $d(G,J) > 0$; *and if* $\hat{\underline{m}}(\underline{n},I,E)$ *exists, then for* $\underline{i} \in I$,

(7.158)
$$m_{\underline{i}}(\underline{n},I,E) = n_{\pi_{E_1}\underline{i}}^{E_1}(I)\, n_{\pi_{E_2}\underline{i}}^{E_2}(I) /$$
$$\{\prod_{j \in J} [n_{\pi_F \underline{i}}^{F}(J)]^{\chi_J(\underline{i})} / \prod_{G \in F(J)} [n_{\pi_F \underline{i}}^{F}(G)]^{d(G,J)\chi_G(\underline{i})}\} .$$

Example 7.30. If $E = \{\{1,3\},\{2,3\}\}$ and

(7.159)
$$\underline{n} = \begin{array}{|ccc|} - & n_{121} & n_{131} \\ n_{211} & n_{221} & n_{231} \\ n_{311} & n_{321} & n_{331} \end{array} \quad \begin{array}{|ccc|} n_{112} & n_{122} & n_{132} \\ n_{212} & n_{222} & n_{232} \\ n_{312} & n_{322} & - \end{array} ,$$

then $F(E) = \{\{3\}\}$, $J_1 = \{2,3\} \times \overline{3} \times \{1\}$, $J_2 = \overline{3} \times \{2,3\} \times \{1\}$, $J_3 = \overline{2} \times \overline{3} \times \{2\}$, and $J_4 = \overline{3} \times \overline{2} \times \{2\}$. The class J is decomposable, and the elements of $F(J)$ are $G_1 = \{2,3\} \times \{2,3\} \times \{1\}$, $G_2 = \phi$, and $G_3 = \overline{2} \times \overline{2} \times \overline{2}$, and $d(G,J) = 1$ if $G \in F(J)$. Then if $\hat{\underline{m}}(\underline{n},I,E)$ exists,

(7.160) $$\hat{m}_{1i_21}(\underline{n},I,E) = \frac{n_{1+1}(I)n_{+i_21}(I)}{n_{++1}(J_2)}$$

if $i_2 \in \{2,3\}$,

(7.161) $$\hat{m}_{i_111}(\underline{n},I,E) = \frac{n_{i_1+1}(I)n_{+11}(I)}{n_{++1}(J_1)}$$

if $i_1 \in \{2,3\}$,

(7.162) $$\hat{m}_{i_1i_21}(\underline{n},I,E) = \frac{n_{i_1+1}(I)n_{+i_21}(I)n_{++1}(G_1)}{n_{++1}(J_1)n_{++1}(J_2)}$$

if $i_1 \in \{2,3\}$ and $i_2 \in \{2,3\}$,

(7.163) $$\hat{m}_{i_1i_22}(\underline{n},I,E) = \frac{n_{i_1+2}(I)n_{+i_22}(I)n_{++2}(G_3)}{n_{++2}(J_3)n_{++2}(J_4)}$$

if $i_1 \in \overline{2}$ and $i_2 \in \overline{2}$,

(7.164) $$\hat{m}_{3i_22}(\underline{n},I,E) = \frac{n_{3+2}(I)n_{+i_22}(I)}{n_{++2}(J_4)}$$

if $i_2 \in \overline{2}$, and

(7.165) $$\hat{m}_{i_132}(\underline{n},I,E) = \frac{n_{i_1+2}(I)n_{+32}(I)}{n_{++2}(J_3)}$$

if $i_1 \in \overline{2}$.

If $E = \{\{1,2\},\{3\}\}$, then the conditions of Theorem 7.4 are not satisfied; however, if $\overline{3} \times \overline{3}$ is identified with $\overline{9}$ through the mapping $f\langle i_1,i_2\rangle = 3(i_1 - 1) + i_2$, then $I = \overline{3} \times \overline{3} \times \overline{2} - \{\langle 1,1,1\rangle,\langle 3,3,2\rangle\}$ may be identified with $I' = \overline{9} \times \overline{2} - \{\langle 1,1\rangle,\langle 9,2\rangle\}$ and $\rho_I^{I*}M(E)$ may be identified with $\rho_{I'}^{I+}M(E')$, where $I^* = \overline{3} \times \overline{3} \times \overline{2}$, $I^+ = \overline{9} \times \overline{2}$, $E' = \{\{1\},\{2\}\}$, and $F(E') = \{\phi\}$. The class $J' = \{J_k': k \in \overline{3}\}$ of maximal hyperblocks of I' is $\{(\overline{9} - \overline{1}) \times \{1\}, (\overline{8} - \overline{1}) \times \overline{2}, \overline{8} \times \{2\}\}$, which is decomposable, with $F(J) = \{G_k': k \in \overline{3}\} = \{(\overline{8} - \overline{1}) \times \{1\}, (\overline{8} - 1) \times \{2\},\phi\}$. One has $d((\overline{8} - \overline{1}) \times \{k\},J) = 1$ if $k \in \overline{2}$ and $d(\phi,J) = 0$. If $J_k = f^{-1}J_k'$ and $G_k = f^{-1}G_k'$ for $k \in \overline{3}$, then $J_1 = \overline{3} \times \overline{3} \times \{1\} - \{\langle 1,1,1\rangle\}$, $J_2 = \overline{3} \times \overline{3} \times \overline{2} - \{\langle 1,1,1\rangle,\langle 3,3,2\rangle\}$, $J_3 = \overline{3} \times \overline{3} \times \{2\} - \{\langle 3,3,2\rangle\}$, $G_1 = \overline{3} \times \overline{3} \times \{1\} - \{\langle 1,1,1\rangle,\langle 3,3,1\rangle\}$, $G_2 = \overline{3} \times \overline{3} \times \{2\} - \{\langle 1,1,2\rangle,\langle 3,3,2\rangle\}$, and $G_3 = \phi$. Thus if $\langle i_1,i_2\rangle \in \overline{3} \times \overline{3} - \{\langle 1,1\rangle,\langle 3,3\rangle\}$ and $\hat{\underline{m}}(\underline{n},I,E)$ exists, then

(7.166) $$\hat{m}_{i_1i_21}(\underline{n},I,E) = \hat{m}_{f<i_1,i_2>1}(\underline{n}',I',E')$$

$$= \frac{n'_{f<i_1,i_2>+}(I')n'_{+1}(I')n'_{++}(G'_1)}{n'_{++}(J'_1)n'_{++}(J'_2)}$$

$$= \frac{n'_{f<i_1,i_2>+}(I)n'_{+1}(G'_1)}{n'_{++}(J'_2)}$$

$$= \frac{n_{i_1i_2+}(I)n_{++1}(G_1)}{n_{+++}(J_2)}$$

$$= \frac{n_{i_1i_2+}(J_2)n_{++1}(J_2)}{n_{+++}(J_2)} .$$

Similarly,

(7.167) $$\hat{m}_{i_1i_22}(\underline{n},I,E) = \frac{n_{i_1i_2+}(J_2)n_{++2}(J_2)}{n_{+++}(J_2)} ,$$

(7.168) $$\hat{m}_{111}(\underline{n},I,E) = n_{111} ,$$

and

(7.169) $$\hat{m}_{332}(\underline{n},I,E) = n_{332} .$$

The identification technique used in Example 7.30 may be applied whenever $E = \{E_1,E_2\}$ and $E_1 \cup E_2 = \bar{d}$, so decomposability provides an effective test for the existence of closed-form solutions when E has two elements and $U(E) = \bar{d}$. When E has more than two elements, then the fact that J is decomposable is not sufficient to ensure that a closed-form solution can be found.

Example 7.31. Suppose that

$$\underline{n} = \begin{array}{|ccc|}\hline - & - & - \\ n_{211} & n_{221} & n_{231} \\ n_{311} & n_{321} & n_{331} \\ \hline\end{array} \qquad \begin{array}{|ccc|}\hline n_{112} & n_{122} & n_{132} \\ n_{212} & n_{222} & n_{232} \\ n_{312} & n_{322} & n_{332} \\ \hline\end{array}$$

and $E = \{\{1\},\{2\},\{3\}\}$. Then $J = \{\{2,3\} \times \bar{3} \times \bar{2}, \bar{3} \times \bar{3} \times \{2\}\}$ is decomposable and $F(J) = \{\{2,3\} \times \bar{3} \times \{2\}\}$. Thus $K_2 = \{2,3\} \times \bar{3} \times \{1\}$ or $K_2 = \bar{1} \times \bar{3} \times \{2\}$. In either case, $\pi^{-1}_{\{2\}}K_2(\{2\}) = \bar{3} \times \bar{3} \times \bar{2}$, so $\pi^{-1}_{\{2\}}K_2(\{2\}) \cap (J_1 \cup J_2) = I$, and $\pi^{-1}_{\{2\}}K_2(\{2\}) \cap J_2 = J'_2$. Thus I is not reducible.

This example reflects the more general result that if $I^* = \bar{r}_1 \times \bar{r}_2 \times \bar{r}_3$ and $E = \{\{1\},\{2\},\{3\}\}$, then if I is reducible and inseparable, then $I = A_1 \times A_2 \times A_3$, where $A_j \subset \bar{r}_j$ for $j \in \bar{3}$. To prove this assertion, suppose that $J = \{J_k: k \in \bar{\ell}\}$ satisfies the conditions of Definition 7.2. Then $G_\ell = \prod_{j=1}^3 B_{j\ell}$ and $J = \prod_{j=1}^3 A_{j\ell}$ have the property that $B_{g\ell} \neq A_{j\ell}$ for some $g \in \bar{3}$. Without loss of generality, suppose $g = 1$. Then $(A_{1\ell} - B_{1\ell}) \times A_{2\ell} \times A_{3\ell} \subset K_\ell$. It follows that if either $i_2 \in A_{2\ell}$ or $i_3 \in A_{3\ell}$ and $\langle i_1,i_2,i_3\rangle \in I$, then $\langle i_1,i_2,i_3\rangle \in J_\ell$. If $A_{2k} \cap A_{2\ell} \neq \phi$, then $A_{3k} \subset A_{3\ell}$. If $A_{3k} \cap A_{3\ell} \neq \phi$, then $A_{2k} \subset A_{2\ell}$. Thus $A_{2k} \cap A_{2\ell} = \phi$ and $A_{3k} \cap A_{3\ell} = \phi$ or $A_{2k} \subset A_{2\ell}$ and $A_{3k} \subset A_{3\ell}$. If the second alternative holds, then $(A_{1k} \cup A_{1\ell}) \cap A_{2k} \cap A_{3k} \subset J_k \cup J_\ell$ and either $A_{1k} \cup A_{1\ell} = A_{1\ell}$, in which case $A_{1k} \subset A_{1\ell}$ and $J_k \subset J_\ell$, or $A_{1k} \cup A_{1\ell} \neq A_{1\ell}$ and $A_{1k} \cup A_{1\ell} \subset B_{1\ell} \subset A_{1\ell}$, in which case a contradiction is obtained. The only remaining possibilities are that $k = \ell$ or $A_{2k} \cap A_{2\ell} = \phi$ and $A_{3k} \cap A_{3\ell} = 0$. Therefore, $J_k \cap J_\ell = \phi$ if $k \neq \ell$. Thus $G_\ell = \phi$ and $K_\ell = \phi$. It now follows that if $i_1 \in A_{1\ell}$, $i_2 \in A_{2\ell}$, or $i_3 \in A_{3\ell}$, then $\langle i_1,i_2,i_3\rangle \in J_\ell$. Thus if $\langle i_1,i_2,i_3\rangle \in J_\ell$ and $\langle i_1',i_2',i_3'\rangle \in J_k$, where $k \neq \ell$, then $\langle i_1,i_2,i_3\rangle \nsim \langle i_1',i_2',i_3'\rangle$. Since I is inseparable, $\ell = 1$ and $I = A_{11} \times A_{21} \times A_{31}$.

The results of this section suggest that reducibility is a rather complex phenomenon which is closely dependent on the generating class E; however, reducible tables can be interpreted in a relatively simple manner, as may be seen from the following theorem:

THEOREM 7.5. *If* I *is reducible, then* $\underline{\mu} \in \rho M(E)$ *if and only if* $\rho_J^I \underline{\mu} \in \rho_J M(E) = M(J,E)$ *for each* $J \in J$.

Proof. The necessity of the condition follows from Lemma 7.1. To prove sufficiency, observe that if $\{J_k: k \in \bar{\ell}\}$ is defined as in Definition 7.2 and Theorem 7.2, and if $\rho_J^I \underline{\mu} \in \rho_J M(E)$ for all $J \in J$, then $\hat{\underline{m}}(\rho_J^I \underline{m}(\underline{\mu}),J,E) = \rho_J^I \underline{m}(\underline{\mu})$ for each $J \in J$. Theorem 7.2 implies that the maximum-likelihood estimate $\hat{\underline{m}}(\underline{m}(\underline{\mu}),I,E) = \underline{m}^{(0)}$, where $\underline{m}^{(\ell)} = \underline{m}(\underline{\mu})$ and for $k \in \bar{\ell}$, $m_{\underline{i}}^{(k-1)} = m_{\underline{i}}(\underline{m}^{(k)},J_k,E)$ if $i \in J_k$, and $m_{\underline{i}}^{(k-1)} = m_{\underline{i}}^{(k)}$ if $\underline{i} \in I - J_k$. A simple induction shows that $\underline{m}^{(k)} = \underline{m}(\underline{\mu})$ for all $k \in \bar{\ell} \cup \{0\}$. Thus $\hat{\underline{m}}(\underline{m},(\underline{\mu}),I,E) = \underline{m}(\underline{\mu})$ and $\underline{\mu} \in \rho M(E)$. ||

Example 7.32. In Example 7.23, the quasi-independence model $\underline{\mu} \in \rho M(E)$ holds for $\underline{n}$ if and only if the independence models $\rho_J^I \underline{\mu} \in \rho_J M(E) = M(J,E)$ hold for $\rho_J^I \underline{n}$ for each $J \in J$. If patient t enters with status X_{t1} and leaves with status X_{t2} and for any $k \in \bar{5}$, X_{t1} and X_{t2} are conditionally independent given that $X_{t1} \le k$ and $X_{t2} \le 6 - k$, then, as shown in chapter 5, $\rho_{J_k}^I \underline{\mu} \in M(J_k,E)$ for $k \in \bar{5}$ and $\underline{\mu} \in \rho M(E)$. Thus a quasi-independence model for an incomplete table is equivalent to several independence models for subtables.

Theorem 7.5 shows that reducible incomplete tables can be interpreted in terms of complete subtables. This observation facilitates computation of dimension, the likelihood ratio, and the asymptotic covariance operator of $\hat{\underline{\mu}}(\underline{n},I,E)$. The following theorems and examples illustrate these consequences of Theorem 7.5.

THEOREM 7.6. *If* I *is reducible, then*

$$\dim \rho M(E) = \sum_{J\in\mathcal{J}} \dim M(J,E) - \sum_{G\in F(\mathcal{J})} d(G,\mathcal{J}) \dim M(G,E). \tag{7.171}$$

Proof. Suppose that $\mathcal{J} = \{J_k: k \in \overline{\ell}\}$ satisfies the conditions of Definition 7.2, and suppose that G_k and H_k are defined as in Definition 7.2. Then H_k is reducible for each $k \in \overline{\ell+1} - \overline{1}$. Suppose that the theorem is valid if $\mathcal{J}$ has fewer than ℓ elements. This assumption is trivial if $\ell = 2$. Since H_ℓ is the union of $\ell - 1$ maximal hyperblocks $\{J_k: k \in \overline{\ell - 1}\} = \mathcal{J}'$, the induction hypothesis implies that

$$\dim \rho_{H_\ell} M(E) = \sum_{J\in\mathcal{J}'} \dim M(J,E) - \sum_{G\in F(\mathcal{J}')} \dim (G,\mathcal{J}) \dim M(G,E). \tag{7.172}$$

Since $\underline{\mu} \in \rho M(E)$ if and only if $\rho_J^I \underline{\mu} \in \rho_J M(E)$ for each $J \in \mathcal{J}$ and H_ℓ is reducible, $\underline{\mu} \in \rho M(E)$ if and only if $\rho_{H_\ell}^I \underline{\mu} \in \rho_{H_\ell} M(E)$ and $\rho_{J_\ell} \in \rho_{J_\ell} M(E) = M(J_\ell,E)$. The linear mapping f from $\rho M(E)$ to $S = \{\langle\underline{\mu}^{(1)},\underline{\mu}^{(2)}\rangle: \underline{\mu}^{(1)} \in \rho_{H_\ell} M(E), \underline{\mu}^{(2)} \in \rho_{J_\ell} M(E), \rho_{G_\ell}\underline{\mu}^{(1)} = \rho_{G_\ell}\underline{\mu}^{(2)}\}$ defined by $f\underline{\mu} = \langle\rho_{H_\ell}^I \underline{\mu}, \rho_{J_\ell}^I \underline{\mu}\rangle$ is one-to-one and onto, so $\dim \rho M(E) = \dim S$. By Halmos (1958),

$$\dim S = \dim \rho_{H_\ell} M(E) + \dim M(J_\ell,E) - \dim M(G_\ell,E). \tag{7.173}$$

The same argument used in (5.118) may now be used to verify that $d(G,\mathcal{J}) = d(G,\mathcal{J}')$ if $G \neq G_\ell$ and $d(G_\ell,\mathcal{J}) = d(G_\ell,\mathcal{J}') + 1$. Thus (7.171) holds and the induction is completed. ||

Example 7.33. In Example 7.22, $E = \{\{1,2\},\{2,3\},\{3,4\}\}$, $F(E) = \{\{2\},\{3\},\phi\}$, $d(\{2\},E) = d(\{3\},E) = 1$, and $d(\phi,E) = 0$. Thus $\dim M(J_1,E) = \dim M(J_2,E) = 2 \times 2 + 2 \times 1 + 1 \times 2 - 2 - 1 = 5$, $\dim M(G_2,E) = 2 \times 1 + 1 \times 1 + 1 \times 2 - 1 - 1 = 3$, and $\dim \rho M(E) = 5 + 5 - 3 = 7$.

THEOREM 7.7. *Suppose that* $U(E_1) = U(E_2)$, $\rho M(E_1) \subset \rho M(E_2)$, $\rho M(E_1) \neq \rho M(E_2)$, *and for* $k \in \overline{2}$ E_k *is decomposable,* $\mathcal{J}_k$ *is the class of maximal hyperblocks of* I *relative to* E_k, *and* I *is reducible relative to* E_k. *Then*

$$(7.174)\qquad -2\Delta(\underline{n},\hat{\underline{\mu}}(\underline{n},I,E_2),\hat{\underline{\mu}}(\underline{n},I,E_1))$$

$$= 2[\sum_{E\in E_2}\sum_{\underline{i}\in I(E)} n_{\underline{i}}^{E}(I)\log n_{\underline{i}}^{E}(I)$$

$$-\sum_{F\in F(E_2)}\sum_{J\in J_2}\sum_{\underline{i}\in J(F)} d(F,E_2)n_{\underline{i}}^{F}(J)\log n_{\underline{i}}^{F}(J)$$

$$+\sum_{F\in F(E_2)}\sum_{G\in F(J_2)}\sum_{\underline{i}\in G(F)} d(F,E_2)d(G,J_2)n_{\underline{i}}^{F}(G)\log n_{\underline{i}}^{F}(G)$$

$$-\sum_{E\in E_1}\sum_{\underline{i}\in I(E)} n_{\underline{i}}^{E}(I)\log n_{\underline{i}}^{E}(I)$$

$$+\sum_{F\in F(E_1)}\sum_{J\in J_1}\sum_{\underline{i}\in J(F)} d(F,E_1)n_{\underline{i}}^{F}(J)\log n_{\underline{i}}^{F}(J)$$

$$-\sum_{F\in F(E_1)}\sum_{G\in F(J_1)}\sum_{\underline{i}\in G(F)} d(F,E_1)d(G,J_1)n_{\underline{i}}^{F}(G)\log n_{\underline{i}}^{F}(G)] .$$

Proof. Equation (7.174) follows from the second equation of (7.112) in Theorem 7.2. The terms involving r_{jk} can be ignored since if $i \in I$ and $r_j(J)$ is the number of elements in $J(\{j\})$, $\prod_{j\in D(E_1)} r_j(J)$ is the number of elements in $\pi^{-1}_{U(E_1)}[\pi_{U(E_1)}(\underline{i})] \cap I$ for each $J \in J_k$ and $k \in \overline{2}$ such that $\underline{i} \in J$.||

Remarks. The most common alternative hypothesis is that $\underline{\mu} \in R^I = \rho M(\{\overline{d}\})$. Any set I is reducible relative to $\{\overline{d}\}$, for in this case, $J_2 = \{\{\underline{i}\}: \underline{i} \in I\}$, $(\{\overline{d}\}) = \emptyset$, and $\pi_{\overline{d}}$ is the identity. If $U(E_1) \neq U(E_2)$, an expression similar to (7.174) results which includes terms based on $r_j(J)$. This expression has been omitted to avoid unnecessary complications. The expression for the likelihood ratio chi-square is most useful when $\hat{\underline{m}}(\underline{n},I,E_1)$ is not explicitly required and a calculator and tables of $n \log n$ are to be used.

Use of Theorem 7.7 is also simplified when $\cap(E_1) = \cap(E_2)$. In this case, $J_1 = J_2$. Since if $E_1 \in E_1$ there exists $E_2 \in E_2$ such that $E_1 \subset E_2$, Definition 7.2 implies that if I is reducible relative to E_2, it is reducible relative to E_1.

Example 7.34. In the triangular table of Examples 7.23 and 7.27, one might test H_0: $\underline{\mu} \in \rho M(\{\{1\},\{2\}\})$ against H_A: $\underline{\mu} \in R^I = \rho M(\{\overline{2}\})$. In this case, $E_1 = \{\{1\},\{2\}\}$ and

$E_2 = \{\overline{2}\}$. As shown in Example 7.23, I is reducible relative to E_1. The remark following the last theorem implies that I is also reducible relative to E_2. Using the results of Example 7.27, one finds that

(7.175) $$-2\Delta(\underline{n},\hat{\underline{\mu}}(\underline{n},I,E_2),\hat{\underline{\mu}}(\underline{n},I,E_1))$$

$$= 2[\sum_{i=1}^{5}\sum_{j=1}^{6-i} n_{ij}\log n_{ij} - \sum_{i=1}^{5} n_{i+}(I)\log n_{i+}(I) - \sum_{j=1}^{5} n_{+j}(I)\log n_{+j}(I)$$

$$+ \sum_{k=1}^{5} n_{++}(J_k)\log n_{++}(J_k) - \sum_{k=2}^{5} n_{++}(G_k)\log n_{++}(G_k)].$$

Since $J_5 = \overline{5} \times \overline{1}$ and $J_1 = \overline{1} \times \overline{5}$, $n_{++}(I) = n_{++}(J_5)$ and $n_{1+}(I) = n_{++}(J_1)$ In addition $n_{51} = n_{5+}(I)$ and $n_{15} = n_{+5}(I)$. Thus

(7.176) $$-2\Delta(\underline{n},\hat{\underline{\mu}}(\underline{n},I,E_2),\hat{\underline{\mu}}(\underline{n},I,E_1))$$

$$= 2[\Sigma\{n_{ij}\log n_{ij}: i + j \in \overline{6}, i \in \overline{4}, j \in \overline{4}\} - \sum_{i=2}^{4} n_{i+}(I)\log n_{i+}(I)$$

$$- \sum_{j=2}^{4} n_{+j}(I)\log n_{+j}(I) + \sum_{k=2}^{4} n_{++}(J_k)\log n_{++}(J_k) - \sum_{k=2}^{5} n_{++}(G_k)\log n_{++}(G_k)$$

$$= 9.60\ .$$

The number of degrees of freedom for this test is 6, as may be seen by noting that $\dim M(E_2) = 15$, the number of elements in the table, and $\dim M(E_1) = 5 + 5 - 1 = 9$ since I is E_1-inseparable. Thus this test provides no evidence to suggest rejection of H_0. Bishop and Fienberg (1969) reach a similar conclusion by use of the Pearson chi-square, which is 8.37 in this example.

THEOREM 7.8. *If* I *is reducible relative to a decomposable generating class* E, *then the asymptotic covariance operator* $P^*_{\rho M(E)}(\underline{\mu})D^{-1}(\underline{\mu})$ *satisfies the equation*

(7.177) $$P^*_{\rho M(E)}(\underline{\mu})D^{-1}(\underline{\mu})$$

$$= \sum_{E \in E}\ \sum_{\underline{i} \in I(E)} [\rho\underline{\nu}(E,\underline{i})] \otimes [\rho\underline{\nu}(E,\underline{i})]/m^E_{\underline{i}}(I)$$

$$- \sum_{F \in F(E)} d(F,E) \sum_{J \in J} \sum_{\underline{T} \in J(F)} [\tau_J^I \rho_J \underline{\nu}(F,\underline{T})] \bullet [\tau_J^I \rho_J \underline{\nu}(F,\underline{T})]/m_{\underline{T}}^F(J)$$

$$+ \sum_{F \in F(E)} d(F,E) \sum_{G \in F(J)} d(G,E) \sum_{\underline{T} \in G(F)} [\tau_G^I \rho_G \underline{\nu}(F,\underline{T})] \bullet [\tau_G^I \rho_G \underline{\nu}(F,\underline{T})]/m_{\underline{T}}^F(G).$$

if $\underline{\mu} \in \rho M(E)$ *and* $\underline{m} = \underline{m}(\underline{\mu})$.

Proof. By (4.12),

$$P^*_{\rho M(E)}(\underline{\mu})D^{-1}(\underline{\mu})\ \underline{x} = d\hat{\underline{\mu}}_{\underline{m}(\underline{\mu})}(\underline{x},I,E) \tag{7.178}$$

for any $\underline{x} \in R^I$. By (7.121), $d\hat{\underline{\mu}}_{\underline{m}(\underline{\mu})}(\underline{x},I,E)$ is equal to the right-hand side of (7.177). The basic results concerning differentials which are used to verify this assertion are that

$$d(\sum_{j=1}^{k} \alpha_j f_j)_{\underline{x}} = \sum_{j=1}^{k} \alpha_j (df_j)_{\underline{x}} \tag{7.179}$$

if $\alpha_j \in R$ and f_j is a differential function from R^I to R for $j \in \overline{k}$, and that

$$d(f\underline{\nu})_{\underline{x}} = f'(x)\underline{\nu} \tag{7.180}$$

if f is a differential function from R to R, $f'(x)$ is the first derivative of f at x, and $\underline{\nu} \in R^I$. Thus if $\underline{\xi} \in R^I$,

$$\{d[\log (\underline{x},\underline{\nu})]\underline{\nu}\}_{\underline{x}}(\underline{\xi}) \tag{7.181}$$

$$= \frac{1}{(\underline{x},\underline{\nu})} (\underline{\nu},\underline{\xi})\underline{\nu} = \frac{1}{(\underline{x},\underline{\nu})} (\underline{\nu} \bullet \underline{\nu})(\underline{\xi}).$$

It is now only necessary to note that $m_{\underline{T}}^E(I) = (\underline{m},\rho\underline{\nu}(E,\underline{T}))$ if $\underline{T} \in I(E)$ and $E \in E$,

$$m_{\underline{T}}^F(J) = (\rho_J^I \underline{m},\rho_J \underline{\nu}(F,\underline{T})) \tag{7.182}$$

$$= (\underline{m},\tau_J^I \rho_J \underline{\nu}(F,\underline{T}))$$

if $\underline{T} \in J(F)$ and $F \in F(E)$, and

$$m_{\underline{T}}^F(G) = (\underline{m},\tau_G^I \rho_G \underline{\nu}(F,\underline{T})) \tag{7.183}$$

if $\underline{T} \in G(F)$ and $F \in F(E)$.||

COROLLARY 7.2. *If* I *is reducible relative to a decomposable generating class* E, *then the estimated asymptotic covariance operator* $P^*_{\rho M(E)}(\hat{\underline{\mu}}(\underline{n},I,E))D^{-1}(\hat{\underline{\mu}}(\underline{n},I,E))$ *satisfies*

(7.184)
$$P^*_{\rho M(E)}(\hat{\underline{\mu}}(\underline{n},I,E))D^{-1}(\hat{\underline{\mu}}(\underline{n},I,E))$$

$$= \sum_{E\in E}\sum_{\underline{i}\in I(E)} [\rho\underline{\nu}(E,\underline{i})] \otimes [\rho\underline{\nu}(E,\underline{i})]/n^E_{\underline{i}}(I)$$

$$- \sum_{F\in F(E)} d(F,E) \sum_{J\in J}\sum_{\underline{i}\in J(F)} [\tau^I_J\rho_J\underline{\nu}(F,\underline{i})] \otimes [\tau^I_J\rho_J\underline{\nu}(F,\underline{i})]/n^F_{\underline{i}}(J)$$

$$+ \sum_{F\in F(E)} d(F,E) \sum_{G\in F(J)} d(G,E) \sum_{\underline{i}\in G(F)} [\tau^I_G\rho_G\underline{\nu}(F,\underline{i})] \otimes [\tau^I_G\rho_G\underline{\nu}(F,\underline{i})]/n^F_{\underline{i}}(G).$$

Proof. The corollary follows from (7.177) since $\hat{\underline{\mu}}(\underline{n},I,E) \in \rho M(E)$, $n^E_{\underline{i}}(I) = \hat{m}^E_{\underline{i}}(n,I,E)(I)$ if $\underline{i} \in I(E)$ and $E \in E$, $n^F_{\underline{i}}(J) = \hat{m}^E_{\underline{i}}(\underline{n},I,E)(J)$ if $\underline{i} \in J(F)$, $J \in J$, $F \in F(E)$, and $d(F,E) > 0$, and $n^F_{\underline{i}}(G) = \hat{m}^F_{\underline{i}}(\underline{n},I,E)(G)$ if $\underline{i} \in G(F)$, $G \in F(J)$, $d(G,E) > 0$, $F \in F(E)$, and $d(F,E) > 0$.||

Example 7.35. Suppose that 95% simultaneous confidence intervals are desired in table 7.10 for the conditional probabilities $p(j|i)$ that a subject with entering status i has final status j, for all $\langle i,j\rangle \in \overline{5} \times \overline{5}$ such that $i + j \le 6$. The maximum-likelihood estimate, $\hat{p}(j|i)$, of $p(j|i) = m_{ij}/\sum_{j'=1}^{6-i} m_{ij'}$ under the quasi-independence model is $\hat{m}_{ij}/\sum_{j'=1}^{6-i} \hat{m}_{ij'} = \hat{m}_{ij}/n_{i+}(I)$. Since $\log p(j|i) = (\underline{\delta}^{(i,j)},\underline{\mu}(I))$ if $I = \{\{k\} \times \overline{6-k}: k \in \overline{5}\}$ and $\underline{\delta}^{(i',j')} = \{\chi_{\{\langle i',j'\rangle\}}(\langle i,j\rangle)\}$ if $\langle i',j'\rangle \in I$, it follows from (4.90) and (7.184) that the estimated asymptotic covariance of $\log \hat{p}(j|i)$ is

(7.185)
$$\hat{w}_{ij} = (\underline{\delta}^{(i,j)},[P^*_M(\hat{\underline{\mu}}) - P^*_R(\hat{\underline{\mu}})]D^{-1}(\hat{\underline{\mu}})\underline{\delta}^{(i,j)})$$

$$= \sum_{j'=1}^{5} (\underline{\delta}^{(i,j)},\rho\underline{\nu}(\{2\},j'))^2/n_{+j'} - \sum_{k=1}^{5} (\underline{\delta}^{(i,j)},\tau^I_{J_k}\rho_{J_k}\underline{e})^2/n_{++}(J_k)$$

$$+ \sum_{k=2}^{5} (\underline{\delta}^{(i,j)},\tau^I_{G_k}\rho_{G_k}\underline{e})^2/n_{++}(G_k)$$

$$= \frac{1}{n_{+j}} - \sum_{k=i}^{6-j} \frac{1}{n_{++}(J_k)} + \sum_{k=i+1}^{6-j} \frac{1}{n_{++}(G_k)}$$

$$= [\frac{1}{n_{+j}} - \frac{1}{n_{++}(J_i)}] + \sum_{k=i+1}^{6-j} \frac{n_k+(I)}{n_{++}(J_k)n_{++}(G_k)}$$

The case of $p(1|5)$ is of no interest since $p(1|5)$ must equal 1, so there are 14 simultaneous confidence intervals to compute. If Bonferroni intervals are used (see chapter 4), then the simultaneous intervals for $\log p(j|i)$ are $[\log \hat{p}(j|i) - \Phi^{(0.025/14)}\hat{w}_{ij}^{\frac{1}{2}}, \log \hat{p}(j|i) + \Phi^{(0.025/14)}\hat{w}_{ij}^{\frac{1}{2}}$ for each $<i,j> \in I$ such that $i \neq 5$, where $\Phi^{(0.025/14)} = 2.92$. The corresponding intervals for $p(j|i)$ are $[\hat{p}(j|i)\exp(-2.92\hat{w}_{ij}^{\frac{1}{2}}), \hat{p}(j|i)\exp(2.92\hat{w}_{ij}^{\frac{1}{2}})$. Results are summarized in table 7.11.

TABLE 7.11

SIMULTANEOUS CONFIDENCE INTERVALS BASED ON $\log p(j|i)$ FOR CONDITIONAL PROBABILITIES IN TABLE 7.10 OF FINAL STATES GIVEN INITIAL STATES[a]

	Final State				
Initial State	A	B	C	D	E
E	0.139 0.369	0.214 0.463	0.095 0.316	0.085 0.325	0.044 0.236
D	0.160 0.411	0.247 0.523	0.108 0.352	0.098 0.364	- -
C	0.202 0.492	0.344 0.624	0.136 0.425	- -	- -
B	0.277 0.626	0.436 0.780	- -	- -	- -
A	1.000 1.000	- -	- -	- -	- -

[a]Top line of entry is lower limit, and bottom line is upper limit.

The construction of confidence intervals by use of $\log \hat{p}(j|i)$ is somewhat arbitrary. Intervals can also be constructed by observing that the estimated asymptotic variance of $\hat{p}(j|i)$ is $[\hat{p}(j|i)]^2\hat{w}_{ij}$. Thus alternative simultaneous intervals for $p(j|i)$ are $[\hat{p}(j|i)(1 - 2.92\hat{w}_{ij}), \hat{p}(j|i)(1 + 2.92\hat{w}_{ij})]$, for each $<i,j> \in I$. These intervals are given in table 7.12. Clearly the conditional probabilities are not accurately determined by the limited data available. The differences between the two types in intervals are noticeable; however, it is not clear which set of intervals is superior.

TABLE 7.12

SIMULTANEOUS CONFIDENCE INTERVALS BASED ON $p(j|i)$ FOR CONDITIONAL PROBABILITIES IN TABLE 7.10 OF FINAL STATES GIVEN INITIAL STATES[a]

Initial State	Final State A	B	C	D	E
E	0.116	0.192	0.069	0.055	0.034
	0.338	0.443	0.277	0.278	0.228
D	0.136	0.225	0.080	0.064	-
	0.378	0.494	0.311	0.312	-
C	0.175	0.291	0.104	-	-
	0.456	0.594	0.378	-	-
B	0.247	0.414	-	-	-
	0.586	0.753	-	-	-
A	1.000	-	-	-	-
	1.000	-	-	-	-

[a]Top line of entry is lower limit, and bottom line is upper limit.

THE DEMING-STEPHAN METHOD

The Deming-Stephan method used in chapter 5 is very similar to the algorithm appropriate to incomplete tables. If $E = \{E_k : k \in \bar{s}\}$, then one cycle of the algorithm is given by the equations

$$m_{\underline{i}}^{(t,k+1)} = m_{\underline{i}}^{(t,k)} \frac{n^{E_k}_{\pi_{E_k}\underline{i}}(I)}{[m^{(t,k)}]^{E}_{\pi_{E_k}\underline{i}}(I)} \tag{7.188}$$

$$= m_{\underline{i}}^{(t,k)} \frac{[\underline{n}]^{E_k}_{\pi_{E_k}\underline{i}}}{[\underline{m}^{(t,k)}]^{E}_{\pi_{E_k}\underline{i}}}$$

for $\underline{i} \in I$ and $k \in \bar{s}$ and

$$\underline{m}^{(t+1,1)} = \underline{m}^{(t,s+1)} . \tag{7.189}$$

It is assumed that $\{\log m_{i}^{(0,1)}\} \in \rho M(E)$. This condition is met if $\underline{m}^{(0,1)} = \underline{e}$. If $\underline{\bar{m}}^{(t,k)} = \tau \underline{m}^{(t,k)}$ and $\underline{\bar{n}} = \tau \underline{n}$, one may write

(7.190)
$$\bar{m}_{\underline{i}}^{(t,k+1)} = \frac{\bar{m}_{\underline{i}}^{(t,k)} \bar{n}^{E}_{\pi_{E}\underline{i}}}{[\bar{m}^{(t,k)}]^{E}_{\pi_{E}\underline{i}}}$$

for $i \in I$ and $k \in \bar{s}$ and

(7.191)
$$\underline{\bar{m}}^{(t+1,1)} = \underline{\bar{m}}^{(t,s+1)}$$

if the convention $0/0 = 0$ is used. Thus the Deming-Stephan algorithm for an incomplete table in which $\underline{m}^{(0,1)}$ is the initial estimate of $\hat{\underline{m}}(\underline{n},I,E)$ is equivalent to the Deming-Stephan algorithm for the complete table $\bar{\underline{n}}$ and the initial estimate $\underline{\bar{m}}^{(0,1)}$. In this case, $\underline{\bar{m}}^{(0,1)} = \tau \underline{e}^{I}$ if $m^{(0,1)} = \underline{e}^{I}$. This reduction to the algorithm for complete tables permits programs for complete tables such as the algorithm of Haberman (1972) to be used with incomplete tables.

Example 7.36. The manifold $\rho M(E)$, where $E = \{\{1\},\{2\},\{3\},\{4\}\}$, has been considered for table 7.1. In this example, if i_1, i_2, i_3, and i_4 are all in $\bar{2}$, then

(7.192)
$$m_{i_1 i_2 i_3 i_4}^{(t,2)} = \frac{\bar{m}_{i_1 i_2 i_3 i_4}^{(t,1)} \bar{n}_{i_1 +++}}{\bar{m}_{i_1 +++}^{(t,2)}} ,$$

(7.193)
$$\bar{m}_{i_1 i_2 i_3 i_4}^{(t,3)} = \frac{\bar{m}_{i_1 i_2 i_3 i_4}^{(t,2)} \bar{n}_{+ i_2 ++}}{\bar{m}_{+ i_2 ++}^{(t,2)}} ,$$

(7.194)
$$\bar{m}_{i_1 i_2 i_3 i_4}^{(t,4)} = \frac{\bar{m}_{i_1 i_2 i_3 i_4}^{(t,3)} \bar{n}_{++ i_3 +}}{\bar{m}_{++ i_3 +}^{(t,3)}} ,$$

(7.195)
$$\bar{m}_{i_1 i_2 i_3 i_4}^{(t,5)} = \frac{\bar{m}_{i_1 i_2 i_3 i_4}^{(t,4)} \bar{n}_{+++ i_4}}{\bar{m}_{+++ i_4}^{(t,4)}} ,$$

and

(7.196)
$$\underline{\bar{m}}^{(t+1,1)} = \underline{\bar{m}}^{(t,5)} .$$

The initial value $\tau \underline{e}^{I}$ may be used for $\underline{\bar{m}}^{(0,1)}$. After five iterations, the maximum value of $|[\bar{m}^{(5,k)}]^{E_k}_{\underline{I}} - \bar{n}^{E_k}_{\underline{I}}|$ for $k \in \bar{4}$ and $\underline{I} \in I^*(E_k)$ is only 0.051. The resulting maximum-likelihood estimate $\hat{\underline{m}}(\underline{n},I,E)$ is given in table 7.13. Given these estimates, the effectiveness of the model may be examined by use of either the likelihood ratio or Pearson chi-square for the null hypothesis $H_0: \underline{\mu} \in \rho M(E)$ and the alternative $H_A: \in R^I$. The two chi-square statistics are, respectively, 47.06 and 47.15, and there are 7 degrees of freedom, so the quasi-independence model is inadequate. Comparison of tables 7.2 and 7.13 suggests that type of female and fourth chromosome interact; consequently, the model $\underline{\mu} \in \rho M(E')$ was tried, with $E' = \{\{1\},\{2\},\{3,4\}\}$. In this case, the algorithm is described by the equations

$$\bar{m}^{(t,2)}_{i_1 i_2 i_3 i_4} = \frac{\bar{m}^{(t,1)}_{i_1 i_2 i_3 i_4} \bar{n}_{i_1+++}}{\bar{m}^{(t,1)}_{i_1+++}} , \tag{7.197}$$

$$\bar{m}^{(t,3)}_{i_1 i_2 i_3 i_4} = \frac{\bar{m}^{(t,2)}_{i_1 i_2 i_3 i_4} \bar{n}_{+i_2++}}{\bar{m}^{(t,2)}_{+i_2++}} , \tag{7.198}$$

$$\bar{m}^{(t,4)}_{i_1 i_2 i_3 i_4} = \frac{\bar{m}^{(t,3)}_{i_1 i_2 i_3 i_4} \bar{n}_{++i_3 i_4}}{\bar{m}^{(t,3)}_{++i_3 i_4}} , \tag{7.199}$$

and

$$\underline{\bar{m}}^{(t+1,1)} = \underline{\bar{m}}^{(t,4)} . \tag{7.200}$$

TABLE 7.13

MAXIMUM-LIKELIHOOD ESTIMATE $\hat{\underline{m}}(\underline{n},I,E)$ FOR TABLE 7.1
IF $E = \{\{1\},\{2\},\{3\},\{4\}\}$

Type of Female	Fourth Chromosome	Male Gamete Type			
		AB	A'B	AB'	A'B'
Y	Marked	802.6	-	1290.8	574.7
	Unmarked	605.8	-	974.3	433.8
B	Marked	-	199.8	721.7	321.3
	Unmarked	-	150.8	544.8	242.5

If $\underline{\bar{m}}^{(1,1)} = \iota\underline{m}(\underline{n},I,E)$, then only one iteration is required to obtain an accurate approximation to $\hat{\underline{m}}(\underline{n},I,E')$. This maximum-likelihood estimate is given in table 7.14. The likelihood ratio and Pearson chi-square statistics are now 8.46 and 8.42, respectively, and there are 6 degrees of freedom, so the model appears satisfactory, particularly in view of the large sample size in this example. Examination of residuals also supports the model, for there is no apparent pattern among the residuals and the standardized residual of largest magnitude is -1.53.

TABLE 7.14

MAXIMUM-LIKELIHOOD ESTIMATE $\hat{\underline{m}}(\underline{n},I,E')$ FOR TABLE 7.1
IF $E' = \{\{1\},\{2\},\{3,4\}\}$

Type of Female	Fourth Chromosome	Male Gamete Type			
		AB	A'B	AB'	A'B'
Y	Marked	838.4	-	1348.3	600.3
	Unmarked	570.0	-	916.8	408.2
B	Marked	-	180.7	652.7	290.6
	Unmarked	-	169.9	613.8	273.3

Example 7.37. Although the Deming-Stephan algorithm for incomplete tables is closely related to the algorithm for complete tables, in the former case maximum-likelihood estimates which have closed form need not be found in a finite number of iterations. For example, if $E = \{\{1\},\{2\}\}$ and

(7.201)
$$\underline{n} = \begin{array}{|cc|} 2 & 1 \\ 1 & - \end{array} ,$$

then $\underline{n}$ is reducible and inseparable. Since $\rho M(E)$ has dimension 3 and I has three elements, $\rho M(E) = R^I$ and $\hat{\underline{m}}(\underline{n},I,E) = \underline{n}$. If $\underline{m}^{(0,1)} = \underline{e}$, then

(7.202)
$$\underline{m}^{(0,2)} = \begin{array}{|cc|} 3/2 & 3/2 \\ 1 & - \end{array}$$

and

(7.203)
$$\underline{m}^{(0,3)} = \begin{array}{|cc|} 9/5 & 1 \\ 6/5 & - \end{array} .$$

In general, $\underline{m}^{(t,1)}$ has the form

(7.204)
$$\underline{m}^{(t,1)} = \begin{array}{|cc|} 2 - \varepsilon_t & 1 \\ 1 + \varepsilon_t & - \end{array} ,$$

where $0 < \varepsilon_t \leq 1$ for all $t \geq 1$. This result holds for $t = 1$. If it holds for t, then

$$(7.205)\qquad \underline{m}^{(t,2)} = \boxed{\begin{array}{cc} 3\,\dfrac{2-\varepsilon_t}{3-\varepsilon_t} & \dfrac{\varepsilon_t}{3-\varepsilon_t} \\ & \\ 1 & - \end{array}}$$

and

$$(7.206)\qquad \underline{m}^{(t,3)} = \boxed{\begin{array}{cc} 2 - \dfrac{\varepsilon_t}{9-4\varepsilon_t} & 1 \\ & \\ 1 + \dfrac{\varepsilon_t}{9-4\varepsilon_t} & - \end{array}}$$

Since $\underline{m}^{(t+1,1)} = \underline{m}^{(t,3)}$, the induction hypothesis holds for $t + 1$ with $\varepsilon_{t+1} = \varepsilon_t/(9 - 4\varepsilon_t)$. Thus $\underline{m}^{(t,1)} \neq \hat{\underline{m}}(\underline{n},I,E)$ for any t.

COMPUTATION OF COMPONENTS

The decomposition of $\underline{\mu}$ into components $\rho\underline{\mu}^B$ suggested by (7.15) involves much more complex issues in the case of incomplete tables than does the corresponding decomposition in (5.38) for complete tables. Questions of uniqueness and estimability now arise and the simple algorithm described by (5.231) and (5.232) no longer suffices for computations.

If $\dim \rho M(E) = \dim M(E)$, then the components $\rho\underline{\mu}^B$, where $B \in H(E)$, are uniquely determined by $\underline{\mu}$. Given the unique vector $\underline{\mu}^* \in M(E)$ such that $\rho\underline{\mu}^* = \underline{\mu}$, $\underline{\mu}^B = (\underline{\mu}^*)^B$ can be found by (5.230) and (5.231) for each $B \in H(E)$. Computation of $\underline{\mu}^*$ may be facilitated by noting that if $J = I^* - I$, and $\underline{c} \in R^{I^*}$, then

$$(7.207)\qquad \begin{aligned} (\underline{c},\underline{\mu}^*)_{I^*} &= (\tau_I\rho_I\underline{c},\underline{\mu}^*)_{I^*} + (\tau_J\rho_J\underline{c},\underline{\mu}^*)_{I^*} \\ &= (\rho_I\underline{c},\rho_I\underline{\mu}^*)_I + (\rho_J\underline{c},\rho_J\underline{\mu}^*)_J \\ &= (\rho_I\underline{c},\underline{\mu})_I + (\rho_J\underline{c},\rho_J\underline{\mu}^*)_J . \end{aligned}$$

The condition $\underline{\mu}^* \in M(E)$ is equivalent to the condition that for all $\underline{c} \in [M(E)]^\perp$,

$$(7.208)\qquad \begin{aligned} (\underline{c},\underline{\mu}^*)_{I^*} &= (\rho_I\underline{c},\underline{\mu})_I + (\rho_J\underline{c},\rho_J\underline{\mu}^*)_J \\ &= 0. \end{aligned}$$

Uniqueness of $\underline{\mu}^*$ is equivalent to the condition $\rho_J[M(E)]^\perp = R^J$. The proof of this observation is straightforward. If $\underline{\mu}^*$ is unique, then $\rho_J[M(E)]^\perp = R^J$, for if $\underline{\mu} \in \tau_J\{\rho_J[M(E)]^\perp\}^\perp$, then $\rho(\underline{\mu}^* + \underline{\delta}) = \underline{\mu}$ and $\underline{\mu}^* + \underline{\delta} \in M(E)$. Conversely, if $\rho_J[M(E)]^\perp = R^J$, then $\underline{\mu}^*$ is unique, for if (7.208) holds for $\underline{c} \in [M(E)]^\perp$ for $\rho_J\underline{\mu}^* = \underline{\mu}^{(1)}$ and $\rho_J\underline{\mu}^* = \underline{\mu}^{(2)}$, then $\underline{\mu}^{(1)} - \underline{\mu}^{(2)} \in \{\rho_J[M(E)]^\perp\}^\perp = \{\underline{0}\}$ and $\underline{\mu}^{(1)} = \underline{\mu}^{(2)}$. To compute $\underline{\mu}^*$, it thus suffices to select $\{\underline{c}^{(j)}: j \in J\}$ such that $\underline{c}^{(j)} \in [M(E)]^\perp$ and span $\{\rho_J\underline{c}^{(j)}: j \in J\} = R^J$. The simultaneous equations

(7.209) $$(\rho_I\underline{c}^{(j)},\underline{\mu})_I + (\rho_J\underline{c}^{(j)},\rho_J\underline{\mu}^*)_J = 0$$

for $j \in J$ uniquely determine $\rho_J\underline{\mu}^*$, and $\underline{\mu}^* = \tau_I\underline{\mu} + \tau_J\rho_J\underline{\mu}^*$. Since $\underline{\mu}^*$ is a linear function of $\underline{\mu}$, the maximum-likelihood estimate $\hat{\underline{\mu}}^*$ of $\underline{\mu}^*$ satisfies

(7.210) $$(\rho_I\underline{c}^{(j)},\hat{\underline{\mu}})_I + (\rho_J\underline{c}^{(j)},\rho_J\hat{\underline{\mu}}^*)_J = 0$$

for $j \in J$, and the maximum-likelihood estimate of the component $\rho\underline{\mu}^B$ corresponding to M_B is $\rho(\hat{\underline{\mu}}^*)^B$. Similarly, the B-interaction vector $\underline{v}^B \in R^{I^*(B)}$ defined by the equation $(\underline{\mu}^*)^B = \{v^B_{\pi_B\underline{i}}: \underline{i} \in I^*\}$ has the maximum-likelihood estimate $\hat{\underline{v}}^B$ defined by $(\hat{\underline{\mu}}^*)^B = \{\hat{v}^B_{\pi_B\underline{i}}: \underline{i} \in I^*\}$.

Example 7.38. In Example 7.36, the model $\underline{\mu} \in M(E)$, where $E = \{\{1\},\{2\},\{3,4\}\}$, was shown to provide a satisfactory fit to the data in table 7.1. To compute the components $\rho\hat{\underline{\mu}}^\phi$, $\rho\hat{\underline{\mu}}^{\{1\}}$, $\rho\hat{\underline{\mu}}^{\{2\}}$, $\rho\hat{\underline{\mu}}^{\{3\}}$, $\rho\hat{\underline{\mu}}^{\{4\}}$, and $\rho\hat{\underline{\mu}}^{\{3,4\}}$, it is first necessary to find $\underline{\mu}^*$. For this computation, the vectors $\underline{c}^{(1)}$, $\underline{c}^{(2)}$, $\underline{c}^{(3)}$, and $\underline{c}^{(4)}$ are employed, where these vectors are defined as in table 7.15. It follows that $\hat{\mu}^*_{i_1i_2i_3i_4} = \hat{\mu}_{i_1i_2i_3i_4}$ if $\langle i_1,i_2,i_3,i_4\rangle \in I$,

(7.211) $$\hat{\mu}^*_{1112} = \hat{\mu}_{1111} + \hat{\mu}_{2112} - \hat{\mu}_{2111},$$

(7.212) $$\hat{\mu}^*_{1122} = \hat{\mu}_{1121} + \hat{\mu}_{2122} - \hat{\mu}_{2121},$$

(7.213) $$\hat{\mu}^*_{1211} = \hat{\mu}_{1212} + \hat{\mu}_{2211} - \hat{\mu}_{2212},$$

and

(7.214) $$\hat{\mu}^*_{1221} = \hat{\mu}_{1222} + \hat{\mu}_{2221} - \hat{\mu}_{2222}.$$

Given $\hat{\underline{\mu}}^*$, the components may be found by use of the equations

(7.215) $$\hat{v}^\phi_\alpha = \frac{1}{16}\hat{\mu}^*_{++++},$$

TABLE 7.15

ELEMENTS $c^{(k)}_{i_1 i_2 i_3 i_4}$ OF VECTORS

SPANNING $[M(E)]^{\perp}$ IN EXAMPLE 7.37

Index	Vector Number 1	2	3	4
<1,1,1,1>	-1	0	0	0
<1,1,1,2>	1	0	0	0
<1,1,2,1>	0	-1	0	0
<1,1,2,2>	0	1	0	0
<1,2,1,1>	0	0	1	0
<1,2,1,2>	0	0	-1	0
<1,2,2,1>	0	0	0	1
<1,2,2,2>	0	0	0	-1
<2,1,1,1>	1	0	0	0
<2,1,1,2>	-1	0	0	0
<2,1,2,1>	0	1	0	0
<2,1,2,2>	0	-1	0	0
<2,2,1,1>	0	0	-1	0
<2,2,1,2>	0	0	1	0
<2,2,2,1>	0	0	0	-1
<2,2,2,2>	0	0	0	1

(7.216) $$\hat{v}^{\{1\}}_{i_1} = \frac{1}{8}\hat{\mu}^{(1)}_{i_1+++} \quad \text{for } i_1 \in \overline{2},$$

(7.217) $$\hat{v}^{\{2\}}_{i_2} = \frac{1}{8}\hat{\mu}^{(2)}_{+i_2++} \quad \text{for } i_2 \in \overline{2},$$

(7.218) $$\hat{v}^{\{3\}}_{i_3} = \frac{1}{8}\hat{\mu}^{(3)}_{++i_3+} \quad \text{for } i_3 \in \overline{2},$$

(7.219) $$\hat{v}^{\{4\}}_{i_4} = \frac{1}{8}\hat{\mu}^{(4)}_{+++i_4} \quad \text{for } i_4 \in \overline{2},$$

and

(7.220) $$\hat{v}^{\{3,4\}}_{i_3 i_4} = \frac{1}{4}\hat{\mu}^{(5)}_{++i_3 i_4} \quad \text{for } i_3 \in \overline{2} \text{ and } i_4 \in \overline{2},$$

where

(7.221) $$(\hat{\underline{\mu}}^{*})^{B} = \{\hat{v}^{B}_{\pi_B \underline{i}} : \underline{i} \in I\}$$

for $B \in H(E)$,

(7.222) $$\underline{\hat{\mu}}^{(1)} = \underline{\hat{\mu}}^{*} - \underline{\hat{\mu}}^{*},$$

and

(7.223) $$\underline{\hat{\mu}}^{(k+1)} = \underline{\hat{\mu}}^{(k)} - (\underline{\hat{\mu}}^{*})^{(k)}$$

for $k \in \overline{4}$. Results are summarized in table 7.16, where $\underline{\hat{\mu}}^{*}$ and the component vectors $(\underline{\hat{\mu}}^{*})^{B}$ are given. The vectors $\underline{\hat{v}}^{B}$ and $\rho(\underline{\hat{\mu}}^{*})^{B}$ may be derived from the table. Since $I^* = \overline{2} \times \overline{2} \times \overline{2} \times \overline{2}$, the B-interaction is determined by $\hat{v}^{B}_{\pi_B<1,1,1,1>}$. Consequently, the interaction structure may be summarized by reporting the vector $\{\hat{v}^{B}_{\pi_B<1,1,1,1>}: B \in H(E)\}$, as is done in table 7.17.

The asymptotic standard deviations reported in the table are derived in the same manner as was used in Example 5.56. If Poisson sampling is assumed, then the estimated asymptotic covariance matrix of $\{\hat{v}^{B}_{\pi_B<1,1,1,1>}: B \in H(E)\}$ with respect to the standard basis is the inverse of the matrix $[M^T D(\underline{\hat{\mu}})M]$, where $M: R^{H(E)} \longrightarrow \mathcal{M}(E)$ satisfies

(7.224) $$M^T\underline{x} = \sum_{B \in H(E)} x_B \underline{c\nu}(B, \pi_B<1,1,1,1>)$$

and

(7.225) $$[M^T D(\underline{\hat{\mu}})M]_{gh} = (\underline{c\nu}(B_g, \pi_{B_g}<1,1,1,1>), D(\underline{\hat{\mu}})\underline{c\nu}(B_h, \pi_{B_h}<1,1,1,1>))$$

for $g \in \overline{6}$ and $h \in \overline{6}$, where $H(E) = \{B_g: g \in \overline{6}\}$. The asymptotic standard deviations are found by taking square roots of the diagonal elements of the inverse $[M^T D(\underline{\hat{\mu}})M]^{-1}$.

To interpret the estimated interactions, it should be observed that given any combination of type of female, fourth chromosome, and second homologue such that A and A' are both possible, the probability of A is $e^{v_1^{\{1\}}}/(e^{v_1^{\{1\}}} + e^{v_2^{\{1\}}}) = e^{v_1^{\{1\}}}/(e^{v_1^{\{1\}}} + e^{-v_1^{\{1\}}})$. The estimated value of this probability is 0.383. Since an approximate 95% confidence interval for $v_1^{\{1\}}$ is $[-0.238 - 1.96(0.014), -0.238 + 1.96(0.014)] = [-0.265, -0.210]$, an approximate 95% confidence interval for this probability is $[e^{-0.265}/(e^{-0.265} + e^{0.265}), e^{-0.210}/(e^{-0.210} + e^{0.210})] = [0.371, 0.394]$. Similarly, given any combination of type of female, fourth chromosome, and first homologue such that B and B' are both possible, the probability of B is $e^{v_1^{\{2\}}}/(e^{v_1^{\{2\}}} + e^{-v_1^{\{2\}}})$, which has a maximum-likelihood estimate of 0.692. The 95% confidence interval for this probability is [0.680,0.704].

TABLE 7.16

COMPONENTS OF ESTIMATED LOG-MEAN VECTOR FOR DATA IN TABLE 7.1

		Effect					
Index	$\hat{\mu}^*$	Main	First Homologue	Second Homologue	Fourth Chromosome	Type of Female	Chromosome × Female
<1,1,1,1>	6.731	6.090	-0.238	0.405	0.112	0.282	0.081
<1,1,1,2>	6.006	6.090	-0.238	0.405	0.112	-0.282	-0.081
<1,1,2,1>	6.346	6.090	-0.238	0.405	-0.112	0.282	-0.081
<1,1,2,2>	5.944	6.090	-0.238	0.405	-0.112	-0.282	0.081
<1,2,1,1>	5.922	6.090	-0.238	-0.405	0.112	0.282	0.081
<1,2,1,2>	5.197	6.090	-0.238	-0.405	0.112	-0.282	-0.081
<1,2,2,1>	5.537	6.090	-0.238	-0.405	-0.112	0.282	-0.081
<1,2,2,2>	5.135	6.090	-0.238	-0.405	-0.112	-0.282	0.081
<2,1,1,1>	7.207	6.090	-0.238	0.405	0.112	0.282	0.081
<2,1,1,2>	6.481	6.090	-0.238	0.405	0.112	-0.282	-0.081
<2,1,2,1>	6.821	6.090	-0.238	0.405	-0.112	0.282	-0.081
<2,1,2,2>	6.420	6.090	-0.238	0.405	-0.112	-0.282	0.081
<2,2,1,1>	6.397	6.090	-0.238	-0.405	-0.112	0.282	0.081
<2,2,1,2>	5.672	6.090	-0.238	-0.405	0.112	-0.282	-0.081
<2,2,2,1>	6.012	6.090	-0.238	-0.405	-0.112	0.282	-0.081
<2,2,2,2>	5.611	6.090	-0.238	-0.405	-0.112	-0.282	0.081

TABLE 7.17

ESTIMATED INTERACTIONS IN TABLE 7.1

Interaction	Estimate	Estimated Asymptotic Standard Deviation
Main	6.090	0.016
First Homologue	-0.238	0.014
Second Homologue	0.405	0.014
Fourth Chromosome	0.112	0.013
Type of Female	0.282	0.013
Fourth Chromosome x Type of Female	0.081	0.013

The problem of recovery of information concerning $\underline{\mu}^*$ and its components has not received much attention in the literature on contingency tables. One exception to this statement is Fienberg (1972), in which multiple recapture censuses are discussed in terms of 2^k contingency tables with one cell omitted. Kruskal (1968b) provides some discussion of this problem in the context of missing values in analysis of variance.

When $\rho M(E)$ and $M(E)$ do not have the same dimension, recovery of information becomes a more complex undertaking. There exists more than one vector $\underline{\mu}^*$ such that $\rho\underline{\mu}^* = \underline{\mu}$, the log-mean vector, so $\underline{\mu}^*$ cannot possibly be estimated. More precisely, in analogy to Scheffé (1959) or Kruskal (1968b), one may say that an expression $\underline{\beta}$ in some vector space R^J is estimable if it is a linear function of $\underline{\mu}$; otherwise, it is inestimable. Thus, $\underline{\mu}^*$ is inestimable since it is not a well-defined linear function of $\underline{\mu}$. Nevertheless, the fact that $\underline{\mu}^*$ is undefined does not preclude the possibility that components $\rho\underline{\mu}^B$ may be estimable for some $B \in H(E)$ or that linear functions $(\underline{c},\underline{\mu}^*)$ may be estimable.

To examine this situation more closely, observe that (7.208) implies that if $\rho\underline{\mu}^* = \underline{\mu}$, then $\rho(\underline{\mu}^* + \underline{\delta}) = \underline{\mu}$ if and only if $\underline{\delta} \in \tau_J\{\rho_J[M(E)]^\perp\}^\perp$. By Lemma 7.1 and (7.207), $(\underline{c},\underline{\mu}^*)$ is a well-defined linear function of $\underline{\mu}$ if and only if $\rho_J\underline{c} \in \{\rho_J[M(E)]^\perp\}^\perp$. The projection $P_{M_B}\underline{\mu}^*$ is a linear function of $\underline{\mu}$ if and only if $P_{M_B}\tau_J\{\rho_J[M(E)]^\perp\}^\perp = \{\underline{0}\}$. This condition is equivalent to the condition $M_B \perp \tau_J\{\rho_J[M(E)]^\perp\}^\perp$, which is equivalent in turn to the condition $\rho_J M_B \subset [\rho_J M(E)]^\perp$. Thus if

(7.226)
$$\mu_{\underline{i}} = \sum_{B \in H(E)} v^B_{\pi_B \underline{i}}$$

for each $\underline{i} \in I$, where $\underline{v}^B \in R^{I*(B)}$ and $\{v^B_{\pi_B\underline{i}}: \underline{i} \in I\} \in M_B$ for $B \in H(E)$, then $\underline{v}^B$ is estimable if and only if $\rho_J M_B \subset \rho_J[M(E)]^\perp$.

To compute maximum-likelihood estimates of estimable components of $\underline{\mu}$, one may proceed by first finding some $\hat{\underline{\mu}}^*$ such that (7.210) holds for some $\{\underline{c}^{(j)}: j \in K\}$ which form a basis of $\rho_J[M(E)]^\perp$. Given this value $\hat{\underline{\mu}}^*$, the algorithm of (5.230) and (5.231) may be used to obtain components $P_{M_B}\hat{\underline{\mu}}^*$ for each $B \in H(E)$. If $\rho_J M_B \subset \rho_J[M(E)]^\perp$ for some $B \in H(E)$, then $P_{M_B}\hat{\underline{\mu}}^*$ is the maximum-likelihood estimate of $P_{M_B}\underline{\mu}^*$. Even when $P_{M_B}\underline{\mu}^*$ is not estimable, some information about $P_{M_B}\underline{\mu}^*$ can be obtained; however, except in cases related to specialized models from the design of experiments such as those discussed in Cochran and Cox (1967), little is known concerning use of this information.

Example 7.39. If $E = \{\{1\},\{2\}\}$, then in table 7.2, $P_{M_\phi}\underline{\mu}^*$, $P_{M_{\{1\}}}\underline{\mu}^*$, and $P_{M_{\{2\}}}\underline{\mu}^*$ are not estimable. This result has been verified already in Example 7.4; however, it is useful to use the methods of this section to obtain the same result. Here $J = \{2,3\} \times \{1,4,7,9\} \cup \{1,4\} \times \{2,3,5,6,8\}$. The linear manifold $\rho_J M_\phi$ is not in $\rho_J[M(E)]^\perp$ since if $\rho_J\underline{\mu} = \underline{e}^J$ and $\underline{\mu} \in [M(E)]^\perp$, then $\mu_{i+} = 0$ for $i \in \overline{4}$ and $\mu_{+j} = 0$ for $j \in \overline{9}$. Therefore, $\mu_{i+}(I_1) = -5$ if $i \in \{1,4\}$ and $\mu_{+j}(I_1) = -2$ if $j \in \{1,4,7,9\}$. Consequently $\mu_{++}(I_1)$ must be both -10 and -8, an impossibility. Similarly if $\underline{\mu} \in [M(E)]^\perp$ and $\rho_J\underline{\mu} = \rho_J[\underline{\nu}(\{1\},1) - \underline{\nu}(\{1\},2)]$, then $\mu_{1+}(I_1) = -5$, $\mu_{4+}(I_1) = 0$, and $\mu_{+j}(I_1) = 1$ for $j \in \{1,4,7,9\}$. Thus $\mu_{++}(I_1)$ must be both -5 and -4, an impossibility. Since $\underline{\nu}(\{1\},1) - \underline{\nu}(\{1\},2) \in M_{\{1\}}$, $\rho_J M_{\{1\}} \not\subset \rho_J[M(E)]^\perp$. Similar arguments also apply to $M_{\{2\}}$. Thus in this example, no maximum-likelihood estimates of components are available.

Chapter 8

QUANTAL-RESPONSE MODELS

In quantal-response analysis the observed response is a nominal variable which takes on $r \geq 2$ possible values. The experiment is designed to investigate the dependence of this response on one or more continuous, ordered, or nominal independent variables. This type of analysis was originally considered by Bliss (1935) and Fisher (1935c) in connection with biological assay. They developed the method of probit analysis to treat this problem when the response is binomial and one continuous independent variable is present. Later Berkson (1944) developed logit analysis for use in the same problem. With the advent of high-speed computation, more complex experimental situations have been examined by means of probit analysis, logit analysis, or related methods. The case of binomial response to several independent variables is considered by Walker and Duncan (1967) and Theil (1970), while multinomial response problems have been examined by Bock (1968) and Theil (1970). Logit models for factorial tables have been explored by Dyke and Patterson (1952) and Bishop (1969), among others. Since, as shown in this chapter, logit and multinomial logit models are log-linear models, the methods of this monograph may be applied to quantal-response analysis. In this chapter, this relationship is used to shed new insight into problems of existence of estimates, computation, and asymptotic properties.

BINOMIAL-RESPONSE MODELS

In a binomial-response model, there are a fixed number $N_j > 0$ of responses to an experimental condition $j \in J$. If the responses are called 1 and 2, then one has a table $\underline{n} = \{n_{jk}: j \in J \text{ and } k \in \overline{2}\}$ of observations and an index set $I = J \times \overline{2}$, where n_{jk} is the number of cases in which response k is observed under condition j. The probability $p(1|j)$ of response 1 under condition $j \in J$ is normally assumed to be $F(\lambda_j)$, the value at λ_j of a known cumulative distribution function F with range $(0,1)$, where $\underline{\lambda} = \{\lambda_j: j \in J\} \in L$, a linear manifold in R^J. The random variable n_{j1} thus has a binomial distribution with sample size N_j and probability $F(\lambda_j)$. The name attached to the method of analysis depends on F. If $F(x) = \Phi(x) = (2\pi)^{\frac{1}{2}} \int_{-\infty}^{x} \exp(-y^2/2)dy$, the distribution function for the standard normal, then the term "probit analysis" is used. The inverse function $\Phi^{-1}(p)$ is called the normit of p, and $5 + \Phi^{-1}(p)$ is the probit of p. If $F(x) = L(x) = 1/(1 + e^{-x})$, the distribution function of the standard logistic, then the term "logit analysis" is employed, and $L^{-1}(p) = \log [p/(1 - p)]$ is the logit of p. The tolerance distribution is the distribution with F as its distribution function. An explanation of this terminology may be found in Finney (1971).

Example 8.1. In the classical problem of biological assay with quantal response, the effects of a drug or poison are assessed by giving a log dosage t_j, where $j \in \overline{r}$ and $r \geq 2$, to each of N_j subjects and observing whether or not the treatment has the intended effect. Response 1 has probability $F(\alpha + \beta t_j)$, and response 2 has probability $1 - F(\alpha + \beta t_j)$. Thus $L = \text{span}\,\{\underline{e},\underline{t}\}$, where $\underline{t} = \{t_j: j \in \overline{r}\}$. To guarantee that α and β are estimable, one assumes that no two t_j's are equal.

Bliss (1935) provides motivation for this model through the idea of a minimum effective dosage. It is assumed that for any subject in the population there is a tolerance t for the drug or poison, where $\alpha + \beta t$ has the distribution function F. This tolerance is the minimum effective log dosage of the drug; that is, response 2 occurs unless the log dosage t_j exceeds the tolerance t. Thus the probability of response 1 is $F(\alpha + \beta t_j)$.

The table in Example 1.6 illustrates this type of problem. The drug digitalis is examined by observing how many frogs out of 15 are killed if the drug is administered at log dosages of 0.75, 0.85, and 0.95. Thus $J = \overline{3}$ and $t = \langle 0.75, 0.85, 0.95\rangle$. Miller, Bliss, and Braun (1939) used probit analysis with these data, while Finney (1947) performed the same analysis with logits. Thorough discussion of this form of quantal-response analysis is given by Finney (1947, 1964, 1971), who also provides extensive references to the enormous literature on this problem.

Example 8.2. Probit and logit analysis may be applied to problems unrelated to drug or poison evaluation. One such example is final standings of major league baseball teams. Such a study was made by Mosteller (1951b) for the American League pennant race of 1948, the results of which are summarized in table 8.1. If the teams are numbered from 1 to 8, n_{ij1} is the number of times team i beats team j, and n_{ij2} is the number of times team j beats team i, then the data may be described by the vector $n = \{n_{ijk}: i \in \overline{j - 1}, j \in \overline{8}, k \in \overline{2}\}$. The index set $I = J \times \overline{2}$, where $J = \{\langle i,j\rangle: i \in \overline{j - 1}, j \in \overline{8}\}$, and $N_{ij} = n_{ij+}$ for each pair $\langle i,j\rangle \in J$. A simple model

TABLE 8.1

RESULTS OF GAMES BETWEEN
AMERICAN LEAGUE TEAMS IN 1948

Winning Team	Losing Team							
	Cleveland	Boston	New York	Philadelphia	Detroit	St. Louis	Washington	Chicago
Cleveland	-	11	10	16	13	14	16	16
Boston	10	-	14	12	15	15	15	14
New York	12	8	-	12	13	16	17	16
Philadelphia	6	10	10	-	10	18	14	16
Detroit	9	7	9	12	-	11	16	14
St. Louis	8	7	6	4	11	-	10	13
Washington	6	7	5	8	6	11	-	12
Chicago	6	8	6	6	8	8	9	-

for these data is one in which each team $i \in \overline{8}$ has a strength α_i and if $<i,j> \in J$

(8.1) $$\lambda_{ij} = \alpha_i - \alpha_j .$$

The probability that team i beats team j is then $F(\lambda_{ij})$, where $\underline{\lambda} \in L$, the space of $\underline{\lambda}$ which satisfy (8.1) for some $\underline{\alpha} \in R^8$. The model arises if it is assumed that in any of the N_{ij} games between teams i and j, team i wins if $x > 0$, where x, the difference in team strength, is a random variable such that $x - \lambda_{ij}$ has the distribution with F as a cumulative distribution function. Mosteller, in his analysis, assumed a normal tolerance distribution. A logistic tolerance distribution can also be used.

This example is just one type of paired comparisons model. Such models are examined in detail in a monograph by David (1963), who provides an extensive bibliography of the subject. In the general model for paired comparisons, r objects are compared by asking N_{ij} judges to state whether they prefer object i to object j, where $1 \leq i < j \leq r$. Object i has a rating α_i for $i \in \overline{r}$, so the difference in rating between object i and object j is $\alpha_i - \alpha_j$. Due to observational error, a judge considers the difference in rating to be $\alpha_i - \alpha_j + x$, where x has the distribution corresponding to F. Thus the probability that i is preferred to j is $F(\alpha_i - \alpha_j)$. In the quantal-response analysis, $J = \{<i,j>: i \in \overline{j-1}, j \in \overline{r}, N_{ij} > 0\}$ and $I = J \times \overline{2}$. The linear manifold L is the set of $\underline{\lambda}$ which satisfy (8.1) for $<i,j> \in J$. The use of the normal tolerance distribution in this analysis is generally associated with Mosteller (1951a, 1951b) and Thurstone (1927), while the logistic tolerance distribution has been employed in this problem by Bradley and Terry (1952). The only peculiarity in the baseball example is a conceptual one; in baseball, the judges are replaced by games between individual teams.

Example 8.3. Yates (1955) examined results of irradiation of spermatozoa of *D. melanogaster*. Two methods of irradiation were used, and their effects were compared. Results are summarized in table 8.2. In the first four experiments, a dose of 960 r was used, while a dose of 3000 r was employed in the remaining two experiments. In addition, it was suspected that unavoidable environmental changes between experiments might affect observed mutation rates. In this experiment, $I = \overline{6} \times \overline{2} \times \overline{2}$ and $J = \overline{6} \times \overline{2}$, where the second set $\overline{2}$ corresponds to the type of spermatozoa observed, the first $\overline{2}$ corresponds to the treatment method, and $\overline{6}$ corresponds to the experiment number.

TABLE 8.2

FREQUENCY OF MUTANTS WITH TWO METHODS OF IRRADIATION

Experiment Number	Method F Mutant	Method F Normal	Method M Mutant	Method M Normal
1	29	815	45	1486
2	78	2622	27	1438
3	110	3175	100	4281
4	25	1038	52	2053
5	31	339	43	507
6	57	543	27	436

Since two variables, experiment and method of irradiation, affect the mutation rate, an appropriate model is that $\underline{\lambda} \in M(J,\{\{1\},\{2\}\})$ and F is the distribution function for the logistic distribution. This model corresponds to the hypothesis that given an experiment $i \in \overline{6}$, the odds $p(1|\langle i,1\rangle)/p(2|\langle i,1\rangle)$ of a mutation under method F are a constant multiple of the odds $p(1|\langle i,2\rangle)/p(2|\langle i,2\rangle)$ of a mutation under method M. A very similar model proposed by Yates on theoretical grounds is that $L = M(J,\{\{1\},\{2\}\})$ and $F(x) = 1 - \exp(-e^x)$. This tolerance distribution corresponds to what Yates calls a complementary log-log transformation. When the probability of mutation is small, the difference between the two models is negligible.

To derive the model proposed by Yates, note that a mutation occurs if there is a mutation at any one of ℓ loci. Suppose that mutations at different loci occur independently and suppose that the probability $p_{jk}(\omega)$ of a mutation at locus k, $k \in \bar{\ell}$, given ω units of radiation administered by method j under experimental condition 1 satisfies the condition $1 - p_{jk}(\omega_1 + \omega_2) = [1 - p_{jk}(\omega_1)][p_{jk}(\omega_2)]$. In other words, it is assumed that the effect of $\omega_1 + \omega_2$ units of radiation is the same as the effect of independent applications of ω_1 and ω_2 units of radiation. Given this assumption, it follows that

$$p_{jk}(\omega) = 1 - \exp(-\Theta_{jk}\omega) \tag{8.2}$$

for some Θ_{jk}. Under experimental condition i, it is assumed that the actual units of radiation administered are equivalent to ω_i units administered under experimental condition 1. Then the probability of a mutation under experimental condition i and method of irradiation j is

$$\sum_{k=1}^{\ell} [1 - p_{jk}(\omega_i)] = 1 - \exp[-(\sum_{k=1}^{\ell} \Theta_{jk})\omega_i] . \tag{8.3}$$

If the complementary log-log transformation is used, then

$$\lambda_{ij} = \log \omega_i + \log \Theta'_j , \tag{8.4}$$

where

$$\Theta'_j = \sum_{k=1}^{\ell} \Theta_{jk} . \tag{8.5}$$

Thus $\underline{\lambda} \in M(J,\{\{1\},\{2\}\})$.

These three examples cannot provide a full indication of the range of applications of binomial response models, but they do suggest the variety of problems which can be examined by the methods developed in this chapter. Much of the rest of the chapter is devoted to examination of the computational techniques and asymptotic theory required to analyze the data in these examples.

MAXIMUM-LIKELIHOOD EQUATIONS

If the tolerance distribution has a density function f which is positive and differentiable at all points on the real line and if both $\log F(x)$ and $\log [1 - F(x)]$ are strictly concave, then maximum-likelihood estimation is straightforward. To see that result, note that the log likelihood $\ell^{(F)}(\underline{n},\underline{\lambda})$ for $\underline{\lambda} \in L$ satisfies

(8.6)
$$\ell^{(F)}(\underline{n},\underline{\lambda}) = \sum_{j \in J} \Big\{ n_{j1} \log F(\lambda_j) + n_{j2} \log[1 - F(\lambda_j)] + \log N_j! - \log n_{j1}! - \log n_{j2}! \Big\} .$$

Thus one may proceed as in chapter 2 and show that for $\underline{\nu} \in L$, the differential at $\underline{\lambda}$ satisfies

(8.7)
$$\begin{aligned} d\ell^{(F)}_{\underline{\lambda}}(n,\underline{\nu}) &= \sum_{j \in J} \left[\frac{n_{j1} f(\lambda_j)}{F(\lambda_j)} - \frac{n_{j1} f(\lambda_j)}{1 - F(\lambda_j)} \right] \nu_j \\ &= \sum_{j \in J} \nu_j f(\lambda_j) \left\{ \frac{n_{j1} - N_j F(\lambda_j)}{F(\lambda_j)} - \frac{n_{j2} - N_j [1 - F(\lambda_j)]}{1 - F(\lambda_j)} \right\} \\ &= \sum_{j \in J} \nu_j \left\{ \frac{f(\lambda_j)}{F(\lambda_j)[1 - F(\lambda_j)]} \right\} [n_{j1} - N_j F(\lambda_j)] \\ &= (\underline{\nu}, \overline{D}^{(F)}(\underline{\lambda})(\overline{n} - \overline{m}^{(F)}(\underline{N},\underline{\lambda}))), \end{aligned}$$

where $\overline{m}^{(F)}(N,\underline{\lambda}) = \{N_j F(\lambda_j)\}$, the mean of $\overline{n} = \{n_{j1} : j \in J\}$, and $\overline{D}^{(F)}(\underline{\lambda})\underline{x} = \{x_j f(\lambda_j)/\{F(\lambda_j)[1 - F(\lambda_j)]\}\}$ for all $\underline{x} \in R^J$. If $\hat{\underline{\lambda}}$ is a maximum-likelihood estimate of $\underline{\lambda}$, then $d\ell^{(F)}_{\hat{\underline{\lambda}}}(\underline{n},\underline{\nu}) = 0$ for all $\underline{\nu} \in L$. Therefore,

(8.8)
$$\overline{P}^{(F)}_L(\hat{\underline{\lambda}})\overline{n} = \overline{P}^{(F)}_L(\hat{\underline{\lambda}})\overline{m}^{(F)}(\underline{N},\hat{\underline{\lambda}}),$$

where $\overline{P}^{(F)}_L(\hat{\underline{\lambda}})$ is the projection from R^J onto L orthogonal with respect to the inner product defined by $\overline{D}^{(F)}(\hat{\underline{\lambda}})$. The maximum-likelihood estimate is unique if it exists since $\ell^{(F)}(\underline{n},\underline{\lambda})$ is strictly concave if $\log F$ and $\log(1 - F)$ are strictly concave.

The condition that $\log F$ and $\log(1 - F)$ are strictly concave is satisfied if the tolerance distribution is logistic or normal. In both cases, since the tolerance distribution is symmetric, $\log[1 - F(x)] = \log F(-x)$. Thus it suffices to show that $\log F(x)$ is strictly concave. In the logistic case,

(8.10)
$$\begin{aligned} g(x) &= \log L(x) \\ &= -\log(1 + e^{-x}) , \end{aligned}$$

(8.10)
$$g'(x) = \frac{e^{-x}}{1 + e^{-x}}$$

and

(8.11)
$$g''(x) = \frac{-e^{-x}}{(1 + e^{-x})^2} < 0.$$

Thus log L is strictly concave. The proof for the normal case is a bit more difficult. Here

(8.12)
$$g(x) = \log (2\pi)^{-\frac{1}{2}} \int_{-\infty}^{x} \exp(-y^2/2)dy \ ,$$

(8.13)
$$g'(x) = \exp(-x^2/2)\Big/\int_{-\infty}^{x} \exp(-y^2/2)dy \ ,$$

and

(8.14)
$$g''(x) = \frac{-x \exp(-x^2/2) \int_{-\infty}^{x} \exp(-y^2/2)dy - \exp(-x^2)}{\left[\int_{-\infty}^{x} \exp(-y^2/2)dy\right]^2} \ .$$

If $x \geq 0$, $g''(x) \leq 0$ since neither term in the numerator is positive. If $x < 0$, the fact that

(8.15)
$$\int_{-\infty}^{x} \exp(-y^2/2)dy < -\frac{1}{x} \exp(-x^2/2)$$

implies that $g''(x) < 0$ (see Feller 1968). Thus $\log \Phi$ is also strictly concave in the normal case. Since the condition that $\log F$ and $\log (1 - F)$ is concave can also be shown to apply if $F(x) = 1 - \exp(-e^{x})$, the assumptions made concerning the tolerance distribution are general enough to include the useful cases. Therefore, it will be assumed in the rest of this chapter that $\log F$ and $\log (1 - F)$ are concave and that $f = F'$ is positive and differentiable.

The logistic tolerance distribution has some advantage over the normal tolerance distribution when computation of maximum-likelihood estimates or asymptotic covariances is considered since the logistic tolerance distribution is essentially the only tolerance distribution for which the second differential of $\ell^{(F)}(\underline{n},\underline{\lambda})$ is independent of $\underline{n}$. In the dosage response problem of Example 8.1, this result was derived by Garwood (1941). To investigate this situation in general, note that if $\underline{\nu} \in L$ and $\underline{\xi} \in L$,

(8.16)
$$d^2\ell_{\underline{\lambda}}^{(F)}(\underline{n},\underline{\xi})(\underline{\nu}) = -(\underline{\nu},W^{(F)}(\underline{N},\underline{\lambda})\underline{\xi}) + (\underline{\nu},V^{(F)}(\underline{n},\underline{\lambda})\underline{\xi})$$
$$= -(\underline{\nu},D^{(F)}(\underline{n},\underline{\lambda})\underline{\xi}),$$

where

$$W^{(F)}(\underline{N},\underline{\lambda})\underline{x} = \{N_j[f(\lambda_j)]^2 x_j/\{F(\lambda_j)[1 - F(\lambda_j)]\}\}$$
$$= \{w_j^{(F)}(\underline{N},\underline{\lambda})x_j\},$$
$$V^{(F)}(\underline{n},\underline{\lambda})\underline{x} = \{[\overline{n}_j - \overline{m}_j^{(F)}(\underline{N},\underline{\lambda})]y(\lambda_j)x_j\},$$
$$y(\lambda_j) = \{f(\lambda_j)/\{F(\lambda_j)[1 - F(\lambda_j)]\}\}',$$

and

$$D^{(F)}(\underline{n},\underline{\lambda}) = W^{(F)}(\underline{N},\underline{\lambda}) - V^{(F)}(\underline{n},\underline{\lambda}).$$

If $f(\lambda)/\{F(\lambda)[1 - F(\lambda)]\}$ is constant for all λ, then $y(\lambda) = 0$ and $V^{(F)}(\underline{n},\underline{\lambda}) = 0$. Thus (8.8) reduces to the equation

(8.17)
$$P_L\underline{\overline{n}} = P_L\underline{\overline{m}}^{(F)}(\hat{\underline{\lambda}}),$$

and the second differential does not depend on $\underline{n}$. Hence the condition that $f(\lambda)/\{F(\lambda)[1 - F(\lambda)]\} = k$ for some $k > 0$ is a desirable one. Since this condition implies

(8.18)
$$\frac{f(\lambda)}{F(\lambda)} + \frac{f(\lambda)}{1 - F(\lambda)} = k,$$

it follows that for some c,

(8.19)
$$\log F(\lambda) - \log[1 - F(\lambda)]$$
$$= \log\left[\frac{F(\lambda)}{1 - F(\lambda)}\right]$$
$$= k\lambda + c.$$

Consequently,

(8.20)
$$\frac{F(\lambda)}{1 - F(\lambda)} = e^{k\lambda + c}$$

and $F(\lambda) = 1/[1 + e^{-(k\lambda + c)}]$. Except for location and scale parameters, this is the distribution function of the standard logistic. Therefore, use of the logistic tolerance distribution results in some unique simplification in the maximum-likelihood estimation problem.

Given the mathematical convenience of the logistic tolerance distribution, use of another tolerance distribution requires justification. The most common alternative is the normal distribution, which differs very little from the logistic except in the tails of the distributions (see Finney 1964). Furthermore, no empirical evidence exists that the normal distribution provides more accurate models than the logistic distribution. Theoretical argüments have been advanced which favor one or the other distribution, but none of them appear convincing, at least to the author. In the context of biological assay, these arguments are summarized by Finney (1964), who also provides substantial references to other authors. Given that evidence in support of other tolerance distributions is limited, the rest of the section will emphasize logit analysis.

If a logit model is used, then the results of the first four chapters of the monograph may be applied, for any logit model is a log-linear model. To verify this statement, it suffices to note that

(8.21)
$$m_{j1} = N_j/[1 + \exp(-\lambda_j)]$$
$$= N_j \exp(\lambda_j/2)/[\exp(\lambda_j/2) + \exp(-\lambda_j/2]$$

and

(8.22)
$$m_{j2} = N_j \exp(-\lambda_j/2)/[1 + \exp(-\lambda_j)]$$
$$= N_j \exp(-\lambda_j/2)/[\exp(\lambda_j/2) + \exp(-\lambda_j/2)]$$

for each $j \in J$. If $\mathcal{R} = \mathcal{L} \otimes \text{span}\{\langle 1,-1\rangle\}$ and

(8.23)
$$\mathcal{N} = \text{span}\{\underline{\nu}^{(j)}: j \in J\}$$
$$= \{\underline{\mu} \in R^I: \mu_{j1} = \mu_{j2}\ \forall j \in J\},$$

where $\underline{\nu}^{(k)} = \{\delta_{jk}: \langle j,i\rangle \in J \times \bar{2}\}$ for each $k \in J$, then

(8.24)
$$\underline{\mu} = \tfrac{1}{2}\underline{\lambda} \otimes \langle 1,-1\rangle + \sum_{j \in J} \log\{N_j/[\exp(\lambda_j/2) + \exp(-\lambda_j/2)]\}\underline{\nu}^{(j)}$$
$$\in \mathcal{R} \oplus \mathcal{N}.$$

On the other hand, if $\underline{\mu} \in \mathcal{M} = \mathcal{R} \oplus \mathcal{N}$, then for some $\underline{\lambda} \in \mathcal{L}$ and $\underline{c} \in R^J$,

(8.25)
$$\underline{\mu} = \tfrac{1}{2}\underline{\lambda} \otimes \langle 1,-1\rangle + \sum_{j \in J} c_j\underline{\nu}^{(j)}$$

Thus for each $j \in J$,

(8.26) $$p(1|j) = \frac{\exp(\mu_{j1})}{\exp(\mu_{j1}) + \exp(\mu_{j2})}$$

$$= \frac{\exp(\lambda_j/2 + c_j)}{\exp(\lambda_j/2 + c_j) + \exp(-\lambda_j/2 + c_j)}$$

$$= \frac{1}{1 + \exp(-\lambda_j)} .$$

Hence the logit model that $\underline{\lambda} \in L$ is equivalent to the log-linear model that $\underline{\mu} \in M$.

The converse to the statement in the last paragraph is also true, for any log-linear model such that $\langle n_{j1}, n_{j2} \rangle$ is a binomial sample for each $j \in J$ corresponds to a logit model. This result follows since M must contain $N = \text{span}\,\{\underline{\nu}^{(j)}: j \in J\}$. If $R = M - N$, then any $\underline{\mu} \in R$ must satisfy $\mu_{j1} + \mu_{j2} = 0$ for all $j \in J$. Therefore, $\underline{\mu} = \underline{\lambda} \otimes \langle 1,-1 \rangle = f(\underline{\lambda})$ for some $\underline{\lambda} \in R^J$. If $L = f^{-1}(R)$, then $R = L \otimes \text{span}\,\{\langle 1,-1 \rangle\}$. The argument of (8.26) applies now, so for some $\underline{\lambda} \in L$,

(8.27) $$p(1|j) = 1/[1 + \exp(-\lambda_j)].$$

On the other hand, if (8.27) holds, then (8.25) holds for the log-mean vector $\underline{\mu}$, which is therefore in M. Thus logit and log-linear models are equivalent.

Example 8.4. The logistic model for the biological assay problem of Example 8.1 corresponds to the log-linear model $\underline{\mu} \in M$, where

(8.28) $$M = \text{span}\,\{\underline{e}^{(r)}, \underline{t}\} \otimes \text{span}\{\langle 1,-1 \rangle\} \oplus \text{span}\{\underline{\delta}(r,j) \otimes \langle 1,1 \rangle: j \in \overline{r}\}$$

$$= M(\overline{r} \times \overline{2}, \{\{1\},\{2\}\}) \oplus \text{span}\,\{\underline{t} \otimes \langle 1,-1 \rangle\}$$

$$= M(\overline{r} \times \overline{2}, \{\{1\},\{2\}\}) \oplus \text{span}\,\{(\underline{t} - \overline{t}.\underline{e}^{(r)}) \otimes \langle 1,-1 \rangle\},$$

$M(\overline{r} \times \overline{2}, \{\{1\},\{2\}\})$ is defined as in chapter 5, and $\overline{t}.$ is the average $r^{-1}\sum_{j=1}^{r} t_j$ of the t_j. Thus this logit model corresponds to one of the trend models discussed at the end of chapter 5.

Example 8.5. In Example 8.3, it is assumed that

(8.29) $$m_{i11}/m_{i12} = c m_{i21}/m_{i22}$$

for each $i \in \overline{6}$. This assumption corresponds to the hypothesis that the interaction

$\mu_{i11} - \mu_{i12} - \mu_{i21} + \mu_{i22} = \log c$ for all $i \in \bar{6}$. Thus the three-factor interaction component $P_{M_{\bar{3}}}\underline{\mu}$ is $\underline{0}$. Therefore, $M = M(I,\{\{1,2\},\{1,3\},\{2,3\}\})$.

The last example illustrates the more general observation that if in a logit model, $J = \prod_{j=1}^{d-1} \bar{r}_j$ and L is a hierarchical manifold, then in the log-linear model, M is a hierarchical manifold. If $E \neq \{\overline{d-1}\}$ and $L = M(J,E)$, where $E \subset \overline{d-1}$ for $E \in E$, then $M = M(I,E^*)$, where $I = \prod_{j=1}^{d} \bar{r}_j$, $r_d = 2$, and $E^* = \{E \cup \{d\}: E \in E\} \cup \{\overline{d-1}\}$. This result follows since, using the notation of chapter 5,

$$M = \left\{\left[\bigoplus_{B \in H(E)} \bigotimes_{j=1}^{d-1} M^{(j)}_{X_B(j)}\right] \otimes \text{span}\ \{<1,-1>\}\right\} \oplus N_{\overline{d-1}} \tag{8.30}$$

$$= \left[\bigoplus_{B \in H(E)} \bigotimes_{j=1}^{d} M^{(j)}_{X_{B\cup\{d\}}(j)}\right] \oplus N_{\overline{d-1}}$$

$$= \bigoplus_{B \in H(E^*)} M_B$$

$$= M(I,E^*).$$

In the one remaining case, $E = \{\overline{d-1}\}$ and $M = M(I,\{\bar{d}\})$. This result also follows from (8.30).

Conversely, if $N_{\overline{d-1}} \subset M(I,E^*)$, the log-linear model $\underline{\mu} \in M(I,E^*)$ corresponds to a logit model $\underline{\lambda} \in M(J,E)$, where $E = \{E \cap (\overline{d-1}): E \in E^*$ and $E \neq \overline{d-1}\}$, $I = \prod_{j=1}^{d} \bar{r}_j$, $J = \prod_{j=1}^{d-1} \bar{r}_j$, and $r_d = 2$. To verify this assertion, note that $M = R \oplus N$, where $N = N_{\overline{d-1}}$ and

$$R = \oplus \{\bigotimes_{j=1}^{d} M^{(j)}_{X_B(j)}: B \in H(E^*), d \in B\}; \tag{8.31}$$

that is, R is the sum of those M_B such that $B \not\subset \overline{d-1}$ but $B \in H(E^*)$. The corresponding manifold $L = f^{-1}(R)$ then satisfies

$$L = \oplus \{\bigotimes_{j=1}^{d-1} M^{(j)}_{X_B(j)}: B \in H(E)\} \tag{8.32}$$

$$= M(J,E).$$

Example 8.6. In Example 8.4, $L = M(\bar{6} \times \bar{2},\{\{1\},\{2\}\})$. Thus $E^* = \{\{1,3\},\{2,3\}\} \cup \{1,2\} = \{\{1,2\},\{1,3\},\{2,3\}\}$ and $I = \bar{6} \times \bar{2} \times \bar{2}$. The condition $\underline{\lambda} \in L$ is equivalent to the condition $\underline{\mu} \in M(I,E^*)$.

Given the equivalence of the logit model defined by L and the log-linear model defined by M, the most convenient formulation may be exploited when questions arise concerning sufficiency, existence of estimates, computation, or asymptotics. There is a one-to-one correspondence between $P_R\underline{n}$ and $P_L\underline{\bar{n}}$, for

$$(8.33)\qquad P_R\underline{n} = P_L\underline{\bar{n}} \otimes \langle 1,-1\rangle - \frac{1}{2} P_L\underline{N} \otimes \langle 1,-1\rangle,$$

where $\underline{N} = \{N_j: j \in J\}$.

This observation may be verified by noting that both sides of (8.33) are in $R = L \otimes \text{span}\,\{\langle 1,-1\rangle\}$ and for any $\underline{\lambda} \otimes \langle 1,-1\rangle$ such that $\underline{\lambda} \in L$, Lemma 5.3 implies that

$$
\begin{aligned}
(8.34)\quad (\underline{\lambda} \otimes \langle 1,-1\rangle, P_M\underline{n})_I &= (\underline{\lambda} \otimes \langle 1,-1\rangle, \underline{n})_I \\
&= (\underline{\lambda}, \{n_{j1} - n_{j2}\})_J \\
&= (\underline{\lambda}, \{2n_{j2} - N_j\})_J \\
&= 2(\underline{\lambda}, \underline{\bar{n}})_J - (\underline{\lambda}, \underline{N})_J \\
&= 2(\underline{\lambda}, P_L\underline{\bar{n}})_J - (\underline{\lambda}, P_L\underline{N})_J \\
&= ||\langle 1,-1\rangle||_2^2(\underline{\lambda}, P_L\underline{\bar{n}})_J - ||\langle 1,-1\rangle||_2^2(\underline{\lambda}, P_L\underline{N})_J/2 \\
&= (\underline{\lambda} \otimes \langle 1,-1\rangle, P_L\underline{\bar{n}} \otimes \langle 1,-1\rangle)_I - \tfrac{1}{2}(\underline{\lambda} \otimes \langle 1,-1\rangle, P_L\underline{N} \otimes \langle 1,-1\rangle)_I \\
&= (\underline{\lambda} \otimes \langle 1,-1\rangle, P_L\underline{\bar{n}} \otimes \langle 1,-1\rangle - \tfrac{1}{2} P_L\underline{N} \otimes \langle 1,-1\rangle)_I .
\end{aligned}
$$

Since $P_M\underline{n}$ is a complete minimal sufficient statistic, $P_L\underline{\bar{n}}$ is a complete minimal sufficient statistic. Comparable sufficient statistics do not exist when the tolerance distribution is not logistic.

The rules for existence of maximum-likelihood estimates in log-linear models may also be expressed in terms of L. The results are given in Theorem 8.1.

THEOREM 8.1. *If the vector* $\underline{\lambda}$ *of logits is assumed to be in a linear manifold* L *contained in* R^J, *then the maximum-likelihood estimate* $\hat{\underline{\lambda}}$ *of* $\underline{\lambda}$ *exists if and only if for some* $\underline{\delta} \in L^\perp$, $0 < n_{j1} + \delta_j < N_j$ *for each* $j \in J$. *Equivalently,* $\hat{\underline{\lambda}}$ *exists if and only if there exists no* $\underline{\lambda} \in L$ *such that* $\underline{\lambda} \neq \underline{0}$, $\lambda_j \le 0$ *if* $n_{j1} = 0$, $\lambda_j \ge 0$ *if* $n_{j1} = N_j$, *and* $\lambda_j = 0$ *if* $0 < n_{j1} < N_j$.

Proof. These results follow from Theorems 2.1 and 2.2. Since $M^\perp = L^\perp \otimes \text{span}\,\{\langle 1,-1\rangle\}$, any element of $M^\perp$ can be written as $\underline{\delta} \otimes \langle 1,-1\rangle$, where $\underline{\delta} \in L^\perp$.

The condition that each element of $\underline{n} + \underline{\delta} \otimes \langle 1,-1\rangle$ be positive is equivalent to the condition that $0 < n_{j1} + \delta_j < N_j$ for each $j \in J$. Thus the first half of the theorem follows from Theorem 2.1. Any element $\underline{\mu} \in M$ satisfies

$$\underline{\mu} = \underline{\lambda} \otimes \langle 1,-1\rangle + \sum_{j \in J} c_j \underline{\nu}^{(j)} \tag{8.35}$$

for some $\underline{\lambda} \in L$, where $\underline{\nu}^{(j)}$ is defined as in (8.12). Suppose that $\underline{\mu} \neq 0$, $(\underline{n},\underline{\mu}) = 0$, and $\mu_{jk} \leq 0$ for $j \in J$ and $k \in \overline{2}$. If $n_{j2} > 0$, then $\lambda_j \leq 0$ and $c_j = \lambda_j$. If $n_{j1} > 0$, then $c_j = -\lambda_j$ and $\lambda_j \geq 0$. Thus $\lambda_j \leq 0$ if $n_{j1} = 0$, $\lambda_j \geq 0$ if $n_{j1} = N_j$, and $\lambda_j = 0$ if $0 < n_{j1} < N_j$.||

COROLLARY 8.1. *If* $0 < n_{j1} < N_j$ *for all* $j \in J$, *then* $\hat{\underline{\lambda}}$ *exists for the logit model* $\underline{\lambda} \in L$.

Proof. This result follows from Theorem 8.1 since $\underline{0} \in L^{\perp}$.||

Example 8.7. In the dosage response problem considered in Example 8.1, $L = \text{span}\,\{\underline{e}^{(r)},\underline{t}\}$. Thus $\{(\overline{\underline{n}},\underline{e}^{(r)}),(\overline{\underline{n}},\underline{t})\} = \{n_{+1},\sum_{j=1}^{r} n_{j1}t_j\}$ is a complete minimal sufficient statistic for $\underline{\lambda}$. If $t_j < t_{j+1}$ for each $j \in \overline{r-1}$, then the maximum-likelihood estimate exists if and only if no $j' \in \overline{r}$ exists such that either $n_{j1} = 0$ if $j < j'$ and $n_{j1} = N_j$ if $j > j'$ or $n_{j1} = N_j$ if $j < j'$ and $n_{j1} = 0$ if $j > j'$. In other words, the maximum-likelihood estimate fails to exist if and only if for some log dosage t_j, all subjects receiving more than this log dosage have one response, while all subjects receiving less than this log dosage have the opposite response. The result is understandable, for in such a situation, no way exists to assess the effect of small changes in the log dosage t if $t_{j'-1} < t < t_{j'+1}$, where $t_{-1} = -\infty$ and $t_{r+1} = \infty$. This conclusion follows from the second part of Theorem 8.1, for any nonzero element $\underline{\lambda}$ of L either satisfies the condition $\lambda_j < 0$ for $j < j'$ and $\lambda_j > 0$ for $j > j'$ or the condition $\lambda_j > 0$ for $j < j'$ and $\lambda_j < 0$ for $j > j'$ for some $j' \in \overline{r}$. Thus the maximum-likelihood estimate exists unless for some $j' \in \overline{r}$, $n_{j1} = 0$ for $j < j'$ and $n_{j1} = N_j$ for $j > j'$ or $n_{j1} = N_j$ for $j < j'$ and $n_{j1} = 0$ for $j > j'$.

If $\hat{\underline{\lambda}}$ does not exist, then the extended maximum-likelihood estimate $\underline{m}^{(e)}$ of $\underline{m}$ is $\underline{n}$, for if $I_1 = \{\langle j,k\rangle \in I\colon n_{jk} > 0 \text{ and } j \neq j'\}$, then $\rho_{I_1}M \supset \rho_{I_1}M(\overline{r} \times \overline{2},\{\{1\},\{2\}\})$, which, since I_1 is inseparable, has dimension $r+1$ (see chapter 7). Since I_1 has $r+1$ elements, $\rho_{I_1}M = R^{I_1}$. If $I_0 = \{\langle j,k\rangle \in I\colon n_{jk} > 0\}$, then $I_0 \subset I_1$ and $\rho_{I_0}M = R^{I_0}$. The maximum-likelihood estimate of $\rho_{I_0}\underline{m}$ is $\rho_{I_0}\underline{n}$ if $\rho_{I_0}\underline{\mu} \in \rho_{I_0}M$, so

$\underline{m}^{(\underline{e})} = \underline{n}$ as a consequence of (B.29). The extended maximum-likelihood estimate $\hat{\underline{\lambda}}^{(e)}$ may be defined as $\{\hat{\underline{\mu}}_{j1}^{(e)} - \hat{\mu}_{j2}^{(e)}: j \in J\}$ if the conventions $\infty - c = \infty$ and $c - \infty = -\infty$ are used for any real c. If all subjects receiving log dosage greater than $t_{j'}$ have response 1 and all subjects receiving a log dosage less than $t_{j'}$ have response 2, then the extended maximum-likelihood estimate corresponds to an estimated probability of 1 that response 1 is observed, given that a subject has received a log dosage greater than $t_{j'}$, and an estimated probability of 0 that response 2 is observed, given that a subject has received a log dosage less than $t_{j'}$. If a subject receives a log dosage $t_{j'}$, the estimated probability of response 1 is $n_{j'1}/N_{j'}$, the observed proportion of subjects receiving log dosage $t_{j'}$ that have response 1.

In the case in which $r = 3$, the problem of existence of maximum-likelihood estimates has been discussed by Berkson (1955) and Silverstone (1957). The maximum-likelihood estimate does not exist if

$$\underline{n} = \begin{array}{|cc|} 0 & N_1 \\ n_{21} & n_{22} \\ N_3 & 0 \end{array}\,, \tag{8.36}$$

$$\underline{n} = \begin{array}{|cc|} N_1 & 0 \\ n_{21} & n_{22} \\ 0 & N_3 \end{array}\,, \tag{8.37}$$

$$\underline{n} = \begin{array}{|cc|} 0 & N_1 \\ 0 & N_2 \\ n_{31} & n_{32} \end{array}\,, \tag{8.38}$$

$$\underline{n} = \begin{array}{|cc|} N_1 & 0 \\ N_2 & 0 \\ n_{31} & n_{32} \end{array}\,, \tag{8.39}$$

$$\underline{n} = \begin{array}{|cc|} n_{11} & n_{12} \\ 0 & N_2 \\ 0 & N_3 \end{array}\,, \tag{8.40}$$

or

(8.41)
$$\underline{n} = \begin{bmatrix} n_{11} & n_{12} \\ N_2 & 0 \\ N_3 & 0 \end{bmatrix} .$$

As Silverstone (1957) points out, in these examples there is no information in the data to suggest any limitation on the effect of a given change in dosage.

Example 8.8. In the logistic model for the paired comparisons considered in Example 8.2, a useful complete minimal sufficient statistic may be found by observing that if a mapping M from R^r to R^J is defined by the equation

(8.42)
$$M\underline{\alpha} = \{\alpha_i - \alpha_j : \langle i,j\rangle \in J\},$$

then M has range L. Since for $\underline{x} \in R^J$ and $\underline{\alpha} \in R^r$

(8.43)
$$\begin{aligned}(\underline{x}, M\underline{\alpha})_J &= \sum \{x_{ij}(\alpha_i - \alpha_j) : \langle i,j\rangle \in J\} \\ &= \sum_{i=1}^{r} \alpha_i(\Sigma\{x_{ij} : \langle i,j\rangle \in J\} - \Sigma\{x_{jk} : \langle j,i\rangle \in J\}) \\ &= \sum_{i=1}^{r} \alpha_i[x_{i+}(J) - x_{+i}(J)] \\ &= (M^T\underline{x}, \underline{\alpha})_r ,\end{aligned}$$

where M^T is the adjoint of M and $x_{i+}(J)$ and $x_{+i}(J)$ are defined as in chapter 7, then

(8.44)
$$M^T\underline{x} = \{x_{i+}(J) - x_{+i}(J)\} .$$

By Halmos (1958), the null space of M^T is $L^\perp$. Thus there is a one-to-one correspondence between $M^T P_L \underline{\bar{n}} = M^T \underline{\bar{n}}$ and $P_L \underline{\bar{n}}$. Therefore $M^T\underline{\bar{n}} = \{\bar{n}_{i+}(J) - \bar{n}_{+i}(J)\}$ is a complete minimal sufficient statistic. If $J^* = \{\langle i,j\rangle : \langle i,j\rangle \in J$ or $\langle j,i\rangle \in J\}$, then the number of times $\bar{n}_{ij}$ that i is preferred to j is $N_{ij} - \bar{n}_{ji}$, where $\bar{n}_{ji}$ is the number of times j is preferred to i. Thus $\bar{n}_{+i}(J) = N_{+i}(J) - \bar{n}_{i+}(J^* - J)$, and

(8.45)
$$M^T\underline{\bar{n}} = \{\bar{n}_{i+}(J^*) - N_{+i}(J)\}.$$

Consequently, the vector $\underline{\bar{n}}^{\{1\}}(J^*) = \{\bar{n}_{i+}(J^*)\}$ is a complete minimal sufficient statistic, where $n_{i+}(J^*)$ is the number of times object i is preferred over some other object. In the baseball example, the element $\bar{n}_{i+}(J^*) = \sum_{j\neq i} \bar{n}_{ij}$ is the total number of victories by team i. Thus to compute $\hat{\underline{\lambda}}$, it is only necessary to know the total number of games won by each team.

Since $M^T P_L \bar{\underline{m}}^{(L)}(\hat{\underline{\lambda}}) = M^T \bar{\underline{m}}^{(L)}(\underline{\lambda})$, the maximum-likelihood equation (8.17) reduces to the simultaneous equations

$$\bar{m}_{i+}^{(L)}(\hat{\underline{\lambda}})(J^*) = n_{i+}(J^*) \tag{8.46}$$

for $i \in \bar{r}$. In (8.46), the estimate $\bar{m}_{ij}^{(L)}(\underline{\lambda}) = N_{ij} - \bar{m}_{ji}^{(L)}(\hat{\underline{\lambda}})$ if $1 \le i < j \le r$. In the baseball case, (8.46) is the condition that the expected total number of victories of each team must equal the observed total.

The second part of Theorem 8.1 provides a procedure which may be used to determine whether the maximum-likelihood estimate $\hat{\underline{\lambda}}$ exists. To apply the theorem, the equivalence relationship $\sim(J)$ is used where $i_1 \sim i_2(J)$ if $i_1 \in J$, $i_2 \in J$, and either $i_1 = i_2$ or for some sequence $\{i^{(j)}: j \in \bar{h}\}$, $i^{(1)} = \min\{i_1, i_2\}$, $i^{(h)} = \max\{i_1, i_2\}$, and for $j \in \overline{h-1}$, $\langle i^{(j)}, i^{(j+1)}\rangle \in J$. If this relationship holds, i_1 and i_2 are said to be comparable (relative to J). This terminology is useful since the difference $\alpha_{i_1} - \alpha_{i_2}$ in the ratings of i_1 and i_2 is 0 is $i_1 = i_2$ and $\sum_{j=1}^{h-1} \lambda_{i^{(j)} i^{(j+1)}}$ if $i_1 < i_2$, provided $\underline{\lambda}$ satisfies (8.1). Thus $\alpha_{i_1} - \alpha_{i_2}$ is an estimable function of $\underline{\lambda}$ (see chapter 7).

Given the equivalence relationship $\sim(J)$, one may find corresponding equivalence classes $\{A_k: k \in \bar{\ell}\}$. If $\underline{\lambda} = 0$, then $\alpha_{i_1} = \alpha_{i_2}$ if $i_1 \sim i_2(J)$. Conversely, if $\alpha_i = c_k$ for all $i \in A_k$ and $k \in \bar{\ell}$, then (8.1) implies that $\underline{\lambda} = \underline{0}$. Thus the kernel of M, the mapping from R^r to R^J defined by (8.1), is $\{\underline{\alpha} \in R^r: \alpha_i = c_k$ for $i \in A_k$ and $k \in \bar{\ell}\} = \text{span}\{\underline{\nu}(A_k): k \in \bar{\ell}\}$, where $\underline{\nu}(A_k) = \{\chi_{A_k}(i): i \in \bar{r}\}$ for $k \in \bar{\ell}$. By Halmos (1958), L has dimension $r - \ell$. If $K = \{\langle i,j\rangle \in J: 0 < n_{ij1} < N_{ij}\}$, then $K \subset J$ and $i_1 \sim i_2(K)$ implies $i_1 \sim i_2(J)$. Thus the equivalence class $\{B_g: g \in \bar{h}\}$ corresponding to $\sim(K)$ is a subpartition of the equivalence class $\{A_k: k \in \bar{\ell}\}$ corresponding to $\sim(J)$. If $\{B_g: g \in \bar{h}\} = \{A_k: k \in \bar{\ell}\}$, and if $\lambda_{ij} = 0$ for each $\langle i,j\rangle \in K$, then $\alpha_{i_1} = \alpha_{i_2}$ if $i_1 \sim i_2(J)$ and $\underline{\lambda} = \underline{0}$. Thus the maximum-likelihood estimate $\hat{\underline{\lambda}}$ must exist.

In the baseball example, the condition that $\hat{\underline{\lambda}}$ exists if $\{B_g: g \in \bar{h}\} = \{A_k: k \in \bar{\ell}\}$ may be applied in a trivial manner, for $J = K$. Thus $h = \ell = 1$ and $B_1 = A_1 = \bar{8}$. Therefore, $\hat{\underline{\lambda}}$ exists and $\dim L = 8 - 1 = 7$. In general, the maximum-likelihood estimate exists if and only if for some $k \in \overline{\ell}$, there exists no $\{\alpha_i : i \in A_k\}$ such that α_i is not constant for $i \in A_k$ and for each i and j in A_k such that $i < j$, $\alpha_i \leq \alpha_j$ if $n_{ij1} = 0$, $\alpha_i = \alpha_j$ if $0 < n_{ij1} < N_{ij}$, and $\alpha_i \geq \alpha_j$ if $n_{ij1} = N_{ij}$. In terms of judges in a paired comparison, $\hat{\underline{\lambda}}$ exists if and only if no set A_k of comparable objects can be ranked so that whenever $i \in A_k$ has a higher ranking than $j \in A_k$ and $\langle i,j \rangle \in J^*$, then all N_{ij} judges comparing i and j prefer i.

Some simple possibilities involving 4 objects with each pair judged by 5 judges can be used to illustrate when the maximum-likelihood estimate exists. If

$$\underline{n} = \begin{bmatrix} - & 0 & 3 & 0 \\ 5 & - & 0 & 2 \\ 2 & 5 & - & 1 \\ 5 & 3 & 4 & - \end{bmatrix} \tag{8.47}$$

where row i and column j represent the number of times object i is favored over object j, then $J = \{\langle 1,2\rangle,\langle 1,3\rangle,\langle 1,4\rangle,\langle 2,3\rangle,\langle 2,4\rangle,\langle 3,4\rangle\}$ and $K = \{\langle 1,3\rangle,\langle 2,4\rangle,\langle 3,4\rangle\}$. Thus $\ell = 1$, $A_1 = \overline{4}$, $h = 1$, and $B_1 = \overline{4}$. Therefore, $\hat{\underline{\lambda}}$ exists. However, if

$$\underline{n} = \begin{bmatrix} - & 0 & 3 & 0 \\ 5 & - & 0 & 0 \\ 2 & 5 & - & 1 \\ 5 & 5 & 4 & - \end{bmatrix} \tag{8.48}$$

then J, ℓ, and A_1 are unchanged, while $K = \{\langle 1,3\rangle,\langle 3,4\rangle\}$, $h = 2$, $B_1 = \{1,3,4\}$, and $B_2 = \{2\}$. Thus the simplest test for the existence of $\hat{\underline{\lambda}}$ fails. Nonetheless, if $\underline{\alpha}$ satisfies the relationships $\alpha_i \leq \alpha_j$ for $n_{ij1} = 0$, $\alpha_i \geq \alpha_j$ for $n_{ij1} = N_{ij}$, and $\alpha_i = \alpha_j$ for $0 < n_{ij1} < N_{ij}$, then $\alpha_1 = \alpha_3 = \alpha_4$, $\alpha_1 \leq \alpha_2$, and $\alpha_2 \leq \alpha_3$. Thus α_i is constant for $i \in \overline{4}$. Consequently, $\hat{\underline{\lambda}}$ still exists. If

$$\underline{n} = \begin{bmatrix} - & 5 & 3 & 0 \\ 0 & - & 0 & 0 \\ 2 & 5 & - & 1 \\ 5 & 5 & 4 & - \end{bmatrix} \tag{8.49}$$

then $\hat{\underline{\lambda}}$ does not exist, for the conditions on $\underline{\alpha}$ are now that $\alpha_1 = \alpha_3 = \alpha_4$ and

$\alpha_2 \le \alpha_i$ if $i \in \{1,3,4\}$. These conditions hold if $\alpha_1 = 1$, $\alpha_2 = 0$, $\alpha_3 = 1$, and $\alpha_4 = 1$. If $\underline{\lambda}$ satisfies (8.1) for this $\underline{\alpha}$, then

$$\underline{\lambda} = \begin{array}{|c|c|c|c|} \hline - & 1 & 0 & 0 \\ \hline -1 & - & -1 & -1 \\ \hline 0 & 1 & - & 0 \\ \hline 0 & 1 & 0 & - \\ \hline \end{array} \tag{8.50}$$

The maximum-likelihood estimate fails to exist since there is no way to assess how undesirable object 2 really is, for it is never favored over other objects.

The results concerning existence of maximum-likelihood estimates may also be applied to other tolerance distributions. Thus the following extension of Theorem 8.1 is available.

THEOREM 8.2. *The maximum-likelihood estimate* $\hat{\underline{\lambda}}$ *of* $\underline{\lambda} \in L$ *for a binomial-response model with tolerance distribution function* F *exists if and only if for some* $\underline{\delta} \in L$, $0 < n_{ji} + \delta_j < N_j$ *for* $j \in J$. *Equivalently,* $\hat{\underline{\lambda}}$ *exists if and only if there exists no* $\underline{\lambda} \in L$ *such that* $\underline{\lambda} \ne \underline{0}$, $\lambda_j \le 0$ *if* $n_{j1} = 0$, $\lambda_j \ge 0$ *if* $n_{j1} = N_j$, *and* $\lambda_j = 0$ *if* $0 < n_{j1} < N_j$.

Proof. Suppose $\hat{\underline{\lambda}}$ exists. By (8.8), if $\underline{\lambda} \in L$ satisfies the condition that $\lambda_j = 0$ if $0 < n_{j1} < N_j$, $\lambda_j \le 0$ if $n_{j1} = 0$, and $\lambda_j \ge 0$ if $n_{j1} = N_j$, then

$$(\underline{\lambda}, \overline{D}^{(F)}(\hat{\underline{\lambda}})\overline{\underline{n}}) = (\underline{\lambda}, \overline{D}^{(F)}(\hat{\underline{\lambda}})\overline{\underline{m}}^{(F)}(\hat{\underline{\lambda}})). \tag{8.51}$$

Thus

$$\sum_{j \in J} \lambda_j[\overline{n}_j - \overline{m}_j^{(F)}(\hat{\underline{\lambda}})]f(\hat{\lambda}_j)/\{F(\hat{\lambda}_j)[1 - F(\hat{\lambda}_j)]\} = 0. \tag{8.52}$$

If $\lambda_j \ge 0$, then $\overline{n}_j - \overline{m}_j^{(F)}(\hat{\underline{\lambda}}) > 0$, and if $\lambda_j \le 0$, then $\overline{n}_j - \overline{m}_j^{(F)}(\hat{\underline{\lambda}}) < 0$. Thus (8.52) can only hold if each summand is 0. Therefore $\underline{\lambda} = \underline{0}$.

On the other hand, if no maximum-likelihood estimate exists, then a sequence $\{\underline{\lambda}^{(k)}\} \subset L$ can be constructed such that $\sup_{\underline{\lambda} \in L} \ell^{(F)}(\underline{n},\underline{\lambda}) = \lim \ell^{(F)}(\underline{n},\underline{\lambda}^{(k)})$ and $\{\ell^{(F)}(\underline{n},\underline{\lambda}^{(k)})\}$ is a strictly increasing sequence. If $0 < n_{j1} < N_j$, then $\{\lambda_j^{(k)}\}$ must be bounded, for each summand in (8.6) is bounded above by $\log N_j! - \log n_{j1}! - \log n_{j2}!$, and

$$\liminf \{n_{j1} \log F(\lambda_j^{(k)}) + n_{j2} \log [1 - F(\lambda_j^{(k)})]\} = -\infty \tag{8.53}$$

if $\{\lambda_j^{(k)}\}$ is not bounded. Similarly, $\{\lambda_j^{(k)}\}$ is bounded above if $n_{j1} = 0$ and $\{\lambda_j^{(k)}\}$ is bounded below if $n_{j1} = N_j$. However, $\{\underline{\lambda}^{(k)}\}$ cannot be bounded if $\hat{\underline{\lambda}}$ does not exist, for otherwise a limit point $\underline{\lambda}^*$ of $\{\underline{\lambda}^{(k)}\}$ must exist such that $\underline{\lambda}^* \in L$ and $\sup_{\underline{\lambda} \in L} \ell^{(F)}(\underline{n},\underline{\lambda}) = \ell^{(F)}(\underline{n},\underline{\lambda}^*)$. Since $\{\underline{\lambda}^{(k)}/||\underline{\lambda}^{(k)}||\}$ is a bounded sequence in L, there is a limit point $\underline{\lambda}^*$ of this sequence which is in L and has norm 1. This limit point is such that $\lambda_j^* \leq 0$ if $n_{j1} = 0$, $\lambda_j^* \geq 0$ if $n_{j1} = N_j$, and $\lambda_j^* = 0$ if $0 < n_1 < N_j$. Thus a maximum-likelihood estimate exists if and only if no $\underline{\lambda} \in L$ exists such that $\underline{\lambda} \neq 0$, $\lambda_j \leq 0$ if $n_{j1} = 0$, $\lambda_j \geq 0$ if $n_{j1} = N_j$, and $\lambda_j = 0$ if $0 < n_{j1} < N_j$. This condition is equivalent to the condition that there exists some $\underline{\delta} \in L$ such that $0 < n_{j1} + \delta_j < N_j$ for all $j \in J$.||

COMPUTATIONAL PROCEDURES

The modified version of the Newton-Raphson algorithm presented in chapter 3 is an appropriate method for computation of $\hat{\underline{\lambda}}$ when both log F and log (1 - F) have negative second derivatives at all points on the real line. If $\underline{\lambda}^{(t)}$ is the estimate of $\hat{\underline{\lambda}}$ at the start of iteration t, then

$$(8.54) \qquad \underline{s}^{(t)} = -[d^2\ell^{(F)}_{\underline{\lambda}^{(t)}}]^{-1} \circ d\ell^{(F)}_{\underline{\lambda}^{(t)}}$$

$$= P_L^{(F)}(\underline{n},\underline{\lambda}^{(t)})[D^{(F)}(\underline{n},\underline{\lambda}^{(t)})]^{-1}\overline{D}^{(F)}(\underline{\lambda}^{(t)}[\overline{\underline{n}} - \overline{\underline{m}}^{(F)}(\underline{N},\underline{\lambda}^{(t)})],$$

where $D^{(F)}(\underline{n},\underline{\lambda}^{(t)})$ is defined as in (8.16) and $P_L^{(F)}(\underline{n},\underline{\lambda}^{(t)})$ is the orthogonal projection on L with respect to the inner product defined by $D^{(F)}(\underline{n},\underline{\lambda}^{(t)})$. To verify (8.54), it suffices to substitute the last expression in (8.54) for $\underline{\xi}$ in (8.16). Thus if $\underline{\nu} \in L$,

$$(8.55) \qquad -d^2\lambda^{(F)}_{\underline{\lambda}^{(t)}}(\underline{n},\underline{\xi})(\underline{\nu})$$

$$= (\underline{\nu},D^{(F)}(\underline{n},\underline{\lambda}^{(t)})P_L^{(F)}(\underline{n},\underline{\lambda}^{(t)})[D^{(F)}(\underline{n},\underline{\lambda}^{(t)})]^{-1}\overline{D}^{(F)}(\underline{\lambda}^{(t)})[\overline{\underline{n}} - \overline{\underline{m}}^{(F)}(\underline{\lambda}^{(t)})])$$

$$= (P_L^{(F)}(\underline{n},\underline{\lambda}^{(t)})\underline{\nu},D^{(F)}(\underline{n},\underline{\lambda}^{(t)})[D^{(F)}(\underline{n},\underline{\lambda}^{(t)})]^{-1}\overline{D}^{(F)}(\underline{\lambda}^{(t)})[\overline{\underline{n}} - \overline{\underline{m}}^{(F)}(\underline{N},\underline{\lambda}^{(t)})])$$

$$= (\underline{\nu},\overline{D}^{(F)}(\underline{\lambda}^{(t)})[\overline{\underline{n}} - \overline{\underline{m}}^{(F)}(\underline{N},\underline{\lambda}^{(t)})])$$

$$= d\ell^{(F)}_{\underline{\lambda}^{(t)}}(\underline{n},\underline{\nu}) .$$

Given $\underline{s}^{(t)}$, the algorithm defined by (3.2) may be used to obtain a new estimate $\underline{\lambda}^{(t+1)}$ such that

(8.56) $$\underline{\lambda}^{(t+1)} = \underline{\lambda}^{(t)} + \underline{\alpha}^{(t)}\,\underline{s}^{(t)}$$

$$= P_L^{(F)}(\underline{n},\underline{\lambda}^{(t)})\{\underline{\lambda}^{(t)} + \alpha^{(t)}[D^{(F)}(\underline{n},\underline{\lambda}^{(t)})]^{-1}\bar{D}^{(F)}(\underline{\lambda}^{(t)})[\underline{\bar{n}} - \underline{\bar{m}}^{(F)}(\underline{N},\underline{\lambda}^{(t)})]\}$$

and

(8.57) $$|(\underline{s}^{(t)},\bar{D}^{(F)}(\underline{\lambda}^{(t+1)})[\underline{\bar{n}} - \underline{\bar{m}}^{(F)}(\underline{N},\underline{\lambda}^{(t+1)})])|$$

$$\le \frac{k}{\alpha^{(t)}} \sum_{j\in J} \{n_{j1}\log[F(\underline{\lambda}_j^{(t+1)})/F(\lambda_j^{(t)})]$$

$$+ n_{j2}\log\{[1 - F(\lambda_j^{(t+1)})]/[1 - F(\lambda_j^{(t)})]\}\},$$

where k is a positive constant chosen to be less than 1. Equations (8.6) and (8.7) have been used in (3.3) to derive (8.57). If the choice of $\alpha^{(t)} = 1$ can be used to satisfy (8.56) and (8.57), then this selection is employed.

As shown in chapter 3, $\alpha^{(t)} = 1$ for $t \ge 0$ if $\underline{\lambda}^{(0)}$ is a sufficiently good estimate of $\hat{\underline{\lambda}}$. In such a case, the algorithm reduces to the conventional Newton-Raphson method. If one calls $\underline{y}^{(t)}$ the vector of working transforms (see Finney 1964), where

(8.58) $$\underline{y}^{(t)} = \underline{\lambda}^{(t)} + [D^{(F)}(\underline{n},\underline{\lambda}^{(t)})]^{-1}\bar{D}^{(F)}(\underline{\lambda}^{(t)})[\underline{\bar{n}} - \underline{\bar{m}}^{(F)}(\underline{N},\underline{\lambda}^{(t)})],$$

then by Kruskal (1968b), $\underline{\lambda}^{(t+1)}$ corresponds to the Gauss-Markov estimate of the mean $\underline{\mu} \in L$ of a random vector $\underline{y}^{(t)} \in R^J$ with covariance matrix $[D^{(F)}(\underline{n},\underline{\lambda}^{(t)})]^{-1}$. Thus computation of $\underline{\lambda}^{(t+1)}$ corresponds to a weighted regression analysis.

If the logistic tolerance distribution is used, then $\bar{D}^{(L)}(\underline{\lambda}^{(t)})$ is the identity and for $\underline{x} \in R^J$, $D^{(L)}(\underline{n},\underline{\lambda}^{(t)}) = W^{(L)}(\underline{N},\underline{\lambda}^{(t)})$ and

(8.59) $$W^{(L)}(\underline{N},\underline{\lambda}^{(t)})\underline{x} = \{x_jN_j\exp(-\lambda_j^{(t)})/[1 + \exp(-\lambda_j^{(t)})]^2\}$$

$$= \{x_j\bar{m}_j^{(L)}(\underline{N},\underline{\lambda}^{(t)})[N_j - \bar{m}_j^{(L)}(\underline{N},\underline{\lambda}^{(t)})]/N_j\} .$$

Thus

(8.60) $$\underline{s}^{(t)} = \tilde{P}_L^{(L)}(\underline{N},\underline{\lambda}^{(t)})[W^{(L)}(\underline{n},\underline{\lambda}^{(t)})]^{-1}[\underline{\bar{n}} - \underline{\bar{m}}^{(L)}(\underline{N},\underline{\lambda}^{(t)})],$$

where $W^{(L)}(\underline{N},\underline{\lambda}^{(t)})$ satisfies (8.59) and $\tilde{P}_L^{(L)}(\underline{N},\underline{\lambda}^{(t)}) = P_L^{(L)}(\underline{n},\underline{\lambda}^{(t)})$ is the projection on L orthogonal with respect to the inner product defined by $W^{(L)}(\underline{N},\underline{\lambda}^{(t)})$. If L has dimension p, and M is a linear mapping from R^p onto L, then by Kruskal (1968b),

(8.61) $$\underline{s}^{(t)} = M[M^TW^{(L)}(\underline{N},\underline{\lambda}^{(t)})M]^{-1}M^T[\underline{\bar{n}} - \underline{\bar{m}}^{(L)}(\underline{n},\underline{\lambda}^{(t)})],$$

where M^T is the adjoint of M.

If the normal tolerance distribution is used, $D^{(\Phi)}(\underline{n},\underline{\lambda}^{(t)})$ and $\overline{D}^{(\Phi)}(\underline{\lambda}^{(t)})$ have somewhat more complex expressions, for $F(\lambda_j^{(t)}) = \Phi(\lambda_j^{(t)}) = (2\pi)^{-\frac{1}{2}} \int_{-\infty}^{\lambda_j^{(t)}} \exp(-x^2/2)dx$,

(8.62)
$$\frac{f(\lambda_j^{(t)})}{F(\lambda_j^{(t)})[1 - F(\lambda_j^{(t)})]} = \frac{\phi(\lambda_j^{(t)})}{\Phi(\lambda_j^{(t)})[1 - \Phi(\lambda_j^{(t)})]}$$

where $\phi(x) = (2\pi)^{-\frac{1}{2}} \exp(-x^2/2)$ is the density at x of the standard normal, and

(8.63)
$$\frac{N_j[f(\lambda_j^{(t)})]^2}{F(\lambda_j^{(t)})[1 - F(\lambda_j^{(t)})]} - [\overline{n}_j - \overline{m}_j^{(F)}(N,\lambda^{(t)})]y(\lambda_j^{(t)})$$

$$= \frac{\phi^2(\lambda_j^{(t)})}{(\Phi_j^{(t)})[1 - \Phi(\lambda_j^{(t)})]}$$

$$+ [\overline{n}_j - \overline{m}_j^{(\Phi)}(\underline{N},\underline{\lambda}^{(t)}]\{\phi(\lambda_j^{(t)})/\{\Phi(\lambda_j^{(t)})[1 - \Phi(\lambda_j^{(t)})]\}$$

$$+ \phi^2(\lambda_j^{(t)})[1 - 2\Phi(\lambda_j^{(t)})]/\{\Phi(\lambda_j^{(t)})[1 - \Phi(\lambda_j^{(t)})]\}^2\}$$

$$= \frac{N_j\phi^2(\lambda_j^{(t)})}{\Phi(\lambda_j^{(t)})[1 - \Phi(\lambda_j^{(t)})]} \left\{ 1 + [\overline{n}_j - \overline{m}_j^{(\Phi)}(\underline{N},\underline{\lambda}^{(t)})] \left[\frac{1}{\overline{m}_j^{(\Phi)}(\underline{N},\underline{\lambda}^{(t)})} - \frac{1}{N_j - \overline{m}_j^{(t)}(\underline{N},\underline{\lambda}^{(t)})} + \frac{\lambda_j^{(t)}}{N_j\phi(\lambda_j^{(t)})}\right]\right\} .$$

Since these formulas are cumbersome, many authors recommend use of $D^{(\Phi)}(\underline{m}^{(\Phi)}(\underline{N},\underline{\lambda}^{(t)}),\underline{\lambda}^{(t)}) = W^{(\Phi)}(\underline{N},\underline{\lambda}^{(t)})$ in place of $D^{(\Phi)}(\underline{n},\underline{\lambda}^{(t)})$, where $m_{j1}^{(\Phi)}(\underline{N},\underline{\lambda}^{(t)}) = \overline{m}_j^{(\Phi)}(\underline{N},\underline{\lambda}^{(t)})$ and $m_{j2}^{(\Phi)}(\underline{N},\underline{\lambda}^{(t)}) = N_j - \overline{m}_j^{(\Phi)}(\underline{N},\underline{\lambda}^{(t)})$ for $j \in J$. Given this simplification,

(8.64)
$$\underline{s}^{(t)} = \tilde{P}_L^{(\Phi)}(\underline{N},\underline{\lambda}^{(t)})\{[\overline{n}_j - \overline{m}_j^{(\Phi)}(\underline{N},\underline{\lambda}^{(t)})]/\phi(\lambda_j^{(t)})\} .$$

In analogy to (8.61), one now has

(8.65)
$$\underline{s}^{(t)} = M[M^T W^{(\Phi)}(\underline{N},\underline{\lambda}^{(t)})M]^{-1}M^T\overline{D}^{(\Phi)}(\underline{\lambda}^{(t)})[\overline{\underline{n}} - \overline{\underline{m}}^{(\Phi)}(\underline{N},\underline{\lambda}^{(t)})] .$$

The replacement of $D^{(\Phi)}(\underline{n},\underline{\lambda}^{(t)})$ by $W^{(\Phi)}(\underline{N},\underline{\lambda}^{(t)})$ dates back to Bliss (1935). It is based on the scoring method used by Fisher (1935a) to compute maximum-likelihood estimates, as may be verified by noting that for any F,

(8.66) $$E[D^{(F)}(\underline{n},\underline{\lambda})] = W^{(F)}(\underline{N},\underline{\lambda}).$$

Thus $W^{(F)}(\underline{N},\underline{\lambda})$ may be described as the information operator. This replacement does not affect the result that $\underline{\lambda}^{(t)} \longrightarrow \underline{\lambda}$ as $t \longrightarrow \infty$, for $W^{(\Phi)}(\underline{N},\underline{\lambda})$ is positive definite and a continuous function of $\underline{\lambda}$. However, the quadratic convergence results of chapter 3 no longer apply. Any association between the scoring method and rapid convergence of $\underline{\lambda}^{(t)}$ to $\hat{\underline{\lambda}}$ is based on the large sample properties discussed later in this section. Since the algorithm for the logit model is somewhat simpler than even the scoring algorithm for the probit model, considerations of computational convenience clearly favor the use of logits.

Given either tolerance distribution, a reasonable starting value $\underline{\lambda}^{(0)}$ can be obtained by letting

(8.67) $$\underline{\lambda}^{(0)} = \tilde{P}_L^{(F)}(\underline{N},\underline{\kappa})\underline{\kappa} \quad ,$$

where $\underline{\kappa} = \{F^{-1}(\bar{n}_j^*/N_j)\colon j \in J\}$ and $n_{jk}^* = n_{jk}$ unless n_{jk} is 0 or N_j. If $n_{jk} = 0$, $n_{jk}^* = \frac{1}{2}$, while if $n_{jk} = N_j$, $n_{jk}^* = N_j - \frac{1}{2}$. This estimate is based on Berkson's (1955) estimate for the dosage response analysis to Example 8.1. As shown later in this section, the estimate is asymptotically equivalent to the maximum-likelihood estimate. In analogy to (8.61), one has

(8.68) $$\underline{\lambda}^{(0)} = M[M^T W^{(F)}(\underline{N},\underline{\kappa})M]^{-1}M^T W^{(F)}(\underline{N},\underline{\kappa})\underline{\kappa} \ .$$

This equation applies whether logits or probits are employed.

Since a logit model is also a log-linear model, it is appropriate to note that the step $\underline{s}^{(t)}$ used in (3.60) for computation of $P_R\hat{\underline{\mu}} = \frac{1}{2}\hat{\underline{\lambda}} \otimes \langle 1,-1\rangle$ is the direct product of the $\underline{s}^{(t)}$ in (8.60) and the vector $\frac{1}{2}\langle 1,-1\rangle$. Thus the modified Newton-Raphson algorithm of this chapter is the same as the algorithm for multinomial sampling proposed in chapter 3. To verify this it is first necessary to show that

(8.69) $$P_{M-N}[P_M^*(\bar{\underline{\mu}}) - P_N^*(\bar{\underline{\mu}})] = \tilde{P}_L^{(L)}(\underline{N},\underline{\lambda}) \otimes P_{\{\underline{e}^{(2)}\}^\perp} \quad ,$$

where $\bar{\mu}_{j1} = \log\{N_j/[1 + \exp(-\lambda_j)]\}$ and $\bar{\mu}_{j2} = \log\{N_j/[1 + \exp(-\lambda_j)]\} - \lambda_j$ for each $j \in J$. The right-hand side is defined as in Halmos (1958) as the direct product of $\tilde{P}_L^{(L)}(\underline{N},\underline{\lambda})$ and $P_{\{\underline{e}^{(2)}\}^\perp}$. Thus if $\underline{x} \in R^J$ and $\underline{y} \in R^2$, then

(8.70)
$$[\tilde{P}_L^{(L)}(\underline{N},\underline{\lambda}) \oplus P_{\{\underline{e}^{(2)}\}^\perp}]\underline{x} \oplus \underline{y}$$
$$= \tilde{P}_L^{(L)}(\underline{N},\underline{\lambda})\underline{x} \oplus P_{\{\underline{e}^{(2)}\}^\perp}\underline{y}\ .$$

Both sides of (8.69) are projections on $M - N$. If $\underline{x} \in N = R^J \oplus \text{span}\ \{\underline{e}^{(2)}\}$, then $\underline{x} = \underline{y} \oplus \langle 1,-1\rangle$, where $\underline{y} \in R^J$. Thus

(8.71)
$$P_{M-N}[P_M^*(\overline{\underline{\mu}}) - P_N^*(\overline{\underline{\mu}})]\underline{x} = \underline{0}$$
$$= \tilde{P}_L^{(L)}(\underline{N},\underline{\lambda})\underline{y} \oplus P_{\{\underline{e}^{(2)}\}^\perp}\langle 1,1\rangle$$
$$= [\tilde{P}_L^{(L)}(\underline{N},\underline{\lambda}) \oplus P_{\{\underline{e}^{(2)}\}^\perp}]\underline{x}\ .$$

Finally, if $\underline{x} \in D^{-1}(\overline{\underline{\mu}})M^\perp = D^{-1}(\overline{\underline{\mu}})(L^\perp \oplus \{\underline{e}^{(2)}\}^\perp)$, then Lemma 5.5 implies

(8.72)
$$m_{j1}(\overline{\underline{\mu}})x_{j1} + m_{j2}(\overline{\underline{\mu}})x_{j2} = 0$$

for all $j \in J$, and $\{m_{j1}(\overline{\underline{\mu}})x_{j1}\colon j \in J\} \in L^\perp$. Since $\underline{x} = \underline{y} \oplus \langle 1,1\rangle + \underline{z} \oplus \langle 1,-1\rangle$, where $y_j = \frac{1}{2}(x_{j1} + x_{j2})$ and $z_j = \frac{1}{2}(x_{j1} - x_{j2})$ for $j \in J$, $z_j = \frac{1}{2}x_{j1}[N_j/m_{j2}(\overline{\underline{\mu}})]$ for $j \in J$. Thus

(8.73)
$$\{2[m_{j1}(\overline{\underline{\mu}})m_{j2}(\overline{\underline{\mu}})/N_j]z_j\} = 2W^{(L)}(\underline{N},\underline{\lambda})\underline{z} \in L^\perp$$

and $\underline{y} \oplus \langle 1,1\rangle \in N$. Since $\underline{y} \oplus \langle 1,1\rangle \in N$, (8.71) implies that it is in the null space of the right-hand side of (8.69). Since $\underline{z} \in [W^{(L)}(\underline{N},\underline{\lambda})]^{-1}L^\perp$, $\underline{z} \oplus \langle 1,-1\rangle$ is also in the null space of the right-hand side of (8.69). Thus $\underline{x}$ is in the null space of both sides of (8.69). Since

(8.74)
$$R^I = N \oplus (M - N) \oplus D^{-1}(\overline{\underline{\mu}})M^\perp,$$

the two sides of (8.69) must be equal.

Given (8.69), it is only necessary to note that if $\underline{x} \in D^{-1}(\overline{\underline{\mu}})N^\perp = D^{-1}(\overline{\underline{\mu}})(R^J \oplus \{\underline{e}^{(2)}\}^\perp)$, then (8.72) holds. If $\underline{x} = \underline{y} \oplus \langle 1,1\rangle + \underline{z} \oplus \langle 1,-1\rangle$, then $z_j = \frac{1}{2}x_{j1}[N_j/m_{j2}(\overline{\underline{\mu}})]$. Thus (8.69) implies that

(8.75)
$$P_{M-N}[P_M^*(\overline{\underline{\mu}}) - P_N^*(\overline{\underline{\mu}})]D^{-1}(\overline{\underline{\mu}})[\underline{n} - \underline{m}(\overline{\underline{\mu}})]$$
$$= \tfrac{1}{2}\tilde{P}_L^{(L)}(\underline{N},\underline{\lambda})[W^{(L)}(N,\underline{\lambda})]^{-1}[\overline{\underline{n}} - \overline{\underline{m}}(\underline{\lambda})] \oplus \langle 1,-1\rangle.$$

Similarly,

$$P_{M-N}[P_M^*(\underline{\nu}) - P_N^*(\underline{\nu})]\underline{\nu} = \tfrac{1}{2}\tilde{p}_L^{(L)}(\underline{N},\underline{\kappa})\underline{\kappa} \otimes \langle 1,-1\rangle , \tag{8.76}$$

where $\underline{\nu} = \{\log n_{jk}^*: j \in J, k \in \overline{2}\}$.

Example 8.9. In Example 8.1, if a logit model is used, then

$$\begin{aligned} \kappa_j &= \log (n_{j1}/n_{j2}) \quad \text{if } n_{j1} > 0 \text{ and } n_{j2} > 0 , \\ &= -\log (2N_j - 1) \quad \text{if } n_{j1} = 0 , \\ &= \log (2N_j - 1) \quad \text{if } n_{j2} = 0 . \end{aligned} \tag{8.77}$$

The operator $P_L^{(L)}(\underline{n},\underline{\lambda})$ may be found by use of a Gram-Schmidt orthogonalization similar to the one used in Example 3.3. One has $L = \text{span}\{\underline{e},\underline{u}(\underline{\lambda})\}$, where

$$\begin{aligned} \underline{u}(\underline{\lambda}) &= \underline{t} - \frac{(\underline{t},W^{(L)}(\underline{N},\underline{\lambda})\underline{e})}{(\underline{e},W^{(L)}(\underline{N},\underline{\lambda})\underline{e})}\underline{e} \\ &= \underline{t} - \bar{t}_\cdot^{(L)}(N,\underline{\lambda})\underline{e} \end{aligned} \tag{8.78}$$

and

$$(\underline{e},W^{(L)}(\underline{N},\underline{\lambda})\underline{u}(\underline{\lambda})) = 0 . \tag{8.79}$$

The term $\bar{t}_\cdot^{(L)}(\underline{N},\underline{\lambda})$ is a weighted average of the dosages t_j, where $j \in \overline{r}$. Thus

$$\underline{\lambda}^{(0)} = \frac{(\underline{e},W^{(L)}(\underline{N},\underline{\kappa})\underline{\kappa})}{(\underline{e},W^{(L)}(\underline{N},\underline{\kappa})\underline{e})}\underline{e} + \frac{(\underline{u}(\underline{\kappa}),W^{(L)}(\underline{N},\underline{\kappa})\underline{\kappa})}{(\underline{u},(\underline{\kappa}),W^{(L)}(\underline{N},\underline{\kappa})\underline{u}(\underline{\kappa}))}\underline{u}(\underline{\kappa}) \tag{8.80}$$

and

$$\underline{s}^{(t)} = \frac{(\underline{e},\underline{\bar{n}} - \underline{\bar{m}}^{(L)}(\underline{N},\underline{\lambda}^{(t)}))}{(\underline{e},W^{(L)}(\underline{N},\underline{\lambda}^{(t)})\underline{e})}\underline{e} + \frac{(\underline{u}(\underline{\lambda}^{(t)}),\underline{\bar{n}} - \underline{\bar{m}}^{(L)}(\underline{N},\underline{\lambda}^{(t)}))}{(\underline{u}(\underline{\lambda}^{(t)}),W^{(L)}(N,\underline{\lambda}^{(t)})\underline{u}(\underline{\lambda}^{(t)}))}\underline{u}(\underline{\lambda}^{(t)}). \tag{8.81}$$

In (8.80), it should be noted that $W^{(L)}(\underline{N},\underline{\kappa})\underline{x} = \{x_j n_{j1}^* n_{j2}^*/N_j\}$, while in (8.81), $W^{(L)}(\underline{N},\underline{\lambda}^{(t)})\underline{x} = \{x_j m_{j1}^{(L)}(\underline{N},\underline{\lambda}^{(t)}) m_{j2}^{(L)}(\underline{N},\underline{\lambda}^{(t)})/N_j\} = x_j N_j \exp(-\lambda_j^{(t)})/[1 + \exp(-\lambda_j^{(t)})]^2$. As should be expected, these formulas, when transformed to the corresponding expressions in $M - N$ in the case $r = 3$ and $\underline{t} = \langle -1,0,1\rangle$, agree with the equations derived in Example 3.3. Thus $\underline{\lambda}^{(0)} = \langle -1.772,-0.796,0.180\rangle$ and $\underline{\lambda}^{(1)} = \langle -1.776,-0.798,0.180\rangle$. Similar expressions may be derived for the normal tolerance distribution. Garwood's (1941) examples suggest that it is not clear whether the faster convergence rate associated with $D^{(\Phi)}(\underline{n},\underline{\lambda}^{(t)})$ compensates for the added computational labor.

Example 8.10. In the logistic model for paired comparisons, computation of $\hat{\underline{\lambda}}$ is facilitated by use of the mapping M defined by (8.42). Since

$$(8.82) \qquad \underline{x} - \tilde{P}_L^{(L)}(\underline{N},\underline{\lambda})\underline{x} \in [W^{(L)}(\underline{N},\underline{\lambda})]^{-1}L^{\perp}$$

for any $\underline{x} \in R^J$,

$$(8.83) \qquad M^T W^{(L)}(\underline{N},\underline{\lambda})\underline{x} = M^T W^{(L)}(\underline{N},\underline{\lambda})\tilde{P}^{(L)}(\underline{N},\underline{\lambda})\underline{x}.$$

The vector $\tilde{P}_L^{(L)}(\underline{N},\underline{\lambda})\underline{x} = \{\alpha_i - \alpha_j : \langle i,j\rangle \in J\}$ for a unique $\underline{\alpha} \in \{\underline{\nu}(A_k): k \in \overline{\ell}\}^{\perp}$, where the notation of Example 8.8 is employed. Thus (8.44) implies that if $x_{ji} = -x_{ij}$ and $w_{ji}^{(L)}(\underline{N},\underline{\lambda}) = w_{ij}^{(L)}(\underline{N},\underline{\lambda})$ for $\langle i,j\rangle \in J$, then for each $i \in \overline{r}$,

$$(8.84) \qquad \alpha_i \sum \{w_{ij}^{(L)}(\underline{N},\underline{\lambda}): \langle i,j\rangle \in J^*\} - \sum \{w_{ij}^{(L)}(\underline{N},\underline{\lambda})\alpha_j : \langle i,j\rangle \in J^*\}$$
$$= \sum \{x_{ij}w_{ij}^{(L)}(\underline{N},\underline{\lambda}): \langle i,j\rangle \in J^*\} ,$$

and for each $k \in \overline{\ell}$,

$$(8.85) \qquad \sum_{i \in A_k} \alpha_i = 0.$$

If $w_{ij}^{(L)}(\underline{N},\underline{\lambda}) = 0$ for $\langle i,j\rangle \notin J^*$ and if $a_k > 0$ for $k \in \overline{\ell}$, then

$$(8.86) \qquad \alpha_i \sum \{a_k + w_{ij}^{(L)}(\underline{N},\underline{\lambda}): j \in A_k - \{i\}\}$$
$$+ \sum \{(a_k - w_{ij}^{(L)}(\underline{N},\underline{\lambda}))\alpha_j : j \in A_k - \{i\}\}$$
$$= \sum \{x_{ij}w_{ij}^{(L)}(\underline{N},\underline{\lambda}): \langle i,j\rangle \in J^*\}.$$

This result follows by addition of (8.84) and a multiple of (8.85). Equivalently, (8.84) may be written

$$(8.87) \qquad M^T W^{(L)}(\underline{N},\underline{\lambda})M\underline{\alpha} = M^T W^{(L)}(\underline{N},\underline{\lambda})\underline{x} ,$$

(8.85) may be written

$$(8.88) \qquad (\underline{\nu}(A_k),\underline{\alpha}) = 0$$

for $k \in \overline{\ell}$, and (8.86) is equivalent to the equation

$$(8.89) \qquad [M^T W^{(L)}(\underline{N},\underline{\lambda})M + \sum_{k=1}^{\ell} a_k[\underline{\nu}(A_k) \otimes \underline{\nu}(A_k)]\underline{\alpha} = M^T W^{(L)}(\underline{N},\underline{\lambda})\underline{x} .$$

Equations (8.86) and (8.89) have unique solutions, for $M^TW^{(L)}(\underline{N},\underline{\lambda})M$ and $\sum_{k=1}^{\ell} a_k\underline{\nu}(A_k) \otimes \underline{\nu}(A_k)$ are both nonnegative definite, so if

$$(8.90) \qquad [M^TW^{(L)}(\underline{N},\underline{\lambda})M + \sum_{k=1}^{\ell} a_k\underline{\nu}(A_k) \otimes \underline{\nu}(A_k)]\underline{\alpha} = \underline{0},$$

then $M\underline{\alpha} = 0$ and $(\underline{\nu}(A_k),\underline{\alpha}) = 0$ for $k \in \overline{\ell}$. Thus $\underline{\alpha} \in \text{span}\,\{\underline{\nu}(A_k): k \in \overline{\ell}\}$ and $\underline{\alpha} \in \{\underline{\nu}(A_k): k \in \overline{\ell}\}^{\perp}$. This condition is possible only if $\underline{\alpha} = \underline{0}$. Thus the projection $\tilde{P}_L^{(L)}(\underline{N},\underline{\lambda})\underline{x}$ can be calculated by means of (8.86). In particular, if $\overline{n}_{ij} > 0$ for each $\langle i,j\rangle \in J^*$, $\kappa_{ij} = \log(\overline{n}_{ij}/\overline{n}_{ji})$ for $\langle i,j\rangle \in J^*$, and $\underline{\kappa} = \{\kappa_{ij}: \langle i,j\rangle \in J\}$, then $\underline{\lambda}^{(0)} = \{\alpha_i^{(0)} - \alpha_j^{(0)}: \langle i,j\rangle \in J\}$, where $w_{ij}^{(L)}(\underline{\kappa}) = \overline{n}_{ij}\overline{n}_{ji}/N_{ij}$ and for $i \in \overline{r}$,

$$(8.91) \qquad \alpha_i^{(0)} \sum \{a_k + w_{ij}^{(L)}(\underline{N},\underline{\kappa}): j \in A_k - \{i\}\} + \sum \{(a_k - w_{ij}^{(L)}(\underline{N},\underline{\kappa}))\alpha_j^{(0)}: j \in A_k - \{i\}\}$$

$$= \sum \{\kappa_{ij}w_{ij}^{(L)}(\underline{N},\underline{\kappa}): \langle i,j\rangle \in J^*\}.$$

Similarly, $\underline{s}^{(t)} = \{\overline{\alpha}_i^{(t)} - \overline{\alpha}_j^{(t)}: \langle i,j\rangle \in J\}$, where for $i \in \overline{r}$,

$$(8.92) \qquad \overline{\alpha}_i^{(t)} \sum \{a_k + w_{ij}^{(L)}(\underline{N},\underline{\lambda}^{(t)}): j \in A_k - \{i\}\} + \sum \{[a_k - w_{ij}^{(L)}(\underline{N},\underline{\lambda}^{(t)})]\overline{\alpha}_j^{(t)}: j \in A_k - \{i\}\}$$

$$= \overline{n}_{i+}(J^*) - \overline{m}_{i+}^{(L)}(\underline{N},\underline{\lambda}^{(t)})(J^*).$$

These equations may be solved by the modified Cholesky decomposition (see Wilkinson 1965). The choice of a_k is somewhat arbitrary. It is best to choose a_k to make $a_k - w_{ij}^{(L)}(\underline{N},\underline{\kappa})$ and $a_k - w_{ij}^{(L)}(\underline{\lambda}^{(t)})$ relatively small in magnitude.

In the baseball example, $\ell = 1$, $A_1 = \overline{r} = \overline{8}$, and $J^* = \overline{8} \times \overline{8} - \{\langle i,i\rangle: i \in \overline{8}\}$. Thus for $i \in \overline{8}$,

$$(8.93) \qquad \alpha_i^{(0)} \sum_{j\neq i} [a_1 + w_{ij}^{(L)}(\underline{N},\underline{\kappa})] + \sum_{j\neq i} \alpha_j^{(0)}[a_1 - w_{ij}^{(L)}(\underline{N},\underline{\kappa})]$$

$$= \sum_{j\neq i} \kappa_{ij}w_{ij}^{(L)}(\underline{N},\underline{\kappa})$$

and

$$(8.94) \qquad \overline{\alpha}_i^{(t)} \sum_{j\neq i} [a_1 + w_{ij}^{(L)}(\underline{N},\underline{\lambda}^{(t)})] + \sum_{j\neq i} \overline{\alpha}_j^{(t)}[a_1 - w_{ij}^{(L)}(\underline{N},\underline{\lambda}^{(t)})]$$

$$= \overline{n}_{i+}(J^*) - \overline{m}_{i+}^{(L)}(\underline{N},\underline{\lambda}^{(t)})(J^*).$$

A reasonable choice of a_1 is 5. Results are summarized in tables 8.3 and 8.4. The initial estimate $\underline{\lambda}^{(0)}$ is very close to $\hat{\underline{\lambda}}$. Only one iteration is required to produce

TABLE 8.3

ESTIMATES OF $\hat{\underline{\lambda}}$ FOR BASEBALL DATA

Winning Team	Iteration Number	Team Strength	Losing Team: Cleveland	Boston	N.Y.	Philadelphia	Detroit	St.Louis	Washington	Chicago
Cleveland	0	0.460	-	0.025	0.051	0.307	0.438	0.838	0.957	1.061
	1	0.472	-	0.025	0.062	0.304	0.446	0.877	0.978	1.082
Boston	0	0.434	-0.025	-	0.026	0.282	0.412	0.813	0.932	1.036
	1	0.447	-0.025	-	0.037	0.279	0.421	0.852	0.953	1.057
New York	0	0.409	-0.051	-0.026	-	0.256	0.387	0.787	0.906	1.010
	1	0.410	-0.062	-0.037	-	0.242	0.384	0.815	0.916	1.020
Phila-delphia	0	0.153	-0.307	-0.282	-0.256	-	0.131	0.531	0.650	0.754
	1	0.168	-0.304	-0.279	-0.242	-	0.143	0.573	0.674	0.778
Detroit	0	0.022	-0.438	-0.412	-0.387	-0.131	-	0.400	0.520	0.624
	1	0.025	-0.446	-0.421	-0.384	-0.143	-	0.430	0.532	0.635
St. Louis	0	-0.378	-0.838	-0.813	-0.787	-0.531	-0.400	-	0.119	0.223
	1	-0.405	-0.877	-0.852	-0.815	-0.575	-0.430	-	0.101	0.205
Washington	0	-0.498	-0.957	-0.932	-0.906	-0.650	-0.520	-0.119	-	0.104
	1	-0.506	-0.978	-0.953	-0.916	-0.674	-0.532	-0.101	-	0.104
Chicago	0	-0.602	-1.061	-1.036	-1.010	-0.754	-0.624	-0.223	-0.104	-
	1	-0.610	-1.082	-1.057	-1.020	-0.778	-0.635	-0.205	-0.104	-

TABLE 8.4

MAXIMUM-LIKELIHOOD ESTIMATE OF
MEAN VECTOR $\hat{\underline{m}}^{(L)}(\underline{N},\underline{\lambda})$ FOR BASEBALL DATA

	Losing Team							
Winning Team	Cleveland	Boston	New York	Philadelphia	Detroit	St. Louis	Washington	Chicago
Cleveland	-	10.6	11.3	12.7	13.4	15.5	16.0	16.4
Boston	10.4	-	11.2	12.5	13.3	15.4	15.9	16.3
New York	10.7	10.8	-	12.3	13.1	15.2	15.7	16.2
Philadelphia	9.3	9.5	9.7	-	11.8	14.1	14.6	15.1
Detroit	8.6	8.7	8.9	10.2	-	13.3	13.9	14.4
St Louis	6.5	6.6	6.8	7.9	8.7	-	11.0	11.6
Washington	6.0	6.1	6.3	7.4	8.1	10.0	-	11.0
Chicago	5.6	5.7	5.8	6.9	7.6	9.4	10.0	-

an accurate approximation to $\hat{\underline{\lambda}}$, and use of $\underline{\lambda}^{(0)}$ rather than $\hat{\underline{\lambda}}$ would have very little practical effect. This conclusion will become even clearer when asymptotic variances are estimated in Example 8.13.

The likelihood ratio and Pearson chi-square statistics for $H_0: \underline{\lambda} \in L$ and $H_A: \underline{\lambda} \in R^J$ are respectively 14.1 and 13.7, and the number of degrees of freedom for the statistics is 21. Therefore, the model fits the data very well. Were $\underline{\lambda}^{(0)}$ used rather than $\hat{\underline{\lambda}}$ in computation of these statistics, the likelihood ratio chi-square would be increased by 0.05 and the Pearson chi-square would be decreased by 0.02. These changes are negligible.

Example 8.11. The logit model considered in Examples 8.3 and 8.5 corresponds to a standard log-linear model for factorial tables. Thus the maximum-likelihood estimates $\hat{\underline{\lambda}}$ and $\hat{\underline{m}}^{(L)}(\underline{N},\hat{\underline{\lambda}})$ may be found by the iterative proportional fitting algorithm described in chapter 5. However, the methods of this chapter are also quite appropriate. The manifold $L = M(\overline{6} \times \overline{2},\{\{1\},\{2\}\})$ has a basis $\{\underline{\nu}(\{1\},i): i \in \overline{6}\} \cup \{\underline{\nu}(\{2\},1)\}$. The first six vectors of the basis are orthogonal with respect to the inner product defined by $W^{(L)}(\underline{N},\underline{\lambda})$. The Gram-Schmidt method can be used to produce an orthogonal basis of L with respect to $W^{(L)}(\underline{N},\underline{\lambda})$. Such a basis is $\{\underline{\nu}(\{1\},i): i \in \overline{6}\} \cup \{\underline{y}(\underline{\lambda})\}$, where

$$\underline{y}(\underline{\lambda}) = \underline{\nu}(\{2\},1) - \sum_{i=1}^{6} \frac{(\underline{\nu}(\{1\},i)W^{(L)}(\underline{N},\underline{\lambda})\underline{\nu}(\{2\},1))}{(\underline{\nu}(\{1\},i)W^{(L)}(\underline{N},\underline{\lambda})\underline{\nu}(\{1\},i))}\underline{\nu}(\{1\},i) \tag{8.95}$$

$$= \underline{\nu}(\{2\},1) - \sum_{i=1}^{6} \frac{w_{i1}^{(L)}(\underline{N},\underline{\lambda})}{w_{i+}^{(L)}(\underline{N},\underline{\lambda})}\underline{\nu}(\{1\},1) .$$

Thus for $i \in \overline{6}$,

$$y_{i1}(\underline{\lambda}) = w_{i2}^{(L)}(\underline{N},\underline{\lambda})/w_{i+}^{(L)}(\underline{N},\underline{\lambda}) \tag{8.96}$$

and

$$y_{i2}(\underline{\lambda}) = -w_{i1}^{(L)}(\underline{N},\underline{\lambda})/w_{i+}^{(L)}(\underline{N},\underline{\lambda}). \tag{8.97}$$

Therefore,

$$(\underline{y}(\underline{\lambda}),W^{(L)}(\underline{N},\underline{\lambda})\underline{y}(\underline{\lambda})) \tag{8.98}$$

$$= \sum_{i=1}^{6} \frac{1}{[w_{i+}^{(L)}(\underline{N},\underline{\lambda})]^2}\{[w_{i2}^{(L)}(\underline{N},\underline{\lambda})]^2 w_{i1}^{(L)}(\underline{N},\underline{\lambda}) + [w_{i1}^{(L)}(\underline{N},\underline{\lambda})]^2 w_{i2}^{(L)}(\underline{N},\underline{\lambda})\}$$

$$= \sum_{i=1}^{6} w_{i1}^{(L)}(\underline{N},\underline{\lambda})w_{i2}^{(L)}(\underline{N},\underline{\lambda})/w_{i+}^{(L)}(\underline{N},\underline{\lambda}).$$

Since

$$(8.99)\quad \tilde{P}_L^{(L)}(\underline{N},\underline{\lambda}) = \sum_{i=1}^{6} [\underline{\nu}(\{1\},i) \otimes \underline{\nu}(\{1\},i)]w^{(L)}(\underline{N},\underline{\lambda})/w_{i+}^{(L)}(\underline{N},\underline{\lambda})$$

$$+ [\underline{y}(\underline{\lambda}) \otimes \underline{y}(\underline{\lambda})]w^{(L)}(\underline{N},\underline{\lambda})/ \sum_{i=1}^{6} w_{i1}^{(L)}(\underline{N},\underline{\lambda})w_{i1}^{(L)}(\underline{N},\underline{\lambda})/w_{i+}^{(L)}(\underline{N},\underline{\lambda}),$$

$$(8.100)\quad \underline{\lambda}^{(0)} = \sum_{i=1}^{6} [\frac{1}{w_{i+}^{(L)}(\underline{N},\underline{\kappa})} \sum_{j=1}^{2} w_{ij}^{(L)}(\underline{N},\underline{\kappa})\kappa_{ij}]\underline{\nu}(\{1\},i)$$

$$+ \frac{\{\sum_{i=1}^{6} [w_{i1}^{(L)}(\underline{N},\underline{\kappa})w_{i2}^{(L)}(\underline{N},\underline{\kappa})/w_{i+}^{(L)}(\underline{N},\underline{\kappa})](\kappa_{i1} - \kappa_{i2})\}}{\sum_{i=1}^{6} [w_{i1}^{(L)}(\underline{N},\underline{\kappa})w_{i2}^{(L)}(\underline{N},\underline{\kappa})/w_{i+}^{(L)}(\underline{N},\underline{\kappa})]} \underline{y}(\underline{\kappa})$$

and

$$(8.101)\quad \underline{s}^{(t)} = \sum_{i=1}^{6} \left[\frac{n_{i+} - \bar{m}_{i+}^{(L)}(\underline{N},\underline{\lambda}^{(t)})}{w_{i+}^{(L)}(\underline{N},\underline{\lambda}^{(t)})}\right] \underline{\nu}(\{1\},i)$$

$$+ \{[\sum_{j=1}^{6} \{[n_{i1} - \bar{m}_{i1}^{(L)}(\underline{N},\underline{\lambda}^{(t)})]w_{i2}^{(L)}(\underline{N},\underline{\lambda}^{(t)})$$

$$- [n_{i2} - \bar{m}_{i2}^{(L)}(\underline{N},\underline{\lambda}^{(t)})]w_{i1}^{(L)}(\underline{N},\underline{\lambda}^{(t)})\}/w_{i+}^{(L)}(\underline{N},\underline{\lambda}^{(t)})]/$$

$$[\sum_{i=1}^{6} [w_{i1}^{(L)}(\underline{N},\underline{\lambda}^{(t)})w_{i2}^{(L)}(\underline{N},\underline{\lambda}^{(t)})/w_{i+}^{(L)}(\underline{N},\underline{\lambda}^{(t)})]]\}\underline{y}(\underline{\lambda}^{(t)}).$$

Just as in the last example, $\underline{\lambda}^{(0)}$ is very close to $\hat{\underline{\lambda}}$. One iteration produces an estimate of $\hat{\underline{\lambda}}$ which is about as accurate as possible for an estimate produced on an IBM 360 with single-precision arithmetic. Results are summarized by tables 8.5 and 8.6. The models fit the data quite well, for the log likelihood ratio and Pearson chi-square statistics are respectively 5.14 and 5.05 and there are 5 degrees of freedom if the null hypothesis is H_0: $\underline{\lambda} \in L$ and the alternative is H_A: $\underline{\lambda} \in R^J$. These hypotheses are equivalent to the hypotheses H_0: $\underline{\mu} \in M(\bar{6} \times \bar{2} \times \bar{2},\{\{1,2\},\{1,3\},\{2,3\}\})$ and H_A: $\underline{\mu} \in R^{\bar{2}\times\bar{2}\times\bar{2}}$. Yates (1955) obtains very similar results with the complementary log-log transform.

ASYMPTOTIC PROPERTIES

The maximum-likelihood estimate $\hat{\underline{\lambda}}$ has the conventional asymptotic properties associated with maximum-likelihood estimates. If a logit model is used, the asymptotic properties of $\hat{\underline{\lambda}}$ may be inferred from the asymptotic results of chapter 4. If one considers a sequence of observations $\underline{n}^{(N)}$ from a logit model $\underline{\lambda}^{(N)} \in L$, where $\underline{\lambda}^{(N)} \longrightarrow \underline{\lambda}^*$

TABLE 8.5
COORDINATES $\lambda_{ij}^{(t)}$
FOR LOGIT MODEL OF DATA IN TABLE 8.2

Experiment Number	Iteration Number	Method F	Method M
1	0	-3.252	-3.551
	1	-3.254	-3.553
2	0	-3.557	-3.856
	1	-3.559	-3.858
3	0	-3.408	-3.708
	1	-3.409	-3.708
4	0	-3.490	-3.790
	1	-3.504	-3.802
5	0	-2.261	-2.561
	1	-2.267	-2.566
6	0	-2.329	-2.629
	1	-2.335	-2.634

TABLE 8.6
MAXIMUM-LIKELIHOOD ESTIMATES $\hat{m}_{ijk}^{(L)}$
FOR DATA IN TABLE 8.2

Experiment Number	Method F		Method M	
	Mutant	Normal	Mutant	Normal
1	31.38	812.62	42.62	1488.38
2	74.72	2625.28	30.28	1434.72
3	105.14	3179.86	104.86	4276.14
4	31.05	1031.95	45.95	2059.05
5	34.74	335.26	39.26	510.74
6	52.97	547.03	31.03	431.97

and the sample sizes $N_j^{(N)}$ are such that $N_j^{(N)}/N \longrightarrow N_j^* > 0$ for $j \in J$, then (8.69) and Theorem 4.1 imply that the maximum-likelihood estimate $\hat{\underline{\lambda}}^{(N)}$ of $\underline{\lambda}^{(N)}$ satisfies

(8.102)
$$\hat{\underline{\lambda}}^{(N)} - \underline{\lambda}^{(N)} \xrightarrow{P} \underline{0}$$

and

(8.103)
$$N^{\frac{1}{2}}(\hat{\underline{\lambda}}^{(N)} - \underline{\lambda}^{(N)}) \xrightarrow{\mathcal{D}} N(\underline{0},\tilde{P}_L^{(L)}(\underline{N}^*,\underline{\lambda}^*)[W^{(L)}(\underline{N}^*,\underline{\lambda}^*)]^{-1}).$$

These results follow since the mean vectors $\underline{m}^{(L)}(\underline{N}^{(N)},\underline{\lambda}^{(N)})$ for $\underline{n}^{(N)}$ satisfy $N^{-1}\underline{m}^{(L)}(\underline{n}^{(N)},\underline{\lambda}^{(N)}) \longrightarrow \underline{m}^{(L)}(\underline{N}^*,\underline{\lambda}^*)$, and the vector $\underline{\mu}^{(N)} = \{\log m_{jk}^{(L)}(\underline{N}^{(N)},\underline{\lambda}^{(N)}): j \in J, k \in \overline{2}\}$ is related to $\underline{\lambda}^{(N)}$ by the equation

(8.104)
$$P_{M-N}\underline{\mu}^{(N)} = \tfrac{1}{2}\underline{\lambda}^{(N)} \otimes \langle 1,-1\rangle.$$

Hence (8.102) follows from (4.6). To verify (8.103) by use of (4.8), note that if $\underline{\mu}^* = \{\log m_{jk}^{(L)}(\underline{N}^*,\underline{\lambda}^*): j \in J, k \in \overline{2}\}$, then the argument used to derive (8.75) shows that

(8.105)
$$P_{M-N}[P_M^*(\underline{\mu}^*) - P_N^*(\underline{\mu}^*)]D^{-1}(\underline{\mu}^*)P_{M-N}$$
$$= \tfrac{1}{2}\{\tilde{P}_L^{(L)}(\underline{N}^*,\underline{\lambda}^*)[W^{(L)}(\underline{N}^*,\underline{\lambda}^*)]^{-1}\} \otimes P_{\{e^{(2)}\}^\perp}P_{M-N} .$$

By Eaton (1970),

(8.106)
$$P_{M-N} = P_{L\otimes\{e^{(2)}\}^\perp}$$
$$= P_L \otimes P_{\{e^{(2)}\}^\perp}$$

and

(8.107)
$$P_{M-N}[P_M^*(\underline{\mu}^*) - P_N^*(\underline{\mu}^*)]D^{-1}(\underline{\mu}^*)P_{M-N}$$
$$= \tfrac{1}{2}\tilde{P}_L^{(L)}(\underline{N}^*,\underline{\lambda}^*)[W^{(L)}(\underline{N}^*,\underline{\lambda}^*)]^{-1} \otimes P_{\{e^{(2)}\}^\perp} .$$

The asymptotic variance of $(\underline{c},\hat{\underline{\lambda}}^{(N)})_J$ for $\underline{c} \in R^J$ may now be found by noting that

(8.108)
$$(\underline{c},\hat{\underline{\lambda}}^{(N)})_J = \tfrac{1}{2}(\underline{c} \otimes \langle 1,-1\rangle,\hat{\underline{\lambda}}^{(N)} \otimes \langle 1,-1\rangle)_I$$
$$= (\underline{c} \otimes \langle 1,-1\rangle,P_{M-N}\hat{\underline{\mu}}^{(N)})_I .$$

Thus the asymptotic variance is

(8.109) $$\left(\underline{c} \otimes \langle 1,-1\rangle, \left[\tfrac{1}{2}\tilde{P}^{(L)}_{L}(\underline{N}^*,\underline{\lambda}^*)[W^{(L)}(\underline{N}^*,\underline{\lambda}^*)]^{-1} \otimes P_{\{e^{(2)}\}^{\perp}}\right] \underline{c} \otimes \langle 1,-1\rangle\right)_I$$

$$= \tfrac{1}{2}(\underline{c},\tilde{P}^{(L)}_{L}(\underline{N}^*,\underline{\lambda}^*)[W^{(L)}(\underline{N}^*,\underline{\lambda}^*)]^{-1}\underline{c})_J(\langle 1,-1\rangle,P_{\{e^{(2)}\}^{\perp}}\langle 1,-1\rangle)_2$$

$$= (\underline{c},\tilde{P}^{(L)}_{L}(\underline{N}^*,\underline{\lambda}^*)[W^{(L)}(\underline{N}^*,\underline{\lambda}^*]^{-1}c)_J \quad ,$$

and the asymptotic covariance of $\hat{\underline{\lambda}}^{(N)}$ is $\tilde{P}^{(L)}_{L}(\underline{N}^*,\underline{\lambda}^*)[W^{(L)}(\underline{N}^*,\underline{\lambda}^*)]^{-1}$.

Similar results are available if the tolerance distribution is not logistic. If $\underline{n}^{(N)}$, $\underline{\lambda}^{(N)}$, $\underline{\lambda}^*$, $\underline{N}^{(N)}$, and $\underline{N}^*$ are defined as in the logit case and the tolerance distribution function F has a positive differentiable density f and $\log F$ and $\log(1 - F)$ have negative second derivatives, then

(8.110) $$\hat{\underline{\lambda}}^{(N)} - \underline{\lambda}^{(N)} \xrightarrow{P} \underline{0}$$

and

(8.111) $$N^{\frac{1}{2}}(\hat{\underline{\lambda}}^{(N)} - \underline{\lambda}^{(N)}) \xrightarrow{\mathcal{D}} N(\underline{0},\tilde{P}^{(F)}(\underline{N}^*,\underline{\lambda}^*)[W^{(F)}(\underline{N}^*,\underline{\lambda}^*)]^{-1}).$$

The proof of (8.110) and (8.111) is very similar to the proof of Theorem 4.1, so details are omitted. The first phase of the proof is the observation that the implicit function theorem may be used to demonstrate the existence of a differentiable function $G(\underline{x})$ with range $B \subset L$ and domain $A \subset R^I$ such that B is an open set including $\underline{\lambda}^*$, A is an open set including $\underline{m}^{(F)}(\underline{N}^*,\underline{\lambda}^*)$, $G(\underline{m}^{(F)}(\underline{N}^*,\underline{\lambda}^*)) = \underline{\lambda}^*$, and $G(\underline{x})$ is the unique element of B such that $d\ell^{(F)}_{G(\underline{x})}(\underline{x},\underline{\lambda}) = 0$ for all $\underline{\lambda} \in L$. The implicit function theorem applies since $d^2\ell^{(F)}_{\underline{\lambda}^*}(\underline{m}^{(F)}(\underline{N}^*,\underline{\lambda}^*),\underline{\nu})(\underline{\xi})$ is negative definite and $d\ell^{(F)}_{\underline{\lambda}^*}(\underline{m}^{(F)}(\underline{N}^*,\underline{\lambda}^*),\underline{\lambda}) = 0$ for $\underline{\lambda} \in L$.

The differential $dG_{\underline{m}^{(F)}(\underline{N}^*,\underline{\lambda}^*)}$ satisfies the equation

(8.112) $$d^2\ell^{(F)}_{\underline{\lambda}^*}(\underline{m}^{(F)}(\underline{N}^*,\underline{\lambda}^*),dG_{\underline{m}^{(F)}(\underline{N}^*,\underline{\lambda}^*)}(\underline{x}))(\underline{\lambda}) + d\ell^{(F)}_{\underline{\lambda}^*}(\underline{x},\underline{\lambda}) = 0$$

for $\underline{\lambda} \in L$. Thus

(8.113) $$-(\underline{\lambda},W^{(F)}(\underline{N}^*,\underline{\lambda}^*)dG_{\underline{m}^{(F)}(\underline{N}^*,\underline{\lambda}^*)}(\underline{x}))$$

$$+ (\underline{\lambda},\overline{D}^{(F)}(\underline{\lambda}^*)\{x_{j1} - (x_{j1} + x_{j2})F(\lambda^*_j): j \in J\}) = 0$$

for $\underline{\lambda} \in L$. It follows that

(8.114) $dG_{\underline{m}^{(F)}(\underline{N}^*,\underline{\lambda}^*)}(\underline{x}) = \tilde{P}_L^{(F)}(\underline{N}^*,\underline{\lambda}^*)[W^{(F)}(\underline{N}^*,\underline{\lambda}^*)]^{-1}\overline{D}^{(F)}(\underline{\lambda}^*)\{x_{j1} - (x_{j1} + x_{j2})F(\lambda_j^*): j \in J\}.$

The next step in the proof involves a demonstration that $\hat{\underline{\lambda}}^{(N)} = G(N^{-1}\underline{n}^{(N)})$ if $N^{-1}\underline{n}^{(N)} \in A$. Since $d\ell_{\underline{\lambda}}^{(F)}(N^{-1}\underline{n}^{(N)},\underline{\nu}) = N^{-1}d\ell_{\underline{\lambda}}^{(F)}(\underline{n}^{(N)},\underline{\nu})$ for $\underline{\lambda}$ and $\underline{\nu} \in L$, if $N^{-1}\underline{n}^{(N)} \in A$, then $d\ell_{G(N^{-1}\underline{n}^{(N)})}^{(F)}(\underline{n}^{(N)},\underline{\nu}) = 0$ for all $\underline{\nu} \in L$. Since $\hat{\underline{\lambda}}^{(N)}$ is the unique solution of the equation $d\ell_{\hat{\underline{\lambda}}^{(N)}}^{(F)}(\underline{n}^{(N)},\underline{\nu}) = 0$ for $\underline{\nu} \in L$, $G(N^{-1}\underline{n}^{(N)}) = \hat{\underline{\lambda}}^{(N)}$. Given this identification, Taylor's theorem and simple asymptotic manipulations show that

(8.115) $$N^{\frac{1}{2}}(\hat{\underline{\lambda}}^{(N)} - \underline{\lambda}^{(N)}) - \tilde{P}_L^{(F)}(\underline{N}^*,\underline{\lambda}^*)[W^{(F)}(\underline{N}^*,\underline{\lambda}^*)]^{-1}\overline{D}^{(F)}(\underline{\lambda}^*)[\overline{\underline{n}}^{(N)} - \overline{\underline{m}}^{(F)}(\underline{N}^{(N)},\underline{\lambda}^{(N)})]/N^{\frac{1}{2}} \xrightarrow{P} \underline{0}.$$

Since

(8.116) $$N^{-\frac{1}{2}}[\overline{\underline{n}}^{(N)} - \overline{\underline{m}}^{(F)}(\underline{N}^{(N)},\underline{\lambda}^{(N)})] \xrightarrow{D} N(\underline{0},T^{(F)}(\underline{N}^*,\underline{\lambda}^*)),$$

where $T^{(F)}(\underline{N}^*,\underline{\lambda}^*)\underline{x} = \{x_j N_j^* F(\lambda_j^*)[1 - F(\lambda_j^*)]: j \in J\}$ for $\underline{x} \in R^J$, and

(8.117) $$\begin{aligned}&\tilde{P}_L^{(F)}(\underline{N}^*,\underline{\lambda}^*)[W^{(F)}(\underline{N}^*,\underline{\lambda}^*)]^{-1}\overline{D}^{(F)}(\underline{\lambda}^*)T^{(F)}(\underline{N}^*,\underline{\lambda}^*)\overline{D}^{(F)}(\underline{\lambda}^*)\tilde{P}_L^{(F)}(\underline{N}^*,\underline{\lambda}^*)[W^{(F)}(\underline{N}^*,\underline{\lambda}^*)]^{-1}\\&= \tilde{P}_L^{(F)}(\underline{N}^*,\underline{\lambda}^*)[W^{(F)}(\underline{N}^*,\underline{\lambda}^*)]^{-1}W^{(F)}(\underline{N}^*,\underline{\lambda}^*)\tilde{P}_L^{(F)}(\underline{N}^*,\underline{\lambda}^*)[W^{(F)}(\underline{N}^*,\underline{\lambda}^*)]^{-1}\\&= \tilde{P}_L^{(F)}(\underline{N}^*,\underline{\lambda}^*)[W^{(F)}(\underline{N}^*,\underline{\lambda}^*)]^{-1},\end{aligned}$$

(8.111) follows from (8.115). Given (8.111), (8.110) follows from the general observation that if $N^{\frac{1}{2}}(\hat{\underline{\lambda}}^{(N)} - \underline{\lambda}^{(N)})$ converges in distribution, then $\hat{\underline{\lambda}}^{(N)} - \underline{\lambda}^{(N)}$ converges in probability to $\underline{0}$.

The properties of $\hat{\underline{\lambda}}$ are shared by the estimate $\tilde{P}_L^{(F)}(\underline{N},\underline{\kappa})\underline{\kappa}$. This observation follows from (8.115) since

(8.118) $$\tilde{P}_L^{(F)}(\underline{N}^{(N)},\underline{\kappa}^{(N)}) \xrightarrow{P} \tilde{P}_L^{(F)}(\underline{N}^*,\underline{\lambda}^*),$$

(8.119) $$\begin{aligned}N^{\frac{1}{2}}(\underline{\kappa}^{(N)} - \underline{\lambda}^{(N)}) &= N^{\frac{1}{2}}\{F^{-1}(n_j^{*(N)}/N_j^{(N)}) - F^{-1}(\overline{m}_j^{(F)}(\underline{N}^{(N)},\underline{\lambda}^{(N)})/N_j^{(N)})\}\\&= N^{\frac{1}{2}}\{[\overline{n}_j^{(N)} - \overline{m}_j^{(F)}(\underline{N}^{(N)},\underline{\lambda}^{(N)})]/[N_j^{(N)}f(\lambda_j^{(N)})]\} + \underline{o}^{(N)},\end{aligned}$$

where $\underline{o}^{(N)} \xrightarrow{P} \underline{0}$,

(8.120) $$\begin{aligned}&[W^{(F)}(\underline{N}^{(N)},\underline{\lambda}^{(N)})]^{-1}\overline{D}^{(F)}(\underline{\lambda}^{(N)})[\overline{\underline{n}}^{(N)} - \overline{\underline{m}}^{(F)}(\underline{N}^{(N)},\underline{\lambda}^{(N)})]\\&= \{[\overline{n}_j^{(N)} - \overline{m}_j^{(F)}(\underline{N}^{(N)},\underline{\lambda}^{(N)})]/[N_j^{(N)}f(\lambda_j^{(N)})]\},\end{aligned}$$

and

(8.121) $$N[W^{(F)}(\underline{N}^{(N)},\underline{\lambda}^{(N)})]^{-1}\overline{D}^{(F)}(\underline{\lambda}^{(N)}) \longrightarrow [W^{(F)}(\underline{N}^*,\underline{\lambda}^*)]^{-1}\overline{D}^{(F)}(\underline{\lambda}^*).$$

Therefore $N^{\frac{1}{2}}(\hat{\underline{\lambda}}^{(N)} - \underline{\lambda}^{(N)})$ and $N^{\frac{1}{2}}[\tilde{P}_L^{(F)}(\underline{N}^{(N)},\underline{\kappa}^{(N)})\underline{\kappa}^{(N)} - \underline{\lambda}^{(N)}]$ are asymptotically equivalent,

(8.122) $$\tilde{P}_L^{(F)}(\underline{N}^{(N)},\underline{\kappa}^{(N)})\underline{\kappa}^{(N)} - \underline{\lambda}^{(N)} \xrightarrow{P} \underline{0},$$

and

(8.123) $$N^{\frac{1}{2}}[\tilde{P}_L^{(F)}(\underline{N}^{(N)},\underline{\kappa}^{(N)})\underline{\kappa}^{(N)} - \underline{\lambda}^{(N)}] \xrightarrow{\mathcal{D}} N(\underline{0},\tilde{P}^{(F)}(\underline{N}^*,\underline{\lambda}^*)[W^{(F)}(\underline{N}^*,\underline{\lambda}^*)]^{-1}).$$

These equations justify use of $\tilde{P}_L^{(F)}(\underline{N},\underline{\kappa})\underline{\kappa}$ as an initial estimate of $\hat{\underline{\lambda}}$. Whether $\tilde{P}_L^{(F)}(\underline{N},\underline{\kappa})\underline{\kappa}$ is as useful an estimate of $\underline{\lambda}$ as $\hat{\underline{\lambda}}$ is not clear. The discussion of chapter 4 concerning $P_M^*(\underline{\nu})\underline{\nu}$ is also relevant when $\tilde{P}_L^{(F)}(\underline{N},\underline{\kappa})\underline{\kappa}$ is examined.

The maximum-likelihood estimate $\underline{\overline{m}}^{(F)}(\underline{N},\hat{\underline{\lambda}})$ also has conventional asymptotic properties. Since

(8.125) $$E^{(F)}(\underline{N}^{(N)},\underline{\lambda}^{(N)})\underline{x} = \{N_j^{(N)}f(\lambda_j^{(N)})x_j\} = W^{(F)}(\underline{N}^{(N)},\underline{\lambda}^{(N)})[\overline{D}^{(F)}(\underline{\lambda}^{(N)})]^{-1}\underline{x},$$

where $\underline{o}^{(N)} \xrightarrow{P} \underline{0}$ and for $x \in R^J$,

(8.125) $$E^{(F)}(\underline{N}^{(N)},\underline{\lambda}^{(N)})\underline{x} = \{N_j^{(N)}f(\lambda_j^{(N)})x_j\}$$
$$= W^{(F)}(\underline{N}^{(N)},\underline{\lambda}^{(N)})[\overline{D}^{(F)}(\underline{\lambda}^{(N)})]^{-1}\underline{x},$$

it follows that

(8.126) $$N^{-\frac{1}{2}}[\underline{\overline{m}}^{(F)}(\underline{N}^{(N)},\hat{\underline{\lambda}}^{(N)}) - \underline{\overline{m}}^{(F)}(\underline{N}^{(N)},\underline{\lambda}^{(N)})] \xrightarrow{\mathcal{D}}$$
$$N(\underline{0},E^{(F)}(\underline{N}^*,\underline{\lambda}^*)\tilde{P}_L^{(F)}(\underline{N}^*,\underline{\lambda}^*)[\overline{D}^{(F)}(\underline{\lambda}^{(*)})]^{-1})$$

and

(8.127) $$N^{-1}\underline{\overline{m}}^{(F)}(\underline{N}^{(N)},\underline{\lambda}^{(N)}) \xrightarrow{P} \underline{\overline{m}}^{(F)}(\underline{N}^*,\underline{\lambda}^*).$$

These results also apply if $\tilde{P}_L^{(F)}(\underline{N},\underline{\kappa})\underline{\kappa}$ is used instead of $\hat{\underline{\lambda}}$. If a logit transform is employed, $\overline{D}^{(L)}(\underline{\lambda}^*) = I$ and thus

(8.128) $$N^{-\frac{1}{2}}[\underline{\overline{m}}^{(L)}(\underline{N}^{(N)},\underline{\lambda}^{(N)}) - \underline{\overline{m}}^{(L)}(\underline{N}^{(N)},\underline{\lambda}^{(N)})] \xrightarrow{\mathcal{D}} N(\underline{0},W^{(L)}(\underline{N}^*,\underline{\lambda}^*)\tilde{P}_L^{(L)}(\underline{N}^*,\underline{\lambda}^*)).$$

Given these results, the estimation procedures discussed in chapter 4 are readily implemented. The only new point to raise concerns the estimation of the asymptotic covariance operator. The obvious estimate is $\tilde{P}_L^{(F)}(\underline{N},\hat{\underline{\lambda}})[W^{(F)}(\underline{N},\hat{\underline{\lambda}})]^{-1}$; however, if the tolerance distribution is not logistic and the Newton-Raphson algorithm has been used to find $\underline{\hat{\lambda}}$, it is more convenient to use $P_L^{(F)}(\underline{n},\underline{\hat{\lambda}})[D^{(F)}(\underline{n},\underline{\hat{\lambda}})]^{-1}$. This estimate is reasonable since

$$(8.129)\quad NP_L^{(F)}(\underline{n}^{(N)},\underline{\hat{\lambda}}^{(N)})[D^{(F)}(\underline{n}^{(N)},\underline{\hat{\lambda}}^{(N)})]^{-1} - N\tilde{P}_L^{(F)}(\underline{N}^{(N)},\underline{\hat{\lambda}}^{(N)})[W^{(F)}(\underline{N}^{(N)},\underline{\hat{\lambda}}^{(N)})]^{-1} \xrightarrow{P} 0.$$

It is not known which estimate is more useful in practice. It should, however, be noted that in large samples in which $\underline{\lambda}^{(0)} = \tilde{P}_L^{(F)}(\underline{N},\underline{\kappa})\underline{\kappa}$, the difference between use of the Newton-Raphson algorithm and use of the scoring algorithm is of slight consequence. If $\underline{\lambda}^{(N,0)} = \tilde{P}_L^{(F)}(\underline{N}^{(N)},\underline{\kappa}^{(N)})\underline{\kappa}^{(N)}$, then

$$(8.130)\quad N^{3/2}\{P_L^{(F)}(\underline{n}^{(N)},\underline{\lambda}^{(N,0)})[D^{(F)}(\underline{n}^{(N)},\underline{\lambda}^{(N,0)})]^{-1}\overline{D}^{(F)}(\underline{\lambda}^{(N,0)})$$
$$- \tilde{P}_L^{(F)}(\underline{N}^{(N)},\underline{\lambda}^{(N,0)})[W^{(F)}(\underline{N}^{(N)},\underline{\lambda}^{(N,0)})]^{-1}\overline{D}^{(F)}(\underline{\lambda}^{(N,0)})\} \xrightarrow{\mathcal{D}} S,$$

where S is a random operator. If f' is differentiable, one may proceed as in chapter 4 and derive equations comparable to (4.104) and (4.105) to show that

$$(8.131)\quad N(\underline{\lambda}^{(N,0)} - \underline{\hat{\lambda}}^{(N)}) \xrightarrow{\mathcal{D}} \underline{r},$$

where $\underline{r}$ is a random vector. It follows after some argument that

$$(8.132)\quad N^{3/2}\{P_L^{(F)}(\underline{n}^{(N)},\underline{\lambda}^{(N,0)})[D^{(F)}(\underline{n}^{(N)},\underline{\lambda}^{(N,0)})]^{-1}\overline{D}^{(F)}(\underline{\lambda}^{(N,0)})[\underline{\overline{n}}^{(N)} - \underline{\overline{m}}^{(F)}(\underline{N}^{(N)},\underline{\lambda}^{(N,0)})]$$
$$- \tilde{P}_L^{(F)}(\underline{N}^{(N)},\underline{\lambda}^{(N,0)})[W^{(F)}(\underline{N}^{(N)},\underline{\lambda}^{(N,0)})]^{-1}\overline{D}^{(F)}(\underline{\lambda}^{(N,0)})[\underline{\overline{n}}^{(N)} - \underline{\overline{m}}^{(F)}(\underline{N}^{(N)},\underline{\lambda}^{(N,0)})]\} \xrightarrow{\mathcal{D}} \underline{s},$$

where $\underline{s}$ is a random vector, and

$$(8.133)\quad N^2\{P_L^{(F)}(\underline{n}^{(N)},\underline{\lambda}^{(N,0)})[D^{(F)}(\underline{n}^{(N)},\underline{\lambda}^{(N,0)})]^{-1}$$
$$\times\ \overline{D}^{(F)}(\underline{\lambda}^{(N,0)})[\underline{\overline{n}}^{(N)} - \underline{\overline{m}}^{(F)}(\underline{N}^{(N)},\underline{\lambda}^{(N,0)})] - \underline{\hat{\lambda}}^{(N)}\} \xrightarrow{\mathcal{D}} \underline{t},$$

where $\underline{t}$ is a random vector.

Hence, the result of the first iteration with the Newton-Raphson algorithm is superior by a factor of $N^{\frac{1}{2}}$ to the result found with the scoring algorithm, but even with the scoring method the approximation to the maximum-likelihood estimate is correct to order $1/N^{3/2}$. Thus it is likely that no more than one iteration will be required whichever algorithm is used, provided a reasonably large sample is present.

Example 8.12. When the classical dosage-response model is examined, the parameters α and β are of considerable interest. Under a logit model,

(8.134) $$\tilde{P}^{(L)}(\underline{N},\hat{\underline{\lambda}})[W^{(L)}(\underline{N},\hat{\underline{\lambda}})]^{-1} = \frac{1}{(\underline{e},W^{(L)}(\underline{N},\hat{\underline{\lambda}})\underline{e})}\,\underline{e}\otimes\underline{e} + \frac{1}{(\underline{u}(\hat{\underline{\lambda}}),W^{(L)}(\underline{N},\hat{\underline{\lambda}})\underline{e})}\,\underline{u}(\hat{\underline{\lambda}})\otimes\underline{u}(\hat{\underline{\lambda}}),$$

where the notation of Example 8.9 is employed. To derive the conventional formulas given by Finney (1947) for asymptotic variances and confidence intervals, one notes that if $\bar{t}. = r^{-1}\sum_{j=1}^{r} t_j$, then

(8.135) $$\hat{\alpha} = \frac{(\hat{\underline{\lambda}},\underline{e})}{(\underline{e},\underline{e})} - \hat{\beta}\bar{t}. = \frac{1}{r}\sum_{j=1}^{r}\hat{\lambda}_j - \hat{\beta}\bar{t}.$$

and

(8.136) $$\hat{\beta} = \frac{(\hat{\underline{\lambda}},\underline{t} - \bar{t}.\underline{e})}{(\underline{t} - \bar{t}.\underline{e},\underline{t} - \bar{t}.\underline{e})} = \sum_{j=1}^{r}\hat{\lambda}_j(t_j - \bar{t}.)/\sum_{j=1}^{r}(t_j - \bar{t}.)^2$$

(see Kruskal 1968b). The estimated asymptotic variance of $\hat{\alpha}$ is then found by noting that

(8.137) $$\left(\frac{1}{r}\underline{e} - \frac{\bar{t}.}{\sum_{j=1}^{r}(t_j - \bar{t}.)^2}(\underline{t} - \bar{t}.\underline{e}),\underline{e}\right) = 1$$

and

(8.138) $$\left(\frac{1}{r}\underline{e} - [\bar{t}./\sum_{j=1}^{r}(t_j - \bar{t}.)]^2(\underline{t} - t.\underline{e}),\ \underline{t} - \bar{t}.^{(L)}(\underline{N},\hat{\underline{\lambda}})\underline{e}\right)$$

$$= \left(\frac{1}{r}\underline{e} - [\bar{t}./\sum_{j=1}^{r}(t_j - \bar{t}.)^2](\underline{t} - t.\underline{e}),\ \underline{t} - t.\underline{e} - (\bar{t}.^{(L)}(\underline{N},\hat{\underline{\lambda}}) - \bar{t}.)\underline{e}\right)$$

$$= -(\bar{t}.^{(L)}(\underline{N},\hat{\underline{\lambda}}) - \bar{t}.) - \bar{t}. = -\bar{t}.^{(L)}(\underline{N},\hat{\underline{\lambda}}).$$

Thus the estimated asymptotic variance of $\hat{\alpha}$ is

(8.139) $$\frac{1}{(\underline{e},W^{(L)}(\underline{N},\hat{\underline{\lambda}})\underline{e})} + \frac{[\bar{t}.^{(L)}(\underline{N},\hat{\underline{\lambda}})]^2}{(\underline{u}(\hat{\underline{\lambda}}),W^{(L)}(\underline{N},\hat{\underline{\lambda}})\underline{u}(\hat{\underline{\lambda}}))}$$

$$= \frac{1}{\sum_{j=1}^{r} w_j^{(L)}(\underline{N},\hat{\underline{\lambda}})} + \frac{[\bar{t}.^{(L)}(\underline{N},\hat{\underline{\lambda}})]^2}{\sum_{j=1}^{r}[t_j - \bar{t}.^{(L)}(\underline{N},\hat{\underline{\lambda}})]^2 w_j^{(L)}(\underline{N},\hat{\underline{\lambda}})}$$

Similarly, the estimated asymptotic variance of $\hat{\beta}$ is found by noting that

(8.140) $$(\underline{t} - \bar{t}.\underline{e},\underline{e}) = 0$$

and

(8.141) $$(\underline{t} - \bar{t}.\underline{e},\underline{t} - \bar{t}.\underline{e} - [\bar{t}.^{(L)}(\underline{N},\hat{\underline{\lambda}}) - \bar{t}.]\underline{e}) = \sum_{j=1}^{r}(t_j - \bar{t}.)^2 .$$

Thus the estimated asymptotic variance is

$$(8.142)\qquad 1/(\underline{t} - \bar{t}^{(L)}_{\cdot}(\underline{N},\hat{\underline{\lambda}})\underline{e}, W^{(L)}(\underline{N},\hat{\underline{\lambda}})[\underline{t} - \bar{t}^{(L)}_{\cdot}(\underline{N},\hat{\underline{\lambda}})\underline{e}])$$

$$= 1/\sum_{j=1}^{r} [t_j - \bar{t}^{(L)}_{\cdot}(\underline{N},\hat{\underline{\lambda}})]^2 w_j^{(L)}(\underline{N},\hat{\underline{\lambda}}),$$

and the estimated asymptotic covariance of $\hat{\alpha}$ and $\hat{\beta}$ is

$$(8.143)\qquad -\bar{t}^{(L)}_{\cdot}(\underline{N},\hat{\underline{\lambda}})/(\underline{u}(\hat{\underline{\lambda}}), W^{(L)}(\underline{N},\hat{\underline{\lambda}})\underline{u}(\hat{\underline{\lambda}}))$$

$$= -\bar{t}^{(L)}_{\cdot}(\underline{N},\hat{\underline{\lambda}})/\sum_{j=1}^{r} [t_j - \bar{t}^{(L)}_{\cdot}(\underline{N},\hat{\underline{\lambda}})]^2 w_j^{(L)}(\underline{N},\hat{\underline{\lambda}}) .$$

In Example 3.3, $t_1 = 0.75$, $t_2 = 0.85$, and $t_3 = 0.95$. Thus $\bar{t}.(\underline{N},\hat{\underline{\lambda}}) = 0.871$, $\hat{\alpha} = -9.11$, $\hat{\beta} = 9.78$, and the estimated asymptotic standard deviation of $\hat{\alpha}$ and $\hat{\beta}$ are respectively 2.92 and 4.39. Thus approximate 95% confidence intervals for α and β are respectively [-14.83, -3.39] and [1.18, 18.38].

While α and β are parameters of interest, there is also interest in estimation of the median tolerance log LD50 = $-\alpha/\beta$ of the members of the population and the standard deviation $\sigma = \pi/(|\beta|3^{\frac{1}{2}})$ of the tolerances of individual subjects in the population. The maximum-likelihood estimate of log LD50 is $-\hat{\alpha}/\hat{\beta}$, and the maximum-likelihood estimate of σ is $\pi/(|\beta|3^{\frac{1}{2}})$. In Example 3.3, these two estimates are respectively 0.931 and 0.185.

The joint asymptotic distribution of $-\hat{\alpha}/\hat{\beta}$ and $\pi/(3^{\frac{1}{2}}\hat{\beta})$ may be found by standard propagation of errors arguments discussed by Rao (1965). Using (8.116), (8.117), and (8.118), one finds that $\langle -\hat{\alpha}/\hat{\beta}, \pi/(3^{\frac{1}{2}}\hat{\beta})\rangle$ is asymptotically normal with asymptotic mean $\langle -\alpha/\beta, \pi/(3^{\frac{1}{2}}\beta)\rangle$ and asymptotic covariance $A(\underline{\lambda})$, where the matrix $[A(\underline{\lambda})]$ with respect to the standard basis satisfies

$$(8.144)\qquad [A(\underline{\lambda})]_{11} = \frac{1}{\beta^2}[1/\sum_{j=1}^{r} w_j^{(L)}(\underline{N},\underline{\lambda})$$

$$+ [\bar{t}.(\underline{N},\underline{\lambda}) + \alpha/\beta]^2/\sum_{j=1}^{r} [t_j - \bar{t}.(\underline{N},\underline{\lambda})]^2 w_j^{(L)}(\underline{N},\underline{\lambda})],$$

$$(8.145)\qquad [A(\underline{\lambda})]_{12} = \frac{-\pi}{\beta^3 3^{\frac{1}{2}}}[t.(\underline{N},\underline{\lambda}) + \alpha/\beta]/\sum_{j=1}^{r} [t_j - \bar{t}.(\underline{N},\underline{\lambda})]^2 w_j^{(L)}(\underline{N},\underline{\lambda}) ,$$

and

$$(8.146)\qquad [A(\underline{\lambda})]_{22} = \frac{\pi^2}{3\beta^4}/\sum_{j=1}^{r} [t_j - \bar{t}.(\underline{N},\underline{\lambda})]^2 w_j^{(L)}(\underline{N},\underline{\lambda}) .$$

In the example, the estimated asymptotic covariance matrix is then

(8.147)
$$[A(\underline{\lambda})] = \begin{bmatrix} 0.00126 & 0.00229 \\ 0.00229 & 0.00694 \end{bmatrix}$$

and approximate 95% confidence intervals for log LD50 and σ are respectively

(8.148)
$$[0.931 - 1.96(0.00126)^{\frac{1}{2}}, 0.931 + 1.96(0.00126)^{\frac{1}{2}}] = [0.861, 1.001]$$

and

(8.149)
$$[0.185 - 1.96(0.00694)^{\frac{1}{2}}, 0.185 + 1.96(0.00694)^{\frac{1}{2}}] = [0.022, 0.348].$$

An alternative way to find an approximate 95% confidence interval for σ is to use the confidence interval for β obtained previously. The confidence interval is then

(8.150)
$$[\pi/18.38(3^{\frac{1}{2}}), \pi/1.18(3^{\frac{1}{2}})] = [0.099, 1.537] .$$

The difference between the two intervals for σ is large since the sample is too small for accurate estimation.

A confidence interval for log LD50 may also be found by the approach of Example 4.19. In this approach, which is based on Fieller's (1940) work, one notes that

$$P(|\hat{\alpha} + (-\alpha/\beta)\hat{\beta}| \le \Phi^{(\gamma/2)} \times \{1/\sum_{j=1}^{r} w_j^{(L)}(\underline{N},\underline{\hat{\lambda}}) + [\overline{t}_{\cdot}^{(L)}(\underline{N},\underline{\hat{\lambda}}) + \alpha/\beta]^2/\sum_{j=1}^{r} [t_j - \overline{t}_{\cdot}^{(L)}(\underline{N},\underline{\hat{\lambda}})]^2 w_j^{(L)}(\underline{N},\underline{\hat{\lambda}})\}^{\frac{1}{2}})$$

is approximately $1 - \gamma$. An approximate level-$(1 - \gamma)$ confidence region for $-\alpha/\beta$ then consists of all c such that

(8.151)
$$(\hat{\alpha} + c\hat{\beta})^2 \le [\Phi^{(\gamma/2)}]^2 \times \{1/\sum_{j=1}^{r} w_j^{(L)}(\underline{N},\underline{\hat{\lambda}}) + [\overline{t}_{\cdot}^{(L)}(\underline{N},\underline{\hat{\lambda}}) - c]^2/\sum_{j=1}^{r} [t_j - \overline{t}_{\cdot}^{(L)}(\underline{N},\underline{\hat{\lambda}})]^2 w_j^{(L)}(\underline{N},\underline{\hat{\lambda}})\}.$$

This inequality holds if $\hat{\beta} \neq 0$ for $c = -\hat{\alpha}/\hat{\beta}$, and it holds if $\hat{\beta} = 0$ for sufficiently large c. Thus the confidence region always contains some points. If the two sides of (8.151) are never equal for real c, then the inequality holds for all c and the confidence region is the real line. By the quadratic formula, this condition occurs if

(8.152) $$d = \{\bar{t}_.^{(L)}(\underline{N},\hat{\lambda})[\Phi^{(\gamma/2)}]^2/\sum_{j=1}^{r}[t_j - \bar{t}_.^{(L)}(\underline{N},\hat{\lambda})]^2 w_j^{(L)}(\underline{N},\hat{\lambda}) + \hat{\alpha}\hat{\beta}\}^2$$

$$- \{[\Phi^{(\gamma/2)}]^2/\sum_{j=1}^{r}[t_j - \bar{t}_.^{(L)}(\underline{N},\hat{\lambda})]^2 w_j^{(L)}(\underline{N},\hat{\lambda}) - \hat{\beta}^2\}$$

$$\{[\Phi^{(\gamma/2)}]^2[\bar{t}_.^{(L)}(\underline{N},\hat{\lambda})]^2/\sum_{j=1}^{r}[t_j - \bar{t}_.^{(L)}(\underline{N},\hat{\lambda})]^2 w_j^{(L)}(\underline{N},\hat{\lambda}) + [\Phi^{(\gamma/2)}]^2/\sum_{j=1}^{r} w_j^{(L)}(\underline{N},\hat{\lambda}) - \hat{\alpha}^2\}$$

$$= \frac{[\Phi^{(\gamma/2)}]^2}{\sum_{j=1}^{r}[t_j - \bar{t}_.^{(L)}(\underline{N},\hat{\lambda})]^2 w_j^{(L)}(\underline{N},\hat{\lambda})}\{[\hat{\alpha} + \hat{\beta}\bar{t}_.^{(L)}(\underline{N},\hat{\lambda})]^2 - [\Phi^{(\gamma/2)}]^2/\sum_{j=1}^{r} w_j^{(L)}(\underline{N},\hat{\lambda})\}$$

$$+ \hat{\beta}^2[\Phi^{(\gamma/2)}]^2/\sum_{j=1}^{r} w_j^{(L)}(\underline{N},\hat{\lambda})$$

$$< 0 .$$

If $d = 0$, then the confidence interval is still the entire line, for the left-hand side of (8.151) is never greater than the right-hand side. If $d > 0$ and $g \neq 1$, then equality is achieved at $\hat{f}_1$ and $\hat{f}_2$, where

(8.153) $$\hat{f}_1 = -\hat{\alpha}/\hat{\beta} + [g/(1-g)][\bar{t}_.^{(L)}(\underline{N},\hat{\lambda}) + \hat{\alpha}/\hat{\beta}] - [\Phi^{(\gamma/2)}/\hat{\beta}g(1-g)]$$

$$\times \{(1-g)/\sum_{j=1}^{r} w_j(\underline{N},\hat{\lambda}) + [\bar{t}_.^{(L)}(\underline{N},\hat{\lambda}) + \hat{\alpha}/\hat{\beta}]^2/\sum_{j=1}^{r}[t_j - \bar{t}_.^{(L)}(\underline{N},\hat{\lambda})]^2 w_j^{(L)}(\underline{N},\hat{\lambda})\}^{\frac{1}{2}} ,$$

(8.154) $$f_2 = -\hat{\alpha}/\hat{\beta} + [g/(1-g)][\bar{t}_.^{(L)}(\underline{N},\hat{\lambda}) + \hat{\alpha}/\hat{\beta}] + [\Phi^{(\gamma/2)}/\hat{\beta}(1-g)]$$

$$\times \{(1-g)/\sum_{j=1}^{r} w_j(\underline{N},\hat{\lambda}) + [\bar{t}_.^{(L)}(\underline{N},\hat{\lambda}) + \hat{\alpha}/\hat{\beta}]^2 \sum_{j=1}^{r}[t_j - \bar{t}_.^{(L)}(\underline{N},\hat{\lambda})]^2 w_j^{(L)}(\underline{N},\hat{\lambda})^{\frac{1}{2}},$$

and

(8.155) $$g = [\Phi^{(\gamma/2)}]^2/\{\hat{\beta}^2 \sum_{j=1}^{r}[t_j - \bar{t}_.^{(L)}(\underline{N},\hat{\lambda})]^2 w_j^{(L)}(\underline{N},\hat{\lambda})\}$$

(see Finney 1971). A number of special cases are possible. If $g < 1$ and $\hat{\beta} > 0$, then the region is the interval $[\hat{f}_1,\hat{f}_2]$. If $g > 1$ and $\hat{\beta} > 0$, then the region consists of the two intervals $[-\infty,f_1]$ and $[f_1,\infty]$. Other cases are possible but less common. As Fieller (1940) points out, the condition that $g < 1$ is equivalent to the condition that $\hat{\beta}$ differs significantly from 0 under the approximate test which rejects the hypothesis $\beta = 0$ when

$|\hat{\beta}/\{\sum_{j=1}^{r} [t_j - \bar{t}_{\cdot}^{(L)}(\underline{N},\hat{\underline{\lambda}})]^2 w_j^{(L)}(\underline{N},\hat{\underline{\lambda}})\}^{\frac{1}{2}}| > \Phi^{(\gamma/2)}$. Thus an interval is obtained when $\hat{\beta}$ is significantly different from 0. In Example 3.3, $g = 0.775$, $\hat{f}_1 = 0.863$, $\hat{f}_2 = 1.411$, and the confidence interval is $[0.863, 1.411]$. This interval differs substantially from the one in (8.148). Again the small sample size is involved. In fact, as the sample size increases, g approaches 0 with probability 1 and the intervals derived by Fieller's technique and the intervals derived by use of the asymptotic variance of $-\hat{\alpha}/\hat{\beta}$ become increasingly similar.

Example 8.13. In the paired-comparisons model,

$$\tilde{P}_L^{(L)}(\underline{N},\hat{\underline{\lambda}})[W^{(L)}(\underline{N},\hat{\underline{\lambda}})]^{-1} = M[M^T W^{(L)}(\underline{N},\hat{\underline{\lambda}})M + \sum_{k=1}^{\ell} a_k \underline{\nu}(A_k) \otimes \underline{\nu}(A_k)]^{-1} M^T , \tag{8.156}$$

where the notation of Examples 8.8 and 8.10 is employed. If $A = \text{span}\,\{\underline{\nu}(A_k): k \in \bar{\ell}\}^{\perp}$, then for $\underline{c} \in R^r$,

$$\begin{aligned}(\underline{c},\hat{\underline{\alpha}})_r &= (P_A\underline{c},\hat{\underline{\alpha}})_r \\ &= ([M^-]^T P_A\underline{c}, M\hat{\underline{\alpha}})_J \\ &= ([M^-]^T P_A\underline{c},\hat{\underline{\lambda}})_J ,\end{aligned} \tag{8.157}$$

where M^- is the inverse of the restriction of M to A. Thus the estimated asymptotic variance of $(\underline{c},\hat{\underline{\alpha}})_r$ is

$$\begin{aligned}&([M^-]^T P_A\underline{c}, M[M^T W^{(L)}(\underline{N},\hat{\underline{\lambda}})M + \sum_{k=1}^{\ell} a_k \underline{\nu}(A_k) \otimes \underline{\nu}(A_k)]^{-1} M^T [M^-]^T P_A\underline{c}) \\ &= (P_A\underline{c}, [M^T W^{(L)}(\underline{N},\hat{\underline{\lambda}})M + \sum_{k=1}^{\ell} a_k \underline{\nu}(A_k) \otimes \underline{\nu}(A_k)]^{-1} P_A\underline{c}) ,\end{aligned} \tag{8.158}$$

and the estimated asymptotic covariance of $\hat{\underline{\alpha}}$ is $P_A[M^T W^{(L)}(\underline{N},\hat{\underline{\lambda}})M + \sum_{k=1}^{\ell} a_k \underline{\nu}(A_k) \otimes \underline{\nu}(A_k)]^{-1} P_A$.

In the baseball example, $\ell = 1$, $A_k = \bar{r} = \bar{8}$, and $a_1 = 5$. One has $\underline{\nu}(A_1) = \underline{e}^{(8)}$ and $\hat{\alpha}_i = (\underline{\delta}^{(i)},\hat{\underline{\alpha}})$, where $\underline{\delta}^{(i)} = \{\delta_{ij}: j \in \bar{r}\}$ and $P_A\underline{\delta}^{(i)} = \underline{\delta}^{(i)} - \frac{1}{8}e^{(8)}$. By use of (8.158), one finds that the estimated asymptotic variances and standard deviations are as shown in table 8.7. This table clearly indicates that a single baseball season provides only a modest indication of the relative strength of the teams involved.

Example 8.14. In Example 8.3, the difference $\log c$ between the log odds $\log [p(1|\langle i,1\rangle)/p(2|\langle i,1\rangle)]$ and the log odds $\log [p(1|\langle i,2\rangle)/p(2|\langle i,2\rangle)]$ is a constant for $i \in \bar{6}$. This difference is $\lambda_{i1} - \lambda_{i2}$ for any $i \in \bar{6}$. By (8.99), the estimated asymptotic covariance of $\hat{\underline{\lambda}}$ is

TABLE 8.7

RELATIVE TEAM STRENGTHS FOR AMERICAN LEAGUE TEAMS IN 1948

Team	Strength	Estimated Asymptotic Variance	Estimated Asymptotic Standard Deviation
Cleveland	0.472	0.0221	0.149
Boston	0.447	0.0220	0.148
New York	0.410	0.0217	0.147
Philadelphia	0.168	0.0210	0.145
Detroit	0.025	0.0209	0.145
St. Louis	-0.405	0.0220	0.148
Washington	-0.506	0.0226	0.150
Chicago	-0.610	0.0232	0.152

(8.159)
$$\tilde{P}_L^{(L)}(\underline{N},\hat{\underline{\lambda}})[W^{(L)}(\underline{N},\hat{\underline{\lambda}})]^{-1}$$
$$= \sum_{i=1}^{6} \underline{\nu}(\{1\},i) \otimes \underline{\nu}(\{1\},i)/w_{i+}^{(L)}(\underline{N},\hat{\underline{\lambda}})$$
$$+ \underline{y}(\underline{\lambda}) \otimes \underline{y}(\underline{\lambda})/[\sum_{i=1}^{6} w_{i1}^{(L)}(\underline{N},\hat{\underline{\lambda}})w_{i2}^{(L)}(\underline{N},\hat{\underline{\lambda}})/w_{i+}(\underline{N},\hat{\underline{\lambda}})].$$

Since

(8.160)
$$\lambda_{i1} - \lambda_{i2} = (\underline{c},\underline{\lambda}),$$

where

(8.161)
$$c_{ij} = \begin{cases} 1 & \text{if } i = j = 1, \\ -1 & \text{if } i = 1,\ j = 2, \\ 0 & \text{otherwise}, \end{cases}$$

(8.162)
$$(\underline{c},\underline{\nu}(\{1\},i)) = 0$$

for $i \in \bar{6}$, and

(8.163)
$$(\underline{c},\underline{\nu}(\{2\},1)) = 1,$$

it follows from (8.95) and (8.159) that the estimated asymptotic variance of $\log \hat{c} = \hat{\lambda}_{i1} - \hat{\lambda}_{i2}$ is

(8.164)
$$1/\sum_{i=1}^{6} w_{i1}^{(L)}(\underline{N},\hat{\underline{\lambda}})w_{i2}^{(L)}(\underline{N},\hat{\underline{\lambda}})/w_{i+}(\underline{N},\hat{\underline{\lambda}}) = 0.00701.$$

Since $\log \hat{c} = 0.299$, an approximate 95% confidence interval for $\log c$ is

(8.165) $$[0.299 - 1.96(0.00701)^{\frac{1}{2}}, .299 + 1.96(0.00701)^{\frac{1}{2}}]$$

$$= [0.255, 0.343]$$

Likelihood ratio tests and Pearson chi-square tests for binomial-response models involve very few new results. The log likelihood ratio chi-square statistic is

(8.166) $$-2\Delta^{(F)}(\underline{n},\underline{\lambda}^{(2)},\underline{\lambda}^{(1)}) = 2 \sum_{j \in J} \sum_{k=1}^{2} n_{jk} \log [m_{jk}^{(F)}(\underline{N},\underline{\lambda}^{(2)})/m_{jk}^{(F)}(\underline{n},\underline{\lambda}^{(1)})],$$

and the Pearson chi-square statistic is

(8.167) $$C^{(F)}(\underline{\lambda}^{(2)},\underline{\lambda}^{(1)}) = \sum_{j \in J} \sum_{k=1}^{2} [m_{jk}^{(F)}(\underline{N},\underline{\lambda}^{(2)}) - m_{jk}^{(F)}(\underline{N},\underline{\lambda}^{(1)})]^2/m_{jk}^{(F)}(\underline{N},\underline{\lambda}^{(1)})$$

$$= \sum_{j \in J} [\overline{m}_j^{(F)}(\underline{N},\underline{\lambda}^{(2)}) - \overline{m}_j^{(F)}(\underline{N},\underline{\lambda}^{(1)})]^2/[m_{j1}^{(F)}(\underline{N},\underline{\lambda}^{(1)})m_{j2}^{(F)}(\underline{N},\underline{\lambda}^{(1)})/N_j].$$

The last equation follows since

(8.168) $$m_{j1}^{(F)}(\underline{N},\underline{\lambda}) + m_{j2}^{(F)}(\underline{N},\underline{\lambda}) = N_j$$

for $j \in J$ and

(8.169) $$1/m_{j1}^{(F)}(\underline{N},\underline{\lambda}^{(1)}) + 1/m_{j2}^{(F)}(\underline{N},\underline{\lambda}^{(1)})$$

$$= N_j/[m_{j1}^{(F)}(\underline{N},\underline{\lambda}^{(1)})m_{j2}^{(F)}(\underline{N},\underline{\lambda}^{(1)})].$$

When a logit model is used,

(8.170) $$C^{(L)}(\underline{\lambda}^{(2)},\underline{\lambda}^{(1)}) = \sum_{j \in J} [\overline{m}_j^{(L)}(\underline{N},\underline{\lambda}^{(2)}) - \overline{m}_j^{(L)}(\underline{N},\underline{\lambda}^{(1)})]^2/w_j^{(L)}(\underline{N},\underline{\lambda}^{(1)})$$

$$= (\underline{\overline{m}}^{(L)}(\underline{N},\underline{\lambda}^{(2)}) - \underline{\overline{m}}^{(L)}(\underline{N},\underline{\lambda}^{(1)}),[W^{(L)}(\underline{N},\underline{\lambda}^{(1)})]^{-1}[\underline{\overline{m}}^{(L)}(\underline{N},\underline{\lambda}^{(2)}) - \underline{\overline{m}}^{(L)}(\underline{N},\underline{\lambda}^{(1)})]).$$

Under a logit model, all results in chapter 4 concerning hypothesis tests may be applied directly. The number of degrees of freedom for the test H_0: $\underline{\lambda} = \underline{\lambda}^{(0)}$ against the alternative H_A: $\underline{\lambda} \in L$ is $\dim L$, while the number of degrees of freedom for the test H_0: $\underline{\lambda} \in L_1$ against H_A: $\underline{\lambda} \in L_2$, where $L_1 \subset L_2$, is $\dim L_2 - \dim L_1$. These results follow since $\dim M = \dim L + \dim N$ if the log-linear model $\underline{\mu} \in M$ corresponds to the logit model $\underline{\lambda} \in L$. Otherwise, these tests require no special remarks. The standard asymptotic properties also apply when other tolerance distributions are used. The arguments of chapter 4 may be applied with minor modifications to verify the following theorems for sequences $\{\underline{n}^{(N)}\}$ of observations with means $\{\underline{m}^{(F)}(\underline{N}^{(N)},\underline{\lambda}^{(N)})\}$ such that $\underline{\lambda}^{(N)} \longrightarrow \underline{\lambda}^*$ and $N^{-1}\underline{N}^{(N)} \longrightarrow \underline{N}^*$.

THEOREM 8.3. *Consider a sequence of null hypotheses* $H_0:\underline{\lambda}^{(N)} = \underline{\lambda}^{(N,0)} \in L$. *If these hypotheses are true, then* $-2\Delta^{(F)}(\underline{n}^{(N)},\hat{\underline{\lambda}}^{(N)},\underline{\lambda}^{(N,0)})$ *and* $C^{(F)}(\hat{\underline{\lambda}}^{(N)},\underline{\lambda}^{(N,0)})$ *are asymptotically equivalent; that is,*

$$-2\Delta^{(F)}(\underline{n}^{(N)},\hat{\underline{\lambda}}^{(N)},\underline{\lambda}^{(N,0)}) - C^{(F)}(\hat{\underline{\lambda}}^{(N)},\underline{\lambda}^{(N,0)}) \xrightarrow{P} \underline{0}\,, \tag{8.171}$$

and

$$\begin{aligned} &\lim_{N\to\infty} P\{-2\Delta^{(F)}(\underline{n}^{(N)},\hat{\underline{\lambda}}^{(N)},\underline{\lambda}^{(N,0)}) > \chi_s^2(\alpha)\} \\ &= \lim_{N\to\infty} P\{C^{(F)}(\hat{\underline{\lambda}}^{(N)},\underline{\lambda}^{(N,0)}) > \chi_x^2(\alpha)\} \\ &= \alpha, \end{aligned} \tag{8.172}$$

where $s = \dim L$.

If $\underline{\lambda}^{(N)} \in L$ *is equal to* $\underline{\lambda}^{(N,0)} + \underline{c}^{(N)}/N^{\frac{1}{2}}$, *where* $\underline{c}^{(N)} \longrightarrow \underline{c}^*$, *then* (8.171) *continues to hold and*

$$\begin{aligned} &\lim_{N\to\infty} P\{-2\Delta^{(F)}(\underline{n}^{(N)},\hat{\underline{\lambda}}^{(N)},\underline{\lambda}^{(N,0)}) > \chi_s^2(\alpha)\} \\ &= \lim_{N\to\infty} P\{C^{(F)}(\hat{\underline{\lambda}}^{(N)},\underline{\lambda}^{(N,0)}) > \chi_s^2(\alpha)\} \\ &= P\{\chi'^2_{s,\delta^2} > \chi_s^2(\alpha)\}\,, \end{aligned} \tag{8.173}$$

where χ'^2_{s,δ^2} *has a noncentral chi-square distribution with* s *degrees of freedom and noncentrality parameter* $\delta^2 = (\underline{c}^*, W^{(F)}(\underline{N}^*,\underline{\lambda}^*)\underline{c}^*)$.

If $\underline{\lambda}^{(N,0)} \longrightarrow \underline{\lambda}^{(0)} \neq \underline{\lambda}^*$, *then*

$$\frac{1}{N}[-2\Delta^{(F)}(\underline{n}^{(N)},\hat{\underline{\lambda}}^{(N)},\underline{\lambda}^{(N,0)})] \xrightarrow{P} -2\Delta^{(F)}(\underline{m}^{(F)}(\underline{N}^*,\underline{\lambda}^*),\underline{\lambda}^*,\underline{\lambda}^{(0)}) > 0 \tag{8.174}$$

and

$$\frac{1}{N}C^{(F)}(\hat{\underline{\lambda}}^{(N)},\underline{\lambda}^{(N,0)}) \xrightarrow{P} C^{(F)}(\underline{\lambda}^*,\underline{\lambda}^{(0)}) > 0. \tag{8.175}$$

Thus

$$\begin{aligned} &\lim_{N\to\infty} P\{-2\Delta^{(F)}(\underline{n}^{(N)},\hat{\underline{\lambda}}^{(N)},\underline{\lambda}^{(N,0)}) > \chi_s^2(\alpha)\} \\ &= \lim_{N\to\infty} P\{C^{(F)}(\hat{\underline{\lambda}}^{(N)},\underline{\lambda}^{(N;0)}) > \chi_s^2(\alpha)\} \\ &= 1. \end{aligned} \tag{8.176}$$

THEOREM 8.4. *Consider a sequence of null hypotheses* H_0: $\underline{\lambda}^{(N)} \in L_1$ *and alternatives* H_A: $\underline{\lambda}^{(N)} \in L_2$. *Suppose that* $\hat{\underline{\lambda}}^{(N,k)}$ *is the maximum likelihood estimate of* $\underline{\lambda}^{(N)}$ *under the hypothesis that* $\underline{\lambda}^{(N)} \in L_k$. *If* $\underline{\lambda}^{(N)} \in L_1$ *for each* N, *then* $-2\Delta^{(F)}(\underline{n}^{(N)},\hat{\underline{\lambda}}^{(N,2)},\hat{\underline{\lambda}}^{(N,1)})$ *and* $C^{(F)}(\hat{\underline{\lambda}}^{(N,2)},\hat{\underline{\lambda}}^{(N,1)})$ *are asymptotically equivalent and*

$$\begin{aligned}(8.177)\qquad &\lim_{N\to\infty} P\{-2\Delta^{(F)}(\underline{n}^{(N)},\hat{\underline{\lambda}}^{(N,2)},\hat{\underline{\lambda}}^{(N,1)}) > \chi^2_{s_2-s_1}(\alpha)\}\\ &= \lim_{N\to\infty} P\{C^{(F)}(\hat{\underline{\lambda}}^{(N,2)},\hat{\underline{\lambda}}^{(N,1)}) > \chi^2_{s_2-s_1}(\alpha)\}\\ &= \alpha,\end{aligned}$$

where $\dim L_k = s_k$ *for* $k \in \overline{2}$.

If $\underline{\lambda}^{(N)} \notin L_1$ *but* $\underline{\lambda}^{(N)} - N^{-\frac{1}{2}}\underline{c}^{(N)} \in L_1$ *and* $\underline{c}^{(N)} \longrightarrow \underline{c}^*$, *then* $-2\Delta^{(F)}(\underline{n}^{(N)},\hat{\underline{\lambda}}^{(N,2)},\hat{\underline{\lambda}}^{(N,1)})$ *and* $C^{(F)}(\hat{\underline{\lambda}}^{(N,2)},\hat{\underline{\lambda}}^{(N,1)})$ *are asymptotically equivalent and*

$$\begin{aligned}(8.178)\qquad &\lim_{N\to\infty} P\{-2\Delta^{(F)}(\underline{n}^{(N)},\hat{\underline{\lambda}}^{(N,2)},\hat{\underline{\lambda}}^{(N,1)}) > \chi^2_{s_2-s_1}(\alpha)\}\\ &= \lim_{N\to\infty} P\{C^{(F)}(\hat{\underline{\lambda}}^{(N,2)},\hat{\underline{\lambda}}^{(N,1)}) > \chi^2_{s_2-s_1}(\alpha)\}\\ &= P\{\chi'^2_{s_2-s_1,\delta^2} > \chi^2_{s_2-s_1}(\alpha)\},\end{aligned}$$

where $\delta^2 = (\underline{c}^*, W^{(F)}(\underline{N}^*,\underline{\lambda}^*)[\tilde{P}^{(F)}_{L_2}(\underline{N}^*,\underline{\lambda}^*) - \tilde{P}^{(F)}_{L_1}(\underline{N}^*,\underline{\lambda}^*)]\underline{c}^*)$.

If $\underline{\lambda}^* \notin L_1$ *but* $\underline{\lambda}^* \in L_2$, *then*

$$(8.179)\qquad \frac{1}{N}[-2\Delta^{(F)}(\underline{n}^{(N)},\hat{\underline{\lambda}}^{(N,2)},\hat{\underline{\lambda}}^{(N,1)})] \xrightarrow{P} -2\Delta(\underline{m}^{(F)}(\underline{N}^*,\underline{\lambda}^*),\underline{\lambda}^*,\underline{\lambda}^{(0)}) > 0$$

and

$$(8.180)\qquad \frac{1}{N}[C^{(F)}(\hat{\underline{\lambda}}^{(N,2)},\hat{\underline{\lambda}}^{(N,1)})] \xrightarrow{P} C^{(F)}(\underline{\lambda}^*,\underline{\lambda}^{(0)}) > 0\,,$$

where $\underline{\lambda}^{(0)}$ *is the location of the maximum for* $\underline{\lambda} \in L_1$ *of* $-2\Delta^{(F)}(\underline{N}^*,\underline{\lambda}^*,\underline{\lambda})$. *Thus*

$$\begin{aligned}(8.181)\qquad &\lim_{N\to\infty} P\{-2\Delta^{(F)}(\underline{n}^{(N)},\hat{\underline{\lambda}}^{(N,2)},\hat{\underline{\lambda}}^{(N,1)}) > \chi^2_{s_2-s_1}(\alpha)\}\\ &= \lim_{N\to\infty} P\{C^{(F)}(\hat{\underline{\lambda}}^{(N,2)},\hat{\underline{\lambda}}^{(N,1)}) > \chi^2_{s_2-s_1}(\alpha)\}\\ &= 1.\end{aligned}$$

Example 8.14. In Example 8.10, the statistics $C^{(L)}(\underline{\kappa},\hat{\underline{\lambda}})$ and $-2\Delta^{(L)}(\underline{n},\underline{\kappa},\hat{\underline{\lambda}})$ were used to test the goodness of fit. These statistics correspond to the null hypothesis $\underline{\lambda} \in L$ and the trivial alternative $\underline{\lambda} \in R^J$. Given the very low value of chi-square obtained, it seems reasonable to inquire whether the sample size taken was large enough to detect errors in the model. This investigation is also motivated by the large estimated asymptotic variances found in Example 8.12. Theorem 8.4 may be employed to check on this difficulty. By Haynam, Govindarajulu, and Leone (1970), $P\{\chi'^2_{21,\delta^2} > \chi^2_{21}(0.10)\} = 0.50$ if $\delta^2 = 9.4$. The values of $w^{(L)}_{ij}(\underline{N},\underline{\lambda})$ are generally about 5 in this example, J has 28 elements, and the noncentrality parameter may be estimated by $(\underline{\lambda} - \tilde{P}^{(L)}_L(\underline{N},\underline{\lambda})\underline{\lambda}, W^{(L)}(\underline{N},\underline{\lambda})[\underline{\lambda} - \tilde{P}^{(L)}_L(\underline{N},\underline{\lambda})\underline{\lambda}])$. Thus an average squared difference between λ_{ij} and $[\tilde{P}^{(L)}_L(\underline{N},\underline{\lambda})\underline{\lambda}]_{ij}$ of $9.4/(5)(28) = 0.067$ would be large enough so that H_0 would be rejected about half the time at the 0.10 level. Such a squared difference corresponds to a difference of about 0.13 between the true probability and the probability obtained if the model were correct. This difference is substantial enough so that the goodness-of-fit test is not likely to detect modest departures from the model, although gross deviations are likely to result in a value of $-2\Delta^{(L)}(\underline{n},\underline{\kappa},\hat{\underline{\lambda}})$ or $C^{(L)}(\underline{\kappa},\hat{\underline{\lambda}})$ larger than $\chi^2_{21}(0.10)$. Therefore, more observations are required before the model can be accepted as an effective descriptive of the behavior of baseball teams, even though American League teams in 1948 certainly provided no evidence that the model might be incorrect.

Example 8.15. Given Theorems 8.3 and 8.4, the simultaneous testing procedures chapter 4 are readily applied. For instance, the birth order data examined in Examples 4.13, 4.14, and 4.15 can be interpreted in terms of logit models rather than log-linear model. In the logit interpretation, the response is the type of child and $J = \overline{3} \times \overline{2}$. The probability $p(1|\langle i,k\rangle)$ that a child is a problem child given that his birth order is i and his mother has status k may be assumed to be $L(\lambda_{ik})$, where $\underline{\lambda}$ is in a linear manifold $L \subset R^{\overline{3}\times\overline{2}}$. To any such manifold L corresponds a manifold M in $R^{\overline{3}\times\overline{2}\times\overline{2}}$ which includes $N^* = \text{span}\,\{\underline{\nu}(\{1,3\},\langle i,k\rangle): \langle i,k\rangle \in \overline{3} \times \overline{2}\}$. This result may be derived by the argument used in (8.27). The manifold M has the property that if the log-mean vector $\underline{\mu}$ is in M, then $\underline{\lambda} \in L$. On the other hand, if $\underline{\lambda} \in L$, then $\underline{\mu} \in M$.

In Example 4.13, the four manifolds L_k, $k \in \overline{4}$, corresponding to the manifolds M_k, $k \in \overline{4}$, are respectively $M(J,\{\phi\})$, $M(J,\{\{1\}\})$, $M(J,\{\{1\},\{2\}\})$, and $R^J = M(J,\{\{1,2\}\})$. The first manifold corresponds to the hypothesis that the probability of a problem child depends neither on the birth order nor on the type of mother. The second manifold corresponds to the hypothesis that the probability of a problem child depends only on the birth order. The third hypothesis specifies that the logit is an additive function of the type of mother and the birth order. The last hypothesis is the trivial hypothesis which makes no assumptions about the dependence of the type of child on the birth order and the type of mother. These models based on L_k, where $k \in \overline{4}$, are not quite conventional logit models since the marginal totals $N_{ik} = n_{i+k}$ are random rather than fixed; however, since all manifolds M_k, $k \in \overline{4}$, contain N^*, inferences may be made conditional on the observed values of N_{ik}. Given this observation, the examples in chapter 4 can be regarded as illustrations of the use of simultaneous testing procedures with logit models.

Simultaneous confidence intervals involve no special difficulties. Arguments like those used in chapter 4 imply that the Scheffé-type approximate level-$(1 - \alpha)$ intervals for all linear combinations $(\underline{c},\underline{\lambda})$ for $\underline{c} \in C$ consist of $(\underline{c},\underline{\lambda})$ such that

$$|(\underline{c},\underline{\lambda}) - (\underline{c},\hat{\underline{\lambda}})| \leq \chi_d(\alpha)(\underline{c},\tilde{P}_L^{(F)}(\underline{N},\hat{\underline{\lambda}})[W^{(F)}(\underline{N},\hat{\underline{\lambda}})]^{-1}\underline{c})^{\frac{1}{2}} , \tag{8.182}$$

where $d = \dim P_L C$. In the case in which the normal tolerance distribution is used, $D^{(F)}(\underline{n},\hat{\underline{\lambda}})$ and $P_L^{(F)}(\underline{n},\hat{\underline{\lambda}})$ may be used in place of $W^{(F)}(\underline{N},\hat{\underline{\lambda}})$ and $\tilde{P}_L^{(F)}(\underline{N},\hat{\underline{\lambda}})$. The conventional Bonferroni intervals for linear combinations $(\underline{c}^{(j)},\underline{\lambda})$, where $j \in \overline{k}$, consist of $(\underline{c}^{(j)},\underline{\lambda})$ such that

$$|(\underline{c}^{(j)},\underline{\lambda}) - (\underline{c}^{(j)},\hat{\underline{\lambda}})| \leq \phi^{(\alpha/2k)} (\underline{c}^{(j)},\tilde{P}_L^{(F)}(\underline{N},\hat{\underline{\lambda}})[W^{(F)}(\underline{N},\hat{\underline{\lambda}})]^{-1}\underline{c}^{(j)})^{\frac{1}{2}} . \tag{8.183}$$

Both results are based on the observation that the estimated asymptotic variance of $(\underline{c},\hat{\underline{\lambda}})$ is $(\underline{c},\tilde{P}_L^{(F)}(\underline{N},\hat{\underline{\lambda}})[W^{(F)}(\underline{N},\hat{\underline{\lambda}})]^{-1}\underline{c})$. Given this observation, equations (4.279) through (4.284) remain valid if λ's replace μ's, L's replace M's, and $W^{(F)}(\underline{N},\hat{\underline{\lambda}})$'s replace $D(\hat{\underline{\mu}})$'s. In the case of logits, one can also derive (8.182) and (8.183) directly from (4.285) and (4.288) by noting that a linear combination $(\underline{c},\underline{\lambda})_J$ satisfies

$$\begin{aligned}(\underline{c},\underline{\lambda})_J &= \tfrac{1}{2}(\underline{c} \otimes \langle 1,-1\rangle,\underline{\lambda} \otimes \langle 1,-1\rangle)_I \\ &= (\tfrac{1}{2}\underline{c} \otimes \langle 1,-1\rangle,\underline{\mu}).\end{aligned} \tag{8.184}$$

Example 8.16. Example 4.19 involves the logit model for dosage response which has been employed several times in this chapter. If one uses results of Example 8.12 to construct simultaneous confidence intervals for the logit corresponding to log dosage t, one observes that the maximum-likelihood estimate of this logit is $\alpha + \beta t$ and the estimated asymptotic covariance is

$$[\sum_{j=1}^{r} 1/w_j^{(L)}(\underline{N},\hat{\underline{\lambda}})] + \{[t - t_\cdot^{(L)}(\underline{N},\hat{\underline{\lambda}})]^2/\sum_{j=1}^{r} [t_j - \bar{t}_\cdot^{(L)}(\underline{N},\hat{\underline{\lambda}})]^2 w_j^{(L)}(\underline{N},\hat{\underline{\lambda}})\}.$$

As in Example 4.19, the Scheffé-type level-$(1 - \gamma)$ intervals for each t on the real line are given by $[g(t),h(t)]$, where

$$(8.185) \qquad g(t) = \hat{\alpha} + \hat{\beta}t - \chi_2(\gamma)\left\{\frac{1}{\sum_{j=1}^{r} w_j^{(L)}(\underline{N},\hat{\underline{\lambda}})} + \frac{[t - \bar{t}_{\cdot}^{(L)}(\underline{N},\hat{\underline{\lambda}})]^2}{\sum_{j=1}^{r} [t_j - \bar{t}_{\cdot}^{(L)}(\underline{N},\hat{\underline{\lambda}})]^2 w_j^{(L)}(\underline{N},\hat{\underline{\lambda}})}\right\}^{\frac{1}{2}}$$

and

$$(8.186) \qquad h(t) = \hat{\alpha} + \hat{\beta}t + \chi_2(\gamma)\left\{\frac{1}{\sum_{j=1}^{r} w_j^{(L)}(\underline{N},\hat{\underline{\lambda}})} + \frac{[t - \bar{t}_{\cdot}^{(L)}(\underline{N},\hat{\underline{\lambda}})]^2}{\sum_{j=1}^{r} [t_j - \bar{t}_{\cdot}^{(L)}(\underline{N},\hat{\underline{\lambda}})]^2 w_j^{(L)}(\underline{N},\hat{\underline{\lambda}})}\right\}^{\frac{1}{2}} .$$

Equations (4.301) and (4.302) give $g(t)$ and $h(t)$ for the case $\gamma = 0.10$ when the data from table 1.3 are used. The simultaneous intervals for the probability of response 1 given log dosage t are then given by $[1/(1 + e^{-g(t)}), 1/(1 + e^{-h(t)})]$. Example 4.19 provides some numerical examples of such intervals.

Examination of residuals is as useful with quantal-response models as with ordinary log-linear models. Some special features arise, however, since $n_{j1} - m_{j1}^{(F)}(\underline{N},\hat{\underline{\lambda}}) = -[n_{j2} - m_{j2}^{(F)}(\underline{N},\hat{\underline{\lambda}})]$. Given this equation and (8.116), it is reasonable to use the standardized residual $\bar{\underline{r}} = [T^{(F)}(\underline{N},\hat{\underline{\lambda}})]^{-\frac{1}{2}}[\bar{\underline{n}} - \bar{\underline{m}}^{(F)}(\underline{N},\hat{\underline{\lambda}})]$. If $\underline{\lambda}^{(N)} \in L$ for all N and $\bar{\underline{r}}^{(N)} = [T^{(F)}(\underline{N}^{(N)},\hat{\underline{\lambda}}^{(N)})]^{-\frac{1}{2}}[\bar{\underline{n}}^{(N)} - \bar{\underline{m}}^{(F)}(\underline{N}^{(N)},\hat{\underline{\lambda}}^{(N)})]$, then (8.115), (8.125), and (8.126) imply that

$$(8.187) \qquad \bar{\underline{r}}^{(N)} \xrightarrow{\mathcal{D}} N(\underline{0}, I - [W^{(F)}(\underline{N}^*,\underline{\lambda}^*)]^{\frac{1}{2}}\tilde{P}_L^{(F)}(\underline{N}^*,\underline{\lambda}^*)[W^{(F)}(\underline{N}^*,\underline{\lambda}^*)]^{-\frac{1}{2}}).$$

Thus the standardized residual $\bar{r}_j$ has an approximate normal distribution with mean 0 and variance $\bar{c}_j \le 1$. This variance may be estimated by

$$(8.188) \qquad \hat{c}_j = (\underline{\delta}^{(j)}, \{I - [W^{(F)}(\underline{N},\hat{\underline{\lambda}})]^{\frac{1}{2}}\tilde{P}_L^{(F)}(\underline{N},\hat{\underline{\lambda}})[W^{(F)}(\underline{N},\hat{\underline{\lambda}})]^{-\frac{1}{2}}\}\underline{\delta}^{(j)}).$$

The adjusted residuals $\bar{s}_j = \bar{r}_j/\hat{c}_j^{\frac{1}{2}}$ then have approximate $N(0,1)$ distributions. Given these observations, the procedures discussed in Draper and Smith (1966) and chapter 4 are applicable to $\bar{\underline{r}}$ and $\bar{\underline{s}}$.

Example 8.17. Finney (1971) performs a standard probit analysis on a study of the toxicity of ethylene oxide on the grain beetle *Calandra granaria*. The results are summarized in table 8.8. In this table the expected number killed at log dosage t_j has been estimated to be $N_j\Phi(8.674t_j - 2.072)$. The Pearson chi-square for the null hypothesis $\underline{\lambda} \in \text{span}\{\underline{e},\underline{t}\}$ and the alternative $\underline{\lambda} \in R^{10}$ is about 33. Since the corresponding number of degrees of freedom is 8, the model clearly fails to fit the data.

TABLE 8.8

TOXICITY OF ETHYLENE OXIDE

Log Dosage	Number of Subjects	Number Killed	Expected Number Killed	Standardized Residual
0.394	30	23	27.3	-2.72
0.391	30	30	27.2	1.78
0.362	31	29	26.6	1.23
0.322	30	22	23.0	-0.44
0.314	26	23	19.3	1.66
0.260	27	7	15.5	-3.31
0.225	31	12	14.0	-0.72
0.199	30	17	11.0	2.27
0.167	31	10	8.3	0.69
0.033	24	0	0.9	-0.97

The standardized residuals provide a way in which the poor quality of the fit can be explored in detail. Even without computation of adjusted residuals, it is clear that standardized residuals at the log dosages 0.199, 0.260, and 0.394 are excessively large in magnitude. If one did wish to use adjusted residuals, it would suffice to note that it follows from the analogue of (8.134) for the case $F = \Phi$ that (8.188) reduces to

(8.189) $$\hat{c}_j = 1 - \frac{w_j^{(\Phi)}(\underline{N},\hat{\underline{\lambda}})}{\sum_{k=1}^{r} w_k^{(\Phi)}(\underline{N},\hat{\underline{\lambda}})} - \frac{[t_j - \bar{t}.^{(\Phi)}(\underline{N},\hat{\underline{\lambda}})]^2 w_j^{(\Phi)}(\underline{N},\hat{\underline{\lambda}})}{\sum_{k=1}^{r} [t_k - \bar{t}.^{(\Phi)}(\underline{N},\hat{\underline{\lambda}})]^2 w_k^{(\Phi)}(\underline{N},\hat{\underline{\lambda}})} .$$

However, this computation appears unnecessary in this example, for it is already evident that the residuals are excessively large.

The residuals exhibit no obvious pattern to suggest any systematic deviations from the model; however, there does exist reason to believe that there are unknown variations in experimental conditions. The strongest evidence in support of this idea comes from an examination of the data corresponding to log dosages 0.391 and 0.394. These log dosages are so similar that the probabilities of both for the two log dosages should be almost identical. In fact, the predicted difference is only 0.004. However, if one compares the number of subjects killed for the two log dosages, the difference is very large. If a

Pearson chi-square test is performed to test the hypothesis that the two probabilities are equal, one finds that the test statistic is

$$\frac{(n_{11}n_{22} - n_{21}n_{12})^2(N_1 + N_2)}{N_1N_2(n_{11} + n_{21})(n_{12} + n_{22})} \tag{8.190}$$

$$= \frac{[(23)(0) - (7)(30)]^2(30 + 30)}{(30)(30)(23 + 30)(7 + 0)}$$

$$= 7.92.$$

Since there is 1 degree of freedom, this statistic is significant at the 0.5% level. Thus there is strong reason to think that variables are present which the model has ignored. Some discussion of such variables is provided by Busvine (1938), who originally obtained the data in this example.

MULTINOMIAL-RESPONSE MODELS

Multinomial-response models have received far less attention in the literature than binomial-response models have received. Bock (1968) has made the most thorough investigation of these models. He employs a multivariate logit transformation with $I = J \times \overline{r}$ and

$$p(k|j) = \exp(\lambda_{jk}) / \sum_{k'=1}^{r} \exp(\lambda_{jk'}) \quad , \tag{8.191}$$

where $p(k|j)$ is the probability of response k given condition j. The number of occurrences of condition $j \in J$ is a constant $N_j > 0$, $\{n_{jk}: k \in \overline{r}\}$ has a multinomial distribution for each $j \in J$, and $\underline{\lambda} = \{\lambda_{jk}: j \in J, k \in \overline{r}\}$ is in some linear manifold $\overline{L}$. Thus the proposed models are obvious generalizations of conventional logit models. It is easily seen that these models are examples of log-linear models. When $r > 2$ they appear to have none of the special properties which simplify analysis in the binomial-response case. Thus no special treatment of these models seems to be needed. A few multinomial-response problems have also been considered in the biological assay literature. Finney (1964) provides some discussion of this literature. Papers by Aitchison and Silvey (1951), Ashford (1959), Cox (1966), and Gurland, Lee, and Dahm (1968) discuss various aspects of this issue.

UNDESIGNED EXPERIMENTS

Traditional asymptotic theory for quantal-response models is based on the assumption that the index set J is fixed and N_j becomes large for each $j \in J$. This assumption is useful when a designed experiment has been conducted. All examples considered so far in this chapter involve such experiments. The dosage-response analyses involve the use of many observations at the same dosage. The comparison of irradiation methods of Example 8.2 involves 6 experiments with large numbers of fruit flies in each experiment. Similarly, the baseball data of Example 8.3 has many comparisons between fixed teams. Situations exist, however, where the index set J cannot be regarded as fixed and N_j does not become large. Such problems have been explored by Cox (1958b, 1966) and Walker and Duncan (1967); however, rigorous discussion of the appropriate asymptotic theory does not seem to be readily available in the literature. This section provides a thorough discussion of the asymptotic theory related to these situations. It is shown that many of the estimation and testing procedures of this monograph can still be applied, although some modifications are required in computational practice.

Example 8.18. Walker and Duncan (1967) analyze records of 5209 participants in the Framingham study of factors associated with coronary heart disease (see Dawber, Meadors, and Moore 1951). The response variable in the study is coronary heart disease, which may be present or absent. The study considers the relationship of this variable to the 10 associated variables summarized in table 8.9.

In the proposed models, some subset of these ten variables is used to predict whether or not coronary heart disease is present. If this subset has k elements and there are N subjects such that all variables in the subset have been observed, then $J = \overline{N}$ and for each $j \in J$, $N_j = 1$ and

$$p(1|j) = 1/\{1 + \exp[-\alpha - (\underline{x}_j,\underline{\beta})]\}, \tag{8.192}$$

where $\alpha \in R$ and $\underline{\beta} \in R^k$ are parameters in the model and $\underline{x}_j$ is the observed vector $\{x_{jh}: h \in \overline{g}\}$ of predicting variables for subject j. For example, if all variables are included as predictors, then $g = 10$ and $N = 2687$. By (8.192), the proposed models are logit models. The vector space $\overline{L} \subset R^N$ is span $[\{\underline{e}\} \cup \{\underline{z}^{(h)}: h \in g\}]$, where $z_j^{(h)} = x_{jh}$ for $h \in \overline{k}$ and $j \in \overline{N}$. Any realistic asymptotic theory for this model must assume that N becomes large but $N_j = 1$ for all $j \in \overline{N}$.

TABLE 8.9

VARIABLES IN FRAMINGHAM STUDY

Name	Abbreviation	Units
Sex		Coded 1 if male 2 if female
Age		Years
Height	HT	Inches
Systolic blood pressure	SYS	mg Hg
Diastolic blood pressure	DIA	mg Hg
Serum cholesterol	SCH	mg/ml
Electrocardiograph abnormalities	ECG	Coded 0 if absent 1 if present
Framingham relative weight	FWT	Weight in pounds divided by median weight in pounds of sex-height group
Alcohol consumption	ALC	Coded according to sex and ounces/month consumed 0 if none 1 if < 4 and male or < 1 and female 2 if 5-14 and male or 1-9 and female 3 if 15-39 and male or 10-24 and female 4 if 40-69 and male or 25-39 and female 5 if 70-99 and male or 40-999 and female 6 if 100-999 and male
Cigarettes smoked	CIG	Coded 0 if none 1 if < 1 pack/day 2 if 1 pack/day 3 if > 1 pack/day

An underlying probability model which corresponds to (8.192) has been proposed by Cornfield, Kannel, and Truett (1967). Unlike previous probability models considered in this chapter, this one assumes, as in linear discriminant analysis with random allocation, that the sampled population consists of subjects described by pairs $\langle \underline{x}, y \rangle$, where $\underline{x}$ is the vector of predicting variables and y is 1 if the patient has coronary heart disease and y is 2 otherwise. Given y, $\underline{x}$ is assumed to have a multivariate normal distribution with mean $\underline{\mu}^{(y)}$ and positive definite covariance operator $\ddagger$. If $P\{y = k\} = p_k$ for $k \in \overline{2}$, then Bayes's theorem implies that the ratio $P\{y = 1|\underline{x}\}/P\{y = 2|\underline{x}\}$ is

(8.193) $$\frac{p_1}{p_2} \exp \{-\tfrac{1}{2}(\underline{x} - \underline{\mu}^{(1)}, \ddagger^{-1}(\underline{x} - \underline{\mu}^{(1)})) + \tfrac{1}{2}(\underline{x} - \underline{\mu}^{(2)}, \ddagger^{-1}(\underline{x} - \underline{\mu}^{(2)}))\}$$

$$= \frac{p_1}{p_2} \exp \{(\ddagger^{-1}(\underline{\mu}^{(1)} - \underline{\mu}^{(2)}), \underline{x}) - \tfrac{1}{2}(\underline{\mu}^{(1)}, \ddagger^{-1}\underline{\mu}^{(1)}) + \tfrac{1}{2}(\underline{\mu}^{(2)}, \ddagger^{-1}\underline{\mu}^{(2)})\}.$$

Since $L^{-1}(p) = \log [p/(1 - p)]$, it follows that (8.192) holds for

(8.194) $$\alpha = \frac{p_1}{p_2} - \tfrac{1}{2}(\underline{\mu}^{(1)} + \underline{\mu}^{(2)}, \ddagger^{-1}(\underline{\mu}^{(1)} - \underline{\mu}^{(2)}))$$

and

(8.195) $$\underline{\beta} = \ddagger^{-1}(\underline{\mu}^{(1)} - \underline{\mu}^{(2)}).$$

As Cornfield, Kannel, and Truett note, this model cannot be entirely realistic in this problem since the predicting variables, two of which are dichotomized, cannot be assumed to have a multivariate normal distribution; nonetheless, the model does suggest that the choice of a logit model is not completely arbitrary. In addition, the model does provide an interesting connection between logit analysis and linear discriminant analysis.

To develop an asymptotic theory appropriate to problems such as the one in Example 8.19, a sequence $\{\underline{n}^{(N)}\}$ of random vectors is considered such that for each N, $\underline{n}^{(N)}$ satisfies a multinomial response model with $I = J^{(N)} \times \overline{r}$, where $\{J^{(N)}\}$ is a nondecreasing sequence of sets. If $j \in J^{(N)}$, then $\{n_{jk}^{(N)}: k \in \overline{r}\}$ is a multinomial sample of size $N_j^{(N)}$ such that

(8.196) $$p(k|j) = \exp(\lambda_{jk}^{(N)}) / \sum_{k'=1}^{r} \exp(\lambda_{jk'}^{(N)})$$

and

(8.197) $$\lambda_{jk}^{(N)} = \sum_{h \in H} x_{jh}\beta_{hk}^{(N)},$$

where $\underline{\beta}^{(N)} = \{\beta_{hk}^{(N)}: h \in H, k \in \overline{r}\} \in B$, a linear manifold in $R^{H \times \overline{r}}$ such that if $\underline{\alpha} \in B$ and $h \in H$, then

(8.198) $$\sum_{k=1}^{r} \alpha_{hk} = 0.$$

It should be noted that $\underline{x}_j = \{x_{jh}: h \in H\}$ is a fixed vector of variables associated with condition j.

The condition (8.198) may not appear obvious. To understand this assumption, note that if $\underline{\beta}^{(N)} \in B$, then

(8.199) $$\sum_{k=1}^{r} \lambda_{jk}^{(N)} = 0$$

for $j \in J^{(N)}$. This result assures that $\underline{\beta}^{(N)}$ is estimable in the sense of chapter 7 if $X^{(N)}$ is nonsingular, where

(8.200) $$X^{(N)}\underline{y} = \{\sum_{h \in H} x_{jh}y_{hk}: j \in J^{(N)}\}$$

for all $\underline{y} \in R^{H \times \overline{r}}$. To verify this observation, note that the assumption that (8.196) holds for $j \in J^{(N)}$ and $k \in \overline{r}$ is equivalent to the assumption that the log-mean vector $\underline{\mu}^{(N)}$ of $\underline{n}^{(N)}$ is in the linear manifold $M^{(N)}$, where

(8.201) $$M^{(N)} = N^{(N)} \oplus \overline{L}^{(N)} ,$$

(8.202) $$N^{(N)} = \text{span } \{\underline{\nu}^{(N,j)}: j \in J^{(N)}\},$$

(8.203) $$\underline{\nu}^{(N,j)} = \{\delta_{jj'}: j' \in J^{(N)}, k \in \overline{r}\}$$

for $j \in J^{(N)}$, and $\overline{L}^{(N)}$ is the set of $\underline{\lambda}^{(N)} = \{\lambda_{jk}^{(N)}: j \in J^{(N)}, k \in \overline{r}\}$ such that (8.197) holds for some $\underline{\beta}^{(N)} \in B$. The vector $\underline{\lambda}^{(N)}$ such that (8.196) holds satisfies

(8.204) $$\underline{\lambda}^{(N)} = P_{L^{(N)}}\underline{\mu}^{(N)} ,$$

and for each $k \in \overline{r}$,

(8.205) $$\underline{\beta}^{(N)} = [X^{(N)}]^{-1}\underline{\lambda}^{(N)} ,$$

provided $X^{(N)}$ is nonsingular. Thus $\underline{\beta}^{(N)}$ is a linear function of $\underline{\mu}^{(N)}$; that is, $\underline{\beta}^{(N)}$ is estimable.

Example 8.19. To formulate Example 8.18 in terms of the general model, let $x_{j(g+1)} = 1$, $r = 2$, and

(8.206) $$\lambda_{jk}^{(N)} = \sum_{h=1}^{g+1} x_{jh}\beta_{hk}^{(N)}$$

for $j \in \overline{N}$ and $k \in \overline{r}$, where $\underline{\beta}^{(N)} \in B$, the set of $\underline{\alpha} \in R^{\overline{g+1}\times\overline{2}}$ for which

$$\alpha_{h1} + \alpha_{h2} = 0 \tag{8.207}$$

for $h \in \overline{g+1}$. The correspondence between (8.195) and (8.206) is obtained by letting $\beta^{(N)}_{(g+1)1} = \frac{1}{2}\alpha$ and $\beta^{(N)}_{h1} = \frac{1}{2}\beta_h$ for $h \in \overline{g}$. In this example, $J^{(N)} = \overline{N}$ and $N_j^{(N)} = 1$ for $j \in J^{(N)}$.

Example 8.20. In the conventional asymptotic models considered in the rest of the monograph, $J^{(N)}$ is equal to J for all N, $N_j^{(N)}/N$ converges to $N_j^* > 0$ for $j \in J$ as $N \to \infty$, and $\beta^{(N)}$ converges to some $\underline{\beta}^* \in B$. The formulation in terms of (8.197) imposes no restrictions on the log-linear model $M^{(N)} = M$, for if $x_{jh} = \delta_{jh}$, the Kronecker delta, and $H = J$, then $\lambda_{jk}^{(N)} = \beta_{jk}^{(N)}$ for $j \in J$ and $k \in \overline{r}$ and $B = \overline{L}$ for each N, where $\overline{L} = \overline{L}^{(N)}$. Hence $\underline{\lambda}^{(N)} \to \underline{\lambda}^* = \underline{\beta}^*$. Thus the general model does include the most conventional asymptotic model.

Given the vectors $\underline{x}_j$, where $j \in J^{(N)}$, one may define a random vector $\underline{V}^{(N)}$ such that the probability that $\underline{V}^{(N)} = \underline{x}$ is

$$s^{(N)}(\underline{x}) / \sum_{j \in J^{(N)}} s^{(N)}(\underline{x}_j) \ , \tag{8.208}$$

where

$$s^{(N)}(\underline{x}) = \sum_{j \in J^{(N)}} N_j \chi_{\{\underline{x}\}}(\underline{x}_j) \tag{8.209}$$

and $\chi_{\{\underline{x}\}}$ is the characteristic function of $\{\underline{x}\}$. Thus $P\{\underline{V}^{(N)} = \underline{x}\}$ is the proportion of observations such that the associated vector $\underline{x}_j$ is $\underline{x}$. The fundamental assumptions of this section are that there exists a random variable $\underline{V}^* \in R^H$ such that

$$\underline{V}^{(N)} \xrightarrow{\mathcal{D}} \underline{V}^* \ , \tag{8.210}$$

$E(\underline{V}^* \otimes \underline{V}^*)$ is positive definite,

$$E(||\underline{V}^{(N)}||^2) = \Big(\sum_{j \in J^{(N)}} N_j ||\underline{x}_j||^2\Big) / \Big(\sum_{j \in J^{(N)}} N_j\Big) \longrightarrow E(||\underline{V}^*||^2) < \infty, \tag{8.211}$$

that there exists a $\underline{\beta}^* \in B$ such that

$$\underline{\beta}^{(N)} \longrightarrow \underline{\beta}^* \ , \tag{8.212}$$

and that the total sample size

(8.213) $$S^{(N)} = \sum_{j \in J^{(N)}} S^{(N)}(\underline{x}_j) \to \infty$$

as $N \to \infty$. The condition that $E(\underline{V}^* \otimes \underline{V}^*)$ be positive definite is equivalent to the condition that for all $\underline{c} \in R^H$, $\underline{c} \neq \underline{0}$,

(8.214) $$\begin{aligned}(\underline{c},[E(\underline{V}^* \otimes \underline{V}^*)]\underline{c}) \\ = E[(\underline{c},\underline{V}^*)]^2 \\ > 0.\end{aligned}$$

Since

(8.215) $$\begin{aligned}E[(\underline{c},\underline{V}^*)]^2 &\geq E[(\underline{c},\underline{V}^* - E(\underline{V}^*))]^2 \\ &= (\underline{c},\mathrm{Cov}(\underline{V}^*)\underline{c}),\end{aligned}$$

$E(\underline{V}^* \otimes \underline{V}^*)$ is positive definite if the covariance operator of $\underline{V}^*$ is positive definite.

Example 8.21. The vectors $\underline{x}_j$ in Example 8.19 may be a random sample from the probability distribution defined by $\underline{V}^*$. The conditions of this section are satisfied if $E(\underline{V}^* \otimes \underline{V}^*)$ exists and is positive definite. These results follow since $\underline{V}^{(N)}$ is the empirical distribution of $\{\underline{x}_j : j \in \overline{N}\}$. By the multivariate generalization of the Glivenko-Cantelli theorem (see Parthasarathy 1967), (8.210) holds with probability 1. If $E(\underline{V}^* \otimes \underline{V}^*)$ exists, then $E(||\underline{V}^* \otimes \underline{V}^*||) = E(||\underline{V}^*||^2)$ exists and (8.211) holds with probability 1 by the strong law of large numbers. The condition (8.218) holds since one may set $\underline{\beta}^{(N)} = \underline{\beta}^*$ for all N. The assumption that $\underline{x}_j$ is fixed for $j \in N$ may appear to be violated, but one may proceed as in ordinary regression and make inferences conditional on the observed independent variables.

Example 8.22. In Example 8.20, (8.212) has been assumed to hold. If $\underline{V}^*$ is a random vector such that

(8.216) $$P\{\underline{V}^* = \underline{x}_j\} = N_j^* / \sum_{j \in J} N_{j'}^* = p_j^* ,$$

then (8.210) and (8.211) hold and $E(\underline{V}^* \otimes V^*)$ is positive definite. The first result follows since

(8.217) $$P\{\underline{V}^{(N)} = \underline{x}_j\} \longrightarrow P\{\underline{V}^* = \underline{x}_j\}.$$

The second result follows since $||\underline{x}_j|| = 1$ for $j \in J$, and the third result follows since if $\underline{c} \in R^J$, then

(8.218) $$(\underline{c},E(\underline{V}^* \otimes \underline{V}^*)\underline{c}) = \sum_{j\in J} c_j^2 p_j^* .$$

Given these assumptions, the following theorem can be proven:

THEOREM 8.5. *Suppose that the assumptions of this section are satisfied. Then the sequence* $\{\hat{\underline{\beta}}^{(N)}\}$ *of maximum-likelihood estimates of* $\{\underline{\beta}^{(N)}\}$ *satisfies the equations*

(8.219) $$(S^{(N)})^{\frac{1}{2}}(\hat{\underline{\beta}}^{(N)} - \underline{\beta}^{(N)}) \xrightarrow{\mathcal{D}} N(\underline{0},B^{-1}(\underline{V}^*,\underline{\beta}^*)P_B)$$

and

(8.220) $$\hat{\underline{\beta}}^{(N)} \xrightarrow{P} \underline{\beta}^* ,$$

where $B(\underline{V}^*,\underline{\beta}^*)$ *is the linear transformation on* $\mathcal{B}$ *defined by*

(8.221) $$B(\underline{V}^*,\underline{\beta}^*) = P_B E[(\underline{V}^* \otimes \underline{V}^*) \otimes W^+(\underline{V}^*,\underline{\beta}^*)] ,$$

(8.222) $$W^+(\underline{V}^*,\underline{\beta}^*) = M(\underline{V}^*,\underline{\beta}^*) - \underline{p}(\underline{V}^*,\underline{\beta}^*) \otimes \underline{p}(\underline{V}^*,\underline{\beta}^*),$$

(8.223) $$M(\underline{V}^*,\underline{\beta}^*)\underline{x} = \{p_k(\underline{V}^*,\underline{\beta}^*)x_k : k \in \overline{r}\}$$

for $\underline{x} \in R^r$,

(8.224) $$\underline{p}(\underline{V}^*,\underline{\beta}^*) = \{\exp[\lambda_k^*(\underline{V}^*,\underline{\beta}^*)]/\sum_{k'=1}^{r} \exp[\lambda_{k'}^*(\underline{V}^*,\underline{\beta}^*)]: k \in \overline{r}\},$$

and

(8.225) $$\underline{\lambda}^*(\underline{V}^*,\underline{\beta}^*) = \{\sum_{h\in H} V_h^*\beta_{hk}^* : k \in \overline{r}\}.$$

Remark. The proof of this theorem is rather intricate. Many readers may find it convenient to omit this proof, at least at a first reading of this chapter.

Proof. The first step in the proof is to interpret the likelihood equations of Theorem 2.3 in terms of $\hat{\underline{\beta}}^{(N)}$. This interpretation is feasible if N is sufficiently large since $\underline{V}^{(N)} \xrightarrow{\mathcal{D}} \underline{V}$ and no linear combination $(\underline{c},\underline{V}^*)$ is 0 with probability 1. Thus $X^{(N)}$ is nonsingular for sufficiently large N. By (1.50) and (2.31), if $\hat{\underline{\beta}}^{(N)}$ exists, then it is the unique $\hat{\underline{\beta}}^{(N)}$ such that

(8.226) $$\hat{\underline{\mu}}^{(N)} = \hat{\underline{\lambda}}^{(N)} + \{\log [N_j^{(N)}/\sum_{k'=1}^{r} \exp(\hat{\lambda}_{jk'}^{(N)})]: j \in J^{(N)},k \in \overline{r}\}$$

$$= \{\log N_j^{(N)} + \log p_k(\underline{x}_j,\hat{\underline{\beta}}^{(N)}): j \in J^{(N)},k \in \overline{r}\}$$

and

(8.227) $$P_{\mathcal{L}^{(N)}}\underline{n}^{(N)} = P_{\mathcal{L}^{(N)}}\underline{m}(\hat{\underline{\mu}}^{(N)}) .$$

Since $\bar{L}^{(N)} = X^{(N)}B$, (8.227) is equivalent to the condition that for each $\underline{\beta} \in B$,

(8.228)
$$(X^{(N)}\underline{\beta},\underline{n}^{(N)})_{J\times\bar{r}} = (\underline{\beta},[X^{(N)}]^T\underline{n}^{(N)})_{H\times\bar{r}}$$
$$= (\underline{\beta},(X^{(N)})^T\underline{m}(\hat{\underline{\mu}}^{(N)}))_{H\times\bar{r}} .$$

Thus if $\hat{\underline{\beta}}^{(N)}$ exists, it is the unique element of such that $\hat{\underline{\lambda}}^{(N)} = X^{(N)}\hat{\underline{\beta}}^{(N)}$, (8.226) holds, and

(8.229)
$$P_B(X^{(N)})^T\underline{n}^{(N)} - P_B(X^{(N)})^T\underline{m}(\hat{\underline{\mu}}^{(N)}) = 0 .$$

The second step in the proof is a demonstration that

(8.230)
$$[P_B(X^{(N)})^T\underline{n}^{(N)} - P_B(X^{(N)})^T\underline{m}(\hat{\underline{\mu}}^{(N)})]/(\sum_{j\in J^{(N)}} N_j^{(N)})^{\frac{1}{2}}$$
$$\xrightarrow{\mathcal{D}} N(\underline{0},P_B E[(\underline{V} \otimes \underline{V}^*) \otimes W^+(\underline{V}^*,\underline{\beta}^*)]P_B)$$
$$= N(\underline{0},B(\underline{V}^*,\underline{\beta}^*)P_B).$$

By Rao (1965), it suffices to show that for all $\underline{\beta} \in R^{H\times\bar{r}}$,

(8.231)
$$[(\underline{\beta},P_B(X^{(N)})^T(\underline{n}^{(N)} - \underline{m}^{(N)}))_{H\times\bar{r}}]/(S^{(N)})^{\frac{1}{2}}$$
$$\xrightarrow{\mathcal{D}} N(0,(\underline{\beta},P_B\{E[(\underline{V}^* \otimes \underline{V}^*) \otimes W^+(\underline{V}^*,\underline{\beta}^*)]\}P_B\underline{\beta})_{H\times\bar{r}} ,$$

where $\underline{m}^{(N)}$ is $\underline{m}(\underline{\mu}^{(N)})$ and $S^{(N)} = \sum_{j\in J^{(N)}} N_j^{(N)}$.

Since

(8.232)
$$(\underline{\beta},P_B(X^{(N)})^T(\underline{n}^{(N)} - \underline{m}^{(N)}))_{H\times\bar{r}}$$
$$= (P_B\underline{\beta},(X^{(N)})^T(\underline{n}^{(N)} - \underline{m}^{(N)}))_{H\times\bar{r}} ,$$

it is sufficient to show that if $\underline{\beta} \in B$,

(8.233)
$$[(\underline{\beta},(X^{(N)})^T(\underline{n}^{(N)} - \underline{m}^{(N)}))_{H\times\bar{r}}]/(S^{(N)})^{\frac{1}{2}}$$
$$\xrightarrow{\mathcal{D}} N(0,(\underline{\beta},\{E_B(\underline{V}^* \otimes \underline{V}^*) \otimes W^+(\underline{V}^*,\underline{\beta}^*)]\}\underline{\beta})_{H\times\bar{r}})$$

Proof of (8.233) is based on the Lindeberg conditions for the central limit theorem (see Loeve 1963). Each vector $\{n_{jk}^{(N)} - m_{jk}^{(N)}: k \in \bar{r}\}$ is distributed as the sum of $N_j^{(N)}$ independent identically distributed vectors $\{z_{jkt}^{(N)} - p_k(\underline{x}_j,\underline{\beta}^{(N)}): k \in \bar{r}\}$, $t \in N_j^{(N)}$, such that $\underline{z}_{jt}^{(N)} = \{\underline{z}_{jkt}^{(N)}: k \in \bar{r}\}$ has a multinomial distribution with sample size 1 and probability vector $\underline{p}(\underline{x}_j,\underline{\beta}^{(N)})$. Thus

(8.234)
$$(\underline{\beta},(X^{(N)})^T(\underline{n}^{(N)} - \underline{m}^{(N)}))_{H\times\bar{r}}/(S^{(N)})^{\frac{1}{2}}$$
$$= (X^{(N)}\underline{\beta},\underline{n}^{(N)} - \underline{m}^{(N)})_{J^{(N)}\times\bar{r}}/(S^{(N)})^{\frac{1}{2}}$$
$$= (S^{(N)})^{-\frac{1}{2}} \sum_{j\in J^{(N)}} \sum_{k=1}^{r} (\sum_{h\in H} x_{jh}\beta^*_{hk}) \sum_{t=1}^{N_j^{(N)}} [z_{jkt}^{(N)} - p_k(\underline{x}_j,\underline{\beta}^{(N)})]$$
$$= (S^{(N)})^{-\frac{1}{2}} \sum_{j\in J^{(N)}} \sum_{t=1}^{N_j^{(N)}} Y_{jt}^{(N)} ,$$

where

(8.235)
$$Y_{jt}^{(N)} = \sum_{k=1}^{r} \sum_{h\in H} x_{jh}\beta_{hk}[z_{jht}^{(N)} - p_k(\underline{x}_j,\underline{\beta}^{(N)})]$$
$$= (\underline{\lambda}^*(\underline{x}_j,\underline{\beta}),\underline{z}_{jt}^{(N)} - \underline{p}(\underline{x}_j,\underline{\beta}^{(N)}))_r .$$

The expected value of $Y_{jt}^{(N)} = 0$, and the variance is

(8.236)
$$(\underline{\lambda}^*(\underline{x}_j,\underline{\beta}),W^+(\underline{x}_j,\underline{\beta}^{(N)})\underline{\lambda}^*(\underline{x}_j,\underline{\beta}))_r$$
$$= (\underline{\beta},[(\underline{x}_j \otimes \underline{x}_j) \otimes W^+(\underline{x}_j,\underline{\beta}^{(N)})]\underline{\beta})_{H\times\bar{r}}$$

Equality holds in (8.236) since both sides are quadratic forms in $\underline{\beta}$ such that for $\underline{\beta} = \underline{\gamma} \times \underline{\delta}$, where $\underline{\lambda} \in R^H$ and $\underline{\delta} \in R^r$,

(8.237)
$$(\underline{\lambda}^*(\underline{x}_j,\underline{\beta}),W^+(\underline{x}_j,\underline{\beta}^{(N)})\underline{\lambda}^*(\underline{x}_j,\underline{\beta}))_r$$
$$= ((\underline{x}_j,\underline{\gamma})_H\underline{\delta},W^+(\underline{x}_j,\underline{\beta}^{(N)})(\underline{x}_j,\underline{\gamma})_H\underline{\delta})_r$$
$$= (\underline{x}_j,\underline{\gamma})_H^2(\underline{\delta},W^+(\underline{x}_j,\underline{\beta}^{(N)})\underline{\delta})_r$$
$$= (\underline{\gamma}\otimes\underline{\delta},[(\underline{x}_j \otimes \underline{x}_j) \otimes W^+(\underline{x}_j,\underline{\lambda}^{(N)})]\underline{\gamma} \otimes \underline{\delta})_{H\times\bar{r}}$$
$$= (\underline{\beta},[(\underline{x}_j \otimes \underline{x}_j) \otimes W^+(\underline{x}_j,\underline{\beta}^{(N)})]\underline{\beta})_{H\times\bar{r}} .$$

It now follows that the expected value of $\sum_{j\in J^{(N)}} \sum_{t=1}^{N_j^{(N)}} Y_{jt}^{(N)}$ is 0 and the variance is

(8.238)
$$\sigma_N^2 = \sum_{j\in J^{(N)}} \sum_{t=1}^{N_j^{(N)}} (\underline{\beta},[(\underline{x}_j \otimes \underline{x}_j) \otimes W^+(\underline{x}_j,\underline{\beta}^{(N)})]\underline{\beta})_{H\times\bar{r}}$$
$$= S^{(N)}E(\underline{\beta},[(\underline{v}^{(N)} \otimes \underline{v}^{(N)}) \otimes W^+(\underline{v}^{(N)},\underline{\beta}^{(N)})]\underline{\beta})_{H\times\bar{r}}$$
$$= S^{(N)}(\underline{\beta}, E[(\underline{v}^{(N)} \otimes \underline{v}^{(N)}) \otimes W^+(\underline{v}^{(N)},\underline{\beta}^{(N)})] \underline{\beta})_{H\times\bar{r}} .$$

The limiting behavior of this variance is now of interest. The basic result needed is that

(8.239) $$E(\underline{\beta},[(\underline{V}^{(N)} \otimes \underline{V}^{(N)}) \otimes W^{+}(\underline{V}^{(N)},\underline{\beta}^{(N)})]\underline{\beta})_{H\times\bar{r}}$$

$$\longrightarrow E(\underline{\beta},[(\underline{V}^{*} \otimes \underline{V}^{*}) \otimes W^{+}(\underline{V}^{*},\underline{\beta}^{*})]\underline{\beta})_{H\times\bar{r}}$$

This result follows from (8.211), (8.212), and the dominated convergence theorem (see Rao 1965) if it can be shown that for all N,

(8.240) $$(\underline{\beta},[(\underline{V}^{(N)} \otimes \underline{V}^{(N)}) \otimes W^{+}(\underline{V}^{(N)},\underline{\beta}^{(N)})]\underline{\beta})_{H\times\bar{r}}$$

$$= (\underline{\lambda}^{*}(\underline{V}^{(N)},\underline{\beta}),W^{+}(\underline{V}^{(N)},\underline{\beta}^{(N)})\underline{\lambda}^{*}(\underline{V}^{(N)},\underline{\beta}))_{H\times\bar{r}}$$

$$\leq ||\underline{V}^{(N)}||_{H}^{2}||\underline{\beta}||_{H\times\bar{r}}^{2} .$$

This inequality follows since by (8.224) and Schwartz's inequality,

(8.241) $$[\lambda_{k}^{*}(\underline{V}^{(N)},\underline{\beta})]^{2} \leq ||\underline{V}^{(N)}||_{H}^{2} \sum_{h \in H} \underline{\beta}_{hk}^{2}$$

and thus

(8.242) $$||\underline{\lambda}^{*}(\underline{V}^{(N)},\underline{\beta})||_{r}^{2} = \sum_{k=1}^{r} [\lambda_{k}(\underline{V}^{(N)},\underline{\beta})]^{2}$$

$$\leq ||\underline{V}^{(N)}||_{H}^{2} \sum_{h \in H} \sum_{k=1}^{r} ||_{hk}^{2}$$

$$= ||\underline{V}^{(N)}||_{H}^{2}||\underline{\beta}||_{H\times\bar{r}}^{2} ,$$

and since for any $\underline{x} \in R^{r}$,

(8.243) $$(\underline{x},W^{+}(\underline{V}^{(N)},\underline{\beta}^{(N)})\underline{x})_{r}$$

$$\leq (\underline{x},M(\underline{V}^{(N)},\underline{\beta}^{(N)})\underline{x})_{r}$$

$$= \sum_{k=1}^{r} x_{k}^{2}p_{k}(\underline{V}^{(N)},\underline{\beta}^{(N)})$$

$$\leq \sum_{k=1}^{r} x_{k}^{2}$$

$$= ||\underline{x}||_{r}^{2} .$$

Given this result, it follows that

$$\sigma_N^2/S^{(N)} \longrightarrow E(\underline{\beta},[(\underline{V}^* \circledast \underline{V}^*) \circledast W^+(\underline{V}^*,\underline{\beta}^*)]\underline{\beta})_{H\times\bar{r}} \tag{8.244}$$

$$= E(\underline{\lambda}^*(\underline{V}^*,\underline{\beta}),W^+(\underline{V}^*,\underline{\beta}^*)\underline{\lambda}^*(\underline{V}^*,\underline{\beta}))_r \cdot$$

$$> 0 .$$

The equation in (8.244) follows from (8.236). To prove the inequality in (8.244), it suffices to note that if

$$E(\underline{\lambda}^*(\underline{V}^*,\underline{\beta}),W^+(\underline{V}^*,\underline{\beta}^*)\underline{\lambda}^*(\underline{V},\underline{\beta}))_r = 0, \tag{8.245}$$

then

$$P\{W^+(\underline{V}^*,\underline{\beta}^*)\underline{\lambda}^*(\underline{V}^*,\underline{\beta}) = \underline{0}\} = 1. \tag{8.246}$$

Since the null space of $W^+(\underline{V}^*,\underline{\beta}^*)$ is span $\{\underline{e}^{(r)}\}$ and $\underline{\lambda}^*(\underline{V}^*,\underline{\beta})$ is orthogonal to $\underline{e}^{(r)}$,

$$P\{\underline{\lambda}^*(\underline{V}^*,\underline{\beta}) = \underline{0}\} = 1. \tag{8.247}$$

If $\underline{\gamma} = \{\beta_{h1}: h \in H\}$, then $P\{(\underline{\gamma},\underline{V}^*)_H = \underline{0}\}$ is 1 and thus $E(\underline{V}^* \circledast \underline{V}^*)$ must be singular, a contradiction. Thus the inequality in (8.243) must be valid.

To prove (8.233), it is now only necessary to apply the Lindeberg condition to (8.234). Thus it suffices to show that for any $\varepsilon > 0$

$$\frac{1}{\sigma_N^2} \sum_{j\in J^{(N)}} \sum_{t=1}^{N_j^{(N)}} E\{(Y_{jt}^{(N)})^2 \chi_{[\varepsilon\sigma_N^2,\infty)}((Y_{jt}^{(N)})^2)\} \longrightarrow 0. \tag{8.248}$$

Since by (8.235) and (8.242)

$$[Y_{jt}^{(N)}]^2 \le \|\underline{z}_{jt}^{(N)} - \underline{p}(\underline{x}_j,\underline{\beta}^{(N)}\|_r^2\|\underline{\lambda}^*(\underline{x}_j,\underline{\beta}^{(N)})\|_r^2 \tag{8.249}$$

$$\le \|\underline{\beta}^{(N)}\|_{H\times\bar{r}}^2\|\underline{x}_j\|_H^2(\|\underline{z}_{jt}^{(N)}\|_{\bar{r}} + \|\underline{p}(\underline{x}_j,\underline{\beta}^{(N)})\|_r)^2$$

$$\le 4\|\underline{\beta}^{(N)}\|_{H\times\bar{r}}^2\|\underline{x}_j\|_H^2 \quad ,$$

it follows that

$$\frac{1}{\sigma_N^2} \sum_{j\in J^{(N)}} \sum_{t=1}^{N_j^{(N)}} E[(Y_{jt}^{(N)})^2 \chi_{[\varepsilon\sigma_N^2,\infty)}((Y_{jt}^{(N)})^2)] \tag{8.250}$$

$$\le \frac{4\|\underline{\beta}^{(N)}\|_{H\times\bar{r}}^2}{\sigma_N^2} \sum_{j\in J^{(N)}} \sum_{t=1}^{N_j^{(N)}} \|\underline{x}_j\|_H^2 \chi_{[\varepsilon\sigma_N^2,\infty)}(4\|\underline{\beta}^{(N)}\|_{H\times\bar{r}}^2\|\underline{x}_j\|_H^2)$$

$$= \frac{4||\underline{\beta}^{(N)}||^2_{H\times\bar{r}}}{\sigma_N^2/S^{(N)}} E\{||\underline{V}^{(N)}||^2_H \chi_{[\epsilon\sigma_N^2,\infty)}(4||\underline{\beta}^{(N)}||^2_{H\times\bar{r}}||\underline{V}^{(N)}||^2_H)\}.$$

As $N \to \infty$,

$$\frac{4||\underline{\beta}^{(N)}||^2_{H\times\bar{r}}}{\sigma_N^2/S^{(N)}} \longrightarrow \frac{4||\underline{\beta}^*||^2_{H\times\bar{r}}}{E(\underline{\lambda}^*(\underline{V}^*,\underline{\beta}),W^+(\underline{V}^*,\underline{\beta}^*)\underline{\lambda}^*(\underline{V}^*\underline{\beta}))_r} \quad (8.251)$$

It is now sufficient to show that

$$E\{||\underline{V}^{(N)}||^2_H \chi^2_{[\epsilon\sigma_N^2,\infty)}(4||\underline{\beta}^{(N)}||^2_{H\times\bar{r}}||\underline{V}^{(N)}||^2_H)\} \longrightarrow 0 \quad (8.252)$$

as $N \to \infty$. To verify this result, note that (8.210) and (8.211) imply that the random variables $||\underline{V}^{(N)}||^2_H$ are uniformly integrable; that is, for any $\delta > 0$, there exists an $a > 0$ such that

$$E\{||\underline{V}^{(N)}||^2_H \chi^2_{[a,\infty)}(||\underline{V}^{(N)}||^2_H)\} > \delta \quad (8.253)$$

for all N (see Loève 1963). By (8.212) and (8.244),

$$\epsilon\sigma_N^2/4||\underline{\beta}^{(N)}||^2_{H\times\bar{r}} > a \quad (8.254)$$

for N sufficiently large. For such N

$$E\{||\underline{V}^{(N)}||^2_H \chi^2_{[\epsilon\sigma_N^2,\infty)}(4||\underline{\beta}^{(N)}||^2_{H\times\bar{r}}||\underline{V}^{(N)}||^2_H)\} < \delta . \quad (8.255)$$

Since δ is arbitrary, (8.252) follows and the proof of (8.233) is now complete. As mentioned earlier, (8.233) implies (8.230).

The third step in the proof is a reduction of (8.229) to the equation

$$P_B[\frac{1}{S^{(N)}}(X^{(N)})^T\underline{n}^{(N)}] - P_B E[\underline{V}^{(N)} \otimes \underline{p}(\underline{V}^{(N)},\hat{\underline{\beta}}^{(N)})] = \underline{0}. \quad (8.256)$$

This operation may be accomplished through the observation that

$$(X^{(N)})^T\underline{m}(\hat{\underline{\mu}}^{(N)}) = \sum_{j\in J^{(N)}} N_j^{(N)}[\underline{x}_j \otimes \underline{p}(\underline{x}_j,\underline{\beta}^{(N)})]. \quad (8.257)$$

This observation is verified by noting that for any $\underline{\gamma} \in R^H$ and $\underline{\delta} \in R$, (8.200) and (8.226) imply that

(8.258)
$$\begin{aligned}&(\underline{\gamma} \otimes \underline{\delta}, (X^{(N)})^T \underline{m}(\underline{\hat{\mu}}^{(N)}))_{H\times\bar{r}}\\ &= (X^{(N)}(\underline{\gamma} \otimes \underline{\delta}), \underline{m}(\underline{\hat{\mu}}^{(N)}))_{J^{(N)}\times\bar{r}}\\ &= \sum_{j\in J^{(N)}} (\underline{\gamma}, \underline{x}_j)_H N_j^{(N)} (\underline{\delta}, \underline{p}(\underline{x}_j, \underline{\beta}^{(N)}))_r\\ &= \sum_{j\in J^{(N)}} (\underline{\gamma} \otimes \underline{\delta}, N_j^{(N)} [\underline{x}_j \otimes \underline{p}(\underline{x}_j, \underline{\beta}^{(N)})])_{H\times\bar{r}}\\ &= (\underline{\gamma} \otimes \underline{\delta}, \sum_{j\in J^{(N)}} N_j^{(N)} [\underline{x}_j \otimes \underline{p}(\underline{x}_j, \underline{\beta}^{(N)})])_{H\times\bar{r}} .\end{aligned}$$

The reduction accomplished by (8.256) is important for two reasons. The first is that

(8.259)
$$\begin{aligned}&P_B[\frac{1}{S^{(N)}}(X^{(N)})^T \underline{n}^{(N)}]\\ &= P_B[\frac{1}{S^{(N)}}(X^{(N)})^T (\underline{n}^{(N)} - \underline{m}^{(N)})] + P_B[\frac{1}{S^{(N)}}(X^{(N)})^T \underline{m}^{(N)}]\\ &= P_B[\frac{1}{S^{(N)}}(X^{(N)})^T (\underline{n}^{(N)} - \underline{m}^{(N)})] + P_B E[\underline{V}^{(N)} \otimes \underline{p}(\underline{V}^{(N)}, \underline{\beta}^{(N)})]\\ &\xrightarrow{P} P_B E[\underline{V}^* \otimes \underline{p}(\underline{V}^*, \underline{\beta}^*)].\end{aligned}$$

The last equation follows from (8.233) and the dominated convergence theorem. This theorem applies since

(8.260)
$$\begin{aligned}||\underline{V}^{(N)} \otimes \underline{p}(\underline{V}^{(N)}, \underline{\beta}^{(N)})||_{H\times\bar{r}} &= ||\underline{V}^{(N)}||_H ||\underline{p}(\underline{V}^{(N)}, \underline{\beta}^{(N)})||_r\\ &\le ||\underline{V}^{(N)}||_H\end{aligned}$$

and since as a consequence of (8.211) and the well-known result that convergence of higher moments implies convergence of lower moments (see Rao 1965),

(8.261)
$$E(||\underline{V}^{(N)}||_H) \longrightarrow E(||\underline{V}^*||_H) .$$

The second feature of this reduction is that $E[\underline{V}^{(N)} \otimes \underline{p}(\underline{V}^{(N)}, \underline{\beta}^{(N)})]$ is a function of the pair $<\underline{\hat{\beta}}^{(N)}, \underline{V}^{(N)}>$, where $\underline{\hat{\beta}}^{(N)} \in R^{H\times\bar{r}}$ and $\underline{V}^{(N)} \in L_2(R^H)$, the Hilbert space of random vectors $\underline{V}$ with range in R^H such that $E(||\underline{V}||_H^2) < \infty$. The norm for this space is

(8.262)
$$||\underline{V}||^2_{L_2(H)} = E(||\underline{V}||_H^2) ,$$

and random vectors $\underline{V}$ and $\underline{V}'$ are identified if $P\{\underline{V} = \underline{V}'\} = 1$ (see Dinculéanu 1967 for details concerning this space). These features permit application of the implicit function theorem (see Loomis and Sternberg 1968).

The fourth step in the proof is an application of the implicit function theorem to construct a function $\underline{\beta}(\underline{V},\underline{x})$ such that for some neighborhoods $A \in L_2(R^H)$ of $\underline{V}^*$ and $B \in \mathcal{B}$ of $\gamma^* = P_{\mathcal{B}}E[\underline{V}^* \otimes \underline{p}(\underline{V}^*,\underline{\beta}^*)]$, the unique $\beta \in \mathcal{B}$ such that

$$(8.263) \qquad F(\underline{x},\underline{V},\underline{\beta}) = \underline{x} - P_{\mathcal{B}}E[\underline{V} \otimes \underline{p}(\underline{V},\underline{\beta})] = \underline{0}$$

is a differentiable function $\underline{\beta}(\underline{V},\underline{x})$ for $\underline{V} \in A$ and $\underline{x} \in B$ such that $\underline{\beta}(\underline{V}^*,\underline{\gamma}^*) = \underline{\beta}^*$. To construct this function, note first that $F(\underline{\gamma}^*,\underline{V}^*,\underline{\beta}^*) = \underline{0}$. Next observe that the first differential of $F(\underline{x},\underline{V},\underline{\beta})$ satisfies

$$(8.264) \qquad dF_{(\underline{x},\underline{V},\underline{\beta})}(\overline{\underline{x}},\overline{\underline{V}},\overline{\underline{\beta}})$$

$$= \overline{x} - P_{\mathcal{B}}E[\overline{\underline{V}} \otimes \underline{p}(\underline{V},\underline{\beta})] - P_{\mathcal{B}}E[\underline{V} \otimes W^+(\underline{V},\underline{\beta})\underline{\lambda}(\overline{\underline{V}},\underline{\beta})] - P_{\mathcal{B}}E[\underline{V} \otimes W^+(\underline{V},\underline{\beta})\underline{\lambda}(\underline{V},\overline{\underline{\beta}})],$$

$$= \overline{\underline{x}} - P_{\mathcal{B}}E[\overline{\underline{V}} \otimes \underline{p}(\underline{V},\underline{\beta})] - P_{\mathcal{B}}\{E[(\underline{V} \otimes \overline{\underline{V}}) \otimes W^+(\underline{V},\underline{\beta})]\}(\underline{\beta}) - P_{\mathcal{B}}\{E[(\underline{V} \otimes \overline{\underline{V}}) \otimes W^+(\underline{V},\underline{\beta})]\}(\overline{\underline{\beta}}),$$

$$= \overline{\underline{x}} - P_{\mathcal{B}}E[\overline{\underline{V}} \otimes \underline{p}(\underline{V},\underline{\beta})] - P_{\mathcal{B}}\{E[(\underline{V} \otimes \overline{\underline{V}}) \otimes W^+(\underline{V},\underline{\beta})]\}(\underline{\beta}) - B(\underline{V},\underline{B})\overline{\underline{\beta}}$$

and $B(\underline{V},\underline{\beta})$ is a nonsingular transformation with domain $\mathcal{B}$. To derive (8.264), one applies elementary procedures of differential calculus to (8.221), (8.222), (8.223), (8.224), and (8.225), together with arguments similar to those used to derive (8.236). To verify that $B(\underline{V}^*,\underline{\beta}^*)$ is not singular, note that for any $\overline{\underline{\beta}} \in \mathcal{B}$, $\overline{\underline{\beta}} \neq 0$, (8.244) implies that

$$(8.265) \qquad (\overline{\underline{\beta}},P_{\mathcal{B}}E[(\underline{V}^* \otimes \underline{V}^*) \otimes W^+(\underline{V}^*,\underline{\beta}^*)]\overline{\underline{\beta}})$$

$$= E(\overline{\underline{\beta}},[(\underline{V}^* \otimes \underline{V}^*) \otimes W^+(\underline{V}^*,\underline{\beta}^*)]\overline{\underline{\beta}})$$

$$> 0 \ .$$

By the implicit function theorem, for $\underline{V} \in A$ and $\underline{x} \in B$, the differential of $\underline{\beta}(\underline{V},\underline{x})$ satisfies

$$(8.266) \qquad d\underline{\beta}_{(\underline{V},\underline{x})}(\overline{\underline{V}},\overline{\underline{x}})$$

$$= B^{-1}(\underline{V},\underline{x})\{\overline{\underline{x}} - P_{\mathcal{B}}E[\overline{\underline{V}} \otimes \underline{p}(\underline{V},\underline{\beta}(\underline{V},\underline{x}))]$$

$$- P_{\mathcal{B}}\{E[(\underline{V} \otimes \overline{\underline{V}}) \otimes W^+(\underline{V},\underline{\beta}(\underline{V},\underline{x}))]\}\underline{\beta}(\underline{V},\underline{x})\} \ .$$

The last step in the proof exploits the observation that without loss of generality, it may be assumed that $\underline{V}^{(N)} \to \underline{V}^*$ with probability 1 (see Breiman 1968). If $\underline{c} \in R^{H \times \bar{r}}$, then Taylor's theorem implies that

(8.267)
$$(S^{(N)})^{\frac{1}{2}}\{(\underline{c},\underline{\beta}(\underline{V}^{(N)},P_B[\frac{1}{S^{(N)}}(\underline{X}^{(N)})^T\underline{n}^{(N)}])) - (\underline{c},\underline{\beta}^{(N)})\}$$
$$= (S^{(N)})^{\frac{1}{2}}[(\underline{c},\underline{\hat{\beta}}^{(N)}) - (\underline{c},\underline{\beta}^{(N)})]$$
$$= (S^{(N)})^{\frac{1}{2}}(\underline{c},d\underline{\beta}_{(\underline{V}^{(N)},\underline{\bar{x}}^{(N)})}(\underline{0},P_B[\frac{1}{S^{(N)}}(X^{(N)})^T(\underline{n}^{(N)} - \underline{m}^{(N)})])),$$

where $\underline{\bar{x}}^{(N)}$ is on the line segment between $P_B[(S^{(N)})^{-1}(X^{(N)})^T\underline{n}^{(N)}]$ and $P_B[(S^{(N)})^{-1}(X^{(N)})^T\underline{m}^{(N)}]$. By (8.259) and (8.230),

(8.268)
$$\underline{\bar{x}}^{(N)} \xrightarrow{P} P_B E[\underline{V}^* \otimes \underline{p}(\underline{V}^*,\underline{\beta}^*)].$$

Thus

(8.269)
$$(S^{(N)})^{\frac{1}{2}}[(\underline{c},\underline{\hat{\beta}}^{(N)}) - (\underline{c},\underline{\beta}^{(N)})]$$
$$- (\underline{c},B^{-1}(\underline{V}^*,\underline{\beta}^*)[(S^{(N)})^{-\frac{1}{2}}P_B[X^{(N)}]^T(\underline{n}^{(N)} - \underline{m}^{(N)})])$$
$$\xrightarrow{P} \underline{0}.$$

The transformation $B(\underline{V}^*,\underline{\beta}^*)$ is symmetric, for

(8.270)
$$(\underline{\beta},B(\underline{V}^*,\underline{\beta}^*)\underline{\gamma})$$
$$= (\underline{\beta},P_B E[(\underline{V}^* \otimes \underline{V}^*) \otimes W^+(\underline{V}^*,\underline{\beta}^*)]\underline{\gamma})$$
$$= (\underline{\beta},E[(\underline{V}^* \otimes \underline{V}^*) \otimes W^+(\underline{V}^*,\underline{\beta}^*)]\underline{\gamma})$$
$$= (E[(\underline{V}^* \otimes \underline{V}^*) \otimes W^+(\underline{V}^*,\underline{\beta}^*)]\underline{\beta},\underline{\gamma})$$
$$= (P_B E[(\underline{V}^* \otimes \underline{V}^*) \otimes W^+(\underline{V}^*,\underline{\beta}^*)]\underline{\beta},\underline{\gamma})$$
$$= (B(\underline{V}^*,\underline{\beta}^*)\underline{\beta},\underline{\gamma})$$

if $\underline{\beta}$ and $\underline{\gamma}$ are in $\mathcal{B}$. Since

(8.271)
$$P_B B^{-1}(\underline{V}^*,\underline{\beta}^*) = B^{-1}(\underline{V}^*,\underline{\beta}^*),$$

(8.230) and (8.259) imply that

(8.272) $$(S^{(N)})^{\frac{1}{2}}[(\underline{c},\hat{\underline{\beta}}^{(N)}) - (\underline{c},\underline{\beta}^{(N)})] \xrightarrow{\mathcal{D}} N(0,(\underline{c},B^{-1}(\underline{V}^*,\underline{\beta}^*)P_B\underline{c})).$$

By Rao (1965), (8.219) and (8.220) follow.||

Given this theorem, estimated asymptotic covariances for $\hat{\underline{\beta}}^{(N)}$ may be computed by use of the observations that

(8.273) $$B(\underline{V}^{(N)},\hat{\underline{\beta}}^{(N)}) \xrightarrow{P} B(\underline{V}^*,\underline{\beta}^*)$$

and that

(8.274) $$B(\underline{V}^{(N)},\hat{\underline{\beta}}^{(N)}) = P_B\frac{1}{S^{(N)}}\sum_{j\in J^{(N)}} N_j^{(N)}(\underline{x}_j \otimes \underline{x}_j) \otimes W^+(\underline{x}_j,\hat{\underline{\beta}}^{(N)}).$$

Thus the right-hand side of (8.274) may be used to estimate the asymptotic covariance. Given the estimated asymptotic covariance of $(S^{(N)})^{\frac{1}{2}}(\hat{\underline{\beta}}^{(N)} - \underline{\beta}^{(N)})$, confidence intervals for linear combinations $(\underline{c},\underline{\beta}^{(N)})$ are readily constructed. Hypothesis tests for such linear combinations and simultaneous confidence intervals involve no special problems.

If a logit model is involved, then $r = 2$ and a number of simplifications are possible. Given (8.198), $\mathcal{B} = C \otimes \text{span}\{<1,-1>\}$ for some linear manifold $C \in R^H$ and one can write

(8.275) $$\underline{\beta}^{(N)} = \frac{1}{2}\underline{\gamma}^{(N)} \otimes <1,-1>$$

for some $\{\underline{\gamma}^{(N)}\} \subset C$. The operator $W^+(\underline{V},\underline{\beta})$ reduces to

(8.276) $$p_1(\underline{V},\underline{\beta})p_2(\underline{V},\underline{\beta})[<1,-1> \otimes <1,-1>].$$

Since $P_B = P_C \otimes P_{\text{span}\{<1,-1>\}}$,

(8.277) $$\begin{aligned} B(\underline{V},\underline{\beta}) &= P_C E[w(\underline{V},\underline{\gamma})(\underline{V} \otimes \underline{V})] \otimes [<1,-1> \otimes <1,-1>] \\ &= 2P_C E[w(\underline{V},\underline{\gamma})(\underline{V} \otimes \underline{V}) \otimes P_{\text{span}\{<1,-1>\}}], \end{aligned}$$

where

(8.278) $$w(\underline{V},\underline{\gamma}) = e^{(\underline{V},\underline{\gamma})}/[1 + e^{(\underline{V},\underline{\gamma})}]^2$$

and

(8.279) $$\underline{\beta} = \frac{1}{2}\underline{\gamma} \otimes <1,-1>.$$

If

(8.280) $$C(\underline{V},\underline{\gamma}) = E[w(\underline{V},\underline{\gamma})\underline{V} \otimes \underline{V}]$$

and $P^+(\underline{V},\underline{\gamma})$ is the projection from R^H to C orthogonal with respect to the inner product defined by $C(\underline{V},\underline{\gamma})$, then

(8.281) $$B(\underline{V},\underline{\beta})[\tfrac{1}{2}P^{+}(\underline{V},\underline{\gamma})C^{-1}(\underline{V},\underline{\gamma}) \otimes P_{span\{<1,-1>\}}]P_C \otimes P_{span\{<1,-1>\}}$$

$$= P_C C(\underline{V},\underline{\gamma})P_C^{+}(\underline{V},\underline{\gamma})C^{-1}(\underline{V},\underline{\gamma})P_C \otimes P_{span\{<1,-1>\}}$$

$$= P_B \ .$$

The last equation holds since for any $\underline{x}$ and $\underline{y}$ in R^H,

(8.282) $$(\underline{x},P_C C(\underline{V},\underline{\gamma})P^{+}(\underline{V},\underline{\gamma})C^{-1}(\underline{V},\underline{\gamma})P_C\underline{y})$$

$$= (P_C\underline{x},C(\underline{V},\underline{\gamma})P_C^{+}(\underline{V},\underline{\gamma})C^{-1}(\underline{V},\underline{\gamma})P_C\underline{y})$$

$$= (P_C^{+}(\underline{V},\underline{\gamma})P_C\underline{x},C(\underline{V},\underline{\gamma})C^{-1}(\underline{V},\underline{\gamma})P_C\underline{y})$$

$$= (P_C\underline{x},P_C\underline{y})$$

$$= (\underline{x},P_C\underline{y}) \ .$$

Given (8.275) and (8.281), (8.280 reduces to

(8.283) $$(S^{(N)})^{\frac{1}{2}}[\tfrac{1}{2}\hat{\underline{\gamma}}^{(N)} \otimes <1,-1> - \tfrac{1}{2}\underline{\gamma}^{(N)} \otimes <1,-1>]$$

$$\xrightarrow{\mathcal{D}} N(\underline{0},\tfrac{1}{2}P_C^{+}(\underline{V}^*,\underline{\gamma}^*)C^{-1}(\underline{V}^*,\underline{\gamma}^*) \otimes P_{span\{<1,-1>\}}) \ .$$

This equation is equivalent to

(8.284) $$(S^{(N)})^{\frac{1}{2}}(\hat{\underline{\gamma}}^{(N)} - \underline{\gamma}^{(N)}) \xrightarrow{\mathcal{D}} N(\underline{0},P_C^{+}(\underline{V}^*,\underline{\gamma}^*)C^{-1}(\underline{V}^*,\underline{\gamma}^*)).$$

In addition,

(8.285) $$\hat{\underline{\gamma}}^{(N)} \xrightarrow{P} \hat{\underline{\gamma}}^* \ .$$

The estimated asymptotic covariance of $\hat{\underline{\gamma}}^{(N)}$ is then $(S^{(N)})^{-1}P_C^{+}(\underline{V}^{(N)},\hat{\underline{\gamma}}^{(N)})C^{-1}(\underline{V}^{(N)},\hat{\underline{\gamma}}^{(N)})$, where

(8.286) $$C(\underline{V}^{(N)},\hat{\underline{\gamma}}^{(N)}) = \frac{1}{S^{(N)}} \sum_{j\epsilon J^{(N)}} w(\underline{x}_j,\hat{\underline{\gamma}}^{(N)})\underline{x}_j \otimes \underline{x}_j$$

$$= \frac{1}{S^{(N)}}[Y^{(N)}]^T W^{(L)}(\underline{N}^{(N)},\hat{\underline{\gamma}}^{(N)})Y^{(N)},$$

for $\underline{\gamma} \in R^H$

(8.287) $$Y^{(N)}\underline{\gamma} = \{(\underline{x}_j,\underline{\gamma}): j \in J^{(N)}\},$$

and $\hat{\underline{\gamma}}^{(N)} = Y^{(N)}\hat{\underline{\gamma}}^{(N)}$.

It is easily shown that this estimated asymptotic covariance is also equal to

$[(Y^{(N)})^T]^{-1}\tilde{P}^{(L)}_{L(N)}(\underline{N}^{(N)},\hat{\underline{\lambda}}^{(N)})[W^{(L)}(\underline{N}^{(N)},\hat{\underline{\lambda}}^{(N)})]^{-1}(Y^{(N)})^{-1}$, which is the conventional estimate of the asymptotic covariance of $\hat{\underline{\beta}}^{(N)}$ if $L^{(N)}$ and $J^{(N)}$ are constant.

Example 8.23. In Example 8.18, a logit model is employed with

$$p(1|j) = 1/\{1 + \exp[-(\underline{x}_j,\underline{\gamma})]\}, \tag{8.288}$$

where $\{x_{jh}: h \in \overline{g}\}$ is some subset of observed values of variables listed in table 8.9 and $x_{j(g+1)} = 1$ for $j \in \overline{N}$. One may set $\gamma_j = \beta_j$ for $j \in \overline{g}$ and $\gamma_{g+1} = \alpha$. There are no restrictions on $\underline{\gamma} \in R^{g+1}$, so $C = R^H$, where $H = \overline{g+1}$. In such a case,

$$N^{\frac{1}{2}}(\hat{\underline{\gamma}}^{(N)} - \underline{\gamma}) \xrightarrow{\mathcal{D}} N(\underline{0},C^{-1}(\underline{V}^*,\underline{\gamma}^*)) \tag{8.289}$$

and the estimated asymptotic covariance of $\hat{\underline{\gamma}}^{(N)}$ is $[(Y^{(N)})^T W^{(L)}(\underline{N}^{(N)},\hat{\underline{\lambda}}^{(N)})Y^{(N)}]^{-1}$. These formulas are consistent with those used by Walker and Duncan (1967). Given these results, they used 4671 observations to obtain the estimated parameters $\{\hat{\gamma}_j: j \in \overline{9}\}$ and corresponding estimated asymptotic standard deviations $\{\hat{s}_j: j \in \overline{9}\}$ for the model based on the first nine predictors in table 8.9. Results are summarized in table 8.10. The Bonferroni simultaneous 95% confidence intervals for each γ_j for $j \in \overline{9}$ are given by the intervals $[\hat{\gamma}_j - \Phi^{(0.025/9)}\hat{s}_j, \hat{\gamma}_j + \Phi^{(0.025/9)}\hat{s}_j]$. The upper and lower limits for these intervals are also given in table 8.10. These results are not easily interpreted. Sex and age have considerable predictive power, but the size of the parameters γ_1 and γ_2 are not well determined. Serum cholesterol, electrocardiographic abnormalities, and Framingham relative weight also appear to be important predictors. An additional problem in interpretation of these data is the omission of data on smoking habits. The data Walker and Duncan have on smoking habits are incomplete, but their analysis of subjects where this variable is recorded does suggest that it is an important predictor.

Example 8.24. If one has the conventional asymptotic model of Example 8.20 and $r = 2$, then $Y^{(N)} = I$, the identity on R^J, and $\underline{n}^{(N)}$ satisfies a logit model with

$$p(1|j) = 1/[1 + \exp(-\gamma_j^{(N)})] \tag{8.290}$$

for $\gamma \in C = L$. Thus

$$N^{\frac{1}{2}}(\hat{\underline{\gamma}}^{(N)} - \underline{\gamma}^{(N)}) \xrightarrow{\mathcal{D}} N(\underline{0},\tilde{P}^{(L)}_L(\underline{N}^*,\underline{\gamma}^*)[W^{(L)}(\underline{N}^*,\underline{\gamma}^*)]^{-1}), \tag{8.291}$$

a formula which is consistent with (8.111).

TABLE 8.10

PARAMETER ESTIMATES FOR FRAMINGHAM STUDY

Variable	Parameter Estimate	Estimated Asymptotic Standard Deviation	Lower Limit	Upper Limit
Sex	-1.59	0.174	-2.07	-1.10
Age	0.0810	0.00798	0.0589	0.1031
HT	-0.0528	0.0232	-1.171	0.0114
SYS	0.00912	0.00365	-0.00099	0.01923
DIA	0.00549	0.00678	-0.01329	0.02427
SCH	0.00663	0.00123	0.00324	0.01004
ECG	0.854	0.171	0.381	1.328
FWT	1.359	0.360	0.361	2.356
ALC	-0.0587	0.0367	-0.1604	0.0429

Example 8.25. In Example 8.18, the response was coded according to presence or absence of coronary heart disease. If desired, the category presence of coronary heart disease could be subdivided into myocardial infarction or angina pectoris. If this is done, then $r = 3$. The model given by (8.206) may be retained, except that B is now the set of $\underline{\alpha} \in R^{\overline{g+1}\times\overline{3}}$ for which

(8.292) $$\alpha_{h1} + \alpha_{h2} + \alpha_{h3} = 0$$

for $h \in H = \overline{g+1}$. Thus $B = R^H \otimes \{\underline{e}^{(3)}\}^{\perp}$ (see Lemma 5.5). Since $P_B = I_H \otimes P_{\{\underline{e}^{(3)}\}^{\perp}}$, (8.221) and (8.222) imply that

(8.293) $$B(\underline{V},\underline{\beta}) = E[I_H(\underline{V} \otimes \underline{V}) \otimes P_{\{\underline{e}^{(3)}\}^{\perp}} W^+(\underline{V},\underline{\beta})]$$

$$= E\{(\underline{V} \otimes \underline{V}) \otimes [I_3 - P_{\mathrm{span}\{\underline{e}^{(3)}\}}]W^+(\underline{V},\underline{\beta})\}$$

$$= E[(\underline{V} \otimes \underline{V}) \otimes W^+(\underline{V},\underline{\beta})].$$

Since the domain of $B(\underline{V},\underline{\beta})$ is B,

(8.293) $$B(\underline{V},\underline{\beta}) = E\{(\underline{V} \otimes \underline{V}) \otimes [W^+(\underline{V},\underline{\beta}) + P_{\mathrm{span}\{\underline{e}^{(3)}\}}]\}$$

on $R^H \otimes \{\underline{e}^{(3)}\}^{\perp}$. Since the right-hand side of (8.293) is positive definite, it is easily seen that

$$B^{-1}(\underline{V},\underline{\beta}) = P_B\{E\{(\underline{V} \otimes \underline{V}) \otimes [W^+(\underline{V},\underline{\beta}) + P_{\text{span}\{\underline{e}^{(3)}\}}]\}\}^{-1} \tag{8.294}$$

and

$$(S^{(N)})^{\frac{1}{2}}(\underline{\hat{\beta}}^{(N)} - \underline{\beta}^{(N)}) \tag{8.295}$$

$$\xrightarrow{\mathcal{D}} N(\underline{0},P_B\{E[(\underline{V}^* \otimes \underline{V}^*) \otimes [W^+(\underline{V}^*,\underline{\beta}^*) + P_{\text{span}\{\underline{e}^{(3)}\}}]\}\}^{-1}P_B).$$

The estimated asymptotic covariance of $\underline{\hat{\beta}}^{(N)}$ is then

$$P_B\{\sum_{j=1}^{N^{(N)}} N_j^{(N)}(\underline{x}_j \otimes \underline{x}_j) \otimes [W^+(\underline{x}_j,\underline{\hat{\beta}}^{(N)}) + P_{\text{span}\{\underline{e}^{(3)}\}}]\}^{-1}P_B.$$

Walker and Duncan (1967) also consider a generalization of their model to a trinomial response. Their model is somewhat different from the one proposed here, and is only usable when responses are ordered.

The approach used in Example 8.25 is easily generalized. For any $B \subset R^H \otimes \{\underline{e}^{(r)}\}$,

$$B(\underline{V},\underline{\beta}) = P_B E\{(\underline{V} \otimes \underline{V}) \otimes [W^+(\underline{V},\underline{\beta}) + P_{\text{span}\{\underline{e}^{(r)}\}}]\}. \tag{8.296}$$

If $P_B^0(\underline{V},\underline{\beta})$ is the orthogonal projection on B with respect to the inner product defined by $D(\underline{V},\underline{\beta}) = E\{(\underline{V} \otimes \underline{V}) \otimes [W^+(\underline{V},\underline{\beta}) + P_{\text{span}\{\underline{e}^{(r)}\}}]\}$, then

$$B^{-1}(\underline{V},\underline{\beta}) = P_B^0(\underline{V},\underline{\beta})D^{-1}(\underline{V},\underline{\beta}), \tag{8.297}$$

as may be verified by noting that if $\underline{x} \in B$, $B(\underline{V},\underline{\beta}) = P_B D(\underline{V},\underline{\beta})$ and

$$\begin{aligned} &P_B^0(\underline{V},\underline{\beta})D^{-1}(\underline{V},\underline{\beta})P_B D(\underline{V},\underline{\beta})\underline{x} \\ &= P_B^0(\underline{V},\underline{\beta})D^{-1}(\underline{V},\underline{\beta})D(\underline{V},\underline{\beta})\underline{x} \\ &= P_B^0(\underline{V},\underline{\beta})\underline{x} \\ &= \underline{x}. \end{aligned} \tag{8.298}$$

Given this relationship,

$$(S^{(N)})^{\frac{1}{2}}(\underline{\hat{\beta}}^{(N)} - \underline{\beta}^{(N)}) \xrightarrow{\mathcal{D}} N(\underline{0},P_B^0(\underline{V}^*,\underline{\beta}^*)D^{-1}(\underline{V}^*,\underline{\beta}^*)) \tag{8.299}$$

and the estimated asymptotic covariance of $\underline{\hat{\beta}}^{(N)}$ is

$P_B^0(\underline{V}^{(N)},\underline{\hat{\beta}}^{(N)})\{\sum_{j \in J^{(N)}} N_j^{(N)}(\underline{x}_j \otimes \underline{x}_j) \otimes [W^+(\underline{x}_j,\underline{\hat{\beta}}^{(N)}) + P_{\text{span}\{\underline{e}^{(r)}\}}]\}^{-1}$. These formulas may not appear consistent with (8.295); however, if $\mathcal{B} = R^H \bullet \{\underline{e}^{(r)}\}^{\perp}$, then the image of $\mathcal{B}$ under $D(\underline{V},\underline{\beta})$ is $\mathcal{B}$. By Kruskal (1968a), $P^0_{\mathcal{B}}(\underline{V},\underline{\beta}) = P_{\mathcal{B}}$ and

(8.300)
$$\begin{aligned} &P^0_{\mathcal{B}}(\underline{V}^*,\underline{\beta}^*)D^{-1}(\underline{V}^*,\underline{\beta}^*) \\ &= P^0_{\mathcal{B}}(\underline{V}^*,\underline{\beta}^*)D^{-1}(\underline{V}^*,\underline{\beta}^*)P_{\mathcal{B}} \\ &= P_{\mathcal{B}}D^{-1}(\underline{V}^*,\underline{\beta}^*)P_{\mathcal{B}}. \end{aligned}$$

Although the estimate $\hat{\underline{\beta}}^{(N)}$ has rather standard asymptotic properties, some modifications are necessary when numerical computation or hypothesis testing is considered. The problem in numerical computations is that, in general, no easily computed approximation $\underline{\beta}^{(N,0)}$ for $\hat{\underline{\beta}}^{(N)}$ is available such that $\hat{\underline{\beta}}^{(N)}$ and $\underline{\beta}^{(N,0)}$ are asymptotically equivalent. The conditioned Newton-Raphson algorithm may still be employed; however, convergence with a starting value such as $\underline{\beta}^{(N,0)} = \underline{0}$ cannot be expected to be as rapid as in the examples presented earlier in this section. Walker and Duncan (1967) propose an alternative computational procedure which they use to obtain the estimates in table 8.10. The numerical properties of their algorithm are not clear, but their approach may prove useful in many problems. It should be noted that in the Framingham study considered by Walker and Duncan, a useful initial approximation to $\hat{\alpha}$ and $\hat{\underline{\beta}}$ may be obtained by use of the linear discrimination approach of Cornfield, Kannel, and Truett (1967). In their approach, α and $\underline{\beta}$ are estimated by means of (8.194) and (8.195). They use the customary estimates in multivariate analysis for $\underline{\mu}^{(1)}$, $\underline{\mu}^{(2)}$, and $\ddagger$ and estimate p_1/p_2 by $\sum_{j\in J} n_{j1}/\sum_{j\in J} n_{j2}$. Their estimates of α and $\underline{\beta}$ are fairly close to $\hat{\alpha}$ and $\hat{\underline{\beta}}$.

Likelihood ratio tests are still available, but Pearson chi-square tests need not have the desired asymptotic properties. For example, if one tests the hypothesis H_0: $\underline{\beta}^{(N)} \in \mathcal{B}_1$ against the alternative H_A: $\underline{\beta}^{(N)} \in \mathcal{B}_2$, where $\mathcal{B}_1$ is properly included in $\mathcal{B}_2$, then if $\underline{\beta}^{(N)} \in \mathcal{B}_1$ for all N, the likelihood ratio chi-square statistic $-2\Delta(\underline{n}^{(N)},\hat{\underline{\mu}}^{(N,2)},\hat{\underline{\mu}}^{(N,1)})$ is asymptotically equivalent to

$$((S^{(N)})^{-\frac{1}{2}}P_{\mathcal{B}_2}(X^{(N)})^T(\underline{n}^{(N)} - \underline{m}^{(N)}),[P^0_{\mathcal{B}_2}(\underline{V}^*,\underline{\beta}^*) - P^0_{\mathcal{B}_1}(\underline{V}^*,\underline{\beta}^*)]$$

$$\times D^{-1}(\underline{V}^*,\underline{\beta}^*)(S^{(N)})^{-\frac{1}{2}}P_{\mathcal{B}_2}(X^{(N)})^T(\underline{n}^{(N)} - \underline{m}^{(N)}))\ ,$$

which converges in distribution to $\chi^2_{\dim \mathcal{B}_2 - \dim \mathcal{B}_1}$. The arguments involved are conventional and are consequently omitted. The basic results used are (8.230), (8.297), and the fact that the function $\hat{\ell}^{(m)}(\underline{n}^{(N)},X^{(N)}\underline{\beta}^{(N)})$ defined as in (2.22) has a second differential $-S^{(N)}(\underline{\bar{\beta}}^{(1)},D(\underline{V}^{(N)},\underline{\beta}^{(N)})\underline{\bar{\beta}}^{(2)})$ at $\underline{\beta}^{(N)}$ for $\underline{\bar{\beta}}^{(1)}$ and $\underline{\bar{\beta}}^{(2)}$ in $R^H \cap \{\underline{e}^{(r)}\}^{\perp}$. The asymptotic equivalence of the Pearson and likelihood ratio chi-square statistics depends on the fact that $J^{(N)}$ does not increase as N increases; consequently, it is in general not valid under the conditions assumed in this section. Thus some care is required when the asymptotic results of this section are employed. Nonetheless, the results of this section do permit a substantial change in the range of applications for logit and multinomial response models.

Chapter 9
SOME EXTENSIONS

In this chapter, the use of log-linear models based on flats is briefly considered. These models appear to have only limited utility by themselves, but they do shed some light on the problem of adjustment of marginal totals considered by Deming and Stephan (1940).

MODELS BASED ON FLATS

The extension to flats involves models in which the log-mean vector $\underline{\mu}$ is in $\underline{z} + M = \{\underline{z} + \underline{x}: \underline{x} \in M\}$. If $\underline{z} \notin M$, then $\underline{z} + M$ is a flat, or affine subspace, rather than a linear manifold. Under such a model, results of the first four chapters are essentially unchanged. The statistic $P_M\underline{n}$ remains a complete minimal sufficient statistic. The likelihood equation remains

(9.1) $$P_M\underline{m}(\hat{\underline{\mu}}) = P_M\underline{n}$$

if Poisson or multinomial sampling is used, and $\hat{\underline{\mu}}$ is unique if it exists. By Theorem 2.6, necessary and sufficient conditions for existence of $\hat{\underline{\mu}}$ are still given by Theorems 2.2 and 2.3, and the computational procedures in chapter 3 still apply, provided starting values are in $\underline{z} + M$. The asymptotic properties in chapter 4 also apply. In both multinomial and conditional Poisson sampling, the basic condition $N \subset M$ is required, where N is defined as in chapter 2.

Example 9.1. The hypothesis testing problem of Example 4.6 can be reformulated in terms of log-linear models based on flats. Under the null hypothesis that the proportions predicted by genetic theory are present, the expected frequencies of the four crosses are given by some multiple of the vector $\underline{z} = \langle\frac{9}{16}, \frac{3}{16}, \frac{3}{16}, \frac{1}{16}\rangle$. Thus the log-mean $\underline{\mu}$ is in the flat $\{\log z_i\} + \text{span}\,\{\underline{e}\}$. Under the alternative hypothesis, $\underline{\mu} \in \{\log z_i\} + R^4$, which is equal to R^4 since $\{\log z_i\} \in R^4$. Under the null hypothesis,

(9.2) $$P_{\text{span}\{\underline{e}\}}\underline{m}(\hat{\underline{\mu}}) = P_{\text{span}\{\underline{e}\}}\underline{n}.$$

Thus if $\underline{\mu} = \{\log z_i\} + a\underline{e}$ and $\hat{\underline{\mu}}^{(1)} = \{\log z_i\} + \hat{a}\underline{e}$,

(9.3)
$$(\underline{m}(\hat{\underline{\mu}}^{(1)}),\underline{e}) = \sum_{i=1}^{4} z_i e^{\hat{a}}$$
$$= e^{\hat{a}}(\tfrac{9}{16} + \tfrac{3}{16} + \tfrac{3}{16} + \tfrac{1}{16})$$
$$= e^{\hat{a}}$$
$$= (\underline{n},\underline{e})$$
$$= 1301.$$

Thus $\hat{\underline{\mu}}^{(1)} = \{\log Z_i\} + (\log 1301)\underline{e}$ and $\hat{\underline{m}}^{(1)} = 1301 <\frac{9}{16}, \frac{3}{16}, \frac{3}{16}, \frac{1}{16}>$. Under the alternative hypothesis, $\hat{\underline{m}}^{(2)} = \underline{n}$. Thus the likelihood ratio $-2\Delta(\underline{n},\hat{\underline{\mu}}^{(2)},\hat{\underline{\mu}}^{(1)})$ is $2\sum_{i=1}^{4} n_i \log (\hat{m}_i^{(2)}/\hat{m}_i^{(1)})$, which is equal to the expression $-2\Delta(\underline{n},\underline{\nu},\hat{\underline{\mu}})$ given by (4.167). Since $\dim R^4 = 4$ and span $\{\underline{e}\}$ has dimension 1, the test statistic has 3 degrees of freedom. The new formulation does not change the analyses in this example, but it is notable that the assumption of a multinomial sample is now unnecessary.

Example 9.2. Suppose $I = \bar{r} \times \bar{s}$ and

(9.4)
$$\mu_{ij} = \alpha + \beta_i + \gamma_j + \delta_{ij},$$

where

(9.5)
$$\sum_{i=1}^{r} \beta_i = \sum_{j=1}^{s} \gamma_j = \sum_{i=1}^{r} \delta_{ij} = \sum_{j=1}^{s} \delta_{ij} = 0$$

and $\{\delta_{ij}\}$ is known. Then M is the simple additive manifold for two-way tables. Since M is spanned by $\{\underline{\nu}(\{1\},i): i \in \bar{r}\} \cup \{\underline{\nu}(\{2\},j): j \in \bar{s}\}$, (9.2) implies that $\hat{\underline{m}} = \underline{m}(\hat{\underline{\mu}})$ must satisfy $\hat{m}_{i+} = n_{i+}$ for $i \in \bar{r}$ and $\hat{m}_{+j} = n_{+j}$ for $j \in \bar{s}$. Theorem 5.1 shows that $\hat{\underline{m}}$ exists if and only if $n_{i+} > 0$ for all $i \in \bar{r}$ and $n_{+j} > 0$ for all $j \in \bar{s}$. If this condition is met, $\hat{\underline{m}}$ may be computed by setting $\underline{m}^{(0,1)} = \{\exp(\delta_{ij})\}$ and defining $\underline{m}^{(t,k)}$ for $k \in \bar{3}$ by

(9.6)
$$m_{ij}^{(t,2)} = m_{ij}^{(t,1)} \frac{n_{i+}}{m_{i+}^{(t,1)}},$$

(9.7)
$$m_{ij}^{(t,3)} = m_{ij}^{(t,2)} \frac{n_{+j}}{m_{+j}^{(t,2)}},$$

and

(9.8)
$$m_{ij}^{(t+1,1)} = m_{ij}^{(t,3)},$$

where $<i,j> \in \bar{r} \times \bar{s}$.

Both Examples 9.1 and 9.2 may be considered to be examples of generalized hierarchical models such that $I = \prod_{j=1}^{d} \bar{r}_j$,

(9.9) $$M^* = \sum_{g=1}^{h} M_{B_g} ,$$

where M_{B_g} is defined as in chapter 5, F is the set of $\underline{\mu} \in M^*$ such that $P_{M_{B_g}} \underline{\mu} = \underline{z}^{(g)}$ for all $g \in A \subset \overline{h}$, and $\{B_g: g \in \overline{h} - A\}$ is hierarchical. Thus

(9.10) $$F = \sum_{g \in A} \underline{z}^{(g)} + M,$$

where

(9.11) $$M = \bigodot_{g \in \overline{h} - A} M_{B_g}$$

is an hierarchical manifold. Since M is hierarchical, iterative proportional fitting may be used to find $\underline{\hat{m}}$, provided $\{\log m_{\underline{i}}^{(0,1)}: \underline{i} \in I\} \in F$. Other features of hierarchical manifolds can also be applied.

Example 9.3. In Example 9.1, $d = 1$, $M^* = M_\phi \odot M_{\{1\}} = R^4$, and F consists of $\underline{\mu} \in M^*$ such that

(9.12) $$P_{M\{1\}}\underline{\mu} = \langle \log \frac{9}{16}, \log \frac{3}{16}, \log \frac{3}{16}, \log \frac{1}{16} \rangle$$
$$- \frac{1}{4} (\log \frac{9}{16} + \log \frac{3}{16} + \log \frac{3}{16} + \log \frac{1}{16})\underline{e}.$$

The manifold $M = M_\phi$ is a trivial hierarchical manifold.

Example 9.4. In Example 9.2,

(9.13) $$M^* = M_\phi \odot M_{\{1\}} \odot M_{\{2\}} \odot M_{\{1,2\}} ,$$

and F consists of $\underline{\mu} \in M^*$ such that

(9.14) $$P_{M_{\{1,2\}}}\underline{\mu} = \{\delta_{ij}\}.$$

The manifold

(9.15) $$M = M_\phi \odot M_{\{1\}} \odot M_{\{2\}}$$

is hierarchical. If β_i were known rather than δ_{ij} in (9.4), then the model would not be a generalized hierarchical model, for M would be $M_\phi \odot M_{\{2\}} \odot M_{\{1,2\}}$, which is not hierarchical. In such a case, the iterative proportional fitting algorithm would not be available.

ADJUSTMENT OF MARGINAL TOTALS

In the problems considered in this section, two parallel tables $\underline{n}^{(1)}$ and $\underline{n}^{(2)}$

in R^I are considered. The log-mean vectors $\underline{\mu}^{(1)}$ and $\underline{\mu}^{(2)}$ corresponding to the two tables are both in a linear manifold M and for some linear manifold $L \subset M$, $P_M\underline{\mu}^{(1)} = P_M\underline{\mu}^{(2)}$. It is assumed that $\underline{n}^{(1)}$ can be observed but that the only information available concerning $\underline{n}^{(2)}$ is that $P_{M-L}\underline{m}(\underline{\mu}^{(2)})$ is known. The sample $\underline{n}^{(1)}$ may be Poisson, multinomial, or conditional Poisson The manifold N describing the sampling method is assumed to be included in L. This section considers the problem of estimation of $\underline{\mu}^{(1)}$ and $\underline{\mu}^{(2)}$.

Example 9.5. Deming and Stephan (1940) consider a population of size N with characteristics $\{X_{jt}: j \in \overline{d}\} \in \prod_{j=1}^{d} \overline{r}_j = I$. The number $n_{\underline{i}}^{(2)}$ of individuals such that $\{X_{jt}: j \in \overline{d}\} = \{i_j: j \in \overline{d}\} = \underline{i}$ is unknown, but a census has determined the marginal totals $[\underline{n}^{(2)}]^{\{j\}}$ for each $j \in \overline{d}$. Given this information, one can describe $\underline{n}^{(2)}$ as a conditional Poisson sample with $\underline{n}^{(2)} = \underline{m}(\underline{\mu}^{(2)})$. In particular, $[\underline{n}^{(2)}]^{\{j\}} = [\underline{m}(\underline{\mu}^{(2)})]^{\{j\}}$ for $j \in \overline{d}$. In addition to $\underline{n}^{(2)}$, a sample $\underline{n}^{(1)}$ is available such that $n_{\underline{i}}^{(1)}$ is known, where $n_{\underline{i}}^{(1)}$ is the number of elements of the sample with characteristics $\{X_{jt}: j \in \overline{d}\} = \underline{i}$. This sample may be Poisson, multinomial, or conditional Poisson. In practice, it may be a sample from the population described by $\underline{n}^{(2)}$.

If no knowledge exists concerning $\underline{\mu}^{(1)}$ or $\underline{\mu}^{(2)}$, one may set $M = R^I$ and $L = M(I,\{\{j\}: j \in \overline{d}\})$. It should be noted that if $i_j \in \overline{r}_j$ and $j \in \overline{d}$, $L = \text{span}\,\{\underline{v}(\{j\},i_j): i_j \in \overline{r}_j, j \in \overline{d}\}$ and

(9.16)
$$\begin{aligned}[n^{(2)}]_{i_j}^{\{j\}} &= [m^{(2)}]_{i_j}^{\{j\}} \\ &= (\underline{m}^{(2)},\underline{v}(\{j\},i_j)) \\ &= (P_L\underline{m}^{(2)},\underline{v}(\{j\},i_j)).\end{aligned}$$

Thus knowledge of $P_L\underline{m}^{(2)}$ is equivalent to knowledge of $[\underline{n}^{(2)}]^{\{j\}}$ for $j \in \overline{d}$. The assumption that $P_{M-L}\underline{\mu}^{(2)} = P_{M-L}\underline{\mu}^{(1)}$ means that the interaction structures of the two tables coincide. If $B \subset \overline{d}$ and B has two or more elements, then

(9.17)
$$P_{M_B}\underline{\mu}^{(1)} = P_{M_B}\underline{\mu}^{(2)} .$$

Equivalently, if for $k \in \overline{2}$,

(9.18)
$$\mu_{\underline{i}}^{(k)} = \sum_{B \in \overline{d}} [v^{(k)}]^{B}_{\pi_B \underline{i}}$$

for

(9.19)
$$[\underline{v}^{(k)}]^B \in \prod_{j \in B} \{e^{(r_j)}\}^{\perp}$$

for $B \in \bar{d}$ (see chapter 5), then

(9.20) $$[v^{(1)}]^{B}_{\underline{\bar{i}}} = [v^{(2)}]^{B}_{\underline{\bar{i}}}$$

for $\underline{\bar{i}} \in I(B)$ if B has two or more elements. If $d = 2$, then one simply assumes that the two-factor interactions in the two tables are identical.

In the example considered by Deming and Stephan (1940), the population consists of the native white persons of native white parentage attending school in New England in 1930. The characteristics examined are state and age of person. There are six states in New England and there are four age groups, so $r_1 = 6$ and $r_2 = 4$. The data consist of the marginal totals $[\underline{n}^{(2)}]^{\{j\}}$ for the population, together with the artificially generated 5% sample $\underline{n}^{(1)}$ summarized in table 9.1. These data are also examined by Stephan (1942), Deming (1943), and Kullback and Ireland (1968). More realistic data with similar structures are examined by El-Badry and Stephan (1955) and Friedlander (1961). Table 9.2 summarizes the data from the 1950 census used by El-Badry and Stephan. In this case, $r_1 = 13$ and $r_2 = 4$.

TABLE 9.1

OBSERVED FREQUENCIES IN 5% SAMPLE OF NATIVE WHITE PERSONS OF NATIVE WHITE PARENTAGE ATTENDING SCHOOL IN NEW ENGLAND IN 1930

	Age				
State	7-13	14-15	16-17	18-20	Population Total
Maine	3,623	781	557	313	105,044
New Hampshire	1,570	395	251	155	47,891
Vermont	1,553	419	264	116	48,633
Massachusetts	10,538	2,455	1,706	1,160	315,316
Rhode Island	1,681	353	171	154	46,608
Connecticut	3,882	857	544	339	113,230
Population Total	457,520	105,698	69,239	44,265	676,722

TABLE 9.2

EMPLOYMENT STATUS ACCORDING TO AGE OF RURAL NON-FARM MALES IN A 20% SAMPLE FOR NEW JERSEY AND THE CORRESPONDING CENSUS COUNTS BY AGE AND BY EMPLOYMENT STATUS FROM THE 1950 CENSUS OF POPULATION

Age	Military Labor Force	Civilian Labor Force		Not in the Labor Force	Sample Total	Census Total
		Employed	Unemployed			
14-19	1,548	952	146	2,867	5,513	27,063
20-24	1,332	2,341	198	644	4,515	22,822
25-29	643	3,089	136	515	4,383	22,761
30-34	434	3,432	101	354	4,321	22,555
35-39	219	3,385	97	346	4,047	21,285
40-44	77	3,134	92	333	3,636	19,388
45-49	34	2,720	88	366	3,208	16,736
50-54	19	2,388	114	506	3,027	15,761
55-59	6	1,934	123	592	2,655	13,845
60-64	2	1,397	97	635	2,131	11,621
65-69	0	8,310	83	835	1,749	9,087
70-74	2	411	29	868	1,310	6,700
75+	3	197	13	1,232	1,445	7,646
Sample Total	4,319	26,211	1,317	10,093	41,940	
Census Total	21,830	137,075	6,532	51,833		217,270

The estimation procedure for $\underline{\mu}^{(1)}$ and $\underline{\mu}^{(2)}$ consists of two parts. If $\underline{n}^{(1)}$ and $\underline{n}^{(2)}$ are independent, then knowledge of $P_L\underline{m}(\hat{\underline{\mu}}^{(2)})$ provides no information concerning $\underline{\mu}^{(1)}$. Thus the maximum-likelihood estimate $\hat{\underline{\mu}}^{(1)}$ of $\underline{\mu}^{(1)}$ satisfies

$$P_M\underline{m}(\hat{\underline{\mu}}^{(1)}) = P_M\underline{n}^{(1)} \tag{9.21}$$

if Poisson or multinomial sampling is used to obtain $\underline{n}^{(1)}$. Since $P_{M-L}\hat{\underline{\mu}}^{(2)} = P_{M-L}\hat{\underline{\mu}}^{(1)}$, $\hat{\underline{\mu}}^{(2)}$ is an element of $L + P_{M-L}\hat{\underline{\mu}}^{(1)}$ such that

$$P_L\underline{m}(\hat{\underline{\mu}}^{(2)}) = \underline{c}, \tag{9.22}$$

where $\underline{c}$ is the known value of $P_L\underline{m}(\underline{\mu}^{(2)})$. Comparison with (9.1) shows that $\hat{\underline{\mu}}^{(2)}$ is uniquely determined by $\hat{\underline{\mu}}^{(1)}$. It is readily seen that $\hat{\underline{\mu}}^{(1)}$ and $\hat{\underline{\mu}}^{(2)}$ exist if and only if the conditions of Theorems 2.2 and 2.3 are satisfied by $\underline{n}^{(1)}$.

Computation of $\hat{\underline{\mu}}^{(1)}$ and $\hat{\underline{\mu}}^{(2)}$ is quite easily accomplished. One finds $\hat{\underline{\mu}}^{(1)}$ by the conventional techniques used to find maximum-likelihood estimates for Poisson or multinomial sampling. Given $\hat{\underline{\mu}}^{(1)}$, one notes that

$$\begin{aligned} \hat{\underline{\mu}}^{(2)} &\in L + P_{M-L}\hat{\underline{\mu}}^{(1)} \\ &= (L + P_L\hat{\underline{\mu}}^{(1)}) + P_{M-L}\hat{\underline{\mu}}^{(1)} \\ &= L + \hat{\underline{\mu}}^{(1)} . \end{aligned} \tag{9.23}$$

If for some $\underline{\mu}^{(0)} \in R^I$, $P_L\underline{m}(\underline{\mu}^{(0)}) = \underline{c}$, then $\hat{\underline{\mu}}^{(2)}$ is the maximum-likelihood estimate of $\underline{\mu} \in L + \hat{\underline{\mu}}^{(1)}$ for the observation $\underline{m}(\underline{\mu}^{(0)})$. One may thus find $\hat{\underline{\mu}}^{(2)}$ by use of the conditioned Newton-Raphson or cyclic ascent algorithms of chapter 3. The initial estimate used for $\underline{m}(\hat{\underline{\mu}}^{(2)})$ may be $\underline{m}(\hat{\underline{\mu}}^{(1)})$.

The asymptotic distributions of $\hat{\underline{\mu}}^{(1)}$ and $\hat{\underline{\mu}}^{(2)}$ are readily determined. As usual, these results also apply if the actual sampling distribution is conditional Poisson. The function

$$F(\underline{x},\underline{\mu}) = P_L\underline{m}(\underline{x} + \underline{\mu}) - \underline{c} , \tag{9.24}$$

where $\underline{x} \in R^I$ and $\underline{\mu} \in L$ has the differential

$$dF_{(\underline{x},\underline{\mu})}(\underline{\delta},\underline{\gamma}) = P_L D(\underline{x} + \underline{\mu})(\underline{\delta} + \underline{\gamma}) \tag{9.25}$$

for $\underline{\delta} \in R^I$ and $\underline{\gamma} \in L$. To approximate $\hat{\underline{\mu}}^{(2)}$ by a linear function of $\hat{\underline{\mu}}^{(1)}$, the implicit function theorem may be applied. One notes that $F(\underline{\mu}^{(1)},\underline{\mu}^{(2)} - \underline{\mu}^{(1)}) = \underline{0}$ and

$P_L D(\underline{x} + \underline{\mu})(\underline{\gamma})$ is a nonsingular linear operator for $\underline{\gamma} \in L$. The implicit function theorem (see Loomis and Sternberg 1968) implies that if $g(\underline{x})$ is defined by the equation $F(\underline{x}, g(\underline{x}, g(\underline{x})) = \underline{0}$, then $g(\underline{x})$ is a well-defined differentiable function such that

$$P_L D(\underline{x}+g(\underline{x}))(\underline{\delta}+dg_{\underline{x}}(\underline{\delta})) = \underline{0} \tag{9.26}$$

for all $\underline{x} \in R^I$ and $\underline{\delta} \in R^I$. A simple calculation shows that

$$dg_{\underline{x}}(\underline{\delta}) = - P_L^*(\underline{x}+g(\underline{x}))\underline{\delta}. \tag{9.27}$$

If $\{\underline{n}^{(N,1)}\}$ is a sequence of observations with log means $\{\underline{\mu}^{(N,1)}\} \subset M$ such that $N^{-1}\underline{m}(\underline{\mu}^{(N,1)}) \longrightarrow \underline{m}(\underline{\mu}^{(*,1)})$, $P_{M-L}\underline{\mu}^{(N,1)} = P_{M-L}\underline{\mu}^{(N,2)}$, and $N^{-1}P_L\underline{m}(\underline{\mu}^{(N,2)}) = \underline{c}^{(N)}$, where $\underline{c}^{(N)} \longrightarrow \underline{c}^*$, then standard asymptotic arguments show that

$$\begin{aligned} N^{\frac{1}{2}}(\underline{\hat{\mu}}^{(N,2)} - \underline{\mu}^{(N,2)}) &= N^{\frac{1}{2}}[\underline{\hat{\mu}}^{(N,1)} - \underline{\mu}^{(N,1)} + g(\underline{\hat{\mu}}^{(N,1)}) - g(\underline{\mu}^{(N,1)})] \\ &= N^{\frac{1}{2}}[\underline{\hat{\mu}}^{(N,1)} - \underline{\mu}^{(N,1)} - P_L^*(\underline{\mu}^{(*,2)})(\underline{\hat{\mu}}^{(N,1)} - \underline{\mu}^{(N,1)})] \\ &\quad + \underline{o}^{(N)}, \end{aligned} \tag{9.28}$$

where $\underline{\mu}^{(*,2)} = \underline{\mu}^{(*,1)} + g(\underline{\mu}^{(*,1)})$ and $\underline{o}^{(N)} \xrightarrow{P} \underline{0}$. Since

$$N^{\frac{1}{2}}[\underline{\hat{\mu}}^{(N,1)} - \underline{\mu}^{(N,1)}] \xrightarrow{\mathcal{D}} N(\underline{0}, [P_M^*(\underline{\mu}^{(*,1)}) - P_L^*(\underline{\mu}^{(*,1)}]D^{-1}(\underline{\mu}^{(*,1)}) \tag{9.29}$$

and

$$\begin{aligned} &[I - P_L^*(\underline{\mu}^{(*,2)})][P_L^*(\underline{\mu}^{(*,1)}) - P_L^*(\underline{\mu}^{(*,1)})]D^{-1}(\underline{\mu}^{(*,1)})[I - P_L^*(\underline{\mu}^{(*,2)})]^T \\ &= [I - P_L^*(\underline{\mu}^{(*,2)})]P_M^*(\underline{\mu}^{(*,1)})D^{-1}(\underline{\mu}^{(*,1)})D(\underline{\mu}^{(*,2)})[I - P_L^*(\underline{\mu}^{(*,2)})]D^{-1}(\underline{\mu}^{(*,2)}), \end{aligned} \tag{9.30}$$

$$\begin{aligned} &N^{\frac{1}{2}}[\underline{\hat{\mu}}^{(N,2)} - \underline{\mu}^{(N,2)}] \\ &\xrightarrow{\mathcal{D}} N(\underline{0}, [I - P_L^*(\underline{\mu}^{(*,2)})]P_M^*(\underline{\mu}^{(*,1)})D^{-1}(\underline{\mu}^{(*,1)})D(\underline{\mu}^{(*,2)}) \\ &\quad [I - P_L^*(\underline{\mu}^{(*,2)})]D^{-1}(\underline{\mu}^{(*,2)})). \end{aligned} \tag{9.31}$$

Thus the asymptotic distribution of $\underline{\hat{\mu}}^{(N,2)}$ does not depend on N and the asymptotic covariance of $\underline{\hat{\mu}}^{(N,2)}$ can be estimated. Since

$$N^{-\frac{1}{2}}[\underline{m}(\underline{\hat{\mu}}^{(N,2)}) - \underline{m}(\underline{\mu}^{(N,2)})] = N^{\frac{1}{2}}[D(\underline{\mu}^{(*,2)})(\underline{\hat{\mu}}^{(N,2)} - \underline{\mu}^{(N,1)})] + \underline{o}^{(N)}, \tag{9.32}$$

where $\underline{o}^{(N)} \xrightarrow{P} \underline{0}$, one also has the equation

(9.33) $$N^{-\frac{1}{2}}[\underline{m}(\hat{\underline{\mu}}^{(N,2)}) - \underline{m}(\underline{\mu}^{(N,2)})]$$

$$\xrightarrow{\mathcal{D}} N(\underline{0}, D(\underline{\mu}^{(*,2)})[I - P_L^*(\underline{\mu}^{(*,2)})]P_L^*(\underline{\mu}^{(*,1)})D^{-1}(\underline{\mu}^{(*,1)})[I - P_L^*(\underline{\mu}^{(*,2)})]).$$

One common special case requires a slightly different analysis. Suppose that $\{\underline{n}^{(N,1)}\}$ is a sequence of random samples from $\{\underline{n}^{(N,2)}\}$ such that the conditions of Example 1.14 are satisfied. Thus

(9.34) $$\sum_{i \in I} n_i^{(N,1)} = n^{(N)},$$

(9.35) $$n^{(N)}/N \longrightarrow f,$$

and

(9.36) $$n_i^{(N,2)}/N \longrightarrow p_i.$$

By (1.127),

(9.37) $$N^{-\frac{1}{2}}(\underline{n}^{(N,1)} - \frac{n^{(N)}}{N}\underline{n}^{(N,2)}) \xrightarrow{\mathcal{D}} N(0, f(1 - f)[P - \underline{p} \otimes \underline{p}]),$$

where

(9.38) $$[P]_{ii'} = p_j\delta_{ii'}$$

and $\underline{p} = p_i : i \in I$.

If $M = R^I$, then $\hat{\underline{\mu}}^{(N,1)} = \{\log n_i^{(N,1)}\}$ and a Taylor expansion shows that

(9.39) $$N^{\frac{1}{2}}(\hat{\underline{\mu}}^{(N,1)} - \underline{\mu}^{(N,1)})$$

$$= N^{\frac{1}{2}}[(n_i^{(N,1)} - \frac{n^{(N)}}{N} n_i^{(N,2)})/(\frac{n^{(N)}}{N} n_i^{(N,2)})] + \underline{o}^{(N)},$$

where $\underline{o}^{(N)} \xrightarrow{P} \underline{0}$. Thus

(9.40) $$N^{\frac{1}{2}}(\hat{\underline{\mu}}^{(N,1)} - \underline{\mu}^{(N,1)}) \xrightarrow{\mathcal{D}} N(\underline{0}, \frac{1 - f}{f}(P^{-1} - \underline{e} \otimes \underline{e})).$$

Since (9.28) still applies, $D(\underline{\mu}^{(*,2)}) = P$, and

(9.41) $$[I - P_L^*(\underline{\mu}^{(*,2)})](P^{-1} - \underline{e} \otimes \underline{e})P[I - P_L^*(\underline{\mu}^{(*,2)})]P^{-1}$$

$$= [I - P_L^*(\underline{\mu}^{(*,2)})]P^{-1},$$

it follows that

(9.42) $$N^{\frac{1}{2}}(\hat{\underline{\mu}}^{(N,2)} - \underline{\mu}^{(N,2)}) \xrightarrow{\mathcal{D}} N(\underline{0}, \frac{1 - f}{f}[I - P_L^*(\underline{\mu}^{(*,2)})]D^{-1}(\underline{\mu}^{(*,2)})).$$

Therefore,

$$N^{-\frac{1}{2}}[\underline{m}(\hat{\underline{\mu}}^{(N,2)}) - \underline{m}(\underline{\mu}^{(N,2)})] = N^{-\frac{1}{2}}[\underline{m}(\hat{\underline{\mu}}^{(N,2)}) - \underline{m}^{(N,2)}] \tag{9.43}$$

$$\xrightarrow{\mathcal{D}} N(0, \frac{1-f}{f} D(\underline{\mu}^{(*,2)})[I - P_L^*(\underline{\mu}^{(*,2)})]).$$

Example 9.6. In the problems examined by Deming and Stephan (1940), $\underline{m}(\hat{\underline{\mu}}^{(1)}) = \underline{n}^{(1)}$ since $M = R^I$. If iterative proportional fitting is used to find $\underline{m}(\hat{\underline{\mu}}^{(2)})$, one sets $\underline{m}^{(0,1)} = \underline{n}^{(1)}$ and lets

$$m_{\underline{i}}^{(t,k+1)} = \frac{m_{\underline{i}}^{(t,k)}[n^{(2)}]_{\pi_{\{k\}}\underline{i}}^{\{k\}}}{[m]_{\pi_{\{k\}}\underline{i}}^{(t,k)}} \tag{9.44}$$

for $k \in \overline{d}$ and

$$\underline{m}^{(t+1,0)} = \underline{m}^{(t,d+1)} \tag{9.45}$$

This algorithm is the original Deming-Stephan iterative proportional fitting procedure.

In the examples given in tables 9.1 and 9.2, $d = 2$ and the equations are $m_{ij}^{(0,1)} = n_{ij}^{(1)}$,

$$m_{ij}^{(t,2)} = m_{ij}^{(t,1)} n_{i+}^{(2)} / m_{i+}^{(t,1)} , \tag{9.46}$$

$$m_{ij}^{(t,3)} = m_{ij}^{(t,2)} n_{+j}^{(2)} / m_{+j}^{(t,2)} , \tag{9.47}$$

and

$$m_{ij}^{(t+1,1)} = m_{ij}^{(t,3)} . \tag{9.48}$$

These equations correspond to (9.6), (9.7), and (9.8). Using these iterations, Deming and Stephan (1940) used three cycles to obtain the estimate of the population totals for table 9.3 given in table 9.4. The true totals are also shown for purposes of comparison. El-Badry and Stephan (1955) obtained the estimates in table 9.4 for the data in table 9.2. The fact that $n_{11}^{(1)} = 0$ results in an extended maximum-likelihood estimate for $\underline{m}(\underline{\mu}^{(2)})$, but this feature does not affect the iteration procedure.

In these examples, (9.42) and (9.43) apply. Thus the estimated asymptotic covariance of $\hat{\underline{\mu}}^{(2)}$ is $[(1 - f)/f][I - P_L^*(\hat{\underline{\mu}}^{(2)})]D^{-1}(\hat{\underline{\mu}}^{(2)})$, where f is the proportion of the population which was sampled. Similarly, the estimated asymptotic covariance of $\underline{m}^{(2)}$ is $[(1 - f)/f]D(\hat{\underline{\mu}}^{(2)})[I - P_L^*(\hat{\underline{\mu}}^{(2)})]$. The asymptotic standard deviations for the entries in table 9.3 are given in table 9.5. Computations use the basis $\{\underline{\nu}^{(k)}: k \in \overline{9}\} = \{\underline{\nu}(\{1\},i): i \in \overline{6}\} \cup \{\underline{\nu}(\{2\},j): j \in \overline{3}\}$ and the mapping from R^9 to L defined by

TABLE 9.3

ESTIMATED AND TRUE POPULATION TOTALS
FOR DATA IN TABLE 9.1[a]

State	Age				Population Total
	7-13	14-15	16-17	18-20	
Maine	72,260	15,620	11,000	6,160	105,040
	70,612	16,983	11,129	6,320	105,044
New Hampshire	31,760	8,020	5,020	3,100	47,900
	32,280	7,722	4,926	2,963	47,891
Vermont	32,160	8,700	5,400	2,380	48,640
	32,756	8,045	4,999	2,833	48,633
Massachusetts	209,840	49,040	33,600	22,820	315,300
	211,031	48,779	32,907	22,599	315,316
Rhode Island	33,240	7,000	3,340	3,000	46,580
	32,910	6,951	4,040	2,707	46,608
Connecticut	78,300	17,340	10,860	6,760	113,260
	77,931	17,218	11,238	6,843	113,230
Population Total	457,560	105,720	69,220	44.220	676,720
	457,520	105,698	69,239	44,265	676,722

[a]Top line is estimated frequency and bottom line is true frequency. Discrepancies in totals are partly due to rounding errors.

TABLE 9.4

ESTIMATED EMPLOYMENT STATUS ACCORDING TO AGE
FOR POPULATION OF NON-FARM MALES IN NEW JERSEY

Age	Military Labor Force	Civilian Labor Force		Not in the Labor Force	Total
		Employed	Unemployed		
14-19	7,598	4,712	680	14,073	27,063
20-24	6,732	11,865	970	3,255	22,822
25-29	3,338	16,073	676	2,674	22,761
30-34	2,264	17,947	497	1,847	22,555
35-39	1,150	17,834	482	1,819	21,285
40-44	409	16,739	465	1,775	19,388
45-49	176	14,214	437	1,909	16,736
50-54	98	12,456	572	2,635	15,761
55-59	30	10,105	623	3,087	13,845
60-64	10	7,635	513	3,463	11,621
65-69	0	4,330	419	4,338	9,087
70-74	10	2,112	139	4,439	6,700
75+	15	1,053	59	6,519	7,646
Total	21,830	137,075	6,532	51,833	217,270

TABLE 9.5

ESTIMATED ASYMPTOTIC STANDARD DEVIATIONS
FOR ENTRIES IN TABLE 9.3

State	Age			
	7-13	14-15	16-17	18-20
Maine	944	304	204	129
New Hampshire	551	238	112	80
Vermont	627	218	133	80
Massachusetts	1857	824	545	463
Rhode Island	559	205	63	70
Connecticut	1079	377	231	207

(9.49)
$$M\underline{x} = \sum_{k=1}^{9} x_k \underline{\nu}^{(k)} \quad .$$

Given M, one has

(9.50)
$$\frac{1-f}{f} D(\hat{\underline{\mu}}^{(2)})[I - P_M^*(\hat{\underline{\mu}}^{(2)})]$$
$$= \frac{1-f}{f} D(\hat{\underline{\mu}}^{(2)}) - D(\hat{\underline{\mu}}^{(2)})M[M^T D(\hat{\underline{\mu}}^{(2)})M]^{-1}M^T D(\hat{\underline{\mu}}^{(2)}).$$

Calculations based on this formula are not difficult. The asymptotic standard deviations are the square roots of the diagonal elements of the matrix of the right-hand side of (9.50) with respect to the standard basis. Comparison of tables 9.3 and 9.5 shows substantial discrepancies between the estimated and true population totals for the states of Maine, Vermont, and New Hampshire. Thus one must wonder how the original 5% sample was artificially generated.

CONCLUSION

This monograph is an attempt to apply the theory of linear manifolds to problems of contingency table analysis. The attempt has produced a substantial increase in the class of models available for analysis of frequency data, and it has provided much information concerning the properties of previously known models. These new results have been applied to data obtained by a variety of investigators in the social and biological sciences. Based on the examples of frequency data considered in this monograph, it appears that the methods developed in this paper make a substantial contribution to the practice of statistics. Whether this conclusion is justified can only be determined as more data are examined by the methods of this monograph. In addition, analysis of data may suggest new ways in which these techniques can be utilized and may provide insight into which results have the greatest usefulness. This monograph provides a new approach to contingency table analysis, but no book can provide a final solution to the problem of examining these tables.

Appendix A

BASIC MATHEMATICAL AND STATISTICAL RESULTS USED IN THE MONOGRAPH

This appendix is a summary of mathematical and statistical results frequently used in this monograph. Results are given without proof. The appendix consists of three parts. The first summarizes results in linear algebra found in Halmos (1958). The second part summarizes some definitions and theorems in analysis found in Loomis and Sternberg (1968). The third part is a summary of statistical results used in the monograph. It is based on material from Rao (1965). In each section, page references for all results are given in brackets. For example, the [3,4] following the definition of vector space in the first section refers to pages 3 and 4 of Halmos (1958).

LINEAR ALGEBRA

Linear algebra involves the study of properties of vector spaces. The following definition of a vector space over a field F may be employed.

DEFINITION A.1. *A vector space is a set* V *of elements called vectors satisfying the following axioms.*

To every pair, $\underline{x}$ *and* $\underline{y}$, *of vectors in* V *there corresponds a vector* $\underline{x} + \underline{y}$, *called the sum of* $\underline{x}$ *and* $\underline{y}$, *in such a way that the following four axioms are satisfied.*

(A.1) $$\underline{x} + \underline{y} = \underline{y} + \underline{x},$$

(A.2) $$\underline{x} + (\underline{y} + \underline{z}) = (\underline{x} + \underline{y}) + \underline{z},$$

there exists a unique vector $\underline{0} \in V$ *such that*

(A.3) $$\underline{x} + \underline{0} = \underline{x}$$

for any $\underline{x} \in V$, *and to each* $\underline{x} \in V$ *there exists a unique vector* $-\underline{x} \in V$ *such that*

(A.4) $$\underline{x} + (-\underline{x}) = \underline{0}\ .$$

To every pair, α *and* $\underline{x}$, *where* $\alpha \in F$ *and* $\underline{x} \in V$, *there corresponds a vector* $\alpha\underline{x} \in V$ *in such a manner that*

(A.5) $$\alpha(\beta\underline{x}) = (\alpha\beta)\underline{x} ,$$

(A.6) $$1\underline{x} = \underline{x} ,$$

for every $\underline{x} \in V$, *where* 1 *is the identity of* F,

(A.7) $$\alpha(\underline{x} + \underline{y}) = \alpha\underline{x} + \alpha\underline{y} ,$$

and

(A.8) $$(\alpha + \beta)\underline{x} = \alpha\underline{x} + \beta\underline{x} .$$

If F *is the field of real numbers, then* V *is a real vector space* [3-4].

Almost all vector spaces considered in this monograph are finite-dimensional. The finite-dimensional vector space depends on the following definitions.

DEFINITION A.2. *A finite set* $\{\underline{x}^{(i)}: i \in \overline{n}\}$ *of vectors is linearly dependent if there exist scalars* $\{\alpha_i: i \in \overline{n}\}$, *not all zero, such that*

(A.9) $$\sum_{i=1}^{n} \alpha_i\underline{x}^{(i)} = 0.$$

If $\{\underline{x}^{(i)}: i \in \overline{n}\}$ *is not linearly dependent, then it is linearly independent* [7].

DEFINITION A.3. *A basis of a vector space* V *is a set* X *of linearly independent vectors such that any element* $\underline{x} \in V$ *can be written as a linear combination* $\sum_{i=1}^{n} \alpha_i\underline{x}^{(i)}$ *of some set* $\{\underline{x}^{(i)}: i \in \overline{n}\}$ *of vectors in* V. *If* X *has a finite number of elements, then* V *is finite-dimensional* [10].

From now on in this section, all vector spaces will be assumed finite-dimensional. In such a vector space V, the number of elements in any basis X is a constant known as the dimension of V, or dim V. All vector spaces of dimension n over a field F are isomorphic to F^n; that is, there exists a one-to-one mapping T from a vector space V of dimension n to F^n such that

(A.10) $$T(\alpha_1\underline{x}^{(1)} + \alpha_2\underline{x}^{(2)}) = \alpha_1 T(\underline{x}^{(1)}) + \alpha_2 T(\underline{x}^{(2)})$$

[13-15].

A subset M of a vector space V may itself be a vector space. In such a case, M is known as a linear manifold or subspace. If $\dim V = n$ and $\dim M = m$, then $m \le n$ [16-18]. A linear manifold M may be specified by describing it as the set of all linear combinations of elements of a set $S \subset M$. In such a case, one says that $M = \text{span } S$. The linear manifold M is then the smallest manifold including S, in the sense that if $S \subset N$, then $M \subset N$ [17].

If M and N are two subspaces of V, then one may define a new manifold $M + N = \{\underline{x} + \underline{y}: \underline{x} \in M, \underline{y} \in N\}$. This manifold is the span of $M \cup N$ [18]. The set $M \cap N$ is also a linear manifold [17], and

(A.11) $$\dim M + \dim M = \dim (M + N) + \dim (M \cap N)$$

[19]. If $M \cap N = \{\underline{0}\}$, then $M + N$ is said to be the direct sum of M and N. It may be written as $M \oplus N$. In such a case, any element $\underline{x}$ of $M \oplus N$ has a unique representation

(A.12) $$\underline{x} = \underline{y} + \underline{z} ,$$

where $\underline{y} \in M$ and $\underline{z} \in N$ [29]. The dimension of $M \oplus N$ is $\dim M + \dim N$ [30].

Manipulations involving vector spaces are facilitated by linear transformations. Halmos (1958) considers only linear transformations from a vector space V to itself. This restriction will be followed in this section; however, no new principals are involved if linear transformations from a vector space V to a vector space W are considered. Loomis and Sternberg (1968) consider this case explicitly.

DEFINITION A.4. *A linear transformation* A *on a vector space* V *is a correspondence that assigns to every vector* $\underline{x} \in V$ *a vector* $A\underline{x} \in V$ *in such a way that*

(A.13) $$A(\alpha\underline{x} + \beta\underline{y}) = \alpha A\underline{x} + \beta A\underline{y}$$

[55]. The set of all such linear transformations is itself a vector space [57]. If the product of two linear transformations A and B is defined by the equation

(A.14) $$(AB)\underline{x} = A(B\underline{x}),$$

then

(A.15) $$A0 = 0A = 0 ,$$

(A.16) $$AI = IA = A ,$$

(A.17) $$A(B + C) = AB + AC ,$$

(A.18) $$(A + B)C = AC + BC ,$$

and

(A.19) $$A(BC) = (AB)C ,$$

where 0 is the zero transformation defined by

(A.20) $$O\underline{x} = \underline{0}$$

for all $\underline{x} \in V$ and I is the identity transformation defined by

(A.21) $$I\underline{x} = \underline{x}$$

for all $\underline{x} \in V$. It should be noted that AB need not equal BA [59].

If a transformation A on V is one-to-one, then A has an inverse A^{-1} such that $AA^{-1} = A^{-1}A = I$ [62]. In such a case, A is said to be invertible or nonsingular. If A and B are invertible, then

(A.22) $$(AB)^{-1} = B^{-1}A^{-1}$$

[63].

A linear transformation A on V may be described by means of its matrix $[A]$ with respect to a basis $\{\underline{x}^{(i)}: i \in \overline{n}\}$. The matrix is an $n \times n$ array $\{\alpha_{ij}\}$ such that

(A.23) $$A\underline{x}^{(j)} = \sum_{i=1}^{n} \alpha_{ij}\underline{x}^{(i)} .$$

The product of two matrices $[A] = \{\alpha_{ij}\}$ and $[B] = \{\beta_{ij}\}$ is $[C] = [AB] = \{\gamma_{ij}\}$, where

(A.24) $$\gamma_{ij} = \sum_{k=1}^{n} \alpha_{ik}\beta_{kj} .$$

The matrix $[I] = \{\delta_{ij}\}$, where δ_{ij} is the Kronecker delta function, and the matrix $0 = \{o_{ij}\}$, where $o_{ij} = 0$ [64-68].

A particular type of linear transformation used extensively in this monograph is the projection.

DEFINITION A.5. *If V is the direct sum of M and N, then the projection E of M along N is the transformation such that for any $\underline{z} \in V$, $E\underline{z}$ is the element of M such that for some $\underline{y} \in N$, $\underline{z} = E\underline{z} + \underline{y}$.*

If E is a projection of M along N, then $E\underline{z} = \underline{z}$ if $\underline{z} \in N$ and $E\underline{z} = \underline{0}$ if $\underline{z} \in N$. A linear transformation E is a projection on some subspace if and only if $E^2 = E$ [73].

Two subspaces may be used to describe a linear transformation A on a vector space V. The range $R(A)$ is the set of $\underline{x} \in V$ such that for some $\underline{y} \in V$, $\underline{x} = A\underline{y}$. The dimension $\rho(A)$ of $R(A)$ is called the rank of A. The null space $N(A)$ is the set of $\underline{x} \in V$ such that $A\underline{x} = 0$. The dimension $\nu(A)$ of $N(A)$ is called the nullity of A. The nullity and rank are related by the equation

(A.25) $$\rho(A) + \nu(A) = \dim V$$

[88-90].

The vector spaces examined in this monograph are all inner-product spaces; that is, they are vector spaces such that a function $(\cdot,\cdot)$ is defined on the Cartesian product $V \times V$ such that

(A.26) $$(\underline{x},\underline{y} = (\underline{y},\underline{x}),$$

(A.27) $$(\alpha_1\underline{x}^{(1)} + \alpha_2\underline{x}^{(2)},\underline{y}) = \alpha_1(\underline{x}^{(1)},\underline{y}) + \alpha_2(\underline{x}^{(2)},\underline{y}) ,$$

(A.28) $$||x||^2 = (\underline{x},\underline{x}) \geq 0 ,$$

and $(\underline{x},\underline{x}) = 0$ implies that $\underline{x} = 0$. This function is known as an inner product. The function $||\underline{x}|| = [(\underline{x},\underline{x})]^{\frac{1}{2}}$ is called the norm of $\underline{x}$ [121]. If $\underline{x}$ and $\underline{y}$ are in V, then Schwartz's inequality states that

(A.29) $$|(\underline{x},\underline{y})| \leq ||x||\ ||y||$$

[125].

Closely tied to the notion of an inner product is the concept of orthogonality. Two vectors $\underline{x}$ and $\underline{y}$ are orthogonal if $(\underline{x},\underline{y}) = \underline{0}$. If X is a set of vectors such that for $\underline{x} \in X$ and $\underline{y} \in X$, $(\underline{x},\underline{y}) = 0$ or $(\underline{x},\underline{y}) = 1$, depending on whether $\underline{x} \neq \underline{y}$ or $\underline{x} = \underline{y}$, then X is called an orthonormal set of vectors. If E is a set of vectors in V, then $E^{\perp}$, the orthogonal complement of E, is the set of vectors in V orthogonal to all elements of E [122-123]. The set $E^{\perp}$ is a linear manifold. If M is a linear manifold in V, then V is the direct sum of M and $M^{\perp}$ and $M^{\perp\perp} = M$ [129].

The adjoint of a linear transformation A on an inner-product space V is the linear transformation A^T such that for $\underline{x}$ and $\underline{y}$ in V,

(A.30) $$(A^T\underline{x},\underline{y}) = (\underline{x},A\underline{y}).$$

This linear transformation exists and the matrix $[A^T] = \{\alpha_{ji}\}$ if $[A] = \{\alpha_{ij}\}$ [132]. If $A = A^T$, then A is self-adjoint or symmetric. In this case, $\{\alpha_{ij}\} = \{\alpha_{ji}\}$ [135].

A symmetric linear transformation A on an inner-product space V is nonnegative definite if $(\underline{x},A\underline{x}) \geq 0$. If in addition $(\underline{x},A\underline{x}) = 0$ implies $\underline{x} = 0$, then A is positive definite. If A is positive definite, then it is invertible and the function defined by $(\underline{x},A\underline{y})$ for $\underline{x}$ and $\underline{y}$ in V is an inner product [140].

The projection P_M on a linear manifold M along $M^{\perp}$ is known as the orthogonal projection on M. A linear transformation E is an orthogonal projection on its range $R(E)$ if $E = E^2 = E^T$; that is, E must be idempotent and symmetric. If $M \subset N$, then

(A.31) $$P_M P_N = P_N P_M = P_M.$$

If M and N are orthogonal, then $M \cap N = \{\underline{0}\}$,

(A.32) $$P_M P_N = 0,$$

and

(A.33) $$P_{M \oplus N} = P_M + P_N$$

[146-149].

ANALYSIS

This section considers two problems, basic properties of a differential and the implicit function theorem.

DEFINITION A.6. *An open ball* $B_r(\underline{x})$ *of radius* r *with center* $\underline{x}$ *defined on a real inner-product space* V *is the set of* $\underline{y} \in V$ *such that* $||\underline{y} - \underline{x}|| < r$ [123].

DEFINITION A.7. *A set* A *is open if for every element* $\underline{x}$ *of* A *there exists an open ball* $B_r(\underline{x}) \subset A$. *If* $\underline{x} \in A$, *then* A *is a neighborhood of* $\underline{x}$ [124,137].

DEFINITION A.8. *If* F *is a mapping from a neighborhood* A *of* $\underline{x} \in V$ *to a real inner-product space* W, *then* F *has a differential* $dF_{\underline{x}}$ *at* $\underline{x}$ *if*

(A.34) $$F(\underline{x} + \underline{\xi}) = F(\underline{x}) + T(\underline{\xi}) + o(\underline{\xi}),$$

where T *is a linear mapping from* V *to* W *and* $o(\underline{\xi})/||\underline{\xi}|| \to 0$ *as* $\underline{\xi} \to \underline{0}$. *The mapping* T *is the differential* $dF_{\underline{x}}$ *and* F *is said to be an element of* $D_{\underline{x}}(V,W)$ [142-143].

The basic properties of differentials are summarized by the following theorem.

THEOREM A.1. *If* F *and* G *are in* $\mathcal{D}_{\underline{x}}(V,W)$, *then* $F + G \in \mathcal{D}_{\underline{x}}(V,W)$ *and*

(A.35) $$d(F + G)_{\underline{x}} = dF_{\underline{x}} + dG_{\underline{y}} .$$

If F *is linear,*

(A.36) $$dF_{\underline{x}} = F .$$

If F *is constant,*

(A.37) $$dF_{\underline{x}} = 0 .$$

[143].

It is also useful to note that if $F^i \in \mathcal{D}_{\underline{x}}(V,W_i)$ for $i \in I$, then $F = \{F^i: i \in I\} \in \mathcal{D}_{\underline{x}}(V,\prod_{i\in I} W_i)$ and $dF_{\underline{x}} = \{dF^i_{\underline{x}}: i \in I\}$ [152].

If F is a mapping from $A \subset V = \prod_{i \in I} V_i$ to W, then the partial differential $dF^i_{\underline{x}}$ is defined as the differential of the mapping $F^i_{\underline{x}}$ from V_i to W defined as

$$F^i_{\underline{x}}(\underline{y}_i) = F(\underline{z}), \tag{A.38}$$

where $\underline{z}_{i'} = \underline{x}_{i'}$ for $i' \neq i$, $\underline{z}_i = \underline{y}_i$, and $\underline{x} = \{\underline{x}_i : i \in I\}$. If F is differentiable at $\underline{x}$, then $dF^i_{\underline{x}}$ exists for $i \in I$ and

$$dF_{\underline{x}}(\underline{\xi}) = \sum_{i \in I} dF^i_{\underline{x}}(\underline{\xi}_i) \tag{A.39}$$

for $\underline{\xi} = \{\underline{\xi}_i : i \in I\}$ [153]. Conversely, F is differentiable at $\underline{x}$ and (A.39) holds if $dF^i_{\underline{x}}$ is continuous at $\underline{x}$ for each $i \in I$ [154].

If $F: V \to R$ has a relative minimum or relative maximum at $\underline{x}$ and $dF_{\underline{x}}$ exists, then $dF_{\underline{x}} = \underline{0}$ [161]. To determine whether a relative minimum or relative maximum is present, one considers the second differential $d^2F_{\underline{x}}$ at $\underline{x}$ if it exists. This mapping is from the space of mappings from V to R to the real line R. It is defined for $\underline{\xi}$ and $\underline{\eta}$ in V as

$$\begin{aligned}[d^2F_{\underline{x}}(\underline{\xi})](\underline{\eta}) &= d[dF_{\underline{x}}(\underline{\xi})]_{\underline{x}}(\underline{\eta}) \\ &= d[dF_{\underline{x}}(\underline{\eta})]_{\underline{x}}(\underline{\xi}).\end{aligned} \tag{A.40}$$

If $[d^2F_{\underline{x}}(\underline{\xi})](\underline{\xi}) \leq 0$ for $\underline{\xi} \in V$, with equality only if $\underline{\xi} = \underline{0}$, then F has a relative maximum at $\underline{x}$. If $[d^2F_{\underline{x}}(\underline{\xi})](\underline{\xi}) \geq \underline{0}$ for $\underline{\xi} \in V$, with equality only if $\underline{\xi} = \underline{0}$, then F has a relative minimum at $\underline{x}$ [186-191].

A basic tool used in this monograph is the implicit function theorem. The following version applies to any vector spaces considered in this monograph. The precise statement of the theorem involves Banach spaces, which are complete normed vector spaces [217].

THEOREM A.2. *Let V, W, and X be Banach spaces, let $A \times B$ be an open subset of $V \times W$, and let $G: A \times B \to X$ be a continuous differentiable mapping such that the partial differential $dG^2_{\langle \underline{v},\underline{w}\rangle}$ is continuous and invertible at $\langle \underline{v},\underline{w}\rangle$. Then there exist open balls M and N including $\underline{v}$ and $\underline{w}$, respectively, such that for each $\underline{\xi} \in M$ there is a unique $\underline{\eta} \in N$ such that $G(\underline{\xi},\underline{\eta}) = \underline{0}$. The function F uniquely defined near $\langle \underline{v},\underline{w}\rangle$ by the equation $G(\underline{\xi},F(\underline{\xi})) = \underline{0}$ is differentiable and*

$$dF_{\underline{v}} = -[dG^2_{\langle \underline{v},\underline{w}\rangle}]^{-1} \circ dG^1_{\langle \underline{v},\underline{w}\rangle} \tag{A.41}$$

[166,230].

STATISTICAL RESULTS

The statistical results needed involve asymptotic theory and the properties of quadratic forms involving normal random vectors.

The first set of results involves a sequence $\{X_n, Y_n\}$ of pairs of random variables. If $X_n \xrightarrow{\mathcal{D}} X$ and $Y_n \xrightarrow{P} 0$, then $X_n Y_n \xrightarrow{P} 0$. If $X_n \xrightarrow{\mathcal{D}} X$ and $Y_n \xrightarrow{P} c$, then $X_n + Y_n \xrightarrow{\mathcal{D}} X + c$, $X_n Y_n \xrightarrow{\mathcal{D}} cX$; and if $c \neq 0$, then $X_n/Y_n \xrightarrow{\mathcal{D}} X/c$. In addition, $(X_n, Y_n) \xrightarrow{\mathcal{D}} (X, c)$ [102-103].

The next result permits consideration of linear combinations of random variables to find limiting properties of random vectors. If $\{\underline{X}^{(n)}\}$ is a sequence of random vectors in R^I and $(\underline{\lambda}, \underline{X}^{(n)}) \xrightarrow{\mathcal{D}} (\underline{\lambda}, \underline{X})$ for all $\underline{\lambda} \in R^I$, then $\underline{X}^{(n)} \xrightarrow{\mathcal{D}} \underline{X}$ [103].

Continuous functions of random variables or random vectors are often of interest. If g is continuous and $X_n \xrightarrow{\mathcal{D}} X$, then $g(X_n) \xrightarrow{\mathcal{D}} g(X)$. If $X_n \xrightarrow{P} X$, then $g(X_n) \xrightarrow{P} g(X)$. In particular, if $X_n \xrightarrow{P} c$, then $g(X_n) \xrightarrow{P} g(c)$. If $X_n - Y_n \xrightarrow{P} 0$ and $Y_n \xrightarrow{\mathcal{D}} Y$, then $g(X_n) - g(Y_n) \xrightarrow{P} 0$ [104].

Quadratic forms of normal random vectors are often encountered. The basic result is that if $y_i \sim N(\mu_i, 1), Y = \{y_i: i \in I\}$, $\underline{\mu} = \{\mu_i: i \in I\}$, the y_i are independent, and $\delta^2 = (\underline{\mu}, A\underline{\mu})$, $(Y, AY) \sim \chi^2_{\rho(A)}(\delta^2)$ if and only if A is an orthogonal projection. If $(Y, A_1 Y) \sim \chi^2_{\nu_1}(\delta_1^2)$ and $(Y, A_2 Y) \sim \chi^2_{\nu_2}(\delta_2^2)$, then they are independently distributed if and only if $A_1 A_2 = 0$ [150-151].

A final result used frequently in asymptotic theory involves a sequence of random vectors $\{\underline{X}^{(n)}\} \subset R^I$ such that

$$n^{\frac{1}{2}}[\underline{X}^{(n)} - \underline{\mu}] \xrightarrow{\mathcal{D}} N(\underline{0}, \ddagger) \tag{A.42}$$

and a differentiable function g from R^I to R^J. One has

$$n^{\frac{1}{2}}[g(\underline{X}^{(n)}) - g(\underline{\mu})] \xrightarrow{\mathcal{D}} N(\underline{0}, dg_{\underline{\mu}} \ddagger dg^T_{\underline{\mu}}) \tag{A.43}$$

[321-322].

Appendix B

PROCEDURES FOR VERIFICATION THAT MAXIMUM-LIKELIHOOD ESTIMATES EXIST

This appendix is a supplement to chapter 2 intended for the statistician uncertain whether or not a maximum-likelihood estimate exists. The first section of the appendix contains useful corollaries for use with Poisson and multinomial models, together with some numerical examples. The second section contains an example of a conditional Poisson maximum-likelihood estimate, while the third section examines extended maximum-likelihood estimates for use when true maximum-likelihood estimates do not exist.

Example B.1. To illustrate the type of problem considered in this appendix, suppose that the table below is given:

6	8	0
4	5	0

.

If M is the additive manifold, then, as in Example 2.3, $\underline{\hat{m}}$ is $\{n_{i+}n_{+j}/n_{++}\}$ if the marginal totals n_{i+}, $i \in \overline{2}$, and n_{+j}, $j \in \overline{3}$, are positive. However, in this example, n_{+3} is 0. Although $\{n_{i+}n_{+j}/n_{++}\}$ still has the same marginal totals as $\underline{n}$, it is no longer the maximum-likelihood estimate of $\underline{m}$ since it corresponds to no finite $\underline{\mu} \in M$. Nevertheless, if $\underline{\mu} \in M$ and $\underline{m}(\underline{\mu})$ approaches $\{n_{i+}n_{+j}/n_{++}\}$, the Poisson log likelihood $\ell(\underline{n},\underline{\mu})$ approaches the supremum of $\ell(\underline{n},\underline{\mu})$ for $\underline{\mu} \in M$. Therefore, it is reasonable to say that $\underline{\hat{m}}^{(e)} = \{n_{i+}n_{+j}/n_{++}\}$ is an extended maximum-likelihood estimate of $\underline{m}$. It should be noted that no regular maximum-likelihood estimate of $\underline{m}$ exists which has some unexpected form since Theorem 2.3 implies that a necessary condition for the existence of $\underline{\hat{m}}$ is that $n_{i+} > 0$, $i \in \overline{2}$, and $n_{+j} > 0$, $j \in \overline{3}$.

THE POISSON AND MULTINOMIAL CASES

Determining whether the maximum-likelihood estimate $\hat{m}$ exists is a serious problem only when some cell counts are 0 but all marginal totals which $\underline{\hat{m}}$ must fit are positive. If all cell counts n_i are positive, Corollary 2.1 implies that $\underline{\hat{m}}$ exists, while if some marginal total to be fitted is 0, then, as noted in the remarks following Theorem 2.3, $\underline{\hat{m}}$ does not exist. In the cases which remain, the difficulty of the problem varies considerably, depending on the complexity of the model. In Example B.1, which treats the independence hypothesis in the 2×3 table, the maximum-likelihood estimate exists whenever the fitted marginal totals n_{i+}, $i \in \overline{2}$, and n_{+j}, $j \in \overline{3}$, are positive. In Example B.2, models for the $2 \times 2 \times 2$ table are given for which $\hat{\underline{m}}$ can fail to exist even though all fitted marginal totals are positive. However, in this example it is still possible to provide simple necessary and sufficient conditions for the existence of $\hat{\underline{m}}$. On the other hand, in the $3 \times 3 \times 2$ table of Example B.3, no simple necessary and sufficient conditions are available. To help deal with such situations, a series of corollaries to Theorems 2.2 and 2.3 are presented which are used in later chapters to determine whether maximum-likelihood estimates exist.

Example B.2. Consider the $2 \times 2 \times 2$ table under the model

(B.1) $$\mu_{ijk} = a_{ij} + b_{ik} + c_{jk}, \ i \in \overline{2}, \ j \in \overline{2}, \ k \in \overline{2}.$$

It is easily seen that the maximum-likelihood estimate satisfies the equations $\hat{m}_{ij+} = n_{ij+}$, $\hat{m}_{i+k} = n_{i+k}$, and $\hat{m}_{+jk} = n_{+jk}$, where i, j, and k are either 1 or 2. Tc show that $\hat{\underline{m}}$ can fail to exist even if each of the marginal totals are positive, the linear manifold $M^{\perp}$ is determined and used to find a necessary and sufficient condition for the existence of $\hat{\underline{m}}$. The manifold $M^{\perp}$ is generated by $\underline{\mu}^*$, where

(B.2) $$\mu^*_{ijk} = -1 \text{ if } i + j + k \text{ is even,}$$
$$= +1 \text{ if } i + j + k \text{ is odd .}$$

Using tabular notation, one may write

(B.3) $\underline{\mu}^* =$

k = 1

i \ j	1	2
1	+1	-1
2	-1	+1

k = 2

i \ j	1	2
1	-1	+1
2	+1	-1

,

Suppose $J = \{<i,j,k>: i + j + k \text{ is odd}\}$. Let $K = \{<i,j,k>: i + j + k \text{ is even}\}$. Then a maximum-likelihood estimate of $\underline{\mu}$ exists if and only if either $I_1 \subset J$ or $I_1 \subset K$, where I_1 is defined as in Corollary 2.3. To verify this result, observe that if $I_1 \subset J$, then $n_{ijk} + \frac{1}{2}\mu^*_{ijk} > 0$ for each $<i,j,k> \in \overline{2} \times \overline{2} \times \overline{2}$. Thus the maximum likelihood estimate exists. A similar result holds if $I_1 \subset K$. On the other hand, if $<i,j,k> \in J$, $<i,j,k> \in K$, and $n_{ijk} = \overline{n_{ijk}} = 0$, then for any c,

(B.4) $$n_{ijk} + c\mu_{ijk} = c ,$$

while

(B.5) $$n_{\overline{ijk}} + c\mu_{\overline{ijk}} = -c .$$

Thus there exists no $\underline{\delta} \in M^{\perp}$ such that $n_{ijk} + \delta_{ijk} > 0$ for every $\langle i,j,k\rangle \in \overline{2} \times \overline{2} \times \overline{2}$. Hence the maximum-likelihood estimate does not exist.

To illustrate this result, it is useful to consider several different values of $\underline{n}$. To do so, the tabular notation of (B.3) is employed. If

(B.6) $$\underline{n} = \begin{array}{|cc|}\hline 5 & 8 \\ 9 & 13 \\ \hline\end{array} \quad \begin{array}{|cc|}\hline 4 & 8 \\ 6 & 10 \\ \hline\end{array} ,$$

then the maximum-likelihood estimate exists. Since the table has no zero cells, Corollary 2.1 may be employed. If

(B.7) $$\underline{n} = \begin{array}{|cc|}\hline 0 & 8 \\ 9 & 13 \\ \hline\end{array} \quad \begin{array}{|cc|}\hline 4 & 8 \\ 6 & 10 \\ \hline\end{array} ,$$

then $I_1 \subset J$. Thus the maximum-likelihood estimate exists. In fact, whenever there is only one zero cell, the maximum-likelihood estimate exists. When there are two cells which are zero, then the maximum-likelihood estimate may or may not exist. If

(B.8) $$\underline{n} = \begin{array}{|cc|}\hline 0 & 0 \\ 9 & 13 \\ \hline\end{array} \quad \begin{array}{|cc|}\hline 4 & 8 \\ 6 & 10 \\ \hline\end{array} ,$$

the estimate does not exist. In fact, $\langle 1,1,1\rangle \in J$ and $\langle 1,2,1\rangle \in K$. The result may also be verified by observing that if

(B.9) $$\underline{\mu}^{*} = \begin{array}{|cc|}\hline -1 & -1 \\ 0 & 0 \\ \hline\end{array} \quad \begin{array}{|cc|}\hline 0 & 0 \\ 0 & 0 \\ \hline\end{array} ,$$

then $\underline{\mu}^{*} \in M$. Another case in which the maximum-likelihood estimate does not exist occurs when

(B.10) $$\underline{n} = \begin{array}{|cc|}\hline 0 & 8 \\ 9 & 13 \\ \hline\end{array} \quad \begin{array}{|cc|}\hline 4 & 8 \\ 6 & 0 \\ \hline\end{array} .$$

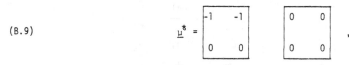

Here $\langle 1,1,1\rangle \in J$ and $\langle 2,2,2\rangle \in K$. The problem is that $n_{111} + c\mu_{111}$ and $n_{222} + c\mu_{222}$ are of opposite signs. However, if

(B.11) $$\underline{n} = \begin{array}{|cc|}\hline 0 & 8 \\ 9 & 0 \\ \hline\end{array} \quad \begin{array}{|cc|}\hline 4 & 8 \\ 6 & 10 \\ \hline\end{array},$$

then the maximum-likelihood does exist. In fact, both $\langle 1,1,1\rangle$ and $\langle 2,2,1\rangle$ are in J. The result also follows directly from Theorem 2.2 since the elements of $\underline{n} + \underline{\mu}$ are all positive.

The manifold M consists of all $\underline{\mu}$ of the form

(B.12) $$\mu_{ijk} = \alpha + \beta_i + \gamma_j + \delta_k + \varepsilon_{ij} + \lambda_{ik} + \nu_{jk},$$

where

(B.13) $$\sum_{i=1}^{2} \beta_i = \sum_{j=1}^{2} \gamma_j = \sum_{k=1}^{2} \delta_k = \sum_{i=1}^{2} \varepsilon_{ij} = \sum_{j=1}^{2} \varepsilon_{ij}$$
$$= \sum_{i=1}^{2} \lambda_{ik} = \sum_{k=1}^{2} \lambda_{ik} = \sum_{j=1}^{2} \nu_{jk} = \sum_{k=1}^{2} \nu_{jk} = 0.$$

Instead of M, one might wish to consider $\overline{M}$, where $\overline{M}$ is the submanifold of M consisting of $\underline{\mu}$ such that $\underline{\mu}$ has the form given by (B.12) and $\beta_i = 0$ for $i \in \overline{2}$. In this case $\overline{M}^{\perp}$ is spanned by $\underline{\mu}^*$ and $\underline{\overline{\mu}}$, where

(B.14) $$\underline{\overline{\mu}} = \begin{array}{|cc|}\hline 1 & 1 \\ -1 & -1 \\ \hline\end{array} \quad \begin{array}{|cc|}\hline 1 & 1 \\ -1 & -1 \\ \hline\end{array}.$$

Suppose $J_1 = \{\langle 1,1,1\rangle, \langle 1,2,2\rangle\}$, $J_2 = \{\langle 2,1,1\rangle, \langle 2,2,2\rangle\}$, $J_3 = \{\langle 2,2,1\rangle, \langle 2,1,2\rangle\}$, and $J_4 = \{\langle 1,2,1\rangle, \langle 1,1,2\rangle\}$. Then a maximum-likelihood estimate exists unless either (1) $J_1 \cap I_1 \neq \phi$ and $J_2 \cap I_1 \neq \phi$ or (2) $J_3 \cap I_1 \neq \phi$ and $J_4 \cap I_1 \neq \phi$. To verify this result, note that if $\underline{\delta} \in \overline{M}$, then $\underline{\delta} = a\underline{\mu}^* + b\underline{\overline{\mu}}$ for some a and b. If $\langle i,j,k\rangle \in J_1$, then $\delta_{ijk} = a + b$. If $\langle i,j,k\rangle \in J_2$, then $\delta_{ijk} = -a - b$. If $\langle i,j,k\rangle \in J_3$, then $\delta_{ijk} = a - b$. If $\langle i,j,k\rangle \in J_4$, then $\delta_{ijk} = -a + b$. Thus δ_{ijk} cannot be positive for both $\langle i,j,k\rangle \in J_1$ and $\langle i,j,k\rangle \in J_2$ or for both $\langle i,j,k\rangle \in J_3$ and $\langle i,j,k\rangle \in J_4$. On the other hand, suppose that neither condition (1) nor condition (2) is satisfied. Without loss of generality, suppose $I_1 \cap J_1 = I_1 \cap J_3 = \phi$. Then if $b = 0$ and $-1 < a < 0$, it follows that $n_{ijk} + \delta_{ijk} > 0$ for every $\langle i,j,k\rangle \in \overline{2} \times \overline{2} \times \overline{2}$. Thus a maximum-likelihood estimate exists if $\underline{n}$ is given by (B.6), (B.7), (B.8), or (B.11). An estimate does not exist if $\underline{n}$ is given by (B.10). It should be noted that a maximum-likelihood estimate does not exist if $\underline{\mu} \in M$ and $\underline{n}$ satisfies (B.8).

Example B.3. The $3 \times 3 \times 2$ table is somewhat more complicated than the $2 \times 2 \times 2$ table, but existence questions are still relatively simple to resolve. Suppose that M is the manifold of $\underline{\mu}$ which satisfy (B.1) for $i \in \overline{3}$, $j \in \overline{3}$, and $k \in \overline{2}$. Suppose

(B.15)
$$\underline{n} = \begin{array}{|ccc|}\hline 0 & 5 & 4 \\ 4 & 0 & 3 \\ 6 & 0 & 2 \\ \hline\end{array} \qquad \begin{array}{|ccc|}\hline 3 & 0 & 2 \\ 3 & 4 & 0 \\ 0 & 7 & 4 \\ \hline\end{array} .$$

To determine whether $\hat{\underline{\mu}}$ exists, it is necessary to proceed in stages. First observe that $\underline{\delta}^{(1)} \in M^{\perp}$, where

(B.16)
$$\underline{\delta}^{(1)} = \begin{array}{|ccc|}\hline 1 & -1 & 0 \\ 0 & 0 & 0 \\ -1 & 1 & 0 \\ \hline\end{array} \qquad \begin{array}{|ccc|}\hline -1 & 1 & 0 \\ 0 & 0 & 0 \\ 1 & -1 & 0 \\ \hline\end{array} .$$

Note now that

(B.17)
$$\underline{n} + \underline{\delta}^{(1)} = \begin{array}{|ccc|}\hline 1 & 4 & 4 \\ 4 & 0 & 3 \\ 5 & 1 & 2 \\ \hline\end{array} \qquad \begin{array}{|ccc|}\hline 2 & 1 & 2 \\ 3 & 4 & 0 \\ 1 & 6 & 4 \\ \hline\end{array} .$$

Next consider $\underline{\delta}^{(2)} \in M$, where

(B.18)
$$\underline{\delta}^{(2)} = \begin{array}{|ccc|}\hline 0 & 0 & 0 \\ 0 & 1 & -1 \\ 0 & -1 & 1 \\ \hline\end{array} \qquad \begin{array}{|ccc|}\hline 0 & 0 & 0 \\ 0 & -1 & 1 \\ 0 & 1 & -1 \\ \hline\end{array} .$$

The vector $\underline{\delta}^{(1)} + \frac{1}{2}\underline{\delta}^{(2)} \in M$ and

(B.19)
$$\underline{n} + (\underline{\delta}^{(1)} + \tfrac{1}{2}\underline{\delta}^{(2)}) = \begin{array}{|ccc|}\hline 1 & 4 & 4 \\ 4 & \frac{1}{2} & 2\frac{1}{2} \\ 5 & \frac{1}{2} & 2\frac{1}{2} \\ \hline\end{array} \qquad \begin{array}{|ccc|}\hline 2 & 1 & 2 \\ 3 & 3\frac{1}{2} & \frac{1}{2} \\ 1 & 6\frac{1}{2} & 3\frac{1}{2} \\ \hline\end{array} .$$

Thus $\hat{\underline{\mu}}$ exists.

In general, rules for existence of maximum-likelihood estimates are more difficult to find than in the preceding examples. Nevertheless, Theorems 2.2 and 2.3 and Corollaries 2.1, B.1, B.2, and B.3 are readily applied to problems in which a specific $\underline{n}$ and M are considered. Further applications are given in later chapters, particularly in chapters 5 and 7. An extended form of the maximum-likelihood estimate is discussed at the end of this appendix. This extended estimate always exists, although it does not have all the properties of the maximum-likelihood estimate.

COROLLARY B.1. *Suppose* M_1 *and* M_2 *are linear manifolds such that* $M_1 \subset M_2$. *Suppose* $\hat{\underline{\mu}}^{(i)}$ *is the maximum-likelihood estimate for* $\underline{\mu} \in M^{(i)}$, $i \in \overline{2}$. *If* $\hat{\underline{\mu}}^{(2)}$ *exists, then* $\hat{\underline{\mu}}^{(1)}$ *exists. If* $\hat{\underline{\mu}}^{(1)}$ *does not exist, then* $\hat{\underline{\mu}}^{(2)}$ *does not exist.*

Proof. If $\hat{\underline{\mu}}^{(2)}$ exists, then there exists $\underline{\delta} \in M^{\perp}$ such that $n_i + \delta_i > 0$ for each $i \in I$. Since $M_2^{\perp} \subset M_1^{\perp}$, $\underline{\delta} \in M_1$. Therefore, $\hat{\underline{\mu}}^{(1)}$ exists. The converse follows immediately.||

COROLLARY B.2. *Suppose* $I_1 = \{i \in I\colon n_i = 0\}$. *Let* $\rho\colon R^I \longrightarrow R^{I_1}$ *satisfy* $\rho\{\mu_i\colon i \in I\} = \{\mu_i\colon i \in I_1\}$. *Let* $\rho(M^{\perp}) = \{\rho\underline{\mu}\colon \underline{\mu} \in M^{\perp}\}$. *If* $\rho(M^{\perp}) = R^{I_1}$, *then the maximum-likelihood estimate of* $\underline{\mu}$ *exists.*

Proof. Suppose that $(\underline{n},\underline{\mu}) = 0$, $\underline{\mu} \in M$, $\underline{\mu} \neq \underline{0}$, and $\mu_i \leq 0$ for every $i \in I$. Then $\mu_i = 0$ for every $i \in I - I_1$. If $((\cdot,\cdot))$ denotes the standard inner product for R^{I_1}, then $((\rho\underline{\mu},\rho\underline{\nu})) = (\underline{\mu},\underline{\nu})$ for $\underline{\nu} \in M^{\perp}$. Thus $\rho\underline{\mu} \perp \rho(M^{\perp}) = R^{I_1}$. Therefore, $\rho\underline{\mu} = \underline{0}$. Thus $\underline{\mu} = \underline{0}$, a contradiction. Hence the maximum-likelihood estimate exists.||

COROLLARY B.3. *Suppose* $I_0 = \{i \in I\colon n_i > 0\}$. *Let* $\pi\colon R^I \longrightarrow R^{I_0}$ *satisfy* $\pi\{\mu_i\colon i \in I\} = \{\mu_i\colon i \in I_0\}$. *Let* $\pi = \{\pi\underline{\mu}\colon \underline{\mu} \in M\}$. *Suppose* π *has dimension* k *and* $I - I_0$ *has* h *elements. If* $p - k = h$, *then the maximum-likelihood estimate of* $\underline{\mu}$ *does not exist. If* $p - k = 0$, *then the maximum-likelihood estimate exists.*

Proof. The kernel of π has dimension $p - k$. This kernel is a submanifold of $\{\underline{\mu} \in R^I\colon \mu_i = 0\ \forall i \in I_0\}$. This latter manifold has dimension h. If $p - k = h$, then the kernel is equal to $\{\underline{\mu} \in R^I\colon \mu_i = 0\ \forall i \in I_0\}$. Hence a $\underline{\mu} \in M$ exists such that $\mu_i \leq 0$ for each $i \in I$, $(\underline{n},\underline{\mu}) = 0$, and $\underline{\mu} \neq \underline{0}$. By Theorem 2.3, the maximum-likelihood estimate of $\underline{\mu}$ does not exist. If $p - k = 0$, then the kernel of π is $\underline{0}$. Since no $\underline{\mu} \in M$ which is not equal to $\underline{0}$ exists such that $(\underline{n},\underline{\mu}) = 0$ and $\mu_i \leq 0$ for $i \in I$, the maximum-likelihood estimate exists.||

THE CONDITIONAL POISSON CASE

An example of maximum-likelihood estimation in the conditional Poisson case is provided by the $2 \times 2 \times 2$ table with M defined as in (B.1). Suppose that sampling is conditional on $n_{ij+} = c_{ij}$ for $\langle i,j\rangle \in \overline{2} \times \overline{2}$ and $n_{i+k} = d_{ik}$ for $\langle i,k\rangle \in \overline{2} \times \overline{2}$, where for $\langle i,j\rangle \in \overline{2} \times \overline{2}$,

(B.20)
$$n_{ij+} = n_{ij1} + n_{ij2},$$

and for $\langle i,k\rangle \in \overline{2} \times \overline{2}$,

(B.21) $$n_{i+k} = n_{i1k} + n_{i2k} .$$

In this case, N consists of all $\underline{\mu}$ such that if $\langle i,j,k\rangle \in \overline{2} \times \overline{2} \times \overline{2}$, then

(B.22) $$\mu_{ijk} = a_{ij} + b_{ik} .$$

This manifold has dimension 6. Consequently, $M - N$ has dimension 1. It is spanned by $\underline{\nu}$, where

(B.23) $$\underline{\nu} = \begin{bmatrix} +1 & -1 \\ +1 & -1 \end{bmatrix} \quad \begin{bmatrix} -1 & +1 \\ -1 & +1 \end{bmatrix} .$$

Since $N^{\perp}$ is the direct sum of $M - N$ and $M^{\perp}$, $N^{\perp}$ is spanned by $\underline{\mu}^*$ and $\underline{\nu}$, where $\underline{\mu}^*$ is defined as in (B.2). By Theorem 2.5, $\hat{\underline{\mu}}^{(c)}$ exists if and only if for some $\underline{\bar{n}} \in S(\underline{c})$, $(\underline{\bar{n}} - \underline{n},\underline{\nu}) > 0$, and for some $\underline{n}^* \in S(\underline{c})$, $(\underline{n}^* - \underline{n},\underline{\nu}) < 0$.

Example B.2. Consider the previous examples of 2 x 2 x 2 tables which were used to examine Poisson maximum-likelihood estimates. If $\underline{n}$ is defined as in (B.6), then $\underline{n} + \underline{\nu}$ and $\underline{n} - \underline{\nu}$ are both in $S(P_N\underline{n})$. Thus the maximum-likelihood estimate exists. This result also follows from Corollary 2.2. If $\underline{n}$ is defined as in (B.7), then $\underline{n} + \underline{\mu}^* \in S(P_N\underline{n})$ and $P_M(\underline{n} + \underline{\mu}^*) = P_M\underline{n}$. Since all elements of $\underline{n} + \underline{\mu}^*$ are positive, it follows from Corollary 2.2 that the maximum-likelihood estimate exists. This result can also be verified by noting that both $\underline{n} + \underline{\mu}^* + \underline{\nu}$ and $\underline{n} + \underline{\mu}^* - \underline{\nu}$ are in $S(P_N\underline{n})$. If $\underline{n}$ is defined as in (B.8), then $\underline{n} + \underline{\mu}^* - \underline{\nu}$ and $\underline{n} - \underline{\mu}^* + \underline{\nu}$ are both in $S(P_N\underline{n})$. Consequently, the maximum-likelihood estimate exists. In contrast, the Poisson maximum-likelihood estimate does not exist if $\underline{n}$ satisfies (B.8). If $\underline{n}$ is defined as in (B.10), then $\underline{n} + \underline{\mu}^* + \underline{\nu}$ and $\underline{n} - \underline{\mu}^* - \underline{\nu}$ are both in $S(P_N\underline{n})$. Hence the maximum-likelihood estimate exists for the conditional Poisson case, even though it does not for the Poisson case. If $\underline{n}$ is defined as in (B.11), then $\underline{n} + \underline{\mu}^* + \underline{\nu}$ and $\underline{n} + \underline{\mu}^* - \underline{\nu}$ are in $S(P_N\underline{n})$. The maximum-likelihood estimate therefore exists. In fact, the maximum-likelihood estimate exists for all five examples.

An example in which neither a conditional Poisson nor a Poisson maximum likelihood estimate exists is the observation vector

(B.24) $$\underline{n} = \begin{bmatrix} 0 & 8 \\ 0 & 13 \end{bmatrix} \quad \begin{bmatrix} 4 & 8 \\ 6 & 10 \end{bmatrix} .$$

In this case $\underline{n} + a\underline{\nu} + b\underline{\mu}^* \in S(P_N\underline{n})$ implies $a \geq 0$. Thus no maximum-likelihood estimate exists for the conditional Poisson model. That no maximum-likelihood estimate exists for the Poisson model may be seen by comparing (B.8) and (B.24).

In this example, whenever a maximum-likelihood estimate exists for the Poisson model, a maximum-likelihood estimate exists for the conditional Poisson model. This result follows since whenever a Poisson maximum-likelihood estimate exists, there exists an f equal to 1/2 or -1/2 such that all elements of $\underline{n} + f\underline{\mu}^*$ are positive. In this case, $\underline{n} + f\underline{\mu}^* + \frac{1}{2}\underline{\nu}$ and $\underline{n} + f\underline{\mu}^* - \frac{1}{2}\underline{\nu}$ are both in $S(P_N\underline{n})$. Consequently, the conditional Poisson maximum-likelihood estimate exists.

The example just employed is unusually simple since $M - N$ has dimension 1. Generally, existence of maximum-likelihood estimates is more difficult to establish. In addition, the need to compute summations to find $\underline{m}(\underline{\mu},\underline{c})$ makes numerical work more difficult than in the Poisson case. Fortunately, an alternative approach exists. The maximum-likelihood estimates corresponding to Poisson sampling may be employed. As shown in chapter 4, these estimates have useful asymptotic properties even under conditional Poisson sampling.

EXTENDED MAXIMUM-LIKELIHOOD ESTIMATES

In the Poisson and multinomial cases, when the maximum-likelihood estimate $\hat{\underline{m}}$ of $\underline{m}$ does not exist, an estimate $\hat{\underline{m}}^{(e)}$ may be found which has many properties associated with $\underline{m}$.

The estimate has the property that as $\underline{m}(\underline{\mu})$ approaches $\hat{\underline{m}}^{(e)}$, where $\underline{\mu}$ is in M, then the log likelihood $\ell(\underline{n},\underline{\mu})$ approaches the supremum of $\ell(\underline{n},\underline{\mu})$ for $\underline{\mu} \in M$.

To find $\hat{\underline{m}}^{(e)}$, let $C = \{\underline{\mu} \in M: \underline{\mu} \neq \underline{0}, (\underline{n},\underline{\mu}) = 0, \mu_i \leq 0 \ \forall i \in I\}$. If the maximum-likelihood estimate does not exist, then C is not empty. If $\underline{\mu} \in C$, let $J(\underline{\mu}) = \{i \in I: \mu_i < 0\}$. Let $I^* = \cup_{\underline{\mu}\in C} J(\underline{\mu})$ and $I_0 = I - I^*$. If $\underline{n} \neq \underline{0}$, then I_0 is nonempty. Let $\rho\{x_i: i \in I\} = \{x_i: i \in I_0\}$. Suppose $M^* = \rho M$. Let

$$\ell^{(0)}(\underline{n},\underline{\mu}^*) = \sum_{i\in I_0} [n_i\mu_i^* - \exp(\mu_i^*)], \tag{B.25}$$

where $\underline{\mu}^* \in M^*$. Then $\ell^{(0)}(\underline{n},\underline{\mu}^*)$ has a maximum at some finite $\hat{\underline{\mu}} \in M^*$. Otherwise, there exists $\underline{\mu} \in M$ such that $(\underline{n},\underline{\mu}) = 0$, $\mu_i \leq 0$ for $i \in I_0$, and $\rho\underline{\mu} \neq \underline{0}$. If $i \in I^*$, there exists $\underline{\mu}^{(i)} \in C$ such that $\mu_i^{(i)} < 0$. Let

(B.26) $$\underline{n} = \sum_{i \in I} \underline{\mu}^{(i)} .$$

Then for large enough $k > 0$, $(\underline{\mu} + k\underline{n}, \underline{n}) = 0$, $\underline{\mu} + k\underline{n} \neq 0$, and $\mu_i + kn_i \leq 0$ for every $i \in I$. For some $i \in I_0$, $\mu_i + kn_i < 0$. Hence $i \in I^*$, a contradiction. Thus $\ell^{(0)}(\underline{n}, \underline{\mu}^*)$ has a maximum at $\hat{\underline{\mu}}^*$.

The maximum of $\ell^{(0)}(\underline{n}, \underline{\mu}^*)$ and the supremum of $\hat{\ell}^{(p)}(\underline{n}, \underline{\mu})$ coincide. In fact,

(B.27) $$\hat{\ell}^{(p)}(\underline{n}, \underline{\mu} + k\underline{n}) \longrightarrow \ell^{(0)}(\underline{n}, \rho\underline{\mu})$$

as $k \to 0$. Here $\underline{n}$ is defined as in the preceding paragraph. Since $\hat{\ell}^{(p)}(\underline{n}, \underline{\mu} + k\underline{n})$ is an increasing function of k, the desired equality follows.

Given this result, one may define $\hat{\underline{\mu}}^{(e)}$ as

(B.28) $$\hat{\mu}_i^{(e)} = \hat{\mu}_i^* \text{ if } i \in I_0 ,$$
$$= -\infty \text{ if } i \in I^* .$$

One may define $\hat{\underline{m}}^{(e)}$ as

(B.29) $$\hat{m}_i^{(e)} = \exp(\hat{\mu}_i^*) \text{ if } i \in I_0 ,$$
$$= 0 \qquad \text{ if } i \in I^* .$$

If $\underline{\mu} \in M$, then

(B.30) $$(\hat{\underline{m}}^{(e)}, \underline{\mu}) = [\hat{\underline{m}}^*, \rho(\underline{\mu})] = [\rho(\underline{n}), \rho(\underline{\mu})] = (\underline{n}, \underline{\mu}).$$

Here $[\cdot,\cdot]$ represents the conventional inner product of R^{I_0} and $\hat{\underline{m}}^* = \{\exp(\mu_i^*)\}$. Thus $P_M\hat{\underline{m}}^{(e)} = P_M\underline{n}$. It therefore follows that $\underline{m}^{(e)}$ has all the properties of $\hat{\underline{m}}$ except that $\hat{m}_i^{(e)} = 0$ for $i \in I^*$. If C is empty, then $\hat{\underline{m}}^{(e)}$ and $\hat{\underline{m}}$ coincide. Thus $\hat{\underline{m}}^{(e)}$ may be regarded as an extension of $\hat{\underline{m}}$.

If $\underline{c}$ is an element of R^I, then the maximum-likelihood estimate of $(\underline{c}, \underline{\mu})$ is $(\underline{c}, \hat{\underline{\mu}})$. If $c_i = 0$ when $i \in I^*$, then $(\underline{c}, \hat{\underline{\mu}}^{(e)})$ is well defined, provided that $0 \cdot \infty$ is assumed to be 0. Thus estimates of linear functions of $\underline{\mu}$ may be obtained from extended maximum-likelihood estimates.

Example B.4. As an example of extended maximum-likelihood estimation, suppose that $I = \overline{2} \times \overline{2} \times \overline{2}$ and M consists of all satisfying (B.1). Suppose $\underline{n}$ satisfies (B.8). In this case, $C = \{a\underline{\mu}^{\#}: a > 0\}$, where $\underline{\mu}^{\#}$ satisfies (B.9). If $\underline{\mu} \in C$, then $J(\underline{\mu}) = \{\langle 1,1,1\rangle, \langle 1,2,1\rangle\}$. Thus $I^* = \{\langle 1,1,1\rangle, \langle 1,2,1\rangle\}$. The problem now reduces to computation of the maximum-likelihood estimate of $\rho\underline{\mu}$ for $\underline{\mu} \in M$ and $\rho\underline{n} \in R^{I_0}$, where $I_0 = \overline{2} \times \overline{2} \times \overline{2} - \{\langle 1,1,1\rangle, \langle 1,2,1\rangle\}$ and $\rho\{x_i: i \in I\} = \{x_i: i \in I_0\}$. This estimate may be found by use of methods developed in chapter 7.

Appendix C

PROOF OF THEOREM 3.1

To prove (a), consider the function $h^{(t)}(\alpha)$ defined by (3.3). Since $\underline{\mu}^{(t)} \neq \underline{\mu}^*$, $\underline{s}^{(t)} \neq \underline{0}$.

It can be shown that $h^{(t)}(\alpha)$ is a strictly concave function of α with a unique maximum for $\alpha = \bar{\alpha}^{(t)}$, where $\bar{\alpha}^{(t)} > 0$. First observe that

$$(C.1) \qquad c = \sup_{\{\underline{\mu}:||\underline{\mu}-\underline{\mu}^*||=1\}} f(\underline{\mu}) < f(\underline{\mu}^*) .$$

The function $f(\underline{\mu})$ is strictly concave, so if $||\underline{\mu} - \underline{\mu}^*|| = k > 1$, then

$$(C.2) \qquad f(\underline{\mu}^*) - f(\underline{\mu}) < k[f(\underline{\mu}^*) - f(\underline{\mu}/k)] \leq kc .$$

Thus as $||\underline{\mu}|| \to \infty$, $f(\underline{\mu}) \to -\infty$. In particular, as $|\alpha| \to \infty$, $f(\underline{\mu}^{(t)} + \alpha\underline{s}^{(t)}) \to -\infty$. Therefore, $h^{(t)}(\alpha)$ is a strictly concave function with a unique maximum at some point $\bar{\alpha}^{(t)}$.

To show that $\bar{\alpha}^{(t)} > 0$, observe that

$$(C.3) \qquad \frac{d}{d\alpha} h^{(t)}(0) = df_{\underline{\mu}^{(t)}}(\underline{s}^{(t)}) = -[d^2f_{\underline{\mu}^{(t)}}(\underline{s}^{(t)})](\underline{s}^{(t)}) > 0.$$

Thus $h^{(t)}(\alpha)$ is increasing at 0. Consequently, $\bar{\alpha}^{(t)} > 0$.

If $\alpha^{(t)}$ is equal to $\bar{\alpha}^{(t)}$, then $df_{\underline{\mu}^{(t+1)}}(\underline{s}^{(t)})$ is 0. Since $f(\underline{\mu}^{(t+1)})$ is then greater than $f(\underline{\mu}^{(t)})$, condition (3.4) is satisfied. By continuity, (3.4) is satisfied for $\alpha^{(t)}$ in some open interval $A^{(t)}$ containing $\bar{\alpha}^{(t)}$.

To prove (b), assume that $\underline{\mu}^{(t)} \neq \underline{\mu}^*$ if $t \geq 0$. Then $\underline{s}^{(t)} \neq \underline{0}$. Since $h^{(t)}(\alpha)$ is strictly concave, $df_{\underline{\mu}^{(t+1)}}(\underline{s}^{(t)}) = 0$ only when $f(\underline{\mu}^{(t+1)}) > f(\underline{\mu}^{(t)})$. By (3.4), $\{f(\underline{\mu}^{(t)})\}$ is a strictly increasing sequence. By (C.2), the set $\{\underline{\mu}: f(\underline{\mu}) \geq f(\underline{\mu}^{(0)})\}$ is bounded. Thus $\{\underline{\mu}^{(t)}\}$ is bounded. Since $\{f(\underline{\mu}^{(t)})\}$ is bounded above by $f(\underline{\mu}^*)$, $f(\underline{\mu}^{(t+1)}) - f(\underline{\mu}^{(t)})$ approaches 0 as t approaches ∞. If $\{\underline{\mu}^{(t)}\}$ does not converge to $\underline{\mu}^*$, then there exists a subsequence $\{\underline{\mu}^{(t)}: t \in K\}$ which converges to some $\underline{\nu} \in M$ such that $\underline{\nu} \neq \underline{\mu}^*$. It follows that $\{\underline{s}^{(t)}: t \in K\}$ converges to $d^2f_{\underline{\nu}}^{-1}(df_{\underline{\nu}})$, where $||d^2f_{\underline{\nu}}^{-1}(df_{\underline{\nu}})|| > 0$. Since $\{\underline{\mu}: f(\underline{\mu}) \geq f(\underline{\mu}^{(0)})$ is bounded, $\{\alpha^{(t)}: t \in K\}$ is bounded.

By Taylor's theorem, for each $t \in K$ there exists $\beta^{(t)}$, $0 < \beta^{(t)} < \alpha^{(t)}$, such that

(C.4) $$\frac{1}{\alpha^{(t)}}[f(\underline{\mu}^{(t+1)}) - f(\underline{\mu}^{(t)})] = df_{\underline{\mu}^{(t)}+\beta^{(t)}\underline{s}^{(t)}}(\underline{s}^{(t)}).$$

A convergent subsequence of triples $\{<\underline{\mu}^{(t)},\alpha^{(t)},\beta^{(t)}>: t \in J\}$ may now be found. If the limit point is $<\underline{\nu},\alpha,\beta>$, then two possibilities exist. If $\alpha > 0$, (3.4) implies that $f(\underline{\nu} - \alpha d^2f_{\underline{\nu}}^{-1}(df_{\underline{\nu}})) - f(\underline{\nu}) > 0$. Thus $\{f(\underline{\mu}^{(t+1)}) - f(\underline{\mu}^{(t)}): t \in J\}$ has a positive limit, a contradiction since $f(\underline{\mu}^{(t+1)}) - f(\underline{\mu}^{(t)})$ converges to 0. On the other hand, if $\alpha = 0$, then $\beta = 0$ and (3.4) and (C.4) imply that

(C.5) $$|df_{\underline{\nu}}(d^2f_{\underline{\nu}}^{-1}(df_{\underline{\nu}}))| \leq - bdf_{\underline{\nu}}(d^2f_{\underline{\nu}}^{-1}(df_{\underline{\nu}})),$$

a contradiction since $b < 1$. The only remaining possibility is that $\{\underline{\mu}^{(t)}: t \geq 0\}$ converges to $\underline{\mu}^*$.

To prove (c), observe that for some $\underline{\xi}^{(t)}$ on the line segment between $\underline{\mu}^{(t)}$ and $\underline{\mu}^{(t)} + \underline{s}^{(t)}$,

(C.6) $$df_{\underline{\mu}^{(t)}+\underline{s}^{(t)}}(s^{(t)}) = df_{\underline{\mu}^{(t)}}(\underline{s}^{(t)}) + [d^2f_{\underline{\xi}^{(t)}}(\underline{s}^{(t)})](\underline{s}^{(t)}).$$

Note that $df_{\underline{\mu}^{(t)}}(\underline{s}^{(t)})$ is $-[d^2f_{\underline{\mu}^{(t)}}(\underline{s}^{(t)})](\underline{s}^{(t)})$ and $d^2f_{\underline{\mu}}$ is continuous in $\underline{\mu}$. Thus

(C.7) $$df_{\underline{\mu}^{(t)}+\underline{s}^{(t)}}(\underline{s}^{(t)}) - o^{(t)}||\underline{s}^{(t)}||^2 ,$$

where $o^{(t)} \to 0$ as $t \to \infty$. By Taylor's theorem,

(C.8) $$f(\underline{\mu}^{(t)}) = f(\underline{\mu}^{(t)} + \underline{s}^{(t)}) - df_{\underline{\mu}^{(t)}+\underline{s}^{(t)}}(\underline{s}^{(t)}) + \tfrac{1}{2}[d^2f_{\underline{\xi}^{(t)}}(\underline{s}^{(t)})](\underline{s}^{(t)})$$

for some $\underline{\xi}^{(t)}$ on the line segment between $\underline{\mu}^{(t)}$ and $\underline{\mu}^{(t)} + \underline{s}^{(t)}$. If the maximum eigenvalue of $d^2f_{\underline{\mu}^*}$ is $-\lambda$, then for sufficiently large t,

(C.9) $$|df_{\underline{\mu}^{(t)}+\underline{s}^{(t)}}(\underline{s}^{(t)})| < \varepsilon \, ||\underline{s}^{(t)}||^2$$

and

(C.10) $$f(\underline{\mu}^{(t)} + \underline{s}^{(t)}) - f(\underline{\mu}^{(t)}) \geq (\tfrac{1}{2}\lambda - \varepsilon)||\underline{s}^{(t)}||^2 ,$$

where ε is chosen so that $\varepsilon < b(\frac{1}{2}\lambda - \varepsilon)$. If (C.9) and (C.10) hold, $\alpha^{(t)}$ may be chosen to be 1.

To prove (d), suppose $\alpha^{(t)} = 1$ for $t \geq t_0$ and $d^3f_{\underline{\mu}}$ exists and is continuous at $\underline{\mu}^*$. Then for $t \geq t_0$,

$$\underline{\mu}^{(t+1)} - \underline{\mu}^* = \underline{\mu}^{(t)} - \underline{\mu}^* + \underline{s}^{(t)} = \underline{\mu}^{(t)} - \underline{\mu}^* - [d^2f_{\underline{\mu}^{(t)}}]^{-1}(df_{\underline{\mu}^{(t)}}). \tag{C.11}$$

Expansion of $[d^2f_{\underline{\mu}^{(t)}}]^{-1}$ about $\underline{\mu}^*$ yields

$$[d^2f_{\underline{\mu}^{(t)}}]^{-1} = [d^2f_{\underline{\mu}^*}]^{-1} - [d^2f_{\underline{\mu}^*}]^{-1}[d^3f_{\underline{\mu}^*}(\underline{\mu}^{(t)} - \underline{\mu}^*)][d^2f_{\underline{\mu}^*}]^{-1} + o_1(\underline{\mu}^{(t)} - \underline{\mu}^*), \tag{C.12}$$

where o_1 is a mapping from M to the space of linear transformations from M^* to M such that

$$\frac{||o_1(\underline{\mu})||}{||\underline{\mu}||} \longrightarrow 0 \tag{C.13}$$

as $\underline{\mu} \to \underline{0}$. Expansion of $df_{\underline{\mu}^{(t)}}$ about $\underline{\mu}^*$ yields

$$df_{\underline{\mu}^{(t)}} = d^2f_{\underline{\mu}^*}(\underline{\mu}^{(t)} - \underline{\mu}^*) + \tfrac{1}{2}[d^3f_{\underline{\mu}^*}(\underline{\mu}^{(t)} - \underline{\mu}^*)](\underline{\mu}^{(t)} - \underline{\mu}^*) + o_2(\underline{\mu}^{(t)} - \underline{\mu}^*). \tag{C.14}$$

Here o_2 is a function from M to M^* such that as $\underline{\mu} \to \underline{0}$,

$$\frac{||o_2(\underline{\mu})||}{||\underline{\mu}||^2} \longrightarrow 0. \tag{C.15}$$

Thus

$$\underline{\mu}^{(t+1)} - \underline{\mu}^* = \tfrac{1}{2}[d^2f_{\underline{\mu}^*}]^{-1} \circ [d^3f_{\underline{\mu}^*}(\underline{\mu}^{(t)} - \underline{\mu}^*)](\underline{\mu}^{(t)} - \underline{\mu}^*) + o_3(\underline{\mu}^{(t)} - \underline{\mu}^*), \tag{C.16}$$

where o_3 is a mapping from M to M such that as $\underline{\mu} \to \underline{0}$,

$$\frac{||o_3(\underline{\mu})||}{||\underline{\mu}||^3} \longrightarrow 0. \tag{C.17}$$

Since $\underline{\mu}^{(t)} - \underline{\mu}^* \to \underline{0}$, it follows from (C.16) that

$$\limsup_{t \to \infty} \frac{||\underline{\mu}^{(t+1)} - \underline{\mu}^*||}{||\underline{\mu}^{(t)} - \underline{\mu}^*||^2} \leq \tfrac{1}{2} ||[d^2f_{\underline{\mu}^*}]^{-1} \circ d^3f_{\underline{\mu}^*}||. \tag{C.18}$$

This proof is now complete. ||

REFERENCES

AITCHISON, J. and SILVEY, S. D. (1951). The generalization of probit analysis to the case of multiple responses. Biometrika 44 131-140.

ANDERSON, T. W. and GOODMAN, L. A. (1957). Statistical inference about Markov chains. Ann. Math. Statist. 28 89-110.

ANSCOMBE, F. J. and TUKEY, J. W. (1963). The examination and analysis of residuals. Technometrics 5 141-160.

ASHFORD, J. R. (1959). An approach to the analysis of data for semi-quantal responses in biological assay. Biometrics 15 573-581.

BAHADUR, R. R. (1967). Rates of convergence of estimates and test statistics. Ann. Math. Statist. 38 303-324.

BERKSON, J. (1944). Application of the logistic function to bioassay. J. Amer. Statist. Assoc. 39 357-365.

--------. (1955). Maximum likelihood and minimum χ^2 estimates of the logistic function. J. Amer. Statist. Assoc. 50 130-162.

BILLINGSLEY, P. (1968). Convergence of Probability Measures. Wiley, New York.

BIRCH, M. M. (1963). Maximum likelihood in three-way contingency tables. J. Roy. Statist. Soc. Ser. B 25 220-233.

BIRKHOFF, G. and MACLANE, S. (1941). A Survey of Modern Algebra. Macmillan, New York.

BISHOP, Y. M. M. (1967). Multidimensional contingency tables: cell estimates. Ph.D. thesis, Department of Statistics, Harvard University.

--------. (1969). Full contingency tables, logits, and split contingency tables. Biometrics 25 383-400.

--------. (1970) Effects of collapsing multidimensional contingency tables. Unpublished MS delivered at Hanover, W. Germany.

--------, and FIENBERG, S. E. (1969). Incomplete two-dimensional contingency tables. Biometrics 25 119-128.

BJORCK, A. (1967a). Solving linear least squares problems by Gram-Schmidt orthogonalization. BIT 7 1-21.

--------. (1967b). Iterative refinement of linear least squares solution I. BIT 7 257-278.

--------. (1968). Iterative refinement of linear least squares solutions II. BIT 8 8-30.

BLACKWELL, D. and GIRSHICK, M. A. (1954). Theory of Games and Statistical Decisions. Wiley, New York.

BLISS, C. I. (1935). The calculation of the dosage-mortality curve. Ann. Applied Biol. 22 134-167.

BLYTH, C. R. and HUTCHINSON, D. W. (1960). Tables of Neyman-shortest unbiased confidence intervals for the Poisson parameter. Biometrika 48 191-194.

--------. (1961). Tables of Neyman-shortest unbiased confidence intervals for the binomial parameter. Biometrika 47 381-391.

BOCK, R. D. (1968). Estimating multinomial response relations. Contributions to Statistic and Probability: Essays in Memory of Sumarendra Nath Roy. Edited by R. C. Bose. University of North Carolina Press, Chapel Hill.

BOROSH, I. and FRAENKEL, A. S. (1966). Exact solutions of linear equations with rational coefficients by congruence techniques. Math. Comp. 20 107-112.

BRADLEY, R. A. and TERRY, M. E. (1952). The rank analysis of incomplete block designs: I. The method of paired comparisons. Biometrika 39 324-345.

BREIMAN, L. (1968). Probability. Addison-Wesley, Reading, Mass.

BUSVINE, J. R. (1938). The toxicity of ethylene oxide to *Calandra oryzae, C. granaria, Tribolium castaneum, and Cimex lectularius*. Ann. Appl. Biol. 25 605-632.

COCHRAN, W. G. (1952). The χ^2 test of goodness of fit. Ann. Math. Statist. 23 315-345.

--------. (1954). Some methods for strengthening the common χ^2 tests. Biometrics 10 417-451.

--------. (1963). Sampling Techniques. 2d ed., Wiley, New York.

--------, and COX, G. M. (1957). Experimental Designs. 2d ed., Wiley, New York.

CORNFIELD, J., KANNEL, W., and TRUETT, J. (1967). A multivariate analysis of the risk of coronary heart disease in Framingham. J. Chron. Dis. 20 511-524.

COURANT, R. and HILBERT, D. (1953). Methods of Mathematical Physics, Vol. 1, Interscience, New York.

COX, D. R. (1958a). Some problems connected with statistical inference. Ann. Math. Statist. 29 357-372.

--------. (1958b). The regression analysis of binary sequences. J. Roy. Statist. Soc. Ser. B 20 215-232.

--------. (1966). Some procedures connected with the logistic qualitative response curve. Research Papers in Statistics: Essays in Honor of J. Neyman's 70th Birthday. Edited by F. N. David. Wiley, London.

--------, and SNELL, E. J. (1968). A general definition of residuals. J. Roy. Statist. Soc. Ser. B. 30 248-265.

CRAMÉR, H. (1946). Mathematical Methods of Statistics. Princeton University Press, Princeton, N. J.

CURTISS, J. H. (1942). A note on the theory of moment generating functions. Ann. Math. Statist. 13 430-433.

DARROCH, J. N. (1962). Interactions in multifactor contingency tables. J. Roy. Statist. Soc. Ser. B 24 251-263.

DAVID, H. A. (1963). The Method of Paired Comparisons. Hafner, New York.

DAVIDON, W. C. (1959). Variable Metric Method for Minimization. A.E.C. Research and Development Report, ANL - 5990 (Rev.).

DAWBER, T. R., MEADORS, G. F., and MOORE, F. E. (1951). Epidemiological approaches to heart disease: the Framingham study. Amer. J. Publ. Health 41 279-286.

DEMING, W. E. (1943). Statistical Adjustment of Data. Wiley, New York.

--------, and STEPHAN, F. F. (1940). On a least squares adjustment of a sampled frequency table when the expected marginal totals are known. Ann. Math. Statist. 11 427-444.

DINCULÉANU, N. (1967). Vector Measures. Pergamon Press, Oxford.

DRAPER, N. R. and SMITH, H. (1966). Applied Regression Analysis. Wiley, New York.

DUNN, O. J. (1961). Multiple comparisons among means. J. Amer. Statist. Assoc. 56 52-64.

DYKE, G. V. and PATTERSON, H. D. (1952). Analysis of factorial arrangements when the data are proportions. Biometrics 8 1-12.

EATON, M. L. (1969). A pseudo-inverse and its application in statistics. Unpublished MS, University of Chicago, Chicago, Ill.

--------. (1970). Gauss-Markov estimation for multivariate linear models: a coordinate-free approach. Ann. Math. Statist. 41 528-538.

EL-BADRY, M. A. and STEPHAN, F. F. (1955). On adjusting sample tabulations to census counts. J. Amer. Statist. Assoc. 50 738-762.

FELLER, W. (1966). An Introduction to Probability Theory and Its Applications, Vol. 2. Wiley, New York.

--------. (1968). An Introduction to Probability Theory and Its Applications, Vol. 1. 3d ed., Wiley, New York.

FIELLER, E. C. (1940). The biological standardization of insulin. J. Roy. Statist. Soc. Suppl. 7 1-54.

FIENBERG, S. E. (1970). Quasi-independence and maximum likelihood estimation in incomplete contingency tables. J. Amer. Statist. Assoc. 65 1610-1616.

--------. (1971). The analysis of incomplete multiway contingency tables. Biometrics 28 177-202.

--------. (1972). The multiple-recapture census for closed populations and incomplete 2^k contingency tables. Biometrika 59 591-603.

FINNEY, D. J. (1947). Principles of biological assay. J. Roy. Statist. Soc. Suppl. 9 46-76.

--------. (1964). Statistical Method in Biological Assay. Griffin, London.

--------. (1971). Probit Analysis. 3d ed., Cambridge University Press, Cambridge.

FISHER, R. A. (1935a). The Design of Experiments. Oliver and Boyd, Edinburgh.

--------. (1935b). The logic of inductive inference. J. Roy. Statist. Soc. 98 39-54.

--------. (1935c). Appendix to Bliss, C. I.: The case of zero survivors. Ann. Appl. Biol. 22 164-165.

--------, THORNTON, H. G., and MACKENZIE, W. A. (1922). The accuracy of the plating method of estimating the density of bacterial populations. Ann. Appl. Biol. 9 325-359.

FLEMING, W. H. (1965). Functions of Several Variables. Addison-Wesley, Reading, Mass.

FREEMAN, M. R. and TUKEY, J. W. (1950). Transformations related to the angular and the square root transformations. Ann. Math. Statist. 21 607-611.

FRIEDLANDER, D. (1961). A technique for estimating a contingency table, given the marginal totals and some supplementary data. J. Roy. Statist. Soc. Ser. A 124 412-420.

GABRIEL, K. R. (1966). Simultaneous test procedures for multiple comparisons on categorical data. J. Amer. Statist. Assoc. 61 1081-1096.

--------. (1969). Simultaneous test procedures--Some theory of multiple comparisons. Ann. Math. Statist. 40 224-250.

GART, J. J. (1970). Point and interval estimation of the common odds ratio in the combination of 2 x 2 tables with fixed marginals. Biometrika 57 471-475.

--------, and ZWEIFEL, J. R. (1967). On the bias of various estimators of the logit and its variance with application to quantal bioassay. Biometrika 54 181-187.

GARWOOD, F. (1941). The application of maximum likelihood to dosage-mortality curves. Biometrika 32 46-58.

GLASS, D. V. (1954). Social Mobility in Britain. Free Press, Glencoe, Ill.

GOOD, I. J. (1958). The interaction algorithm and practical Fourier analysis. J. Roy. Statist. Soc. Ser. B. 20 361-372.

--------, GOVER, T. N., and MITCHELL, G. J. (1970). Exact distribution for χ^2 and for the likelihood-ratio statistic for the equiprobable multinomial distribution. J. Amer. Statist. Assoc. 65 267-283.

GOODMAN, L. A. (1961). Modification of the Dorn-Stouffer-Tibbitts method for "testing the significance of comparisons in sociological data." Amer. J. Sociol. 66 355-363.

--------. (1964). Simultaneous confidence limits for cross-product ratios in contingency tables. J. Roy. Statist. Soc. Ser. B 26 86-102.

--------. (1965). On the statistical analysis of mobility tables. Amer. J. Sociol. 70 564-584.

--------. (1966). On estimating the logit and its variance in binomial and multinomial populations and in contingency tables. Unpublished MS, University of Chicago.

--------. (1968). The analysis of cross-classified data: independence, quasi-independence, and interactions in contingency tables with or without missing entries. J. Amer. Statist. Assoc. 63 1091-1131.

--------. (1969a). How to ransack social mobility tables and other kinds of cross-classification tables. Amer. J. Sociol. 75 1-40.

--------. (1969b). On partitioning χ^2 and detecting partial association in three-way contingency tables. J. Roy. Statist. Soc. Ser. B 31 486-498.

--------. (1970). The multivariate analysis of qualitative data: interactions among multiple classifications. J. Amer. Statist. Assoc. 65 226-256.

--------. (1971a). A simple simultaneous test procedure for quasi-independence in contingency tables. Appl. Statist. 20 165-177.

--------. (1971b). Partitioning of χ^2, analysis of marginal contingency tables, and estimation of expected frequencies in multidimensional contingency tables. J. Amer. Statist. Assoc. 66 339-344.

--------. (1972a). A general model for the analysis of surveys. Amer. J. Sociol. 77 1035-1086.

GOODMAN, L. A. (1972b). Some multiplicative models for the analysis of cross-classified data. Sixth Berk. Symp. Math. Stat. & Prob. 1 649-696.

GROSSWALD, E. (1966). Topics from the Theory of Numbers. Macmillan, New York.

GURLAND, J., LEE, J., and DAHM, P. A. (1960). Polychotomous quantal responses in biological assay. Biometrics 16 382-398.

HABERMAN, S. J. (1971). A conditioned Newton-Raphson algorithm for function minimization. Unpublished MS, University of Chicago, Chicago, Ill.

--------. (1972). Log-linear fit for contingency tables. Appl. Statist. 21 218-225.

HALMOS, P. R. (1958). Finite Dimensional Vector Spaces. 2d ed., Van Nostrand, Princeton.

HARRIS, J. A. (1910). On the selective elimination occurring during the development of the fruits of *Staphylea*. Biometrika 7 452-504.

HAYNAM, G. E., GOVINDARAJULU, Z., and LEONE, F. C. (1970). Tables of the cumulative non-central chi-square distribution. Selected Tables in Mathematical Statistics. Edited by H. L. Harter and D. B. Owen. Markham, Chicago.

HOEL, P. G. (1962). Introduction to Mathematical Statistics. 3d ed., Wiley, New York.

HOFFMAN, K. and KUNZE, R. (1961). Linear Algebra. Prentice Hall, Englewood Cliffs, N.J.

HUREWICZ, W. and WALLMAN, H. (1941). Dimension Theory. Princeton University Press, Princeton.

KALLIANPUR, G. and RAO, C. R. (1955). On Fisher's lower bound to asymptotic variance of a consistent estimate. Sankya 15 331-342.

KAVAN, G. (1937). Factor Tables Giving the Complete Decomposition into Prime Factors of all Numbers up to 256,000. Macmillan, London.

KRUSKAL, W. (1968a). When are Gauss-Markov and least squares estimators identical? A coordinate-free approach. Ann. Math. Statist. 39 70-75.

--------. (1968b). Notes on analysis of variance. Unpublished MS, University of Chicago, Chicago, Illinois.

KULLBACK, S. (1959). Information Theory and Statistics. Wiley, New York.

--------, and IRELAND, C. T. (1968). Contingency tables with given marginals. Biometrika 55 179-188.

LEHMANN, E. L. (1959). Testing Statistical Hypotheses. Wiley, New York.

--------, and SCHEFFÉ, H. (1950). Completeness, similar regions, and unbiased estimation. Sankya 10 305-340.

LESLIE, P. H. (1951). The calculation of X^2 for an $r \times c$ contingency table. Biometrics 32 284-293.

LEWONTIN, R. C. and FELSENSTEIN, J. (1965). The robustness of homogeneity tests in $2 \times n$ tables. Biometrics 21 19-33.

LOÈVE, M. M. (1963). Probability Theory. 3d ed., Van Nostrand, Princeton, N.J.

LOOMIS, L. and STERNBERG, S. (1968). Advanced Calculus. Addison-Wesley, Reading, Mass.

MANTEL, N. (1970). Incomplete contingency tables. Biometrics 26 291-304.

MILLER, L. C., BLISS, C. I., and BRAUN, H. A. (1939). The assay of digitalis. I. Criteria for evaluating various methods using frogs. J. Amer. Pharm. Assoc. 28 644-657.

MILLER, R. G. (1966). Simultaneous Statistical Inference. McGraw-Hill, New York.

MITRA, S. K. (1958). On the limiting power function of the frequency chi-square test. Ann. Math. Statist. 29 1221-1233.

MOSTELLER, F. (1951a). Remark on the method of paired comparisons. I. The least squares solutions assuming equal standard deviations and equal correlations. Psychometrika 16 3-9.

--------. (1951b). Remark on the method of paired comparisons. III. A test of significance for paired comparisons when equal standard deviations and equal correlations are assumed. Psychometrika 16 207-218.

MULLER, T. and MAYHALL, J. T. (1971). Analysis of contingency table data on *torus mandibularis* using a log linear model. Amer. J. Phys. Anthropol. 34 149-153.

NOETHER, G. E. (1955). On a theorem of Pitman. Ann. Math. Statist. 26 64-68.

NOVITSKI, E. and SANDLER, I. (1957). Are all products of spermatogenesis regularly functional? Proc. Nat. Acad. Sci. 43 318-324.

ODOROFF, C. L. (1970). A comparison of minimum logit chi-square estimation and maximum likelihood estimation contingency in 2 x 2 x 2 and 3 x 2 x 2 contingency tables: tests for interaction. J. Amer. Statist. Assoc. 65 1617-1631.

PARTHASARATHY, K. R. (1967). Probability Measures on Metric Spaces. Academic Press, New York.

PATNAIK, P. B. (1949). The noncentral χ^2 and F distributions and their applications. Biometrika 36 202-232.

PEARSON, E. S. and HARTLEY, H. O. (1966). Biometrika Tables for Statisticians. 3d ed., Cambridge University Press, Cambridge.

PEARSON, K. (1900). On a criterion that a system of deviations from the probable in the case of a correlated system of variables is such that it can be reasonably supposed to have arisen in random sampling. Phil. Mag. (5) 50 157-175.

PERLMAN, M. D. and DAS GUPTA, S. (1974). On the power of the noncentral F-test: effect of additional variates on Hotelling's T^2-test. To appear in J. Amer. Statist. Assoc. 69.

PLACKETT, R. L. (1962). A note on interactions in contingency tables. J. Roy. Statist. Soc. Ser. B 24 162-166.

RALSTON, A. (1965). A First Course in Numerical Analysis. McGraw-Hill, New York.

RAO, C. R. (1963). Criteria of estimation in large samples. Sankya Ser. A 25 189-206.

--------. (1965). Linear Statistical Inference and Its Applications. Wiley, New York.

REIERSØL, O. (1961). Linear and non-linear multiple comparisons in logit analysis. Biometrika 48 359-365.

ROY, S. N., and KASTENBAUM, M. A. (1956). On the hypothesis of "no interaction." Ann. Math. Statist. 27 749-757.

SCHAFFER, R. S. (1971). Personal communication.

SCHEFFÉ, H. (1959). The Analysis of Variance. Wiley, New York.

SILVERSTONE, H. (1957). Estimating the logistic curve. J. Amer. Statist. Assoc. 52 567-577.

SNEDECOR, G. W. and COCHRAN, W. G. (1967). Statistical Methods. 6th ed., Iowa State University Press, Ames, Iowa.

STEPHAN, F. F. (1942). An iterative method of adjusting sample frequency tables when expected marginal totals are known. Ann. Math. Statist. 13 166-178.

SVALASTOGA, K. (1959). Prestige, Class, and Mobility. William Heineman, London.

THEIL, H. (1970). On the estimation of relationships involving qualitative variables. Amer. J. Sociol. 76 103-154.

THURSTONE, L. L. (1927). A law of comparative judgement. Psychol. Rev. 34 273-286.

TOIVANEN, P. and HIRVONEN, T. (1970). Sex ratio of newborns: preponderance of males in toxemia of pregnancy. Science 170 187-188.

TUKEY, J. W. (1962). The future of data analysis. Ann. Math. Statist. 33 1-67.

VAN EEDEN, C. (1963). Conditional limit distributions for the entries in a 2 x k contingency table. Classical and Contagious Discrete Distributions. Edited by G. P. Patil. Pergamon Press, Oxford.

--------, and RUNNENBURG, J. T. (1960). Conditional limit distributions for the entries in a 2 x 2 table. Statistica Neerlandica 14 111-126.

WAGNER, S. S. (1970). Maximum likelihood estimate for contingency tables with zero diagonal. J. Amer. Statist. Assoc. 65 1362-1383.

WALKER, S. H. and DUNCAN, D. B. (1967). Estimation of the probability of an event as a function of several independent variables. Biometrika 54 167-179.

WILKINSON, J. H. (1965). The Algebraic Eigenvalue Problem. Oxford University Press, London.

WILKS, S. S. (1938). The large-sample distribution of the likelihood ratio for testing composite hypotheses. Ann. Math. Statist. 26 64-68.

--------. (1962). Mathematical Statistics. Wiley, New York.

WILNER, D. M., WALKLEY, R. P. and COOK, S. W. (1955). Human Relations in Interracial Housing: A Study of the Contact Hypothesis. University of Minnesota Press, Minneapolis, Minn.

WORKING, H. and HOTELLING, H. (1929). Application of the theory of error to the interpretation of trends. J. Amer. Statist. Assoc. Mar. Suppl. 73-85.

YARNOLD, J. K. (1970). The minimum expectation in X^2 goodness of fit tests and the accuracy of approximations for the null distribution. J. Amer. Statist. Assoc. 65 865-886.

YATES, F. (1948). The analysis of contingency tables with groupings based on quantitative characters. Biometrika 35 176-181.

--------. (1955). The use of transformations and maximum likelihood in the analysis of quantal experiments involving two treatments. Biometrika 42 382-403.

ZANGWILL, W. I. (1969). Nonlinear Programming: A Unified Approach. Prentice-Hall, Englewood Cliffs, N.J.

INDEX

Adjusted replication number, 174
Adjustment of marginal totals, 376-386
Aitchison, J., 351, 408
Anderson, T. W., 102, 186, 408
Anscombe, F., 139, 408
Ashford, J. R., 351, 408
Asymptotic properties, 7, 14, 18-27, 74-146, 205-212, 288-292, 331-351, 354-373, 380-386
    accuracy of approximations, 144-146
    asymptotic confidence intervals, 81-84, 85-91, 257, 290-292, 339-342, 343-344 (see also Simultaneous confidence intervals)
    asymptotic equivalence, 97, 99, 102, 108, 324, 336, 345
    asymptotic power, 102-107, 110, 345-347
    asymptotically efficient estimates, 95-97
Attitudes toward Negroes, 119, 201-202, 204-205, 207
Bahadur, R. R., 97, 102, 408
Baseball, 304-305, 318, 328-330, 342-343, 347
Berkson, J., 63, 93, 303, 316, 324, 408
Billingsley, P., 408
Biological assay, 304, 312, 315-317, 337-342, 348-351
Birch, M. M., 34, 39, 149, 180, 408
Birkhoff, G., 235, 408
Bishop, Y. M. M., 3, 14, 46, 64, 58, 149, 180, 184, 190, 228, 266, 268, 274, 288, 303, 408
Bjorck, A., 49-50, 408
Blackwell, D., 38, 409
Bliss, C. I., 5, 303, 304, 323, 408, 412
Blyth, C. R., 30, 409
Bock, R. D., 46, 303, 351, 409
Bonferroni inequality, 117, 122, 125, 131
Borosh, I., 234, 266, 409
Bradley, R. A., 306, 409
Braun, H. A., 5, 304, 412
Breiman, L., 366, 409
Busvine, J. R., 351, 409
Chinese remainder theorem, 236
Closed-form maximum likelihood estimate, 149, 166-187, 266-292
Cochran, W. G., 2, 15, 25, 27, 104, 105, 106, 107, 119, 145, 203, 301, 409
Coin tossing, 1, 3
Complementary log-log transformation, 306, 331
Complete factorial table, 147-214, 260-261
Complete minimal sufficient statistic, 7, 9, 11, 12, 16, 314
Components in models for factorial tables, 200-205, 296-302
Conditional Poisson model, 14-27, 42-45, 95, 105-106, 107, 108, 400-402
Contiguous alternatives, 103
Cook, S. W., 119, 414
Cornfield, J., 354, 372, 409
Courant, R., 235, 409
Cox, D. R., 15, 139, 352, 409

Cox, G. M., 301, 409
Cramér, H., 22, 78, 146, 409
Cross-product ratio, 5, 51, 82-84
Curtiss, J. H., 20, 24, 409
Cyclic ascent, 64-73, 190-200, 292-296, 375-376 (see also Deming-Stephan algorithm)
Dahm, P. A., 351, 412
Darroch, J. N., 46, 180, 409
Das Gupta, S., 105, 413
David, H. A., 305, 409
Davidon, W. C., 47, 410
Dawber, T. R., 352, 410
Decomposable generating class, 166-167, 175-176, 178-190, 192-197, 208-212, 266-292
total decomposability, 192-197
Deming, W. E., xi, 64, 190, 374, 377, 410
Deming-Stephan algorithm, 64-73, 114, 149, 190-198, 203, 292-296, 375-376, 378, 383 (see also Cyclic ascent)
Differential, 34, 35, 40, 42, 76, 289, 308, 380, 392-393
Digitalis, 5, 304
Dinculéanu, N., 365, 410
Direct products, 150-156, 324
Draper, N., 138, 139, 349, 410
D. melanogaster, 228-229, 294, 299-300, 306
Duncan, D. B., 303, 352, 369, 371, 372, 414
Dunn, O. J., 133, 410
Dyke, G. V., 46, 303, 410
Eaton, M. L., 12, 126, 150, 333, 410
El-Badry, M. A., 378, 383, 410
Estimability, 301-302
Exact confidence intervals, 29-33
Exponential families, 7, 12, 16
Extended maximum-likelihood estimate, 271, 315, 383, 402-404
Feller, W., 9, 145, 309, 410
Felsenstein, J., 145, 412
Fieller, E. C., 340, 341, 410
Fienberg, S. E., 3, 34, 228, 245, 265, 266, 268, 274, 288, 301, 408, 410
Finney, D. J., xii, 5, 46, 304, 311, 322, 338, 341, 349, 351, 410
Fisher, R. A., 15, 16, 30, 113, 303, 323, 410
Fisher-consistent estimate, 95-97
Flats, 374-386
Fleming, W. H., x, 411
Fraenkel, A. S., 234, 266, 409
Framingham study, 352, 369-370
Freeman, M. R., 139, 411
Friedlander, D., 378, 411
Frogs, 6, 85
Gabriel, K. R., 119, 411
Garwood, F., 309, 326, 411
Gart, J. J., 146, 411
Gaussian elimination, 234
Generating class, 159, 166-167, 172 (see also Decomposable generating class)
Girshick, M. A., 38, 409
Glass, D. V., 215, 411
Good, I. J., 145, 203, 411
Goodman, L. A., 50, 82, 85, 102, 105, 112, 116, 119, 120, 122, 126, 127, 132, 133, 134, 146, 149, 166, 168, 171, 180, 184, 186, 187, 215, 216, 227, 228, 230, 245, 248, 261, 263, 266, 270, 275, 277, 281, 408, 411, 412
Gover, T. N., 145, 411
Govindarajulu, Z., 105, 347, 412
Gram-Schmidt orthogonalization, 26, 49
Grosswald, E., 236, 412
Gurland, J., 351, 412
Haberman, S. J., 47, 65, 190, 412
Hadamard inequality, 235
Halmos, P., x, 7, 49, 100, 132, 150, 151, 186, 208, 262, 286, 317, 318, 324, 387, 389, 412

Harris, J. H., 229, 412
Hartley, H. O., 30, 413
Haynam, G. E., 105, 347, 412
Hierarchical model, 156-198, 313-314, 375-376
Hilbert, D., 235, 409
Hirvonen, T., 1, 414
Hoel, P. G., 32, 412
Hoffman, K., x, 13, 412
Homework, 139-142
Hotelling, H., 135, 414
Hurewicz, W., 185, 414
Hutchinson, D. W., 30, 409
Hypergeometric distribution, 17
Hypothesis tests, 84, 85, 90, 97-131, 258-261, 286, 288, 344-348, 372-373 (see also Likelihood ratio chi-square and Pearson chi-square)
Implicit function theorem, 76, 334, 365, 381, 393
Incomplete factorial tables, 228-302
Inseparable table, see Separable table
Intersection class, 174
Ireland, C. T., 46, 378, 412
Iterative proportional fitting, see Deming-Stephan algorithm
Kallianpur, G., 95, 412
Kannel, W., 354, 372, 409
Kastenbaum, M. A., 46, 413
Kavan, G., 237, 412
Kruskal, W. H., ix, 7, 10, 49, 84, 206, 301, 322, 338, 372, 412
Kullback, S., 46, 188, 378, 412
Kunze, R., x, 13, 412
LD50, see Median lethal dose
Lee, J., 351, 412
Lehmann, E. L., 7, 14, 28, 30, 32, 145, 412
Leone, F. C., 105, 347, 412
Leslie, P. H., 189, 412
Lewontin, R. C., 145, 412
Likelihood ratio chi-square, 97-131, 187-189, 247, 258-259, 260-261, 286-288, 344-347, 372-373 (see also Hypothesis tests and Pearson chi-square)
Loève, M. M., 359, 363, 412
Logits, logit analysis, 5, 28-29, 31-33, 60-64, 72-73, 85-87, 134-138, 213, 214, 304, 308-320, 326-334, 336, 337, 344, 347-351, 352-354, 367-370
Loomis, L. S., x, 2, 76, 365, 387, 389, 412
MacKenzie, W. A., 113, 410
MacLane, S., 235, 408
Maize crosses, 106, 374
Mantel, N., 228, 412
Markov estimate, 186-187
Mayhall, J. T., 54, 413
Meadors, G. F., 352, 409
Median lethal dose, 138, 340-342
Miller, L. C., 5, 304, 412
Miller, R. G., 117, 135, 136, 138, 413
Minimum-variance unbiased estimate, 28-29, 94
Mitchell, G. J., 145, 411
Mitra, S. K., 78, 413
Modified Newton-Raphson algorithm, 47-64, 93, 321, 332, 337
Moore, F. E., 352, 409
Mosteller, F., 304, 306, 413
Muller, T., 54, 413
Multinomial model, multinomial sampling, multinomial response, 9-14, 39-41, 78, 95, 105-106, 107, 351-373
Newton-Raphson algorithm, see Modified Newton-Raphson algorithm
Noether, G. E., 102, 413
Nonhierarchical model, 198-200
Novitski, E., 228, 250, 413
Odoroff, C. L., 145, 413
Ordered classifications, 213-214

Paired comparisons, 305-306, 317-320, 327-330, 342-343
Parole violation, 51, 82-84
Parthasarathy, K. R., 357, 413
Patnaik, P. B., 105, 413
Patterson, H. D., 46, 303, 410
Pearson, E. S., 30, 413
Pearson, K., 25, 98, 413
Pearson chi-square, 25, 97-131, 141, 246-247, 260-261, 288, 344-347, 372-373 (see also Hypothesis tests and Likelihood ratio chi-square)
Perlman, M. D., 105, 413
Pitman, E., 102
Plackett, R. L., 82, 85, 413
Poisson model, Poisson sampling, 6-9, 34-38, 78, 95, 105, 107, 260
Probits, probit analysis, 304, 308-309, 311, 323, 349-351
Quantal response, 5, 303-373
Quasi-independence, 229, 230, 245, 261-263, 265-266, 268, 270, 277-282, 285, 294
Ralston, A., 32, 413
Rao, C. R., x, xi, 7, 13, 27, 77, 78, 94, 95, 97, 108, 117, 125, 132, 251, 339, 359, 361, 364, 367, 387, 412, 413
Raw replication number, 124
Reducibility, 266-292
Reiersøl, O., 131, 413
Residuals, 138-144, 247, 257-258, 349-351
Roy, S. N., 46, 413
Runnenburg, J. T., 27, 414
Sandler, I., 228, 250, 413
Schaffer, R. S., 145, 146, 413
Scheffé, H., 28, 131, 165, 301, 412, 413
Scoring algorithm, 323, 337
Separable tables, 245-266, 285
Sex ratio, 1, 4, 82, 169
Silverstone, H., 93, 316, 317, 413
Silvey, S. D., 351, 408
Simultaneous confidence intervals, 131-138, 290-292, 348-349
Simultaneous testing, 116-131, 347-348
Smith, H., 138, 139, 349, 410
Snedecor, G. W., 2, 106, 119, 413
Snell, E. J., 139, 409
Social-mobility tables, 215-227, 270
Staphylea, 229-230
Stephan, F. F., xi, 64, 190, 374, 377, 378, 383, 410, 414
Sternberg, S., x, 2, 76, 365, 387, 389, 412
Stroke patients, 268-269
Svalastoga, K., 215, 222, 414
Terry, M. E., 306, 409
Theil, H., 303, 414
Thornton, H. G., 113, 410
Thurstone, L. L., 306, 414
Toivanen, P., 1, 414
Tolerance distribution, 304
Torus mandibularis, 54-56, 57, 113, 147, 213, 214
Toxemia, 1, 4, 82, 90-91, 147
Truett, J., 354, 372, 409
Tukey, J. W., 139, 242, 408, 414
Undesigned experiments, 352-373
Uniformly-most-accurate unbiased confidence intervals, 29-30
Van Eeden, C., 27, 414
Vector spaces, properties of, 387-392
Wagner, S. S., 228, 414
Walker, S. H., 303, 352, 369, 371, 372, 414
Walkley, R. P., 119, 414
Wallman, H., 185, 412
Wilkinson, J. H., 49, 328, 414
Wilks, S. S., 13, 17, 98, 414
Wilner, D. M., 119, 414

Working, H., 135, 414
Yarnold, J. K., 145, 414
Yates, F., 139, 203, 306, 331, 414
Yates algorithm, 203
Zangwill, W., 64, 414
Zweifel, J. R., 146, 411